The Thought of
Teilhard de Chardin

ÉMILE RIDEAU

The Thought of
Teilhard de Chardin

TRANSLATED BY RENÉ HAGUE

Harper & Row, Publishers
NEW YORK AND EVANSTON

La Pensée du Père Teilhard de Chardin
was first published in France by Editions du Seuil in 1965

Library of Congress Catalog Card Number: 67-21558

The Thought of Teilhard de Chardin
was published in England under the title
Teilhard de Chardin: A Guide to his Thought

Original French edition © 1965 Editions du Seuil
English translation © 1967 William Collins Sons & Co., Ltd., London
Printed in Great Britain by William Collins Sons & Co., Ltd., London and Glasgow

Nihil obstat, LIONEL SWAIN, STL, LSS, *Censor*;
Imprimatur ✠ PATRICK CASEY, VG; Westminster, 17TH JULY 1967

The Nihil obstat *and* Imprimatur *are a declaration that a book*
or pamphlet is considered to be free from doctrinal or moral error. It is
not implied that those who have granted the Nihil obstat *and* Imprimatur *agree with the contents, opinions or statements expressed.*

Contents

INTRODUCTION   9

CHAPTER 1   FORMATIVE INFLUENCES   15
   I PHYSICAL HEREDITY AND CHARACTER   15
   II FAMILY INFLUENCES   18
   III SECONDARY EDUCATION   18
   IV THE SOCIETY OF JESUS   19
   V THE 1914 WAR   21
   VI SCIENCE   22
   VII SOCIOLOGY   23
   VIII FRIENDSHIPS   24
   IX TEILHARD'S READING   25
The Stages of Teilhard's Life and Thought   27
Conclusion   28

CHAPTER 2   THE INTUITION AND THE PROJECT   31
   I THE MODERN CRISIS OF CONSCIOUSNESS   31
   II THE HUMAN CONDITION   35
   III CHRISTIANITY AND THE MODERN WORLD   36
The Operative Method   38
   I A UNIVERSAL PHENOMENOLOGY   38
   II A DIALECTICAL PHENOMENOLOGY   44
   III THE PLANES OF THE PHENOMENON:
     PHILOSOPHY AND THEOLOGY   48
Conclusion   49

CHAPTER 3   A PHENOMENOLOGY OF HISTORY   51
   I MATTER   51
   II LIFE   52

5

III MAN   52
IV MANKIND TODAY   53
 V THE END OF HISTORY   56
Omega Point   57
The Universal Christ   60
A New Apologetics   62
Conclusion   64
  I THE TRANSCENDENCE OF GOD   65
 II THE TRANSCENDENCE OF FREEDOM   68
III COMPLEXITY OF HISTORICAL FACTORS   70

CHAPTER 4 COSMOLOGY   74
  I THE METHOD AND VALUE OF SCIENCE   74
 II THE FORMS   76
III ENERGY   78
    a: *Apparent duality of the forms of energy* 78
    b: *Unity of the forms of energy*   79
    c: *The dialectic of union and dissociation* 82
    d: *Discussion*   84
    e: *Comparison with modern scientific concepts* 88
IV THE INTERIORITY OF THE REAL   90
 V SCIENCE AND PHILOSOPHY   92
Note on Transformism   95
Conclusion   98

CHAPTER 5 ANTHROPOLOGY   100
  I THE HUMAN CONDITION   100
    a: *Man's transcendence of the universe*   100
    b: *Man's involvement in the universe*   102
    c: *Man's psychic structure*   104
 II PERSONALISM   108
III THE EXISTENTIAL DISTRESS   110
    a: *Multiplicity*   110
    b: *Man's passivity*   111
    c: *Time*   111
    d: *Death*   112

e: The magnitude of the universe 112
f: Man's isolation 113
g: Man's distress: the problem of evil 114
IV EXISTENTIAL VALUES 118
 a: The quest for knowledge and technology 119
 b: Philosophy 124
 c: Art 124
 d: Society 126
 e: Morality 135
 f: Religion 140
Conclusion 144

CHAPTER 6 THEOLOGY 146
 I THE EXISTENCE OF GOD 146
 II CREATION 152
 III THE HISTORY OF CREATION 156
 IV CO-OPERATION OF GOD AND HIS CREATION 159
 V NATURE AND THE SUPERNATURAL: DISTINCTION
  AND COINCIDENCE OF THE TWO ORDERS 160
 VI THE INCARNATION 162
 VII SIN AND REDEMPTION 169
 VIII IS THERE PROGRESS IN HISTORY? 174
 IX THE CHURCH AND THE EUCHARIST 179
 X THE PAROUSIA 179
 XI THE UNITY OF THE MYSTERIES 180
Eschatological Problems 180
 I CONNECTION AND DISSOCIATION OF THE TWO ORDERS 181
 II THE TRANSITION TO THE FINAL LIMIT 183
 III THE HISTORICITY OF ESCHATOLOGY 185
 IV THE RESURRECTION OF THE BODY AND THE
  DIVINIZATION OF THE COSMOS 185
 V THE DIVINIZATION OF THE COSMOS 186
 VI THE PROBLEM OF EARLIER GENERATIONS 187
 VII THE JUDGMENT 187
Conclusion 188

CHAPTER 7 SPIRITUALITY 192
 I FAITH 193
 II ACTION 195

III PASSIVITIES 200
IV THE CHURCH 202
V THE EUCHARIST 205
An Introduction to Spirituality 208
I THE THREE CHOICES 208
II THE THREE PHASES OF PERSONALIZATION 209
III TOWARDS THE LIVING GOD 210
Teilhard's Spirituality and the
    Spiritual Exercises of St Ignatius 211
Critical Comments 221
I HUMAN VALUES AND CHRISTIAN VALUES 221
II ACTION AND PRAYER 224
III THE MEANING OF THE CROSS 225
IV HUMANIZATION AND THE KINGDOM OF GOD 228
V CHARITY AND POVERTY 229
VI HISTORY OF CHRISTIAN MYSTICISM 229
Conclusion 230
CHRISTIANITY AND OTHER RELIGIONS 237

CONCLUSION 237

APPENDIX: VOCABULARY AND LANGUAGE 255
I FUNDAMENTAL IMAGES 258
II BEING AND REALITY 259
III AFFIRMATION AND NEGATION 260
IV SPACE 261
V MOVEMENT 262
VI FORMS 265
VII QUALITIES AND OBJECTS 266
VIII LIFE 268
IX THOUGHT 269
X GOD 272
XI CONCLUSION 273

Teilhard's style 273

NOTES 277

INDEX 661

Introduction

When the history of our time comes to be written, it will certainly record the 'phenomenon of Teilhard'.

In every circle of society, in every nation that respects culture, among unbelievers and among Christians, a keen interest has been aroused by the personality and writings of Père Teilhard de Chardin. They are in some way in tune with what many people have been feeling, deeply but inarticulately, and they meet aspirations that are widely shared.

We live in a time of tragedy and crisis. In spite of his triumphs, man's pride is shaken and his security threatened by despair: for he sees some of our greatest thinkers accepting the notion that the world is an absurdity; men who are eminent in literature and the cinema seem to delight in blackening life as a useless agony, and ridiculing man himself as a mere mechanical puppet. With human activity robbed of all hope and nobility, men are turning to Teilhard in order to find out whether man's labour is vain and without justification, or whether it has indeed an absolute value; whether it contains the assurance of a certain and triumphant end or whether it can only peter out in a trackless waste and meet a catastrophic end; whether the long wagon-train of man will emerge from the tunnel or plod on in unending darkness.

We want to know whether it is worth while carrying on with the vast adventure of history. We have our technical skills, our science, inventions and discoveries, our cities; we have the natural beauties of our earth; we can speak to one another and communicate with one another across continents and oceans; we know the joy of living and creating; we can see and hear the intense activity of the human hive—and we ask whether all these have a meaning and a direction. Will they take on eternity, or are they fated to disappear, forgotten and annihilated, as the ship's wake is lost among the waves?

9

Are we building up on earth the kingdom of God, in the midst, admittedly, of all the vicissitudes and uncertainties of a developing history, and is some astounding cathedral emerging here below in the strident but fruitful turmoil of builders and labourers? Or are we working in a Babel, with the workers, at cross-purposes, divided by hate?

Finally, is it possible to be truly Christian and fully a man, faithful to one's own day and faithful to the Gospel? Is it possible to hold the crucified God before one's eyes, while still being passionately devoted to human enterprise and the full development of man? Can one love both the world and God? Is secular history inseparable from sacred history?

There is a general feeling that Teilhard can answer these agonizingly urgent questions.

'Tell this fair kingdom of the world how deeply I have loved it.' Bernanos' dying words might well have been spoken by Teilhard. The two men differed greatly in their spiritual option in face of the Christian mystery, but both shared the same passion for man, for life, and for the world.

Teilhard, however, is also a symbol of contradiction. The attitude he adopted towards some of the most fundamental of problems, arouses violent opposition, bitter controversy, and contradictory interpretations. In consequence, many minds are at a loss to know what they should think about him, and are looking for information and a decisive judgment of his position.

A great deal has already been written about Teilhard, some of it extremely valuable.[1] The present study has profited from this pre-

---

[1] I owe a great deal to a number of excellent accounts of Teilhard's life, thought, and writings: in particular, C. Cuénot's *Pierre Teilhard de Chardin: les grandes étapes de son évolution*, Plon, 1958 (English version, London, 1965), and his *Teilhard de Chardin*, Editions du Seuil, in the series 'Ecrivains de toujours', 1962; N. M. Wildiers, *Teilhard de Chardin*, Editions Universitaires, 1961; G. Crespy (Professor in the Protestant faculty of Montpellier), *La pensée théologique de Teilhard de Chardin* (*ibid.*, 1961); H. de Lubac, *La pensée religieuse du Père Teilhard de Chardin*, Aubier, 1962 (English translation, London, 1967, *The Religion of Teilhard de Chardin*); Madeleine Barthélemy-Madaule, *Bergson et Teilhard de Chardin*, Editions du Seuil, 1963; P. Smulders, *La vision de Teilhard de Chardin*, Desclée de Brouwer, 1962. A complete bibliography of Teilhard's writings has been published in *Essais sur Teilhard de Chardin* (Recherches et débats du Centre catholique des intellectuels français, *Cahier* No. 40, October 1962, Fayard).

paratory work of clearing the way, and offers an over-all and synthetic examination, corresponding to all the multiple aspects of Teilhard's own work.

It has been based on as complete as possible a study of all his writings, both published and unpublished, and it attempts to reconstitute the *logic* of his thought in the dialectical balance of its complementary aspects.

The long sequence of Teilhard's essays calls, in fact, for the bringing out of the coherent structure that gives them unity.[2] Although he made no claim to present a system, he puts forward an all-embracing view, from which nothing essential is missing, and whose elements are bound together by an inner inevitability. There is no important problem that Teilhard did not deal with and on which he failed to throw new light. In particular, he built up a positive science of man and described the existential mediations of his fulfilment.

In as much as it seeks to be strictly objective and rigorously scientific, the present attempt suffers from the disadvantage of presenting in schematic form a living thought that developed over a period of forty years: it remains for some exact and scrupulous historian to bring out all the initial emergence of Teilhard's thought, the broadening of its expression, and even his complete changes of

[2] Teilhard was too aware of the complexity and mystery of the real in the sum of its 'orders', to attempt the elaboration of a definitive system. 'I do not believe, absolutely, in any system' (Letter of 2 February 1920). Following the example of Bergson, and of Pascal, too, who proceeded by convergent 'digressions' ('this order consists principally in a digression on each point, which is related to the end, so as continually to bring it out') he illuminates the real from a number of different and complementary angles, and advances towards various aspects of the truth along 'lines of approach'. 'The important thing in existence is not to mark out the limits of the Real ... but to determine, within the Real, certain assured lines of advance and arrangement' (Letter of 17 November 1947). Teilhard seeks primarily to develop a spirit and stimulate an attitude. Moreover, in his loyalty to positive scientific method, he remains in the order of the 'phenomenon' and eschews a deductive and abstract metaphysics. Christianity itself is to him in the first place an evidential datum, a fact.

At the same time, and with full justification, he took as his basis the value of reason and the analogical capabilities of language and so endeavoured, throughout his life, to organize his thought logically and present it as a coherent whole: thus he arrived at the structure that informs a philosophy and a theology.

mind. This difficulty, however, is greatly lessened by Teilhard's extreme fidelity to his original intuition.

The unusual length of the notes, which must, I fear, be an inconvenience to the reader, calls for an explanation. Two considerations were behind this: it made it possible to relieve the body of the book from encumbrance, and at the same time allows the reader to make direct contact with Teilhard's thought and personally to verify the view expressed in the text.[3]

The integral structure that runs through the whole of Teilhard's thought facilitates a critical appraisal, and this I have done my best to present. While he carried his interpretation of the mystery of being and existence as far as possible, by giving the effects of the Incarnation their full import, he was well aware, as were his great predecessors, of the inevitable gulf between reason and faith. We shall see, however, that he sought to establish between Christianity and man, between sacred history and 'natural' history, a dialectical balance that would conform as closely as possible both with tradition and with the new demands of the modern spirit.

Whatever may be said about any shortcomings in his thought, they are outweighed by the great value of his positive contribution. Teilhard clears the way for a restatement of the philosophy of science and religion. He forces us to revise our mental categories and to invent a new language that will correspond to the present change in consciousness. He lays down the irrevocable conditions that the expression of the truth must satisfy if it is to be acceptable. In virtue of this, at least, Teilhard stands on a level with the greatest thinkers in history.

I owe a great debt, which I now acknowledge, to those who have

---

[3] The notes (sometimes preceded by a descriptive title) bring together passages that relate to a particular subject. Generally speaking, they are arranged in chronological order, which makes it possible to follow the evolution of Teilhard's thought. In the case of Teilhard's three major books (as opposed to collections of essays) the date of publication is not given in the notes. These three are *Le Milieu Divin* (1927), *The Phenomenon of Man* (1940), and *Man's Place in Nature* (1949).

It is important always to bear in mind an essential principle in the interpretation of Teilhard's writings. In judging them, one must consider to what degree they contain a final and complete expression, and to how wide or narrow a circle they were addressed. Much that he wrote represents an unfinished study or enquiry, or a stage in the development of a theme.

already written about Teilhard, and to friends who have generously helped me by comment and criticism; and I am grateful to Mlle Jeanne Mortier for her kindness in allowing me to quote so freely from Teilhard's writings.

Quotations from *The Phenomenon of Man* are taken from the revised edition, 1965; from *Le Milieu Divin*, from the 1964 paperback edition.

Chapter I

Formative Influences

Highly original and personal though it undoubtedly was, Teilhard's quest for truth was nevertheless subject to a number of influences that made their mark upon it. These provide, to some degree, an explanation of certain aspects of his thought that were peculiar to him.

I PHYSICAL HEREDITY AND CHARACTER

Constitutionally, Teilhard possessed physical *health* and an intense *vitality*, a well-balanced nervous make-up, great capacity for effort and great power of resistance, marked virility. Organically, there was no weakness or delicacy, and at the same time this was accompanied by the refinement that comes from good breeding. Increasing years, moreover, in no way blunted the youthfulness of his soul and energy.

His intelligence was clear and swift, inventive, creative, ready to receive all that was real; it was, perhaps, better adapted for synthesis than for the patient work of analysis. It was keenly aware of the need for logic and unity, for rational structure and continuity, even between the different orders of the real, anxious to understand and explain, with complete faith in the mind's cognitive capacity. The great need, Teilhard felt, was for 'coherence'.[1] From this was derived a pronounced *intellectual vocation*. Teilhard was very well equipped for scientific and philosophical research, for handling ideas and expressing them in words.[2] At the same time he had little liking for an *a priori* and purely abstract dialectic, with no foundation in facts.

Teilhard had a vivid imagination, predominantly visual. It made great use of the multiplicity of sense-impressions, giving them rich verbal form in a variety of metaphors and symbols. It seems to have been unusually fascinated by a widening of frontiers and horizons, by an infinite extension of the contours that delimit beings.[3]

We find exceptional sensibility, in two ranges, at once alternate and complementary and interdependent (in which the psychologist recognizes the marks or modes of *emotion* and *passion*) the one more passive and briefer, the other more active and lasting.

Affectivity, with a capacity for sympathy with the *real*,[4] but also for intense vibration, for ardent exaltation and inspired enthusiasm; and which, while preparing to purify and sublimate them, does not shrink from sharing the truth of certain natural aspirations.[5]

An ardent dynamic energy, capable of enduring activity in carrying out far-reaching projects.[6] This dynamism, a psychological and conscious form of the need *to be*, is, in Teilhard, the source of a constant questioning of reality, of a refusal to be satisfied with immediate evidence, of a search for God in depth.[7]

To this we may add a strong *will*, which enabled him not only to be master of his interior self, but also to pursue his aims with perseverance and courage, and to retain his serenity in suffering and his liberty in obedience.[8] This strength of will contributed to the nobility of his character, the solidity of his personality and the independence of his judgment.

All these qualities are clearly inseparable from and involved in one another, and, taken all together, they gave Teilhard's personality an unusually high degree of *harmony*.

At the same time, owing to the *dominance of sensibility*, this harmony brought with it an imbalance, itself fruitful and dynamic but the source of a number of problems.

Teilhard's sensibility explains his love for things and for man: it may be that this is a debatable point,[9] and that his feeling of compassion is sometimes threatened by a certain hardness or by a preference for general ideas, but at the same time Teilhard was spontaneously *kindly*. It was said of him, with truth, that he had a 'genius for friendship'.

His sensibility explains, too, both his intuitive fellow-feeling with the world and the ease with which he found, beneath the transparency of symbols, mystical communion with God.

It is the source of his precocious appetite, even as a child, for the absolute and for plenitude, for what has consistence and is incorruptible,[10] of his love of danger and adventure,[11] of his intrepidity, of his intellectual curiosity, of his 'generosity' in the Cartesian meaning of the word.

Sometimes, we must admit, it would have benefited by subjecting its exuberance to a critical toning-down, in favour of a more austere discipline of thought and language, of greater prudence in some lines of approach or conclusions. Teilhard's passion for truth inhibited in him the birth and development of a certain irony, that would have modified the vigour of his assertions and the assurance of his theses. Sometimes his thought, for lack of a sense of humour, from being insufficiently relaxed and withdrawn, comes close to dogmatism.

It is to Teilhard's ardour, again, that we should attribute his *extraversion*:[12] his interest in the external world, his eagerness to embrace the universe, and his passionate concern for the problems it raises, and, even more, his consciousness of his own individual vocation, his sense of his apostolic responsibility. While it made for stability and mental health, this open receptiveness somewhat distracted his attention from existential problems, at any rate in the way they are approached by St Augustine, Pascal, Kierkegaard or Blondel. It ruled out the search for a direct intuition of the ego, as it had been conducted by Bergson; and, *a fortiori*, the habitual introspection that examines the states of one's soul, the turning-in on oneself, the delight in egocentrism. Fidelity to a task and a mission saved Teilhard from any display of the ego and also from the excesses of intimate analysis; the richness of his interior life came from concentration on the real.

This extraversion, or realism, this love of being, were a happy counterbalance to a temptation to *anguish*, whose roots lie deep in the feeling of the fragility and lack of consistence of the real, the mystery of the future.[13] The need for the absolute, characteristic of Teilhard since childhood, might perhaps be seen as a dialectical compensation, to which grace was to give added force and weight.[14] The serenity of the man thus seems to have been the result of a *contradiction* that was solved.

Every aspect of Teilhard's personality is reflected with astonishing clarity in his handwriting.[15]

Photographs of Teilhard, at different ages, and in all sorts of circumstances, also show the same constant characteristics of his ego: refinement, virility, kindness, liveliness, delight in living and creating, peaceful serenity.

II FAMILY INFLUENCE

On the religious level, his mother's influence affected him profoundly, in particular by awakening in him a devotion to the Heart of Jesus.[16] His father's influence, too, left his mark on him, both by giving him, as Teilhard recognized, 'a certain fundamental balance on which all the rest was built', and by awakening his vocation to science.

The family atmosphere was peaceful and warm, undisturbed by disagreements or rivalries—the unruffled happiness of the young who are troubled by no problems. Living a rather sheltered life, Teilhard was indifferent, it seems, to the problem of sex, which he was late in meeting, when he was about thirty.

His background was the comfortable setting of the provincial gentry, rooted in tradition and not very receptive of modern ideals, and, as a result, with little awareness of the problems of social justice. Privileged by birth and education, Teilhard was never to experience the tragedy of the life of the poor, and, though he was in no way reactionary, he was never to feel intensely the need to question the established order or institutions. This can only make one admire the more the broadening, if not the complete change, of mind that later enabled him to write so well about democracy.

III SECONDARY EDUCATION

At Mongré (1892–8) the young Teilhard received a sound classical education, primarily literary, in accordance with an ideal based on reason, order and strictness, on intellectual and moral discipline.

The social climate of the school was distinctly self-contained and middle-class, and no doubt hostile to democracy and the existing regime, but loyal to the Church in the humiliating position imposed on her by the modern world—the 'sad years of the eighties and nineties' of which Claudel speaks.[17]

Teilhard's ardent piety and exemplary behaviour point to an important characteristic, whose consequences were to make themselves apparent in his theology and spirituality. Everything would seem to suggest that Teilhard never had the deeply-felt experience of a *conversion* that must start from a sense of sin (this is a word we seldom find him using). In this he differed greatly from St Augustine, Pascal, Kierkegaard and De Foucauld: his general evolution took the form of maturing through an expansion of personality. Sharply aware of human anguish though he was, one cannot imagine that he was ever able to exclaim with St Paul, 'Who will deliver me from this body of death?'

IV THE SOCIETY OF JESUS

First there came an intensive training for the spiritual life, following the method and ideal of St Ignatius: a deepening of personal love for Jesus Christ, directed towards the apostolate. This apostolic vocation was fundamental to Teilhard, and to answer it, it was continually and primarily his concern to carry the good news of salvation to the modern world and bring it back to the Church: it is worth noting that his first essay, after coming out of the war of 1914, was entitled, 'Note for use in the evangelization of the new era'.[18]

There was the influence, too, of the *Spiritual Exercises*, with their grandeur and generosity of manner, but also with their sense of history, and their closing invitation to love God in all things.[19]

This religious ascesis was demanding, but rational and humane, being regarded not as an end in itself but as an opening towards communion with God. Teilhard was very soon faced with the problem of reconciling humanism and grace, nature and the Cross, prudence and heroism, freedom and obedience: the long dramatic confrontation of Eros and Agape, and their final Christian confluence, of vitality and grace, of ardour and submission. The impulse towards being, considered as an absolute to be mastered, was subordinated to attention to a Word: 'consistence' was seen to be 'charity'.

There was the early, and lasting, encouragement Teilhard received to pursue his vocation to science. Though by no means exceptional in the Society's traditions, at that time such encouragement was still relatively rare. Moreover, a scientific vocation was regarded primarily as a way of serving the Church and as a means to missionary expansion, rather than as a disinterested contribution to the human effort.

Teilhard's literary, philosophical and theological studies were solid and serious, even brilliant, under teachers who were at times outstanding.[20] In philosophy and theology, it seems, they taught within the framework of a classical Thomism, which has the advantage of harmonizing the relations of nature and grace, and also

(with its theory of matter and form) of defining the substantial
relationship of matter and spirit, body and soul. This relationship was to remain fundamental in Teilhard's thought.

Theology was to supply Teilhard with many formal elements and
implicit stimuli: his personalism derives from the dogma of the
Trinity and the notion of the Mystical Body; his concept of a global
history of creation is borrowed even more from the Bible than from
biology; the mystery of the Incarnation, as interpreted by St Paul
and the Greek Fathers, disclosed to him the eminent and central
position of Christ in the world; from Christianity, again, he drew his
rejection of Manicheanism and Jansenism, the creature's relationship to God by analogy and image, and hence the value of participated being; from the same source he drew, together with the
category of hope, the certainty of Catholicism's ability to assimilate
all things.

On the other hand the theological disciplines he was taught were
lacking in a readiness to face modern problems. Apologetics was
chary of embracing Maurice Blondel's recent attempt to demonstrate
the correspondence of revelation with man's interior problem.[21]
Clinging to a literal interpretation of the Bible, apologists were still
maintaining theses that conflicted with the science of the origins of
man or which contradicted established historical facts. Exegesis was
suffering from the repercussions of the measures taken in 1908
against modernism and was not trying to bring out the religious
message of the Scriptures: the problem raised by the language of the
Bible was not to be solved until 1943 by the encyclical *Divino
afflante Spiritu*.[22] Theology still made little attempt to revitalize itself
by getting back to biblical and patristic sources. Placed one after
the other, in sequence, and with no internal connexion, the
Christian mysteries appeared in the setting of a static world which
was not deeply involved in them. Finally, the study of dogma was
seen as an abstract discipline, a body of theses, with no relation to
personal life or to human history. 'Frigid scholasticism', Teilhard
was later to call it.[23]

Teilhard was to suffer all his life from these deficiencies. The Old
Testament remained somewhat unfamiliar to him,[24] and was to
raise for him problems that were distorted by the way in which the
questions involved were normally framed. Even his reading of the
New Testament was incomplete. His polemical attitude towards

some theological positions was to be to some degree warped by the very inadequacy of the synthesis he had received.

Finally, official teaching gave little room to social applications of Christian principles. Faithful to their family origins, the majority of Teilhard's teachers and companions were men who supported the established order and tradition. A certain number of them were ready to accept the ideas of the *Action Française*.[25] The condemnation of the *Sillon* took place in the middle of Teilhard's theology years (1910).

More generally, throughout all Teilhard's youth and during part of his adult life, the Church, as a whole, was drawing in on itself, adopting an attitude of opposition and defence. In spite of its evident fervour, it was maintaining or even increasing its distance from the modern world. This situation, of which he was painfully conscious, was to react on Teilhard's thought: the new approach, which he witnessed, and to which he contributed, came too late for him to benefit by it. The era of the 'counter-Reformation' and even, in a sense, of the 'counter-Renaissance' was not to come to an end officially until the second Vatican Council was in session.

V THE 1914 WAR

'Baptism in the real',[26] in his own phrase, the 1914 war gave Teilhard an opportunity for making an extensive contact with men, and also for intense personal reflexion and mystical illumination. The war made him become conscious for the first time of the collective, when he saw great masses of human beings combining their diverse elements into a composite whole. He saw the history of today running on in continuity with the history of the whole of nature.[27] Apostolic problems emerged from the vision of a humanity, Christian by its origins, but widely separated from the Church and indifferent to its message, that was yet capable of virtue and heroism. It was then that the essential core of Teilhard's thought came into being: the idea of a world in process of genesis, of a universal matter permeated, animated and unified by Christ.

Although Teilhard found in the war an opportunity for a heightened stimulation of energy, stretched 'to the very limit',[28] the impact of this experience was, nevertheless, not strong enough to awaken him to the most profound of the problems presented by history, in particular to that of man's social estrangement; and the great comprehensive view he was beginning to work out, of a global progress of mankind, sometimes seems to have left him insensitive to, or at any rate detached from, the mass of individual suffering brought about by the outbreak of war. In his anxiety to understand it, he did not, initially, take up an attitude of revolt or disgust towards the horror he saw; what he tried to do was to integrate human unhappiness in the rising flood of history.[29] Here we already find an indication that suggests some bias towards the majestic sweep of rational syntheses, in which the particular is included in the general.

Some of his remarks, finally, reflect the influence of the traditional, not to say reactionary, education Teilhard had received, and indicate errors of judgment. The most disturbing are with reference to the distinction between the élite and the masses[30] or to the necessity for the use of force in society.[31] On the other hand, it is significant to see Teilhard becoming personally, and sharply, aware of human injustice in connexion with a question of leave.[32]

His remarks about the enemy, too, ('the Boche') will be noted, and about the justice of the allied cause. These reflect the pseudo-patriotic conformism of the time; we find a certain veneer of charity towards others in his 'condescending' attitude to sometimes rough fellow-soldiers; an appreciation, correct in principle, but too cut and dried, of the moral effects of non-religious and secular education 'in line with the principles of the republic';[33] and, after reading Daudet's *Salons et Journaux*, the unattractive dream of spending a large part of one's life in the creative intimacy of coteries of intellectuals and artists, of a chosen circle of 'decent' people, at the heart of events and ideas (though one should add that Teilhard also dreamt of spending the rest of his time 'in the austerity of study or conflict').[34]

His joy, too, in a heightening of energy through fusion in the collective soul is not without some ambiguity.[35] Finally, his magnanimous wish for a combatant posting, in order that he might share more effectively in the men's activities and hardships, may seem questionable, if one knows that at the time Teilhard was the semi-official regimental chaplain.[36]

VI SCIENCE

Practical scientific training developed in Teilhard the scientist's normal qualities: a respect for facts, exactitude, accuracy. It gave him, too, a sense of the magnitude, complexity and richness of the universe, a sense of an objective world, existing as one whole, as an organism of inter-dependent elements.

More profoundly, science left its mark on Teilhard by making him demand a *rationality* in regard to a real that it had to express in logical, necessary, and unified relations. He shared the faith of his time in the value of positive phenomena, as the only way in which man can apprehend sensible reality, but at the same time, like Bergson, he extended this positivity to spiritual phenomena.

His originality in philosophy consists specifically in this, that he attempted a total generalization of this ideal of unity, extending it to the progressive movement of history, but at the same time to the whole of the orders of the real: meeting the natural demand of thought, Teilhard's philosophy is *unitary* and tries to embrace the totality of being in one logical coherent structure. Problems of extreme difficulty were to arise from this passion for the rational that sometimes comes close to rationalism and tends to devalue the concrete, individual existence of beings and at the same time to minimize the discontinuities between the orders of being.[37]

His specializing in geology and biology gave Teilhard a sense of *time* and of history, seen in their widest dimensions. Biology provided him, too, with the evidence that showed the irresistible power of spiritual energy. It seems finally to have confirmed in him the persistent notion of a hierarchy of values in beings, of an inequality in men and races, and of the aristocratic role of the élites.

VII SOCIOLOGY

Teilhard became more and more interested in the transformations of the world in the direction of unity. In particular, he had in his own life had experience of the new conditions of research carried out in collaboration and as a team.

Standing apart, geographically, from what was going on in the world, he was all the better in a position to observe the general movement of contemporary history. His travels, and his contact, starting in 1923, with the masses of the Far East, developed in him a sense of the collective that had already been born during the war of 1914.

It is odd, too, that this aristocrat and patriot, impregnated with a

class culture and little brought by education into contact with the
social problem, should have arrived, through his own intuition of
world-currents, at a vision of mankind that gradually embraced its
differences and divisions in a universal humanism. Even more, in
fact, than his questionable theories about the end of the world, it is
this invitation to the common, organized, effort for man's development, that explains why Teilhard found so wide an audience. And
this mysticism he drew, as Claudel perhaps did, from his experience
as a traveller.

We may add that eastern religions, after momentarily attracting
him by their pantheism, in the end confirmed him, by reaction, in
his preference for western humanism and in his religion of the
Personal.

Prolonged contact with the Anglo-Saxon mind had made it
familiar to him; his taste for the positive made him very much at
home with it, and it may have left its mark on him through its
pragmatic criterion of truth.[38]

VIII FRIENDSHIPS

Edouard Le Roy (1870–1954); a disciple of Bergson and his successor
at the Collège de France, was an intimate friend of Teilhard, and for
some time worked in close collaboration with him. Le Roy made
him realize, in particular, the reality of biological and psychic
'invention', and helped him to become aware of the ideal of the
'conspiration' of persons to counter their totalitarian mechanization.

A small group of other friends should be mentioned, who all, in
different capacities, had an influence on Teilhard.[39]

Foremost was *Père Auguste Valensin* (1879–1953). He was an
intimate and confidential friend, his spiritual director and intellectual guide, a restraining influence as an adviser, and an intermediary between Teilhard and Blondel.[40]

At Louvain, there were *Père Pierre Charles* and *Père Joseph Maréchal*,
both philosophers and theologians, and both at once traditional and
receptive.[41] At the same time Teilhard soon became conscious of
differences with his friends (Valensin, Charles): with his positive
mind, he distrusted abstraction and wished to keep in contact with
facts.[42]

At Paris, where he was editor of *Etudes*, there was *Père Léonce de*

Grandmaison (1868–1927). A classical scholar, a theologian and spiritually minded. He, too, though with some caution, was receptive of Teilhard's ideas.[43]

In England, there was *Père Pierre Rousselot* (1878–1915). For a year at least he must have been one of Teilhard's companions when studying theology, if not an intimate friend. Rousselot was a man of exceptional intelligence and he contributed, in particular, to rediscovering in St Thomas the mind as a force fundamentally related towards being.[44]

In Paris, and especially between 1920 and 1925, there was *Père Paul Doncoeur* (1880–1961) who shared Teilhard's open-hearted temperament, and his passionate love of the world, and who was delighted by his friend's theology of the Incarnation.

At Lyons, *Père Victor Fontoynont* (1880-1958), in the front rank of classical scholars, a philosopher, theologian, a discriminating intellectual and spiritual director. He shared Teilhard's years of religious training, and was his constant friend.[45]

In the scientific field, there were *Marcellin Boule*, who introduced Teilhard to palaeontology, in which he was the leading expert; and the *Abbé Henri Breuil*, a great authority, also, in prehistory, of which he held the chair at the Collège de France. Both were older than Teilhard, and helped him to understand scientific method and its demands.

IX TEILHARD'S READING

Although he was reluctant to admit it (for he was conscious of his differences with him) Teilhard was nevertheless strongly influenced by Bergson, whose works he had studied, in particular *Creative Evolution* in 1908[46] and *The Two Sources of Morality and Religion* during the 1939 war. It was the first of these two books, above all, that awoke the young Teilhard from his 'fixist slumber' and introduced him to the idea of a creation that continues in duration and ascends towards spirit. Bergson will always be recognized as the original discoverer of a scientific metaphysics of cosmic history. In borrowing many elements from it, Teilhard corrected it by the notion, at once rational and religious, of unification and universal convergence.

Although Teilhard may not have read *Maurice Blondel* during his formative years, towards the end of 1919 the two came into contact; it was at the time when Teilhard was intensely concerned with the relationship between humanism and Christianity. Blondel emphasized for him the demands of detachment and renunciation. It was to Blondel, too, that Teilhard must have been indebted for being confirmed in the notion of a 'pan-Christism'. From him, again, he seems to have received, as he did from Edouard Le Roy also, the idea of an *action*, directed towards the existential transcending of the person by the community of inter-personal relations.[47]

Both in quantity and sometimes in quality, it must be admitted, Teilhard's reading was somewhat deficient. His four years of philosophy and four of theology were no doubt academically planned and disciplined, but they do not seem to have been filled out by a study of modern thinkers or by the history of the progress of ideas. Descartes, Kant, Hegel, Marx,[48] and many others, appear only as 'opponents' who call for refutation. Later, the war of 1914, his scientific activities, and the distance at which he lived, all prevented Teilhard from coming sufficiently in contact with contemporary movements in literature, philosophy and theology. To some extent, however, an intellectual contact with individuals made up for this. During the 1914 war he got a great deal from reading Newman's *Apologia*, where he found a number of views on the development of dogma that coincided with his own thought. He responded to the Christian humanism of Père Sertillanges, which he found in the *Revue des Jeunes*, and in 1933 he was to write Sertillanges a cordial letter about his book *Dieu ou rien*. Some other books that came his way were comparatively poor.[49] Even Péguy he knew only through Joseph Lotte's little book. In about 1938 a lecture to students at the Ecole Normale refers to the subject matter of André Gide's *Nourritures terrestres*. Teilhard's enforced leisure during the 1939 war had one fortunate result, in that it gave him the opportunity to do a great deal of reading, as several notebooks indicate. By this time, however, he was already sixty years of age. Back in France, he no doubt learnt something about contemporary existentialism. In the course of his life, too, he read a good many English or American books that agreed with or contested his own line of thought, in particular those by his friend Julian Huxley. All this, however, should not be taken as belittling Teilhard's wide culture: we have, in fact, little information about how he kept it up. Without in any way diminishing Teilhard's originality, all these influences, taken together, contributed to the birth and development of his thought.

The Stages of
Teilard's Life and Thought

No study of Teilhard's thought can, in fact, demarcate the stages of its progress. Remarkably unified and self-consistent as it was, it was subject not so much to a series of deviations as to a continuous maturing and development.[50]

1908–12: During his years of theology, Teilhard became aware of 'a deep current of the universe, ontological and total'.[51]

1913: Discovery of the 'feminine', of the reality and importance of the problem of sex. There is no need to close our eyes to the fact that at this time Teilhard's chastity was put to the test, on the emotional plane.[52] The temptation was to reappear during his time in Paris, 1927–8, but was soon overcome.

1915–18: The war. It was from 1916[53] onwards that the essays of capital importance were written; these bring out the progressive coincidence of the universe in movement and Christ, in particular the Christ of the Eucharist. It was not, however, until 1923 that the problem of the one and the multiple emerged from the field of philosophic abstraction and became a problem of life and history.[54]

1924: Teilhard began to direct his attention to the problems of human history today.[55]

1930: After successfully passing through a spiritual crisis, Teilhard was becoming aware of the importance of *man* in the phenomenon of evolution. Soon after this, he discovered the law of complexity-consciousness. Thus this date marks the end of a period that was still centred on metaphysical or purely spiritual problems, and a more pronounced entry into the problem of the history of the cosmos as it approaches unity through convergence. With this new stage Teilhard evolved a more clear-cut picture of the universe.[56]

1935: An even sharper awareness of the importance of the collective and of the phenomenon of socialization. With this, Teilhard's orientation finally becomes predominantly towards the future.[57] From this point onwards, he becomes progressively more *committed*

to a refashioning of history and to the service of a world that now
has to be built.

1945–55: These last years are characterized by the vision of a
collective ultra-human, the term of history in time; during these
years also he came up against the recently discovered existentialist
pessimism.

Thus, there was a shift in Teilhard's centre of interest: from the
abstract to the concrete; from metaphysics to history; from the past
to the present, and from the present to the future; from theory to
practice (from speculation to commitment).

From Teilhard's writings and correspondence we can give a date,
also, to a certain number of events in his interior life.

1916–18: An outstanding period of mystical exaltation. *The Mass
on the World* serves as a sort of musical coda to this.

1918–20: These years were dominated by the problem of the place
of attachment and detachment in the Christian life.

1926–9: A painful crisis, following on Teilhard's being obliged to
cease teaching at the Institut Catholique in Paris (May 1925), and
which is reflected in the bitter criticism of *Le Sens humain* (1929).

Teilhard's most active years, in the field of scientific research,
were between 1930 and 1939. During that period he produced
84 articles or notes (there were 17 in 1930 alone); 1921–9 brought
46 of which one, in 1922, was his doctoral thesis (in 1926 there were
10 articles). Starting with 1940 his scientific writing became less
prolific (33 articles from 1940 to 1955). On the other hand, during
these years he wrote numerous essays, sociological, philosophical and
spiritual.

Nevertheless it is interesting to note that, unlike Pascal, Teilhard's
closing years brought a return to strictly scientific work, accompanied, too, by a 'personal elaboration' of his ideas.[58]

CONCLUSION

To conclude, we may attempt an over-all interpretation of Teilhard's psychology, as related to his thought.

It seems that his reserves of exceptional *sensibility*, itself made up
of intuitive emotivity but also of passional energy, were mobilized
to serve an *intellectual* vocation, of which it was the soul. There was
a twofold dialectical tension, the one between the two components
of the heart, the other between heart and thought.

Teilhard's concern was to confront the apparently contradictory terms of a dramatic problem: the opposition between Christianity and man, between God and the world, between sacred and secular history.

In virtue of an absolute logical necessity, checked by the facts, he strove to establish that the whole of the reality of becoming is governed by the same law, to embrace the whole of history in the continuity of one and the same structure, to unite in synthesis all the orders of the real: everything converges towards the one, everything is creative communion, everything is a bringing together of beings and persons in the unity of love.

To demonstrate this as a Fact, known in the first place by personal response and as something personally lived, was Teilhard's constant preoccupation, his *idée fixe*, the passion of his life. It was fostered by a religious enthusiasm, since, in the final unanimity for which he looked, he saw Christ.

However, in so far as he had to make use of ideas and words, this intellectual effort was abstract; and the psychological mobilization he brought into play could be achieved only by partially inhibiting the normal movement of sensibility in relation to individual persons and things.

It is clear that Teilhard retained his power of being interested in the individuality of beings: his whole life is evidence of his capacity for friendship, for resolute devotion, for perceptive tenderness. He could love, and was loved.

At the same time, it is clear—and this we know from Teilhard's own admission—that his intellectual and, in a sense, his mystical passion, impeded the opening-up—the output, we might say—of his sensibility. His bias was towards the 'universal' and the 'general'. Science and philosophy had 'eaten him up'. The more so, in that he had, to his loss, been subjected to influences that were at once valuable and fraught with danger: his education at home and at school, his aristocratic background, his geographic, with which went his spiritual, exile. Here, indeed, privilege worked both ways.

It is hardly astonishing, therefore, that these factors sometimes should have prevented him (as he admits, again, himself) from feeling as much pity as he might have done for human suffering, and from devoting himself above all to justice and the immediate service of his fellow-men. Although he was the complete converse of the ultra-conservative or reactionary, Teilhard, wrapped up in his own vocation, did not have the soul of a Mounier.

Prophet and seer, poet of history, building on a vast and comprehensive scale, clearing the way for others and creating extensive and forward-looking projects, Teilhard is the leader, the director of the work to be done. Living in the heights, he dominates us. And he is almost alone, moreover: he stands aside from, or ahead of, or above, the mass of men, even his friends. Yet he was happy to accept this adventure, exacting and full of danger though it was, for it was Another that led him.

Two images, both chosen by Teilhard himself, and both equally favoured by him, taken together as complementary to one another, symbolize his life: *iron* and *fire*. Both envisage the absolute; but the absolute of truth is in tension with the absolute of love.[59]

Chapter 2

The Intuition and the Project

Two subjects must first be examined, Teilhard's fundamental intuition and his project.

If, as Bergson[1] would have it, a central intuition is the soul and leaven of a thought that, seeking to recapture it, expresses itself in many different verbal forms, then, in the case of Teilhard, it sprang from an *existential* experience, from a profound awareness of the drama of his own days, from a certainty that Christianity and man, at present dissociated from one another, are in fact indispensable to, and complementary to, one another.

I THE MODERN CRISIS OF CONSCIOUSNESS

Deeply involved in the modern world by his scientific commitment,[2] Teilhard shared its deep-seated aspirations at the same time as he was aware of its disorder and the crisis it was passing through. With close sympathy, he felt its unrest and was sharply aware of the causes and reasons that produced the prevalent despair.

A number of discoveries, marked and symbolized by the names of Galileo, Darwin and Freud, have, in fact, completely revolutionized the consciousness of modern man.

In earlier times there was something reassuring in our view of the universe, as being centred on the earth, with no knowledge of the infinite dimensions of time and space, confined within a series of concentric spheres, static and with no global evolution.[3] The existence of God and his attributes were apparent in the visible order of beings, in the timeless stability of structures and essences, and in the rationality of all things. A supernatural hope opened up spontaneously for man's desire and offered him a transcendent conclusion, after the wretchedness that is normal to his existence. The feeling of the liberty of the person was warranted by its very naiveté. Living within comparatively restricted and familiar groups, in an unquestioned social hierarchy, man had not yet

31

fully experienced the critical emancipation of individual reflexion.[4]

However, a progressive re-orientation took place under the influence of the following factors:[5]

Between God and man, hitherto directly juxtaposed, a 'new star' had made its way, the *World*, which drains off mankind's religious energies.[6]

This world is not simply a physical reality: it is also a spiritual *value*, and, even more than an existing entity, it is an objective to be realized. 'The *deep* religious movement of our time seems to be characterized by the appearance in human consciousness of the *universe*—the universe seen as a *natural whole more noble* than man, and therefore equivalent for man to a God (finite or not). The features of this God are still indistinct. More clearly than the God himself we can distinguish his dawning radiance: we see it shining from the direction in which Life, and Truth, and Spirit are moving. Of that irradiation there can be no doubt.'[7]

The static cosmos has become a moving cosmos, characterized by a *genesis*, and progressing towards an end. The universe, possessing not simply a local but a substantial, deep-seated, movement, has a *history as a whole*. This history is convergent. 'The modern world . . . is born, body and soul, from the discovery of the organic time of evolution. The nebula of monads climbs in a spiral, and as it climbs is compressed upon itself.' In this history there is, too, something of the divine; it is 'a gesture charged with the absolute and the divine, in which the spiritualizing activity of beings emerges as a sacred energy'.[8] Moreover, the reservoir of vital forces is inexhaustible.

As a result, man has awoken 'apparently once and for all to the consciousness of his planetary *responsibilities* and planetary future.'[9] 'In earlier times, a hundred and fifty years ago, we used to think that we were like passive and irresponsible spectators, looking at the magnificent scene of the earth that surrounded us: we were still children. Now we understand that we are men with work to do, dedicated to a vast enterprise; we feel that we are the living atoms of a universe in forward progress: we have grown to manhood'.[10] In earlier days, the fate of the individual obscured the collective destinies of the whole. 'There were plenty of tasks for men, but there was no human task, and still less any specific universal task, involved in creation.'[11] Today, 'the existence of the smallest monad is seen to be bound up with and synchronous with the whole evolution of things'.[12] Moreoever, 'the forces of self-evolution, once they have been appropriately stimulated, are ready to leap into action and are even now beginning to do so'.[13]

Science and technology asserted man's *mastery* of the world, while at the same time *economic* advances, 'throwing men together', were making them conscious of their unity.

Thus mankind, 'in a world that had suddenly become too big and too organized, temporarily lost its God'.[14]

And yet, in spite of appearances, this new humanism—this sense of the human—has a religious nature, and within it a Presence lies hidden: from its faith, it derives the spirit of universalism, of the absolute, of sacrifice, the need to pursue some aim that is greater than man, the aspiration towards unity and unanimity, the pre-sentiment of an all-embracing harmony.[15] Even in its atheism, mankind still experiences the influence of a formative period that included God, and is animated, in its earthly projects, by a spiritual fire hidden in the earth.[16] How, indeed, could the religious spirit grow weaker, when we remember that the capacity for religion is essentially linked to hominization?

Moreover, in contrast to eastern mysticisms (which are all more or less Manichaean)[17] this mysticism, which fits in with the con-sciousness of the West, is *directly derived from Christianity* and the spirit of the Incarnation: this is by virtue of the value it attributes to time, to history and to matter, of the effort it makes to preserve the multiple in unity, and, finally, of its concept of some fulfilment that will be possible for man and of a convergence of all things.[18]

If, then, the World-god, the God of earthly hopes, is far from answering man's deep-seated desires, or fulfilling his boundless vocation, he is none the less the expression, imperfect no doubt, of an absolute, the witness of a quest and a need. Modern conscious-ness lays down certain *a priori* conditions for the delineation of the true God that it awaits:[19] the most fully alive section of humanity would refuse to accept a transcendent hope unless it included the legitimate values of humanism and nature, and the hope of a success-ful outcome, within time, to history.

Nevertheless, this transformation of man, this new 'slant' to his mind,[20] is accompanied by crises and heart-burnings:

The feeling of internal liberty, that gave man the illusion of being completely his own master, is threatened by the discovery of the unconscious: 'And now Analysis, after relentlessly dissecting the substance of our bodies, is beginning to disclose a complex, fragile, tissue in what we thought was the most spiritual part of our substance, . . . to our horror, we are discovering that we are made up, even in that part of ourselves we thought so lofty and sacred, of a monstrous web woven from all sorts of strands.'[21]

Even more hopelessly than Pascal imagined, man feels that he is lost and has been robbed of all significance in the spatial and temporal vastness of the world, wandering in 'an obscure corner of nature', and at the same time carried along by a torrent of energy towards a future wrapped in mystery.[22]

He feels isolated and lost, too, in a humanity that has become inordinately enlarged; the flexibility of social relations has been transformed into impersonal and 'concentrational' mechanical devices; and the conflict between the emancipated individual person and social or political pressures has become more acute.[23]

Modern man is beginning to envisage, more clearly than before, the possibility of a collective disappearance—of the death of the species.[24]

Moreover, there have been dramatic episodes and tragic conflicts in the political and social field to make man realize that his contradictions are permanent.

Operating together, all these factors have produced an 'existential fear', a 'cosmic anguish', a 'panic crisis', as though under the 'psychological shock of a sudden awakening in the night'.[25]

In the very midst of his triumphs, modern man finds himself at a loss, and is vaguely conscious of the nihilistic logic of his atheism and of his powerlessness to use for the fulfilment of man the forces that he claims to have made his own. Abandoned to despair,[26] a mankind without God has no valid reasons for anticipating a future and an end for itself. With the increased vulnerability that comes with its increased critical insight, it is now in a position where it may attempt to dam the stream of life. Man's great project is unrealizable without the presence, as a permanent stimulus, of a living absolute, without the hope, too, of a transcendent outcome to sanctify and finally restore significance to his effort.[27]

II THE HUMAN CONDITION

In the form it now takes, this experience stems, too, from man's ontological condition. 'The horror of the terrifying machine he is caught up in,' the agony of feeling imprisoned in the 'cosmic bubble', the despair of seeing himself ringed in with no possible outlet, claustrophobia, 'the essential distress of the atom lost in the universe', the strain of time that brings disintegration and corruption, the contradiction between the 'fragmentation of beings' and the need for the absolute, the incorruptible and final, man's inability to stand up against the blind brutality of determinist forces, and, above all, the stumbling block of death ('the dark impenetrable wall'). 'What is the reason for this bondage of toil in which we are imprisoned? Why should we pursue our quest any further? Why should we go on building? Why even continue to reproduce our kind? It does not call for much experience of life to realize how widely, and how agonizingly, such questions are asked even by the humblest folk.' We meet the sadness 'that comes from the splitting up of our lives and their lack of significance', dispersion, routine and, above all, boredom: 'Oh, if only we could feel that we were doing something that mattered!'[28]

Enslaved and imprisoned, man feels that his future is a dead-end, and that he must find some escape. Quite apart from sin, which is an 'historic' accident, all this is part of the 'penalty of individuation', and by that very fact it is linked with thought, conscious of the natural limits of existence. Sometimes one catches an echo of Pascal, but a modern thinker would find in such sentiments the concept of estrangement. It may not be rash, perhaps, to attach them to a biblical source, in particular to the anthropology expressed in the Psalms.

As we shall note later, this panoramic view suffers from the lack of a more exact analysis of man's economic, social and political estrangement—of the individual and collective violence that is expressed in permanent oppressive systems and inhuman institutions. Although not directly applied to these mechanically applied forces, the cry of the prophets might well have stimulated Teilhard to a more clearly expressed examination of one of the most shocking forms of 'human misery'.[29] Pascal's irony, for all his gentility, did not spare 'the bloated armies whose hands and strength are only for the rulers', or the contingent nature of the strength and origin of property.[30]

III CHRISTIANITY AND THE MODERN WORLD

The only spiritual force that could both answer the problem that man has always been faced with, give new life to modern man, and restore his faith in his destiny, is *Christianity*. Unfortunately, a deep gulf cuts it off from the whole body of contemporary mankind.

In the first place, there must inevitably be a conflict between the World-God and the transcendent God of Christianity.[31] God, who formerly could be seen clearly, is now obscured or eclipsed. 'The natural power of adoration is now directed towards an object, the universe, which, to modern man, appears to be opposed to the Christian God.'[32]

The world, boundless yet 'hermetically sealed', self-sufficient, is a watertight compartment, with no supernatural outlet. The human mind finds it impossible to 'enter *phenomenally* into direct contact with any trans- or super-human'.[33]

Nevertheless, for all its custody of the spiritual truth and the conditions of salvation, Christianity is, in a number of ways, responsible for the attitude taken by the modern mind. Teilhard is not sparing in his analysis of these, and they may be enumerated as follows:

— A lack of receptiveness to modern humanism and the aspirations of the new consciousness; narrowness of outlook; a lack of a Catholic capacity to assimilate contemporary values.[34]

— The persistence of Manicheanism, Jansenism and dualism in doctrinal teaching and piety.[35]

— A defective concept of charity.[36]

— An incomplete, if not obsolete, notion of God.[37]

— Predominance, over a concrete and physical concept of the Incarnation, of juridical and moralistic concepts.[38]

— An incorrect interpretation of original sin, of the mystery of the Cross, of resignation to suffering, and of renunciation and detachment.[39]

— An unrealistic attitude towards the world and lack of any real contact with it.[40]

— The treating of salvation simply from the point of view of the individual.[41]

— A static concept of the universe: 'The spirit is no longer under way, it is not going anywhere, it is simply hanging on: nature is complete. Perfection can consist, for men, only in an individual ascent towards the supernatural.'[42]

As a result, Christianity suffers from a lack of appeal;[43] and for the same reasons Christians feel a certain uneasiness.[44]

These criticisms, which are sometimes expressed too strongly, but without rancour or partiality, are not aimed at Christianity but only at the attitude of some of the faithful; they derive from a deep love of the Church and share the freedom of the manner of the prophets. They coincide with much[45] that has commonly been remarked and in fact, sometimes even lag behind the development of contemporary theological thought (with which Teilhard was not in a position to keep abreast); nor do they seem surprising to the bulk of Catholics since the latter have awoken to a sense of clear-minded and courageous self-criticism, the prelude to a remarkable readjustment. In analysing modern atheism, Teilhard correctly emphasizes its essential factors.

Deeply and essentially attached to his faith as a Christian, and loyal to his Church, Teilhard is convinced that Christianity is the *only* salvation of the world in history. This, however, is only provided it regains, both by a complete rediscovery of its mystery and a modification of the terms it uses, its power of attraction, and regains its youth in contact with and in its action on the world: and this while remaining completely true to tradition and in an effort of Catholic universalism to assimilate, baptize and Christify the legitimate values accepted by modern consciousness.

For Teilhard, a *mystical* experience[46] is the intimately personal source of this faith and of the apostolate it impels him to: the experience, in fact, of St Ignatius's *Spiritual Exercises*, in which the different aspects of the Christian mystery are re-lived in prayer, and in which, accepting the Incarnation by which we are redeemed, man, now converted and anxious to pass on the evangelical message, seeks to share with his fellow-men his enamoured vision of a transfigured universe, of a history in which God becomes all in all, of a mystical body in which God is willing to grow in his children until they meet in a final communion.[47]

Teilhard's concern, therefore, was, while using the language and forms of thought of his contemporaries,[48] to show that man's

existence in history is unjustified and unjustifiable unless it includes
the fact, and the recognition, not only of a divine absolute but also of
an incarnation in time of that absolute, as expressed in Christianity.
A human universe is absurd, unreal and inacceptable, if it does not,
in its essence, involve a *victory over death*; time makes no sense if it
does not emerge into eternity. And man is faced by a tragic
dilemma, 'suicide or adoration'.[49] 'Must we, yes or no, recognize a
direction, a future, a way out to the universe?' 'Is life a through
road or a dead-end?' How are we 'to set men's minds at rest?' 'By
what hope can we preserve in the heart of the human mass the
blessed appetite for research and progress?'[50]

It was thus that, as a Christian scientist, a seeker and a priest, as
a man with a passionate love for the world and for God, that Teilhard felt that he was called to restore contact between modern man
and the Church, between humanism and Christianity,[51] between
'those who worship Christ and those who worship the world',
between 'the two great currents that today share the world between
them: the passion for the earth that is to be built up, and the
passion for the heaven that is to be attained'.[52] This double vocation
as child of the earth and child of heaven is the soul of Teilhard's
work.[53]

The Operative Method

It was from this determination that the method we find in Teilhard's work was derived: starting with the assumption of universal
reality, it seeks to understand it in order to transform it.

I A UNIVERSAL PHENOMENOLOGY

Reality presents itself to experience as an immense sum of phenomena, belonging to different levels of beings, and forming one
organic structural whole, potentially intelligible.

His first approach to truth is made by scientific methods, adapted
to each sector of the real: as geologist and biologist, Teilhard left an
important body of work.

From that starting point, however, he moved up to a higher form
of knowledge, *philosophical* in order, to express the nature and

meaning of reality: his books and essays are part of this quest, whose object and method we must now examine.

In the widest and deepest sense of the word, this philosophy may be called '*phenomenology*'.[54] It seeks for a 'vision' of the real,[55] but a vision that is intellectual and logical, governed by all the mind's resources.

This phenomenology is *positive* and scientific: it is based on factual data, on the truth-content of phenomena[56] and on experimental verification of hypotheses.[57]

At the same time it is not positivist, nor simply descriptive, since it expands, by interpretation, the observation of the whole of the immediate evidence:[58] conscious of the value of thought and language, it seeks the logical *reason* for the real, and finds even the ultimate criterion of truth in the 'total coherence of the universe'.[59] It believes it can translate and express objective reality in *idea*; it goes beyond analysis in a constructive synthesis, which is seen as the theoretical picture of the real.

This phenomenology is inspired by a fundamental choice, which consists in the *affirmation of being*;[60] though initially vague and rudimentary,[61] this affirmation becomes consciously explicit in the recognition and affirmation of an absolute reality, of a plenitude that is at once undefined and perfect, sufficient and necessary, and manifested in phenomena. There is the having of being, but there is also being. The 'significance' of being, and its intuitive emotive power, produce, according to Teilhard, a dynamic act of will, which is tension and intention, demand, commitment, preference, intellectual love.[62] What has to be done is both to define more exactly the nature of this being and vindicate its spontaneous affirmation.

This phenomenology is positive, logical and ontological; but it is also *historic*, because the real presents itself, both to intuition and to reflexion, as within time:[63] in the form and shape and manifestation of phenomena, being is seen as a movement and a progress towards an *end*, and evolutionary time can be understood through its term, and vindicated by the syntheses attained in successive stages, which are the prelude to an absolute and unsurpassable end. The time of the world, far from being an indefinite oscillation or flow, is a genesis; and its passage is not the logical unfolding of something pre-contained but the creative new production of an increase of being.[64] Finally, the movement of time is not manifested only in localized or partial sectors: the world proceeds towards its end in its totality.[65]

Teilhard's phenomenology seeks to discover the significance and the laws of this movement of the whole of history. Cardinal in his thought is the assertion that pinpoints the dialectic of science and philosophy, and thus of theology: it is *in as much as* and *because* the world of phenomena is historical in nature (both in movement and with a final purpose) that it can be grasped by a reflexion that reaches out beyond it, even while forming part of it: a reflexion that simply makes explicit what is already implicit in the evidence, and so discloses rather than invents: and which, accordingly, always seeks to be based on experience and scientific.

This phenomenology must necessarily be *universal* and synthetic, and must take the whole of reality into account: truth would cancel itself out if it failed to take into account the concrete totality of the elements of the real.[66]

In the first place, accordingly, it rejects any dissociation of the real, and, in consequence, the *dualism* of matter and spirit: it insists on the fundamental link between man and the world, that makes a valid discovery of the truth possible.[67] The substantial connection of body and soul is even the criterion and the type of all reality.[68]

If we break down Teilhard's phenomenology and reconstruct it in a hierarchy of sections, it includes a cosmology, an anthropology, a metaphysics, and an ontology. In an order distinct from these, it is associated with a theology.[69]

— *Cosmology*, or the natural philosophy of matter and life: itself founded on a reflexion on the data provided by science.[70]

— *Anthropology*, or the science of man, his nature and existential vocation.

— *Metaphysics*, or the science of the origin of being and the absolute conditions of existence: it is here that philosophy arrives at the affirmation of God by reason.

— *Ontology*, or the science of being, of its degrees or levels ('spheres' is the word that Teilhard liked to use).

Theology, the science of what we receive from revelation, is in one sense part of this science of phenomena, of this philosophy of phenomena or phenomenology, in as much as the revelation of God comes about through the facts of history; the 'logic' of reason continues to operate, with some degree of autonomy, even though working on a content that is supernatural in origin.

In Teilhard, theology is carried further by a *spirituality*, the science of the activity to be put in motion in order to bring about the ultimate fulfilment of man's destiny in the universe.

Finally, the whole of this quest has an *existential* character, since it centres on the problem of man's fulfilment in solidarity with the universe, and defines the conditions of that fulfilment. The affirmation of being, whether spontaneous or reflective, cannot be dissociated from a negative experience of distance and separation: present or absent, it is apprehended in the fragility, individuality and multiplicity of phenomena; located by its very attempt to elude us, and experienced through a fundamental dissatisfaction.

For all its intended universality, this logic of the real does not claim to be a complete and detailed science of each of its sectors; Teilhard is content to extract their essence and treat them in their outstanding features.

Moreover, apart from two full-length books,[71] forty years of a busy life was not long enough to allow Teilhard to produce a real synthesis of his thought: confident of the value of his initial intuitions, he developed it in a series of separate, overlapping, essays, representing a continual search for and approach to a truth that always eluded complete expression.

Finally, although this admission does not diminish its objective relevance, Teilhard often presents his thought only as a witness, as an attempt to reconcile the demands he recognized as a scientist with those of his faith.[72] We should remember, however, that one of the properties of every philosophy is that it bears the mark of one man's character, and reflects a personal choice.

In the very width of its scope, which makes it akin to the great systems, in particular to those of Hegel and Marx, the originality of Teilhard's phenomenology is apparent. At the same time he used a highly classical method: the passage from fact to theory, from experience to idea. His procedure is close to the traditional progress, that recognizes being in its manifestations, the infinite in the finite, the absolute in the relative, the necessary in the contingent, the end in the intention: and which seeks to make the real intelligible and rational. It is thus, as we shall see, that the experiential and scientific recognition of a structural complexity and of a progress of that complexity, *points to* and leads by induction to, an interior spiritual reality and a progress of that reality: there is a *passage* from the less real to the more real. More generally, the notion of *analogy* or correspondence plays an essential part in Teilhard, and being is conceived in depth,[73] as a network of unified planes: this is a profoundly human concept, which is the essence of knowledge, poetry and religion. Unlike Pascal, who in at least one well-known passage separates the 'orders' more effectively than he unites them, Teilhard brings out the metaphysical and religious fertility of science,[74] the note of being and of the absolute that can be read in it.

Again, Teilhard's refusal to consider his work as a 'final explanation of things—a metaphysics'[75] seems to have been dictated by an insufficiently bold appreciation of his undertaking as a whole. After all, what he gives us is an all-embracing system of thought that, although it uses the medium of particular conceptions and 'representational' schemata, leads to the whole of truth that man can attain. In the 'system', Teilhard rejects only the rigid framework of conceptualism; in the method of approach to truth, only the supposed pride of a rationalism that is not receptive of experience; in certainty, only the claim to exhaust the infinity of the real.[76]

Metaphysics, from which Teilhard disassociates himself, represents for him a purely abstract and *a priori* science of being, a geometrical deduction of conclusions from premises. Whatever may be the position of such metaphysics in the history of thought, we may well ask whether, even in the most deductive idealism, it is as divorced from experience as Teilhard imagines: and there can be no doubt that its value is derived only from its starting point in the concrete (material or spiritual), by its reference to the concrete and its correspondence with the real. Although Descartes and Kant, Hegel or Hamelin, were obviously unable to extract the lesson of facts from its source to the extent that Teilhard could, yet they certainly claimed to express man's experience of the world; and the Thomistic proofs of the existence of God undoubtedly bring out the affirmation of the absolute that is part and parcel of man's condition. We shall see that the discovery of Omega Point, which is the Teilhardian absolute, does not differ essentially from the classical approaches: nor, indeed, could it. 'Profound' causality is indeed found by Teilhard *in the heart* of the phenomenon and by reflexion on facts; and he would be making a mistake himself if he thought that this affirmation of the absolute is independent of a requirement of thought, for the latter is embodied in his vision.

More generally, in spite of his avowed claim to remain strictly within the limits of natural experience (for the non-theological part of his thought), Teilhard could not avoid introducing all the great categories that are specifically philosophical: being and non-being, absolute and relative, unity and multiplicity, order (or finality) and disorder, necessity and contingence, eternity and temporality, interior and exterior, object and subject, liberty and determinism, consciousness and unconsciousness, condition, relation, identity, analogy, person.

Thus, while it retains the appearance of a cosmology, of a physical study of nature, Teilhard's quest inevitably extends itself to become what in fact it is: a philosophical phenomenology, an 'ultra-physics'.[77] It lies between science and philosophy; the distinction is both respected and transcended, for the knowledge of the world in so far as it is a *history* brings reflexion to a grasp (intellectual, at least) of being and value.[78] Being emerges as truth in the discovery of the movement of phenomena towards a maximum of unity, in the expression of this movement by thought, and in man's participation in the movement: thought operates the passage from the manifesta-tion of things to their law and their reality. The appeal, at a later stage, to faith, will only give a new consistence and new certainty to this truth of the real that has come from reason.[79]

Later on we shall see in what this *real* consists, for Teilhard: it is the world or the universe, but *in so far* as this world is itself united to man and thought by him, and *in so far* as man himself, the thought of the world, is united to God, his present and future term. There are levels or degrees of being, some more concrete, some less, connected vertically by a network of relationships; there are unities, some more unified, some less, and therefore more spiritualized and interiorized or less, that are associated even in their discontinuity; there are liberties, defined by their internal tension, and moving towards the supreme liberty.

And man's knowledge of the real proceeds *from the abstract to the concrete*. Still abstract, sensible knowledge of qualitative multiplicity is transcended in the knowledge of *phenomena*; and the logical coherence of scientific representation, in one sense, and in its own order, certainly arrives at the essence of the real. *Philosophical* speculation, too, starting from the world, also attains, in its own field, a knowledge of the absolute, but in an abstract mode.[80] Already stimulated by these earlier activities, knowledge of the subject by himself, in reflexion, develops through his knowledge of other human subjects, within social relations and love: a higher and more concrete mode. It remains for the ensemble of practical experience, which reaches its highest point in religious experience (itself conceptualized in theology) to give concrete embodiment to the ensemble of knowledge already gathered by man. This is what gives full authority to his personal affirmation of reality. This, finally, is what enables him to arrive at *concrete possession* of being, at least to such possession as is compatible with the conditions of existence in time.[81] In this sense, Teilhard's thought (as is true, moreover, of all thought), while including some certainties—and whether it reflects on natural data or enriches itself as it proceeds by revealed data—is always at a distance from its goal, and is never complete: it is enough for it to be not only a moment of knowledge of the truth of being, but a *mediation* of it.

II A DIALECTICAL PHENOMENOLOGY

Comprehension of an experienced fact that is essentially historic, and therefore creative of something new, could be expressed only in a dialectic.

While the normal approach of thought to a static reality is to *enclose* ideas in a continually more general idea, to include them in a continually wider theory, in which they appear as particular cases, to arrange them in a logical structure, the expression of a history of progress calls for an original method that brings out the relation between being and becoming.

Teilhard's phenomenology develops the convergent movement of the whole history of the cosmos only by disclosing its successive supersessions: from the primitive turning about of material energy to that turning about of spiritual energy and ecstasy in God,[82] new and higher realities arise through an opposition that nevertheless preserves those from which they emerge.[83] Consubstantial with the world and the spirit, whose movement it stimulates, *negation* is fulfilled in an affirmation that confirms and continues what it supersedes.[84]

The spirit maintains identity in negation in the principle both of being and of becoming, linking the same and the other, the continuous and the discontinuous.[85] The *constant* (or recurrent) coincides with the *new*, being simply superseded, without being contradicted, by it: through 'critical thresholds' and breaks, the conditions and preparations for a coming event are radically metamorphosed. This structural dialectic may be reasonably well expressed by the term *transformation* or transfiguration, for it connotes both negation and affirmation.[86]

To this objective reality there corresponds, on the plane of thought and by virtue of its fundamental connexion with the real, a sort of dialectical *category*,[87] that is to say a capacity to understand and express the forming-anew of phenomenal being: a category that is a personal and living *act* of the mind.

Thus the universe, as conceived by Teilhard, is as far as it could be from a peaceful fulfilment in the positive plentitude of being through spontaneous passage from potentiality to act. While it clearly manifests an overall harmony, and a mutual implication of man and things, and while it is permeated by an unconquerable spiritual energy, at the same time it bears on all sides, and since its very beginning, the marks of the rupture between matter and spirit; and all unification is the fruit of a struggle against dispersion.

Like the dialectic of Hegel and Marx, and above all like that of Christianity, this dialectic, whose *dramatic* and tragic[88] character should also be emphasized, makes it possible to express also the *tension* between the complementary and inseparable aspects of reality. In particular:

— The relation between the *degrees of being* (matter, life, man): the relation between emergence and the new, identity and negation, continuity and transcendence.

— The relation between *man* and the *universe*, the personal and the universal: 'It is through what is most incommunicably personal in us that we make contact with the universal.'[89]

— The relation between the real, as *objective*, and the real, as thought or interior to the subject.

— The relation between *natural reality* and *Christianity*: a relation of disjunction and subordinated unification.

— The relation between *Omega Point*, in as much as it fulfils and makes total the evolution of the universe, and in as much as it is distinct from it (or in as much as it transcends it): it must necessarily be at once total and incomplete.

While this dialectic is less abstract and scholarly than that of Hegel, and Marx or Hamelin, and while even its author (who avoids the word) hardly realized it consciously, it is none the less real; and it is this dialectic, by integrating propositions that are sometimes discontinuous or presented in succession, that amply vindicates them.[90]

It is implicit in the whole body of Teilhard's work, and it makes it possible, in particular, to dispel the disquiet aroused by the apparent one-sidedness of the biological representation of the history of the universe: for Teilhard, in fact, the history of man overlaps, on a transcendent plane, biological history, while still remaining closely bound up with it, and gives it significance.

Finally, Teilhard's dialectic is reminiscent of Pascal's and closer to it than one might imagine.[91]

Idealism and realism

The relation between objective reality and reflective reality is a particular case of the Teilhardian dialectic, and is clarified by it.

From Teilhard's constant attribution of personality to the world, it might appear that the universe is endowed with autonomous existence: the world exists in itself, as the global unity of a whole, progressing in history in its own being and towards being.

This *realism* reflects the spontaneous attitude of the scientist who is obediently receptive of the message contained in facts and formulates their data: an initial impulse, violent and passionate, that takes the form of a loving embrace, drives Teilhard to the heart of things, in the light of an intuitive illumination and with an ear ready to listen to what they can tell him.

While it coincides (though perhaps with some difficulty) with the idea of a single and universal spiritual energy and of a consciousness that extends to every being, this fundamental realism which Teilhard shares with Bergson, divides him, on this point, from his friend Edouard Le Roy, whose idealism recognizes only thought.[92]

It is also *methodological* and deliberate: Teilhard refuses to be tied down to a system and retains the liberty of elementary commonsense and of an unsophisticated straightforward approach. He does not

put forward the problem of the conditions that allow man to perceive and affirm objectivity; he does not draw up a table of mental
categories; like Bergson, he rejects from the outset the Kantian
enquiry 'What can we know?' The world, *given* to man in a primitive, constitutive relation of existence, in a substantial interconnexion coextensive with the totality of space and time[93]—the
world is presented to knowledge, subject to the necessary methods;[94]
and truth, in degrees that differ but are absolute in their own order,
is patient of being affirmed by man and possessed by man. And
history, in which this truth is to be found, has its own laws and
objective determinism.[95]

At the same time an essential *reversal* takes place in this specially
favoured prospect, for the universe involves *man*; and at the term
of vital evolution, man may picture the universe to himself and
think, in Julian Huxley's phrase, that 'Man is nothing else than
evolution becoming conscious of itself', and that 'the consciousness
of each one of us is evolution looking at itself and reflecting on
itself'.[96] Man, 'the centre of perspective' is also the 'centre of construction': he 'imposes on the cosmos first a certain stuff, and then
a certain structure'. He 'occupies a position in nature at which the
convergent lines are not only visual but structural'.[97] He seeks, in
particular, *meaning* for the past 'so that the world may be true for us
at this moment'.[98] And 'the truth about man is the truth about the
universe for man, that is to say simply the truth'.[99] The very
progress of science shows the superseding of unsophisticated realism
in favour of an idealism that recognizes the indispensable part
played by the constructive activity of thought.[100]

To take it still further, the universe is without value except
through man and *in man*, who is its consciousness and its fulfilment:
the universe is a universe of man, and its past exists only for man,
who projects it into the past as a condition of its present being. If
man is *relationship to the universe*, he also transcends it; he is the only
true value. And all that matters is to define the *significance of man*
and his history, a history that is tied up with that of the world but
is henceforth human.[101]

Although Teilhard often speaks of the universe as a *thing*, he
never forgets, implicitly, the *act* of objectifying operated by man.[102]
By introducing a man-world *dialectical relationship*, the presence of
man avoids the objections of Kant or Valéry,[103] and the philoso-

phical difficulties that would arise from the idea of an autonomous whole.

It seems, therefore, that in spite of an objectivist terminology, when Teilhard speaks of the 'world', he means—closely related to things—a spiritual reality: persons and the organism they make up.

Thus Teilhard provides a dialectical solution to the opposition between *realism* and *idealism*: it is true that the world is real, and it is true that it is thought of as an object by man. And, unlike Engels, the 'dialectic of nature' constructed by Teilhard represents together a real movement of things and a movement bound up with man's becoming conscious of it. Even more, man's emergence in history introduces for Teilhard a new dialectic, characterized by liberty.[104]

Underlying Teilhard's lyrical attitude towards the universe[105] we must always therefore disclose a *human* reality: if man is placed in the universe, the universe is placed in man, and the history of the universe is ultimately the history of man. If the world contains and goes beyond man, it is also true to say that man contains and goes beyond the world.

III THE PLANES OF THE PHENOMENON: PHILOSOPHY AND THEOLOGY

Teilhard's dialectical method comes into its own in his expression of the relationship between nature and grace, reason and faith. Rejecting entirely the facile alternative of a logical synthesis, it makes it possible to retain both their distinction and their union.

The Christian phenomenon appears at the heart of the pheno-menon and at the centre of history: the natural reality of the phenomenon of man in the perspective of science coexists with the supernatural reality of the same phenomenon in the perspective of Christian revelation.

Distinct from one another, these two realities would be abstract and unreal if they remained in separation: the reality of man-in-the-world (and of the world-in-man) is, in fact, supernatural, by virtue of the infinite charity of God and the act of the redemptive Incar-nation;[106] at the same time the action, at once human and super-natural, of liberty, is indispensable to the world and to the fulfilment of 'natural history'. While the order of nature, accordingly, deserves a special study, with the data supplied by observation, this order is, in fact, *assumed* by Christianity, and action in the world is, in fact, an action governed by the supernatural. Nature is the image of grace,[107] and between the two distinct orders there exists a *correspondence* that gives them a common solidarity: their divergence, like that of the meridians on a sphere, is converted into coincidence at their pole.[108]

Although they were never completely successful, perhaps, in doing so, Teilhard's writings respected in principle this double requirement of *separation* and *unity*. His most fully-worked out book, *The Phenomenon of Man*, appeals only to a philosophical reflexion on the evidence provided by the ascertainable facts of science. Similarly *Le Milieu Divin* is an essay in Christian spirituality, that obviously belongs to the order of revelation. Other unpublished works belong more to theology: the same is true of the last section of *The Phenomenon of Man* ('the Christian phenomenon').

Nevertheless, as Teilhard himself recognized,[109] his Christian vision influenced his philosophical interpretation of the natural history of the world: in one sense, while remaining scientific, *The Phenomenon of Man* belongs to 'Christian philosophy'.[110] Implicitly or explicitly, the whole of Teilhard's work is inspired by faith. And it is, in any case, the pervasive influence of Christianity that makes him reject out of hand Plato's and Plotinus's notion of a material universe that has fallen from the divine harmony, and accept the contrary fundamental idea of a *history* in time, extending to the totality of things, of the subordinate value of a *nature* that is capable of rejoining its origin.

CONCLUSION

Apart from certain external appearances, Teilhard's realist objectivism makes common ground with the reflective philosophy that starts from the *cogito* and continually questions every datum in order to include it in a truth, progressively more fully disclosed, that man is truly conscious of re-creating or reconstructing. But, in arriving at a synthesis, he refuses any compromise with the dualism that continually threatens the reflexion upon itself of the ego: there is no trace in Teilhard of a dissociation of thought and content, body and soul, matter and spirit.

We shall see later how fully Teilhard was committed to the *personalist* current, which he had the merit of attaching firmly to history and to the world, while at the same time he tinged it with a dramatic anxiety about the meaning and direction of existence and offered it universalist projects and goals.

Finally, the place of Teilhard's philosophy in French tradition is defined by the affirmation of *liberty*, by the search for the conditions that allow man to build himself up in action on the real, to make being exist for him while at the same time welcoming the gratuitousness of its generous gift.

The introduction to the supernatural universe (itself the answer both to man's original condition and to his place in history), presents man's liberty with a new problem; but at the same time it gives it the concrete means of fulfilling itself, and fulfilling the universe as it moves with Christ towards its supreme end.

Chapter 3

A Phenomenology of History

Teilhard's phenomenology, like that of Hegel and Marx, is *historical*. It examines and describes the main developments of a *genesis*—that of the material world, of living forms, and of man—and points out both its continuity and the thresholds which it crosses. The reality of the world, essentially incomplete, is *temporal*: directed towards an end, it flows in a becoming which is at once change and progress. Just as an organism, the totality of the world is capable of growth; and time, far from being a passive framework or container, is the living and creative energy of that development.

A fundamental constant, a law of recurrence, governs this becoming: the *growth of unification*. Not only is the world at each stage a unity of elements, themselves unified and structured, but this global unity advances in quality: in mathematical language, its derivative is positive.[1]

This history is not a turbulence;[2] it is not only metamorphosis, but also a directed growth of beings towards more being through increase of unity. The universe is convergent in structure. And 'to be more, is to be more fully united'.[3]

A series of *five* successive, mutually complementary, *propositions* allows Teilhard to describe what we might call the epic of this history in the progress of unity.

I MATTER

Here we meet a curious and inexplicable contrast with the inertia of determinisms, in other words with the normal stability of structures and movements; in particular, it runs counter to the regressive tendency produced in all forms of energy under the 'majestic and inflexible influence of entropy'.[4] Normally, that tendency is to loss and dissipation, to a movement towards the homogeneous and the most probable, and to uniformity in distribution. And yet, since matter created for itself structures of greater complexity which were the prerequisite condition of life, we already find in it this con-

tradictory 'spiral' phenomenon of involution, infolding or convergence.

Matter has always had a history;[5] it is subject to a genesis; it is in
process of ascending towards higher states. Matter is a limitless
source of energies, with the potentiality to produce forms in which it
will go beyond itself. It is the 'matrix of spirit'.[6] 'The world, says
Teilhard, 'seems to me to "fall" forwards and upwards upon the
spiritual.'[7] And this is because it is already, in its heart, permeated
by vital energy and endowed with a minimum degree of consciousness and interiority.[8]

II LIFE

Unification is seen most clearly in the order of appearance of the
biological forms that, after lengthy preparatory stages, have emerged
from material structures; in the multiple deployment of its divergent
lines and the intricacy of the specialized forms in which it is stabilized
and passed on,[9] the history of life discloses a transformation of
organisms in a determined direction.[10]

From tentative explorations and hesitancies, and in the course of
innumerable attempts,[11] an *increased structuration* is produced, and in
this the elements are continually more ordered and arranged; more
complex[12] and more sophisticated, the anatomical and psychological syntheses seem to condition and to reflect a progress both in
consciousness and in the autonomy that accompanies them; it is as
though a constant pressure, dominating and bringing together the
forces of determinism, were striving to bring about more spiritual
interiorities, as though the driving force of this animal upsurge was
the demand not only to think but also to act with more freedom.[13]

III MAN

The coming of man, prepared on a specially favoured axis, on a
central stem, by a more advanced structuration of the nervous
system and of the brain, but also by other morphological conditions
and, indirectly, by a mobilization of the whole universe,[14] the coming
of man,[15] in spite of being an 'infinitesimal morphological leap',[16]
introduces, paradoxically, a radical supersession. We now find not
only consciousness but reflective thought,[17] turned back upon itself,
emerging from a personal centre of freedom and capable of conscious creation, of indefinite newness, and receptive of the universal
absolute of values.

Though rooted in animality, the phenomenon of man is not comparable with it and transcends it: in spite of many analogies with the animal, man's biological structures, the hand in particular, indicate the absence in him of specialization, his indeterminism, and his potential universalism.[18]

Man is not a fortuitous or accidental[19] phenomenon, but one obviously prepared and, in a sense, willed—evolution's crowning success. Far from being an anomalous aberration, he is the key, the head, the growing point of the universe,[20] the 'supremely characteristic form of the cosmic phenomenon', 'the front-line of life', 'evolution become reflexively conscious of itself'.[21] Here we have a fact of planetary and even universal importance: the noosphere is grafted once and for all on the biosphere. A new physical energy has emerged, that is capable of renewing the very face of the earth: thought.[22]

IV MANKIND TODAY

Leaving aside what concerned Hegel and Marx—the dialectical process of the human advance of civilization[23]—Teilhard's phenomenology of history leaps across the centuries and proceeds by a study of the present phase of man's development: young though mankind is, Teilhard knows enough about its past to read in it the way its future is built.

Thus, in the continuation of the great transformation of the Renaissance and the more recent rediscovery of history, an important phenomenon is taking place:[24] a sloughing-off of man's old concepts, as he suddenly becomes conscious not only of the objective coherence of the whole development of space-time but also of the fact that he is the subject of anthropogenesis, and that it continues in him.[25] 'Zoologically and psychologically speaking, man, seen in the integration of his destiny with the cosmos, is still only at an embryonic stage—beyond which looms a wide fringe of the ultra-human.'[26]

Our present age is still, in fact, characterized by a dispersion of conscious minds, separated by their individual and collective egoisms, and is hardly emerging as yet from a phase of exaggerated respect for autonomy;[27] nevertheless it shows many signs that herald a coming together of men. Evolution, that seems to have come to a halt on the biological plane and to be marking time, is taking a fresh leap forward, like a multi-stage rocket,[28] in a *social* form, through the creation of mechanisms and metabolisms and of an 'indivisible' network of interdependence; these are being stimulated both by technical progress and also by extensive collective movements towards unification,[29] of which totalitarian regimes are simply aberrant exaggerations. 'An informed organization imposes a geometric order on the masses and seeks to give each individual a specialized function.'[30] Mankind progressively develops its structure and accepts the laws of a common order that assembles its different elements.

In the domain of *thought*, scientific effort is not only giving reality to a vision of a world transformed by work, but is bringing about co-operation in a common approach to intellectual problems, in the exchange of knowledge and inventions, the reduction of chance, the enriching of a collective hereditary memory, the general increase of 'grey matter'. The advance of automatic processes provides leisure, which can be employed in creative research. What is more, under the inspiration of collective research, the organized progress of science produces simultaneously a convergence of minds, a global increase of *psychic* energy and (through the development of instrumentation) a sort of interiorization of matter itself.[31]

In the order of the *heart*, too, the network of human inter-relationships is beginning to be charged with more intimacy and sympathy. 'From the moment when men have woken to an explicit consciousness of the evolution that carries them along, and begin to fix their eyes, as one man, on one same thing ahead of them, by that very fact they must surely begin to love one another.'[32] 'Relationships become ties of friendship.'[33] 'The atmosphere in which man lives becomes sustaining, warm and consistent.' 'With the sense of "universal unification" to which he is now alive, a wave of new life penetrates to the fibre and marrow of man's most trifling activities and desires. Everything lights up. Everything expands. Everything is filled with an essential flavour of the absolute . . . And everything is animated by a sweet breath of presence and love— which, rising from the supreme pole of personalization, sustains and nourishes the mutual affinities of individual existences as they move towards convergence.'

Moreover, mankind's internal conflicts cause it to seek more complete unity. 'The whole of history shows us this: after every revolution, and after every war, mankind has always emerged a little more cohesive, a little more united, in closer forms of organic relationships and with a stronger expectation of its common emancipation . . . After each crisis we find it more differentiated and yet more one . . . So how will it work out this time? If we are not already today witnessing the last convulsion of discord, then it must be here any moment: the hour is at hand when the human mass will close in on itself and gather all its members together within a finally achieved unity, with one and the same governance, mind, and orientation, reaching out to embrace the never-ceasing diversity of individuals and peoples. A little while still, and we shall form but one bloc. The whole mass is *setting*.'[34]

What is still more, mankind, imprisoned within inelastic limits[35] and compressed by the growth of population, is being forced by the very problems it has to face, to take the peaceful road of friendship, called on to transform itself into a community of brothers, constrained to organize itself.[36] This folding back on itself, in contrast again with the indefinite, strife-producing divergence of the animal species, is in conformity with man's biological nature.[37]

Thus to forced unification, produced by the energies generated by *compression*, is added free unification by consent, the latter stimulated by the energies of *attraction*, and by internal affinities: to the curve imposed by geography is added the curve imposed by the mind. In short, we have a universal phenomenon of *gravity*.[38]

In spite of efforts to resist it, in spite of crises and threats and dangers[39]—indeed, through its dissensions and conflicts[40]—humanity is closing in on itself and, in a word, becoming 'planetary' urged on by the demands of coexistence and collaboration. A spiritual current of love is forcing its way through, painfully but rich with promise, and a slow change of consciousness is being produced which is coming to grips with the future.[41]

This spiritual *co-reflexion*, of which socialization is only the visible sign, marks the crossing of a threshold, the emergence of a new state of man. Man is beginning to be raised to a higher level, not in the elevation of the individual of which Nietzsche dreamed, but in a completely new synthesis in which liberties are enriched and personality unfolds, and which testifies, in anticipation, to man's supreme vocation.

Here we meet again a fundamental metaphysical law of progress, already recognized in the earlier stages of the evolution of being: the convergences of matter and life were only the half-hidden symbol of this structural organization of society. Initiated at the very origin of man and persisting throughout his history, it has now, thanks to a number of favourable circumstances, reached a new level, or taken on a more rapid pace.[42]

The present crisis of growth through which mankind is passing is a realization both 'of what it lacks and of what it is capable': 'Mankind anticipates and expects'.[43] Man is beginning to react to the universe as a whole and feels that in some undefined way he is linked to the totality of beings. Thus the temperature of the noosphere (or, in scientific terms, its potential of energy) is continually and increasingly rising: 'the universe is heating up, is opening itself to the forces of love.'[44] The curve of the human phenomenon is becoming 'exponential'. *Man*, once more a spectator of evolution than an agent, is becoming the creative subject, and is forcing science itself to take him as the major object of its enquiry.[45]

Thus, 'painfully, through and by virtue of the activity of man' the new earth is emerging.[46] 'Like a huge flower,' mankind is closing in on itself. 'The true man is the man who gathers up, or will gather up, in himself the consciousness of the whole human layer.'[47]

V THE END OF HISTORY

There still remains a *last stage* to be gone through. Modern man is without doubt open to two temptations: that of selfish autonomy, which arises from intellectual loss of balance or from intoxication with freedom, and which fragments or disintegrates;[48] and that, again, of mechanical socialization which stifles personality and reduces it all to the same level in the anonymity of the mass. The serious dangers inherent in progress can be overcome only by 'a know-how-to-do, sufficiently expert to avoid the various traps and blind alleys' and a 'will-to-do strong enough not to retreat before any tedium, any discouragement or any fear met on the road'.[49]

Man, it is true, will always remain master of his own choice; but in the long run (so far at least as mankind as a whole is concerned)[50] love, under the influence of the spirit and through its gratuitous action, cannot fail to win the battle against hate, unity to triumph over disintegration, the person over the pressures exercized on it.[51]

'Spirit will always, as it has so far, succeed in standing up to determinism and chance. It represents the indestructible part of the universe.' 'The world contains in itself the warrant of ultimate success'; 'it must, by its very structure, emerge into the absolute.'[52]

Thus, by an infallible extrapolation, we may foresee, after the requisite states of maturity have been achieved, and in contrast to some vague becoming, a final state, a paroxysm,[53] an historical fulfilment that nothing can suppress. 'In virtue of its convergent nature,' the progress of socialization 'necessarily determines at a finite distance in the future, a critical meeting point or peak.'[54]

This new critical point will be defined by the inauguration of a *perfect community of persons*, linked together by a mutual recognition of their freedom and their collective adherence to an absolute ideal of love.[55] It is in the direction of a single 'heart' even more than in that of a single brain that we must look if we wish to picture to ourselves the final 'super-mankind'—that 'higher biological state that mankind seems destined to attain if . . . it succeeds in totalizing completely upon itself'.[56]

But this 'end of the whole', higher in order than the 'ends of the elements', is by nature incapable of being 'halted and closed in on itself'.[57] Thus, once mankind has reached its term and is incapable of any further synthesis, and at the same time is more eager than ever for the absolute and for eternity,[58] then it will be ready to 'break through the experiential framework of time and space to escape somewhere towards an ultra-centre of unification and consistence, where there will finally be assembled, comprehensively and in detail, everything that is irreplaceable and incommunicable in this world'.[59] 'Happy the world whose end is in ecstasy.'[60]

Omega Point

Teilhard's thought, which here takes a more metaphysical turn, though without ceasing to be scientific and to be based on facts, infers that this necessary term implies God as its *condition*: on the phenomenal plane, a divine term can and must be inferred by reason as the *end* (pole, or summit) of the genesis of the world and of man.

The emergence of material units, biological and human (persons and groups) continually more structurally complete, more centred on themselves and more conscious—the maturing of the personal and collective organization of mankind—reciprocal love between person and person[61]—these are inexplicable and impossible without the existence of an ultimate and ultra-human *focus* of convergence or meeting-point. This, borrowing the term from the Greek alphabet, but primarily in allusion to the Christ of the Apocalypse to whom it will be assimilated, we may call *Omega*:[62] the prime mover, but one that lies ahead of us.[63]

Here we find that there are two different ways of looking at the existence and nature of this Omega Point. From the point of view of immanence, the centre of cosmic and human convergence is engendered from within 'by simple grouping of the elements among themselves'.[64] It is, accordingly, still impersonal. In this option, the evolutionary process is emphasized; more justly, however, another option, that of *transcendence*, attributes a divine reality to Omega Point.

This term-end, which lies in the future, which is progressive and, *in as much as it is participated in by finite being*, is finite, must, then, be:

— *actual* and present now,[65] so that it can exercise an attraction, and an attraction of love,[66] on beings and minds.

— *stable*, eternal, free from any threat of material disintegration and temporal retrogression, so that it can be the basis of the demand for survival and immortality formulated by man in the name of the irreversibility of evolution—and so that it can bring together in itself, without confusing them, all persons, when the concentration of the spirit[67] has reached its term.

— *transcendent*, unique, and outside time and space, so that it can dominate, control and give coherent form to history: it is impossible, too, to conceive it 'as being born from some sort of aggregation of elementary personalities', since the nature of the ego is such that it cannot be de-centred and cannot add to itself.[68]

— and, finally, it must be *personal*, endowed with spiritual interiority, with thought, freedom and love, so that it can be the absolute type of finite being and its pole of fulfilment.[69] An anonymous ideal, as conceived, for example, by contemporary humanists who reject God, is incapable of being a sufficiently active motive force behind the progress of the world. If it is to be fully intelligible, the absolute, towards which history advances, must be *someone*. Only a personal being has the warmth and radiant power that enable it to be loved and to constitute the meeting-point of a communion of persons. And, if in man the person is the summit of biological evolution, then the person must exist in the fullest form as the summit of the whole of history. The materialist and pantheist illusion of the diffusion or dispersion of the absolute in space cannot stand up against the fact of the world's concentration, in time, in the direction of the spiritual.[70]

Thus, for Teilhard, so far from the existence of God being *produced* by the dynamism of the world, it is *demanded* by it as a necessity; the generating lines of the cone of universal ascent call for an apex, and that apex is also an origin and a foundation. As for man, he is urged to *recognize* explicitly the end towards which he tends, in solidarity with the universe, and the ultimate point that can be discerned in the signs of convergence. Being incapable of producing his own fulfilment, either as a person or as a collective body in history, he *receives himself* in his entirety from a divine personality, he is given to himself, in history and at the end of history, by the absolute-God.

This supreme fulfilment, however, is prepared and progressively matured in time, by the co-action of man's liberties with the action of Omega. Even under the disguise of modern atheism, the religious vitality of the earth is continually increasing; though apparently eclipsed by the world, 'God is becoming manifest to our consciousness as greater and more necessary than ever.' The more man is man, the more inevitably he feels the need to adore, and, if the hope that animates his activity is to be legitimate, it must imply a living absolute. 'It appears, then, that as mankind's expectation grows more marked, so, correspondingly, does the face of God gradually loom greater through the world.'[71]

It is God, essentially distinct from the finite spiritual energy[72] that has been the moving force in history and stimulated the progressive development of beings, who—actively assisting but never encroaching on initiative and freedom—gives this energy, as he gives every element in the world, being and activity. It is he who is the supreme author of a creation that is itself inventive, if not creative, and that he united to himself in giving it being. Far from being the sum and final integration of the progress of persons and things, he is not comparable to them: he is the founder of their existence and of their subordinate freedom, and he is also the principle of their fulfilment and the giver of a survival into eternity to which everything that is mortal aspires. And, if we must recognize that the energy that builds the universe, and still more the universe of man, is an energy of love, then there is only one name that can rightly be given to God, the name of love. It is, then, only through him and in him that man and the universe attain their end.

In fact, however, they are already, and by anticipation, attaining this end. History, accordingly, has an absolute and divine value: in spite of the problems it appears to raise, life is fully vindicated. If *'when all is said and done*, all the forces of the world work together to bring about our fulfilment', then 'our terror of matter and of man is transformed, and reversed, to become peace and trust, and even *existential love . . . and all this is so, because the world has a heart'*.[73] Human activity is not useless and sterile, but infinitely fruitful, if it conforms to the good, for then it is 'physically' linked to God. If the cosmos unravels as we look back and is woven together as we look forward,[74] then it is well worth while to contribute to a spiritual movement that can and must culminate in a triumph of the universe: man's adventure has a final outcome and death is conquered.[75]

The Universal Christ

This conclusion, arrived at solely in the light of an honest appraisal of the scientific evidence, is strikingly confirmed by an appeal to another source of information besides facts of the natural order: if these may be regarded as the first way in which God speaks to us, he has gratuitously offered us a more direct word, a more concrete confrontation. By revealing himself in person, God 'reflects himself' says Teilhard, in the very heart of human reflexion and co-reflexion. History bears the mark, in its very centre, of the coming in time and birth of one sent by God: none other, in fact, than his own son. To the Christian this is evident, and so it should be to every man of good will; though it cannot be demanded nor determined in its mode, it is the effectual fulfilment of a desire.[76] God is come, in person, loyally and fully to share the existence of man. Henceforth he belongs to man's world and links his own destiny to that of man.

Further, the localized Jesus of Nazareth and Calvary, when considered theologically, particularly in the light of some of the epistles of St Paul, is seen to be the king of the universe, its creator, as he is its end and its centre. 'It is he who fills, it is he who consummates, and it is he who gives its consistence to the building up of matter and spirit.'[77] 'He is . . . the first-born of all creation; for in him all things were created . . . all things were created through him and for him . . . in whom are hid all the treasures of wisdom and knowledge.'[78] The whole world, in bondage to sin through its solidarity with man, yearns for a spiritual liberation, and its history is the bringing to birth of a divine reality.[79] There is nothing in the universe, except sin, which is not part and parcel of the scheme of infinite love which, with the co-operation of man's free will, seeks to achieve the supernatural communion of men with God, within the community of the body of the Church. A directive plan, inaugurated from the beginning of time, and matured by long preparation, is being implemented; it has for its aim the fulfilment of all things in God, and the entry of man (and in him, of all that has value and reality) into the eternal life of the Trinity. Within history the Church, which continues the mission of Christ and is animated by his spirit, works at the same task as her master: the communion of every man and of the whole of man with perfect being. Coincident, though subordinate, with the universal Christ, she grows to the full perfection of her stature until the consummation, both quantitative and qualitative, of the Pleroma.[80]

And, marked, as it will be, by a judgment that will appraise and sanction both the individual choices of men's free wills, and the final choice that adult man will make between revolt and adoration, the end of all man's days may be seen as the ultimate triumphal success of the divine enterprise: 'in a burst of fire', the conjunction of Christ with Omega Point will produce the 'astonishing phenomenon of a general conflagration of the world—through *total amorization*'.[81] The Easter of the risen Christ will be that of man and of the universe: 'God, gathering to himself not only the scattered multitude of souls, but also the solid organic reality of the universe, taken whole and entire in the extension and total unity of its energies—is it not precisely to that that we are striving to feel our way?'[82]

Henceforth, despair, if not anguish, can have no justification,[83] and hope opens out to the clear vision of faith: life is fully vindicated, the universe is good, history is worth-while. And man is sure that his own activity co-operates, if he consents, in the realization of a divine end, with which no temporal value and no purely earthly happiness can compare, but in which all things can be transfigured and in which every valid work will be re-assumed, consummated, and transcended. It is not a nameless thought nor a blind force that made the universe and directs it, but a *love*: the vastness of the world is transformed 'into a centre of loving energy', and the risen Christ is already the victor.[84]

A New Apologetics

There is a manifest analogical *correspondence*, if not identity, between the order of 'natural' history and the evidence of Christian revelation, 'allied and hierarchically arranged phases of one and the same event': between the genesis of mankind in the world and the genesis of Christ, through the Church, in mankind, there is a coherent subordination.[85]

Although, indeed, 'the universe cannot have two heads', 'the two centres meet or at least overlap: Christ would not be the only driving force behind, the only issue open to, the universe, if the universe were not able, in some way, to centre itself, even at a lower degree, outside him'.[86] Thus the temporal term of the world's movement and of man's, *coincides* with the plenitude of the mystical body—a plenitude that nevertheless is not the result of a natural evolution: the moving sphere of beings calls for a personal centre, and this centre exists for faith and is Christ.[87] The emergence of Christ answers the convergence of the cosmos.

'If the world is convergent and if Christ occupies its centre, then the Christogenesis of St Paul and St John is nothing else and nothing less than the extension, both awaited and unhoped-for, of that noogenesis in which cosmogenesis—as regards our experience— culminates. Christ invests himself organically with the very majesty of his creation. And it is in no way metaphorical to say that man finds himself capable of experiencing and discovering his God in the whole length, breadth and depth of the world in movement.'[88] 'Instead of the vague centre of convergence envisaged as the ultimate end of this process of evolution, the personal and defined reality of the Word Incarnate, in which everything acquires substance, appears and takes its place.'[89] 'Here, indeed, there is a remarkable coincidence of what we receive by faith and what we arrive at by reason. What seemed a menace becomes a magnificent confirmation.' 'A marvellous coherence, introduced by Revelation, in the whole system of our thought and action.'[90] 'The appearance of a summit of unification at the higher term of the cosmic ferment, has the *objective* effect of providing man's aspirations (for the first time in history) with an absolute direction and goal.'[91]

Already impregnated though it is with the grace of Christ, nevertheless 'nature' is only an image of the supernatural: and it is a vision illumined by faith that gives a complete solution to the mystery of being, of which a natural vision could offer only a rough outline or anticipation. Thus a supremely important *approximation* is established between science and faith, and modern man is on the road that leads to a religious choice—even, indeed, to a religious commitment—prepared and induced by logic and reason.[92] The act of faith, while still entirely free, is made easier by the discovery that there is a concrete connexion between man's secular aims and the hopes of the Christian: Christianity shows man the deep-rooted reality of what, without knowing it, he is seeking, and the conversion to which it summons him—difficult though it may seem—is found to consist in an extension of the values that he finds the most authentic. The communion of man, which is the end of history, though desired by all, can be realized only in Christ: and we cannot take man and history seriously unless we are receptive to Christianity. If Christianity goes beyond history and attributes to it a transcendent vocation, it begins by being of service to it.[93]

The phenomenology we have just outlined is summed up in the four following propositions:

In the material universe, life is not an epiphenomenon, but the central phenomenon of evolution.

In the organic world, reflexion is not an epiphenomenon but the central phenomenon of vitalization.

In the domain of reflective life, socialization is not an epiphenomenon, but the essential phenomenon of hominization.

In the genesis of the human social organism, the Church is not an epi- or para-phenomenon, but constitutes the very axis (or core) of concentration.[94]

CONCLUSION

Extremely simple in its general form and its main lines, this pheno-menology of history represents the governing principle or heart of Teilhard's thought. The analyses given in later chapters are based on this and form no more than a logical recapitulation of it, aimed at bringing out its structure and framework.

If Teilhard seems to have derived from Christianity the notion of a history that reaches its term in God, his own contribution is, using a positive approach and basing himself on a consideration of the facts, to have expressed the indispensable convergence of the world's time and man's time on a supreme, unsurpassable unity.

At this point, to dispel the uneasiness produced by the vague, nameless, idea of universe or totality, we should first recall the dialectic noted earlier: the universe that reaches its term in God is not the universe in itself, but the universe *of man*. What is even more important, it is man, the thought and consciousness of the universe, who moves towards the absolute-God and attains him in the com-munity, finally realized, of persons. And the world is saved only in man, who transcends its forms and energies.

Teilhard's philosophy of history has in its favour an extreme *rational necessity*: while it makes full allowance for the thresholds that mark a break in continuity, it has the boldness, the rashness even, maybe, to bring together in a single *idea* the most diverse orders of the real and, in the end, the world and God, the nothing and the infinite. In the allied progress of complexity and consciousness, observed first in biology and later in sociology and then generalized for the whole of history, it claims to have found, more clearly even than Einstein, a *constant in the universe*, a universal law of being and of the phenomenon.

So far from there being anything left that is irrational or anoma-lous, there is nothing that is not embraced in the unity of one single movement, directed towards the absolute: all chance and all con-tingence, all resistance and contradiction is eliminated, axiomati-cally, by the triumph of a spiritual necessity that is at the same time freedom. In consequence, the return of the world to its origin is achieved harmoniously: everything finds salvation and reaches its goal. History acquires fullness and substance: the night in which we have had to feel our way opens out into the dawn of the final end.

Thus history, involved in its end even more than in its origin, attains being and value: in as much as it is attached, in its term, to the absolute, it is already divine, and its vast range of manifestations, its innumerable contingencies, the wide dispersion of its successive instants, are justified by the end it attains, the unity in which it culminates. Traversed by a wind of spirit, it gradually realizes (in man, its consciousness) that the spirit which animates it is none other than the spirit of God and that it leads it to communion with God: thus history is seen to be an affirmation of God, who is its end.

The *difficulties* of this view of history derive from its very rationality, from its passion for unity. They relate to a threefold transcendence: that of God in relation to man, that of individual freedom in relation to the world of matter and of life, and finally to the plurality of the effective expressions of history in relation to the plan of unification.

I THE TRANSCENDENCE OF GOD

The first difficulty arises from the problem of the *fusion* of history, at its term, with God—of man's final access to God.

From a purely scientific point of view, this access does, in fact, present an ambiguity, even, indeed a contradiction.

On the one hand, unless it is to be lacking in authenticity, the progressive, and later final, convergence of the noosphere must already, through its own effort, achieve an absolute, conquer a totality, fulfil history in an insurpassable state of thought and love, and so coincide with being and value. Already, in fact, our thought can affirm the absolute as the end of history.

And yet what is emerging is not yet, and cannot be, the true absolute. This affirmation of the absolute still lacks its real object. The final unanimity of every consciousness is only the prerequisite condition of their passage to God: it is still infinitely removed from his transcendence. The moral, spiritual and religious maturing of mankind, the progress of the growth of God in man, of the participation in God by the consciousness of man, can indeed attain their zenith: but this term still remains a *falling-short*. As to the present affirmation by man of the absolute, it must recognize much more than this—its personal interiority; and man must recognize his inability to communicate with the mystery of God without a gratuitous approach on the part of God.[95]

Teilhard says, too, and very justly, that if it is to participate fully 'in the cosmic properties of Omega', 'the organized totality of the reflective elements of the world' must become irreversible 'within a super-ego' which is 'the heart of matter'. Only then will the universe of man attain its 'ultimate consistence'.[96]

Thus the natural movement of history can end only in an absolute 'of the first species' (if one may use such an expression), at an 'end' rather than a 'goal'; and so, by a radical negation, Teilhard preserves the distance and supreme autonomy of God.[97] For all that, the problem is still not solved.

The difficulty just referred to was inevitable and only to be expected in the purely scientific approach of *The Phenomenon of Man*. Teilhard is well aware of the fact that this point of view is abstract, and that the reality of history is supernatural, as indeed, he points out in his *Postscript*.

In this case, while man's final passage to God still remains a mystery, the difficulty contained in its content is partly removed by two factors that (in some way) lessen the gap between man and God. — In the first place, by the idea of *creation*, which makes man an image of his creator. This analogy *pre-adapts* him to a vocation that is higher than his nature; and if he is able, some day, to attain the fulness of communion with God, in the spiritual organism of persons, it is because it has been granted to him, from the very beginning, to possess a germ of desire for it.

Until man, spiritual energy, immanent in matter and emerging from it, is still confined within the limits of animal consciousness; suddenly, however, man can think and will the infinite, can project himself towards the absolute and the whole. He is the first reality, the absolute beginning of history.

By deliberately refusing, as a matter of method, to have recourse to a decisive *creation* for the historical origin of man, Teilhard thus deprived himself also of the power to appreciate his real stature: at the most, all he could do—and that from outside—was to distinguish the signs of a transcendence of man over nature. In consequence, he was equally unable to avoid difficulties involved in the destination of history.

— The final distance between man and God can be partly closed up, again, by the notion of *participation*: this, already included in the idea of creation, is more fully realized in the supernatural order.

The divinizing process that reaches back in time right to the very origins of man, confers on him, as it does on his universe, not only a receptivity to the infinite, but also a more profound pre-adaptation. While maintaining, with Teilhard, the necessity for some supreme gratuitous gesture if mankind is to be saved and enter into divine life, we can envisage more clearly the possibility of man's attaining God at the peak of his journey through time, if real history is the history of sons of God, and above all if it is traversed by the breath of God, if it bears the mark of his supernatural interventions, and is cultivated by the Church of men of good will.

Thus, at the risk of allowing the final gap between the unified term of natural history and the transcendence of God still to remain, Teilhard does not shrink from developing the progress of that history in a natural and scientific perspective. At the same time he realized perfectly well that the problem was still unsolved, and was even obliged, as we shall see, to introduce the necessity, for mankind in its final stage, of consenting to a death, an annihilation, an excentration.

And, as we noted earlier, for Teilhard a natural phenomenology stands only as *a first moment of a total dialectic of history and being*, a dialectic that becomes effectively supernatural and Christic through the grace of the Incarnation. This moment, in a certain sense real and autonomous, can, nevertheless, never be isolated from the synthesis: it is in just this paradox, however, that the whole problem lies.

At the same time this positive development of the stages of history had to be attempted, in the first place for the benefit of unbelievers, in virtue of being a *sign* of, and a correspondence with, a mysterious reality whose content is revealed only to faith. Although it cannot be imagined, the consummation of history must show a *preparation* in time. And it is important, and legitimate, to construct a theory of this advance, from an experiential point of view, and to distinguish the natural signs of a religious significance in history. The movement of cosmic and human evolution towards its end is not inauthentic, but it will be called upon to recognize that it is itself a gift and that it can reach fulfilment only thanks to a gratuitous descent of the absolute towards man: the desire of Eros will have to abandon any claim to conquest and transform itself into an attitude of receptivity and submission in relation to Love; and the super-abundance of the Mediator's grace will transform *natural aspiration* into *supernatural hope*.

Thus temporal history is fulfilled at an absolute term, but must nevertheless pass through into something else. In the same way, knowledge of God by the way of science is real: it must, nevertheless, be complemented by the act of faith. Such is the paradox of religious reflexion.[98]

II THE TRANSCENDENCE OF FREEDOM

A second difficulty in Teilhard's philosophy of history arises from the emergence of individual *freedom* in the history of the world.

The 'constant' of unification is obviously important for an understanding of the convergent ascent of matter and of life, but can it be extended to the global movement of history? Does not the coming of man introduce a break in continuity that rules out the certainty and predictability of the laws of the cosmos? Until man, the dynamism of spiritual energy is irresistible, but can it now be halted, or contradicted, by the chance options made by individual persons? Can a history of active liberties be entirely subject to the demands of reason? Finally, can the order of the *event*, that comes in with man, be subject to the order of the *idea*?

We shall see that the certainty of a victory of spirit has been impaired or reduced by the recognition of a possible schism in the noosphere, and that Teilhard has restored to history its tragic character.

Taken even more seriously, this recognition would have re-introduced, at the very foundation of his theory, the role of individual freedom as an 'infinite' power of negation, always in a position to stand out against the unifying pressure of spirit and, through the choices it makes, to snap the thread of history. Without underestimating the importance of personal freedom, Teilhard was too convinced of the scientific necessity of a convergence of history to admit the ultimate consequences of this emergence of freedom: he had to embrace the whole of history in the unified sweep of one and the same synthesis.

There is no doubt that the problem of history is still obscure: the freedom of persons does not rule out their interdependence nor the possibility of a victory of the spirit.

It must, however, be recognized that even if spiritual energy was in fact all-powerful in the order of biology, so powerful, indeed, that it could bring about the miracle of the emergence of man, this birth entails a radical *break*. Henceforth we have spirit standing absolutely helpless before its own success, with no answer to, if not completely baffled by, the moral resistance of the person (and of a person whose otherness is affirmed by Christianity). The fundamental unity of mankind exists side by side with the singularity, and plurality, of individuals and their decisions: so many separate worlds in which the destiny of history is privately worked out.

However, if this is so, any unifications that may be realized by history, lose much of their significant value and remain largely superficial and formal phenomena. Our present socialization (of organization, of thought, of collective life), undeniable and remarkable though it is, cannot constitute a link between primitive man, still dispersed, and final man, unified in the absolute. The evidence found by Teilhard on the sociological map of the world is important because of the difficult problems it raises, but it cannot provide serious grounds for our hope in final unanimity. A coincidence of minds in the use of the same methods, or the inclusion of persons in a more functional or even a more democratic social system, is a long way from the real communion of souls in love. The present phenomena of unification can work in either direction: they can stimulate freedom, but they can equally well stifle it—the more so that science, technology and socialization, for all their value, belong to the lower levels of the existential order.

Thus the progress of mankind, real though it may be, is not patient of scientific observation: and, if it is to hold good, the extrapolation of the movement of history must be based on data that belong in fact to another dimension: that of 'salvation'.

This criticism applies only to too imaginative a conception of Omega Point: it still holds good as the condition of the movement of history, as the ultimate and absolute finality of individual liberties but also of the spiritual body that they constitute. In any case, the question of the progress of history will be examined again in the chapter dealing with Teilhard's theology.

Finally, the vision of the final term of history, the theoretical perfection of the ideal of communion, comes up against the difficulty of reconciling the concrete conditions of unanimity, which is such that it must be at once universal and intimate, widespread and deep-seated. The other, essentially characterized by difference, conceals an inexpressible mystery which withdraws and hides it from the very love of which it is the object. And while the continuous network of roles and functions links those who are close to those who are distant, the social gap or the material distance that separates the personal centres of a progressively more numerous mankind is a serious obstacle to their true communion. Moreover, without a supernatural eschatological intervention, the most advanced human organization on the juridical plane still allows the passions that govern men's minds and the tensions created by their situations to persist. However necessary it may be, obedience to rules, loyalty to directives, is still no more than a palliative, or a substitute for a total harmony of hearts, for the power of minds to see into and think with one another.[99] Thus the analysis of the concrete conditions of the final coming together of men raises difficult problems for Teilhard's position.

III COMPLEXITY OF HISTORICAL FACTORS

Teilhard's scheme of unification, characterized as it is by a certain simplification—indeed over-simplification—is in itself no doubt, incapable of fully accounting for the movement of history. It has to be filled out by dialectical elements borrowed from Hegel, Marx, and Bergson and from Christianity. The analysis of the effective factors of history brings out, in fact, the following points.

1 The permanent problem with which man is faced because of his natural condition of *incompleteness*, and hence of lack and distress in relation to possible values, and in his threefold relationship to nature, to other men, and to God: the contradictions produced by sexual fertility, economic laws, social privilege, political situations, conflict of interests, multiplicity of ideals, etc.

Here we have to recognize the importance of the different determinisms, that sometimes have the appearance of a closely-linked *fatality-sequence*, as we see them in the great crises of history (revolutions, wars): mysterious underground forces that, in spite of being partly the effect of human decisions, nevertheless pursue their course independently. These determinisms emerge as problems presented to freedom, which they stimulate to fresh options. Faced by hitherto unknown situations, man reacts as best he can, but always with final reference to his natural condition, his ontological structure; and that is of infinite desire and hence of negativity. And the advance of consciousness, encouraged by spiritual factors, finally emerges from the immensely complicated aspects of situations: the successive facts—technical in nature, economic, social, political, cultural—would be no more than a meaningless and valueless sequence of episodes if they did not, in some hidden way, contribute to the rise of spirit.

2 Man's *power of invention*, the factor that rejects the received, that creates afresh, at all levels and in all domains: man, ready to receive the infinite and perpetually disappointed, constantly refuses to be only what he is, to have only what he has. Continually aroused and stimulated by the contradictions of history, it is he and he alone who can find a dialectical solution for them.

3 The immanent action of *spirit*, in an extension of the spiritual energy already active in nature: this point was strongly emphasized by Teilhard.

4 The action, still more intimate and effective, of the *living God*, the educator and enlightener of consciousness, the force behind its spiritual advances: in an imperfect form in paganism, but more fully in Israel and in Christianity. God's successive 'covenants' with man, and his decisive interventions, in a spirit of increasing fidelity and generosity; the prophetic pre-figuring of the future and the impact of its realization. And here Teilhard's historical vision might well have been more concentrated, more minute and exact in examining the sacred symbolism provided by the people of Israel. We might well wonder whether they do not supply a *key* to universal history, more valid than the scientific and logical scheme of unification; and they should perhaps be regarded as the *type* of the dramatic relationship between God and man for all time: God's victory, no doubt, in mankind through the pouring out of love, but at the same time in the shattering of liberties.

Moreover, as Paul Ricoeur has well pointed out,[100] unlike peoples that live on primitive myths that have become stabilized and cannot be given new forms, Israel, by its unremitting spiritual activity and with the help of its great inspired minds, re-thought out and re-interpreted its traditions in continually more religious terms, until it finally built them up into a theology. While Israel was living through real events and experiencing the interventions of God, it was developing its history through faith and was transforming itself internally through this creative fidelity to God's teaching. Israel may therefore be regarded as the *prototype of the movement of history*, the model of an advance of human time through a dialectic that takes up, renews and transposes the past: all that will then be left for it to do will be to hand over to the Church.

In other words, if by history we mean not the empirical succession of facts but the progress of consciousness, then Israel (in as much as it is orientated towards Christ and in relationship with him) discloses the secret of history: the *synchrony* of structures and situations, in itself inert and repetitive, is not truly overcome except by the *diachrony* of a creative tradition, fed by the past and looking forward to a future for which it hopes.[101] Any naturalist phenomenology, however highly spiritualist, entirely by-passes the mystery of history and can never succeed in deciphering it.

5 The indispensable role of the *great man*: the sages, heroes, prophets, and mystics. At their head stands Christ. His importance has been fully recognized by Teilhard, in the theological part of his theory; but he does not seem to have paid as much attention as Bergson to the activity of historical *personalities*, dwelt-in and visited by the spirit in a specially favoured way, in assisting the progress of history. This results in a certain neglect of the capital *master-disciple* dialectic and a certain failure to recognize the important thresholds of history that it produces.

6 *Society:* through the reliability of its memory, through its organs of preservation and transmission; through the problems raised by the development of its technology and organization; through the spiritual demands of its present and its future. Here Teilhard makes a valuable contribution. He recognized the importance of the fact of society and agrees with Marx in his appreciation of modern technology.[102] At the same time, it is not certain that he allowed sufficiently for the economic and political factor.

7 Evil and *sin*; and the collective ill that results from them: the phenomenon of *estrangement* that, without changing man's natural condition, aggravates his problems and upsets his normal relations with nature, with other men, and with God.

Although Teilhard was obviously aware of the evil in man and the lack of discipline in his options, yet, as a result of a number of influences, he does not seem to have introduced with sufficient force into his theory of history the dialectic of the master and the slave: the individual and collective oppression of man by man, violence and injustice, the lagging behind of institutions compared with the demands of conscience, and finally the progress-factor represented by a questioning of the established order. Even without turning to Marx, a more attentive reading of the Old Testament could have made Teilhard appreciate the capital role of 'the poor' in history.

At a deeper level, the spiritual advance of history seems to be realized through successive *returns* of God, whose education uses, to benefit man, the experience of the unhappiness that his faults produce. The patient generosity of his mercy strives to overcome man's resistance, by forming élites who understand the significance of events and transmit to one another the current of the spirit: these élites are always arbitrarily persecuted by the social body but they nevertheless succeed in disseminating their witness and gradually modifying the collective consciousness.

Teilhard's phenomenology of history, then, is incomplete: it is far from constituting a screen fine enough to make its progress intelligible. Nevertheless, leaving behind the inertia of pagan times, it has the merit of vindicating the reality of historical development by the presence of God in the world and by the final direction of all things towards him. It has the fairness of recognizing the relative autonomy of secular history, while taking it up into the heart of sacred history, centred upon Christ. Finally, in a magnificent vision, it unifies the aspects and phases of the entire unfolding of history. And it is not to be wondered at that in his search for rational unity Teilhard should be tripped up by the mystery of liberty, both God's and man's, whose dialogue and inter-relationship constitute the mystery of history.

This phenomenology of history, which has followed the development of being, leads to an *ontology*, which studies it in the hierarchy of its degrees; the synthesis of the two forms a logic of the real:

> The world of matter and of life, in a cosmology.
> Man, in an anthropology.
> God, in a theology.[103]

Chapter 4
Cosmology

The whole of Teilhard's work is based initially on a scientific philosophy of the material and biological universe. The essence of this cosmology has already been briefly explained, but it calls for some more exact treatment and raises problems that are worth looking at more closely.

I THE METHOD AND VALUE OF SCIENCE

From Teilhard's work there emerges in the first place a consideration of the method and value of science.

The possibility of scientific knowledge is based on the *correspondence* between the universe and thought: a correspondence that is more certain than in Descartes, and that raises no problem if it is true that man cannot be dissociated from the universe; the whole man is a co-presence with being, and perception is an immediate resonance to the world. The capacity of thought responds to the fundamental intelligibility of the real, thought being receptive of the absolute and the infinite of truth, and organized in functional structures that adapt it spontaneously to the world. Although Teilhard never studied the *a priori* conditions of knowledge, he would be ready to admit, going further than a somewhat rigid Kantism, that it is from within and actively, in the course of an indefinite dialogue with the world, that the mind forms *its own* structure in the quest for truth. Faith in reason is founded on an act of *freedom*, itself directed towards the truth of being.

Energy, however, and *thought* cannot be dissociated from one another. 'A priori,' says the philosopher 'only what is thinkable can exist': 'a priori,' says the scientist, 'only what conforms to energy can come to light.'[1]

In the real 'everything holds together':[2] the multiple whole of phenomena, in time and space, forms a totality, physically held together by an organic inter-dependence of the elements. From

74

this follows 'the vanity of any solution . . . that seeks to account for the elements independently of the whole'.[3]

Observation of the whole, then, which collects the crude elements of the datum and analyses them, is continued by a synthesizing activity that reassembles them in a logical order through the medium of a sign-language and the establishment of a network of relationships. It is here that *idealism* wins, but its truth is limited by its very choice and its field of action.[4]

The truth of science is derived from the agreement, continually more fully verified by experiment, following on an initial hypothesis, between the logical coherence of the theory and the facts. But this coherence, a fundamental law of thought as it is of the real, is already in itself a sign of truth.[5] Here Teilhard might well have brought out the *operational* character of modern science, which arrives at truth only through instrumental verifications of theories that are themselves plans for possible action upon a sector of the real.[6] He was, however, involved in specialized biological research and field-work and was not sufficiently alive to the universal importance at present of mathematical explanation.

Now, knowledge of the real may be arrived at by two complementary roads.

The first is the *classification* of the forms, or ideas, of reality, themselves defined by their characteristics, in an organic system whose embrace is continually more extensive.[7] Physics and biology succeed in establishing a *systematics* of beings and species, but also of laws: an entity is understood by being included in a wider intelligible group, of which it is seen to be one particular case.[8] This is the classical logic, whose origin goes back to Aristotle, and which is still imperative for every science, including mathematics.

The second way considers the movement in time that makes of the real a *history*. It determines the order of successive geneses and the causes of transformations. Biological transformism is simply the application of a universal law that obliges thought to relate forms to their antecedents. This is a new classification that makes it possible to determine the place that every phenomenon must occupy in the order of its appearance.[9]

Here, the experiential fact of the *progress* of this history obliges science, if it is to understand the real, to use a *dialectical* plan of conjunction and disjunction which expresses logically the continuity and discontinuity of forms. 'True scientific advance consists in . . . (thus) disclosing the underlying connexions that link together orders that are apparently the most widely separated.'[10]

The whole of this process is *gradual*, because knowledge itself is a historical fact: under the inspiration of curiosity—and curiosity is a passion for the true—it operates through a victory over obstacles,[11] through a dramatic offensive that proceeds from appearance, illusion and incoherence, to a continually more valid truth.[12]

Finally, it is *man* who is the author of this knowledge, the creator and the centre of the picture. Fully involved in his act and, through his act, in the world, his thought cannot be dissociated from the real, from which it cannot receive anything except by projecting itself into it and so illuminating it.[13]

Further, if man is to know the world and to know himself in the world, he must possess certain powers of recognition, of which Teilhard gives a list.[14]

II THE FORMS

The theory of scientific knowledge referred to the *forms*, that is to say the structures of the real. Teilhard's cosmology attributes a fundamental position to them.

The pure *multiple* is nothingness: 'Where there is complete disunion of the cosmic stuff (at an infinite distance from Omega), there is *nothing*'.[15] The problem of creation, which involves the freedom of God, could be introduced at this point, but will be dealt with later when we examine Teilhard's contribution to theology.

As Bergson has shown,[16] absolute disorder is unthinkable; at every degree of being there is nothing that is not a 'unity of plurality'.[17] And a thought, which is unifying oneness, is immanent in the world, of which it makes a *cosmos*; 'in its roots, the substance of the cosmos has a primordial disposition, *sui generis*, to organize itself and involute upon itself'; 'beyond and above the *curve-of-convergence* there is the curve-of-arrangement'.[18]

Matter, then, in so far as it tied to multiplicity, does not exist, has never existed and cannot exist as an absolute of dispersion and incoherence. The extreme concept of pure matter, though impossible to represent in itself, is nevertheless dialectically necessary, as a relationship to spirit, which is an act of unification: it is a contradiction of spirit, but it is also the point of purchase and the content of that unification, which is the real.[19] On the *metaphysical* plane (which is concerned with the origin of being), it will appear as a pure potentiality, an abstract possibility of existence;[20] on the *moral* plane, as an inertia, a dead weight, a temptation, when presented with freedom, to dissociation.

We must, however, get back to the *real* and effective order of phenomena. Matter,[21] a lower level of the universe, at every stage of its history and in each of its elements as well as in its sum total, is already organized: everywhere it has an intelligible form. And it is organized *because it organizes itself and its structure.*[22] Once beyond aggregations that show no arrangement, and undefined geometric repetitions (such as crystals) it exists only tied to a definite internal structure,[23] limited and relatively autonomous, whose unity gathers together, combines and gives order to elementary entities: the degree of complexity being determined by the organization of a larger number of elements.[24] Thus Teilhard, by implication, restates a traditional philosophical category: the fundamental dialectical connexion of the one and the multiple, of form and matter.[25]

However, as science finds when it comes to analyse things more and more closely, we are obliged to abandon the idea of an ultimate substratum: here we have the mystery of the indefinable, that baffles representation without discouraging the attempt:[26] with science uncertain whether it is inventing or discovering the primary elements of matter. The latter, in any case, cannot be thought of, whether at the level of the senses or at the atomic level, except as *plurality-and-unity*—as unified plurality. In other words there is no form or structure that is not defined as an internal *relation* of its elements; moreover, this relation is always open and 'undefined'.

But this 'relational' structure of the elements itself exists only *in its relation* to other structures and, ultimately, in solidarity with the entire universe. The similarity and homogeneity of the elements indicate the collective unity that embraces and holds them together.[27] The sum total of the cosmos, indivisible and inseverable, forms an organized system, of which each element 'is positively woven from all the others'. And yet, within this, orders can be distinguished, and levels and zones (atom, molecule, stars, galaxies) superimposed upon or included in one another, without completely imitating one another.[28]

As for *living forms*, considered first from without, these are situated at a higher point on the curve of corpusculization, and are differentiated from matter only by an infinitely higher degree of structural complexity, comparable in fact with the 'thread of Ariadne' in the advance of cerebration. This means that life is 'a property of the cosmos' and the 'mark of a universal process'[29] —a property of matter that is not partial or limited, 'analogous to some vibratory or molecular effect', but rather an inversion in relation to it, which so constitutes it that its mechanical arrangements cannot be reversed. Life appears to be a precarious and minute phenomenon in the immensity of the heavenly bodies, 'a speck of mould on a grain of dust', an improbable anomaly and chance by-product, but it is in fact the 'characteristic and specific higher aspiration of the universal phenomenon of evolution'.[30] And what matters the rarity of living substance if its quality reaches such a height?

The factual classification of the elements is tied up, it seems, with the historical order of their genesis. 'To push anything back into the past is equivalent to reducing it to its simplest elements'.[31] But while the series of possible atoms is relatively rigid and reaches its upper limit comparatively quickly,[32] the world of living molecules presents very great flexibility: preceded by the body of proteins, it is, right from its lower forms (viruses and bacteria) patient of an indefinite increase of organized complexity.[33] Teilhard points out, too, the importance of the planets, vital points in the universe, for all their insignificance and darkness.

III ENERGY

With the notion of form is essentially linked that of *energy*: this constitutes the internal structure of beings, while it is also the principle of their movement in history. Thus, in one sense, it constitutes the bridge between unity and plurality, for it is only by energy that the multiple is organized.

a: Apparent duality of the forms of energy

It appears just as though the 'stuff of the universe' were divided between two forms of energy, both finite and limited, but united even in their separation.[34]

The first is *tangential* energy: mechanical and external, superficial and peripheral, constant and subject to law, this energy is, in conformity with the second law of thermodynamics (extended and generalized),[35] one of dissipation and dissociation. Entropy, 'the mysterious involution of the world' tends to fold back 'the layer of cosmic energy'[36] toward unorganized multiplicity, and to neutralize it. Thus, in one whole aspect of itself, the universe 'follows irreversibly a branch whose development is limited'; it is included 'among the realities that are born, grow and die'.[37]

The other is *radial* ('axial' or 'centric') energy. Spiritual and internal, increasing and irreversible, this is an energy of ascent, of arrangement and unification: unification of structures, but, creation, too, of the progressive complexity of beings.[38] Unlike tangential energy, 'radial' energy is not 'operational': it does not lend itself to precise and planned verification.

While this distinction has an overall validity, it needs to be modified. Tangential energy is capable of syntheses, of forming structures and combinations. It can increase and grow more intense. In the end, however, it is bound to wear itself out. 'A rocket rising in the wake of time's arrow, that bursts only to be extinguished: an eddy rising on the bosom of a descending current—such then must be our picture of the world.'[39] Radial energy relies for its progress on the flow of tangential energy, part of which it 'shrewdly' uses.[40] In the light of what will be said in the next paragraph, it may not be impossible to interpret the structures and combinations of matter as initial effects of radial energy, of which Teilhard says that it is a factor in arrangement.[41] Moreover, this energy works primarily by 'informing': it brings together by arousing, at different levels, the consciousness of the reciprocal relationships of the elements.

b: Unity of the forms of energy
In reality, both these forms of energy, which should not be conceived as things but as an action,[42] belong to a *single* energy which is psychic in nature.[43]

With 'spatiality', which 'gives extension' to material beings, but whose absolute character is no more than an abstraction,[44] is associated a *temporality*, organic and orientated, creative of unities of an ever higher quality.

Associated one with the other like the foci of an ellipse, but of opposite mathematical signs, the two sorts of energy are engaged in a sort of duel.[45] Quite apart from any appraisal of the value of its essence and action, a 'wind of spirit' can be distinguished in the world.[46] The spiritual energy of convergence, present in the whole universe and also interior to every structure, makes itself manifest in a movement of the real, a vital movement, but still blind, towards the supreme absolute unity,[47] which is God. Thus it transforms reality into living history, directed towards an end.[48] The 'focus' of the ellipse, which represents the energy, is destined to an infinite development, until it becomes, at its term, completely autonomous. Thus the world that is, is in fact, a world that is *being born*; and the 'primacy of spirit', is identical with the 'primacy of the future': 'the higher form of being and the final state of equilibrium for the stuff of the cosmos is to be an object of thought'.[49] Until that term is attained, at every level and in every domain, material energy is an obstacle of resistance, a dead weight; but in itself it is no more than the shadow and reverse aspect, provisional and indispensable, of the single spiritual energy.

Further, spiritual energy is by nature irreversible:[50] in its totality, the universe 'can never bring itself to a halt, or turn back in the movement that draws it towards fuller liberty and consciousness'.[51] Moreover, 'it is a constantly *increasing* physical magnitude: there is, in fact, no appreciable limit to the expansion of consciousness and love'. 'The fundamental law of the universe appears to be that *everything that is possible* is realized.'[52] 'The world does not hold together from below, but from above. There is nothing apparently more lacking in stability than the syntheses that life gradually produces. And yet it is towards these fragile constructions that evolution advances, never to turn back.'[53]

Thus a concrete infinity, an infinity of *complexity*, [54] is introduced, that complements but is primarily a reaction against the indefinitely extensible and divisible spatial infinity of Pascal[55] and Descartes. At the heart of the real, the principal 'abyss' is the 'abyss of synthesis'.[56] Parallel with material gravity runs a 'gravity of the second species' which causes beings to fall (rise) towards a more advanced centration, or concentration. Thus beside the mechanical principle of 'least effort' we have 'the great biophysical principle of "maximum arrangement" of matter'.

As soon as concentration, a universal property of nature and

therefore of matter, reaches a certain degree, it appears in the form
of the *phenomenon of life*. Life, then, is simply 'the property peculiar
to large organized numbers'.[57] 'The phenomena of life and consciousness, so difficult to localize in the universe, might well be
nothing more than the properties peculiar to matter when carried
to a very high degree of arrangement and centration.'[58] Driving on
in the same direction life will bring about the phenomenon of
increasing cerebration (or cephalization).[59] Thus one may speak,
in the course of the world's evolution towards Omega Point,
of *isospheres* of consciousness[60] sometimes more, sometimes less
centred.

The world, therefore, is far from being a 'dust made up of unconscious elements, on which life blossoms in some incomprehensible
way—as though it were an accident or a mould': it is '*fundamentally*
and *initially* living, and its whole history is basically just one vast
psychic operation: the slow but progressive concentration of a
diffuse consciousness, which gradually escapes from the material
conditions in which an initial state of extreme plurality, as a
secondary operation, disguises it'. Life, 'a possibility held in reserve
throughout the universe', found on the earth the conditions in which
it could be realized. Man was to be the last thing to emerge from that
movement, the flame that suddenly leapt up from a general ferment
of the universe.[61]

Thus spirit and matter, in one sense, are 'indeed fundamentally
one and the same thing, as the neo-materialists claim; but between
the two there lies a reversal that makes them in some way opposed
to one another, as the ancient philosophers of the spirit maintained':
'Spirit's true name is spiritualization.' 'Spirit is not something superimposed on, or a by-product of the cosmos, but represents simply the
higher state assumed in us and outside us by the first, indefinable,
thing that we may for lack of a better name, call "the stuff of the
universe". It is nothing more than that, but it is also no less than
that. Spirit is not a meta-, nor an epi-phenomenon; it is *the* phenomenon.' 'Before our eyes, in ourselves, it is not just the earth that is
concentrating *itself* in thought; it is the universe—precisely as at the
other end, symmetrically, it disintegrates *itself* in amorphous
energy.'[62] 'Everything becomes, if not spirit, at least a distant
preparation for, "matter" for, spirit.'[63]

Further, the laws of nature are no more than the superficial projection, or 'statistical echo', of a deeper energy:[64] determinism, though valid in its own order, and founded on a certain inertia or stability of the real,[65] can provide only an *approximation* of reality. Quantic indeterminism, the interior finality of the living, man's decisions in history, these, in their respective degrees, are signs that demonstrate the immensity or the super-extension of a reality that is incommensurable with the mechanism of physical chemistry.

These propositions are not a mere assertion or description: they stem from the logical necessity of giving an acceptable explanation of the fact of *invention*, and organizing invention, to be found more and more in the totality of the real.[66] Determinism is the law of repetitions, the expression of identities and inertias: in itself, it can create nothing. And yet, since all time, the universe has without any doubt been in movement and has been ascending, inventing *the new*, creating more fully organized forms. 'All the accumulated determinism can never give even the shadow of freedom.'[67] 'We shall be struck by the necessity in which we shall find ourselves of resorting to the continuous and dominating influence of an "inventive— that is to say psychic—power" as a *physical* explanation both of the constant upward movement of elementary terms to build always more mechanically improbable groups; and, in the course of this upward movement, the astonishing expansions of spontaneity that we witness.'[68] And the most accurate picture of this movement is not 'the progressive curve of the sinusoid but the upward screw of the spiral'.[69] Nature's apparent turmoil is, in reality, comparable to a 'swarm of bees attracted to the daylight', or again to the pressure of elementary particles against the wall of their isosphere as they look for a crack: the attraction of Omega 'can operate only by lying in wait for and grasping as they pass by', the probabilities of an emergence of spirit.[70]

c: The dialectic of union and dissociation

Spiritual energy is first expressed historically in matter: the geometrical arrangement of crystals,[71] and the formation of continually more complex molecules in conformity with the laws of thermodynamics, are also the result of an interior drive that itself takes advantage both of more favourable sets of conditions and of the opportunities it grasps.[72] It next succeeds in crossing the difficult threshold that introduces it to the kingdom of biology and then to reflective thought and freedom, while continuing to obey the material determinisms that provide it with a foundation to work on. The whole of this development takes place in a perfect coincidence, a sort of marriage, between the 'radial' and the 'tangential', whose relationship is at once one of solidarity and of subordination; or, again, between the identical and the different, between the same and the other. In the kingdom of life, transformation, in particular, coexists and co-operates with the tendency towards repetition—which is seen in 'reproduction'.

A dialectic of *relation* and *rupture* thus connects and disconnects matter and life, in the order of their appearance in history. A *common element* unites them—spiritual energy, already present in matter as an organizing activity and a potentiality of advance. 'In the world, nothing can ever burst forth as final across the different thresholds (however critical they be) which has not already existed in an obscure and primordial way.'[73] But this continuity is subject to the domination of a *discontinuity* which embraces it as it goes beyond it: 'A metamorphosis of this sort (the emergence of life) could not be the result of a simple continuous process. By analogy with all we have learnt from the comparative study of natural developments, we must postulate at this particular moment of terrestrial evolution a coming to maturity, a sloughing-off of the old, a threshold, a crisis of the first magnitude, the beginning of a new order.'[74] Still imperfectly closed-in on itself and characterized above all by its exteriority, the material entity attains, in the biological cell, an individual interiority.

As a specialist in biology, Teilhard did not fail to point out the distinguishing characteristics of the living being and the originality of life: its capacity to add and invent, its vector in opposition to material energy (or, at any rate, its way of using it for its own constructions), its orientation towards the improbable[75] . . . And the order of complexity of the living stands at a higher level than that of material beings. Moreover, while material elementary entities, because of their number and relative simplicity, or their quasi-identity, can only be the object of statistical laws, the living must be considered above all in its individuality.

Finally, in an attempt to solve the problem of the *activation* of human energy, Teilhard has most perceptively noted that while the dynamic state of a living mass is initially defined in thermodynamic quantities, it is also determined by 'a certain capacity imparted to this energy of using itself, with greater or less rapidity, in the direction of survival, of multiplication, or of some super-arrangement of organized matter': this latter goal being 'based on imponderables'.[76]

d: Discussion

1 Teilhard neither formulated nor solved the no doubt insoluble problem of the metaphysical origin of the co-existence, at once antagonistic and associated, of the two forms of energy; but his position is the logical result of a desire for complete fidelity to the real. It could not be further from the concept of matter, as held by the ancients, as an inconsistent degradation of spirit, an explosion of being in the multiple. At once, and inevitably, dualist and anti-dualist, Teilhard takes into account the two aspects of the datum: the indissoluble connexion of matter and spirit, and their opposition. There is an obscurity here that nothing can completely dispel: that is how the world is. Thus the opposition between spiritualism and materialism, both fascinated by an abstract aspect of the real, is overcome.

Whatever, nevertheless, may be the apparent scientific basis of the idea of the dissipation of material energy, we must recognize the obscurity it displays when it is extended beyond closed systems to the universe as a whole. Should one, too, with Bergson or Teilhard, attribute such an antithesis-value to the dissipation of energies, if it contributes (impregnated, no doubt, with spirit) to the creation of centres of unity that proceed precisely in the direction followed by the positive movement towards the summit of being?

We may wonder, moreover, whether the criterion of complexity is sufficient in itself to warrant the assertion of the qualitative discontinuity of the living in relation to material being, for this criterion is still based on a quantitative enumeration. All that the form or formula of the living assembles is simply a larger number of elements. Teilhard, however, makes use of these signs only to assert interiority and its progress. Moreover, it is certainly true that life is expressed only in physical and measurable manifestations.

2 While the attitude of the scientific world to Teilhard's work is generally favourable, science, particularly in fields of research still affected by materialism, is chary of recognizing the fact of a spiritual

energy at the origin of evolution and history, and fears the threat to determinism contained in irrational forces.

The difficulty that science (and physics and biology especially) finds in admitting a *spiritual energy* should not be overlooked, for scientific method essentially presupposes the measurement of phenomena, their anticipation, and the definition of what is invariable in them.

Science has the right to maintain the necessity for a positive verification of hypotheses and theories by experimental methods, by objective operational processes, that lead to precise definitions, quantitative measurements, laws or numerical functions: the whole being founded on the principle of determinism, that is to say on the invariability of a nature that is entirely free from any arbitrary and unforeseeable interventions, and on the complete rationality of the real. By reason of the universality of extension and of matter, the ideal of this mathematical method holds good for the totality of the real: there is no phenomenon that has not a quantitive aspect and that cannot, at least partly, be subjected to numerical analysis and to measurement, expressed in mathematical laws. In contrast with the physics of the ancients and the middle ages, Descartes laid down the definitive principle of the possibility of a reduction of all reality to the laws of extension and movement: as Plato had said before him, everything is 'geometry'.

Nevertheless the legitimacy and fruitfulness of this method are limited by the abstraction of its *dualism*: this, indispensable though it is to science, belongs to the order of representation and can only signify or symbolize, in terms of abstract truth, a concrete reality that continually escapes it. This method is justified for the purely material sectors or levels of reality, but is no longer so, by itself, at least, for those levels of the real that bring about the appearance of life and thought.

Life and thought, in fact, introduce both syntheses of extreme *complexity* and a *progress* in time, a higher finality and a history: the organization of living beings cannot be reduced to pure mechanism, and their transformations are the very antithesis of the invariability of material phases.

In the first place, *every physical structure*, as is every regularity, is already a mystery that implies much more than a play of material energies: what, then, shall we say of the complexities of the living?[77]

As to the *temporal becoming* of matter itself, this is just as great a mystery: no purely mechanical material cause can explain why the primitive universe evolved, in fact, towards living forms. The Marxist's introduction of a dialectic immanent in things is here no more than a flight from the real.[78] *A fortiori*, the evident progress of the living kingdom, and still more the fact of human history imply a factor of propulsion and invention, an active principle of emergence, different from determinism: Teilhard, adopting a Bergsonian expression, calls it 'spiritual energy'.[79]

By this he does not mean some 'occult force', reminiscent of medieval verbalism, but a fact, necessitated by respect for a total and indissociable reality, as called for by phenomenological method, in which matter and spirit are inextricably knit together. If, in the order of man, body and soul form one and the same substantial reality, in reciprocal action, in which spiritual energy (sometimes called 'morale') is a true concrete reality, in some way physical —then why should it not be admitted for the totality of the universe?[80]

Thus, without taking spiritual energy to be a 'thing'[81]—nor (as in vitalism) for an intermediate and distinct entity capable of pre-science and caprice—and explaining its effectiveness less through direct action than through a process of organization and arrangement[82]—Teilhard considers it a fact and a physical reality. He induces it from its observable and phenomenal effects, from the manifest invention it brings about, reversing, though without violating, natural determinisms. What is more, his logic leads him to expect that science may be able to appraise it in numerical terms.[83]

The positivist concept, too, of a strictly analytical method is being, if not superseded, at all events made more flexible, and completed by a method that can account for all the phenomena of the real and is adapted to each of its levels. Biology, in particular, has been obliged to call upon other principles than pure mathematical formalism and physical mechanism to explain and express the facts of finality, organization,[84] evolution, psychism, and psychosomatic interaction.[85] Here the work of Dr Chauchard reflects that of Lucien Cuénot and many others, as it does that of Bergson. In rejecting the dualism of matter and spirit and taking as the core of his thought the complexity-consciousness connexion, Teilhard's phenomenological work belongs also to a science that is faithful to the real and tries to find a total explanation of it.

Teilhard's realism makes it possible to attempt a conjunction. In the first place, he attributes great importance to *determinism*, to the effects of chance, to statistical laws, to nature's hesitant advances. 'We can only bow before this universal law whereby, so strangely to our minds, statistical necessity is mingled and confounded with a final purpose.'[86] It is essential that the probabilities of an opportunity for the emergence of spirit be infinitely multiplied.

Moreover, as we have seen, Teilhard does not hesitate to recognize that life 'presents itself experientially to science as a *material effect of complexity*'.[87] Modern research is making us familiar with the idea that matter contains fundamental *properties* that, once certain conditions of complexity have been attained, allow it to pass 'naturally' into life. With varying success, but always with hope, scientists are trying to simulate these conditions experimentally.[88] Already we have strong indications that show the natural possibility of the appearance of life from matter. In short, Teilhard's notion of a genesis of spirit is basically positive.

Accordingly, without seeking to reduce the opposition between spiritualism and materialism to a mere argument about words, we may hold that the real imposes the same obligations on both: the transition from one register to the other is effected by a system of equivalences. To explain the fundamental data represented by structures, constants, movement, and the progress of the movement towards unity—we must necessarily introduce a principle of unification and a principle of progress: what is called by one party a 'natural property' is called by the other active thought or spirit.[89] As for the 'dialectical power of negation' on which the Marxists, following Hegel, rely, this too is closely akin to spirit, which is defined by the very activity of negation.

Teilhard remained at the same time faithful both to the ancient notion and to the Cartesian (and modern) notion of matter. He retained, but as an unreal *abstraction*, the Platonic idea of an undefined, unorganized matter, a pure disorder of the multiple. He retained, too, the Aristotelian idea of a matter, the universal substratum, in potentiality (or desire?) for actualization, but in fact always given reality by its intelligible form, its organization of its elements. Finally, he accepted the Cartesian notion of a matter, a divisible and figurable extension, whose movement is a state of nature: it being understood, as we have already seen, that in this we have a dualist abstraction, necessary for the representation of the real and for effective action on the real. It is impossible to escape from this threefold aspect of matter, if we are to order and seriate its complementary phases.[90]

e: Comparison with modern scientific concepts

A comparison of Teilhard's views on matter and life with modern scientific concepts disclose numerous analogies. For contemporary science:[91]

1 Matter is, as a whole, *structure* and *energy*. The continuous medium of space-time has physical properties: geometry is physics, just as physics is geometry. The whole universe, then, is structured, in an organic inter-dependence of its elements. But matter is only the sensible manifestation of energy and may be reduced to energy by a system of equivalence.[92] Thus the element of the structures is seen only as an *incident* in an energy-system.

2 The two preceding categories of matter-energy are found again in two contrary but inseparable aspects:

— a tendency towards maximum *disorder*, through dissipation and disintegration: transition to the homogeneous, the uniform, to repetition, to identity, to inertia, to death; a levelling-down process. This tendency is seen in the macroscopic order in the dissipation of useful energy in heat; in the microscopic order, in radiation, that transforms material electrons into photons, or quantified grains of light; in the astronomical order, in the phenomenon of expansion.

— a tendency towards maximum *order* (unity, form, structure, architecture, organization, internal finality) through the integration of the elements in individual defined systems. This tendency, apparent at all levels through the influence of forces of convergence and attraction, is seen, in particular, in the atomic field. In conformity with Pauli's exclusion principle, two particles cannot exist simultaneously with the same set of quantum numbers, if their spin is taken into account. This exclusion, in which Louis de Broglie sees 'the least interpretable of the laws of physics' seems to be the first appearance at the heart of matter of the universal tendency towards diversified individualization (or singularity), the ascending progress towards the heterogeneous.[93]

Thus, against anti-finality there always stands a finality, against disorder an order.

3 Life, held back and paralysed in matter by the dominance of hostile forces, lies in an extension of this latter tendency: minuscule in the universe, but majuscule in its own order, it represents a victory of organized structure, of diversity, of variation and variety, of a stepping-up of energies. In Schrödinger's phrase, it is a 'negative entropy' a 'negentropy'. It is seen, in particular, in the photosynthesis effected by chlorophyll, the indefinite branching out of species and the mutations of their history, the variety of individuals and their mutual exclusivism,[94] the complexity of their structure, the autonomous interiority of their formation and development. It is a precarious victory, and constantly threatened: death being the return of the living to the homogeneous and to disintegration.[95]

4 The life-matter whole is knit together by a dialectic of *continuity* and *discontinuity*, which makes it into a system of correspondences.

If the biological order is marked by specific characteristics, it is foreshadowed, in the order of the quantum, by Pauli's principle, which postulates the 'singularity' of the particles; it is still more clearly announced at the molecular stage, where each DNA controls the formation of an individual enzyme.[96] Life would thus appear to be in potentiality everywhere in the universe—the characteristics of the higher living being becoming progressively impoverished and attenuated as we gradually get closer to matter.

Moreover, it would seem as though once the lower structures have been integrated in more fully structured systems, they are retained: all the elements of the living appear in Mendeleyev Periodic Table; but the energies of the lower structures, provisionally absorbed by the living, continue to threaten it with disintegration.

5 Finally, as Stéphane Lupasco has shown, a logic of *complementarity* controls, through a dialectic of potentiality and act, the contrary aspects of the universe: attraction and repulsion, unification (cohesion) and diversification, homogeneity and heterogeneity, identity and otherness, equilibrium and disequilibrium, symmetry and dissymmetry, variation and invariability, repetition and novelty, loss and accumulation, continuity and discontinuity. Thus it is that the corpuscle, the discontinuous stationary phenomenon, is tied to the continuous field of the wave. Everything goes to show that the realization or favoured emergence of one of these aspects causes the

other to pass into a condition of potentiality, and vice-versa, but without ever annihilating it: knowledge being powerless to attain exactness in relation to one except at the cost of exactness in relation to the other.[97]

IV THE INTERIORITY OF THE REAL

The twofold associated notion of organized form and spiritual energy implies that of interiority, which the unitary coherence of the world makes universal in the whole extension of the phenomenon. To this argument will be attached, if man is indeed the centre and the key of the universe, the invitation to make of life a distant and incomplete adumbration of reflexion.

It is essential that we admit, at the heart of what is most physical in the real, and in matter itself, the existence not only of an impersonal 'seed' of thought, to use the Stoic phrase, but of a concrete thought which possesses a beginning, minute though it may be, of consciousness, if not of personal reflexion. Thus there is no reality that has not both a *without* and a *within*;[98] and the entire cosmos is an interaction of these elements, of these seeds of interiority. The fact is that 'properly observed, even if only at one spot, a phenomenon necessarily has an omnipresent value and roots by reason of the fundamental unity of the world'.[99] 'Consciousness reveals itself as a cosmic property of variable size subject to a global transformation . . . Refracted rearwards along the course of evolution, consciousness displays itself qualitatively as a spectrum of shifting shades whose lower terms are lost in the night.'[100] 'If a piece of iron is heated to 500° it gives off red radiations: this does not, however, prove that before that there was no radiation in it.'[101]

Comparing the corpuscles of matter to a sphere that is not fully closed at each end, Teilhard points out, too, that matter has no true 'within' but only the predisposition to produce one, once the segments close up and come together: the corpuscles 'are still only fragments of immanence'.[102]

Teilhard wonders, incidentally, how consciousness can be passed on and communicated in the course of evolution. He finds that he should distinguish two sorts of *ego*: the first, which forms the kernel, more or less complete and rudimentary, is incommunicable; the other, peripheral and incompletely individualized, is divisible and transmissible.[103]

He formulates, too, the cardinal law of parallelism, or rather of *correspondence*, between the without and the within of beings; this law provides an experimental parameter of their growth of value in time. External complexity is always a sign of the advance of consciousness. 'Spiritual perfection (or conscious "centricity") and material synthesis (or complexity) are but the two aspects or connected parts of one and the same phenomenon.'[104] Although it is not possible to quote precise passages where it is stated, we are justified even in thinking that the correspondence in question expresses, in fact, a *causality*: there is no material form that is not the work of spirit, no biological structure that is not the effect of an action of the life to which it is linked, and is not expressed in it.

The hypothesis of a matter that is animated even in its energies and in its elementary forms by a hidden consciousness, coincides with some propositions of Leibnitz, Schelling, Ravaisson and Bergson.[105] 'Matter,' says Bergson, in a comment on his master, Ravaisson, 'cannot be anything but dormant spirit ... We must picture to ourselves an initial distension of spirit, a diffusion in time and space, which constitutes materiality.'[106] Borrowing again, the idea from Ravaisson, the author of *Creative Evolution* compares matter to a 'habit',[107] developed by mind, but partially deprived of consciousness, and defines it as a creative action which unmakes itself.

Behind Teilhard's position lies the logical necessity for continuity and connexion between life and its antecedents, but there is an even deeper basis in his fundamental proposition of the correspondence, and even the identity, between *unity* and *spirit*. This is a classic metaphysical notion, but Teilhard brings out the full depth of its physical consequence. The mutual affinity of the material elements in the unity of a structure seems to him even to be governed by some sort of aspiration, analogous to love.[108]

As Père Maréchal has rightly seen, it is possible, too, that Teilhard wished 'to interpret nature, in its ascending movement towards man, by analogies suggested to us by the immediate perception of our conscious life'; and he justifies his having, 'from the origins of natural evolution' introduced 'latent potentialities, sorts of *rationes seminales* that are already "thought' or "liberty", but the thought is in embryo and the liberty still held in check'.[109]

Teilhard, moreover, by no means accepts, as do some interpreters of the indeterminism of atomic phenomena, the illusion of elemen-

tary liberties that arbitrarily influence the real. Agreeing with
Bergson's view, in *Matter and Memory*, he attributes psychism to
matter only in a state of 'distension', 'in a way that is infinitely
diluted and unobservable'.[110]

The successive reductions that modern science has imposed on the
notion of matter, make it easier to accept the notion of a relatively
dematerialized matter. At the end of its analyses, 'physics is no
longer sure whether what is left in its hands is pure energy or, on the
contrary, thought'.[111] It is not beyond the bounds of possibility to
imagine lowerings of the degree of consciousness below the biological degree. And, for all its obscurity, St Paul's famous passage
(Rom. 8. 18–23) on 'the eager longing of creation', may well hint
at a diffused presence of spirit. Moreover, as E. Borne has shown,
the legitimate conclusions of the great philosophers, those of Plato,
Aristotle and Descartes, for example, do not rule out the necessity,
built into things, of thinking the real in its twofold and indivisible
aspect of separation and unity.[112] Here again, an attitude (we may
call it phenomenological) that respects the mysterious factual
connexion of matter and spirit that man's experience, at least, discloses, *cannot escape* the logical necessity of the interiority of the real
and of its spiritual energy: full scope, once again, being allowed to
the necessity for 'representation', in the form of extension and
mechanism.[113]

Finally, Teilhard's attitudes may be related to the modern notion
of 'information'. It would appear that, at every level, the structures
are informed both by their past through a sort of memory, by their
own capacities for combination with defined elements to produce
new syntheses, and by the entire universe. And the living being may
be regarded as a higher 'stock-pile' of information.

V SCIENCE AND PHILOSOPHY

For many modern scientists, the great difficulty lies in extending into
philosophy the scientific laws Teilhard extracted from the facts.
Moreover, Teilhard's avowed aim was to 'build a bridge' between
science and philosophy.[114]

On the whole, biologists would no doubt be ready to accept the
following propositions:

— The increase of unification in structures: as the advance of life is achieved, so more elements are collected in the unity of the same being.

— The correspondence between external complexity and level of interiority: a more evolved consciousness corresponds to a nervous system and a brain that are made up of more numerous and more sophisticated inter-relationships.

— The dialectic of continuity and discontinuity: matter, life and mankind, though bound together as one, none the less constitute three distinct entities, defined by new and uncomparable characteristics; they are three sectors separated by an absolute threshold.

For the majority of scientists these laws, which imply a belief in transformism, hold no difficulty in principle. Except perhaps in some fields of research, where positivist prejudices are still marked, there seems to be no serious objection to the assertion of man's transcendence over the animal kingdom, to his key position in the universe, or to his exclusive 'singularity'. The science of the phenomenon is justified in determining levels of value that can obviously be seen in the facts: experience is never really total and provides 'a homogeneous and coherent picture' only when it includes man, who alone can 'enable man to decipher the world'.[115] Observation of the convergence in history of biological forms (and through them of the whole of cosmic history) towards man may be regarded as a positive fact, one that is even to some degree measurable.

The real quarrel comes when these propositions are taken to their extreme limit, when we make an extrapolation that consists in the affirmation of the final point of cosmic evolution, Omega Point; this is contested not only by materialist atheism but, at least for a certain number of scientific minds, by scientific method itself.

Teilhard obviously attaches great importance to this affirmation and is at pains to justify it logically: the dynamic finality of the ascending movement of the cosmos implies a transcendent being, without which it cannot be explained.

In fact, compared with the laws referred to above, it constitutes a more philosophic position, apparently less directly related to facts. It steps boldly into an order that differs from sensible reality. Like every practical affirmation of God, it seems to carry with it a moral option, and implicit in it, no doubt, is the influence of Teilhard's religious faith.

We shall shortly have to discuss Teilhard's proposition of an ultimate unification of mankind and, included in it, of the ascent of history. Even when questioned, it still allows the affirmation of a transcendent absolute, the motive force and end of all reality.

There is nothing in this to hamper the autonomy of science's positive research; on the contrary, it provides it with the foundation that justifies its relative truth, the term towards which it strives, the supreme value it seeks, the soul of its curiosity, the hope that inspires its activity:[116] like every human action, it needs to be stimulated and maintained by a certainty of immortality, of which God is the warrant.[117] Purified, as we shall see, of any mythical imagery, of a spatial representation of becoming, Omega Point, accordingly, is not for science an irrelevant construction, an arbitrary option, but a necessity. Science can exist only when supported by its historic and concrete relation to an ultimate absolute, and when it has the guarantee of its implicit recognition.[118] Père Daniélou was right in congratulating Teilhard on having, in the face of modern scepticism and the crisis that threatened truth (even scientific), laid down the metaphysical basis of truth.[119]

Moreover, science can have no serious objection to seeing itself extended by a phenomenological examination of the significance of history. Does not science itself belong to history, part and parcel of it in countless ways, and is not science subject to the intimate influence of the spirit that is the motive force of history, the soul of all invention and all progress?

Finally, science, even in its most physical sectors, is never purely analytical: on the contrary, its essential approach is to proceed to progressively larger *syntheses*, to theories whose application is progressively wider and include all that went before as particular cases. In introducing a consideration of the totality of the real, Teilhard's approach simply pushed to the limit, carried to the limit, the natural movement of science. It leads spontaneously to the philosophical assertion that, for all its belonging to another order, is none the less intimately linked with the scientific act. The 'veil of phenomena',[120] which it is impossible to pierce with only the resources of science, is thus drawn aside—partially at least—and exposed to the total effort of thought; and so discloses their significance and meaning. Nevertheless, this thought itself will have to go beyond its abstraction in a real possession of truth and being.

Thus, while it does not belong to science properly so-called, the central approach of *The Phenomenon of Man* is still physical: experimental and adhering to the real, in contact with facts, it sets out to reveal what is implicit in them, to disclose what they have wrapped up in them, to induce the law of their being. This is indubitably philosophy, but it is positive philosophy: a new sort of philosophy that unites theory and reality in an intimate connexion. It is scientific phenomenology, and an indispensable basis for science.

Note on Transformism

We have reached the point where it becomes necessary to examine, even if in a summary fashion, the theory of transformism, which is the scientific basis of Teilhard's thought.

1 The transformist theory, which considers the history of the world in the dialectical scheme of a differentiated and progressive unity in time, rests on *the convergence of a large number of facts*: palaeontological (order of appearance and connexion of living forms); anatomical and physiological (survivals of transformations); embryological (ways of development of living beings); biogeographical (present distribution of living beings). Advances in palaeontology, in particular, are giving us a continually more complete picture of the last third of the history of life, from about the beginning of the vertebrates, including the history of the vegetable kingdom.

2 Nevertheless, these complementary facts are not a *sufficient basis* for the absolute certainty of the theory of a progressive genetic transformation of living beings. In the field of evolution, a phenomenon that belongs to history and occupies a vast period of time, there can be no real experimental proof, for direct experiment is impossible.[121] As Teilhard often stressed, we must expect to be unable to discover the peduncles that evidently linked a species to an earlier different species: precarious and indecisive, the birth of new forms has been blotted out by time. 'You never find a fossilized embryo.'[122] It is moreover, a general law of history that it is impossible to get hold of any authentic origin: because of the scarcity and scattered nature of the evidence, evolution appears discontinuous and full of gaps. Many links between species are still lacking and will probably never be determined.

At the same time, life shows an astonishing stability. Jean Rostand, himself nevertheless a transformist, goes so far as to say that 'the normal rule of life is invariability: for life, change is something quite unusual'. Teilhard himself notes, as a consequence of the animal's effort to ensure its survival as a species, 'the sharpness, the resistance to admixture, and the remarkable length (broken only here and there by some explosive mutation) of the phyletic lines in palaeontology'.[123]

3 Nevertheless, in spite of its gaps, transformism remains not only an acceptable but an *indispensable* explanation.

In the first and most important place, this is because of an *a priori necessity* that the real shall be intelligible, because it is impossible to conceive a fact that is not linked to an earlier fact by a chain of causality. This intellectual necessity corresponds, moreover, to the universal *interdependence* of phenomena in time and space, in particular to the interdependence of living beings; it corresponds, too, to the fact that their order of succession reveals a *progress*. The existence of living beings appears 'emerging from a background of chance events, of progressively more complex spatio-temporal structures tending towards a concentration, an ordered convergence, of phenomena whose character is not explicable in terms of chance',[124] —the phenomena of orthogenesis.

4 The search for *mechanical* and measurable *explanations*, if possible physico-chemical, is legitimate and necessary.

As we have said earlier, science is obliged to accept the *dualist* abstraction, that chooses the search for the laws of extension and movement: while the idea of finality, in so far as it is identified with organization, is scientific, it is unacceptable to science when it claims to designate the directing activity of a vital force, the 'prophetic preparation of the future'.[125]

Historically, various theories have therefore tried to interpret the facts: *Lamarckism* puts forward the hypothesis of an adaptation of the interior needs of the living being, and then of its structure, to modifications in the external environment. *Darwinism* puts forward the theory of vital competition that ends in the elimination of the ill-adapted and the selection of the better adapted.

Modern science, using the evidence of genetics, no longer looks, like Lamarck and Darwin, to the hypothesis of exclusive exterior influences, but to the experimental study of the *internal structure* of living nuclei: penetrating as far as the molecular level, it attributes the modifications of species to accidental disturbances of the molecule of DNA. Just as moving around the letters of the alphabet produces new words and new meanings, so a permutation of the order of the elements of DNA can produce new bacteria. Re-adopting, then, the theories of Lamarck or Darwin, all we have to assume is that a modification of environment or selective competition was able formerly to determine and amplify the permutations of the molecule: 'selection favours characteristics that gradually spread to the whole population'[126] and species end by diverging through the progressive accumulation of genetic differences.

The search for the mechanisms of evolution is being conducted more and more with the aid of mathematical procedures. It was thus that Gaylord Simpson was able to determine the statistical laws of evolution: rate of mutation, duration of generations, sizes of populations. In their study of the primitive chemism of the earth's crust, Miller and Calvin have accepted the possibility in theory of a progressive differentiation of organic combinations that could be seen as forerunners of the chemical structures proper to living structures.[127]

If, for Bergson himself, there can be no questioning 'the fundamental identity of inorganic matter and organic matter', analysis will undoubetdly resolve the process of organic creation into an ever-increasing number of physico-chemical phenomena; [128] and if 'to measure a thing will sometimes disclose its nature',[129] then mathematical expression can to some extent give us the very essence of life.

5 Nevertheless, while physico-chemical mechanism can, up to a point, account for *how* things happen and the way in which phenomena appear, it cannot by itself illuminate them fully or explain them completely: analytical description of the micro-causalities that condition the progress of life cannot reconstruct the general directed significance of evolution.[130]

Mechanism, which reduces the higher to the lower, cannot completely explain the *structure* of the living (its unity of elements, its complexity of organization) any more than it can its *interiority* (its autonomy, its consciousness). It is baffled, too, by the fact of its *history*, that is to say the ordered movement of its increasing complexification: the more so that, as we saw earlier, determinism by itself is a factor of repetition, of preservation, of imitation—and not of progress, innovation and invention. 'The significance of man reacts as an influence on the whole of the universe that conditions him.'[131]

Thus, to explain the directed dynamism of life, its trend towards more organized and improbable forms, many philosophers and scientists come to accept the notion of *spiritual energy*: an activity of a different order from that of mechanical causality and one which integrates, without doing violence to, determinisms.[132]

In any case, few would reject the idea of *levels of explanation* (physical, chemical, philosophical, religious) at once autonomous and complementary, each recognizing what is valid in the others.[133]

CONCLUSION

Looked at in this way, in isolation from the whole body of his work, Teilhard's cosmology obviously represents no more than an abstraction: leaving that aside for the moment, it needs to be taken further by a study of the phenomenon of man and by theology. The world of matter and of life was an anticipation and gestatory period of man, whose root and background, and the condition of whose liberty, it still remains. It can have no justification except in its ultimate end, and no basis except in its culmination. Though real and existing in itself, it is nevertheless interior to man, who recognizes it and projects it as an object; and the substance of its being, made up of structures and energies, is given to it by God, from whom it depends.

At the same time, this world, even when considered in isolation, merits the attention given to it by Teilhard: and this because it already displays the higher realities that are to develop and derive all their impulse with the world of matter as their starting point: the evolution of life, and the matter that precedes it, reveal at the very heart of their mechanisms, and beyond, the presence and action of a spiritual energy that is responsible for the organization of their forms and of the movement of invention that converts them into an ordered and intelligible history.

What is more, scientific observation cannot really 'respect the phenomena' (*salvare apparentias*) except by going beyond them in the metaphysical affirmation of a reality that is greater than the phenomena. In a later discussion we shall try to determine the value of the line of argument that postulates Omega Point as the fulfilment of the unification of man. There can be no doubt, however, that the existence of a transcendent absolute should not be inferred rationally, starting from the phenomena of matter and life, as a complete explanation of their being and progress, and an answer to the problem presented by their structure and movement. This, no doubt, is an abstract problem, if it is cut off from the real living man, but it is one that the universe itself calls on us to answer.

There are some who may feel that the hypothesis of a hidden consciousness, or of spirit in the heart of things, is indeed precarious; nor can there be any doubt that Teilhard's intuitions suffered from his not submitting them to a rigorous criticism that would examine the relationship of the picture he gave to the meaning he intended, of the language he used to the idea behind it. Though impossible to represent, it must be admitted, and going beyond pure science, the hypothesis is none the less necessary to define the unity of different orders, the highest of which are the basis and warrant of those they are superior to. And, if spirit exists in man, why should it not be found also deep in the heart of things? Teilhard's cosmology, moreover, without succumbing to the temptation to 'realize' or 'thing-ify' the consciousness and energy it discloses in the real, is at least fully justified in reflecting the mystery of a cosmos which oversteps mechanical categories and in which, most important of all, a mystery of love will soon be disclosed.

Chapter 5
Anthropology

Teilhard's phenomenology has brought out man's position in the global history of the universe, and revealed his supreme finality; at the same time there are implicit in it the basic propositions of an anthropology, or science of man. These, too, need to be examined and filled out in a more wide-reaching and precise analysis. It is worth noting, too, how a scientific outlook, for which man is in the first place a 'phenomenon', opens out so readily into an existential view in which man is no longer simply a source of wonder to himself but a problem.[1]

I THE HUMAN CONDITION

An examination of the human condition reveals in turn man's transcendence of the universe and his implication in it: it reveals, too, his psychic structure.

a: Man's transcendence of the universe

If man is observed *from outside*, scientifically, as a phenomenon in history, we see that on the biological plane, but even more in the active means he disposes of, in what he does and makes, he transcends matter and animality.[2]

He represents a *negation of the determinisms* that enslave instinct to immediately useful ends; an advent of the indeterminate; an undefined field open to action; a potential emergence of leisure and freedom;[3] a limitless potentiality for thought.

The phenomenon of man is in the first place the victory of improbability; even more than life it runs counter to the downward regression of material energies and the inertia of mechanisms. It creates 'within the universe a continually deeper and wider centre of indeterminacy and information'.[4]

Situated in the world, whose centre of perspective and construction he is, man represents a fixed point in, and gives significance to, the becoming of the universe;[5] and, if all the aspects of animality are still to be found in him, they are at the same time metamorphosed in him.[6] Man 'appears as a continuous zone of spiritual transformation, in which all lower realities and forces, without exception, are exalted into sensations, ideas and powers of knowing and loving'. Using another metaphor, we will find Teilhard saying that the phenomenon of hominization is the transition from a diffuse state (of consciousness) to a state that is strictly concentrated at one point; or, again, that it is concentration of the circle of living beings in its own centre.[7]

Man, however, has also the unique privilege of being able to arrive at himself *from within* and to provide evidence about his own self. He then emerges, no longer as consciousness in general, but as personal interiority: in the very process of acting, this turning back upon himself which constitutes reflexion enables him to see himself as a subject, distinct from the object he knows or pursues; he affirms himself in this relationship and sees himself standing as a creative centre; he endows himself with a permanent unity.[8] Unique in his biological and psychic characteristics, man gradually acquires an individual personality which distinguishes him from others and which, through the sum total of the choices he makes, takes on responsibility for his destiny.[9]

An even closer exploration can disclose to him the depth of an unfathomable abyss, from which rises the mysterious fact of life.[10] This exploration, which is associated with his experience of the universal interconnexions that are necessary to his existence, gives him a glimpse of the creative activity by which he is sustained. Taken all together, these experiences give him the consciousness of being a person, universal in value and absolute in dignity.

At the same time man is in fact *incomplete*, unstable, and, as though cantilevered without apparent support.[11] He is in tension, too, towards God, his origin, whom he seeks to rejoin as his end. Infinite in capacity, of unbounded receptivity, he feels a thirst for fulfilment and eternity, an eagerness for 'continually more-being';[12] he strives to go beyond himself, and the driving force behind his actions is his desire for 'a result that nothing can destroy'.[13] Finally, he has 'the sacred appetite for being'.[14] The need for the absolute comes with the very first awakening of consciousness and the confrontation with death involved in it, and, as hominization progresses, that need continually grows greater: 'From the moment when consciousness, by reflecting upon itself, begins to *foresee*, every being, no matter how primitive, starts to reject as shocking the idea that it can ever *entirely* disappear.'[15]

This spontaneous tendency towards God first shows itself in relation to absolute *values* of truth[16], beauty, good (justice and love), which man finds incarnated in the concrete beings around him: these concrete beings are the envelopes in which God reveals himself in terms of these absolute values. In spite of a certain barrier, man discovers in himself a natural sympathy with these ideal values; the next step is to recognize, under the signs and veils, the reality of a personal God. Corresponding analogically, the planes of being are successively ranged *in depth*. Knowledge is invited to go through these stages until their term is reached.[17] In all these orders of values, man has a capacity for the absolute.

Particular mention should be made, but this time on the plane of history, of the desire for *totality* and the universal, which seeks to give 'to the extensions of the world . . . a concentration that embraces everything that is beautiful: individuals, thoughts, things.'[18]

This desire to attain the absolute and the universal is the underlying basis of man's *freedom* and his power of choice, coexistent both with the determinisms it overcomes and with the spirit or spiritual energy of the world that is immanent in it. In man, consciousness of freedom is 'the advanced and distinct expression' of a universal reality hidden under physical mechanisms.[19]

Thus even when Teilhard's thought relies only on scientific observation or interior reflexion, it brings out with sufficient emphasis man's absolute discontinuity in relation to nature (material and biological); and the dialectic it establishes stresses similarly the *negative* aspect of the rupture: man is not entirely in nature, he escapes from the conditions that determine him. Religion will simply confirm and sanctify his innate attitude to freedom and extend to its utmost his own development as a person.[20]

b : Man's involvement in the universe

Man's transcendence, however, is dialectially bound up with his insertion into the universe.

Man, including his thought, is a *natural* phenomenon, an event occurring in the series of facts: he 'must be looked at in the same way as other phenomena . . . he is the expression, seen by us from within, of a property that is universal in the world',[21] of a fundamental current of things.

'Born of the earth',[22] initially 'isolated and defenceless', man remains passive and determined; through the medium of biology, he is in solidarity with, and indissociable from, the whole of the universe, to whose influences he, too, is subject. 'It is only through the extreme peak of our own selves that we can emerge into reflexion and freedom.'[23]

Man is a *microcosm*, corresponding to and in tune with the entire universe: no wonder, then, that the universe can be understood by observing and knowing man. In particular, man's experience of invention and freedom is the higher form of the invention, working in obscurity, that brings about the progress of matter and life.[24]

Man's situation, and that of thought itself, is essentially *within time* and history. Man is involved in the history of the universe, and appears at a moment determined by the laws that control a process of cosmic and biological maturing: he rests on a vast accumulation of physical and biological entities without which he could never have emerged. Here Teilhard introduces an interesting but unusual idea, a relationship which he calls the 'yield' of cosmogenesis.[25]

However personal it may be, the flow of consciousness is itself a participation in world-time: 'Space-time, like some subtle fluid, first absorbs our bodies and then penetrates our souls, too. It fills the soul, it impregnates it, and is so involved with its powers that it soon becomes impossible to distinguish it from the soul's own thoughts.'[26]

But how can we 'conceive a cosmogenesis that extends to spirit without at the same having to recognize the existence of a *Noogenesis*?' Spirit, too, is 'the structured term of a determined operation'; mankind is 'the leading wave of a universe that is illuminated as it closes in on itself'; hominization is 'the particular form assumed, and the final term—so far as we can see at present—arrived at by the molecULIzation of the universe, when it has reached the extreme limit of complexity'.[27] 'It is in the form not, I would say, of concepts but of *thought* that the stuff of things gradually concentrates, in the pure state, at the peak of the cosmos—in the most stable form, which means the form that has become most completely irreversible.'[28] 'Evolution is a continual process of personalization.'[29] Although it appears utterly insignificant compared with thermodynamic forces, the 'hominized quantity of energy' nevertheless represents the hope of the world.[30]

Stage by stage, and crisis by crisis, noogenesis continues in history; as the result of various factors history is punctuated, along its route, by profound *mutations* of human consciousness; these have repercussions in every field and necessitate radical readjustments: 'Surely, as man becomes adult, he must become aware of this or that primary "demand" that hitherto, for lack of a stimulus, has remained dormant deep within him?'[31]

c: Man's psychic structure

For the attainment of his end man is provided with a complex psychic structure, in which we can see both his spiritual greatness and his biological origin.

His *thought* can attain the true: at the same time, to do so, it must free itself from appearance and illusion; it must accept the necessity of an indefinite analysis and, in its syntheses, it must overlook no element of the real.[32] Closely linked with the absolute of being, in which it shares, and with the existence in time of the world, it possesses the structures (or categories) necessary for understanding and expressing reality. There is nothing that cannot or should not be thought: far from having a direct intuition of himself, man knows himself, comes into his own consciousness, only in the act of objectivizing, in the activity that judges truth.[33] There is no devaluation of the understanding in Teilhard, no tendency to separate the intuitive and intellectual functions, no neglect of 'representation'. In its own degree and in its respective order, all speculation (in science, philosophy or theology) shares, through abstraction, in the spirit's ascent towards fulfilment and possession of the concrete; this will be attained, in religious existence, at the term of an existential journey. And an informed observer can already see that the very sensitivity through which the world reaches man is surrounded by a radiant aura in which can be discerned the essential mystery of the universe.[34]

At the same time Teilhard, still faithful to his evolutionary outlook, refrains from defining man as 'rational', as fully constituted reason. He prefers, as we saw, to dwell on the historical advance represented by *reflexion*, which is a transition into centred, personal, consciousness.

In order to understand the real, man has at his disposal a *language*; this enables him, through the medium of signs and images, to express not only the truth of phenomena but also, through analogy and correspondence, that of spiritual realities. The sign in its mediative function is an *incarnation* of the idea: the mediation operates both in the inner content of words and in the complementary overtones added by symbols, which enrich the idea by evoking the different aspects of the sensible world.[35] It has the advantage of arousing an affective emotion, which facilitates the understanding of the idea. Nevertheless, in every field, the expression is still *inadequate* to the reality. It can even happen that men 'are submerged in the words they have created', lose sight of the real problems and fail to grasp the meaning of their experiences.[36]

Man's activity, through the medium of the *tool*, is another factor in knowledge of the real. While an animal can act on the world only through its body and the specialized transformations of its limbs, man has succeeded in winning and keeping his freedom by the creation of artificial instruments, separate from himself and designed for every sort of function. But if the tool is homologous with the brain and the hand—in fact an extension of nature—once it appears, progress in instrumentation replaces progress in the development of organs.

Man's bodily and biological character involves a complex *affectivity*.[37] Although this is ambivalent, and can produce disorder, in its higher forms it is of the utmost value, for, in addition to the contact it ensures with the world,[38] it is the energy behind rational action, and the instrument of the intellectual curiosity and love that takes the person beyond itself: the will never acts except in the hope of obtaining some joy.[39] It has a continually increasing need to be stimulated by 'the appeal of the future', by the incomplete, the unexpected, the ideal.[40]

Affectivity is, simultaneously and alternately, emotion and passion. *Emotion*, which is shorter-lived and concentrated like some source of potential energy, is the principle of creation, in which it expresses, spreads and disperses itself, and so converts itself into

work. Passion is lasting and true to itself, and is the permanent
dynamism that maintains the pursuit of some value.

Comprehending both emotion and passion, *love* is the supreme
form of human energy. When it is at least linked to Omega, penetrated and animated by God, it unifies all the powers of the ego; it
fulfils and totalizes personality in a total commitment that consists
in an adherence to being, while at the same time it produces
communion of persons.[41]

One particular aspect of this universal love, *sexuality*, is of special
importance: 'The energy that feeds and elaborates our interior life
is originally passionate in nature. Like every other animal, man is
essentially an urge towards the union that brings completeness; he is
a capacity to love. Plato pointed this out a long time ago. It is from
this primordial impulse that the rich complexity of intellectual and
emotional life develops and builds up and assumes different forms.
However lofty and widespread the ramifications of our spirit, their
roots still reach down into the physical. It is from man's deep
reserves of passion that the warmth and light of his being arise,
transfigured. It is in them that is initially concentrated, like a seed,
the highest and most subtle essence, the most sensitive motor, of
our whole spiritual development.'[42]

Affectivity, again, makes man capable of *suffering*; though this,
indeed, is 'the natural condition of life and progress'.[43]

We should recognize, moreover, several *levels* or layers of consciousness in man: while consciousness, through affectivity, reaches
down into the obscure depths of life, at the same time, as it
approaches its highest peaks, it is linked also to God; God acts upon
it, in a trans-experiential way, through its keenest extremity,[44]
giving solidity to its natural fragility and instability.[45] And, even
though the faculties or functions of the ego operate in relative independence, they are bound together in a spiritual centre of
synthesis that is capable of intuitions of a higher order.[46]

With this affiliation to cosmic energy to support and strengthen it,
the ego is capable of *creative invention*;[47] in every field it can start from
what exists, and then act otherwise, do more or better, make some
real addition to being, and in so doing, itself gain in stature. Here
we have a personal act, in which the whole ego is involved and
rises up into freedom. Following Bergson and some of Edouard Le
Roy's suggestions, Teilhard emphasizes this personal act.

Although the free act is not seen, on the lines of Bergson's *Time and Free Will*, as a return to the authenticity of the underlying ego, it is thus deeply involved in the various stages of the development of personality, in particular in moral and spiritual life; and it is seen in the choice that is offered by the alternative of fidelity to spiritual energy or its rejection in individualism. Thus authenticity is achieved not by direct intuition but by an existential act of invention and self-conquest, an act that is continually reinitiated but will never be completed until the end of duration.[48]

Teilhard's analysis of freedom, however, is somewhat over-concise, and stops short of a more subtle examination that would have disclosed the 'abnormal' and almost miraculous emergence of a 'decisive' act which, starting from a datum (interior and objective) commits itself totally to a future that it itself determines: the pure occurrence of an instant, both in time and outside time, a dramatic *ekstasis* or breakthrough that causes man, through a dying, to be born and re-born into existence, and that culminates in religious conversion.[49]

We should note that Teilhard, in contrast with Bergson, says nothing, or relatively little,[50] about memory. Memory, however, is involved in the fact of invention, both psychic and cosmic, since creative innovation can arise only on the foundation of the past, preserved and recalled in and for the very advance that is made upon it. On the other hand Teilhard is with Bergson in emphasizing the fact and danger of *habit*, which, in the individual, is the homologue of, or corresponds to, life's relaxation of effort or acceptance of routine, and in the face of which freedom has continually to be reconquered.[51]

For Teilhard, *intuition* of the concrete real—which must be clearly distinguished from other as yet theoretical, abstract and partial intuitions—is effected by travelling through the complete range of values (which we shall examine shortly), a range that culminates in loving knowledge of God and the world, in consciousness of self as freedom given to the conscious self by God for a work of cooperation with him in history. It is this fulfilment, desired, at any rate, in hope, that will justify and give their respective values to the different types of knowledge of the real, and to the different, partial, perceptions of things and persons. In other words, while Teilhard is far from denying the reality and fruitfulness of the creative emotion that underlies a particular theory or global vision of the world, he seems, with reason, entirely to abandon Bergson's utopia of an intuition of life or movement (through return and coincidence). *The real can be attained only in the totality of the organic stages through which man passes in order to fulfil himself in being*, and which culminate in spiritual existence.[52] Scientific knowledge leads directly into philosophical knowledge (which is still intellectual), and the latter is normally continued in moral and religious 'action' this last alone can give true knowledge of being, but at the same time it reacts, in order to 'authenticate' them, on the earlier modes of grasping the real.

II PERSONALISM

These propositions bring out the central importance Teilhard attributed not only to man in general, but to the human *person*, in its irreplaceable and incommunicable uniqueness.[53] The personal is the cardinal fact in a universe that is advancing towards maximum unity, and whose term is the communion of persons in God: it is the 'mesh' of the cosmos.[54] The hypothesis of 'person' and 'personalization' is progressively verified by the coherence it gives to the whole of the movement of the real.

In language that comes extremely close to that of the modern philosophy of the *pour soi* and the *pour autrui*, Teilhard analyses the threefold property possessed by every consciousness: (1) of centring *everything* to some extent around itself; (2) of being able to centre upon itself continually more fully; and (3) of being drawn by this self-concentration *into conjunction with all other centres* that surround it.[55]

The '*person*' is a distinct *individual*; but, in as much as it is so, it is tempted to an isolation that impoverishes it. On the other hand, communion in love heightens its uniqueness and increases its value. 'What makes a centre "individual" is its distinctness from the other centres that surround it. What makes the "personal" is being profoundly itself . . . Individuality decreases with centrogenesis, and is completely lost (in Omega) when personality reaches its maximum.'[56] Persons then, without losing their separate identity in one another, are in fact released from all excessive selfish isolation.[57]

Observation of man, no doubt, is primarily conducted from

outside him, regarding him as a phenomenon, for an objective science of man is today possible. Thanks, however, to Père Auguste Valensin, Teilhard kept abreast with the writings of Maurice Blondel and also with the Thomistic revival, inaugurated by Pères Sertillanges and Rousselot and developed by Père Maréchal. He accepted, accordingly, the possibility of a study of man that would analyse his thought and will, study the moral alternative presented to him, and so bring out his spiritual transcendence, his power to affirm being, and his duty to go beyond himself through the life of religion. He was familiar with the enquiries of existential personalism and its rediscovery of man as relation with the other, as dramatic freedom in the face of moral options.

While Teilhard provides the philosophies of the spirit with an indispensable complement by emphasizing man's relation with the universe and with history, at the same time there is less of a gulf between the two points of view than might be imagined, for a philosophy of the spirit can disclose the spirit only *in its incarnations* and creations, in its intentions and projects, from which consciousness arises:[58] and, for Teilhard, positive, phenomenal observation of man also works back *from the sign to being*.

Thus it is that, while bringing out man's evident incorporation in animality and also the fundamental relationship between the person and the world through the activity by which the former is personalized and fulfilled,[59] Teilhard at the same time brings out man's absolute transcendence: this he does by examining, from the outside, his power and his *works*: his use of tools, his language and culture.

The scientific point of view adopted in *The Phenomenon of Man* could not, no doubt, reveal the mystery of man's appearance, for that goes far beyond its conditions and expressions; at the same time, however, Teilhard was aware of the inexpressible character of the soul: 'Man's secret . . . lies in the spiritual nature of the soul. Now this soul, entirely synthetic in its activities, escapes science, the essence of which is to analyse things into their elements and material antecedents. Only insight and philosophical reflexion can find it.'[60]

Similarly, Teilhard is ready to make his way down into the inmost depths of the ego, as the following passage (oddly reminiscent of *Time and Free Will*) illustrates: 'I took the lamp and, leaving the zone of everyday occupations and relationships where everything seems clear, I went down into my inmost self, to the deep abyss whence I feel dimly that my power of action emanates. But as I moved further and further from the conventional certainties by which social life is superficially illuminated, I became aware that I was losing contact with myself. At each step of the descent a new person was disclosed within me of whose name I was no longer sure, and who no longer obeyed me. And when I had to stop my exploration because the path faded from beneath my steps, I found a bottomless abyss at my feet, and out of it came—arising I know not from where —the current which I dare call my life.'[61]

It is worth noting, too, that the problem of the activation of human energy (which we shall soon have to discuss) should have led Teilhard to an 'introspection' of evolution in its social form: what he aimed at was a 'spectroscopy of the energy of evolution from within'.

III THE EXISTENTIAL DISTRESS

Once again Teilhard meets the philosophers of existence on a plane that they have made their own. His personalism is by no means simply one of principle and affirmation: it develops through an exploration in depth of the human person, in which it reveals a fundamental suffering. A number of factors contribute to this. As such, man is so constituted that his condition, which makes him a problem to himself, cannot but bring distress. Existence is essentially incomplete, a mixture of being and non-being, of bond and free; it is alive to the appeal of an infinite value that it must desire and pursue but that continually escapes it; it is responsible for the whole of the universe and history; it can never be certain of its own personal success or of the world's success; existence, then, must be justified. This, as we have seen, is the stimulus behind Teilhard's enterprise.

An analysis of his work enables us to bring together in a synthesis, at least in some sort of tabular form, the scattered elements of an interior analysis that he constantly sought to extend.

a: Multiplicity

In the first place, man is cut off from the unity he passionately desires, 'the multiplicity of the flesh, the dualism of man's nature, the

very complexity of the soul as it forces its head above the swirling
dust of a world that is hardly consolidated; the misery of the personal
multitude within us.'[62]

b: Man's passivity

The passivities, internal or external, of diminishment: strokes of
misfortune, personal inferiorities: 'collapse, rebellion, inner
tyranny.'[63]

More widely, there is man's weakness and subjection in relation
to the impersonal forces of the universe: 'on certain days the world
seems a terrifying thing: huge, blind and brutal. It buffets us about,
drags us along, and kills us with complete indifference. Heroically,
it may truly be said, man has contributed to create a more or less
habitable zone of light and warmth in the midst of the great, cold,
black waters—a zone where people have eyes to see, hands to
soothe, and hearts to love. But how precarious is that habitation.
At any moment the vast and horrible thing may break in through the
cracks—the thing we try hard to forget is always there, separated
from us by a flimsy partition: fire, pestilence, storms, earthquakes,
or the unleashing of dark moral forces—these heartlessly sweep away
in one moment what we have laboriously built up and made
beautiful with all our intelligence and all our love'.[64]

c: Time

The passage of time is one aspect of these fundamental passivities:
'there still remains that slow, essential deterioration which we cannot escape: old age little by little robbing us of ourselves and
pushing us on towards the end. The passing of time, which postpones possession, which tears us away from enjoyment, which
condemns us all to death—what a formidable passivity is that'.[65] We
find this same thought in a war-time letter: 'Time that carries us
along and gives rhythm to our lives, time that passes too slowly or
too quickly, time that separates us mercilessly from a longed-for
date, or makes the hours of reunion go by too fast: time which stands
in our way to prevent us from achieving in the twinkling of an eye
the improvements we dream of in ourselves or in those around us:
time which makes us grow old.'[66] In a letter of 27 August 1931,
Teilhard is planning an essay entitled 'Prayer in duration'. It was
to be 'at the same time an interpretation, a making one's own, an

acceptance and a transfiguration of the world, put forward in the context of the deepest and most commonly shared of man's questionings, anxieties and emotions: those of discovering, enduring, growing old and waiting—all of which are effects or forms of duration'.[67]

d: Death

'In death, as in an ocean, all our slow or swift diminishments flow together and merge. Death is the sum and consummation of all our diminishments: it is *evil* itself—purely physical evil, in so far as it results organically from the manifold structure of that physical nature in which we are immersed—but moral evil too, in so far as this disordered plurality, the source of all conflict and all corruption, is produced, both in society and in our own selves, by the wrong use of our freedom.'[68]

The agony of death, something unknown to the animal, is the fruit of *reflective thought*: the more highly this develops, the more does it tend to question itself about the reason for being and the goal of existence:[69] since man can foresee his own death, he asks himself whether it is worth while living and creating. 'Tomorrow? But who can guarantee us a tomorrow anyway? And without the assurance that this tomorrow exists, can we really go on living, we to whom has been given—perhaps for the first time in the whole story of the universe—the terrible gift of foresight?'[70]

e: The magnitude of the universe

Characterizing the 'infinitely great and the infinitely small' as two 'abysses', Teilhard adds: 'What is the first effect on our minds of the appearance of these immeasurable depths? Clearly, to make us feel that we are engulfed, annihilated. Squeezed between the vast and the very small, life and humanity seem lost and insignificant.'[71]

His own travels suggested to Teilhard the thought that 'our domain is absurdly constricted. We feel increasingly driven to find some way out. Nothing but the earth, that is not enough.'[72] 'The universe is a vast thing in which we should be lost if it did not converge upon the person.'[73]

In his examination of the sources of his existence and in his reflexions on the countless physical conditions of his personality, Teilhard adds, 'At that moment, as anyone else will find who cares to make this same interior experiment, I felt the distress characteristic to a particle adrift in the universe, the distress which makes human wills founder daily under the crushing number of living things and stars.'[74]

Sometimes again, this distress comes out in the form of prayer: 'To some of your servants, Lord, the world, our new world, the world of nuclei and atoms and genes, has become a source of cease-less anxiety—for it now seems to us as though, being about to cast itself into the wide ocean of matter, it yet hesitates for fear that in acquiring a new dimension it should see its God suddenly dis-integrate.'[75]

'The more, Lord, the years pass by, the more I believe that I can see in me and around me that the great, hidden, concern of modern man is far from being to quarrel over the possession of the world: it is to find some way of escaping from it. The agony of feeling that one is not only spatially but ontologically imprisoned in the cosmic bubble! The heart-rending search for some way out, or rather some centre, for evolution!'[76]

f: Man's isolation

Even deeper, because more intimate and more a denial of the long-ing for intercommunion of persons, is the 'agony of isolation'. Torn asunder in his own self, man is constituted also in a state of social separateness: the autonomy of the person arises only from the foundation of a totality, from which it severs itself, but which it must nevertheless regain.

As early as 1917, Teilhard came to recognize this agony and so introduced one of existentialism's favourite propositions: 'It seems to me that terrestrial beings, as they become more autonomous, psychologically richer, shut themselves up in some way against one another, and at the same time become *strangers* to the cosmic environment and currents, *impenetrable* to one another, and *incapable of exteriorizing themselves*.'[77] He goes on, very rightly, to attribute this to a necessity in nature, that splits up the vital current among individuals, and to the fact of moral responsibility, as a structure of consciousness, which can 'become intoxicated by independence and seek to dominate or repel others'.

He goes on to describe the psychic consequences of such a dis-sociation: nostalgia for fusion with the whole, the horror of ice-cold solitude, the bewilderment of freedom and choice, the fear that history may be simply one great failure, endangered by the very development of personal thought.[78] This is a most penetrating passage, which throws a new light on Teilhard's position and brings out the existential character of his project. It is no surprise, again, to see him, without denying the gratuity of Christ's intervention, appealing to him as the *solution of unity*, for man and for history.[79]

Later, developing this in a more organized way, Teilhard was to return to this analysis, describing in turn the 'agony of plurality' and the 'agony of differentiation'.[80]

Further, his own personal experience was more than once to make him realize the unbridgeable gulf between both intellectual points of view and moral options, and the part played by incompatibilities of temperament.

g : Man's distress : the problem of evil

All these complementary factors are summed up in the existential experience of man's distress. Like the whole world, and in company with the world, man is an infinite yearning that is denied: 'O men, in whom heart-rending agony and gnawing desire have been implanted as by vocation!'[81]

In 1918 Teilhard had described the groaning of the universe: 'All around us we can see nothing but irreconcilable division and innate antagonism: everywhere the worthless is mixed up with the precious —the wheat growing up with the tares. Everywhere we see uselessness, wastage, loss . . . superficial incoherence . . . deceptive appearances . . . the universal lament of creatures imprisoned in inert matter' . . . organic isolation and deliberate egoism (among the monads).'[82] One cannot but be reminded of the famous passage in St Paul where he speaks of the groaning of creation. And, in fact, man's groaning is the groan of the entire universe, the very soul of the world.[83]

The subject comes up again, of course, in *Le Milieu Divin*: 'Man is constantly torn by the separations which set distance between bodies, which set the impossibility of mutual understanding between souls, which set death between lives. Moreover, at every minute he must lament that he cannot pursue and embrace everything within the compass of a few years. Finally, and not without reason, he is incessantly distressed by the crazy indifference and the heartbreaking dullness of a natural environment in which the greater part of individual endeavour seems wasted or lost, where the blow and the cry seem stifled on the spot, without awakening any echo.'[84]

These numerous and emphatic observations—the product of no limited mind—are a sufficient answer to the criticism of Teilhard as a thinker who paid less attention to the personal conflicts inherent in consciousness, to the activity of consciousness as something lived, and to its unique universe, than to cosmic forces, to the great aggregations of men, and mass phenomena.[85] They may serve, too, to blunt the accepted Pascal–Teilhard contrast.

No doubt, too, Teilhard's over-all vision, his embrace of time, and his bias towards synthesis, may sometimes give the impression that he was blind to individual realities.[86]

Similarly, he admits that he is more sensitive to the aspirations of his time than to human pity.[87] In contrast, it would seem, with the emphatic demands of the Christian revolution and the teaching of the encyclicals, the common good (including the common good of the future) interests Teilhard more than today's immediate problem of the emancipation and free development of the person. His plan to mobilize energies for the collective advancement of man seems rather to evade the issue when one considers how urgently the problem of justice here and now is sometimes discussed, and how deeply committed to it some of us are.

Moreover, for all Teilhard's insistence on the value of personality, his concern to reject individualism and offer man the prospect of a communal vocation may well have prevented him from vindicating with sufficient profundity the individuality of each person's consciousness and freedom. His theory of history as centred on the universal unification of beings and orientated towards the Omega in which men will be brought together, should, no doubt, have been more fully counterbalanced by the affirmation of *the primacy of the person* over the whole. However, the scientific viewpoint of *The Phenomenon of Man* made it impossible to appeal to the mystery of a creative love or to introduce the Incarnation of God. The frequent repetition of the phrase 'union differentiates' never goes beyond the expression of an empirical statement. Finally, some passages exalt the superseding of the individual in mass-movements that are often confused.[88]

Strictly existential philosophies, though they are liable to overlook the objective laws of the real, to neglect the external world and history, and to accept an irrational individualism, are nevertheless more concerned, in their description of the human, to bring out the full content of every physically experienced moment—the agony of the ego confronted by the infinite of freedom and the uncertainty of the future, the dramatic crisis of decision, the precariousness or incompetence of reason, the fragmentation of the ego faced with incompatible mirrorings of itself, and the difficult problem of encounter and communion with others. Some existentialists will even claim to find in man a substantial and hopeless contradiction, an almost inevitable bad faith. Such thinkers, by their rejection, too, of system and coherent explanation, show their anxiety not to petrify or immobilize consciousness, or to neutralize man's permanent contradiction in some purely logical reconciliation.

Teilhard's thought, on the other hand, is a philosophy of history: and every great philosophy of history, whether it is Hegel's or Marx's or Bergson's, has to pay this price: the person is affirmed only in union with totality or the universal; it is swallowed up in a movement in which it shares. Even more than his predecessors, Teilhard counterbalances this over-all view by his respect for the *individual* person: in contrast with eastern theories of complete absorption or western forms of technical and utilitarian rationalism, he constantly asserts the unique value of the 'difference' in souls, and the possible preservation of 'personalities' within their conjunction. 'Our own soul—in itself and in its being at the heart of the universe—is the first of the tasks calling for our efforts.'[89] In what follows we shall soon see the existential importance that Teilhard attached to humble 'forms of sympathy'—comradeship, friendship, and love. As for things, his *Letters*, with their wonderful descriptions of nature and natural objects, are sufficient proof that Teilhard's love of the earth we live on was as strong as that of Bernanos or Saint-Exupéry.[90]

Teilhard attaches the whole of man's agony to the wider fact of human *suffering*: 'Of all things, the epic of man is most like a way of the Cross.'[91] It is a vast problem and, at different levels of profundity, the whole of Teilhard's work is an answer to it.

The foregoing remarks derive from an appreciation of man in his natural condition, in his fundamental finiteness. Physical evil is inherent in the very structure of the universe and of man.[92] It is ontologically linked with the fact of a multiplicity that achieves unity as it passes from less-being to more-being. In every living being it is linked with the existence of a sensibility that is a prey to determinisms that nothing can escape; in man, with the permanent hiatus between non-fulfilment and fulfilment, with the infinity of desire, the painful task of personalization, and the inevitability of transformations, in particular that of death.[93] Another aspect, inseparable from the first, will later introduce the historical fact of moral and spiritual evil, of sin, which so aggravates man's condition as to lend a further significance to suffering and death: responsibility for this is linked with consciousness and freedom, and increases as they increase.

Apart from the supernatural solution, there is no solution to the problem of evil other than the *immortality* of persons and of collective mankind at the term of a history that converges on a transcendent end.[94]

This immortality—a vindication of existence against the absurdity of a prospect of annihilation or of the complete halting of the movement already under way—is an *a priori* condition of the universe of man: it is a victory over the existing biological situation, demanded by the irreversibility, necessary to the fulfilment, of cosmic and human history.[95] In contrast with the materialist or pantheist illusion, the final transcendent centre on which history converges and in which the universe culminates, does not confuse the person with itself, or absorb it into itself; it must, by giving them immortality, preserve 'the properties of our own centre and so of this centre itself'.[96] This certainty for the future is sufficient immediately to take us beyond phenomenism, since the very being of the real is attained: and the consciousness of belonging to a universe in genesis, moving infallibly towards an absolute and divine end, should be sufficient not only to alleviate man's distress and suffering but to convert it into joy.[97] The boredom of living, the *taedium vitae*, that possesses man—all the more overpoweringly now that technical progress has released him from constant activity—this, too, can be dispelled only by that same hope and by the eagerness it arouses to make a generous creative effort to fulfil history.

There is, however, a further point that should be noted: immortality must first be conceived as a participation in God's eternity and his existential plenitude. It cannot, indeed, be dis-

sociated from the notion of indefinite prolongation; but this is only
a secondary aspect and may well be no more than a provisional
necessity, to help us in forming a picture of it.

IV EXISTENTIAL VALUES

Here we meet Teilhard's theory of existential values, a logical continuation, summary in form and found in disconnected scattered
notes, of his description of man: 'from the point of view of action,
what place is held by values in a personal universe?'[98]

Unlike both the Marxist and the (atheistic) existentialist concept,
and, possibly, unlike the Lutheran explanation of sinful man, Teilhard does not start his existential enquiry from a denial of meaning
or value in man or history (a denial of meaning from which no act
of freedom, and no divine intervention either, could enable
him to emerge). Dialectically bound up, no doubt, with man's
thought and action, the world in which man develops, and in
which every man continually develops, is already *meaning* or at least
an unfolding of meaning. Man rooted in the eternal before being
rooted in the world, is presented to himself as already *meaning*, as
spirit directed towards and summoned by the absolute. And yet at
the same time this initial meaning has still to be created or invented
in its entirety—in a way with nothing to start from—and every man
is entirely responsible for himself. It is true, indeed, that he
receives gratuitous assistance from the world (at every moment of
history, and ever increasingly)—and thus from the physical circumstances that condition him—and even more from other men: but
nevertheless he is completely responsible for his own development.
In other words, inadequate though they are to express the mystery
of man, the initial meaning is incomplete: man is given to himself
as a problem of *freedom* inside time, and called on to perfect himself, personally and collectively, through the encounters of his
existence, until he has invented and discovered (the two go together) the *total* meaning of being: and by that very fact he transforms, and so gives a total meaning to, the world.

Great and wretched, imperfect but yet capable of the infinite,
man is therefore called, through particular encounters, to complete
himself and recover fullness of being and value: and this not only for

the full development of his own person, but also within the general history of the world. 'What is the purpose of man's work, in the interest even of life in general, what is man's supreme work, if not to establish, in and by each one of us, an absolutely original centre in which the universe reflects itself in a an unique and inimitable way? And those centres are our very selves and personalities.'[99]

Teilhard did not explicitly use the technical dialectical terms of the modern existential vocabulary that expresses the appearance of freedom through its detachment from the *en-soi* of nature; but he had a perfectly clear view of the problem of man's ascent to consciousness. Although he directed himself primarily to the 'natural' study of the phenomenon of man, he was not satisfied with generalities and did not overlook existential mediations: research and technology, art, social life, religion.

Thus within the collective history of mankind lie individual histories, in which the wills of men express their deep-rooted projects and pursue their ends: the ego seeks for itself as it unfolds in the world, and an examination of the methods it uses can help us to grasp its mystery.

a : The quest for knowledge and technology

To research, which is science's pursuit of the true,[100] Teilhard accords a respect[101] that gives it, if not a specially privileged position, at least one of cardinal importance.[102] Appearing originally as what seems to be no more than some superfluous private fancy, scientific research is first an active exuberance, the curiosity of a handful of dreamers and men of leisure; it is stimulated, later, by the prospect it offers of making life easier; and then, among the élite, it is inspired by a more fundamental passion: the passion for *more-being* and for going beyond man, the passion for the augmentation and fulfilment of the world.[103] 'Originating in childish diversions', it has become 'the serious, central, vital, occupation of the grown man', 'the form under which is hidden the creative power of God and in which that power is most intensely active in the nature that surrounds us'.[104] 'Once undertaken,' it 'goes forward like a rocket, fed and accelerated by the logic and stimulus of its own success.'[105]

As the earth's impetus builds up, a day will come when concern for production with a view to well-being will give way 'to the passion for discovery with a view to more-being';[106] then, too, the passion for discovery will absorb the energies now devoted to war: 'War, the great open sore (could one not say?) which draws off the overflow of energy engendered by anthropogenesis.'[107] 'A true "geopolitics" will finally replace the wretched parish-pump disputes which is all that history has so far amounted to.'[108] And, if this is to happen, it is urgently necessary that man should channel and organize the undisciplined super-abundance of his industry and production.[109]

At the same time, for all the importance of the role of technology, 'machines and industry are already here and now taking second place to an even more powerful agent. Not only . . . are the differences between laboratory and factory rapidly disappearing, but, in the coalescence of the two, it is the laboratory that has the dominant position. All in all, it is not an industrial age we have entered, but an age of research'.[110]

Moreover, if the aim of science is to construct a complete picture of the universe, coherent in all its parts, not by simply illuminating a datum but by extracting new being from it, then the peak of evolution will coincide with a systematic completion of world-knowledge, 'in a supreme act of collective vision'.[111]

In the light of this ideal, science's most powerful creations are both the symbol and the leading expression of the concentration of spirit that is produced in the course of history. The apparently scattered elements of research are so many stars in a vast spiralling galaxy. Initially 'absorbed and captivated by the object to which his effort is directed', man the worker is ultimately 'transformed (ultra-unified) by the combination of *his work* and *his own working*'.[112]

Science, however, is closely linked with *technology*, with the rational organization of the earth. Normally, it progresses only under the stimulus of practical problems, and 'its most sublime theories would never have taken root in human thought if they had not been immediately converted into, or embodied in, some way of mastering the world'.[113] Moreover, it is through work and in the ingenuity of the solutions he finds for his needs that man creates and develops himself. 'Increased power for increased action' but at the same time 'increased action for increased being'.[114] The automatic functioning of the machine, again, produces the leisure essential 'to creation, to love and to thought', and, in spite of its dangers industrialization follows the line of vital energy's progress towards interiority.[115] Finally, technology is in a position to augment and complete man's mental capabilities, not only by electronic computers but also through the possibilities, that may well be realized at some time, of a higher development of the brain.[116]

Technology is also becoming progressively more *collective*: 'For a long time past there have been neither isolated inventors nor machines . . . every machine comes into being as a function of every other machine, and all the machines on earth, taken together, tend to form a single, vast, organized machine.' 'Accelerating and multiplying their own growth,' they form 'a single gigantic network, girdling the earth'; and the 'inventive core of this vast apparatus' is 'the thinking centre of the noosphere'. From being an appendage to the human body, the tool is 'transformed into a mechanized envelope (coherent within itself and immensely varied) appertaining to all mankind'. 'All these material instruments, ineluctably linked in their birth and development,' are 'the manifestation of a particular kind of super-brain, capable of obtaining mastery over some super-sphere in the universe and in the realm of thought.'[117] Thus even what would appear to be the most dangerous and two-edged inventions, such as the applications of atomic energy, indicate 'the birth into the world of a mankind both inwardly and outwardly at peace . . . the coming of the *spirit of the earth*'.[118] This is the more emphatically so in that 'nothing brings souls more closely together than a common pursuit of the same truth: in the course of genesis, knowledge links together not only brains but inevitably hearts as well'.[119]

Technology has a special application in the field of human *biology*: health, improvement of the race by wise eugenics, 'controlled selection' at once free and planned,[120] determination of the optimum population-level. Technology is itself linked with *economics*.

More widely, there is no limit to the target research sets itself. 'It is fundamentally that of mastering, beyond all atomic or molecular affinities, the ultimate energy of which all other energies are merely servants; and thus, working as one man, to grasp the very mainspring of evolution and so seize the tiller of the world.'[121] Nothing is impossible to science, not even 'the vitalization of matter by the creation of super-molecules', the 're-modelling of the human organism by means of hormones' . . . 'Cannot every kind of effect be produced by a suitable arrangement of matter?'[122] And the discovery of the applications of nuclear energy shows plainly that, as Descartes thought, 'not only can matter be expressed in terms of geometry, it can be subjugated by geometry'. 'Nothing in the universe can resist the converging energies of a sufficient number of minds sufficiently grouped and organized.'[123] 'Is it beyond the bounds of possibility that we may sometime succeed in constructing apparatus capable of registering the rays emitted by thinking brains and concentrating their energy when they are is directed in a given direction?'[124]

Science must pursue its enquiries and their applications, including the human field, to their furthest possible limit. It is love, rather than any abstract moral system, that will prevent such research from being harmful;[125] but the awakening of this love is itself an integral part of the advance of science. 'Morality and the machine cannot get on without one another.'

The dialectic of the relations between *science and religion* is contained in the following formula: while science, in as much as it takes history for its object, leads thought to the affirmation of an absolute, and should therefore culminate in adoration, at the same time it is, in its method, entirely independent of religion. 'In no field and at no point do science and revelation encroach on one another or duplicate one another.'[126]

From this examination of science and technology there emerge the essential elements of the encounter they constitute.

It has, however, done little more than lay the foundation of a *philosophy of work*. One would have liked to see a development of the profound remark on the detachment practised by man in relation to *immediate* perception and action, 'in order to roam in the domain of the distant reaches of the possible'. Here, indeed, Teilhard could have introduced the operational *encounter* by which man objectifies and universalizes himself in a world that is continually more human, at the same time constantly withdrawing himself from the object opened up, in the consciousness of his creative subjectivity.[127] But he saw very clearly the difference between the compact and undetachable mechanism of animal activities, and the reflexive freedom of human work, as he did the problem, as existential as it is social, presented by the fundamental detachment of *leisure*.[128]

At the same time these elements in Teilhard's thought are still abstract. He would have profited by including an analysis of the mechanics of economic and social *estrangement*, in which freedom is abandoned, but through which it can be recovered.[129] Absorbed by the manifest spectacle of scientific and technical progress, he is somewhat inclined to overlook the *political* conditions that provide the framework for work and determine its history. The normal division of working functions, already disturbing in itself, has been transformed, under the influence of human passions—violence in particular—into phenomena of social domination, which produce mutual antagonism between unequally privileged groups; the authority necessary to collective industry has become a slave-mastery; the inertia inevitable in any institution has hardened into ultra-conservatism and a refusal to keep up with the progress made both in consciousness and in methods of production. In short, from the very beginning, tragedy has forced its way into the core of human work, giving it a fundamentally disruptive character. Now, the history of scientific and technical progress cannot be explained simply by the peaceful action of spiritual energy, but by the various reactions and consequences of the struggle between social forces, which stimulate the spirit of invention and enquiry, continually adapting structures to new situations, projecting and channelling man towards the future in the hope of achieving a harmony.

Although it meant that he might appear to pay little attention to the element of hardship in man's labour and at the same time to overlook the real factors of a history that advances only through contradiction, Teilhard refrained from examining this dramatic aspect of human reality. His interest lay so much in the promise held by the future and was so concentrated on the end of history, and he was so certain of the triumph of unanimity, that he was inclined to neglect the forms now assumed (and continually with fresh vigour) by human oppression and degradation—those being the price that must inevitably be paid for the advance of consciousness. His overall grasp, or bird's eye view, of the situation was too far removed for him to be shocked into a realization of the humiliation of the weak, to hear the cries of the vanquished, or to make him insist that the first duty of those who have legal or political power is to busy themselves on their behalf. Man's existential fulfilment entails not only a conversion of attitudes but a structural transformation, and both these belong to the order of love and justice: work is as much a factor of degradation as of advancement, and can humanize the worker only if it accepts another law than that of pride and selfishness.[130]

b: Philosophy

This is the logical place, as an extension of science and *through reflexion on science*, for an existential value of a more general order: philosophy. The whole body of Teilhard's work is evidence of his faith in the value of thought, and in man's capacity and vocation to attain the absolute of truth through intellectual representation of 'the whole phenomenon' and of the phenomenon considered in its totality. This, as we have seen, is the normal step— the transition to the metaphysical plane that, by making explicit what is implicit in the real (as thought by man) recognizes both its foundation and its underlying intention. Teilhard's originality would seem to have consisted simply in disclosing, *in the actual analysis of the movement of cosmic history*, the unity towards which it is directed: spirit, being.

This indispensable, but still abstract,[131] appreciation must now introduce a series of progressively more *concrete* values, capable of giving man not simply knowledge but actual *possession* of the real: art, intercommunion of persons, moral and religious life. Thought, itself a necessary stage in man's journey towards fulness of existence, already participates in the following stages: in one sense, it is already love, just as it is already impregnated with poetry, involved in social life, and given discipline by morality; and it will necessarily continue to be present in every stage, even religious and mystical experience. Only when the term is reached, however, will it be fully vindicated.

c: Art

Although the role of art is treated less fully by Teilhard, he does not neglect it.[132] As an artist and poet himself, he could hardly overlook the essential part played by creation and contemplation of the beautiful in the spiritual development of consciousness and in the progress of mankind.[133] A craftsman in words, like every great philosopher, he is an example of the intimate union of matter and form, of word and idea. Divorced from the style of expression, truth would be dead and incommunicable. Without the magic of symbolism and imagery, a world-philosophy, inexpressible in ordinary language, could never have been made intelligible. Moreover, Teilhard's theory of the value of matter and the incarnation of spirit is the basis of every aesthetics: at their different levels, scientist, artist, and philosopher all share in the harmony of creation and augment it by their personal contribution.

For Teilhard art, rooted in the instinct for unity, in the awareness of a universal presence and in resonance with the whole,[134] is 'the perfection of expression' in sensible forms. In virtue of this, it is to be found in the wonders of plant and animal life: 'There is supreme art in the fish, the bird, the antelope.'[135] In man it corresponds, as does science, to a superabundance or exuberance of spiritual energy 'gradually released from the fetters of matter' by the progress of mechanization. At first, in its creative fancy, it seems, like the colours of flowers and butterflies, to serve no purpose. However, far from being a parasitic activity or mere luxury, it fulfils a function that is necessary to man's existence. In the first place, aesthetic form gives material incarnation and body to man's feelings (anxieties, hopes, enthusiasms) and enables them to be intimately communicated to others. Moreover, art, though it does not directly set out to do so, disseminates ideas that may be fruitful. And finally, as a reaction against the impersonality of science and thought that lose the worker in his work, it preserves the unique individuality of the person: 'The more the world is rationalized and mechanized, the greater its need of poets as the guardians and leaven of personality.'

This line of thought shows Teilhard's appreciation of a value that is indispensable to the person and to history. In so far, however, as it is based only on pragmatic and functional considerations, it leaves untouched much of the mystery of artistic creation: a notable aspect of this is the intimate communion with the absolute that it makes possible,[136] through the transformation or recreation of a sensible harmony whose multiple forms and mechanism also call for analysis. Teilhard was satisfied to experience in his life and express in his work the transition of creative emotion into its incarnation through the selective interposition of images and symbols, and so to seek for communion with others in the harmony of beauty and through the clarity of truth.

d : Society

Although Teilhard is comparatively guarded on the subject of the role of art, on the other hand he elaborates that of the inter-personal and *social* values within which, as the extension of biology—and integrating without being reduced to biology[137]—the unification of man is brought about.

For Teilhard, society does not of course possess an autonomous consciousness; at the same time not only is society as objective as its members but, as for Max Scheler and personalist philosophy, sympathy and reciprocity play a great part in man's development.[138]

Co-reflexion is, in fact, implied in the appearance of reflexion: the human species, the fulfilment and the term (so far as we can see) of biological evolution, no longer needs to be relieved by another species, and is therefore called upon—unless we prefer to say condemned—to find in itself the structural links that hold it together: thus evolution is faced with a new task, or enters on a new phase, as it rebounds upon itself.[139] *Hominization*, too, leaves behind its origin in history and its individual aspect, to introduce the global and progressive vocation of the whole of mankind: with man, 'an "excentric" or at any rate unconcentrated way of coming together, is replaced for the cosmic corpuscles, by the possibility of "centre to centre" contacts between complete centres. And, at the same time, it is their unified totality that begins to be animated in a sort of common personality'.[140] The awakening of a sense of mankind is, indeed, even the necessary preliminary to a victory of charity.[141]

Teilhard first brings out the fundamental interconnexion of persons: without introducing the Hegelian notion of recognition or the appeal to the *thou*, he suggests that the person is completed only in union with other persons and in the hope of a universal and absolute communion.[142] Personal consciousness does not arise only from a confrontation with nature in work, but from encounter and dialogue, from the welcome extended by others, from awareness of, appeal to, and response to this free gift. When the paths or trajectories of individuals diverge, there is no personalization; it is when they come together that it is realized. Unable to find equilibrium and repose in himself, man constantly escapes from himself; and what ultimately he loves, in himself, is always 'another' that lies ahead of him. The contact or fusion of beings is always an 'infinite mystery': 'Some sort of coming together, or at any rate some sort of bond within matter, lies at the root of union. But the stages in the interiorization (the progress) of co-penetration are infinite: each within the other, the two beings can be tossed indefinitely, like a pebble in the ocean.'[143]

The progress of human unity, then, goes hand in hand with that of interiority: while egoism or isolation harden and stultify the stuff of man, 'union differentiates',[144] provided it be the expression of a gift; for the ego that loves, far from wishing to assimilate the other in an identity that confuses the two, seeks to preserve the initial identity of the other and helps him to become personalized in order that both together they may try to attain new syntheses. Similarly, 'what is most incommunicable in every being, and therefore most precious, is that which makes him one and the same with all the others'. Communion of persons, however, implies *frameworks* and mechanisms in which their exchanges are made objective and incarnate.[145] In short, the personal is associated with the universal:[146] and if man is to re-discover the truth of his being, he must awaken in himself the cosmic sense of a spirit of the earth, in which all individual thoughts 'are steeped and react upon one another'.[147]

This spirit has always been active: here and now its action is becoming more marked, in the activity that Teilhard calls 'conspiration',[148] which tends to unanimize the human mass in a common environment, while at the same time heightening individual values. Geographical concentration, too, carried further by the numerical increase of men on a closed surface, encourages the interpenetration of consciousness, while unlimited inter-breeding contributes to the anastomosis of mankind in a 'single organic membrane'. Here we have the phenomena of involution, of clustering, of agglutination, of synthesis, under the influence of forces of attraction—the direct converse of the phenomenon of dispersion—which attraction is combined with a phyletic orthogenesis characteristic of animal species. Nor is it beyond the bounds of possibility that this phenomenon may be measurable.[149]

In more detail, Teilhard points out the importance assumed in the 'human zoological group' by *educative heredity* and the accumulation of acquired knowledge and skill,[150] the connecting thread in biological history and the history of today, the new vigour instilled into what has proved successful in life by present forms of human intercommunion.[151] In his account of the 'energy of personalization', he speaks of the comradeship of work and research, and of friendship.[152]

Above all, he discusses *sexual love*, 'the most universal, most formidable and most mysterious of cosmic energies': regretting its waste, he asks that it shall go beyond not only the selfishness of undisciplined passion, and the more subtle temptation of enclosed possession in a universe of two persons,[153] but also the immediate functional end to which its fertility is directed, in order to elevate itself, by sublimation, to the vocation of consummating the universe; and to do this he urges it to introduce God himself as the mediator of love. *Woman*, 'the charm and symbol of the world' stands before man, as the first requirement of this fulfilment.[154] Teilhard was to return later to this theme: 'It seems to me beyond dispute (both in logic and fact) that however devoted a man may be to the service of a cause or a God, he can never attain spiritual maturity and fullness of stature, without some "emotional" influence to sensitize the intelligence and to stimulate in him, at least initially, the powers of loving. Man—any man—and this is every day more unmistakably obvious—can no more do without the feminine any more than he can do without light or oxygen or vitamins.'[155]

In a number of key passages Teilhard touches on some of Claudel's themes,[156] though they are more reminiscent of, and may well be inspired by, some well-known paragraphs in Maurice Blondel's *L'Action*. Without examining it very profoundly, they introduce also the dialectic of man and woman, analysed by Père Fessard, which, rising above that of master and slave, is the type of all human unifications.[157]

If to love is to rediscover and complete oneself in someone other than oneself,[158] then the distress and anguish of isolation can be alleviated, and, sometimes, overcome. With great penetration, Teilhard describes 'this psychological reversal whereby, in the case of all intelligent creatures, joy in action imperceptibly melts into desire for submission, and the exaltation of being one's own self into the zeal to die in another'.[159] And if the description of inter-personal relationships seems to emphasize their ultimate finality in history, yet such remarks show that one can go beyond the moments of human encounter only if one *preserves* them in their original warmth.[160]

We can only regret that, unlike Bergson, Teilhard, while accepting the role of the élite, did not include in his theory of the development of history the influence of the great *personalities*, the heroes and the mystics who, raised up by the spirit, initiate all progress and are the specially favoured channel through which it flows. History does not advance in one homogeneous layer, converging uniformly, but in knots in which spiritual energy concentrates, the better, then, to diffuse itself.

Obstacles
At the same time Teilhard is far from underestimating the difficulty of human unification.

In the first place, 'fragmentation and divergence seem to dominate the history of life'. This in particular was the impression made on Teilhard by his first contact with the Far East.[161]

Moreover, both in principle and by instinct, man normally keeps apart from man. 'What we know as social man feels at his ease with any jungle animal. But as soon as another man like himself appears, he starts to bristle up.'[162] He withdraws from the plurality that disconcerts him.

With the Bergson of the *Two Sources*, Teilhard notes, too, that 'the appearance of reason marks an organic crisis in life': 'the monads refuse any longer, rightly or wrongly, to submit to the laborious task of extending life blindly and with docility. Either they look only for enjoyment, and follow the line of least resistance; or else they try to break the links that attach them to others: they have a constitutional urge to exist proudly and selfishly.'[163] Individualism is more pronounced in civilized man: even though he has at his disposal a richness of life that augments immeasurably his incommunicable values, yet it 'isolates him among his fellows, it "absolutizes" and "autonomizes" him to such a degree that it makes him lose his sense of the species.' 'There is then only one way open to our impulse as individuals if we are to survive and attain super-life, and that is resolutely to plunge back into the general current from which, for a moment, we thought we could escape.'[164]

Side by side with the danger of this 'Brownian movement' goes that of the termitary. The unification of society can stifle the person in the tyrannical *mechanization* of the community. Here again, as though to shatter the egoism of individuals, we meet the necessity for God to save man from the menace of enslavement to organization:

if it is not to cease to be human, the sense of man must be of the order of love.

Finally, the anticipation of *death* is a formidable contradiction, in the very heart of history, not only of the effort to survive, which is common to all living beings, but also of the mysterious lure of the future, and of the ideal of a collective fulfilment, both characteristic of mankind today.[165]

The activation of human energy

This brings us to the central problem of the *activation* of human energy. Teilhard, particularly in his last years, was always haunted by this problem, and it has close links with his theology. If man is 'the only being for whom the stimulus that moves him to action is not confined to the perception of some immediate end, but comes from his *confrontation with the whole of the future*' how will he ever 'have the *heart* to press on to the end of, to go right through with, the ever more demanding work of his co-reflexion?'[166] It is not, moreover, simply a matter of saving man from lack of heart, but of getting him to put his whole heart into the work, so that he may attain his end not as a survivor but as a victor.[167]

At first, among persons who are scattered, the sense of a world to be completed may provide the irresistible pressure that binds them together in a common passion.[168] Then, 'in a universe that is drawing together, the *other*, terrifying though it be in the ever more penetrating light of our consciousness, ceases to terrify us, and for the very good reason that from being alien and hostile it is becoming *patient of unification*'.[169] 'Everything makes a fresh start; everything is in motion; everything continues, in a higher mode, to evolve even more fully. And, at the same time, everything in the desperate multitude of men in which we might well have thought ourselves lost, falls into place in the general pattern.'[170]

Thus the general principle of morality emerges from the duty to fuel the energy of man: 'We must learn to direct ourselves unceasingly (in our decisions, in what we make and in what we believe) along those lines in which the universe, by the opportunities presented for the unification and unity of its elements, shows the *maximum activation*.'[171]

Teilhard sees *sexuality*, disciplined by reason, in the light of this activation of spiritual energy for the service of the world, as though the main function of the senses were to free or make available an ever greater 'quantity of love'.[172] The future of mankind depends largely on a useful application, sublimated by chastity, of sexual energy. 'Not in flight from (by suppressing them) but in mastery of (by sublimating them) the unfathomable spiritual forces that still lie dormant beneath the mutual attraction of the sexes—there lie the hidden essence of chastity and the grand task it will have to face.'[173] Teilhard envisages, too, 'a gradual increase in the spiritual function of the sexes, accompanied by a gradual cutting down of the "reproductive" aspect and of the physical acts that lead up to it (this transformation coinciding with an *end* that awaits a mature mankind—or perhaps simply *limiting* the multiplication of the species to the optimum required by eugenics)'.[174]

It is, however, the *problem of religion* that is most closely and directly involved in the science of man through the indispensability of a 'powerful field of stimulation'. Sooner or later we must become conscious of 'an objective, whose appeal is both undeniable and in-exhaustible: a goal whose driving force . . . will satisfy the physical conditions needed to activate the human species'. 'Since mankind has, biologically, only a limited number of thousands or millions of years in which to complete its evolution, we are compelled to envisage ahead of us, *at some finite distance* in time, the existence of some *ultimate point*, or peak, of organic coordination, of intellectual co-reflexion, and finally (step by step) of unanimity.'[175] 'There can be no future for man without a neo-sense of the species; but there can be no neo-sense of the species outside a universe that, by its very nature, converges irreversibly on some ultra-personalizing centre.'[176]

'It is psychologically impossible for anything but a true *super-love* (and that means the eager anticipation of a true "super-person") to dominate, absorb and synthesize the multiplicity of other terres-trial loves': without this, 'there can be no coherence in a totalized mankind, and in consequence, no consistence'.[177]

Christianity will be seen to be, indeed, the saviour both of the personal and of the universal, for these are united and centred in the person of Christ; and revelation as the 'reflexion of the supreme consciousness on the consciousness of the elements it gathers into one'.[178]

From this analysis Teilhard draws the bold but irrefutable conclusion that 'THE PHYSICAL UNIVERSE IS BUILDED OF A GREAT LOVE.'[179]

It is not a difficult step from this to the anticipation of the appearance, under the planetary pressure of concentration, of a universal solidarity, 'a new kind of love, not yet experienced by man'.[180] and to seeing the end of the world as the supreme triumph of unanimity. 'What love can achieve daily on a small scale, in the couple or the team we work with, can it not repeat one day on world-wide dimensions?'[181]

Even so, Teilhard points out again that a successful issue to this depends on freedom and cannot be achieved without suffering,[182] and notes, rightly, that it is for *education* to ensure 'the psychic continuity of this vast development':[183] education that has continually to start afresh with each person but that has the benefit of a new form of heredity, a constantly richer spiritual inheritance.[184] Thus Teilhard rediscloses the essential category of the master-disciple relationship, central in the Bergson of the *Two Sources* and emphasized by Père Fessard.[185] At the same time he considers and appreciates education much more from the point of view of its collective results than from that of its effect on the consciousness of individuals. Since Teilhard looks more to the global influence of spiritual energy for the progress of history than to the privileged individuals in which it is embodied, he pays little attention to the personal transmission of an experience or a truth, or to the stimulation of free will by authority.

Similarly, although he never succumbed to the least form of racialism,[186] yet in Teilhard's ideal of a social structure controlled by an élite, we can distinguish a certain corruption of the biological laws of selection and of aristocratic hierarchy: this is so pronounced as to blind him to the fundamental viciousness of Nazism and its criminal contempt for human personality.[187] He may, again, have been underestimating the fundamental opposition between contradictory mystiques when he hoped that they might be reconciled in a common effort to 'exalt and unify the earth'.[188] After all, however in accordance with tradition it may be to see the truth contained in error and to recognize the 'positive' characteristics of totalitarian ideals, and however much justification there may be for an optimistic view of man's future,[189] one cannot help wishing that Teilhard had more emphatically insisted on their monstrous distortion, their abominable caricature of the collective ideal. Liberal, individualistic, democracy may well seem by no means perfect; but it still has more to offer than its opposites: in such democracy, the rights of the person may often be neglected in practice, but they are not categorically denied by some doctrinal system.

It would have been most interesting if Teilhard had completed his theory of personalism by an analysis of the relationship between persons when they make the choice of working together for communion: it involves the necessary humility of attitude, the refusal to treat others as things or slaves, or to pass judgment on them, the acceptance of their limitations (even, indeed, their culpability), the readiness to welcome the other person and to receive what he has to say, respect for his inexhaustible uniqueness, a progressive understanding of his mystery, trust in his future and the promise he holds, stimulation of his spiritual progress, and finally the value, but at the same time the insufficiency, of ethical norms and moral virtues.[190] In short, a more penetrating examination of the interior life behind personal contacts would have counterbalanced a perhaps one-sided and exaggerated emphasis on the importance of realizing our personal involvement in a history of convergence, in which the future counts for more than the present.

So far as *politics* are concerned, Teilhard's thought included an examination of *democracy* and its conditions; while he was critical of liberal democracy,[191] he recognized that 'apart from Christianity, perhaps no social movement had better understood the human person or valued it more highly than the Revolution'.[192] He rightly insisted that every possible opportunity of development should be given to the person and that, while being included in collective organizations, sufficient outlet should be provided for its own initiative. He recognized the right of the individual to share in any claims that are made; he saw the basis of fraternity to lie in the increasing sense of universalism; he realized that democracy must be animated by a spirit of unanimity, a desire for a cohesion that still respects individual differences and the variety of opinions and groups; finally, and realistically, he noted that the lack of uniformity in the maturity of different sections of mankind called for great flexibility and variety in the forms taken by democracy.[193] In this field his conclusions, always valuable, were to some extent in line with those of contemporary philosophers and jurists[194] and of recent encyclicals.

In the *international* field—and again following his proposition of unity in difference—Teilhard looked for an order that would integrate individual aspirations while at the same time it respected rightful liberties. 'Only a powerful polarisation of human wills, after each fragment of humanity has been led to the discovery of his own particular form of freedom, can ensure the unified working of this plurality in a single, co-ordinated planetary system.'[195]

Nevertheless, Teilhard's political sociology is always somewhat sketchy. He almost entirely overlooks the necessity for the state as providing, in its function of deciding the common good, the best-equipped link between the personal and the universal; he neglects, too, the at least partial alienation of a power that is itself captive to dominant social groups or to a business technocracy. While he clearly points out the danger that the person may be stifled by mechanical organizations,[196] he does not stress the need for this to be met by democratic forces, which would counterbalance the will to power of economic, social and political pressure-groups and fore-stall totalitarian ambitions. He failed, again, to note the present critical position of a democracy that is still only formal and still held back by inertia and the cult of prosperity and comfort. More widely, nowhere in Teilhard's thought will one find vigorous and detailed criticism of the shortcomings of modern civilization. His early education as a member of a privileged class, his scientific calling, and a certain natural simplicity of mind were perhaps responsible for a partial blindness to the seamy side of an economy that is enslaved to the passion for money, is indifferent to man, inevitably produces more marked divisions, and is directed towards a purely materialistic end.

On the other hand, Teilhard boldly and forcibly insisted on the importance of a *rational planning* of the collective effort, provided it was capable of preserving and advancing the freedom of the person. Finally, we should note the essential coincidence, in Teilhard, of *action* and theory: the ethics of respect for man, the spirituality of commitment to the service of human progress, the generous readiness to welcome the spirit of love, all these are introduced to correct the faults inherent in concrete history and to humanize the harshness of the biological process of development. Teilhard's teaching is one of *freedom*: the constant intervention of freedom is designed to neutralize the negativity of mechanical determinisms, and to stand out against an even more formidable entropy than the dissipation of material energy: hope can be realized infallibly only through the continually direct mediation of action—an action that draws its vigour from the fire of the spirit and is mystical in motivation. The mutations of history are achieved only at the cost of a revolution against degraded forms of the human.[197]

e : Morality

A total synthesis such as Teilhard's was bound explicitly to include morality among the existential values. Since in every domain it ensures the ideal rightness of every act of freedom, it enables man (and, in him, the universe) to attain its end. It is at once the discipline of action, which it brings into conformity with the law of reason, and the medium that, starting from a particular datum, operates man's transition to the universality of the good, in which he finds fulfilment.

In fact, Teilhard first lays down, 'it is impossible in practice to push the progress of consciousness beyond a certain level without this power of reflective arrangement having *automatically* to accept internal obligations and bring into play new spiritual demands'.[198] This means that the appearance of thought is linked with that of ethics and moral choice: the order of speculative presentation, of abstract 'theory', gives place to that of should-be or should-do.

1 The origin of morality

As René Le Senne has already made clear, this 'should' emerges within consciousness from the problem raised by the gulf between what is and what should be, from the obstacle, that is, presented to value.[199] The fact and the feelings of obligation are linked together, for Teilhard, first by the essential *incompleteness* of the finite being, and secondly by the permanent temptation presented by *multiplicity*, multiplicity being inertia, a check or break, a drag, and a tendency towards dissociation: 'matter' is not only external material energy; it is present and immanent in spiritual interiority.[200]

Moreover, even though the appearance of thought has initiated a new era in the history of nature, man is still substantially rooted in *animality*, and biological forces are still to be found in him, 'recognizable even if hominized: hunger, for example, love, belligerence, the hunting instinct. To control these inherited forces on a higher plane is the work of morality and the secret of super-life'.[201]

Moreover, as we have already seen, the emergence of *thought*, by introducing the indetermination of freedom and making leisure possible, is a dangerous threat to the balance of the vital impulse: it can bring with it lack of discipline, disorder, and the pursuit of worthless ends and can neutralize or annihilate spiritual energy through the objections and refusal of the individual. This refusal is directed, in particular, against unity of consciousness and the general movement towards unification.

Here, perhaps, Teilhard might well have followed St Augustine and noted the awakening of consciousness to which disobedience to the law contributes: man, *in fact*, attains autonomy only through a resistance that releases him from a servitude he cannot clearly define.

2 The metaphysical basis of morality

Moral obligation is the check devised by spiritual energy to ensure its survival, its increase and its success, with the collaboration and consent of personal freedoms: it is a new force that henceforth takes charge, under the responsibility of persons, of the movement of history. This check is first expressed in a juridical system of rights and duties designed by society to meet the threat of individualism; since Christianity, however, and the modern awakening of consciousness, social obligation has been developing into a spiritual summons to universalism.[202]

Obligation retains the pressure that characterizes the biological impetus, but, now that it is conscious and no longer blind, it rests on the choice that freedom decides upon. Henceforth everything depends on man's responsibility,[203] on the daily drama of the wager he makes—the side to which he commits himself.[204]

Thus morality is deeply involved in the *cosmic current*, of which it is the formal expression. Although it is 'too often looked on as a purely artificial (infra- or para-physical) organ' it is 'in fact the experience more or less rudimentary, of an energetics of thought'.[205] 'The cosmos is built up physically, starting with man, by moral magnitudes . . .; no longer do we live in a physical sphere and a moral sphere—there is nothing but the *physico-moral*.'[206] 'Duty, from its very origin, is nothing but the reflection of the universe in the atom.'[207] 'Just think of the awe-inspired emotion of the atom that sees in the depths of its own being the face of the universe!'[208] 'By the very structure of things, we can move only within the current of the universe. We have the right to move only in what coincides with the legitimate, authentic, direction of that current.'[209] If the fibres of the cosmic stuff knit themselves together in the individual only in order to extend themselves—then, 'to continue to run true (i.e. in coherence with the world), we must try to unite in achieving some further synthesis'.[210]

Thus Teilhard comes back to the *fundamental structures* of morality: rational coherence, universality, the absolute imperative of obligation: if 'in the widest sense we may give the name of "morality" to every coherent system of action, accepted either by necessity or by convention', then, 'in the strict sense of the word a "morality" is a coherent system of action—universal (controlling the whole of human activity) and categorical (involving some form of obligation)'.[211]

Although some prejudice or misconception was always a barrier between Teilhard and traditional *metaphysics*, he coincides with it (though he may not have realized this) when, by intellectual examination and scientific observation of the movement of history, he brings out the absolute that is immanent in it and towards which it moves. This is because, as a result of the dialectical relation between man and the world, this observation from the outside *coincides* exactly with what must, internally, hold good: the world's movement towards unity, known from outside by science, is also apparent at the same time in the very heart of consciousness and in the same act, and acquires its full significance from thought. The good that is manifest to man as the absolute value is identical with that pursued by the objective history of the world: if, as we have seen, Teilhard's phenomenology is primarily philosophical, his morality, though derived from life, also depends on an absolute summit, immanent in and transcendent to consciousness.

This reflexive *expression* of the absolute and the universal in the man-world datum avoids the absurdity of a *biological morality*, while it still retains the fact of the inclusion of value in life, and of life's paving a way to morality: ethics takes over responsibility for cosmic unifications. It rejects the impossible notion of an absolute *autonomy*, while retaining the necessity for man's invention of morality: value is really given to consciousness and 'discovered' by it, but man has still to accept it and adapt it to every problem he meets, on his own responsibility. Finally, it avoids the abstract *heteronomy* of a deduction that is powerless effectively to coincide with the human act and give it the strength to carry itself through. It is cosmic energy, become conscious and morally controlled in man, that makes action possible. And this 'physical' value is none other than love:[212] in one sense, it is already 'grace', since this love is given and all that it still needs is to be taken over and transfigured by the supernatural.

3 The spirit and content of morality

Before morality is reduced to particular precepts, it is, then, governed by a *spirit*: 'Strictly speaking, nothing is sacred or profane, pure or impure. All there is is a *good direction* and a *bad direction*: the direction of the spirit, and the downward direction, the direction of narrow selfishness, of material pleasure. If we follow them in the direction that leads upwards, all creatures are luminous: if we take them in the direction that leads downwards, they become dimmed, and as though they were diabolical. As they go by they will either make our ship lose way or drive her ahead, according to the skill with which we set our sails to their breeze.' And while the risks involved should not be underestimated, it is often necessary to take them: 'In every field of the real (the physical, the emotions, the mind) danger is a symptom of power.' This morality, from being static in the juridical stage of social obligation, becomes a dynamic morality of movement; open and undefined, it has no law other than the participation of freedom in the progress of history towards final unity, the fulfilment of the world in the communion of persons.

The *main lines* of morality can then be drawn: its 'chief law is the greatest useful effort', the struggle against every check and all inertia.

Thus it is that, 'from a true understanding of the phenomenon of man we can appreciate somewhat more exactly the gravity of the sin of interior *laziness*, of desertion'. Similarly, *avarice* is a 'sin against the world', since 'if mankind is to live and develop and produce spiritual value', it must have wealth, and to halt its circulation is to damage the whole.

But it is *selfishness* above all that calls for condemnation: 'the individual cannot find his fulfilment in himself: his supreme and final personality must be realized in the way in which he is able to unite himself with other persons in order to form with them a continually more developed and better organized subject'.[213]

The human monad, therefore, must overcome the intoxication of autonomy and the temptation of isolation, and, if he is to fulfil himself, he must leave himself behind in the service of mankind and work to complete hominization in unity: if he is to exist he must, therefore, excentrate himself in a greater than himself.

Now that man has reached adult stature, he must answer the call of a new spirit that takes him out of all the watertight compartments in which he has lived and leads him towards unanimity. The only way to unite men is to offer them a goal commensurate with this new consciousness and with the overwhelming abundance of resources they have acquired or the forces they have released: 'The age of nations is past: what we now have to do, if we are not to perish, is to shake off ancient prejudices and start building the earth.'[214] 'As a result of the ever vaster organizations that are forming or emerging in the world, a new category of duties is coming into force, and these must be fitted in side by side with the ancient commandments. Hitherto, morality has been primarily individualist (between one individual and another): in future it will have to take into account more explicitly *man's obligations towards the universe*—political, social, one might even say cosmic duties; and foremost among these is *the law of work and research.*' Progress does not mean in the first place ease or well-being or peace: nor is it rest after labour, nor even, directly, virtue. Progress is essentially a *force*, and the most dangerous of forces. It is the consciousness of all that is and all that can be. Though it may encounter every sort of prejudice and resentment, this must be asserted, because it is the truth: to be more is in the first place to know more.[215]

In a phrase that calls for more exact qualification, Teilhard goes so far as to say: 'Everything should be tried—and the trial carried through to the end.'[216] He analyses at length the elements that make up the programme for the organization of human energy: science, technology, harnessing and control of sources of energy, economic control, eugenics, sublimated application of sexuality, fostering of a sense of the cosmos, development of a common human soul. This programme is based on the hope of finally attaining a supreme and

unsurpassable form of mankind.[217] 'As things are going now it will
not be long before we run full tilt into one another. Something will
explode if we persist in trying to squeeze into our tumbledown huts
the material and spiritual forces that are henceforward on the scale
of a world.'[218] Teilhard urges, therefore, the necessity of tracing out
'as soon as possible the main lines of spiritual energetics'; graphs
must be drawn up showing 'the psychogenic convergence of the
universe', 'the curve of speciation (or cerebration), the curve of
expansion, the population curve, the curve of planetary compression'. 'We have to make up our minds and get to work *without
delay, here and now*.'[219]

While personal existence is made dramatic by the inevitability of
making this choice, it is *tragic*, too. The tragedy consists not only
in the dilemma of absolute optimism or absolute pessimism,[220] 'but
also in the alternative of eternal success or failure. It is continually
subject to the judgment of Christ; since it is he who unites, it is he
who selects his own, and his sword mercilessly cuts off the unworthy
or decayed members'.[221] We may go further and say that the
whole of human history should be thought of as the battleground of a
cosmic struggle.[222] Though he extends Blondel's view even further,
Teilhard is implicitly in agreement with him in his belief that the
choice in favour of the absolute gives significance to being and
justifies its affirmation.[223]

To be real, however, freedom must be exercized in a dialectical
relation to its objective *conditions*. It is not surprising, then, that
Teilhard should have pointed out the mediative function of social
structures, and the importance of environment and education in the
advance of consciousness and in man's fulfilment in history. His
latest writings even show that he believed that the determinist
forces in an organization of mankind could be largely effective in
gradually bringing about the unanimity of consciousness in mankind: so convinced, indeed, was he of this that he was ready to
admit the statistical inevitability of a favourable evolution of
history.[22]

f: Religion[225]

'However, no morality can be viable without religion or, to put it
more exactly, without a surrounding aura of adoration. The
measure of an ethic is its capacity to blossom into mysticism.'[226] In

that statement, which at once links together and divides morality and religion, Teilhard may well have given a hint of all that Kierkegaard brought out: the existential insufficiency of a morality that, as a form of reason, never goes beyond the 'general' and abstract. And, in fact, a purely human action, even virtuous and good, can never be completely divorced from some will to power, or from the realization that the action comes from and belongs to oneself: an inevitable pride contaminates self-mastery, obedience to the law and the norm.[227] Morality calls for a going beyond oneself in love, and is fully justified only by a dispossession of the ego in another.

Religious existence precisely meets the need to worship that lies at the heart of man and is activated by the sense of the cosmos, now so generally awake. The phenomenon of religion is 'nothing other than the reaction of man's collective consciousness and activity, as they develop, to the universe as a universe'; it is certainly not 'a primitive and transitory phase that mankind goes through in its infancy' but simply 'one of the aspects of hominization and, as such, it represents an irreversible cosmic quantity'. Even though religion can become an opiate, 'even though it is taken to be a mere anodyne', 'its true function is to maintain and spur on life's progress'.[228] And 'the more man becomes man, the more necessary will it be for him to have the power and knowledge to worship'.

More exactly, religion is a positive counter to the danger we noted earlier of aimless freedom. If morality brings order and discipline, religion offers the impetus that drives souls towards 'a universal and final goal', a 'divine pole' of attraction and equilibrium, a source of energy.[229] The function of religion increases in importance in relation to the same end and with the same speed as 'hominization'.[230]

'To crown my convictions and my growing sense of "wonder", in this business of human energy, I am at this very moment seeing more clearly the formidable value and the function of the love of God . . . in the building up of the world of man—love of God that has hitherto been studied chiefly as an individual relationship between man and the summit of the world, but should now be understood as the highest and most universal form of activity'.[231]

Science in particular, valid though it is in its own order, is only a relative channel to an act that goes beyond it; and only that act

makes it possible to attain, beyond the veil, 'all the real that lies
deep down in the real'. Science is not, in itself alone, 'a sufficient
goal for existence', it is no more than preliminary to a 'fuller discovery of God'.[232] What is more, it can neither maintain its impetus nor justify its effort without recognizing that the end it
pursues is none other than God, and without seeing that God is the
warrant for the preservation of its results.[233] Similarly it cannot
'reach its own limits without being imbued with mysticism and
charged with faith'. 'By the very fact that science is led to foresee
and bank upon the future and the whole, it is taken beyond itself
and emerges into option and adoration.'[234]

Again, the problem of *communion* of consciousness and 'unanimization of man' cannot be solved without the intervention of
religion: 'only a super-love can dominate, possess, and synthesize
the host of earthly loves'.[235]

We have seen, too, that the utilization of the forces of sexuality
in the order of reason and love releases the underlying tendency
towards an absolute term.[236]

More widely, the appetite for living, which is threatened by
critical reflexion on life itself, cannot be maintained without the sure
hope of an absolute, a living absolute, that eternally gathers up man
and all his efforts,[237] both after each individual's death and at the
term of man's collective history.

A mediator of this absolute can be anticipated by reflexion even
though he cannot be deduced from it, and will be recognized by
faith. Thus Teilhard's anthropology is carried on into a Christology
that also gives it its basis: light is shed on the mystery of man only
by his movement towards God through Christ; man is fulfilled,
both in his personal and his common history, only through and in
Christ.

The peak of the development of the person, the synthesis that sums
up, without superseding, all human activities, is *mysticism*: 'the
supreme science and the supreme art' that attains simultaneously
'the universal and the spiritual'.[238] Even more than science, which
at the same time it extends and to which it presents itself as a
special subject of study,[239] it is mysticism that enables us to 'disclose
the secret of the real and reach its source'. It takes us into fullness and totality, into unity, into the presence and the mystery.[240]
It is the 'total human experience' that embraces and extends,

though still discontinuous with, the others.[241] 'We are brought to the absolute not by a journeying but by an ecstasy.'[242]

This last sentence, that stresses the element of severance in the religious life, should be counterbalanced by the notion of the continuity of values: a dialectic that Teilhard did not overlook. For Teilhard, the real, which is offered to man for his knowledge, may be represented by a series of concentric *circles* or *spheres* attached to one another by a common stem or axis. Teilhard's universe has height or depth and includes planes that are distinct from one another but have a homothetic similarity in their construction, and passage from one to another is both possible and obligatory.[243] Teilhard conceives the journey of existence only as subject to all the *forces that determine it*, still present when they have been superseded.

Nevertheless, in the time within which the person moves, the whole of this process does not lead to complete success, and the alienations of freedom are not entirely overcome: suffering and setback, finiteness and error. Desire fails to obtain the full satisfaction it seeks. Human existence can, however, at least start upon the solution of its problem, while still awaiting or hoping for a definitive solution. Even sorrow, which appears to be a formidable obstacle, can be understood and accepted as a specially effective medium for the fulfilment of the person and the world.[244] The man of good will starts, if not from non-sense and despair, at least from anxiety and puzzlement; he is urged on by confidence in life and hears the summons of being; so, in solidarity with the world and humanity, he attains the joy of *sense*, the discovery of the *real*, and the loving *wisdom* of peace.[245] But this sense, and this real, and this wisdom exist at the heart of history as an effective, concrete *participation* in God, who communicates himself freely in the form of signs, to the soul that is receptive and detached, not only from disorder, but also from its own self-sufficiency and freedom. The discovery of the whole, accordingly, does not result, as Bergson thought, from a mere psychological 'deepening' of self but from a step that brings a different demand: receptiveness to the integral life of the spirit. Taken to its extreme by the inner demand of the spirit, the existential step that is also the experience of liberty, thus reaches the 'basis of things', the supreme secret, the truth of the 'noumenon'. Without, however, ceasing to be active and creative, at a given moment it has had to reverse its attitude, to become passive to its love and to adopt a 'feminine' role—to see itself, as Claudel would say, as *Anima*. At the same time, this ill-defined plenitude has but one kind of duration, and, looking at it with new eyes, man returns to the determinations of the real, the imperatives of the should-be, and the fulfilment of history, with the knowledge, henceforth, that there is something divine in what he handles and that everything *has a basis.*

CONCLUSION

We can, then, gather from Teilhard's writings an anthropology that is complete, even if summary.

Though founded on scientific observation of the phenomenon of man, it goes far beyond this, and is enriched by a great variety of evidence drawn from more intimate and deeper reflection. It is also linked with and backed by metaphysics and theology.

It is not surprising that Teilhard should have rediscovered the classical propositions, the dialectic of man's greatness and pettiness, the transcendence of his nevertheless incarnate condition. What is more significant is that though Teilhard did not, as did Pascal and Blondel, take as his central theme the study of man in his spiritual movement towards his end, or the analysis of the moral alternative, yet his anthropology can still fairly be called *existential*, since it introduces the problem of man's destiny and does not neglect either the channels through which the person is fulfilled or the drama of the option that decides the value of being. Similarly Teilhard's spirituality is the culmination of the means that enables man to reach his fullest development.[246]

What Teilhard has to tell us about man, however, goes beyond the narrow framework of existentialism, for it sets man at the heart of the movement of the cosmos and of the history of the universe, and calls on him to perfect the unification of the world in unanimity of persons. The individual's progress in 'existence' goes hand in hand with the global fulfilment of history, and the person finds its full self only by projecting itself in the service of others and uniting itself to the movement of spiritual energy, which is love.

Thus Teilhard's thought avoids the dangerous exclusiveness of both some philosophies of being and some modern philosophies of existence, while including the positive aspects of both. It recognizes the interconnexions of man and the universe, as it does the uniqueness and the tensions in the person; but it refuses both to include the latter in the whole, and to overlook its vocation and power to rejoin and participate in the whole.

All that is lacking in this account is a clear statement and development of the fundamental difference between man's *normal* severance from being and the *abnormal* dissociation introduced by error. Man's 'condition' is not the same thing as his 'situation', and *objectivation* is not of the same order as *alienation*: the ontological gap between thought and its object, between man and man, and between man and God, must be distinguished from the historical and contingent rupture that tragically divides them, to their cost and their misfortune. This lack results in a certain blindness to the tragic element in man's situation, to certain lines of force in history and to the conditions in which man can attain freedom.

Chapter 6
Theology

Teilhard's cosmology and anthropology are completed by a theology that expresses in a logical system the evidence provided by a supernatural revelation. God is known through a rational investigation that starts from facts, but he is known more profoundly by faith. God, the triune love, calls man to communion with him; and, through Christ, God has entered history, in order to redeem man the sinner and allow him again to accept his divine calling.

Teilhard's theology is not a mere patchwork nor an appendix to the main body of his work, but an integral part of it; for it corresponds to a fundamental *datum*, though one that has a different source from the phenomenon of science. And in that lies the ultimate basis of the totality of the real.

As developed afresh by Teilhard, with the intellectual background of a modern scientific mentality, and therefore with new questions to be answered,[1] theology raises many problems. In examining these, each of its principal mysteries must be looked at in turn.

This chapter will introduce some nicer problems than those we have already considered, and before we go any further an important point must be emphasized. When we use anything that Teilhard wrote we must appraise it, according to the degree of publicity that he intended for it (this applies particularly to his letters); moreover, we should remember that sometimes Teilhard is speaking as a philosopher, and sometimes as a theologian.

I THE EXISTENCE OF GOD

The process that leads, through reflection on the experience of cosmic history, to the affirmation of God, is maintained by an intellectual imperative, at once ontological and axiological: being is, and is value. 'If we admit that being is better than its contrary, then it is difficult to stop without proceeding as far as God. If we do not admit it, then no further discussion is possible.'[2] That theoretical consideration, moreover, is intimately bound up with a relation of being to the value of being, which is equally an objective affirmation of an absolute,[3] and with an imperative and dramatic dilemma between the all and the nothing, between God and nothingness.[4] As it is for Blondel, it is an 'energetics of the spirit' that posits God; but for Teilhard the spirit is simultaneously, and in a dialectical relationship, that of man and of God. This affirmation is integrally akin to the Kantian proof,[5] to the powerful Hegelian notion that the idea of the all contains in itself its objective truth, and to the (re-formulated) ontological argument, in which Jacques Paliard, following Maurice Blondel, saw the great proof of the existence of God. It is an affirmation, too, that involves the whole of man's being, and that in consequence is at once affective, intellectual, moral and religious: scientific, in the fullest sense of the word.

At the peak, then, of the hierarchy of being, in an impassable beyond, there exists *Being-God*: perfection of existence, spiritual unity, transcendent freedom, consistence and plenitude. Transcendence of personality.[6]

The perfection of being is not that of an inert substance: the divine unity is the act by which God unifies, interiorizes, and concentrates himself: it is the perfection of a spirit that knows itself and wills itself. It is the supreme type and unification, which gives structure to the elements of finite beings and guides their development towards final unity.

It may have been observed that in the purely experiential and rational part of his phenomenology Teilhard does not start by positing God as the origin of the world, as the starting point of evolution. This is because his method seeks to remain faithful to scientific experience. As we have seen, however, he arrives at the necessary existence of God as the *end* of history, as the absolute condition of final unity, as the focus of personalization: Omega is, above all, the assembler of consciousness.[7] From this Teilhard deduces his animating presence here and now, at every moment of history. Known in the first place as 'the prime mover ahead of us', God is then known as the universal source of being; '*in a first stage*, we have to begin by assuming, as a gratuitous datum, the irreversible and self-sufficing presence of a "first being" (our Omega Point).'[8]

We shall shortly have to discuss the value of Teilhard's eschatology; and, without denying the progress of history towards its fulfilment, we shall have to question the strict application to human history of the biological plan of unification, and the unmistakable character of present indications of spiritual progress. From Teilhard's point of view these provide an argument that is essential to the affirmation of God. One might, then, wonder what remains of his thesis.

It would seem, however, that once the necessary transpositions have been made, the thesis holds good in its entirety, akin as it is to some of the classical proofs of the existence of God: the proof from degrees of being, or the proof from final purpose, which makes explicit use of finite being's tension towards the absolute. If we take our stand initially, as Teilhard does, on the objective plane, it is perfectly true that the universe, in process of becoming in time, posits God 'by intention', 'wills God', is directed towards God: and that the true significance of its upward progress entails nothing less than a personal absolute. Even more imperatively, perhaps, from a subjective point of view, also adopted by Teilhard, it is man, as part and parcel of the universe whose consciousness he is, who posits God (both through his personal thought and his collective reality) as the necessary life and the ultimate convergence of a total history: closely linked with an antecedent history of which he is the leading shoot, man recognizes that it is advancing, with him and through him, towards a supreme unity.

Subject to this correction and transposition, which still allows it to retain its particular slant, Teilhard's proof harmonizes with the metaphysical potentialities of reason, as defined by the first Vatican Council: and it is all the more valid and important in that like Bergson in the *Two Sources*, it directly reveals the nature of the absolute, which is the energy of *love*, the active unity of a communion of consciousness.[9] We have seen, too, that in a second and quite distinct stage, Teilhard identifies Being, thus recognized, with the Christ of Christian revelation.

Teilhard rightly accepts and makes use of the results of Blondel's examination of the moral conditions of this approach and this recognition: the affirmation of Omega, he says, implies 'a fundamental option, a postulate that cannot be proved but from which everything stems'.[10] It demands the total effort of man's mind and heart. 'Today the whole of human activity is called on to face the problem of God: it is a problem that can be approached only by the total effort of human research and experience. It is not only that God gives lasting value to human effort, but also that his revelation is a response to the combined total of that effort.'[11]

Further, as this passage shows, the problem of God takes on for Teilhard, particularly in the last papers he wrote, a continually more *practical* or even pragmatic emphasis: with the existence of God being postulated by the successful fulfilment of history, or, more exactly, by the activation of the human energy necessary for that success. Moreover, for Teilhard the God in question is, in fact, the Christian God, the universal Christ.

Teilhard cannot fairly be accused of pantheism, for he is manifestly careful not to assert that history is creative of God: he emphatically asserted the transcendence of God.[12] His view is summed up in a succinct and carefully worded phrase: 'God is complete for himself, while for us he is continually being born'.[13] He saw very clearly that the love of the Christian God for persons reinforced Christianity's rejection of any loss of individuality in God. At the same time, at least when he was confining himself to a consideration of the facts of nature, the unanswerable logic of his thought brought him to a crucial point from which emerged what was at least an apparent contradiction.[14] If finite, Omega Point does not satisfy the demands of plenitude and totality; if infinite, it would be in itself transcendent and divine. Being the *nec plus ultra* of the world's unification in the unanimity of love, it must both coincide with God and be distinct from him: it must be what it cannot be, must have acquired what it still lacks for its consummation, must make actual what by nature it possesses only as a possible potentiality (or, rather, what can only be given to it). In fact the scientific and naturalist attitude of *The Phenomenon of Man*, while it recognizes from external signs the transcendence of man, still does not fully bring out the notion of man as the creature and image of God, 'capable of God'. Thus communion of consciousness can appear only as natural and finite, and therefore at a distance from God. The theological view, however (and in fact the only real view), that identifies this communion with the organism of the mystical body of Christ, gives the former gratuitously a divine reality by participation. In any case, Omega Point belongs to something that is beyond representation and can be expressed only in the dialectical couple finite—infinite. And this couple itself, in as much as it is still an effort of reason, cannot express the mystery of the religious union of man and God. In other words, again, Teilhard's Omega is at once God and not God: the final coming together of conscious minds, while absolute, no doubt, in as much as it is a totality that cannot be exceeded, is only the preliminary condition, necessary, but not in itself sufficient, of their divinization.[15]

It should be noted, moreover, that the notion of Omega Point does not entirely avoid a certain *ambiguity*. On the one hand, as we saw in the chapter on phenomenology, Omega seems to possess the attributes of divinity: personality, presentness, transcendence, unity, distinctness.[16] On the other hand, some passages speak of it as 'partially actual', 'partially transcendent', and 'of maximum complexity'; and its eternity coexists with a temporal act of emergence. Without being born 'from the confluence of human egos', it emerges over their organized totality as a spark that leaps between the transcendent aspect of Omega and the peak of a partially unified universe.[17] The language used is obviously contradictory, and we can see that Teilhard was aware of the difficulty. It can, we believe, be resolved only by interpreting it in the light of the sentence quoted earlier. 'God is complete *for himself*, while *for us* he is continually being born.'[18] What, moreover, that sentence does is simply to express the mystery of the union of Christ the Word with his mystical body, and the preparatory stage foreshadowed by gratuitious and progressive, though partial and incomplete, participation in a final super-transposition.

Similarly, one should certainly be careful not to underestimate the force of the language Teilhard uses about the 'transformation' that God consents to undergo in his creative and unifying (by grace) activity: at the same time one should note with equal care the very deliberate modifications to be found in his writings.[19] The interpretation of Teilhard's thought is in no way assisted by diluting the bold realism of a language that uses a very individual approach forcibly to emphasize the extraordinarily close link between God and man, and that is not satisfied with classical modes of expressing it.

In so far as it had to bring out the underlying reality of a mystery, this contradiction was inevitable; it is even more so when it has to deal with a *linear* (or conic) view of history, which considers the transcendent end as succeeding to a progression within time, and therefore as to be expected after a series of determined events: God then has to fill the gaping void between his eternity and the term of history. In order to express man's final religious transition to God, Teilhard chose to represent it as a biological movement. So impressed was he by the final instant of a convergent history that he concentrated his attention on it and gave it a very special position, at the expense of the present and actual.

Now, it is possible and necessary to conceive God as revealing himself at the heart of history, through signs, both natural and supernatural, in the *actuality* of the present. Totally complete in himself, absolute reality, plenitude of life, God yet consents freely and generously to manifest himself and communicate his infinite mystery to man, and to guide man towards him, in so far as man has faith, under the veil and through the medium of symbols. Thus there is a progressive revelation, both individual and collective, whose peak was represented by Jesus Christ, and to which there will be no end, not even in the Beatific Vision. Man's knowledge always falls short of the reality, but is always really present, eternity being in some way adapted to human time.

The problem, then, and the mystery of man's *transition* to God is no longer relegated to the future, conceived as at the term of a geometric movement: it is thought and lived in the *nunc* of a spiritual present. This, moreover, does not exclude an even more generous act of a total fulfilment, a collective consummation—the Parousia. In other words, God can appear and act at the term of history only if he does so throughout the course of history: he must *already* be here, already be seen, already be revealing himself.

This essential concept seems to rule out the possibility of a purely scientific and secular phenomenology, which does not, and in itself cannot, embrace the religious problem. Man can, in truth, be described only as the object of a revelation that culminates in the revelation of Jesus but at the same time is, and always has been, operative through signs.

At the same time Teilhard's attitude, like that of Blondel, remains valid and *necessary*, but only as *abstract*, as a self-conscious abstraction, as one moment of a wider phenomenology and logic of history. It was this relationship, so difficult to express, he was continually striving to explain more clearly. He constantly sought to maintain the autonomy of science and of scientific reflection and at the same time to crown his phenomenology with a theology.[20]

Here Blondel's dialectic is more coherent and exact: it, too, starts (though on a subjective plane) from the being's natural movement towards God, but is careful not to let it arrive, if not at an intellectual discovery, at least at a possession. It accepts man's fundamental inability to achieve his desire, and leaves it to the freedom of transcendence to reveal itself in answer to good will, to operate the encounter and determine its forms. It is true that Teilhard, too, speaking as a *theologian*, was careful to point out the conditions for a total encounter with God.[21]

We may conclude, then, that while Teilhard rightly sought to balance the immanence and transcendence of God by a correspondingly balanced series of affirmations, he was unable to escape from the dilemma of a contradiction. At the same time, that contradiction is undoubtedly inherent in the very terms of a problem that is also a mystery.

II CREATION

God freely confers a finite and participated existence on the universe and the beings that make it up. He is their initial and permanent principle, their consistence and energy, their heart. Everything stems from him, just as everything rises up to and returns to him. Everything depends on him and everything proceeds towards him.[22] And the immanence that makes him present in everything, and which allows him to be recognized in his signs, is not one of confusion or inter-absorption but of transcendence, in other words, of negation.[23]

When he is speaking as a *philosopher*, Teilhard limits himself to asserting the preliminary condition (if one may so put it) of nothingness,[24] the gratuitousness of the creative act and the total dependence of the finite being, in its existence and its becoming, in relation to God. In his phenomenological reflection he avoids formulating the question of a 'beginning' for the universe, since scientific thought cannot express it without paradox.[25] This 'limitless elasticity of time' must be given a real value; it is not simply a way of looking at it, but is a necessary consequence of 'the very structure of the universe' and reflects the '*absolute* conditions of participated being'.

The notion of creation, which is metaphysical, or rather 'meta-experiential', 'expresses the absolute dependence (the essential relationship) of the universe *in globo*', in as much as it forms a whole: it cannot be applied to anything but the whole.[26]

In fact, if time is inaugurated with the world, God does not create the world in time: in its transcendence, the creative act cannot be contained in history or be subject to observation—it is not an event. It appears experientially to a reflection on the scientific datum only under the sign and the veil of the phenomenon of unification (of individual beings and their temporal totality).

In his desire to form some sort of picture of the origin of the universe, Teilhard, following (as he is perfectly justified in doing) current scientific ideas on the subject, imagines a state of matter that is very loosely held together and has very little structure. To this he attributes, necessarily though paradoxically, a condensed potential of spiritual development, since this matter is the 'matrix of spirit'.[27] Teilhard realizes, however, that it is impossible to push this un-organized and tension-less character to the *extreme limit*, for the absolute multiple is nothingness: matter, however primitive it may be, must have some structure. Ascending, then, to the *trans-experiential* or metaphysical plane, he believes that he can posit as though presenting itself to God, a sort of pure potency—pure nothingness, no doubt, but at the same time a 'passive potentiality'. The imagery of his language is sufficient evidence of the absence of any trace of Manicheanism, of the suggestion of God's coexistence with an eternal matter.[28] Teilhard is trying, obviously enough, to connect the evidence of science with a plane that goes beyond experience; unless the expression 'passive potentiality' designates both the sovereign freedom of God and the 'transcendental' con-dition of a creation, that consists in submitting to the 'matrix' of the unification of the multiple. In any case, the mystery of the origin of the world remains intact.

When Teilhard introduces the *Christian datum*, he is at pains, in line with the teaching of dogma, to attribute to Christ not only the creative decision but also the existence of the universe in its being and becoming.

One point, however, should be noted: the total freedom of creation is associated with the rejection of its arbitrary character. How, asks Teilhard, can we seriously envisage a universe that emanated from a mere whim of generosity. Such a view would destroy the appetite for action and even more, strike at man's dignity.[29]

On the philosophical plane, again, he proposes to add to the metaphysics of *Esse* a metaphysic of *Unire*, to the notion of pure act that of union, to define being by its internal movement of self-unification—a movement that can be carried further by that of uniting other beings to oneself, these latter being patient (actively patient) of the supreme unifying activity.[30] The importance, more-over, of the idea of unification is derived for Teilhard from *experiential* observation: we find that no being exists except by de-veloping its own structure and integrating itself in an all-embracing history of unification: it is not surprising that he makes of this the type of being and builds it up into a general philosophy.[31]

Speaking as a *theologian*, and applying this principle to the evidence of revelation, Teilhard suggests that bound up with the trinitarian movement by which God posits himself and affirms him-self in the communion of the persons, is a movement of loving expansion, by which God, completely freely and gratuitously, unites his creation with himself:[32] creation itself, as we noted earlier, standing initially 'at the antipodes of God' as a pure potentiality, a 'yearning for being', but now invited to rise up to the real existence of participating in God's interior communion, and, once it has developed within time, to attain fulfilment in him. Thus creation, with its content of progressive unification, is seen to be 'a sort of replica or symmetrical copy of trinitisation', by which, no doubt, we should understand that it is its image or analogical corres-pondence.[33]

Although this dialectic is difficult and possibly overbold it is no doubt justified in employing the profound resources of the meta-physics of *Being*, or *Esse*: neither supreme abstraction nor static thing, but a concrete and personal act of unification of self by self, a rich and living interiority.[34] It comes close, however, to the rationalism of a logical and necessary deduction of created being from absolute existence. And yet by the unavoidable device of com-plementary verbal contradictions, that correct one another, Teil-hard seeks to preserve the sovereign sufficiency of God, while at the same time emphasizing the relationship, as intimate as it can possibly be, of participated being to its origin. And, when he considers the fact—*the only historically real fact*—of man's supernatural vocation, then, in his eagerness to synthesize, he in some way anticipates the *abstractly discontinuous* stages of God's plan, and so telescopes them together at the heart of transcendence. It would, no doubt, have been better to suggest that the act of creation and the act by which God unites his creation to himself are an *image* and a correspondence of the act by which God unites himself to himself.

Nevertheless, it remains true that Teilhard was sharply aware of the problem raised more urgently today than at any time by the mystery of creation, and that he presented it boldly and forcibly: even though there are no perfectly valid formulas to take its place, it was worth stressing the relative character of classical philosophy and criticizing the picture of 'efficiency'. While we cannot affirm a 'need'[35] or a 'propensity' in him who is all sufficiency and freedom, and without attempting in any way to dismiss the fact of contingency, yet some gleam of light may perhaps illuminate the paradox: not only by introducing the notion of God *diffusivus sui* but also by that of the eternal pre-existence of things in the Word of God and, still more, by the predestination of Christ, who links the triune God to his own creation.[36] In other words, Teilhard's view may imply the inter-connections, as close as possible, of the mystery of the Trinity and the mystery of the Incarnation—as though the Word could not be begotten except with his humanity, the whole process existing in eternity and in freedom.

Equal prominence is rightly given to God's great plan, as described in the Epistle to the Ephesians, of uniting men in communion with himself. It is not enough for him, says Teilhard, to envelop us in an omnipresence of creative action: 'Under what form and with what end in view, has the creator given us, and still preserves in us, the gift of participated being? Under the form of an essential aspiration towards him—and with a view to the unhoped-for cleaving which is to make us one and the same complex thing with him. The action by which God maintains us in the field of his presence is a unitive transformation.'[37]

Still following St Paul, Teilhard adds that God's ultimate aim is 'the quantitative repletion and the qualitative consummation of all things: it is the mysterious pleroma, in which the substantial *one* and the created *many* fuse without confusion in a *whole*, which, without adding anything essential to God, will nevertheless be a sort of triumph and generalization of being . . . *The divine omnipresence* (thus) *manifests itself* within our universe *in the network of the engendering forces of the total Christ.* God exerts pressure, in us and upon us . . . only in the act of forming and consummating Christ who saves and super-animates the world.'[38]

Thus Teilhard's thought, in agreement with Christianity, leads to the notion of an infinite *love* that, through an immanence of grace, draws its free creation to itself. 'Suddenly cosmogenesis takes on, even in its most ineluctable and deeply-hidden determinacies, the aspect of a limitless contact with a supreme pole of attraction and completion. A current of love gushes out and spreads over the whole breadth and depth of the world: and this it does not like some added warmth or fragrance—but like some basic essence that will transform everything, assimilate and take the place of everything.'[39]

There is one final lack that we may note: Teilhard accepted in their original simplicity the great concepts of God, the creation and the world. It is a pity that he did not subject these to a more mature and up to date criticism, examining them with an attention focussed more closely on interiority and inspired by more dialectical requirements: not, indeed, in order to weaken their value, but, after any necessary corrections, to accentuate it. The realist and scientific outlook could have been transferred to the plane of the subject in the act of reflexion; and an 'apophatic' negation introduced to reduce the objective representations and images of the absolute. As for the creative act, it becomes manifest to the ego in its own existence, before being imposed on the 'world' or the 'universe'.

III THE HISTORY OF CREATION

Creation has its laws and conditions that are freely respected by God, though they are not imposed on him from without.[40]

Leaving aside, of course, the case of the angels, Teilhard believes that, in our world, God can create and wishes to create only beings that exist in *history* and in time, freely endowed by him with the desire to be united to him, and situated within a history (cosmic and human) that is itself also freely endowed with the desire progressively to unify itself in order to be united with God and coincide with its end.[41]

Moreover, it is just as possible and necessary, Teilhard says, for modern theology to embrace this notion of a God who creates an historic world (meaning a world capable of progress in time towards unity) as it was for the theology of Saint John and the Alexandrians to embrace the notion of a logos, the creator of a world that was at that time regarded as static. Creation is necessarily coextensive with time, and 'the world is incessantly, though imperceptibly, emerging a little above non-being'.[42]

From this idea stems a consequence that we shall later return to and examine: the essential precariousness of created being, the inevitable and statistical necessity of error and fault, the probability of a disorder consubstantial with the progressive development of order and unity. However, God, impelled by his infinite charity, intervenes immediately, even in the order of matter, to counter the evil he had permitted.[43]

Bound up with the historical character of creation in general is that of the creation of *man*, appearing as such, within world-time, conditioned by the entire cosmos, and prepared by the evolution of biological forms towards fullest consciousness—and at the same time the specially favoured object of an act that establishes him as transcendent of the universe, as the unique image of God, and that summons him to a matchless vocation.[44]

Here we meet a first problem, that of the apparent contradiction between the notion of a creation of the soul *ex nihilo subjecti* (=with nothing antecedent or preliminary), and the phenomenal evidence of the interconnexion of man and the universe. Modifying the idea of passive 'potency' in relation to 'act', Teilhard holds, on the contrary, that the former contributes to the latter the elements of a unification. In consequence, 'the soul cannot be created *outside* a world, since it can exist only *by acting* upon a subject of action in its own degree (this action consisting in *unifying* around itself a universe that, without it, would sink back into plurality). The soul is not created *with* some matter or some pre-existing life, but *on* that life and matter—but in such a way, however, that it forms, with that life and matter, one and the same organic and "hierarchic" whole— the higher and lower elements not being confused with one another but conditioning one another—the higher (because the more united) *holding up* the lower, and the lower *contributing to the higher* what it requires to release its unifying power (or act). This amounts to saying that there is a sort of "metaphysical" continuum, that is to say a *complex*, hierarchically *structured chain* of even the most spiritual essences. In this view, the physical *elements* of a thing said to be composite are not the *constituents* of that thing, but its specific *sub-jacents* (the "sub-jacency", moreover, being *essential*, since the monads exist only in "chain-formation", in "series", in "universe").'[45]

Another problem turns on the multiplicity of God's creative acts. It is clear enough that, looked at from the point of view of God, creation takes place in an eternal and transcendent act that cannot but be unique. From man's point of view, it appears both continuous and multiple: continuous, because God's assistance is indispensable to every being and every movement, to every stable form and to every innovation and every change: multiple, because it is possible limitlessly to recognize divine acts as the source of finite being and its mutations. God's assistance seems in some way to be more active through new advances that bring about some progress in cosmic history, for example for the coming of life and for the emergence of new species. It is absolutely indispensable not only for the transition from animal to man, but for the appearance of every human soul in history. At the same time, this divine action, apparently discontinuous, accepts the causality of nature and the dependence of an event upon its antecedents and conditions. The human soul, in its partly 'animal' aspect, remains subject to this law. Thus the creative act respects the working of evolution, in which it intervenes only by successive 'jerks'.[46] As we shall be seeing shortly, one may even regard God as endowing the spiritual energy of the universe with a certain potential, a certain capacity to invent new forms, a certain responsibility.

Because of the point of view that Teilhard adopted in *The Phenomenon of Man* and in many other essays, he did not deal with this problem of philosophy, which lies outside a scientific phenomenology.[47] But, as we noted earlier, the inevitable failure to recognize an Act of Creation in the case of man burdens Teilhard's phenomenology with a fundamental difficulty, which becomes apparent as soon as it seeks to complete the history of man in God. However wide the allowance one makes, as Teilhard does, for the powers granted to evolution, and therefore to natural causality, in the creation of human nature (in its origin) and of all men in their individuality (this can be seen, in particular, in one of the passages quoted in note 47), it is difficult to get away from the notion (inevitably spatial) of a creative act that brings about the existence of the person—as a 'subject', that is to say as endowed with an infinite capacity for development of self by self. The purely phenomenal or scientific point of view, while legitimate in its own order, is radically incapable of explaining man's transcendence: behind the emergence of existence lies the mystery of a total datum.

IV THE CO-OPERATION OF GOD AND HIS CREATION

Having established the complete dependence of beings in relation to God, simultaneously with the absolute character of their existence, Teilhard then sets out to explain the movement of the world, within the progress of its history. Here again, philosophical considerations are complemented by reference to revealed sources.

The temporal dynamism of the world is explained in the first place by the attractive force of *unity*. As far back as one can look into the past, what one sees is *multiple proceeding towards unification*: or, more exactly, multiple, already unified, proceeding towards greater unity. This universal unification, which can be seen in cosmic and biological progress, can be explained only by the attraction, present and active, of a *personal and transcendent unity*.[48] Thus the spirit of God is the motive force, though through a transcendent action, of creation, since it is its end.

This act is operated, however, *with the co-operation of the finite being*. In line with the Thomist theory of the consistence of nature and the autonomy of secondary causes, Teilhard notes that 'God does not so much make things as make them make themselves'.[49]

'For the Christian transformist, God's creative action is no longer conceived as an intrusive thrusting of His works into the midst of pre-existent beings, but as a bringing to birth of the successive stages of His work in the heart of things. It is no less essential, no less universal, no less intimate either on that account.'[50] At the same time, Teilhard makes it clear that 'evolution is certainly not "creative" as science for a brief moment believed, but it is the expression of creation, for our experience in time and space.'[51]

Thus, through an act of his transcendence God gives it to every being, according to its degree, both to exist and to have structure, and to *act*. This gift is given, in particular, to life, in its evolutionary impulse and in the activity by which it invents new forms. It is given to man, too, in the exercise of his freedom. This gift involves a permanent *co-operation*. Precisely to the extent that, according to Teilhard's cosmology, things involve unification of their elements, God gives it to them, not only to be but also to act for the sake of their own unity.[52]

Introducing a *theological consideration*, Teilhard adds that the unity that moves and attracts the world is none other than *Christ* in his eternal and historical reality. It is even in and through Christ, directly and originally willed, that God operates in the world.

V NATURE AND THE SUPERNATURAL:
DISTINCTION AND COINCIDENCE OF THE TWO ORDERS

A true interpretation of Teilhard must endeavour, as he does, to express with exactness the distinction between the order of nature and the supernatural order, and their union.[53]

Teilhard was very alive to this problem, and was at pains to assert the eminence of the supernatural order and the absolute gratuitousness of God's gift: as we have seen, to obtain the data of a total phenomenology, he looked in turn to two distinct sources of information.[54] He defines the 'Christian phenomenon' as 'the reflection onto what is ascending of that which is already on high', 'the palpable influence on our world of *another* and supreme someone'.[55] And, while emphasizing that the supernatural cannot dispense with nature, he adds that it transforms nature.[56]

'All our work ultimately culminates in forming the offering upon which the divine fire is to descend.' 'Every human enrichment, no matter what it be, is but dust, unless, by uniting itself to a centre of immortal love, it becomes the most precious and most incorruptible of all things.'[57] 'Since by nature he is an element, man has to recognize that, in the definitive act that is to unite him with the whole, the two terms of the union are incommensurable. On his side he, the lesser, has more to receive than to give. He finds himself taken up by what he thought to possess.'[58] And Teilhard speaks of 'the universal and unremitting advances of the divine contact' that man has to accept, 'the kiss that God is continually offering us through the world' and that faith must return to him.[59] Comparing knowledge of God by reason and by faith, he says, 'I made my way to Omega Point through the cosmos and biology, but it was still at arm's length—and that as a result of a dialectical reconstruction that presented me with a "deduced and conjectured" entity rather than one undergone and experienced centre to centre, heart to heart; with one anticipated rather than realized. It was indeed, on my part, a movement of intense passion—but it was still not real love: and thus there was still a whole world between the two.'[60] He adds that the appetite for the invisible has been 'given to him from heaven' and, after first nourishing deep within him his 'innate appetite for the earth' has ended by forming one with it. Elsewhere Teilhard says, 'I attribute no definitive and absolute value to the various constructions of man. I believe they will disappear, recast in an unimaginable new whole . . . What I love in them is not their form but their function, which is, in the first place, to produce what can be divinized—and then, through the grace of Christ applied to the effort we make, to produce the divine . . . I attach no "divine stability" to the natural order. Rather would I say that it is characterized by a radical *instability in Christum*, everything being "cantilevered", apparently unsupported, in tension, on the *real* centre of the Pleroma.'[61] 'The only *stable* factor of life that every creature contains in its whole make-up, is its being destined (in a way that is sometimes more and sometimes less fully realized) to enter into the Pleroma, or for a time to co-operate with it.'[62] Finally, 'Every human enrichment, no matter what it be, is but dust, unless, by uniting itself to a centre of immortal love, it becomes the most precious and most incorruptible of all things'.[63]

While subordinating nature to grace, Teilhard had at the same time to assert with equal emphasis the *correspondence* and analogy of the two orders. Nature, the first legible communication and initial revelation of God, not only 'symbolizes' with the supernatural order, but constitutes its basis and substructure, its conditioning and its preparation.[64] We may go further, in fact, and say that it is penetrated through and through by the influence of the redemptive Incarnation and that, since all time, it has been orientated towards Christ, its creator, its ambience and its end: at the same time, Christ will give it gratuitously a transfiguration, a fulfilment and an exaltation which it could never claim for itself.[65]

This finality or 'ordination' becomes apparent, psychologically, in the person as the *desire for God*: a desire that, by reason of man's supernatural vocation, is the desire for the living God: moreover, the gift of faith effectively satisfies the yearning, often unexpressed and vague, underlying all man's activities.[66] The grace of faith presupposes 'a special sensitizing of the eyes and ears of the soul'.[67]

Linked with the question of the relations of nature and the supernatural, is that of the relationship between the mystery and its *expression*, which is the problem of the possibility of a theology. On this cardinal point, the whole of Teilhard's philosophy, confirmed by the fact of the Incarnation, is conclusive evidence for the ability of human language positively to express, in analogical correspondence, a reality that at the same time goes beyond it, and to give it a content of intelligible truth. Image or symbol, however, cannot do more than reflect what cannot be represented or contained in word.[68] Even so, one may regret the absence, in Teilhard's thought, of an explicit consideration of the negativity of the formulas that endeavour to express the aspects of the mystery.

This transcendence of the mystery in relation to its expression involves also the subordination and relativity of the intellectual forms of the revealed message, in relation to its catholicity. From this arises the problem of a theological search for structures continually more independent of the historicity of cultures and civilizations.[69]

Although Teilhard devoted much thought to the relationship between nature and the supernatural, we should note that he has nothing to say about the allied problem of grace and free will: he does not seem to have investigated the nature of the indispensable co-operation and assistance of God in making the human act possible, effective, and valid.

VI THE INCARNATION

First, we may summarize the chief propositions of Teilhard's Christology.[70]

Christ, eternal God and man appearing within time, has a fundamental relation to the world and to evolution. He is at once its author and creator, animator and mover, director and leader, centre and head, its consistence and consolidation (active unity), its gatherer and assembler, purifier and regenerator, crown and consummation, spear-head and end. Though immanent in the universe, yet Christ transcends it. 'Christ is not a supernumerary added to the world as an extra, an embellishment, a king as we now crown kings, the owner of a great estate . . . he is the alpha and the omega, the beginning and the end, the foundation stone and the keystone, the fulfilment and the fulfiller. It is he who consummates and he that gives its consistence to all. It is towards him and through him, the life and light that lie within the world, that the universal convergence of all created spirit makes its way, in toil and suffering.'[71]

Thus the existence of Christ meets a sort of demand of the universal: 'By constructional necessity there must be in the cosmos (if it is to keep going) some specially favoured place, where—as though at a universal cross-roads—everything sees, feels, directs, animates, *touches* everything else: would that not be a wonderful point at which to place (or rather to recognize) Jesus?'[72]

The recognition of Christ as the centre of the universe meets a demand of thought, too, and gives it something that it urgently needs to allay the distress it feels when it contemplates the immensity of our universe.[73]

The divine influence of Christ, which, both by natural right and through the Resurrection, is universal, radiates not only in souls but through the totality of all beings, penetrating to the heart of material and biological forces.[74]

This radiation is also the kindling of a *fire*, burning deep in the world: for if the 'fire from heaven' can come down to us and consume us it is because, by virtue of the Incarnation, it has first set fire to the world: 'so that it is, to some degree, *fire of the earth*—and that the universe, *having become fire, now* implies fire by "constitutive" right—analogical but real'.[75]

This radiation and kindling stimulate and co-operate with a progress of the entire world, through man and in man: it belongs essentially to Christ to be complete, total, and self-consistent, and equally essentially it belongs to him to 'be able to grow indefinitely, without distortion or discontinuity' in as much as he gratuitously makes himself one with man and the world; and this fundamental note is also his 'mark of recognition'.[76] Far from being finished, creation 'is continuing still more markedly, and in the highest reaches of the world' in the building up of the Pleroma, of the body of Christ.[77] The growth of creation is the growth of the Incarnation.

Teilhard sees the Incarnation as a 'prodigious biological operation'.[78] To create, to fulfil and to purify the world, St John and St Paul tell us, is for God to unify it by making it organically one with himself. How, then, does he unify it? By to some degree immersing himself in things,[79] by making himself an 'element', and then, using this purchase-point found deep within the heart of matter, taking over the direction and leadership of what we now call evolution. Christ, the principle and vital inspiration of the universe, by appearing as man among men, has taken up his specific position and since all time has been subordinating to himself, purifying, directing and super-animating the general rise of consciousness in which he has included himself. Through a perennial action of communion and exaltation he makes one with himself the whole of the earth's psychism. And when he has thus gathered all together and transformed all, he will re-unite himself in a final act with the divine centre from which he never emerged and close in upon himself and what he has won as his own. Then, St Paul tells us, 'there will be nothing but God all in all'.[80]

In contrast with an extrinsicist view of the Incarnation, Teilhard distinguishes in it three characteristics that associate it intimately with man's universe: '*Tangibility*, in the order of experience, through Christ's historic entry (by birth) into the actual process of evolution; *expandibility*, universal in order, given to the Christic centre as an effect of "resurrection"—and finally *power of assimilation*, organic in order, potentially integrating in the unity of a single "body" the totality of human kind.'[81] Thus the Incarnation has an essentially *physical* character.

The modern concept of a universe in evolution[82] or of the intimate association of time and space makes it easier to vindicate the kingship of Christ and to reconcile harmoniously 'the two domains of experience and faith'.[83] 'In a universe of "conical" structure Christ has a place (the apex) ready for him to fill, whence his spirit can radiate through all the centuries and all beings; and because of the genetic links running through all the levels of time and space between the elements of a convergent world, the Christ-influence, far from being restricted to the mysterious zones of "grace", spreads and penetrates throughout the entire mass of nature in movement. In such a world Christ cannot sanctify the spirit without (as the Greek Fathers intuitively perceived) uplifting and saving the totality of matter.'[84]

The notion of the universal Christ, world-wide in dimensions, and in intimate relation to its history, provides the answer to the modern criticism levelled against a religion that has no concrete relation to a universe in evolution.[85] In short, what Teilhard is doing is simply to develop to the full the notion of the mystical body by giving it a fully concrete physical meaning and linking it to all that gives the universe its solidarity. 'Such seems to me in our days,' he says, 'the role reserved for the grand notion, so essentially dogmatic, of the Christian *Pleroma*. The Pleroma: the mysterious synthesis of the uncreated and the created—the grand completion both quantitative and qualitative, of the universe in God.'[86]

The contemplation of the magnificent figure of Christ, king of the world, does not rule out for Teilhard, any more than it does for St Paul, the contemplation of the human features of the Christ of the Gospels, for it is the incarnate image of the Word that gives the cosmic Christ and the Christ of the Parousia his true lineaments. 'The mystic Christ, the universal Christ of St Paul, can have neither meaning nor value for us except as an expansion of the Christ born of Mary and dying on the Cross. It is from the latter, that the former derives essentially his fundamental quality of being indisputably concrete. However far we allow ourselves to be drawn into the areas of the divine open to Christian mysticism, we never leave behind the Jesus of the Gospels. On the contrary, we feel an ever greater need to envelop ourselves even more closely in his human truth.'[87]

In emphasizing so forcibly the all-embracing dimensions of the mystery of the Incarnation, expressed in physical,[88] and 'universal' rather than juridical terms, in emphasizing its conditions and conditioning factors,[89] and in linking it with the creation and history of the world, Teilhard conforms with the evidence of Scripture, and adheres to the tradition of the Greek Fathers, in particular St Irenaeus and St Gregory of Nyssa.[90] What he does is simply to give a more concrete, more experiential significance to the classic notion of the new Adam, of universal man.[91] The implications of the liturgical feasts (Christmas and the Epiphany, Easter and the Ascension, the Feast of Christ the King) bring out Christ's cosmic role, which, moreover, is essentially linked with his appearance in history.

Here Teilhard's thought has the great merit of reasserting the importance of the mystery of the *Resurrection*, which is called for in particular by the contemporary liturgical movement, and whose significance for salvation has been obscured and weakened, since the middle of the medieval period, by a juridical theory that is more concerned with the mystery of the Cross than with the mystery of Easter. Teilhard brings out forcibly the role of the risen Christ in the divinization of man and, with man, of all creation, at least at an initial stage. [92]

The expression 'Super-Christ' is no doubt an unfortunate one, but in the context in which it is used it involves no suggestion that the real Christ is purely relative: it invites us, rather, to distinguish more clearly the features of the total Christ, enriched by his mystical body and gradually, *for men who can see* his radiance, becoming the *very truth* of God. [93]

Just as he rejected the arbitrary character of the creation, Teilhard seems to combine, in a dialectical paradox, the complete freedom of the Incarnation and its quasi-necessity: for, he believes, creation can consummate the unity it seeks only through the intervention of a God-man. This argument is close to the view held by many of the Fathers and many theologians, particularly of the Franciscan school, who accepted the 'fittingness' of the Incarnation, by which they meant its conformity with God's infinite love for man. [94] From a different point of view, Karl Rahner, again, demonstrates that both God and man have some sort of reciprocal *aptitude* for a common encounter. [95]

As he does for the creation, here again Teilhard takes his stand in the concrete order of *fact*, of effective concrete reality: it is only after the factual event, and once it is part of the evidence, that the existence of the Incarnation is seen to be necessary for the achievement of God's aims; it forms an integral part of a whole, it is the realization of an indivisible design; [96] it makes manifest, and is the source of the ultimate significance of creation, and also of the significance of man. If creation is for Christ, man and his history are the condition of Christ: man, then, in Christ and through Christ, is God in as much as God freely wills to be finite; he is the expression of the Word in nothingness, just as the Word is the expression of God in the infinite. [97]

And it is the human-divine connexion brought about by the Incarnation, it is the idea of union revealed by it, that makes it possible to reformulate and enrich the usual theology of the creation and the current concept of God.[98]

Similarly, while a static view of the universe could in earlier days justify discussion about the motives of the Incarnation, the modern, definitively established, concept of a world in process of organic evolution, makes it possible to combine the two points of view: it is both possible and necessary that 'a salvation of sinful man should be also the sanctification of the world'.[99]

Teilhard is ready to see the Incarnation as designed to serve the world, and to see in Christ a function of the universe;[100] while at the same time he balances that statement by its complement, for the universe is the basis of the Incarnation. In fact the extraordinary 'humility of God' (in Bergson's phrase)[101] makes him consent to this loving service, this seemingly impossible alliance, and Christ wills himself to the service of his bride.

There is, however, some danger attached to this interconnexion, so close in Teilhard's view, of creation and Incarnation, and to this inversion that makes of Christ the medium through which the *universe* attains its goal. Teilhard's point of view, always synthetic and concrete, rejects any splitting up of the economy of God's plan, of which St Paul speaks. But, *taken literally* and *without reference to this supernatural context*, his ideas would in fact tend somewhat to rationalize the mystery by regarding it as the consequence of a principle, the unfolding of an antecedent fact.[102] Wherever its roots may lie, and whatever benefits it may confer on man's history, the Incarnation is above all a gratuitous intervention of the Word, a break with history, singular and unique: it establishes and sets up a new order, and is in fact a new creation. And, similarly, the *Bible*, which is at the same time the voice of God speaking to the world, and an account of the preliminaries to the Incarnation, and of the Incarnation itself, is not simply included *within* the earlier context of a first and fundamental expression of God, represented by the universe; it, too, bursts out into the wide waters of the world: a new and gratuitous gift, the writing and reading of a text of salvation, that goes beyond the bounds of the history of the universe. Teilhard's Christology practically disregarded this history of *fidelity*, in which, through the interpretation of events, human consciousness becomes progressively more alive to the inspired notion of an *alliance* between God and man: an alliance already universal in its aim, but individual and incomplete in its form, and whose symbolism was to reveal the fullness of its significance in the Incarnation.

Père Maréchal, whose point of view was perhaps insufficiently appreciative of the substantial interconnexion of matter and spirit and of the gratuitous interconnexion of the supernatural and nature, felt that he was justified in pointing out to Teilhard that Christ's 'universal' and cosmic function was less important than his supernatural function of sanctifying souls: '. . . Surely, to be thus the key to the whole of nature and the "saviour of cosmic evolution", necessary and splendid though that be, is only a secondary perfection for Christ the saviour of souls? To "see" it and explicitly to inspire our "practice" by it seems to me to belong more to the elaboration of our religion than to its *essence*.'[103] He added that some of Teilhard's expressions seemed to him 'to invert, at least "affectively" the necessary order of the two aspects—supernatural and cosmic—of Christian salvation'.

Continuing on the lines of that criticism, one could add that far from being a stage (a capital stage, admittedly) in history, the historical Incarnation of the Word terminates history—in this sense, at least, that Christ's paschal act solved for ever the opposition between man and God. In manifestly transferring the centre or summit of history towards the Parousia, Teilhard may have failed to find the necessary terms for expressing the dialectical tension of a history which, though completed, nevertheless continues, for it manifests and accomplishes the progressive triumph of Christ in his mystical body. And it is precisely in virtue of the release of freedom by Christ that freedom can be fully exercized, in a way to be initiated in a series of dramatic choices, by participating (if it so wishes) in Christ's Redemption. Against the heretical temptation to deny value to time, it was Teilhard's mission to emphasize the importance of the Parousia and of the road that leads to it: if history ended with Easter, at the same time it was immediately *given back* to man by the virtue of Easter.

Nevertheless, with his never-failing *realism*, Teilhard accepts Christ as an objective historical fact: Christ, meeting the world's undeniable need for a centre and a unity, and man's for a channel to the absolute and a redemption, is immediately recognized by Teilhard as God from his own testimony to himself. Although he is not blind to certain difficulties of the historical order in the Gospels,

Teilhard finds no distinction between the real Christ and the Christ of faith: there is no problem, as there is for Bultmann, of demythologizing,[104] for the subordinate value of the *image* is recognized as a consequence of the Incarnation itself. The most that Teilhard does is to note the non-representable character of certain facts that faith can arrive at only through their expression.[105]

Finally, it might seem surprising that the Person of the Holy Spirit is not mentioned in Teilhard's writings. The reality, however, of his action is always present in it, at different levels: it is from the spirit that the spiritual energy at the heart of matter and life proceeds, and the energy that later, in the course of man's history, brings persons together. And this energy is a love, light, and fire, which constitutes the divine ambience in which all things and all souls dwell. This love proceeds in its entirety from Christ: it 'spreads out over all the breadth and depth of the world; and this it does not simply like some added warmth or savour—but like a basic essence that will transmute, assimilate and replace everything'.[106] For Teilhard, then, it is indeed the spirit—not 'the spirit of philosophers and scientists', but the Holy Spirit, the Spirit of Christ, who is active in history and in the world until they achieve their fulfilment.

VII SIN AND REDEMPTION

The Redemption is bound up with sin, from which it emancipates man. To what extent, on this point, was Teilhard faithful to the data of Christianity?

In connexion with *original sin*,[107] he noted that some excesses of evil could not be explained except by the hypothesis of a grave primordial responsibility.[108] Without denying that the interconnexion of individuals is 'of a type strictly and lineally hereditary', he suggested as a 'simple and fruitful interpretation' of this sin, 'the genetic solidarity of all men within a humanity impregnated by sin'.[109] Developing this idea, and thinking no doubt of the mysterious character of original sin, he refused to regard it 'as a mere link in the chain of historical facts', as an event that could be strictly localized and as one individual phenomenon in the series of phenomena. He held that, 'in its cosmic basis, if not in its historical realization among the first human beings', original sin tended 'to merge into the mechanism of creation, in which it represents the action of the negative forces of "counter-evolution" '.[110] He attached, moreover, to this theological expression two conditions: the maximum aggrandisement of the role of Christ, and the acceptance of maximum 'activation' by the spirit.[111]

These passages display in the first place a legitimate and necessary care to respect the mystery of a sin that goes beyond the order of representation, to associate it firmly with its redemptive and victorious antithesis,[112] and to emphasize its cosmic repercussion on the whole history of man.[113] What he says, moreover, agrees substantially not only with Scripture (which sees in Adam primarily the antithesis of Christ, the universal prototype of man the sinner, and which often stresses the collective character of sin)—but also with the basic significance and evident intention of dogmatic formulas: these, if we look beyond an expression that is necessarily coloured by the culture of the time, imply the common solidarity of all men in sin and their need for redemption.[114] At another level, however, the same passages show a less successful effort to *rationalize* sin in the logical perspective of a system, though without at the same time abandoning the biblical notion of an original revolt: it is evident that 'the mechanism of creation' that constitutes man in a state of fragility is only a *factual condition* that facilitates sin, without excusing it or coinciding with it.[115]

Natural observation of phenomena is incapable of exploring the mystery of *sin*: it can only reveal *evil*. From the point of view of Teilhard's non-theological writings, evil may rightly be interpreted as a cause of the slowing down of history or of a running to waste:[116] sometimes even, with a suggestion of dualism, it appears as a return to material multiplicity, a dissociation. While it is always a fault against love, through an undue preference for some individual advantage that is exalted into an end, it does not in itself involve the notion of a rupture of friendship between man and God, of a religious estrangement so serious that it can be made good only by a divine redemption. Again, in his *Phenomenon of Man* Teilhard is justified in interpreting evil as a statistical loss, a by-product of history, a check to the rise of spirit. Free though it is, and serious, the fault appears as the consequence of human fragility, the counterpart of an order that is in process of formation: 'Our freedom of choice may be imprudent or vicious, and that is to blame for what was no more than a *delicate stage* in the synthesis of the spirit suddenly becoming an *acute and almost deadly crisis*.'[117]

Teilhard's theology of sin has no difficulty in rising up from this still 'natural' line of thought to the classic notion of the 'mystery of iniquity'. As we can see in a cardinal passage in *Le Milieu Divin*,[118] it accords an important place to evil. It is no longer a notion simply of the moral order: an inversion of good, a deviation or retreat, a disintegration into multiplicity, an 'abyss opening out into nothingness'. History, both individual and collective, experiences the drama of confrontation with a living adversary; it is swept by the fire of an attack, building up afresh, inexplicable and gratuitous, against man and against God.

At the same time it would certainly seem that, reacting against some Jansenist attitudes prevalent at the time, and also because he wished to present his apostolic message in a form more acceptable to the modern world, Teilhard did not develop the full depth of the traditional teaching of a sin whose gravity (involving a divorce between, and a rupture of friendship between, God and man) calls for a tragical redemption, God's passage through death.

In consequence, he failed, again, sufficiently to express the unfathomable depth of a mystery in which the whole of mercy is engaged (in a struggle of infinite intensity) to reconcile man and God. The prospect of nature's elevation to the supernatural takes precedence of that of its reparation, and the austere and triumphant grandeur of the paschal dialectic is somewhat overshadowed by the continuity of history's line of advance.[119] Christ's baptism in death does not appear as the death of death, the abolition of man's estrangement, the demolition of the wall that, in separating man from God, deprived him also of true communion with his fellows. Teilhard does not seem sufficiently to have retained, in the Redemption, its aspect of God's judgment of history, of condemnation of evil, and at the same time of the *re-creation* of man and, in a sense, of the universe.[120] He looks at it in a way that is more faithful to the logic of his thought than to the biblical evidence.

The mystery of the Cross, however, is not only 'the sublimation of the law of all life', the royal road of the Cross is not only 'the road of universal progress' or 'the path followed by human effort' supernaturally corrected and extended.[121] This mystery represents also a break in the line of progress: it is fault and abyss, the excessive and the inordinate, the unjustifiable extremism of love. It resists every attempt to rationalize it as a means to attain an end, or as a stage in history. It introduces a new criterion and a new law; it creates a wisdom that is the converse of a reason mutilated by sin. Finally, it is the condition for man's transition to a higher sphere and his entry into the ineffable intimacy of God.[122]

Both the justification of *history* and its understanding suffer from this relative shortcoming in the appraisal of sin, and Teilhard's phenomenological interpretation is affected by it. Even though it is balanced by the dialectic of continuity and discontinuity, the scheme of unification and convergence is too simple and too univocal to express both biological progress and the progress of humanity. Starting with man, the real key to the progress that constitutes history is the continual correction applied by the spirit to the individual and collective deviations of sin: God's struggle with man, the intervention of mercy into the situations created by evil, the succession of punishment and forgiveness, the constant recovery by God's education of what man has surrendered. If, as it appears primarily to be, history were no more than revolt, injustice and violence, it would be simply an indefinite oscillation or closed circle, and, without doubt, it would ultimately be disaster and suicide. Since the beginning of time however, in paganism and still more in Israel, the Spirit has been incarnate in the utterance of the prophet and, at long intervals, has won some advance from man. To the dialectic of the slave who is dominated has been opposed a dialectic of love and justice, and the evolution of cultures and cities in the end reflects some small degree of his victory, modest and precarious though it always remains. Only so has man had a real history. However, since everything was still imperfect and degraded, and since Israel was only a partial success, then a definitive redemption was brought about at one stroke in the person of Christ—the culmination of the preparations that led up to it. The son of God, himself become a slave, freed masters and slaves from the burden of their dialectic. And so history was fulfilled. Nevertheless, history continues, for, since Christ, it has been given gratuitously to man to benefit, in a wider outpouring, from the eternal pardon; and under the influence of the same divine education, man's development, as recounted in his records, is always made up of experiences that have been overcome, of abandonments and returns, of deviations and corrections. With the coming of man, then, the convergence of history does not work—indeed less than ever does it—as it did in the progress of biological forms; or rather it still works, but within the mystery of free options.

With such considerations is linked Teilhard's interpretation of contemporary *atheism*. He was influenced by a natural kindliness that led him to see the proportion of truth buried in error, and by the missioner's desire to bring Christianity to the modern world. As a result, Teilhard sometimes seems to concentrate on only the positive values of modern atheism.[123] This attitude is justifiable, but only provided one does not overlook the satanic aspect that is also to be found in the absolute denial of God and the gratuitous hostility to Christianity that often accompanies it. One may doubt whether Teilhard was sufficiently careful to balance the two points of view, and his hope of reconciling Christian and atheist sometimes seems to suffer from an excessive simplicity.[124]

Moreover, what Teilhard strove to do, particularly in his latest writings, in his treatment of the problem of the relation of the Incarnation to the Redemption, produced a recoil or reaction, which *reversed* the primacy normally attributed, both in theology and in piety, to the second mystery. The present change in human awareness, the humanist revival, the Church's need for a fresh contact with modern man, these seemed to him to postulate an *insistence* on the positive function of Christ, which is to divinize man and his collective history. It was not that he wished to minimize or reject Christ's role of salvation, reparation or restoration, but 'to remove them from the foreground of attention'. So that what Christ does is 'not in the first place to expiate and then, as a further step, to restore; but *in the first place* to create (or super-create) and, in order to do so, inevitably but incidentally, to fight against, and pay the price of, evil'. 'A baptism in which purification becomes the subordinate element in the overall divine act of raising up the world; a Cross that symbolizes not so much the expiation of the fault as the rising up of creation through effort; a blood that circulates and gives life, even more than it is shed; the lamb of God who bears not only the sins but the burden of the world's progress; the idea of Parousia and sacrifice being transmuted, through an enrichment of itself, into the idea of consummation and conquest.'[125]

This choice of emphasis fits in not only with the whole body of Teilhard's system but also with a theological current and spiritual approach to be found particularly in Eastern tradition. Similarly

God's plan envisages as its first objective the divinization of man in Christ, and his attainment of communion with God. 'The final goal of the Incarnation is communion with God.'[126] And Teilhard rightly points out that 'Christ's essential message is wholly contained in the pronouncement of divine fatherhood; in other words, in the assertion that God, personal being, offers himself to man as the term of a personal union'.[127]

To meet the needs of a mankind that is as profoundly contaminated by sin as it is elevated by an ideal of humanism and temporal achievement, we may well look, along these lines, for a dialectical *balance* between reflexion on the mysteries of the Incarnation and the Redemption and the permanent validity allowed in the Church of two possible attitudes and approaches in theology and spirituality, each fitted to a particular vocation.[128]

VIII IS THERE PROGRESS IN HISTORY?

Teilhard's view of history is based on the principle that mankind achieves a progress which, even if not biological, is at all events moral and spiritual.[129] Mankind as a whole, in the extension of vital energy that it consciously takes over, is progressing, infallibly and irreversibly, towards greater consciousness, but also towards greater love.

This proposition belongs largely to the domain of faith,[130] and rests on the following considerations:

The spontaneous complicity of nature, which cannot but pursue to the end the work begun by the creation of man, for which nothing can be a substitute.[131]

The statistical infallibility of an evolution, involved in the law of numerical magnitude, which, without encroaching on freedom, impels 'the totality of mankind' towards the final unity of all consciousness.[132]

The changes that can be observed in human consciousness, particularly at the present time.[133]

And finally, the presence and supernatural activity of the spirit of God, working for the fulfilment of its task.[134]

As Teilhard concludes, 'We may say with certainty that it would be easier to halt the revolution of the earth than to prevent the totalization of mankind'.[135]

May we say that this view of history meets the demands of truth or conforms to the Christian view?

Teilhard, it is true, saw very clearly that there are two sides to the modern organization of society, on the observation of which he based his hopes.[136] He realized that it vacillated between impersonal and personal forms, between 'mechanization' and 'conspiration'. 'For one form of synthesis that brings freedom, there are hundreds of others that drive us into the vilest slavery.'[137] Teilhard was well aware that the compression 'of the human mass' was not in itself sufficient to raise its temperature. Accordingly, he was at pains to link the forces of attraction to an ultimate transcendent centre, and, further, maintained that 'the success of anthropogenesis contained, in spite of the rigour of its external conditions, what was essentially a basic element of indeterminacy and uncertainty'.[138] Estimating the chances of the universe's spiritual concentration, he admitted that the dangers inherent in freedom, 'the dangerous principle of undisciplined emancipation', were 'menacing and vital'.[139] He pointed out the temptation offered to man, more acute today than ever before, by autonomy and self-sufficiency,[140] and the temptation, too, of a cosmic intoxication in surrender to matter.[141] More widely, he recognized the existence of sin and its consequences for society. Moreover, just as he accepted that suffering increases 'throughout the ages in step with the rise of consciousness',[142] so he did not shrink from envisaging the probability that evil would increase, side by side with good.[143] Teilhard's view of history, accordingly, has nothing in common with a mere waiting for an inevitable 'happy ending': the 'suspense' is continuous and, so long as any power of free choice is active, the curtain will not fall.

Nevertheless, Teilhard's concept of a progressive evolution that extends into the world of spirit, comes up, in the first place, against the discontinuity—relative if not basic—of this spiritual universe in relation to the material and biological world. This was pointed out to Teilhard, from a perhaps too narrowly Aristotelian standpoint, by Père Maréchal.[144]

We must, moreover, admit the weakness of a line of argument, emphatic though it is, that exaggerates the importance of present signs of human progress and then uses them as a basis to extrapolate the curve of the ascent of history towards a communion of persons.

The persistence of evil does not allow us to forecast with reason, on the basis of the facts, a happier future; and the Christian, who, better than anyone else, knows how deep run the roots of sin, hesitates to envisage a progressive reduction or destruction of selfishness. Influenced in particular by his reading of the Psalms, which represent the type of a universal anthropology, he can look at man and society only within the structural frame of a fundamental cleavage; and it is always from the utmost depths, in the last extremity of anguish, that mankind's cry rises up to God. This is ever man's condition, and this the inner truth of his being.

Thus the indeterminacy inherent in freedom makes the application of the biological scheme to human history problematical and uncertain. The progress of consciousness towards unanimity is not simply a continuation of the progress of organisms towards unity: the latter is no more than an image of the former.

Although one should not overlook the indications of the spirit's action, any such symptoms are bound to be deceptive, and their interpretation is arguable: the concentration of the human mass does not operate in depth, and though the unification of humanity is indisputable on the scientific plane, it is accompanied by divisions in other domains.[145] The Church itself shows no obvious signs of a collective progress, other than those of an expansion that is constantly endangered, and the growth of the mystical body is an almost complete mystery. Light and darkness seem to balance one another, and Satan, though he is and will be conquered, is still historically present and still confronts God. True enough the universe is ascending towards its term, and the ascent of humanity is as much in the Church as it is personal, but it is effected primarily in the interiority of each man's spirit. It is in the hidden places of consciousness, and even more in the hidden places of God, that the battle of history is won or lost: the totalization of the world is not patient of man's observation.

Although exegesis has not, perhaps, yet been able to provide a conclusive interpretation[146] of St Paul's remarks about the orientation of the world towards Christ as its end (Col. 1.16; Rom. 8.21), and the unification of the Church (Eph. 4. 12-16), Teilhard rather gives the impression of having strained their historical import in order to bring out an apparent conformity with his own view of a convergent universe. Now, it is not impossible to conceive the unification of the mystical body as the continual gathering together, effected by God, of his elect, up to a *numerical* limit determined by him, starting from a history whose transformations, however profound they may be in the psychic or social order, yet do not substantially affect the dramatic and contradictory persistence of human nature.

Similarly, the notion of a general drift of history toward unity, is a rational idealization, *a myth of reason*: it applies to the movement of mankind a mental category, an intellectual demand for synthesis and symmetry which is the law of the spirit. The hope, natural enough in man, of a communion of persons in time, to follow on from their present dissociation, takes over this scheme, and colours it with affective elements. Historical time, represented in linear form, is then compared to a convergence on a point or terminal peak, to be effected in the course of a measurable lapse of time. Dialectical considerations sometimes support this concept, which at times seems to be adopted by theology; but the true history of souls on the road to spiritual concentration does not conform with the picture presented.

Although there is no lack of images of growth in Scripture, the idea of a natural progress of history is foreign to it: and, while it is impossible to deny the influence of the spirit on the advance of mankind, man's progress towards a communion of consciousness with consciousness is only an *analogy* of that of the mystical body. And as to the final totalization of the mystical body, referred to by St Paul, this is a mystery of religion, shrouded in obscurity; and it cannot, without incurring the charge of concordism, be regarded as on the same footing with perceptible representations.[147]

Teilhard's faith as a Christian, indeed, seems to react on his phenomenological thought and colour his interpretation of history with a supernatural optimism.[148] His affirmation of Omega, as the ultimate point of personal communion in love, is based primarily on the energy of the spirit—of a spirit itself animated by a transcendent love that can overcome all resistance. For man's adventure to suffer a reverse would be 'God's bankruptcy'.[149] Without doubt the fact of Christ, the fact of the Virgin Mary, the fact of Pentecost, the fact of the holiness (ordinary or extra-ordinary) in the Church, all these, in different degrees and with varying force, point to the effective possibility of God's victory in history. Moreover, when all is said and done, we cannot fail to note a correspondence between the invisible progress of the mystical body and the progress of humanity: on the phenomenal plane, there must be some evidence of God's grand effort. And, if historical time is real, if it is subject to the energy of the spirit, Teilhard was justified in envisaging an indefinite progress of man in love, and even in conceiving the end of all time as mystical unanimity; even when their outward appearance is secular and temporal, advances in the communion of persons have had an undeniable spiritual impact. Nevertheless such evidence does not justify us in concluding *by reason* that there will be a final temporal triumph of the spirit; the most lively hope is a supernatural category, resting on the certainty of a faith, all the more ill-defined in that it is not easy completely to reconcile the various New Testament texts.[150] Within these limits, however, it is both praiseworthy and advantageous for man to make the *optimistic choice* about his future and his end. It is not utopian to look forward to, coexisting with the fundamental permanence of human nature (wounded by sin), an improvement in man's ways, a better social order, and such an advance in consciousness and institutions that violence will be radically excluded as a solution for social groups and for nations.[151] It must be admitted, too, that Teilhard's argument that allows and counts on a vast expanse of time, 'some millions of years, maybe',[152] is not without force. Finally, Teilhard's optimism can be defended by its agreement, at least in part, with a certain biblical tradition—itself also one form of choice or interpretation—to be found both in the Old and in the New Testament.[153] It is significant that Pope John XXIII's encyclicals *Mater et magistra* and *Pacem in terris* noted many signs of a progress of history.[154]

Thus the kinship Teilhard suggested could be found between the data (problematical though they are) of the *phenomenon* of man's ascent and the *mystery* of the growth of the Church, can be interpreted only in terms of analogy: any legitimate attempt to represent them must remain alive to the gulf between the image and the reality. Reason's unification or unity is not of the same *order* as that of the supernatural order.

IX THE CHURCH AND THE EUCHARIST

What Teilhard has to say about the Church and the Eucharist will be dealt with in connection with his spirituality.

One point, however, should be noted here and now: the *development* of the fundamental and immutable content of the Christian message, through its intellectual unfolding, under the action of the Spirit, who animates and nourishes the Church's consciousness: *Nova et vetera*. It is inherent in the normal economy of the Christian life that, in the domain of Revelation, certain elements, long dormant, suddenly develop—branching out vigorously, in step with and to meet the needs of new times and new requirements. Thus it is that 'recently, in a gesture that represents a decisive stage in the development of dogma, Rome has expressed and sanctified, in the figure of Christ the King the irresistible forward advance of Christian consciousness towards a more universalist and realist statement of the Incarnation'.[155]

Similarly, the emergence of new ideas provides a wholesome stimulus to the Church, calling on the 'catholicity' of her transcendent mystery to assimilate the rise of the young sap. 'For all its divineness and immortality, the Church cannot escape the universal compulsion common to all organisms, no matter what they be, periodically to find new youth . . . through the infusion of new elements.' Today the Church is presented with the opportunity for this—is even challenged to do so—by the noticeable change in consciousness that has caused the emergence of the notion of *cosmogenesis* and, with it, of the value of *humanization*. Thus 'the humanist revival', 'the irresistible rise of a Christian optimism', seem to Teilhard to call on the Church to re-think the mystery of the Incarnation and the Redemption and to emphasize the creative and animating function of the Word rather than his function as saviour.[156]

X THE PAROUSIA

The importance of the problems raised by Teilhard's eschatology calls for treatment in a separate section.

XI THE UNITY OF THE MYSTERIES

In conformity with the thought of St Paul,[157] Teilhard adds that in spite of the distinction between them, the mysteries form but one single mystery of which each is a phase: everything is governed by God's eternal plan to unite with himself, in Christ, the whole of his creation.[158] In one single flash, at one span, connexion is established between God in his original condition (if one may use the phrase) and God freely but really enriched (again if one may use the phrase) by the whole of mankind and the whole of the universe.

The search for the bond that links the two mysteries is encouraged by the first Vatican Council which sees in it, for 'reason illuminated by faith', an 'analogical' correspondence of their truth.[159] Nevertheless, it would be well to note that each of the two phases shows an unpredictable *further passage* of love in the direction of an ever more gratuitous generosity. In this connexion, moreover, all Teilhard had to do was to develop an idea contained in one of his first essays: 'Creation, Incarnation, Redemption, while each marking one more degree in the beauty of the divine operation—are they not at the same time three indissolubly linked acts in the appearance of *participated being?*'[160]

Eschatological Problems

The evolution of Teilhard's thought shows a continually more pronounced emphasis on *man's future*. Interest in the discovery of the past takes second place to exploration of the future:[161] as 'a pilgrim of the future' it is in terms of what is *to be* that he studies what has been, what is, and what is growing. The directive force in history, which is man-in-the-world and the-world-in-man, is to move towards an absolute and divine end.

The essential point in Teilhard's theological thought is his bringing together the demands of scientific philosophy that postulate the ultimate unity of cosmic history, and what Christian hope has to tell us about the end of all time: Omega Point, which reason accepts as God, is, for faith, none other than Christ in his glory, the head of the mystical body.

The day will come that will bring, together and within the same unity, the fulfilment of the history of the universe, the coming together of the consciousness of the elect, the consummation of the mystical body in the plenitude of Christ, and the revelation of his presence.[162] In St Augustine's words, 'There will be but one Christ, Christ loving Christ', *erit unus Christus, amans seipsum.*'[163]

Teilhard's eschatology obviously raises problems of great interest. A number of points call for separate discussion, the disconnected nature of which will, I hope, be excused.

1 CONNECTION AND DISSOCIATION OF THE TWO ORDERS

A dialectic of *continuity* and *discontinuity* is essential to an intellectual expression in Christian terms of the end of history, and this Teilhard sought to do.

In his view, the final communion of all consciousness, which is the peak to which man and the cosmos ascend, is the necessary preliminary condition for the act by which the heart of God opens itself to redeemed mankind in order to introduce it into his bliss: 'For his consummation Christ has to find a summit to the world, just as for his conception he had to find a woman.'[164] In fact, God will make use of man's effort and will gather up the whole of his work, the sum total of a regenerated universe.[165] Moreover, the transition cannot be effected except through an ultimate acceptance by persons of the grace of vision. Thus there is continuity between human history and eternity.

Nevertheless, as we have seen, the final communion of consciousness is, in the first place, still a *finite* entity, and cannot logically be identical with the Christ-God. Even if nature (which is in fact the whole development of the world and of man) is gratuitously penetrated by Christ and invited to communion with the living God, the final transition of redeemed humanity to God cannot be conceived as the approach of an asymptotic curve: it must introduce an ultimate intervention, even more gratuitous than its predecessors, coming as an even more unexpected surprise. Even though everything has already been given to man to the highest degree in the Word, yet it is only by transformation that man discovers his riches: the Parousia is not inevitable.

Moreover, there is no proportion between the gift and the merit, and every right vanishes in the face of the incomparable ultimate, the pearl without price, the superabundance of the happiness that is offered, and the final plenitude of seeing God face to face. There is a yawning gulf between the ultimate temporal state of the human community, even at its highest degree of psychic and spiritual maturity, and the mystery of intimacy with God. The convergence of the cosmos does not entail, as by right, the Christic emergence: it is no more than the preliminary symptom. The ultra-human, inferred by extrapolation of the curve of man's growth, is only the temporal and earthly aspect of a mysterious and religious reality which transforms it into the 'trans-human'.

Teilhard, of course, did not overlook this problem, which, in another form, is again the problem of the *supernatural*. Here again, he seeks to bring together the terms of a dialectic.

On the one hand, he insists on the *link* between temporal history and the Parousia: the latter, like the first Christmas, implies, as a necessary condition and preliminary, a maturing of man.[166]

On the other hand, the entry of redeemed humanity into intimacy with God cannot be effected by itself; it calls for a completely gratuitous intervention to fill the gap between God and man: 'The whole of hominization is no more than a preparation for the final Parousia.' Moreover, after saying, 'To confirm the presence at the summit of the world of what we have called Omega Point, do we not find here the very cross-check we were waiting for?' Teilhard corrects himself in a footnote: 'Or, to be more exact, to confirm the presence at the summit of the world *of something in line with, but still more elevated* than, Omega Point. This is in deference to the theological concept of the "supernatural" according to which the binding contact between God and man, *hic et nunc* inchoate, attains to a super-intimacy (hence also a super-gratuitousness) of which man could have no inkling and to which he could lay no claim by virtue of his "nature" alone.'[167] Elsewhere he adds, 'Before passing into the beyond, the world and its elements must attain what may be called their point of annihilation':[168] and this, without doubt, implies a complete and agonizing recognition, analogous with the sacrifice of Christ, of the eminent freedom of God. 'The whole world,' he wrote earlier, 'is concentrated and uplifted in expectancy of union with the divine; yet at the same time it encounters an insurmountable barrier. For nothing can come to Christ unless he himself takes it and gathers it into himself.'[169] 'Because the term towards which the earth is moving lies not merely beyond each individual thing but beyond the totality of things; because the world travails, not to bring forth from within itself some supreme reality, but to find its consummation through a union with a pre-existent being; it follows that man can never reach the blazing centre of the universe simply by living more and more for himself, nor even by spending his life in the service of some earthly cause, however great. The world can never be definitively united with you, Lord, save by a sort of reversal, a turning about, an *excentration*, which must involve the temporary collapse not merely of all individual achievements but even of everything that looks like an advancement for humanity.'[170] 'The critical point of maturation envisaged by science is simply the physical condition and empirical aspect of the critical point of the Parousia postulated and awaited in the name of revelation.'[171] Finally, in his discussion with Maurice Blondel (conducted through Père Auguste Valensin) he wrote: 'In the first place I readily agree that the universal effort of the world can be understood as the *preparation of a holocaust*. Through its spiritual acquisitions (in which all the others are summed up) the world develops, in its essence, a capacity or power of adoration, in other words of renunciation. The ultimate purpose it is developing for all consciousness, both individual and collective—the supreme act in view of which it fosters, refines, and emancipates them—is their voluntary return to God and the freely accepted sacrifice of their apparent (or immediate) autonomy—the only milleniarist prospect, then, that I can envisage is that of an age in which men, having at last become conscious of their unity *with all beings*, and of their intimate links with everything else, will hold the *plenitude of their souls* available to cast, of their own free choice, into the divine centre. All our work, ultimately, amounts to producing the sacrifice upon which the fire of God is to descend.'[172]

Teilhard's bringing together of cosmological philosophy and Christian eschatology is interesting in its attempt to link reason and faith, nature and grace; nevertheless, as we pointed out earlier, the plenitude of the mystical body, as it emerges from the scriptural texts, lies in another plane.

II THE TRANSITION TO THE FINAL LIMIT

As we have seen, Teilhard envisages the end of history as the culmination of the unification of the cosmos in communion of consciousness.

In the first place, this line of thought implies two preliminary conditions; the validity of these has already been discussed and we concluded that it was somewhat questionable. It must be shown that although we find at present that there are powers of choice, inherent in men's freedom, which counter it, the movement of history does in fact proceed towards unity. Secondly, if this spiritual unification should at any time be observable, it must be possible to extrapolate it into the future.

Moreover, we may well wonder why there must be an end, why the process of unification does not continue indefinitely, as is theoretically possible on the phenomenal plane.[173] Can it totalize itself, can it by itself build up to a 'paroxysm', can it reach an absolute point of perfection beyond which it is impossible to go, a saturation of its energies? Will mankind come one day to 'reflect upon itself at a single point', 'in a total and final reflection, to reduce in it everything to a common idea and a common passion',[174] and so escape from time and space?

Again, does the permanence of the structures and discursive categories of thought allow us to envisage the crowning of evolution by 'a supreme act of collective vision obtained by a pan-human effort of investigation and construction',[175] by a complete mastery of cosmic energies, by controlling 'the mainspring of evolution',[176] by 'the unanimous construction of a spirit of the earth?'[177]

To take only the first two phases, human thought, in virtue of its very structure and its obedience to the laws of representation, can never be more than an approximation to the real, through the medium of abstract language; and so far as technology is concerned, its intimate connexion with thought makes it impossible for it to conquer more than successive fragments of the universe. It seems extremely difficult to admit the idea of an omni-science or omni-potence, or more widely that of the total or the all-inclusive, applied to man's evolution in history. In short, man's condition implies the permanence of the dialectical relation of subject and object, man and world. Man is essentially made 'confronting the world' and cannot 'become universalized' without being submerged in it and vanishing.

Mankind's transition to a stage that transcends its natural condition can be achieved only through an eschatological and religious metamorphosis, through God's gratuitious and miraculous intervention.

III THE HISTORICITY OF ESCHATOLOGY

As Christians see it, the end of the world is overshadowed by a great mystery, and its date cannot be calculated in relation to the present moment.

Wisely refusing to speculate on 'the hour of this event and the forms it will take',[178] Teilhard's views can readily be reconciled with the normal picture that places it at the end of an evolution of history in time. They do not, however, touch the philosophical problem raised by the imagery necessary to their expression.[179]

Here again, a dialectic reinforces thought. In one whole aspect of itself, the terminal point belongs to history, to the experiential world of phenomena, to which it is bound by an indissoluble continuity: it emerges as a result, and it sums up an effective task. At the same time, it lies beyond history; it transcends and breaks away from history, in rupture and dissociation. As Père Jeannière says, 'the term of history is not the last event in the series of events; Omega Point is, more truly, the plenitude of reflection, the totality of the spirit's folding-back upon itself . . . the making total of history'.[180]

In Teilhard, these two aspects are not so much thought out in their dialectical relation, as coexistent: he tried to retain the representational picture and at the same time to abandon it by introducing the idea of a total spiritualization of man.[181] It is true this mystery cannot but be a stumbling block to thought; even so it is fair to say that Teilhard's geometric picture of a conic time made its intellectual expression difficult; it over-emphasized the image of a temporal term lying ahead at the expense of the eternal present of a spiritual event that is going on in the hidden places of God, an event in which the mystical body is invisibly attaining the perfection of its stature.

In any case, in contrast with the Marxist concept of a history that is consummated simply in man's temporal and natural perfection,[182] Teilhard holds that history is fulfilled and totalized only in and through Christ, and that it rises beyond itself into a transcendent supernatural universe.

IV THE RESURRECTION OF THE BODY, AND THE DIVINIZATION OF THE COSMOS

Teilhard conceives the end of historical man as a full maturing of the 'spirit of the earth', of the noosphere 'which has simultaneously reached the uttermost limit of its complexity and its centration',[183] and 'is abandoning its organico-planetary support, to focus itself upon the transcendent centre of its increasing concentration'. 'The ultimate break-up of the complexity-consciousness partnership to release, in the free state, a thinking without brain. The escape of some part of the *Welstoff* from entropy.'[184] 'The centre throwing off its original shell of complexity.'[185] Is such a 'take-off' possible?

So long as Teilhard remains on the plane of philosophy, he cannot be blamed for not mentioning the resurrection of the body.[186] At the same time, the unexpectedly 'spiritual' expression raises a problem: it seems to reintroduce into his eschatology the dualism that was initially rejected.

For Teilhard, however, the idea of man's interconnexion with the universe is so essential that he cannot regard it as impossible that it should extend into eternity. In that case, the resurrection would simply be a coincidence, final indeed and definitive, of man and the world, beyond the present frontiers of the body. Such, moreover, is the condition of the risen body of Jesus.[187]

V THE DIVINIZATION OF THE COSMOS

Teilhard, moreover, has little to say about the participation of the cosmos in the collective transfiguration of the consciousness. The material substructures of the universe, it would seem, have fulfilled their part by *releasing* spirit, which, in a sort of coincidence, becomes one with Omega-Christ.

How are we to picture the final transformation of matter, of all the 'elements of the world' that make up the substructure of spirits? Should we envisage the entry of these elements into the spiritual (i.e. the personal), should we see it as a sort of emancipation from determinism and from serfdom, on the lines of one possible interpretation of the famous Pauline passage?[188] Here again, we are beyond the limits of what can be represented.

Mutual charity has so important a place in Teilhard's eschatology that it would justify the concept of the universe re-born through the mediation of conscious minds that have opted, in time, for the ideal of communion and justice. Every advance in human relations (whether close or distant), every improvement in social structure, is not simply an image and preparation of, but an anticipation of the eternal kingdom of charity. Only sin can prevent this approximation from being carried to its limit. Thus the 'divinization of the cosmos' should be taken as applying to matter only in so far as matter has an integral share in the progress of the spiritual communion of minds, in particular through technical transformations.[189] In emphasizing the liberation of spirits rather than a transfiguration of matter, Teilhard may have intended to focus attention on the ideal of the union of men in the mystical body of Christ.

VI THE PROBLEM OF EARLIER GENERATIONS

A further problem is raised by the apparently specially favoured position of the last generation of men, in their access to Omega through the transition, now finally effected, into universal communion in love.

The point is that earlier generations should not be sacrificed: rather should they be associated with this triumph and share actively in it by being present.

Another point is that at any moment of history it should be possible for every consciousness to rise above itself and really attain, for itself, a fulfilment that already in some way represents, by anticipation, an end of history.

Here we come up against the difficulties and limitations of the eschatological concept.

VII THE JUDGMENT

In *The Phenomenon of Man*, Teilhard, without introducing the theological evidence, stated two hypotheses to cover the situation of mankind at the end of its history: either unanimity of agreement and the triumph of good, or the division of men, in a spasm of blinding clarity, between love and selfishness, adoration and revolt: and he presents the second hypothesis as being 'more in conformity with traditional views of the apocalypse'.[190]

On another occasion, in connection with Christian revelation, Teilhard describes the 'rending of the noosphere that allows a portion of mankind to be excluded from love'.[191] 'In this there may be some loss,' though it would never be as much as '100%'. Some elements of mankind, condemned for all time, will be 'banished to the antipodes of God'. Thus God's victory, total though it is in Christ, may be only partial for man.

Teilhard adds that the alternative of 'all or nothing' 'respects the importance of life and the dignity of man'; and, while he believes it to be impossible to form any picture of eternal damnation, he holds, and rightly, that hell is 'the opposite pole from God', the reverse of heaven, the notion that must correspond to freedom's denial of love.[192]

Thus, in contrast with Origenism,[193] and at the risk of being inconsistent with the logic of a total harmony, Teilhard does not hesitate to accept the possibility of eternal damnation. History ascends and converges, but its limit is defined by a judgment that sanctions the options made by freedom. He is at pains, moreover, to 'make the ever-threatening gravity of damnation part of his normal view of the world and his practical attitude to it'.[194] There could be no better evidence that he did not allow his system to run away with him and that his personalism outdistanced his purely biological views. At the same time it must be admitted that he had difficulty in making up his mind on this point.[195]

Similarly, Teilhard holds that, far from being a catastrophe or a disintegration, the end of the world is the triumph of the divine enterprise, the successful realization of God's plan, through the fulfilment of man and his collective emergence into the life of God: this concept of a supreme Pentecost, effecting the purification and final exaltation of the Church, was borrowed by Teilhard from the theology of St Paul.[196]

This question, we may conclude, of Teilhard's eschatology, which completes and sets the seal on the whole body of his work, is difficult and even crucial, for it goes beyond the order of what can be represented; and it leaves us with many problems to be solved.

CONCLUSION

Teilhard's theology, which, *in virtue of its supernatural sources*, is entirely independent of his cosmological system, expresses the essence of the whole content of tradition, to which on *a priori* grounds it is absolutely faithful. There is no fundamental dogmatic statement that is not affirmed and maintained in its entirety: the transcendence and freedom of the triune God; the freedom of the creative decision; the immanence and transcendence of the creative act;

man's relative transcendence of nature; the mystery of the Incarnation, mediating between God and man, God and the universe; the mystery of the Redemption; the mystery of the Church and the Eucharist; and, lastly, the mystery of the Parousia, linked with and yet transcending history, and of the judgment that reads and sanctions man's options.[197]

In particular, Teilhard's theology has the great merit of being centred on Christ, and of emphasizing his total dimensions and his physical relation to the history of the universe and of man. This history, again, he read and interpreted as the radiation and diffusion, the action and the invitation, of a love.

These dogmatic statements can be found in Teilhard's work, but their expression is sometimes sporadic and disconnected; they assume their true form only within a dialectic whose function it is to bring them together and allow each to serve as warrant for the others.

Moreover, Teilhard was sharply aware of the shortcomings of some modern expressions of Revelation, affecting nearly all the essential dogmas,[198] and he tried to think them out again in order to adapt them to the change in men's consciousness and so make their truth more readily accepted.

We should always remember, too, that while Teilhard never abandons the scientific idea of the progress of the universe, at the same time he deliberately adopts the supernatural (and only effectively useful) point of view of the growth of the mystical body. The scientific point of view then becomes a natural *correspondence* to the divine reality, which embraces and governs it in a dialectical relationship.

In so far, however, and only in so far, as Teilhard sought to effect too close a *rational synthesis* of cosmology and dogma, his theology necessarily became somewhat more precarious: the rigidity of the system then becomes apparent and, although it gives his thought its vital originality, at the same time it tends to undermine its validity.

In so far, again, as Teilhard's theology depends upon an evolutionary concept of history and a *Weltanschauung* of total unification, there is some difficulty in reconciling it completely with the legacy of tradition. A tendentious critic might well accuse him of being more concerned to emphasize the continuity of the different orders than their distinctions,[199] of blurring the gap between God

and man, and between sacred and secular history; of not fully
including the mystery of sin and thereby failing to bring out the full
import of the Redemption; of exaggerating the signs that indicate the
progress of human history; and finally of claiming to identify the
convergence of history, postulated by reason, with the final unity of
the mystical body.[200]

On the other hand, although this synthesis appears to be so
prominent and even in the very foreground of his thought, Teilhard
never regards it as anything more than a hypothesis, as the reflection
of a personal experience; and he is not so convinced of its truth as to
be blind to the gap that separates it from the mystery.

In any case, theology is always obliged to present the religious
problem in terms of rational *categories* and intellectual schemes,
whose value as truth must at the same time fall short of the depth of
the mystery. Theology must express the communion of God and
man through a dialectic of such complementary ideas as finite–
infinite, human freedom and divine freedom, nature and grace (or
nature and the supernatural), time–eternity; and any affirmations
it makes must be completed by negations that correct them. It
would be fair to say that sometimes with less success and accuracy,
sometimes with more, Teilhard satisfies this requirement, 'keeping
hold' in Bossuet's phrase 'of both ends of the chain'.[201]

Moreover, theology cannot escape from the condition inherent
in history that brings about the evolution of human consciousness
and makes it alive to new values.[202] As Pope John XXIII reminded us, in particular in his opening address to the Council, it is
the essential duty of theology, while retaining the whole of Revelation in its integrity, to become apostolic and to meet the religious
needs of men by taking up a *pastoral* attitude.[203]

The emergence of the idea of evolution brought with it the
problem of *the communion of God and man at the term of cosmic history*:
it is Teilhard's great merit that he stated this problem, and it does
him honour that, with all its risks, he was the first to do so with such
force. Nor could he, any more than any other thinker, escape from
the inadequacy of verbal expression; from the connection and
at the same time the antinomy of the continuous and the
discontinuous; from the contradiction of a summit that has to be
exceeded, of a plenitude that has to be completed, of a fulfilment
that has to be fulfilled, of a closing-in that is open, of an 'already'

and a 'not-yet', of a 'for-us' and a 'for-God'. Such, however, is the Christian fact; but such, too, is the law of a thought that is limited and yet, if faithfully exercised, can already, under signs and through correspondences, in the image we see in the mirror, and in the riddle we seek to read, attain the truth of the mystery.

Chapter 7
Spirituality

Teilhard's view of the world and of history, and the theology to which it leads up, would never go beyond abstract speculation if they did not open the road to an *action* that enables man's freedom effectively to realize the ideal. What has been, and what is known, have no meaning except as a preparation of the future through a transformation of the present.[1]

In fact Teilhard's thought, continuing on from morals, immediately introduces a *spirituality* which is inseparable from it. It calls for an art of living, in perfect conformity with the truth that has been disclosed: a truth, that now has to be 'put into practice', to be made to exist in ourselves and in the world.[2]

If we are fully to understand and pin-point this spirituality, we must bear in mind Teilhard's initial intuition and his over-all project, which is *existential* in order. Behind this there is a twofold awareness: of man's natural condition, aggravated by sin, and the present reciprocal situation of the Church and the world. On one side there is man's finiteness and his spiritual alienation in history: natural constraints, physical and moral evil, death. On the other, the problem raised by the awakening of modern consciousness to the dimensions of the world and its 'reaction on religion'.[3] Teilhard's intention, which is both philosophical and biblical, is to facilitate man's transition[4] to his end, the fulfilment of the person and of society, the plenitude of existence in the regeneration of being and communion with God.

This essentially *Christic* spirituality is based on an intense participation in the mystery of the Incarnation, in the existence and the life of Jesus Christ.[5]

Christ is first of all placed in his context, determined and marked off. By virtue of his individuality he is a particular being in the world and in history. But, in as much as he is king of the universe and risen from the dead, he is also involved in the reality of the

192

cosmos, through which his radiance is carried and in which he is prolonged. Since he is the plenitude of being and of beings, 'the sum and peak of all human and cosmic perfection',[6] he has the whole world for his body. He is the source and the term of the universe and all its elements, the active unity and ambience, the centre and nucleus, the energy and the stimulant; and through his Passion he knows the burden of all determinisms. He has a new claim to boundless faith and love; man's love for the world may now coincide with his love for Christ.

Thus the spiritual life participates in Christ in his design for the salvation of universal history, and co-operates with him in the fulfilment of the world, in the plenitude of the mystical body[7] and in the supreme unification of all things in love.

This co-operation of freedom with Christ's work is achieved through the following integrated and complementary means.

I FAITH

It is hardly surprising that the fundamental attitude adopted by Teilhard is *faith*: not simply intellectual adherence to religious truth, but total communion with God: a God represented by the figure of Christ, one whose love, as in the Scriptures, is seen under the symbolism of fire.[8]

As in the *Spiritual Exercises* of St Ignatius, and also as in the tradition of St John of the Cross, this faith, which involves the normal passage through all the mysteries of Christ, takes as its object God himself in all the signs under which he reveals himself.

Going beyond fragmentary or disjointed appearances, 'through the worthless husk of every shape and every physical attribute',[9] under veil and image, faith reveals the living and active reality of God, the genesis of the divine, in the world and in history. Man must have eyes made sensitive to the light of God, be the source lowly or grand; he must be open to God's radiance and incandescence, receptive of his diaphany, manifest in his work; for there is nothing that does not emanate from God, depend upon him, and that is not his 'sacrament'.[10] God spreads out from the centre, to fill the sphere, with neither increase nor loss of his own being, as universal existence, as the unity diffused through the immensity of the world, as the ultimate element in which everything finds its definitive consistence.[11] The *milieu divin* is, precisely, this spiritual ambience, this inner kingdom, deep within which man discovers the face of God, revealed in signs and yet ungraspable. And this discovery is made, not so much in the contemplation of a picture as in the recognition of an objective movement, in which the whole world, penetrated by God and as though one body with him through Christ, advances towards its absolute fulfilment in unity;[12] more inwardly still, he makes this discovery in a direct encounter in friendship.[13]

This faith must even recognize God and the face of Christ, as though under the 'matter of one and the same sacrament', in the horror of the universe, in the apparent blindness of the world, in its chances, its threats and its catastrophes. There, too, God lies hidden, and this, too, is his body. As in the storm on the lake of Galilee, Jesus comes in person, under the appearance of a spectre, to meet his friends: *Ego sum, nolite timere*. Thus, too, he gives us the true solution to the problem of existence.[14]

When we come to a crisis of sorrow and our hearts fail, this, too, we must overcome with patience, in absolute trust in God and in complete surrender to his will.[15]

This calls for an agonizing effort, that leads to a mystical awareness of the omnipresence of God, whose loving providence controls the entire universe for the well-being of every creature.[16] We have to accept the hazards of this adventure over the ocean of the divine, of this apparent loss of self in the universal Being.

It is at the heart of God, too, the centre and bond of the world, in never-ending adoration of simplicity, that lies the point where man makes contact with every reality, every force and every soul:[17] a point that cannot be contained in boundaries of space or time, and that human words are powerless to express. The natural links that hold beings together are left intact, but a new principle is superimposed upon them, a new soul; and this has the power to give them a new orientation, to combine them in a new way, and sometimes even to give them greater flexibility.[18] With the power to influence even the future, a bold and living faith 'forces the barriers of determinism and brings order to chance'; it is 'an operative power'; it is creative of being.[19]

It goes without saying that this faith is *love*: love appears as the unique higher form towards which all the other types of spiritual energies converge as they are transformed. Charity breaks down isolation, the bulkheads that enclose the individual microcosms, and, going beyond natural affinities, facilitates the coalescence, the communion, the welding together of all men in the mystical body.[20] Allying itself with all the values of the world, it is a spiritual energy that concentrates the universal ascent of beings towards final unity, which is communion of persons.[21] Leaving the domain of feeling, it enters into the heart of history as a new force, purged of violence, but 'emerging from sweetness and kindness as their ecstatic climax', and fights then to win 'earth's great battle'.[22]

Faith is love, but it is hope, too, for it holds what it has not yet fully disclosed. Within the setting and limits of human categories, it anticipates a transparent vision that it still awaits. The Christian is a 'pilgrim of the future'.

Thus, man's inclusion in the divine ambience through this God-centred attitude, is the more than sufficient solution of all his problems and the answer to all his demands. Already within time, it hopes for the paschal transition that transfigures and fulfils his condition.[23]

II ACTION

However, as with St Paul long ago, the very desire for communion with God obliges man to turn back to the world.[24]

Faith would be vain and sterile if it did not immediately inspire an action in which it is incarnate. Creation, long and lovingly contemplated, is not completed nor perfect. Human history, which continues the evolution of life, and which is the history of God in man, is not accomplished but still in genesis or birth. It must be continued, and carried further, and brought to an end, until everything is total and totalized.

The Christian, then, must, like Christ, throw himself into the world; he must make himself one with the universe, open himself to it, master and welcome its energies, so that he may realize their latent potentialities. He must 'extract from things, by making them his own, to the very last fragment, all that they hold of eternal life, so that nothing may be lost'. He must never cease from 'working to extract from the world all that this world can hold of truth and energy . . . We must try every road, "plumb all things"'.[25]

Rejecting any retreat or desertion, and paying for it by a costly effort of detachment,[26] the Christian must boldly commit himself to all that has human value, and he must not hesitate to attempt anything that is legitimate in order that he may co-operate with the creative spirit, who sets a high target for man's initiative. 'He must not be content with soothing pain and easing suffering; he must, by love, by every form of effort and discovery, drive the forces of humanity to their upper limit.' 'He must urge on the whole operation of cosmic forces within which the cosmic Christ is born and fulfilled.'[27] The world will never be vast enough, nor mankind strong enough, to be worthy of him who created them and was incarnate in them.[28] Knowing that matter, in spite of its equivocal character, is good,[29] and that the world has been sanctified and renewed by the Incarnation, the Christian must therefore 'co-operate even in the natural maturing of all things—though obviously preserving a hierarchical order of precedence'—and so 'the new earth must emerge from the fulfilment of the old earth'.

The Christian is called upon to augment the stature of man and the world, to cause them to rise up to their peak, so that they may receive God more amply; it is for him to make ready the holocaust upon which the fire of God will descend;[30] he must 'encourage the awakening of spirit in the world' in order to 'allow the influence of Christ to grow more palpable'. It is his mission to Christify history, to bring about a consecration of the world, and above all to promote the communion of men, so that amorization may reach its term.[31] And this obligation, in virtue of which man no longer belongs to himself, entails a permanent urge towards indefinite extensions of his horizon.

The supernatural is not a separate entity, an autonomous organism, but a leaven;[32] and the growth of the kingdom of God is brought about by the 'world's great three-fold effort: the effort to dominate the real, the effort to organize society, and the effort to endure suffering'.[33] In short, it is the actual *work*, in as much as it is objective, it is the real that must be sanctified.[34]

The spiritual progress of persons is, no doubt, a break away from and a break in continuity with the biological progress which made possible the emergence of man; and the release of spirit lies 'in a completely different order from that of the slow working upon matter that led up to the development of the brain'. At the same time 'we have to bring to the task of sanctification all the spirit that has instinctively animated and still irresistibly raises all terrestrial life: We have to transfer to heaven (go to heaven with) all our zest for the earth . . . make directly for God without leaving the line of all truly natural effort, the line that runs through the aspiration immanent in the whole of our cosmos'. 'Neither moralization nor sanctification are a break; they are a purification, careful as they must be to reject no fragment of legitimate human effort and never to forget the fundamental unity of all the particles of our creation.' The universe is linked with the ego and centred on it, and in the ego the whole destiny of the world is worked out.[35] It is 'no longer the carefully laid-out garden to which a whim of the creator has for a time exiled us it has; become the great task that is moving towards its achievement, and whose salvation we must win with our own'.[36] The action of the supernatural cannot be dissociated from all that conditions and paves the way to it in nature.[37] The sanctification of the world, accordingly, in as much as it is objective and real, and the sanctification of man, must be operated in one and the same indissoluble synthesis.[38]

Thus no work is wholly profane: everything is sacred.[39] 'God, in all that is most living and incarnate in him, is not far away from us, altogether apart from the world we see, touch, hear, smell and taste about us. Rather, he awaits us every instant in our action, in the work of the moment. There is a sense in which he is at the tip of my pen, the point of my pick, in my brush, my needle—in my heart and my thought. By pressing the line or the stroke or the stitch on which I am engaged to its ultimate natural finish, I shall lay hold of that last end towards which my innermost will tends.'[40] 'We serve to complete creation even by the humblest work of our hands . . . in virtue of the interrelation between matter, soul and Christ, we bring part of the being which he desires back to God, *in whatever we do*. With each one of our works, we labour—as individual atoms but no less really—to build the Pleroma: that is to say, we bring to Christ a little fulfilment.'[41] There is no human value (science, beauty, justice) that has not absolute value; and what the Christian must do is to realize how they are related to faith.

In short 'a vast concrete aim' must plunge us into the heart of the real, in the service of God's kingdom in all things, and give practical expression to our intentions in acts operated 'as perfectly as possible.'[42] The humblest effort, exerted with God behind it, reacts upon the world and upon history more effectively than any human force, however massive. 'We can lose ourselves in God only by prolonging the most individual determinations of beings far beyond themselves';[43] and it is always from the specific point determined by his own situation that man 'must climb towards the light, passing through, in order to attain God, a given series of created things', regarded not as obstacles but rather as hand-holds or intermediate steps.[44]

Detachment, in principle and in spirit, must be absolute, since it expresses the choice of the *unum necessarium*: even so, it must be reconciled and harmonized with the obligation to retain an active attachment to the positive values of nature. For such detachment to be first possible, and then extended to the scale of the universe, it must do all it can to encourage the development of the world and the realization of its potentialities. 'Thus the formation of the supernatural Pleroma operates, with the natural universe as its starting point, according to a law not of rupture but of transformation. Transformation means that the supernatural in a real way refashions the elements of the world, and so makes them truly *more* and *other*; but it means also that these natural elements are absolutely necessary to feed the work of salvation and supply it with an appropriate matter. The plenitude of Christ rests upon a natural and concrete plenitude . . . As spirit appeared in man by in some way making use of the primitive attempts of instinct, so the supernatural is continually being formed by super-creation of our nature . . . I attribute no final and absolute value to the various constructions man has built up. I believe that they will disappear, recast in some new thing that we cannot even imagine. But I admit that they have an essential role for the time being—that they are indispensable, inevitable, *phases* through which we (we or our race) must pass in the course of our transformation. What I love in them is not their particular form, but their function; and that is, in some mysterious way, to construct first what can be divinized, and then, through the grace of Christ that adds itself to our effort, to construct the divine.'[45] '*The whole of my being enters into the act by which I decide to give myself to God*: it enters in, not only with all my underlying personality, but with every shade and detail of my past. If, then, it is my "living" choice that is to be divinized (and "our deeds that follow us" are, at any rate, such an option) by the fire that is to re-cast me, it is equally true to say that the fire will consume me and fulfil me. We must say of these flames that they devour if we wish fully to emphasize the unprecedented magnitude of the process of renewal, and to bring out the persistence, within the sublimation experienced by our nature, of even the smallest elements of what has been accumulated by the use of our human freedom. For grace, to consume and to transfigure are one and the same thing.'[46]

Unity, accordingly, enters into spiritual life under the sign of love: 'Eating and drinking, work and study, the creation of truth or of beauty, or of happiness: all these may hitherto have seemed to us simply a number of heterogeneous, unconnected activities, impossible to reduce to a common denominator—with love as no more than one of many branches in this divergent psychic stream. But now, under the guidance of the super-Chirst, the fascicle is drawing itself together . . . Love stands at the head, not simply love as the common factor by virtue of which the multiplicity of human activities are succeeding in knitting themselves together—but love as *the higher and universal form and symbol of spiritual energy*, in which all the other energies of the soul are transformed and exalted the very moment they enter the field of Omega.'[47]

It is true that an inevitable risk is inherent in action;[48] but this risk must be accepted, in faith and detachment 'because charity lives also by constant maintenance of human enthusiasm' and 'the very logic of man's development stimulates in him the desire to enter into one greater than himself'.[49] Thus, even when it appears to be secular, human effort 'plays the part in Christian life of a holy and unifying operation . . . Concern with personal fulfilment and improvement is simply the first stage of an act of self-giving'.[50] Action allows man to be continuous with God's creative power, to serve as its instrument, its living extension:[51] by making man ally himself with the creative effort, it merges him in the very heart of God. This is what is behind the first form of *ascesis*, which aims 'at the perfection of human effort through mortification'. 'It is not enough to establish the reign of peace and silence in the body, so that the soul may be free to devote itself to the things of God. To be perfect, what matters most of all is to extract from the body all the *spiritual power* it contains: moreover, not simply from this body that is confined within the narrow limits of its physical members, but from the whole vast "cosmic" body formed for each one of us from the surrounding mass of the evolving *Weltstoff*.'[52]

Thus work cannot be regarded as an imposition that breaks up our existence: it assists man's spiritual progress and corrects his balance. 'Just think what solidity, what consistence, what interest, every life holds for a man who has understood that the infinite reality of God is apprehended (is apprehensible) at the term of every work of conquest, of every act of social charity, of every suffering endured.'[53]

Finally action, so understood, allows us conclusively to answer the objection, frequently met in modern times since Marx and Nietzsche, that the Christian seems to turn his back on human endeavour.[54]

III PASSIVITIES

Teilhard is always careful to retain, side by side with action, as an accompaniment to, and in, action, the value of suffering for, the Christic fulfilment of the world: the more so, in that inherent in action is the danger of being bewitched or hypnotized by the values it pursues.[55]

Suffering is in the first place at the very heart of faith, whose act of adherence comes about only through *negation* of the finite, which must continually be 'traversed' in the direction of the beyond represented by God, and which can be loved only in relation to its source and its end. Teilhard was very aware, too, of faith's inevitable lack of clarity, and also of the basic helplessness of man in the face of the divine transformation he seeks.[56]

Suffering is also the suffering of *asceticism*, which makes man more free and less encumbered, more flexible and responsive, and, through detachment, makes it easier for him to be more fully one with the world and with other men.[57] The demands of action already force him into perpetual detachment; but if he is to be truly pure, he must renounce every satisfaction and every backward look, and *traverse*[58] all things without any slackening of his drive towards God. The virtue of purity, which is the bond of morality and religious existence, unites the powers of the soul in a passion for the simplicity of God.[59]

In his correspondence, through Père Auguste Valensin, with Maurice Blondel, Teilhard emphasized the necessity 'for renunciation and ascesis and the capital and definitive part it has to play—

certainly not "a purely penitential" function—in the construction of the new universe.' '*Fundamentally,* I admit that the fulfilment of the world can be consummated only through a death, a "night", a turning about, an excentration, almost a de-personalization of the monads. The integration of a monad with Christ presupposes some sort of internal disintegration in the monad, that is to say a re-fashioning of the whole of its being as a condition of recreation and integration in the Pleroma. Union with Christ presupposes as essential that we transfer to him the ultimate centre of our existence—and that means a radical sacrifice of self-hood.'[60]

The man of faith, drawn from darkness to the light, from a stifling prison to the free wind of God, throws off his self-engrossment and is seized by a feverish passion for active dependence, for a total sensitivity that answers the pulsing rhythm of God: unceasingly, he purges his affections, and becomes obedient to the least hint uttered by the spirit, while at the same time he expands his powers and intensifies his activity, in order to command a little more creative energy. 'There are no limits to the right ordering of his approach, nor to the flexibility of his will, nor to the translucency of his mind and heart.' The more he adheres to God the more, indefinitely, he becomes one with the divine action. 'Yet a little while, it seems, and God himself, who now finds no resistance as he guides the tool according to his plan, will no longer be able to distinguish the tool he holds and his own almighty hand.'[61]

Moreover, the Christian has not only to fight against his own egoism, to cleanse himself of sin and gradually to master the 'incurable mutability' of his soul,[62] but also to take part in the struggle that God wages, in history, against his adversaries, the forces that act as a brake and bring disorganization.

However, while the Christian must habitually live in a state of 'flexibility', of absolute docility towards God, and under his domination,[63] he must also, with still greater love and still more complete surrender, accept *suffering,* when suffering is inevitable; most of all, he must accept *death,* for death is communion.[64] And to accept them means that he must interiorize them, assimilate them and make them his own. The night of faith is continued into the night of agony. Blessed be a universe in which suffering is natural and inevitable, for it is 'a fit setting for the growth of the saintly qualities that are born in the shadow of the Cross'.[65]

Although these passivities seem in no way to advance the progress of history and the development of personality, since they involve rupture and deprivation, nevertheless they are immensely fruitful; they allow God's education to obtain from man a transition into love and a transformation, through a recasting that transfigures what it preserves,[66] and to complete the construction of the world.[67] What is more, it is the function of death to operate man's turning about and excentration in God.

Thus physical and moral evil are regenerated. Even more than the creative man (of whom Bergson said this) the Christian is possessed by joy, nor is youth the slave of time, for 'the real value and happiness of existence consists in passing into something greater than self'.[68]

IV THE CHURCH

These activities or passivities, both sanctifying, operate in the Church, which is 'the greatest collective centre of love that has ever appeared in the world',[69] 'The Christic pole of the world', the 'axis or nucleus of universal concentration'.[70]

It is a spiritual Church, but one that demands structures and institutions, to serve as the medium of mystical communion.[71]

It is a Church that preserves and keeps distinct the infinite variety of persons, each responsible for their own salvation, but at the same time unites them in the organism of a mystical body: a body that grows, and within which a collective consecration of the world is brought about, and which is the principle of an ever more close intercommunion of souls, and the stimulus that arouses their mutual charity.[72]

This Church, moreover, is mother and teacher; and in her, through the words and the radiating influence of her members, faith and love are aroused and handed on.[73] In dwelling on this educative aspect, associated with his own experience, Teilhard is reminiscent of the Bergson of the *Two Sources*, and of the role he attributes, if not to the Church as such, at least to its charismatic or mystical elements.[74] It is thus that existence, already capable of rational invention and autonomous culture, attains, with no loss of freedom, to a higher and infinitely enriching plane.

Within the Church, different and complementary *vocations* divide Christians into particular categories, according to the emphasis laid on the practice of the active life or of detachment, of prayer or human work.[75] While stressing the prayer that is immanent in the duty appropriate to a man's state, Teilhard does not overlook the importance of explicit prayer, which in some way constitutes an encounter with God in its full purity.[76]

The priestly vocation is a specially privileged vocation in this forward-moving Church.[77] Similarly the specialized life of contemplation renders most valuable service to the world.[78]

At the same time Teilhard justifies the entry, in special cases at least, of the priest or the religious into the field of scientific research 'where every truth and every new power is to be found: so that Christ may inform everything that, through man, assists the growth of the universe as it moves ahead'. Realizing, however, the spiritual problem raised by the absolute demands of research, he would like to see special seminaries established that would train the 'young research students or practical workers of tomorrow in a theology that is more concerned than our present theology to bring out the interconnections that link together, genetically, the kingdom of God and man's effort', and teach them to rethink their whole view of religion.[79]

In the same life, a number of phases follow in succession and fit in smoothly with one another. 'For each one of us, there is a time for growth and a time for diminishment. At one time it is the human constructive effort that predominates, at another it is mystical annihilation.'[80] Spiritual sensitivity and prudence will ensure that each individual, to the extent that is appropriate to him, will attain the highest possible level of personal development and detachment:[81] for 'vocations are infinite in number . . . In the Church we find St Thomas Aquinas and St Vincent de Paul side by side with St John of the Cross'. Yet 'these different forms of holiness are all shades of the same spectrum'.[82]

The progress of history will perhaps bring with it a wider extension of the mystical life.[83] It should logically arouse also not simply a greater love of chastity, properly understood, but a preference, too, for *virginity*, conceived as a spiritual energy indispensable to the convergence of the world,[84] a preparation for mankind's eschatological transition to God.

Finally, the Church is the axis, the centre or spiritual nucleus of the whole universe, in the historical movement that carries it to its

fulfilment: the Church presses on towards the heavenly Jerusalem
which will also be the new earth.[85] 'Expectation—anxious, collective and active expectation of an end of the world, that is to say of
an issue for the world—that is the supreme Christian function . . .
The Lord Jesus will come soon only if we ardently expect him.
It is an accumulation of desires that must cause the Parousia to
burst upon us.'[86] But this expectation is, to some degree, entertained
in darkness and anxiety.[87]

The growth of the Church

The apostolic growth of the Church depends in the first place on a
clear recognition of the cleavage that divides her from men, and,
with this, a study of her shortcomings and an acceptance of her
responsibilities. It entails, too, an awareness of the change that man
is now experiencing, in his attempt to attain a collective fulfilment
of his history and of the history of the world.

Henceforth the Christian, in an initiatory phase, will strive to
arouse or foster around him a spirit of disinterestedness and
generosity in this creative activity. Intimately associated with this
work of moral education will be a personal sharing, as physically
real as possible, in the hopes and sorrows, desires and anxieties, of
his fellow-men. Like them, the Christian will have to devote himself
wholeheartedly, to science, technology and social progress, and take
an active part in the work of the world.[88] In all this activity, however, and through the audience he has won for his teaching, he
will show, as much by example as by word and thought, that Christ
continues and sets the crown upon human effort, and that nothing
can attain its full development or flowering except in him. He will
make his fellows feel that the Christian God is identical with the
God of whom the earth dreams, but is even greater and more
mysterious, more immediate and more concerned in man's progress
even than man himself. He will exalt human effort by leading it to
the higher forms of activity represented by purity, prayer and
detachment for the sake of God.

Thus the Christian apostolate will not aim solely at converting a
nation or a social category, but at sanctifying the very axis of human
thought and at bringing the kingdom of God into the inmost core
of mankind. He will offer human action, which seeks to be total,
a task infinitely greater than its apparent aim—the quest for and the

acceptance of the divine gift, of communion with God. 'Tomorrow
the world will belong to those who give the earth (even here on
earth) a greater hope.'[89]
The expansion of the Church among mankind thus depends on
the radiating influence of its members, and in the witness they
provide of the perfect concord of nature and grace, of the human
and the divine;[90] at the same time, however, it is ensured by the
expansive power of spirit: 'For a truth to appear just once in one
single mind is sufficient to ensure that nothing will ever be able to
prevent it from spreading in a universal blaze.'[91] 'Catholicism has
an extraordinary power of penetrating and re-shaping souls.'[92]

As in the scriptural metaphor, *scintilla in arundineto*, the Christian
must ask of life that it give him the 'great joy of falling like a "spark
on the bush", and so spreading the fire that is within him; but
even though we "spend our lives waiting for the great day, the
great battle, or the deed of power" this external consummation
is not granted to many: nor is it necessary. So long as our being is
tensed, directed with passion, towards that which is the spirit in all
things, then that spirit will emerge from our own hidden, nameless
effort.'[93]

V THE EUCHARIST

The Church, however, stems from the eucharistic mystery: and
reflection on the Eucharist plays a large part in Teilhard's spirituality.

The Eucharist, the type and anticipation of the divinization of
man and the world, does more than effect the change, in one particular place, of one fragment of matter: indirectly, too, it influences
the whole universe and steeps its energies in the divine—not,
indeed, by an automatic action but by vital transformation of the
Christian.[94] It involves, in fact, an action of the spirit, 'proceeding'
from the Incarnate Word, which, through all the Church's sacramental mediations, seeks to embrace the whole world and restore it,
purified, to communion with God.[95]

At the same time the Eucharist is also the sacrifice that allows the
Christian, and above all the priest, to effect, in union with the
oblation of Christ, the offering up of 'all the labours and sufferings
of the world' and to satisfy the universal desire for unity.[96] Moreover, 'from the hands that knead the dough, to those that consecrate

it, the great and universal host should be handled and prepared only in a spirit of worship'.[97]

In a magnificent panoramic vision, Teilhard notes the conjunction of the Incarnation and the Eucharist, in the oneness of the whole history of salvation: 'From the beginning of the Messianic preparation, up till the Parousia, passing through the historic manifestation of Jesus and the phases of the Church's growth, a single event has been developing in the world: the Incarnation, realized, in each individual, through the Eucharist. All the communions of a lifetime are one communion. All the communions of men now living are one communion. All the communions of all men, present, past and future, are one communion.'[98]

Although Teilhard's treatment of the Eucharist is magnificent, we may regret that he failed to deal with the *sacraments*, of which the Eucharist is the centre. There are some references to baptism, but he has nothing to say about penance, in particular; and the union of the sexes, in his treatment of it, is not explicitly centred on sacramental marriage. His philosophy of matter, however, and his theology of the Incarnation would have provided him with ample material for reflection.

It is of the essence of all these aspects that they should not be dissociated, or applied in practice in succession or alternation, for they interlock and complement one another in a vital unity.[99] In the subordination, then, of the secular to the supernatural, the whole of human existence becomes orientated towards God and based on religion. The distinctions disappear between prayer and action, between attachment and detachment; and we can, without any ambiguity, accept the programme of 'attaining heaven by fulfilment of the earth'.[100] 'Under the attraction of Christ, there is no danger that the faithful may forget heaven, and let themselves succumb to a pagan naturalism and be drawn to a materialist conquest of the world. Does not the universal Christ, in all his glory, ever rise from the Cross?'[101]

'A more passionate detachment, a more militant resignation, a more creative charity, a humility that takes more pride in its subjection to the universe, a tenderness that is more animated by the spirit of conquest, a virtue that is less akin to ineffectiveness or mediocrity, a view of salvation as something more resembling a

victory for the effort of the universe than a lifeline thrown to the
individual, a propagation of the faith more clearly differentiated
from sectarian proselytism—those are the modifications we look for
if we are to feel that Christianity can meet our new requirements;
they are already in the air, and there can be no doubt that they will
be realized.'[102] 'I dream,' wrote Teilhard in 1921, 'of a new St
Francis or a new St Ignatius, who will bring us the new sort of
Christian life we need—one that is at the same time more involved
in and more detached from the world.'[103]

When God is understood and loved as 'the supreme reality of the
universe', in pain and labour he takes the place of our own being,
thereby giving it a deeper and more stable happiness. A rhythmic
movement 'carries the soul away from (and in turn drives it back to)
the Divine Milieu, homogeneous and essential, the vehicle being the
particular determined forms of the real that we have to know and
love and fulfil'.[104] In obedience to a mystical summons, man plunges
into the deepest layers of being and follows the road of a dialectic of incarnation in, and negation of, the world:[105] The universe,
that had been an object of temptation or terror, becomes the
expression, the word and the parable of God: the blaze of its sun
ceases to dismay and is merged in the sun of the spirit.[106] God is
not jealous of man, of his strength and greatness, but, as he did
with Jacob, loyally accepts a struggle that leads up to a closer embrace and a more intimate gift of self.[107]

History, too, is divinized. The Christian may suffer and die, but
he knows that his existence, in union with that of his fellow-men and
of every individual man, gradually brings about the consecration of
the world, brings the final term closer, calls down from heaven and
raises up from earth the new Jerusalem.[108] The world was not
given to man simply 'to keep him busy', 'like a wheel he has to
keep in motion'; it fulfils Christ by uniting in him the original
types of all perfections, realized in the exercise of many different
activities;[109] and the virtue of the Resurrection makes possible the
transformation of evil into good.[110] Thus the significance of history,
the key to its mystery, is a progressive *amorization*, that transforms
the still untamed energy of the earth into divine charity.

Existence, then, and in it and with it all that is real, is *founded* on
the *practical* acknowledgement of him who is the foundation of all
things: united with the divine act, man can say, IT IS.[111]

An Introduction to Spirituality

While these spiritual rules, and this method of mystical ascent, are addressed to Christians and at the same time reflect Teilhard's own experience, he always had in mind also a universal audience and wished his message to reach every man. Thus, just as in his apologetics he sought to establish a correspondence between a positive view of history and Christianity, so he sought also to outline an approach to an authentic spiritual life that would be suitable for all men, and to construct the ground-plan of a spirituality that would be acceptable to all men of good-will. He invited his contemporaries, even non-Christian, to accompany him on a common journey in the hope that it would, when completed, carry them beyond a purely human moral system. A lecture he gave in Peking in 1943, to a mixed audience, admirably elaborates a sort of *propaedeutics* or introduction to the spiritual life.[112]

As it is for Blondel, the starting point can only be the will towards happiness—universal, infinite, happiness,—which transcends and takes over from the biological desire for well-being and animates every human being.

I THE THREE CHOICES

Rising above the animal level, freedom introduces the possibility of three choices as an answer to life: the choice of weariness and pessimism, that of enjoyment, and that of ardent acceptance.

The tired and pessimistic. There are some who, like incompetent mountaineers, are soon discouraged by hard work, and regard existence as bad and not worth living: the wisdom of the Hindu, the pessimism of Schopenhauer, even Christianity when, as sometimes, it is regarded as an escape.

The good-timers who look for enjoyment. Epicurus, in the new version of André Gide, incites man to enjoy, intensely and subtly, all the good things the earth has to offer, to appreciate every source and every ramification of flavour: the fleeting moment is so rich that it dictates a policy of enjoyment, careless of the hierarchy of values, and liable to break up the ego in emotional disorder.

The ardent. Thirdly there are those who are faithful to the desire for fuller being and, in spite of evil and suffering, stake all upon life, projecting themselves into the future and answering every summons from the world and from man. Without seeking happiness directly, they find it added to them in the joy of creation and fuller development of self, of sacrifice and generosity, and of the inexhaustible plenitude of being. Their choice, vindicated by experience, is equally vindicated by reflection.[113]

II THE THREE PHASES OF PERSONALIZATION

If we are looking today for a *scientific* and positive solution of the problem of happiness, we can find it only by examining nature itself and the facts it provides, in the light of physics and biology.

Running counter to the material current represented by the dissipation of energy, life has chosen to rise up towards an ever more interiorized and personal *consciousness*. This rise of consciousness in the universe reaches its peak in man. Obedience to this factual development makes it impossible to cut oneself off from the movement, for it has no issue except ahead and above: 'to retreat towards less being, to halt for enjoyment' is to take a meaningless step 'against the stream of the universal current'. The only solution to the problem of man and to the problem of happiness is spiritual growth, collaboration with the impulse that drives history towards its end. Three phases may be distinguished in the process to which man is called: centration, decentration, and super-centration.

Centration on self. In the first place, each individual must get away from the dispersive, restless confusion that brings servitude and alienation; he must attain the maximum of *being*, must grow and increase in stature, must emancipate himself and possess himself. This involves an effort to develop a total, hierarchic *culture*, which will result in giving his personality more order, more unity and more value.

Decentration upon others. Personal culture might well become a subtle form of self-love, if it did not open out into love and place itself at the service of others.[114] Here again, our lesson comes from nature, where everything shows us the interconnexion, interdependence and solidarity of elements, directed towards the unification of individuals. Love is coexistence and collaboration, acceptance and gift, sacrifice and renunciation: the only love that brings happiness is expressed in a spiritual progress realized in common.

Super-centration on the absolute. Once the earlier movement has got under way, it moves out, beyond closed circles and groups, towards the creation of a perfectly unified and single-minded humanity. Once again, this effort consorts with the evident fact of the present increase in the unity of man. 'We may anticipate the time when men will know what it is all together, as though with one heart, to desire, to love the same thing at the same time.' It consorts too, with a recent spiritual phenomenon that is drawing the élite of mankind towards a value that overtops them: the epic of the explorer, the technologist and the scientist.

Although we can yet give no name to this value, it is already an absolute. The secret of joy is thus to lose oneself in 'one who is greater than oneself'; it is to do greatly even the smallest of things, 'to add a single stitch, no matter how small, to the grand tapestry of life, to see in it the formation of the immense, to merge one's interests and hopes in those of the world and, more particularly, in those of mankind; it is to be the ready servant of progress'.

III TOWARDS THE LIVING GOD

To unify oneself, to unite oneself through love with others, to subordinate self to an absolute ideal, is still only a beginning. When man has reached this term he is still unsatisfied, and his problem not completely solved.

If man's ideal is not personal, and if an infinite centre of love does not really exist, his enthusiasm may well flag, and lacking warmth and a sure warrant, men will lose heart.

Only Christianity reveals to modern man the meaning and end of his effort, by showing him the figure of a universal Christ, the soul and peak of the world, who makes of evolution a history of love. The modern world can win through only by recognizing Christ as the end of its hesitant quest.

The youthful surge of the earth's energies must, therefore, enrich and stimulate the Christian life-sap; but the figure of Christ as a person must lie at the heart of men's dreams of progress, in order to define them more clearly, to humanize them, and realize them. The complete solution to the problem of happiness is thus a Christian humanism, or a human Christianity which enables us not only to serve the world of man but to cherish it and transform it.

Teilhard's Spirituality and the Spiritual Exercises of St Ignatius

Teilhard's spirituality is linked to that of the *Spiritual Exercises* and through them to the general tradition of the Society of Jesus. It is worth noting both the points where the contact is most evident and where it is less marked.

From the Ignatian spirit, Teilhard's spirituality inherits in the first place the *grandeur* of its outlook and aims, the universality of its style, and the largeness of its horizons. Like his master's, Teilhard's thought is on the scale of the world, which is filled by Jesus Christ and in which man must recognize him and establish his kingdom. The totality of time and space is the domain over which the divine action extends, through which God's glory radiates and his being shines, all the more vigorously and clearly in that this diaphany is realized within a history of progress.[115] Teilhard's spirituality is first an adoring receptiveness of this immense sacramental affirmation and interpretation of his Word. A plan and a task are being accomplished in the world; these must be understood and men must fall into line with them; the eternity of interior love projects itself into time, to unite with the whole of its creation, once the latter has found consummation in unity. The God who is, is also the God who is coming and who accompanies the movement he animates, and so links together beginning and end; and man is invited to share in the grandeur of this task. Man must escape from the limitations of his condition, he must overcome its constrictions and shortcomings. In vision and action he must extend his horizons, and be ready to answer a summons that knows no limit. All this, however, goes beyond the *Exercises* to Scripture itself, the written evidence of sacred history. Teilhard makes his way back to Scripture because of a spontaneous community of thought, and the passionate cry that concludes the opening prayer in *The Mass upon the World* echoes the wish expressed in Christ's priestly prayer, 'Lord, make us one'.

This call to greatness is embodied in the first place by *docility* in practice, the obedience which is applied 'attention',[116] fidelity to the least indications of the divine will.[117] Under Teilhard's counsel of surrender, it is easy to recognize a transposition of loving indifference,[118] governed by the *Foundation*[119] of the *Exercises* and directed by the development of the Ignatian method: everything must be subordinated to God, just as this creation is, which exists only in as much as it is dynamically related towards its end; every worldly task, no matter how humble, must be made into a sacred act; the whole world must be gathered up into an eucharistic offering; going beyond passive resignation, we must give a passionate assent to every divine influence and pressure, in suffering and even in death we must, in the name of the universe, allow ourselves to be moulded by the hand of God; by deliberate detachment we must disencumber ourselves, so that our freedom may advance more readily towards its end. Finally, and in complete agreement with the Gospel and the *Exercises*[120] any self-satisfaction is ruled out, any falling back upon self is forbidden, by a permanent orientation, theological (in the sense of the theological virtues) and theocentric, of the spiritual life towards God and his work.[121] Here again we meet the full biblical spirit, and in particular the attitude of the Israel of the 'poor', *ad amussim*, in the precise demands of faithfulness in all things: Teilhard's spirituality, like that of Ignatius, is characterized by honesty, straightforwardness and nobility.[122]

It is, however, a difficult effort that is called for, and man finds little to assist him in a rebellious and wounded nature. It would be easy, in this connexion, to illustrate the *Exercises* by a large number of references made by Teilhard to man's *temptation* and his *sin*. There is the personal temptation to an idolatrous worship of nature and absorption into the whole, to autonomy and to revolt:[123] there is the threat of pride that sets itself up against God; of lust that squanders the energies of love; of laziness that shirks effort and checks the noble impulse that drives life forward; of the intelligence that stands critically aloof; of the pessimism that makes men lose heart, and of the selfishness that shrinks from others . . . There is the temptation of society, that seeks to put the collective and the mechanical before the person and freedom. Teilhard's universe is a dramatic confrontation of man and the anti-forces of the evil spirit, which carries further and takes over from the inherent tendency of matter to dissipate and disintegrate. Teilhard does not hesitate to contradict his spontaneous optimism, when he considers the possibility of man's total loss in an eternal refusal of love; and he confesses that to meditate upon hell 'gives the spiritual life an emphasis, a gravity, a sharpness, a depth that it would otherwise lack'. By adding that 'the peak can only be measured correctly in relation to the abyss it looms over' he takes up the deeply perceptive view that damnation is the antithesis of love, and that its dreadful possibility is linked to the revelation of supreme charity and the full development of freedom.[124] More widely, Teilhard's particular contribution can be seen as the right ordering of the passage from non-existence to existence, from lack of authenticity to the truth. In seeking, however, to commit rebellious man to the project of life, which is the projection of God's design, it is closely akin both to the impulse of the Bible and to that of the *Exercises*. Thus Teilhard's work is orientated towards the Resurrection.

The most striking point common to Teilhard and the *Exercises* is the *primacy of Christ*, through the part he plays both in the heart of the world and in that of human persons.[125] Teilhard does not, indeed, any more than St Paul, unfold in detail the mysteries of the life of Jesus. He is content with saying and thinking that the king of the universe was first an 'element' of the world, a being of flesh, existing in history, with a place in the linked series of 'phenomena'. Teilhard seems to concentrate his attention on the great mysteries of Christmas and Easter.[126] Following, however, the essence of St Ignatius's thought, he has the power to bring out, more fully than other writers, their sublime meaning: that nothing can exist without Christ as its axis or centre, the creator and unity of the world, the alpha and omega of history, the beginning and end of all things, the ambience and plenitude of creation, the soul of its progress, the point of convergence of universal concentration. It is this unique being, who is worthy of a passionate attachment, of a devotion that knows no reserves, of an imitation that is at once clear-sighted and blind, and communion in God with whom constitutes the fulness of man's development. It is this being, too, who is the principle and model of human action, since the only end this can hold out to itself is to Christify the whole content of things and of history; and in that being everything, now and in the future, must find its fulfilment and transfiguration. It is, lastly, Christ who is the crucial option of man's existential and historical choice.[127] As in the

exhortations of the *Exercises*, every reader of Teilhard will have come
to feel how boundless are the limits of a love that has no reservations,
that extends to the furthest extreme of constancy, that chooses an
ever-wider horizon and unquestioningly prefers the communion of
sacrifice.[128] Like Ignatius, Teilhard is well read in the Gospel of
renunciation and the Cross, and accepts without hesitation its
absolute demands, as he does the practical applications of
Vince teipsum:[129] not in order to achieve a natural progress of the
person, but as a preparation for communion with God.[130] In both
Ignatius and Teilhard, an accelerating impulse carries their initial
adherence to the heights of generosity of spirit. And, like Pascal in
the *Memorial*, Teilhard, too, comes back to the key symbol of the
Bible, fire.[131]

The celebrated Ignatian meditation 'to obtain love'—*ad amorem*—
which is the culmination of the *Exercises*, is an anticipation on earth
of the soul's attitude in eternity. Here again, by establishing himself
definitively in this advanced position, Teilhard coincides with the
Exercises. Teilhard's writings are a brilliant commentary on this; in
them we meet again all those aspects that make of the universe a
divine ambience; and in his phenomenology, which is at first purely
scientific and later takes in Revelation, it is not difficult to recognize
those precise touches by which Ignatius describes the effusion and
radiation of God in his creation, in which he makes himself present,
in which he works, and into which he distils his superabundance, as
in the intimate heart of one great body.[132] For Ignatius, in fact, as
for Teilhard, the universe is the body of God: not, indeed, in a
pantheist and naturalist sense, for it remains wholly distinct from
the transcendent being; and yet it is his body in virtue of a concrete
communion that the mediation of Christ makes possible for God.
And it is the Paschal transfiguration of Christ, itself the completion
of the Incarnation, that effectively operates this transition of the
world into God. Man, however, must still, in the course of his
history and, first of all, through individual spiritual life, participate
of his own free choice in Christ's victory and introduce creation
into it, so that at the term God may be all in all. By temperament
and by vocation Teilhard was deeply attached to the universe and
its values, and made this favoured theme very much his own: himself committed, as a follower of Christ, to this marriage of nature
and the supernatural, he calls on us to plunge into the heart of the

real, there to contemplate the presence of God and there to read the *sign-post* that directs creatures towards their source and their centre; but thereby, too, to open up a wider road for the total penetration of God.[133] Although Ignatius, maybe, was still forced to accept the closed spheres of the Ptolemaic universe, he would have welcomed with enthusiasm the explosive dilation of the cosmos into the infinite dimensions of time and space, and the concept of an expanding world, secretly animated by Christ, drawn by his attractive power and developing according to the free dispositions of God until the *apocalypse*: that apocalypse being not a cataclysm but, as the imagery of the word implies, a revelation, a final discovery.[134] Nor would Ignatius have repudiated the objective realism of his disciple, in attributing such importance to the *development* of Christ in his own creation, and the progress in the formation of his mystical body, until its fulfilment in the unity of love.[135] But while this ideal is to be attained here and now, Teilhard does not forget, any more than did Ignatius, the hard road and the painful vicissitudes that made it possible for its joy to be born. The light of Easter could spring only from the night of Calvary. In spite of some analogies Christian mysticism is the antithesis of the pagan attitude to the world.[136]

It is this Christic approach that fully vindicates the *optimism*, even more supernatural than spontaneous, shared by Teilhard and his master when they look at the universe and at history. Throughout the whole of Ignatius's spiritual handbook, as throughout Teilhard's writings, there runs an ever-swelling current of hope. Their universe is dramatic, no doubt, but in virtue of its character as an image of God, it is good, and it is, moreover, already penetrated by Christ: in contrast with Jansenism or Manicheanism, and equally far removed from Pelagianism or quietism,[137] they see the universe as summoned to communion with God, open to the free play of liberty, subject to the triumphant influence of a love that makes light of determinisms and of evil because it disposes of an infinite spiritual energy and of all the patience of compassion. Expecting much from man, while recognizing his impotence without grace, Teilhard makes his own the Ignatian maxim: 'do everything as though success depended on you alone, but expect nothing save from God'. The practical scheme of the *Exercises* presupposes a limitless potentiality for God in man and relies upon it, just as Teilhard recognizes in the material, biological and human world the irresistible impulse of a vitality that only sin can stand in the way of, and that must triumph. For Ignatius, as for Teilhard, nothing is excluded, in principle, from this universal consecration that is operated in history; they both see that, under the divine action, a great coming together of the multiple is being effected and, what is more, a new and more startling conjunction of what was cut off by evil, until, as St Paul and St John foretold, the unity of Church and cosmos, finally completed, attains to the unity of infinite love.

Further, Teilhard's spirituality, like that of the *Exercises*, is characterized by *apostolicity*: if the torch, kindled by Ignatius, is essentially destined to be handed on, and if interior experience is immediately projected into action, Teilhard also does not turn his attention to the Christian life nor develop his theological thought, except in close relation to the missionary problem of man's salvation.[138] As we have seen, the stimulus behind his life's work was the intolerable and shocking position of a Church and a world, each made for the other and with everything to bring them together, and yet separated by misunderstanding and enmities. The whole of Teilhard's message is aimed at bringing together two energies—the pagan vigour of the earth and the surge of the Christian spirit: or, to put it in another way, the synthesis of a legitimate but in itself insufficient hope looking *ahead*, and a hope, directed *above*, of what is promised supernaturally. In the spiritual life, as presented by Teilhard, there is no turning back of the soul upon itself, no self-satisfaction, but a permanent impulse towards the objectivity of a history that must be fulfilled, a mobilization of the whole being on the urgency of a problem to be solved, an absolute tension towards the completion of the task of divinizing the world. Here again, Teilhard is faithful to the spirit of the Bible (both that of Israel and that of Christ) and to the spirit of Ignatius. It is the entire universe, and the whole of man, that must make one with the plenitude of Christ; and Christ looks to man for the effective action that will bring about his *kingdom*.[139]

Finally, the similarity between the two spiritualities culminates in their *mystical* character and vocation. If that would appear to be putting it too strongly, the phrase should be understood at least as the perfection of a life directed towards God, which seeks to embrace the whole man in order to bring about his communion with God. It is common knowledge that the *Exercises* reflect a mystical experience, inaugurated at Manresa, whose peak is probably represented by the vision of the Storta. That all might follow the same road, Ignatius put forward the method that leads up to the *ad amorem*. The *suscipe*, which is an answer to the outpouring of God, indicates the depth of the intimacy between God and man, of their coming together through transition beyond (and at the same time preservation of) the created. Teilhard's writings, too, are the expression of an interior life that is dissatisfied with constrictions and servitudes and is eager to rejoin the absolute of love at its very source, by overcoming the contradiction of the personal and the universal. He describes the ascent of the mystic who rises up, from what fills him with wonder as much as from what repels him, through signs and symbols, and giving full play to his passion *to see*, to the diaphany of God.[140] Through the mediation of Christ, and of the host, he opens himself to the immensity of a life whose flames encompass him, and strives to raise himself to the level of the gratuitous gift, beyond all measure, that overwhelms him as he is folded in the embrace of a divine ambience. In the imperishable plenitude and sufficiency of God, whose 'solidity' is made up of fidelity to himself and his creatures, he finds the answer to his yearning for 'consistence'.[141]

His highest activity, however, comes from the freely accepted passivity of 'suffering' God:[142] receiving more than he can give, 'he finds himself in the grip of what he thought he could grasp'.[143] His awareness of the beyondness of God, his realization of the inexhaustible depths of his discovery and of the necessity for a supernatural transfiguration, guards him against the temptation to pantheism and at the same time makes him accept the dark night of passivities and the transition through the annihilation of death. If Teilhard is more alive than Ignatius could have dreamt to the temporal progress of creation towards the supreme unity, he still shares the same movement and accepts the same rhythm: the only meaning of existence and its only justification, is to associate oneself with the return of all things, enriched by consciousness and love, to the God from whom they proceed. Following, however, his master and mystical tradition, Teilhard realizes that everything is given back to him, that everything in the world already belongs to him, that he shares and co-operates both in the exuberance of the creative act and of the reuniting that it operates.[144]

Nevertheless, for all the evident kinship between Teilhard and the *Exercises* as his source, there are certain aspects of them that he sometimes failed fully to assimilate.

In the first place, we find in Teilhard no method of the spiritual life; he makes no attempt to set out a rational order of progress or to define the stages of a process. *Le Milieu Divin*, in particular, provides only a series of general propositions indispensable to life: the sanctification of activities, the useful application of passivities, co-operation in God's work through implication in and detachment from the world.

From this it follows that Teilhard's spirituality is incomplete and does not claim to cover everything that should be said. On his own admission, all he wishes to do is to testify to a personal and individual experience. This, indeed, was less limited than is sometimes supposed, since it includes the essence of life directed towards God and even extends into mysticism; nevertheless, it is characterized by a particular slant, an emphasis on the central importance of man's work, and a summons to assist in the fulfilment of creation.

The most striking lack in this spirituality, and its chief divergence from the *Exercises*, may well lie in the exact study of the problem of conversion.[145] It need hardly be said that Teilhard cannot conceive a spiritual life that does not include a difficult effort on the part of freedom to attain the ideal of perfection and fully to meet the demands of God: he lays great stress on the transformation, and even the reversal that the person and the whole of mankind must effect, the annihilation they must suffer, if they are to be fulfilled in communion with God. He speaks of 'the crying need for purity the universe suffers from'.[146] He points out the break that must be made with self-love, pride and laziness, the conflicting aspects of social progress and spiritual progress. Nothing, in his view, is assured or given in advance. Finally he emphasizes the two-fold dialectical temptation of immersion in and escape from the world, the conflict between the God of the above and the new God of the ahead, and at the same time the danger of a 'dehumanizing spiritualization'.[147] In short, existence, whether individual or

collective, is dramatic and tragic: it is confronted with the yes or
no, adoration or revolt, that decide man's fate. Nevertheless Teilhard was not greatly concerned with a methodical treatment of
the sin of man or to describe the threats that menace him.[148] He
might, indeed, have profited from a detailed analysis of the classic
dialectic of Jew and pagan that is built into the history both of
individuals and of mankind. On this point Marx, in particular,
brings out much more clearly the development of the forms of
social violence that overwhelm the weak. Even though Teilhard was
far from being blind to human misery and the alienation of man's
condition, some barrier would seem to have prevented him from
realizing the depths of personal concupiscence, and the gulf of contradiction between sinful man and God. Not being really familiar
with the whole of St Paul, he paid too little attention to his description of man's fundamental cleavage and the deviation of his
impulses. This accounts for a certain inadequacy in his treatment
of the problem of *conversion*,[149] the decisive break that allows the
person to pass, by repentance, into communion with God, through
his boundless mercy, and that enables the prodigal to return home
to the arms of the father. There is some neglect of the *re-creation* of
man, by which he is re-born from sin and rises again (body and
soul, both here and now and in hope), as it unites him to the Resurrection of Christ. It accounts, too, for a certain over-shadowing of
the mystery of the Redemption, which is somewhat merged into the
mystery of the Incarnation and interpreted primarily as the
generous gift of a new contribution of energy to the movement
towards final unity. This latter, again, coinciding with the
Parousia of the Lord, somewhat obscures its aspect of ultimate
purification in favour of the glory of his victory.

It should be added that in spite of what Teilhard asserts in
principle, his thought is so centred on the glorious mysteries that
consummate the Incarnation, that it seems, by contrast, to be less
concerned with the concrete content of the *Gospel*. It leaps directly
to the Paschal, the Eucharistic Christ, the Christ above all of the
Parousia. It is so wedded to the rational and scientific view of
the historical evolution of the world that it tends to emphasize the
still 'incomplete' character of Christ (in his mystical body) at the
expense of his already actual and total character. The very ardour
of Teilhard's contemplation of the burning heart of Christ soon

leads to an imprecision that identifies it with the universal presence of Christ in the world.[150] In the tradition of the *Exercises*, however, the spiritual transformation is in fact effected only in diligent contemplation of the person of *Jesus* in the acts and events of his historical existence, by assimilating his mysteries and imitating his behaviour. On the other hand, Teilhard's spirituality, though it never excludes this, does not go further than to pre-suppose the journey of the faithful soul on the roads of Galilee and the hill of Calvary. One may well wish, too, that Teilhard's entrancement with the greatness of the universe had been balanced by a more loving examination of the *humble* station, and the negation of greatness chosen by the Word.[151]

More widely, Teilhard does not seem to have paid much attention to the purifying and illuminating influence of the *Bible*. In fact, he seldom uses the word. He was content to take a number of passages —not many, but admittedly of capital importance—from the New Testament, to confirm his theory of the convergence of history towards unity; but he does not consider the present efficacy of the sacrament of the Word of God for the spiritual progress of consciousness. The *Church*, again, to whom Teilhard asserts his loyalty and to whose growth he is devoted heart and soul, is not presented in the first place as the means of salvation, as the sacrament of Christ in history, or as the mother who brings into life the sons of God.[152] In short, the primacy accorded to the *universe* (a universe that, no doubt, when one re-reads Teilhard, is theologically recognized as Christic), to which everything is related, tends to relegate to the background the act of theological submission to the supernatural sources of the revealed message, and the acceptance of the historical forms which determine the relationship between man and God.

Such then, in sum, would appear to be the relation of Teilhard's spirituality and that of the *Exercises*: an absolute fidelity in principle is coloured, if not weakened, by a special outlook manifestly derived from Teilhard's great vision of a universe progressing from the multiple to unity. Nevertheless, the inevitable faults, of omission or emphasis, to be found in his spiritual writings are swallowed up in and outweighed by his appreciation of the totality of the mystery of Christ, which came to him through the *Exercises*.

Critical Comments

A few general observations will suffice to fill out the comparison just made.

I HUMAN VALUES AND CHRISTIAN VALUES

Teilhard sought to express the essential dialectic of Christian spirituality, which must at the same time assert the *unity* and the *disjunction* of secular realities and supernatural values.

In contrast with gnostic Manicheanism, which devaluates the material world, with ancient and modern pantheism, which leads to confusion of man and nature, and with contemporary atheism, which has no foundation on which to base its humanism—in contrast with all these, Christianity, following the line of the Old Testament, recognizes in the world an image of its creator, and accords to man, in the uniqueness of his person, an eminent value as son of God. Christianity does not separate in Christ the attributes of creator and redeemer. The Word, the mediator between man and God, is first affirmed by St John as the mediator of creation. So authoritative an interpreter of Christianity as St Thomas accords to nature, and to human nature in particular, a real 'consistence', an authentic even though subordinate autonomy. Man, both as an individual and a historical collectivity, is necessarily incomplete, but he is endowed with a dynamic freedom and is open to the infinite absolute; thus he is called upon to *complete* himself in his ultimate end, by a personal act that gradually gives his being (and through it gives the world) the maximum of value and significance. All existential activities, in so far as they contribute to this completion, are rightly exercised, in their own order, so that they may attain the respective values to which they are directed. Christianity in no way denies this completion (personal, collective, historical) in principle: on the contrary, it preserves and elevates man and the human. It does not ask man to lose and annihilate himself, but offers him a super-creation which already, in time, is transfiguring and exalting his being.

While terrestrial values can be sanctified and divinized, and while they are a preparation for the kingdom and contribute to the building up of the mystical body, at the same time they are no more than

a beginning and an initiation: it will be for a gratuitous act of God
to crown them, when once they have been purified and transfigured.
In comparison with Judaism, and *a fortiori* with pagan religions, the
new and original contribution of Christianity is precisely the revelation of the divine *interiority*, which is love. Although this widening
of outlook in no way justifies a devaluation of earthly existence, the
life of the Trinity is *incomparable*, incommensurable with finite reality
and even with the limitless embrace of man's desire. Moreover, the
'living God' and even more the God of the new revelation, cannot
come to man except through an explosive invasion that revolu-
tionizes him and introduces him into a new universe, and in
paradoxical ways that are completely at variance with rational
wisdom. Unlike any secular behaviour, even legitimate, which is
defined by the pursuit, the creation and the achieving of the values
of humanism, the spiritual life is above all a hearing of the Word,
a welcoming of it, a ready receptivity and fidelity to the spirit.[153]

Moreover, in consequence of man's sin, the spontaneous openness
of human nature to the infinity of being, and its impulse towards the
absolute of value, are inhibited not only by man's biological or
animal character but also by the deviations of even his highest
spiritual activity. It is not only man's sensibility that is impaired,
but also his spirit; and the temptations he has to face are not simply
from involvement or engrossment in the flesh, but from pride, too,
and self-sufficiency, from deceit and seduction. The devotion that
secular values can arouse may as easily lead man towards the living
God as drive him away. It can even happen that they are made into
idols and imprison man in a closed universe: in such a case, they
cease to be mediations and stimulants, and check spiritual development. Science and technology, philosophy and poetry, even the
values of social life, can all succumb to this temptation.

Thus a scientifically inexplicable perversity prevents man from
fulfilling or completing himself in his end through a spontaneous
movement that originates only in himself: the harmony of nature is
disturbed. The road towards fuller being is blocked, and nothing
can be perfectly pure, nothing can succeed solely by force of wisdom
and reason.

From this arises the necessity not only of vigilance and an educative ascesis—any moral system would demand as much—but for a
transition through death, for a destruction of being, on the model of

Christ. This destruction, desired by the subject, but which cannot be effected by him in an absolute mode without disorder or pride, comes to man through the trials of existence, sometimes even through the horror and darkness, through the heartbreak and utter desolation of terrible sorrow, and in any case through death. Moreover, it is in fact only this apparently negative attitude that is capable of restoring to man full possession of the human, existential plenitude.

Although the road to holiness may be prepared by a heightening or broadening of personal culture, or by an increased flexibility of nature, and although it may sometimes even lead to a new harmony, it is not always to be found in a direct and normal prolongation of the human: it is largely independent, and belongs to another order.[154]

Teilhard preserved the essence of this dialectic, and was careful to point out the transcendence of spiritual values and the painful road that leads to them. Partly, however, for polemical reasons and as a reaction against mistaken attitudes, he emphasized the importance of the temporal term of the dialectic: what he puts forward is a work to be done, a structure to be built up, and even 'passivities' are presented as a medium through which history triumphs.[155] Being much concerned with the logic of the situation, and not as receptive as he might have been to all the lessons of the Bible and the history of God's interventions, he failed to describe God's relations with man in the terrible realism of their forthrightness, their novelty and their assumption of a chasm to be bridged.

These remarks may perhaps detract from Teilhard's somewhat hasty criticism of the 'Heaven and Earth' image, in favour of the discovery of God in historical time, and, as a collective discovery, at its term; for we cannot dispense with the vertical symbolism we have inherited from the Bible, to express both God's transcendence and his possession: indeed, Teilhard himself retained the above side by side with the ahead. The God of 'heaven' is attained by the man of good will in the theological act of charity, in an ill-defined and veiled form. But this incomplete encounter immediately directs action towards the temporal future, and the desire of hope towards the plenitude of eternal possession.

Further, if the reader of Teilhard is not to be carried away by an enthusiasm that is natural enough, he should study with care those passages in which, after having shown the importance of temporal values and the necessity of integrating them in religious existence, he then emphasizes their ambivalence.[156]

Teilhard's spontaneous and legitimate sympathy with the great driving forces in the contemporary world may sometimes have drawn him into an excessive optimism and a certain confusion of the *sacred* with the *religious*. Evidence, however, that human values appear to be worshipped is not in itself conclusive proof that in that worship there is a Christian reality. Such worship is no more than an approach, sometimes distant from its end, and it needs to be purified, transfigured, and re-created.[157]

It is not inconceivable that some readers may be so inordinately attracted by Teilhard's hope in an earthly end awaiting mankind and by his mystique of action, as mistakenly to assimilate his thought to Marxism and succumb to the temptation of the Marxist ideal. They could, however, do so only by being blind to another aspect of Teilhard's thought and to the subordination it establishes of earthly to supernatural values, of temporal history to its transcendent end. Even so, Teilhard's concept of the end of time is still open to criticism.

II ACTION AND PRAYER

The reader should be equally careful to retain the correct balance in studying what Teilhard wrote about action and prayer.

It may appear that action is specially favoured. He summons men to mobilize energies for the construction of the world, and to fill the factories and building sites. The increased leisure so won by technical progress is to be devoted to scientific discovery.[158]

This is a perfectly sound point of view: the interior life, which would be lost in speculative dreams, and would come to a halt in the fallacy of isolation, involves a passage into *objectivity*: there it is enriched by contact with the real and vindicates itself by the gift of self in charitable work.

What is more—though Teilhard may not have realized it—on this point he coincides with one whole side of biblical spirituality, which is directed, as we can see in the Psalms, towards God's aims in the history of men, towards the temporal and spiritual salvation of Israel and the fulfilment of its history. He coincides, too, with the major ideal of the New Testament, which is the incarnation of charity in the heart of the real: of this the Lord's Prayer is evidence, in its intimate association of heaven and earth, of man's practical problems and the coming of the Kingdom of God.

Teilhard would readily have accepted this remark of Pierre Emmanuel's: 'The interior life is not, as it is often represented to be, a sort of private study into which one can retire to think things out alone: it is a way of living everything from inside oneself, of being in the world as though we were in ourselves.'[159]

One should, however, study the carefully worked out synthesis in *Le Milieu Divin* to appreciate the subordination of activities to their supreme end and their beginning. In this we are invited to an act of constant faith, nourished by eucharistic prayer. Action has value only in so far as it is shot through with a theological attitude instinct with silence and expectation, acceptance and receptivity, with total involvement in God and communion with the mystery. What is more, Teilhard goes so far as to say: 'As humanity is Christianized, so it should feel less and less the need for certain earthly nourishment. Contemplation and chastity should thus tend, quite legitimately, to supersede anxious work and direct possession.'[160]

Teilhard's own life was a witness to this communion: in it we see the ebullience of an undying enthusiasm for all the manifold harmonies of the universe, for all the music of things; and his own writing often reads like a psalm.[161]

III THE MEANING OF THE CROSS

Teilhard attached great importance to the useful application of passivities, and devoted much thought to the spiritual value of suffering and death. He emphasized not only the spiritual combat but also the annihilation that is a necessary preliminary to the mystical life. Nor did he overlook the essential cleavage between the kingdom of God and the material world.[162]

Nevertheless, he seems to be inclined to merge the mystery of the Redemption in that of the Incarnation: he sees the Cross primarily as the supreme means, used by Christ, more effectively to urge on the world towards its term. 'Jesus on the Cross is both the symbol and the reality of the immense labour of the centuries which has, little by little, raised up the created spirit and brought it back to the depths of the Divine Milieu. He represents (and in a true sense he is) creation, as, upheld by God, it reascends the slopes of being.'[163]

And this it is that gives life 'a gravity beyond understanding'.

Had Teilhard thought more deeply about the Bible and Christian tradition it would have helped him to discern how unique and inexpressible in human terms is a mystery which, though orientated, no doubt, towards Easter and the Parousia, cannot be embraced in the logic of a synthesis with human realities, and which presents itself above all in terms of a rift between God and man. We can see how the Cross is a source of good for creation and history, but it is first and foremost a *salvation*, in the strongest sense of the word: it is a transition from a situation of loss to one of recovery. The core of the Bible is undoubtedly the revelation of man's relation to God, or, again of the relation of misery to mercy. And the whole of the Bible story is surely the history of God's intervention as liberator, in answer to man's cry. We cannot begin to discover the world nor to admire the wonders of creation except within this history of salvation.[164]

There is no trace in Teilhard of the Pauline dialectic of death, of death through the death of God, of the final destruction of a fundamental alienation and a collective existential regeneration through Christ's priestly act. The Cross is never interpreted as a pardon and a return to grace.

This neglect has consequences in other fields. In the first place, it is interesting to note that Teilhard does not appear to have adopted from the Old Testament the essential figure of the *poor man*, oppressed by his fellows, in argument with God, who seems, in spite of his promises, to be abandoning him; the poor man unjustly held in subjection, drowning in deep waters, who, with Isaiah and Jeremiah, comes in the end to recognize his vocation and mission as redeemer for universal sin. This omission may well be linked with a certain lack of appreciation of the dialectical function of the poor in the progress of history. Teilhard's concern for them was limited to including them in the global system of unification and social concentration, without taking specifically into consideration the awakening of a collective conscience, aroused, sometimes dramatically, by the existence of injustice.

Similarly, Teilhard's fine spirituality of work would have benefited by integrating the *redemption* constituted by offering up its never-ending toil in expiation for the sin contained in human activity and its historical deviations. The Christian, powerless to escape from inhuman structures, is forced to accept and be an accessory to the arrogation of privilege, the various forms of selfishness, collective pride and will to power. He endorses and contributes to universal alienation. The suffering, however, inherent in all work has the power to pay the price of its own infidelity: the most valuable element, accordingly, in work is not its participation in the fulfilment of the world, in bringing it victory and joy, but may well be its very difficulty and exhaustion, the enslavement to its constraints and disciplines, and even the thwarting of its aims. It is this suffering, even more than the results of his work, that enables the Christian to associate himself with the redemptive work of Christ. A mysterious transmutation is brought about, which not only gives value to what seemed lost but effectively corrects the distortions of history. Admirable though his theory of passivities is, Teilhard gave little attention to this practical application of it.

He seems, again, to have felt little attraction to the retrospective images of Christ in his individual mysteries, in particular to that presence at the foot of the Cross which, following the example of Mary, was shared by so many of the saints, and of which Pascal, in his 'Mystery of Jesus' has, after so many others, left us an unforgettable commentary. For all his closeness to Pascal on many points, Teilhard did not sufficiently make his own the moving words: 'Take comfort: you would not be seeking me if you had not found me. In my agony it was of you that I thought, and for you the blood streamed from me. Would you have it even now cost me blood of my humanity, while your eyes are dry?'[165] One can well understand the reaction of François Mauriac,[166] who was disconcerted by a certain lack of intimate, physical, feeling for the Jesus of the Gospel, with a corresponding emphasis on an encounter —admittedly no less personal—with the great risen one of the world. Never having sufficiently intense personal experience of a conversion such as that of Augustine or Pascal, Teilhard did not express, as they did, the impulse that, going beyond merely rational considerations, freely flings the soul into the arms of the Lord, there to find the radiant joy of a new-won communion. If, again, we cannot reach the final 'solution' to the enslavement of spiritual and moral evil until the end of time—which means the end of the evolution of time—it is to be found nonetheless in loving encounter with Christ, in participation in his death and resurrection.

Much can be learnt from a comparison with the religious universe of Bernanos. Exaggerated though they sometimes are, his favourite characters, Donissan or the anonymous curé of Ambricourt, Chantal and her saintly director Chevance, live in the familiarity of an authentic spiritual world. In this, although there is no trace of Jansenism or rigorism, there is nevertheless hardly any emphasis on enthusiasm for human tasks and the fulfilment of creation. Confronted by Satan, and alive both to the sin of the world and the agony of Christ, they keep up a hard-fought battle and find no rest until they fully share in their Master's Redemption. Their vocation is not to build up the earth, but to relive in their own bodies and souls the agony of Christ and his very weaknesses. In so doing they also bring about the Kingdom of God on earth, but by other roads than those of activity: hell is overcome, not by a fresh surge of life's impulse, by fidelity to the spirit who creates and animates the world, but by sinking into the lowest depths of suffering, into the total passivity of agony and death. Holiness consists not in the generous application of every energy to the service of the world of man, but in the transparent simplicity of a child-like soul, in the unsullied sincerity of a lovingly resigned consciousness. These, no doubt, are exceptional and stylized characters, but they serve as an example to all, in as much as they represent and emphasize a fundamental aspect of the Christian attitude, total fidelity to the mystery of the Redemption.

Valuable though the message of Bernanos is, it makes no claim, in the form in which it is presented, fully to express the scope and complexity of Christianity, in particular the complete significance of the Paschal mystery. Like every artistic form and every spirituality, it depends for its effectiveness upon the choice of one particular form of representation. We must also remember that Teilhard's triumphant vision is continually modified by a concentration on the drama of man and the crucial gravity of his choice when faced by the tragic terms of his destiny.

IV HUMANIZATION AND THE KINGDOM OF GOD

A further point of some importance again raises a difficulty: the close interconnexion between the establishment of the Kingdom of God and the completion of humanization.[167] It is a concept somewhat reminiscent of some post-war theories of the social and political conditions required for a successful preaching of the gospel.

As against a concept of the Kingdom that tends to see it as a triumph, it is salutary to remember that the gospel identifies it with the sorrow of the Beatitudes. While the progress of the Church may well depend upon certain special conditions, it is certainly not governed by them.

V CHARITY AND POVERTY

Teilhard was rightly anxious to counter a narrow concept of love of one's neighbour, and to promote the ideal of mankind's collective success. Here, again, however, he is not in full agreement with the precepts of the gospel nor with the Church's tradition of a charity that is primarily concerned with immediate and individual cases, and with personal failings and destitution.[168]

Mankind's attainment of a collective consciousness and structure, the discovery of its common vocation, the methods that are indispensable to progress and action, none of these should make us forget the pre-eminent value of acts of personal charity, nor the eternal mystery of a poverty that is more necessary to the Church and the world than any success.

VI HISTORY OF CHRISTIAN MYSTICISM

Finally, Teilhard would appear to be mistaken in holding that Christian spirituality, after having been originally permeated by Oriental influences, gradually threw them off, and must continue to do so. 'The mystical history of the West,' he writes, 'could be described as Christianity's long effort to distinguish and separate within itself the two roads to spiritualization, the eastern and the western: to *suppress* or to *sublimate*.'

'The Gospel is based upon a number of fundamental affirmations, such as the Resurrection of the body. When these are developed in their full significance, they lead directly to the western concept of the universe.' 'The whole profound logic of the Incarnation, and the instinct of the emergent world, proceed in the direction of divinization by sublimation.'

'Use and abstention: Jesus and John the Baptist. In this duality some have sought to see two essential and mutually reconcilable components of holiness. They are, in reality, evidence of two conflicting attitudes. The time has come to clarify and simplify

Christian mysticism . . . The Christian should henceforward think and speak, unequivocally and exclusively, the language of the West. He should no longer be passively resigned but move into the attack, no longer close his eyes but busy himself in discovery. He should not despise the tangible universe but lose himself in contemplation of it and its action.'[169]

We saw earlier to what extent this programme, which insists on the retention of an ascesis, conforms to tradition.

We need only note that Teilhard's attack is, in fact, directed primarily against the infiltration of *manichean* ideas into Christianity, in the form of some extreme interpretations of the evangelical counsels of renunciation.

It should, however, be added that in many passages Teilhard does not do justice to extreme forms—exceptional but valuable and authentic—of a renunciation that itself can also assist the progress of the world.

CONCLUSION

In spite of Teilhard's attempts to integrate his spirituality into the main body of Christianity, it is still characterized by a deliberate personal style and is still a special vocation.[170] For this reason, it is liable to produce distortions and misunderstandings. It can, in particular, give rise to or encourage a certain naturalism, a neglect of the supernatural, and stimulate the flow of the world's 'life-sap', without thereby divinizing it.[171] It is not sufficient therefore to take it as a whole; it must be balanced and filled out, both by contributions from other types of spirituality and, even more, by a thorough immersion in the universe of the Bible.

These comments and warnings should not be allowed to obscure the value of Teilhard's spirituality.[172] It can be isolated from a system some aspects of which must remain problematical.

As we have seen, it has the unique merit and inalienable originality of firmly attaching human activity to religious existence, to the pursuit and achievement of the kingdom of God, and of affirming the essential importance of the human act and human history in their divine vocation.[173] Rejecting a fatal dissociation, Teilhard makes full use of all the resources of the mystery of the Incarnation to summon man to total involvement in the world and to a sanctification of earthly values: the Christian's main vocation is to assist, with all his strength, God's plan, which is the divinization of man and the universe, and the triumph of Christ in history through the plenitude of the mystical body.

Subject to the reservations already suggested, Teilhard's spirituality has a further merit, its undeniable *timeliness*. There is a certain type of Christianity that tends to withdraw into itself and live behind a barrier, that hesitates to embrace and sanctify earthly values, and that ultimately finds itself not completely in line with the great tradition of the Church and the message of the Incarnation. It is essential today that such Christians should be reminded that even if the Kingdom of God stands outside temporal barriers, it is on earth that it is initiated and made ready, within the framework of the human city and in the service of the ideals that condition the spiritual life and the spread of the Gospel, and that human labour in particular can become a part of God's work.[174] This is a time, too, when atheism, by its contradiction of history,[175] brings despair and stagnation, and materialism, by concentrating on selfish interests and immediate enjoyment and refusing to worship, produces hostility between men and war between nations. At such a time, men must be shown that human activity can be maintained and can achieve its end only in the context of God, the only warrant and only salvation for a technological civilization. On the other hand an age that is impregnated with the idea of evolution will find in Christianity the religious support and stimulus for its effort to carry through the task it is undertaking. Once the spirit of Christianity has corrected antiquated ideas and has made men both respect matter and realize their responsibility to the world, and has given them a real sense of temporal history, then man's progress will be assured by this recognition of the mystery of the Incarnation.[176]

Teilhard's spirituality rounds off the whole body of his work. As in Hegel, the logic of history (or phenomenology) continues into a logic of being (or ontology). This latter, however, produces a science of action, or spirituality, which puts the seal upon and vindicates the earlier stages.

The real is known first as a *development* of the world—the world essentially bound up with man—towards its end, through a series of dialectical transitions or transformations. Here the Christian fact is recognized not only as a phenomenon within this process, but as its transcendent term. Thus rational phenomenology emerges as an analogical correspondence to Christian phenomenology.

A further logic is then initiated, that traces the outline of the picture of *being*. The sum of the real appears as a series of hierarchically arranged, and yet continuously linked, planes or levels. The world (matter and life), man, and God are studied in a cosmology, an anthropology, and a theology.

The lower planes of being, surveyed by knowledge from their lowest to their highest levels, depend on their higher term: each of them represents some degree of *the absolute*, which can be attained as such by man, but which, in its own degree, participates in God-the-Absolute.

It is *action*, however, moral and spiritual life, that, combined with thought, opens up for man the true secret of the real, which always lies beyond things. At the same time, man must wait for the emancipation of death to attain the highest level of knowledge.

Teilhard's thought, then, may be summed up as an *affirmation of being*, spontaneously initiated by an ingenuous *sense* of reality and truth, that then develops, becomes explicit, and finds its justification in the *coherence* it finds in all the elements of the real. Teilhard gives the name of *faith* to this adherence to totality, to this communion of mind and heart with the universal, to this acceptance of the given: initially a natural faith, it becomes a religious faith at the supreme point where what is given is seen to be God's personal word.

CHRISTIANITY AND OTHER RELIGIONS

This total phenomenology now disposes of the evidence needed to appraise the various religions or the systems that serve as substitutes for them.

While *eastern* religions, those of India, for example, and Buddhism, can prove attractive in their sense of the cosmic universal, they are blind to the reality of the multiple, of matter and person, which they absorb into the whole, as 'dead weight and illusion'. They provide no foundation or justification for human activity.[177]

Islam, again, in spite of its retention of the oneness of God, is equally powerless to give value to this activity.[178]

On the other hand, the *atheistic humanisms*, another form of pantheism, are ready to accept nature and the earth and to recognize the values of progress and action; but they can offer only an impersonal ideal, without warmth or appeal; their universe is closed, unfeeling, icy, holding out to man no hope of survival in immortality.[179]

Christianity, however, always provided it is not confined to an individualist concept of salvation and a purely juridical view of the Incarnation, is manifestly supreme over all other religions, the highest peak attained by the history of spirit. While it includes and integrates all that is valuable in different forms of pantheism, it makes up what they lack; while it is a religion of the whole, at the same time it is a religion of the person; and while it is a religion of hope, it is also a religion of terrestrial and temporal values.

What Christ does is to unite the *universal* and the *personal*; taking it to himself in his grace and raising it up to himself, he identifies himself with the cosmic centre, the summit on which history converges. Omega Point, which is known through rational reflexion on the ultimate significance of evolution, makes possible and recognizable the plenitude of Christ, in which he attains the fulness of his stature.[180] Being physically involved in the universe, Christ makes it possible to love it as a person and to recognize, beneath the signs, the presence of a living love.

Himself a person, the universal Christ is the foundation of the reality of *persons* and of their infinite value, and at the same time of the *universality* of their communion: his resurrection inaugurates an organic expansion of his body, which allows the whole of the human species to be integrated, without being lost, in it.

Finally, he consecrates all human *values*, and all the reality of matter. He stimulates man's temporal activity, and at the same time invites man to pass beyond himself into the eternal: he makes existence infinitely worth-while.[181]

Thus Christianity, in perfect congruity with man,[182] supplies the absolute answer to all that is in him; it sets before him an objective that is indestructible and supremely desirable, and gives him the means to fulfil himself and his history by victory over death and entry into life. Instead of being an 'alien growth', it is what gives the universe its significance and truth. If there were no Christianity, 'the presence of a loving God would cease to be included among the earth's psychological reserves: a depth of darkness and cold beyond anything we can imagine'.[183] In rivalry with other religions, the Christian faith stands above all, in virtue of its power to activate, which makes the whole of history and the whole world infinitely worthy of love:[184] Christ is the intrinsic physical condition of their fulfilment. 'More organically and realistically than any other psychological current we know, Christianity continually persists—as practically nothing else in the world does—in maintaining and heightening in itself the ardent vision of a universe that is not impersonal and closed but opens out beyond the future upon a divine centre.'[185]

No wonder, then, that for those who really practise Christianity, it is an intense focal point of warmth and vitality.[186] Sooner or later, the currents that run counter to it will turn towards it and flow with it.[187] The star awaited by the world is none other than Christ, the 'truth of life'.

Meanwhile, to meet the threats of history and to 'save mankind', it is urgently necessary to establish a *common spiritual front*, which will bring together the values contained in, but scattered among, the ideals and trends that now divide the world among themselves.[188]

Democracy, communism, nationalism, all embody, though each with its own one-sided emphasis, man's essential aims and fundamental ambitions. *Democracy* expresses his desire for never-ending progress; *communism* the desire for universal and global success in perfecting the earth; *nationalism* the full development of what is most valuable in individual ethnic groups, controlled by their most advanced elements.

Unfortunately, the temptations they have to meet and the internal contradictions they develop make them fall tragically short of their objectives. Democracy is threatened by the anarchism of individuals, by the conflict between individual interests, and by egalitarian demagogy. Communism succumbs inevitably to a totalitarianism that may well stifle personal freedom; nationalism is reactionary, narrow, and sometimes racialist, and its elevation of the élite often tends to produce a contempt of the individual.

If one could get beyond such hard and fast divisions, party loyalties and violent expressions of mutual hostility, the authentic values of these currents could be reconciled in a common creed, and work together in a grand collective project: the 'conquest of the trans-human', the search for a total humanism, and the development of spiritual energies in the service of man's fuller being.[189]

In point of fact, Christianity can provide each of these three components of the human project with a solution and a transition to a higher level. To the 'futurism' of boundless hopes, which Christianity, too, embraces, it gives the hope of eternity; to universalism which, again, it accepts, it gives the mystique of a definitive 'catholic' communion; and finally it founds the person and personality on a supremely personal being who has the power to gather them to him.

Thus, if man consents, the future lies open for him. 'The sceptics, the agnostics and the false positivists are wrong. Within all this shift of civilizations, the world is neither moving at random nor marking time; beneath the universal turmoil of living beings, something is being made, something heavenly, no doubt, but first something temporal. Nothing here below is lost to man, nothing of his toil.'[190]

The two loves that now sustain history must inevitably come together in the end; the love of the universe and the love of the living God. After the appearance of the biosphere and the noosphere, a final transfiguration is bringing about the coming of the 'theosphere', the new religious consciousness that will represent the meeting of Christianity and man in worship of the universal Christ.[191] We are witnessing the 'rise of God'. The future will undoubtedly make it plain that history cannot succeed without him.

A final critical comment should be added. Teilhard was not always successful in expressing with sufficient accuracy the universal *transcendence* of a Christianity that can assimilate the religious values of the modern world without sacrificing any part of its own message. For example, he says, though we should remember that he was giving an informal address, 'the problem that faces us now is accordingly the problem of the *two faiths* (faith in the world and faith in God): a synthesis of these two in the total Christ. A solution that is not simply remedial, but creative. What we have to produce from it is a new attribute, an impregnable spiritual principle, stronger than those at present in force'.[192] On another occasion Teilhard speaks of what we may hope for from the combining of a transcendent super-human and an immanent ultra-human, present in two forms of faith, as they continue indefinitely to clarify and reinforce one another.[193]

It is evident that the word *faith* is not used with the same meaning in each case. The context, taken in connexion with other passages, allows us to interpret the view expressed as a hope that Christians will become more fully aware of the richness of their unalterable faith, and as a call to Christianity to promote human values.[194] 'It seems indisputable that a difference and a revolutionary advance can readily be distinguished, which permanently divide the "Christian phenomenon" from all other "religious phenomena" among which it has appeared, but from which it has, ever since its origins, continually sought to detach itself . . . It is no exaggeration to say that, in virtue of its very individual ultra-monotheism, the religion of Jesus has a special quality: in the first place it shows itself to our experience as capable of standing up to the new temperatures and tensions produced in the human mind by the appearance of the idea of evolution; and, what is more, it finds in this transformed field the best environment in which to develop and make mutually rewarding contacts. For this reason it asserts itself as henceforward the only stable religion for a world that has suddenly become conscious of its true dimensions and of the direction in which it is moving, both in space and time.'[195] 'Only the Christian (and this *to the degree that* he makes the human properties of the universal Christ his own) is in a position nowadays to meet the complex demands of nature and grace by an incredibly rich yet simple act: it is an act of complete synthesis in which there is a conjunction, mutually completing and elevating, of the spirit of detachment and the spirit of conquest, of the spirit of tradition and the spirit of adventure, the spirit of the earth and the spirit of God.'[196] 'By disclosing a pole that continually exercises a stronger pull on the convergent forces of the universe, a progressively more "Christified" monotheism will always be at hand—even if everything else must change—to "work like yeast in" and amorize evolution.'[197] 'There can be no solidity in faith in the world, without an answer given since all time by that which is promised to Faith in the World. The thinking spheres of the universe must have a principle of cohesion and *spiritual* energy. If the whole is to win our love, it must have heart and face. All our experience teaches us that a Christ who has both a sensible history and divine attributes is the only principle we can see capable of giving the sense of the human its authenticity and consistence.'[198]

Conclusion

Teilhard's work, taken as a whole, is seen to be a *phenomenology* of the whole of reality, that is to say an attempt to understand the whole datum, and a synthesis of all the aspects of being. Based on a profound faith in truth, it seeks to understand and express that which is. It is a science of the *world*, considered in its convergent history, and a science, too, of *man*, determining his vocation and term and studying the conditions of his existence. Building on these foundations, it constructs a *metaphysics* which determines the origin of finite being and the motive forces that govern its progress. To this it adds an *ontology*, which brings out the hierarchy constituted by the degrees of being. The whole of this treatment is *dialectical*, in that it expresses the relations of identity and opposition in being and its becoming.

In its endeavour to be all-embracing this phenomenology is presented with a twofold datum—that provided by *nature*, and that provided by *Christian revelation*. Again it aims, sometimes with more success, sometimes with less, at producing a synthesis of the two or at any rate to define their dialectical relationship.

One part of Teilhard's work is purely *philosophical*; using only the resources of experience and reason,[1] it seeks to discover the laws and the final end of the phenomena of matter, life and man. Profoundly *rational*, it looks for the reason behind the datum: confronted with the objective totality of the world, it deciphers the idea hidden within it by following the indications given by a coherence of relationships and so constructing the formula that 'expresses' it. The phenomenon, the universal mode in which the real is made manifest, does not belong to a lower domain: rather is it reality presenting itself to be read as truth, as 'theory'—and at different levels. Science's reading, initially explanatory, has only to be carried deeper to bring out its value as absolute, its ontological fecundity, and its tension towards existence. Yet, while the real is essentially historical, the meaning of phenomena must also take account of their metaphysical structure. Now, our experience of the temporal process confirms what thought had already discovered as the metaphysical structure of things: a tendency in the world towards maximum unity, the creation of ever fuller unity and, on the human plane, the creation of ever greater unanimity among the centres represented by persons. Thus everything is thought of as order, structure, and necessity: everything becomes intelligible and everything is vindicated. Teilhard, therefore, is much *more classic* than at first would appear, or than he himself claims. Like his great predecessors in the ancient world,[2] in medieval and in modern times, but with much wider scientific experience behind him, he presses on towards the truth and has faith in the word that expresses it.

At the same time this basic rationalism seeks, though only as a secondary aim, to integrate the principal elements of an *existential philosophy*. While Teilhard avoids any excess of individualistic exhibition (though personal testimony is not excluded) he deals appropriately with the problems of interiority, with man's uneasiness and the conflicts and crises of the ego. Above all he sees *freedom* not only as the motive force behind history but also as the constant possibility of a break with the world or with reason, as a questioning of the datum. He attributes to man a total responsibility that makes him answer for the entire world, and makes the success of history depend on the contingence of his options. Finally, he enumerates the chief stages in the existential journey, which must lead not man in general but the individual person to fulness of value.

It would appear, then, that Teilhard sought to reconcile dialectically the duality of the philosophies that divide between them the aspects of the real: world and person, reason and freedom, totality and existence.[3] There is even for him so intimate a connexion or interdependence between the world and man that rational knowledge cannot operate from outside *on* a static reality to which thought holds up a mirror or for which it provides a framework: it must do so in the course of a *creation* total, and at all levels (technology, science, art, love, spirituality), in which man, by action, interiorizes for himself a reality which nevertheless pre-exists him, resists him and gives itself to him.[4] This integral experience, itself included in that of mankind, implies (and the more so, the more it rises towards the zenith) not only a stretching of the will to its limit, but, even more, self-renunciation, 'decentration', in the opening of the personality towards a reality that can never be possessed by man.

While Teilhard's work is in the first place philosophical and autonomous, it also, in as much as it is an approach to the supernatural and preparatory to the act of faith, constitutes an *apologetics*. It shows that nature, through the impulse of its internal energy, is orientated towards God. It explains the movement of living beings and of man's history as given finality by a transcendent term. It *suggests* that the final unity of history corresponds to the final unity of the mystical body. Thus, in his sense of *nature* and of man, Teilhard follows in the steps of *Saint Thomas*, who also based his thought on the analogy of being, on the correspondence between the 'orders' and on nature's pre-adaptation to the supernatural. He has links, too, with the philosophic humanism of *Maurice Blondel*, in that he shows, as Blondel does, but by an analysis of objective phenomena, the impulse that drives finite being towards God, and the necessity to affirm God as the absolute End of the movement of the universe and of man's striving:[5] more clearly even than in the development of *action*, and in conformity with an initial existential experience of man's condition, God is seen to be the necessary answer to the problem and mystery of man.

Nevertheless, again like Blondel, Teilhard is careful not to assert the necessity of the supernatural: while recognizing it as a fact that he includes in his phenomenology, he does not go further than to note the *correspondence* between the rational demands of secular history and the evidence of sacred history, between the God who is the necessary term of evolution and the God of revelation. He leaves it to faith to bring the two together, and also to accept the historical *determination* represented by Christianity, as affecting the natural relationship between man and the absolute.

This correspondence is presented by Teilhard not as an abstract datum, but in the full force of its *tension*, in the confrontation of its two terms: it is essential to human existence both that it be realized by an act of freedom and at the same time that it be received in its entirety from God. In this he reminds us of Péguy in his defence of Corneille's Polyeucte before God and his assertion that grace takes nothing away from man.[6]

On the *theological* plane, Teilhard made an important contribution: his thought is based essentially on the mystery of the Incarnation, all the doctrinal and spiritual consequences of which he developed. Making use in particular of certain aspects of the cosmic Christology of St Paul and St John, he brought out the full scope and depth of the Christian fact, the complete revolution initiated in the world and in human consciousness by the Incarnate Word. While not forgetting man's vocation to a transition beyond himself, he emphasized the physical bond and conjunction of man and God which were brought into being by Christ and which give history a divine value.[7] He took to heart the hope expressed in the Lord's Prayer that earth may be 'as in heaven', that it may become the kingdom of God, and that man's condition on earth may be so transformed that he is completely delivered from evil.

For Teilhard, Christ's position is even such as to make it possible, at least implicitly, to satisfy anything that is valid in contemporary atheist criticism of the idea of God: the negativity involved in the condescension of the Incarnation and Redemption in fact forces religious thought to undertake a radical purification of its objective representations of God, substituting for a crude realism a sense of the divine reality. It is unfortunate that Teilhard did not continue further in this direction, which called for a more idealist and dialectical type of thought than his own. He may even have overemphasized certain aspects of the greatness and power of God without seeing them sufficiently in the light of the New Testament.

He appreciated, too, the problem presented to modern minds by the dogma of the Creation: although he did not reject the gratuitous act of a supreme cause, the notion of *union* (borrowed simultaneously from science, human existence and Christianity) seemed to him more important than the metaphysic of being, and to harmonize better with the possibility of God's going outside himself. Moreover, the equally acute and urgent problem raised by evil, seemed to him less formidable if it was seen as a necessary consequence of an historical creation.

We see, then, that while the form in which Teilhard's thought appears may be diffuse, it is both coherent and comprehensive. It claims our assent by its universal appeal and its conformity with the whole of man, whose truth it discloses. While Teilhard's work bears the stamp, no doubt, of its author's personality, and is characterized by the individuality of his style, it is in no way capricious or arbitrary. The apparent novelty springs from loyalty to tradition, from concentration on the essence of the Christian mystery, which is the redemptive Incarnation—the divine enterprise undertaken for the elevation of man to the supernatural, and for the healing of his wounded nature, which is at the same time a consecration of the primitive soundness of that nature. However deep their lines of preference, and however marked their habitual tendencies, Teilhard's writings, taken as a whole, and qualified or complemented by one another, discover and finally enclose the sum total of the Christian datum. His message is all the more easily read in that, following the ideal and the practice of the great thinkers, he puts it forward in simple language, with comparatively little technicality, and in a form that all can assimilate. Teilhard's thought fulfils Martin Heidegger's requirement for philosophy, that it should not be the preserve of experts.[8]

By its very clarity, this great synthesis is a conclusive answer to a number of modern errors, whose illusory fame is sometimes derived simply from a partial borrowing from Christianity. In conjunction with Bergson's work, it discredits positivist *materialism* by showing that spiritual energy is active in the world and is responsible for all structure and progress. Although man is certainly tied to nature, he transcends, through his personal interiority, its conditions, and his history is explained and justified by its movement towards an absolute and divine end.[9] Secondly, Teilhard's synthesis reinstates the authentic values distorted by *Marxism*:[10] while recognizing the value of technical and social mediations, it asserts the primacy of the person, and at the term of history it places not a purely temporal human success, but a transcendent love that unifies persons in communion with God. To the *forward* impulse that presses on to a successful issue to history and a regeneration of man, it adds the *upward* impulse provided by supernatural hope: and it is precisely because Teilhard reaffirms temporal values that he makes it impossible any longer to criticize Christianity as a religion that claims to do no more than console the weak and calm the oppressed. Atheistic *existentialists* see that their passion for freedom is recognized, but they, too, are convincingly answered both by Teilhard's rejection of an individual existence that, from a foundation in non-being or non-meaning, draws its absolute origin from itself, and also by his relation of man to a prior biological reality, to a physical nature. History, being orientated towards value, acquires an objective meaning that rules out anarchy and despair. And Nietzsche's challenge is answered by bringing out the conditions of an authentic Christianity: the voice of Zarathustra urging his fellows to be 'faithful to the earth' is swallowed up in that of the Christian. In short, abstract visions are eliminated by the unfailing resources of the concrete, reminding one of Claudel's phrase, 'A horse is true because it has four legs and all its other organs'.[11]

On the *apostolic* and missionary plane, Teilhard has the merit of seeing clearly the change in modern consciousness and, by analysing simultaneously the root causes of contemporary atheism and the shortcomings in the Christian attitude, of providing a masterly diagnosis of the present religious crisis. He is well qualified, moreover, to facilitate contact between the Christian and the nonbeliever: he reminds the former of his duty, based on the demands of the mystery of the Incarnation, to be true to man, and he shows the latter how limited and narrow is his point of view. Here Teilhard's contribution is of the utmost importance, in its restoration of value to man's physical condition, in its championing of temporal existence, and in its summons to achieve man's success in history. Valuable again, is his insistence on a transcendence, both actually present and waiting in the future, which that physical condition is to attain, at the peak of its successful fulfilment, through death and inversion, and through a surrender of the self-sufficiency it claims. In this way Teilhard re-includes an essential Old Testament value that is sometimes dangerously neglected by Christians: attachment to the earth, with firm roots in time. Alive to the gravity of the warnings of modern atheism (Marx and Nietzsche in particular) he urges his fellow-men not to make of their faith a rival to man but a summons to incarnation and service. Without, no doubt, realizing it, in this he anticipated the most recent tendencies of a Church that is now officially getting rid of any superiority or inferiority complex, that is neither seeking to assert its power nor to stand on the defensive, but rather to enter into a constructive dialogue with the world, speaking its own language and taking over, in order to consecrate it, all that is valid in its new conceptions and developments.[12]

In view of his own experience of apostolic work, and in virtue, too, of the eternal transcendence of the Christian mystery over its historical expressions, Teilhard was justified in hoping for a theological interpretation of the mystery that would be more receptive of, and more adapted to, the new structure of human thought. Modern man is physically incapable of accepting a formulation of religion that does not take into account the radical change in his relationship with the world that has been brought about by the scientific revolution.

Teilhard lays down the long-term conditions that must be satisfied if the project that inspired him is to be successful: the gulf between the Church and the modern world must be closed, and the godless energy of the earth and the energy of the spirit must combine their two dynamic currents and so revitalize one another.[13]

This programme, of which Teilhard himself provided a by no means unsuccessful example, is far from being a 'shattering revision': it is simply an intelligent elaboration of the deposit of faith, through a study of the *language* of revelation, of the way in which the Word of God is expressed, of the historical context that governs its development, and of the analogy in the symbols it uses. This, in fact, is already happening, particularly in scriptural studies. Being cut off from the world and working in isolation, theology used formerly to have comparatively little knowledge of man: by the very nature of its apostolic vocation and in order to obtain a hearing, it is now called on to present its unalterable heritage in a pastoral setting.

What is more, Teilhard went beyond the problems that concerned his Church, and influenced the world of his time at its most sensitive spot, where its spiritual hunger asserted itself most urgently. With the stern sword of the prophet in his hand, he first attacked the falsehood, as unacceptable as it is arrogant, implied in an abstraction that severs man from his basic links with the world, with other men, and with God. He cut the ground from under that schizophrenic autonomy that mutilates and diminishes man until he is reduced to nullity, and plunges him into a universe of non-being or fatality. He demolishes man's attempt to wipe out his fundamental mystery by 'reducing' it to physical or social mechanisms. Teilhard's teaching is essentially a sweeping assertion of the universal *bond*, of solidarity and communion; it is the initial and unshakeable option for being and value; it is the assent to existence *with* and *by* the world, other men, and God. It is faith in *meaning* and the word in which it is expressed: and all this, not in consequence of an act of abstract speculation, but through a recognition that is at once objective and interior, scientific and intuitive, of the great movement of ascent and convergence manifested by the real: a movement from which, under the breath of the spirit, there emerge in sequence ever more irreducible *mysteries* and uniquenesses. In these days, when language is so loosely used, when there is so much empty verbosity and men turn their backs on the real, Teilhard asserts, as central to our times, the principle of a true *culture*, which consists in loving service of the word, in setting free the word in the name of the world.[14]

In a more positive way, Teilhard has the further merit of stimulating a mysticism and outlining a practical programme that meet a universal need for unity and yearning for communion: in contrast with abstract or materialist forms of humanism, his religious humanism holds out the hope men have been looking for. His profound intuition diagnosed the soul of his time at a critical moment, and was in tune with the aspiration that animates nations, overriding their divisions: and his optimism for the future, almost unjustifiable and shocking though it might appear, echoes the 'utopia' proposed in an encyclical on peace, in which a pope proposed to a distraught humanity nothing less than a total and immediate disarmament that would allow men to concentrate on really urgent tasks. And, just as that encyclical touched the heart of human problems and urged men towards singleness of mind, so Teilhard brings together the most different types of men in agreement on the absolute priority of the great problems of the day: men's daily bread, their culture, their advancement, their unity in a common brotherhood. Nor can there be any formula for collaboration and coexistence of groups and nations, other than that which he puts forward: pluralism in unity. Whatever the value of his theory of history's final convergence on the absolute, Teilhard certainly convinces us of the possibility of some temporal emergence to a higher level, even though it may be *finite and limited*; and this less ambitious but still magnificent hope is sufficient to set men's energies in motion and arouse their enthusiasm. He was alive to the many currents that flow independently of the Church and yet are animated by the same spirit, and in which the efforts of the world are today mobilized: and on that ground we may say that he belongs to all mankind.[15]

The difficulties in Teilhard's thought have often been pointed out by the very writers who have shown the most friendly interest in it, have studied it with the most sympathy, and recognized its outstanding value.[16] These difficulties, moreover, are inherent in all Christian philosophy and all Christian humanism, and that because of the inevitable gap between the mystery and its expression in human terms. It is not surprising, too, that so original a thought should be embodied in a *style* that is coloured by personal emphasis and prepossessions. Finally, we should remember the missionary aim that always governed Teilhard's message: it is addressed primarily to the Gentiles and uses language deliberately adapted to the modern world.

The root of all these difficulties, apparently so diverse, may well lie in this, that Teilhard's statement of the dialectic was not unmistakably clear, and that he failed to integrate his whole phenomenology into one complete and balanced construction; the result was that, in spite of many attempts to do so, he was not perhaps completely successful in bringing out the extraordinary, almost inexpressible, *tension* contained in the relationship, at once continuous and discontinuous, between nature and the supernatural, between history seen in the light of positive reason and history seen in the light of revelation. He did not, of course, deny man's supernatural end, but by making religion a function of life,[17] a privileged organ of cosmic history, he tended to transpose the 'kingdom of heaven' to the terrestrial plane, as something to be hoped for in world-time. Again, while retaining God's transcendence in relation to his work and the gratuitous character and newness of the Christian mystery, all his intellectual and emotional bent led him to emphasize the connexions and continuities between creation and creator, between the world and Christ. His logical insistence on unity and his aspiration for the universal caused him, while retaining the distinction between them, to unite in *synthesis*[18] and in theory orders or planes that are separated by their distance from the mystery. The ascent of the universe, in which he was passionately interested, so fascinated him that it tended to harden into a system a thought that, in Kierkegaard's phrase, should have been expressed in *paradox* and have modified by *irony*, even by humour, the rigour of an inflexible logic.

To this temptation we may attribute the general use, extended to every field, of scientific method. While it is well adapted to the contemporary change in consciousness, once its demands of rationality and logical coherence are removed from their own plane, they come into conflict with the fundamental demands of religious consciousness; they meet the wall behind which lies the mystery, and are held up at the threshold of transcendence: man is not completely attached to the world, and still less is he to God. The dialectical *negations* that separate the orders of the real or the degrees of being are infinitely stronger than those that distinguish ideas or the terms in which they are formulated.

Teilhard was a romantic, and his keen sensibility was so excited by the immense spatial dimensions of the universe, by the power and complexity of cosmic energies, without qualifying that emotion by a critical assessment, that he made of 'the world' an initial, paramount, primordial entity. No doubt this 'world' is dialectically linked with man and ascends towards a fuller degree of spirit; but, in its very development, it is affirmed as absolute and governs his whole view of being and existence.

After all, however, the world that concerns man is less the universe in the vastness of its extension and the power of its energies, than the universe of *man*—than the immediacy of his personal and social problems, the endless repetition of his dramatic encounters, and the transformations which must be effected in the heart of man and the form of his institutions. Once it is correctly interpreted, the 'totality' of the universe is simply the environment (useful and necessary) of this immediate world in which man's distressful story is endlessly unfolded. When seen from this angle, the universe is none other than the infinite depth of each man's consciousness, gradually linked to the totality of being, of which Teilhard says, very well, that it is 'something infinitely vaster and more moving than we would care to imagine'.[19]

Valuable and full of promise though it may be, we cannot, again be certain that the place now accorded to nature and to action upon nature, represents an irreversible and final form of human consciousness, or that the philosophies of becoming will retain their hold. In Bergson's phrase, there are in history laws of 'twofold frenzy' that can lead men to different positions and interests; and it is not impossible that mankind may turn one day to spiritual culture, to the development of interior and mystical potentialities that are at present held in check by the passion for action. That was what Bergson wished and hoped for.[20] Though the force and usefulness of some of Teilhard's criticism should not be overlooked, this hypothesis would weaken the case he made out against a theological system and a Christian attitude that is not sufficiently receptive to the modern spirit.

Difficulties arise particularly in connexion with Teilhard's concept of history. What Teilhard tried to do was, in principle, praiseworthy and in conformity with a long philosophical tradition: he sought to use science (particularly in its biological branches, essentially linked with history) in order to induce from it, almost experimentally, the existence of God, and from that a religious apologetic. Nevertheless, the biological law of unification, backed by the rational demand for unity, cannot be fully transposed to the plane of a human history, for the latter is subject to the indetermination of moral freedom, to the alternative of the spiritual option, as it is to God's loving battle with sinful man.

Even though the action of spiritual energy enables history to escape from the naturalist, pagan, cycle of endless re-beginnings, it is not in itself sufficient fully to explain the concrete economy of the progress of consciousness through stages that include not only the surmounting of problems and the emergence of spirit and structure, but also God's interventions in man's failures, and the unforeseeable outpourings of grace. Moreover, the homogeneous scheme of unification needs to be completed by an analysis of the conflict that opposes the baneful dialectic of master and slave, and later of pagan and Jew, to the beneficent dialectics of master and disciple, man and woman. The negations of man that, by cutting off his fundamental relationship to others and to the world, threaten to arrest or even destroy him, are then gradually neutralized by the interventions of an educative Fidelity which culminate in the redemptive Act: man's disruptions and constraints are wiped out by the Personal Absolute, who shares them, and history is re-born to freedom in the movement of Spirit.

A further point: in likening history to the ascent of the generating lines of a cone to their apex, Teilhard was perhaps too influenced by the geometrical picture and the spatial illusion. Although it is eminently concrete and in a sense temporal, the end of history cannot be reckoned as coming on D-day or H-hour.[21] It cannot be expressed in concordist or representational terms, for it is not getting closer as a date waited for on the calendar of time, or as a meeting point at the end of mankind's long journey. Remarkable and important in their own order though the signs of man's progress may appear to be, they are but a distant and vague reflection of the spiritual growth of the mystical body; and it is doubtful whether one can see a correspondence or coincidence between what St Paul says about the final unification of the Church and the convergence of cosmic history deduced from scientific reflexion. Here, perhaps, Bergson, although he does not introduce the notion of the mystical body, has the advantage over Teilhard, in that he leaves the end of time an open question and confines himself to dealing with the divine transformation of persons.[22] Everything in fact is in some way won for history and for universal history, by the existential victory of a single man, especially if, like that of a saint, it is an indisputable victory: the world arrives at its term in that man. No doubt, in so far as it can be realized and verified, mankind's progress, particularly in the order of intellectual and social life, is of great importance to the kingdom of God; but it still remains the image and projection of invisible spiritual progress: and, if we assume that it arrives at an ultimate term beyond which no progress is possible, then that end of history does no more than symbolize a religious mystery. Finally, since Omega[23] cannot be defined except by assuming that between one consciousness and another there will be so intimate a contact that each is transparent to the other, we meet the difficulty that persons are physically separated in a way that nothing can alter.

Thus the attraction of a temporal Parousia, to be hoped for in some future, blurs and weakens the Johannine idea that it is already being realized in the *here* and *now* of history, by man's present entry into spiritual transfiguration, or his rejection of it. Teilhard gives more weight to the scheme of the *ahead* than to that of the *beyond*,[24] to the *still-to-come* than to the living eternity of the moment, to the vectorial movement of time than to the mystery of an 'immobile' enrichment of the spirit. While, again, the final coming of the kingdom of God implies conditions and preparations, the conception of a global unanimity of the human mass at the end of history as a necessary preliminary to the Parousia, is purely hypothetical. The realism of the beatitudes, modelled on the long, austere and dramatic experience of Israel, can hardly be reconciled with this triumphalism. Rather than this hypothetical vision, some would prefer—and rightly—that of a humanity or a Church that is constantly staggering under a burden, constantly road-weary, constantly, but always with greater hope, crying out to the divine mercy to take pity on it. Christianity, we must remember, is above all *salvation*, which means liberation—God's enterprise to extract man from a condition of loss and despair; and the true picture of man is always that of the wounded traveller, more dead than alive, lying by the roadside and awaiting the charity of the Samaritan. Moreover, by recognizing the liberty of the person and the spiritual alternative, Teilhard is obliged to strain his basic theory and admit that man's option can run counter to the ascent of spirit and bring it to a halt. The abstract logic of a phenomenological reason is not, and cannot be, reconciled with a philosophy of 'existence'.

Teilhard was justified in his belief in a world that has been supernaturalized by Christ and moved by the spirit since its very beginning, but he failed to perfect the formulas that would accurately express the transcendence of the divine freedom and the gratuitous character of its historical intervention into finite and fallen nature. He had difficulty, in particular, in including the breaks represented by sin and by the Redemption in a theory of history which is based on a continual concentration of unity, and progress towards communion. Careful though he was to preserve the difference of individuals, it is fair to say that problems of personal options and the eternal destiny of individual persons are blurred by an outlook that is primarily concerned with wholes. The glare of the sun at the end of the road makes it difficult to distinguish details of the advance.

In short, the influence of a scientific ideal of coherence and harmony hampered the expression of a truth that, without being alien to reason, cannot be wholly grasped by it. Too great an anxiety to satisfy the demands of thought and the logic of an organic structure weakens the emphasis on the mutual exclusiveness of the degrees of being, just as it somewhat obscures the rendings of existence, the concrete and immediate heart-searchings of the person.

Thus, Teilhard's work makes one feel the lack of a phenomeno-logy of man at once more classical and more logical. This would have started with a consideration of *the condition of man*, then de-veloped the dialectic of the existential orders or stages in the fulfil-ment of man, and proceeded finally to the affirmation of the God-Absolute and to the religious problem of the mediations that operate his concrete possession. This was the approach adopted by Maurice Blondel, many elements of whose thought reappear in Teilhard.[25] A second stage would then have approached it from the Christian standpoint (accepted as certain by the believer, as a possible hypothesis by the unbeliever of good will), to unfold the whole development of *history* in time: that of the cosmos, of life, and of man. It would have integrated in this history both the con-sequences of sin and the successive moments of Revelation and the redemptive intervention:[26] the pagan world, Israel, Christ, the Church, the hope of the Parousia. It would have been perfectly feasible to take, as Teilhard did, the scheme of the progressive unification of inanimate and animate beings, followed by that of the hidden progress of human unanimity until the attainment of unity, and use it as a connecting thread or signpost, treating it as a hypothesis that calls for verification. A final stage in this process of reflection would have *compared* the results of the analysis of man's condition and the evidence of history: history would have emerged as penetrated and illuminated by the answer, gratuitous and pro-gressively defined, to the problem and mystery of man. The act of *faith* (already accorded by the believer) would have been vindicated at this point by the coherence between man's helpless aspiration and the signs of God in history. Man's *activity*, too, in promoting the progress of history would have been vindicated, so that the world may attain the term, both transcendent and temporal, to which it is called.[27]

Most of the elements in this plan, which determines the logic of a philosophy of religion, are to be found in Teilhard. In particular, *he laid the foundation of a philosophy of history based on experience, and scientific*, which would now appear to be indispensable to religious thought.

Although the ecclesiastical authorities were always careful to ensure that the form in which their 'warning' was expressed avoided any solemn condemnation, their action was justified by the danger presented to uninformed Christians by reading Teilhard and becoming familiar with his thought.[28] Not only do some of his propositions call for reservations and critical modification, but his teachings can be made unexceptionable only by a dialectical synthesis that balances and completes points of view that are otherwise one-sided.[29]

Moreover, Teilhard himself was more anxious to stimulate a climate of thought than to propagate ideas. 'The rather hazardous over-systematized points in my "teaching" are in fact of only secondary importance so me. It's not nearly so much ideas that I want to propagate as a *spirit*; and a *spirit* can animate almost all external presentations.'[30]

It is all the more remarkable that, when freed from too close an association with the scientific theory of the convergence of the universe, Teilhard's theology loses nothing of its essence and gains in richness. The existence of God can be affirmed as the demand for finality of the whole cosmic process and the source both of nature's inventions and man's. It is indeed in truth that the Paschal Christ arises as king of the world, in the whole depth and extension of his physical reality. The redemptive Incarnation did much more than free man from every servitude; it gave to the earth, to the time of the earth and of history, and to man's activity, a divine value. A concentration is effected that brings together in the invisible unanimity of the mystical body the consciousness of all men of good will —that being the prelude and inauguration of the final union of Mankind-Church in love. In spite of the unavoidable paradoxes and difficulties of verbal expression, it was well worth embarking on a theology in which the continuities between God and man balance, dialectically, the infinite distance that separates them. Similarly, there was much to be said for concentrating on a Christology that was perhaps more alive to the exaltation of man and the world than to the self-abasement of God.[31]

To turn to Teilhard's apologetics: it retains the fundamental notion of an analogical (and mysterious) *correspondence* between nature and grace, between temporal and sacred history: to register, with circumspection, signs of God in the history of mankind is perfectly permissible, since it remains true (though hidden from direct observation) that history rises towards its fulfilment through the action of the spirit. In man and in social structures progressive advances are both possible and necessary, conditioning the supernatural progress of persons and of history. There is a progressive maturing of consciousness, and there is a tide that carries man along, albeit slowly. In so far, therefore, as Teilhard's optimism proceeds from his hope and faith, it is justified; the secret of history is the infinite love of which it is the object and by which it is saved. Human existence, too, is vindicated against every form of pessimism or escapism, for it is in a very real sense the history of God in man.

Teilhard's *spirituality* lacks the subtlety, and perhaps even the depth, of other spiritual experiences, nor does it claim to describe the complex movement of the spirit. Nevertheless, and largely independent though it is of his general system, it has an inestimable gem-like beauty, and reflects an authentic Christianity. Provided it accepts the conditions of detachment and subordinates itself to a transcendent hope, humanism shares in supernatural divinization, and all secular values lend themselves to a consecration which transfigures them while leaving them intact.[32] Without prejudice to the mystery of a consummation of history, we may say that it is here and now that God becomes all in all. Thus, by a dialectical reversal, speculation on the end of time comes back finally to the option *of the moment* which decides man's ultimate destiny. It is today that that destiny, individual and collective, is worked out for eternity.

It should be added that the theologian has the honour and the vocation of undertaking a great enterprise; at the summons of the spirit, in the light of and under the guidance of the Church—and in spite of the risks inherent in the task and of the shortcomings of human language—he must attempt a synthesis of reason and faith that men will be able to grasp: *quaerens intellectum*, faith seeks to understand. The history of theology shows that whenever it has reached its highest peaks it has always sought to rejuvenate itself and re-adapt itself in order to fulfil its apostolic mission to new generations. And has human consciousness ever experienced so profound a change as that we are now witnessing? Has any period before our own known so urgent a need or so heart-felt a yearning for God—or a need, at least, to reconcile its intellectual climate with the mystery of Christianity? As, of old, the people of God sent out spies into the country of the infidels,[33] so the Good Shepherd sends out chosen sheep into the wilds of nature, deep into new universes, and gives them the task of reconnoitring the road the flock will follow, of clearing the way, of opening up difficult lines of communication. To hold up the temple, Peter welcomes the assistance of the troubadour of Assisi as much as that of the great Parisian doctor, sound and solid but a disturbing ally, who has no patience with the sluggards and hastens to confront the thinkers of heathendom and baptize them with the light of the Word.[34]

The questions raised by Teilhard, and those that are asked of him, bring out, finally, the depth of the Christian mystery; at the same time they show its 'catholic' receptiveness of what is new in modern consciousness and its generous readiness to accept its demands. Man is continually sensitive to the appeal of the absolute, which through pride he denies, and advances tentatively towards the fulfilment of a history which he feels within himself must be divine; but his option, rejecting God, throws him back on the banality of a hope that is purely temporal, on the heroic effort to attain the power of a superman, or on the gnostic illusion, and today his continual experience of bitter disappointment is filling him with scepticism and despair. Now he has a fellow-man from whom he can accept the message, a man in tune with his own time, who has tried to give him back a sense of direction and to guide him out of the darkness by showing him the appeal of a Christianity that, without being in any way untrue to itself, rejects nothing that is human.

Although some may be puzzled by the language[35] in which Teilhard expressed his thought, his great claim to recognition will always be that he went as far as possible to express the physical bond between man and God effected by the Incarnation; that he tried to raise up the great cathedral of a universal humanism, whose vast nave would hold the whole of sacred and secular history, whose windows would be filled with the glowing transparency of heaven and earth, and whose vaulting would meet in the keystone who is Christ.[36]

At the same time, more precisely adapted though it is to modern man than any other synthesis in history (as such in fact it is irreplaceable),[37] Teilhard's synthesis discloses no less a hiatus between the infinity of the Christian mystery and the rational thought that sought to express it.[38] His vision was inevitably, as he himself foresaw, limited in this way, but it nevertheless retains its value as an approach and as establishing a correspondence.[39]

We may add, finally, that Teilhard brings us back to the purity of the Gospels, the attitude of the small child, the simple candour, of which he himself was so excellent an example. The least we can say is that he was true to his mission to preach Christ to a stricken world, to show it what conditions might bring it hope, and, as a lonely pioneer in the van, to be a worthy and effective representative of his Church in the midst of living men. Many already are the souls who are finding the way to her through him.[40]

APPENDIX

Appendix
Vocabulary and Language

Teilhard's thought cannot be fully understood without a study of his language.

In 1951, realizing that there were a number of neologisms in his vocabulary, and anxious to make his meaning perfectly clear, he started to plan a dictionary of his principal terms. Two have been compiled by experts who are familiar with his work.[1]

The problem is more than one of practical utility: it leads into the field of the metaphysics of being and of the conditions determining both its truth and our knowledge of it.

The analysis that follows contains, it is true, a summary of the choice of words peculiar to Teilhard, of his preferences and shades of emphasis, the result of the internal and external influences he experienced.

It has, however, a wider range, in that it enables us to draw up step by step a table or list of the *categories of the real* (or the normative structures of being), the *mental categories* that apprehend and comprise it, and finally the *existential categories* that ensure and control man's fulfilment.[2]

For all his originality, Teilhard did not do more than use the essential, universal and commonly accepted structural concepts of reality which no thought can escape from and no philosophy can neglect.

Given the world (matter in extension, forms, movement, history), with the problem of intelligibility to man that it raises, one has to rely on a vocabulary, a symbolism of imagery and logical rules of a grammar, in order to express what is. The notion of correspon-

[1] Claude Cuénot, *Lexique Teilhard de Chardin*, Editions du Seuil, 1963; Hubert Cuypers, *Vocabulaire Teilhard*, Editions Universitaires, 1963.
[2] The table of Teilhard's categories has been drawn up by Madame Barthélemy-Madaule, *op. cit.*, pp. 649–53. Its multiplicity, however, can be reduced by relating them to wider categories.

dence, moreover, or analogy, makes it possible to connect the different planes of being by the meaningful use of signs.

What is more, 'every human language, and language itself as such, is so essentially symbolic in the full traditional meaning of the word, that its very structure reflects nothing less than the union of the two natures in the Incarnate Word'.[3]

Although, as we shall see, there is a great variety of detail, the modes of expression are comparatively few, for they may be grouped together and connected as synonyms. A similar analysis would find the same in any thinker, conditioned by the shades of emphasis and peculiarities of his personal style. No one in future, we may well suppose, can afford to neglect the line marked out by Teilhard. A world in genesis must become an integral part of our thought.

I FUNDAMENTAL IMAGES

Our analysis begins with a summary of the fundamental, initial images expressed by grammatical *prepositions*, which are indispensable to the expression of the great mental categories. Each represents an act or movement of the mind. Teilhard used them not simply in line with common usage, but sometimes more deliberately and advisedly.[4] If we give these prepositions in the Latin form from which they are etymologically derived, we find:

Cum: unity of the multiple, synthesis of elements, significance of a whole, consistence, order. This preposition must come first, because it expresses the universal and capital act of thought, which is one

---

[3] G. Fessard, *La vision religieuse de Teilhard de Chardin* in *L'homme devant Dieu* (*Mélanges offerts au Père de Lubac*), *op. cit.*, p. 235. The mediation of sensible being by language, he adds, 'not only has a meaning for *natural* appetite but takes on a *theoretical* significance and, further, introduces a *practical* orientation that aims *beyond human nature* pure and simple' (*ibid.*, pp. 235–6).

[4] A typical example is found in this synthesis of human evolution: 'power of reflexion', 'power of *co*-reflexion', 'critical point of *ultra* (or *supra*)-reflexion' (*The singularities of the human species*, 1954, in *The Appearance of Man*, p. 232). Similarly, in *Réflexions sur le bonheur* (*Cahiers Pierre Teilhard de Chardin*, No. 2) we find this programme of moral life: centration, *de*centration, *super*centration. Or again, *in*flexion, *circum*flexion, *re*flexion (*The formation of the Noosphere*, 1947, in *The Future of Man*, p. 159). In *L'étoffe de l'univers*, 1953 (in *L'activation de l'énergie*, p. 398) Teilhard gives a hierarchical order to the three zones of interiority: the 'reflexive', the 'co-reflexive', and 'the pan-reflexive'.

of *relation* and unification. It is implicit in the other prepositions.
In, inter, intra, intro: interiority, intermediary (mediation), intimacy.
Ab, ex, extra, de: origin, exclusion, separation, dependence. *Ab*
occurs again, with particular force, in the important notion of
absolute. Teilhard uses, for example, excentration, ecstasis, deploy-
ment, dematerialization, emergence.
Dis: dispersion, divergence, distribution, disjunction, difference.
Ad: movement towards an end: the notion of use, of fulfilment or
achievement ($= ad\text{-}caput$).[5]
Per: means, mediation, instrument of realization (sometimes complete or total: per-fection).
Ob, pro, prae (Greek *para*): objectivity, project, prolongation,
presence (reality), representation.
Sub, super; infra, supra: relative position in altitude.[6]
Circum:[7] position as surrounding, envelope, *milieu* (environment,
ambience, climate).
Re, retro: backward movement (in reverse). Relation (correlation),
reflection, reciprocity, response, replacement, folding back (*reploiement*), return, revolution, dialectical change, 'back to square
one'.
Trans: traversing or transition (*traversée*),[8] passage, transcending
(*dépassement*), mutation, metamorphosis, transmission . . . across,
transverse.
Ultra: beyond.
Contra (anti): encounter, opposition, antinomy, antagonist.

II BEING AND REALITY

The above prepositions help to express, in different modalities,
reality and being.

This reality becomes apparent: it is *phenomenon*. The phenomenon
is asserted as *objective*, as the object of the subject.

[5] The movement that culminates in the unity of the organism represented
by the head.

[6] Applied to God and Christ, the image and idea of 'super' involves a
dialectic of negation.

[7] Teilhard frequently uses, when they are hardly needed, the expressions
'around' (us, them) or 'that surround': an indication of his constant awareness of the solidarity of all beings.

[8] The image and idea of 'traversing' or passage plays an essential part in
Teilhard's spirituality.

A group of similar phenomena is grouped (included, framed) in an *idea*, an essence (type, exemplar): the idea has characteristics, features, or properties that determine it. The biological species (the phylum) is a particular instance of the idea.

The idea includes *individuals* (atoms, grains, corpuscles, particles, bits (*brins*), specimens, fragments) which are in some degree unique and elementary.

The elements of the whole may be enumerated exhaustively: they are 'all' present (stock, swarm, series, whole, phalanx (*phalange*).

They can be regarded as *numerous* (abundance, proliferation).

The sum total of phenomena is expressed by: nature, the world, the universe, cosmos, *Weltstoff* (reality of the universe).

Reality includes degrees: matter—life—spirit; essence—accidents; substance; appearance—truth. It has more or less consistence.

It can be affected by *negation*: non-being, unreality, elimination, disappearance, exclusion, absence, void, 'without'.

III AFFIRMATION AND NEGATION

The phenomenal appearance of reality is answered by an act of affirmation, which is the recognition of its relation to being and truth.

This act of affirmation is dialectically linked with an act of negation or exclusion: a being can be known only by being determined, distinguished, separated from and related to what is not that being, what is 'other' (different).

All mental acts, expressed in the foregoing prepositions, imply this dialectical act: both those that do not involve movement (synthesis, unification) and those that do (origin, separation, transcending).

Essentially, we shall see, Teilhard plays upon the two ideas of synthesis (internal unity) and transcendence or transition (*dépassement*), the creation of a new synthesis whose unity is of a higher degree.[9] Thus his whole thought is dialectical, in the form of Yes and No. A constant negation leads the syntheses beyond and above themselves, to the final and supreme unity. The mutation, however, (metamorphosis, transformation), creating afresh, is effected in

[9] The modern development of the idea of evolution consists essentially in the appreciation of this *dynamic unity* (*Du cosmos à la cosmogénèse*, 1951, in *L'activation de l'énergie*, p. 265).

connexion with (in continuity with) the lower synthesis which it takes over and recovers in a higher synthesis. The very notion of *new* implies an associated negation and affirmation.

IV SPACE

Spatial realities provide abundant and fundamental material for images that are indispensable to the expression of higher realities.

Magnitude (amplitude, scope, dimension, quantity): long–short, wide–narrow, immense (colossal, enormous, gigantic, excessive, exaggerated)–minute, finite–indefinite, limited–limitless, equal–unequal. Macro–micro; hyper, mega (mega-molecule). Fuller-being, better-being (*plus-être*, *mieux-être*). Order of magnitude. Shred, section. To increase, amplify, swell, vary, rectify.

Position (situation, localization): within–without; facing to (forward, ahead)–facing away (backwards, in the rear); high (super-imposed) –low (deep, abysmal); ceiling–floor; median (mediate, interpolated, intermediate)–immediate, contiguous (juxtaposed)–separate; lateral, transverse, askew; near (approximation)–far (removed), gathered together (close, concentrated)–dispersed (disseminated, scattered), divided, isolated–linked (in anastomosis); concentric, nuclear, peripheral (envelope); encircled (embraced), parallel–intersecting, overlapping, interference; marginal (edge, rim, contour, side); symmetrical–asymmetrical; eminent (supreme); spaced out . . . Threshold, zone, region, slope, latitude, antipodes . . . Cardinal, 'dorsal'.

Distance: near–far; direct–indirect. Hiatus (separation, dividing), interval, gap, fault, crevasse, breach, lacuna, hole, void, ditch; severing, cutting, fissure; break (dislocation, fragmentation); compartment, partitioning, segregation; dispersion, displacement, spacing-out, bottle-neck . . . Inseparable.

Line: straight or curved (curvature), axis, segment, outline, spoke, ray (radial, radiation), vector; circle (encircle), envelope (contour), limit (horizon), profile (to be outlined), tangent (tangential), asymptote, fork (bifurcation); meridian, equator; front, alignment, prolongation, intersection; orthogenesis.

The setting-out of lines: drawing, diagram, graph, triangulation.

Point: (intersection or crossing of lines): centre, pivot, focus, point, pole (to polarize), peak, highest point (of trajectory), apogee, summit, crown. Meeting-point, dotted, pointed.

Plane: produced by unfolding, expansion, extension; modifiable by distortion, bending, folding-back. Base, plane, surface, field, stratum, level, ground, terrace . . . Flatness, relief. Precipitous.

Superimposed planes: surface, base (foundation)—ceiling ('to ceiling'), 'landing,' level, stage.

Volume: relief, calibre.

Shapes: covering every sort of shape and construction. Teilhard uses particularly the following images: frame, side, pyramid, ellipse, cone, spiral, spindle, sphere (hemisphere),[10] globe (englobe), dome, cupola, ring or girdle (to ring, to girdle, *boucle*, *boucler*), orbit, calibre. Concave, convex.

Number: measure (dimension) of spatial realities: number (to be numbered), zero, infinite (incommensurable), unity, duality (couple, to double, doubling), half (dichotomy), multiplicity (abundance, profusion, accumulation, proliferation, teeming, swarming, myriad, crowd, mass, richness); diversity, variety, mosaic; positive–negative; maximum–minimum; parameter; vector, coefficient, power-index ('to the square'); series, indefinity; degree (value, level, gradient); equal–unequal, equivalent; remainder (residue).

Mathematical *operations:* determination (indetermination); addition (accumulation, sum, integration, totalization), multiplication, division (subdivision), distribution, decomposition, reduction, cancellation; complement, growth, modification, variation; extrapolation. Chance, hazard, statistics, large numbers, probability. Equation, function, formula, result.

Ideal *relationships:* identity (same), coincidence, difference (other). Likeness (analogous, similar, conformable, homologue, homogeneous) participation, proportion, concordance (discordance). Reciprocity; variation (invariance); exaggeration, excess.

V MOVEMENT

Teilhard takes the following essential images from mechanics.

Action (reaction): activity (passivity, to undergo), enterprise, adventure, operation, creation, innovation (newness), transformation (mutation), transience, construction, shift. Mechanism, auto-

---

[10] Evolution ascends to its peak, as the generating lines of a cone to the apex. The spiritual focus of the ellipse of the real tends to develop at the expense of the material focus. Biosphere, Noosphere, Christosphere.

matism, contrivance, process, regime, factor (component), cause, effect, consequence (to stem from, to follow), aim (target). Possible, impossible (non-viable), effective. To counteract.

Force (energy): capacity, potential, power, potentiality, reserve; kinetic energy, field of forces, impetus (*élan*), dynamism; tension, propulsion, urge, impulse, repulsion; current (maelstrom), counter-current, fluid, flux, influx, efflux, tide, flow, ebullition, profusion, exuberance, effervescence; weight, ballast (to ballast); attraction, gravitation, entropy; pressure, compression, explosion; projection, injection, unfurling; irradiation; elaboration, effort, spring, in-fluence; shock, impact; attack, combat; maintenance; balance, compensation, preponderance, repugnance; complicity; stimula-tion, activation, spur, stimulus; to galvanize, electrify; irresistible.

Movement: negation of a stable state (stationary, static), fixed, dormant (torpor)—of equilibrium (repose, inertia, fixation, per-manence). Agitation, instability, precipitancy; spontaneity. At one blow, to the end.

Origin: source (to spring from, fontal), point of support.

Beginning: prelude, initiation, inauguration, priming (*amorce*, and as verb, *s'amorcer*), starting-up, disturbing, releasing, take-off, launch-ing, departure (point of departure), setting in motion, motive force, quivering, soaring, springing forth, surging, escape, evasion, migra-tion, emersion (emergence), uprooting; draft, novelty; to be detached, to get out of one's depth, to venture.

Progress: advance, course (route), voyage, march (approach), step (fairway, passage, transition), gradation, drift, fluence (conflu-ence), flow (flowing), pursuit, propagation, expansion, extension, deployment, ascent, sliding, leap, jolt, approach (coming together, approximation), groping, growth (excrescence, recrudescence, accretion), enlargement, dilating, inflation, rolling, (in-folding), re-leasing, racing. To move, run to, cross, overflow, draw along, toss about, climb, raise oneself, hoist, spur on, prolong, bear down on, plunge into.

Direction: direction, orientation (orient), polarization (pole), tension, intention, project, aim, goal, inversion.

Track (trajectory), path, road, rail, canal, wire, drawing-plate, drawing out (as of wire), circuit, circulation, cycle (cyclic), laby-rinth (network), centripetal, centrifugal, relay.

Deviation: diversion, twist, veering, undulating, flexion (bending, to fold, to turn), inflexion (= folding-in), warping, going astray, losing the way, distortion, crisis, perturbation, distraction, derailment.

Access (accession), contact, encounter (meeting point), impact, irruption, intrusion, penetration, invasion, impregnation, reverberation (repercussion), revolution, metamorphosis, endomorphosis. To push aside, supplant, establish oneself, maintain oneself, culminate.

Decline: shrinking, failing (defection), wastage, diminishment, weakening, depletion, deterioration, attenuation, relaxation, rarefaction, stagnation, numbing (ankylosis), retreat, retrogression, regression, narrowing, disintegration, dissolution, decomposition, fall. To give way, to get out of order, vacillate, check, hinder, mark time, weaken, deflower.

End: goal, term, outcome, dead-centre (of piston), fulfilment, development, perfection, consummation, paroxysm (peak of trajectory), winning the game, issue, peak, crown (culminate), success, achievement, apotheosis, triumph (trophy), victory, destiny, stop.

Exhaustion, satiety, fading away, extinction, effacing, volatilizing, bursting, stifling, dissipation, disappearance, destruction, elimination, corruption, engulfment, submersion, absorption, loss, overthrow, catastrophe, shipwreck, condemnation, neutralizing, check, rout, miscarriage, dead-end. To drive back, disfigure, depose, wear away, checkmate.

Rebeginning, leap, resurrection, recasting, renewal. To start again. Interminable, inexhaustible, untiring.

The order of movement is *law* (rule, regulation, norm, recurrence, invariance, constant). Determination, determinism, condition. Automatic, implacable, inexorable. The contrary of law is chance–anomaly, exception, whim, absurdity, hazard, miracle.

The notion of *time* is introduced by movement:

Before–after; past–present–future; yesterday–today–tomorrow; old–new; simultaneous–successive; primitive, initial, preliminary; earlier, later; precocious, premature, backward; young–old.

Chronology: hour, date, age, era, epoch, period, season.

Momentary, ephemeral, precarious, passing, provisional (definitive), reversible–irreversible. Short–long (a long time), rare–frequent, lasting, eternal (always–never), urgent.

Continuity–discontinuity, (jolt, shake, spasm, leap, range). Halt, pause. Sudden, brusque, gradual.

Progress, outdistancing, development, evolution, overflowing.

Speed (gait): slow–fast, constant, accelerated, decelerated, monotonous–varied.

Rhythm (phase, period, wave, pulsation, oscillation, shudder, pendulum, alternation), modulation, vicissitude.

Anticipation, foresight, prognostic, promise, expectation.

History is the movement of being towards an end. It includes appearance, event, phenomenon, fact, incident, occurrence, emergence, datum, crisis, consequence. Ordinary, extraordinary, fated.

VI FORMS

A reality cannot exist, nor be an object of thought, without associating the multiple and the one, the elements and the whole. A being exists only by unifying its elements. It can be known only through and in a synthesis.[11] Absolute chaos and disorder cannot be objects of thought.

A lesser order is expressed by the following terms: confusion, dust (pulverulence, pulverized), scattering, fragmenting, teeming, jungle, tangle, magma, nebula, impenetrable forest . . . Amorphous (polymorphous).

Thus every finite being is a structure (framework, edifice), a form, a shape; it organizes, combines, harmonizes, articulates, a certain number of elements which converge into its unity (a unity that may be more, or may be less, simple or complex). It possesses an essence and is represented by an idea: it is determined by an internal law of constant unity, which gives it an identity and allows it to carry a name.

The multiplicity of beings in space and time is subject also to temporal forms or structures of unity: the laws of regular patterns of invariability (cf. above). Teilhard made much use of this notion of form, combining it with that of movement: the basic theme of all his work is the *progress of the unity of forms*, the increase in unification,

[11] Teilhard justly says: 'Following Greek thought—following all thought in fact—are not 'to be' and 'to be one' identical?' (*The Phenomenon of Man*, p. 294 note). 'The mind is power of synthesis and organization' (*ibid.*, pp. 259–60). 'In virtue of the very structure of the universe we are forced—condemned—to unify ourselves, if we are to become fully alive' (*Man's Place in Nature*, p. 117).

the impulse of elementary and imperfect unities, through complexification, towards an absolute terminal unity. His fundamental idea of the world or universe is that of an organized whole in process of fulfilment.

It is hardly surprising, therefore, that Teilhard should have used such a remarkable variety and number of terms to express unification. Even the list that follows is no doubt incomplete:

Complexity, centration, concentration, convergence, confluence, coalescence, concrescence; compression (*reserrement*), folding back (*reploiement*), condensation, accumulation (gathering-up), assembling; in-folding (*enroulement*, involution), implosion; coming together (*rapprochement*) interpenetration, overlapping, interlocking; embrace, grip; bond, cementation, fusing, knot, buckle, attachment, linking, fascicle; agglomeration, aggregation, incorporation; corpusculization, molecwith, planetization, constellation; junction (conjunction), adhesion, connexion (annexation, connective), conjugation, agglutination, to cluster; synthesis, form, stuff, tissue, texture, stitch, braid, anastomosis, network, procession (*cortège*); group, whole, phylum, bloc; association, socialization, collectivization; unanimization, unanimity; consistence, coherence, cohesion, harmony, co-ordination, organization, arrangement, disposition, adjustment, articulation, ordering, combination, assemblage, architecture; totalization, integration, sum, consummation, completion.[12]

VII QUALITIES AND OBJECTS
As metaphors, sensible qualities can be used to designate higher qualities, Teilhard takes abundant advantage of this.

Sight. Light (luminous, luminescent)–night (darkness); bright (to light up)–dim (dark, shade, to blur, to befog, cloud, to eclipse); sharp (distinct, precise)–confused, vague, muddled, woolly, involved, intricate). Fire,[13] spark (scintillation), star, lightning, flash, brilliance, to shine; spectrum, colour (refracted), tint, shade, iridescence, fluorescence, shimmer, motley, glow, purple, gold,

---

[12] As collected in this list, the terms relating to unification express inequalities of value and differences of order. Thus Teilhard confines the word 'aggregation' to accidental or non-organic groupings.

[13] On the essential metaphor of Fire (and its derivatives or analogues) cf. Chapter VII, note 131.

empurpled. Radiation (irradiation); spangle, dazzling; lighting (extinguishing); spectacle, perspective, prospect, vista, point of view; blindness (blind); translucent. Visual imagery plays an important, indeed a completely predominant part, in Teilhard's writing. This comes out with special force in his descriptions of nature, for example in his *Lettres d'Egypte* (as noted in Père de Lubac's preface to the volume) and in all his later correspondence.

Hearing: resonance, tuning, harmonic, tonality, scale, rustling, to grate.

Smell: fragrance, scent.

Touch: solid (robust, vigorous), consolidate (consolidation), strengthen, indestructible;[14] fragile (frail), delicate (refinement), coarse; hard (hardened); dense, compact, consistent, concentrated, compressed; rigid, elastic, flexible; slack (distended, relaxed,

---

[14] Recalling some childhood memories and his naive predilection for iron, Teilhard comments, 'And why in fact, *iron*? and why, more particularly, *this or that* special piece of iron (it had to be as thick and massive as possible)? Simply because nothing, in my childhood experience, was harder, heavier, more tenacious, more durable than this wonderful substance grasped in its *fullest* possible form . . . *Consistence*: that without any doubt has been for me the fundamental attribute of being . . . the sense of plenitude, already sharply individualized and already seeking satisfaction in the possession of a definite object in which the essence of things was *concentrated*' (*Le coeur de la matière*, unpublished, 1950).

In this connexion, a comparison, only apparently paradoxical, might be made with the ideal of Jean-Paul Sartre: Teilhard would share Sartre's horror of the viscous, the sticky, the flabby, the muddy, the insipid, the shapeless and his preference for the hard, the metallic, the compressed, the dry. Both agree in a quest to transcend nature, in the deliberate emergence of liberty through an advised rejection of the determinisms of the datum. Teilhard, however, seems to have failed to criticize, as Sartre does, the teeming, natural proliferation of life—a proliferation that is readjusted both by aesthetic and rational action, to conform with order, exactness, and abstraction (compare nature's confusion and its metamorphosis in the artist's composition).

Teilhard's Christian name was *Pierre*: is it over-fanciful to read a symbolism into the name? Finally, there is no paradox in noting the coincidence (unnoticed by Teilhard himself) between his preference for the hard and solid, and a fundamental *biblical* attitude. God is the Rock; truth (which is also fidelity) is identical with solidity ('emeth', 'amen'); consistence is the primary quality of being, and the basis of the continuance it seeks; vanity or non-being are synonyms of smoke and wind.

diffuse), tension (taut); thin, thick; tight; contracted; viscous (viscosity); palpable, tangible, touchable.

Heat: cold, hot; cool, icy, lukewarm. Fire, hearth, burning, effervescence, temperature, igniting. To light, to enflame.

Dry, wet; light (alleviation), heavy; pure, impure; full, empty; closed, covered; penetrable, impermeable (impervious, hermetic); healthy, sick; corruptible.

Teilhard also used as symbols a number of *substantives*, borrowed from natural, artificial or scientific realities.

Breath (spirit); water (to bathe, inundate, swallow up); flux (influx), stream, river, bank (strand), drift; layer, ripple, swell (of the sea), wave; eddy, whirlpool, vortex; foam, boiling; ocean, tide, flood; storm, cataclysm; climate, atmosphere; fog, snow; flame, fire, flash, combustible, ash; stone, mineral, clay, crystal, metal; crown, peak; reef; film, spot, nebula.

Tool: wheel, mechanism, chain, gearing, coupling; spanner, nut; brick (imbricate); wall (bulwark), barrier, enclosure; scaffolding; architecture, keystone; bridge, road, canal; vessel, ship, boat, prow; wire (conductor), thread, skein, knot, chain; stuff, linen, fold, veil, curtain, felt (felting), cloth (to drape), clothing; fan, mask, breastplate, seat, support, block, fork, picture, film, store, frame, sheath, bunch, sheaf, target, spindle, filter, debris, outlet, anchor (to anchor), platform, support, welding, crossroads, bread, key, tunnel . . .

Saturation, critical point (or threshold), ebullition, volatilization, evaporation, distillation, sublimation, crystallization, solidification, osmosis, isotonic, isostasy, dosage, interference, isosphere.

viii LIFE

Life is, inevitably, designated by images borrowed from the order of space and matter: form, structure, organization, organism, unity, complex, finality, evolution.

To these external realities there corresponds a relative interiority, by which the living being is *consciousness*, if not reflexion: the image in consciousness is that of unity or unification (*cum*).

The cardinal term of *evolution* may be broken down into an image of origin and separation (*ex*) and an image of circular movement or rotation (*volvere*). In as much as it is a dialectic, evolution involves a negation and an affirmation, a discontinuity and a continuity:

the mutation it effects rejects past reality, while at the same time it recovers and assumes it.

Life, too, introduces its own images: body, cell, sex, matrix, generation, genesis (child-bearing, birth, childhood, growth, adolescence, youth, maturity, adulthood, development, senescence, longevity, death), (abortion, suicide, poisoning, asphyxiation). Anatomy, organ, function, envelope. Nourishment (autotrophic), feeding. Fecundation (sterility–fertility). Proliferation. Respiration. Awakening, re-awakening. Ferment. Flourishing, wilting. Contamination, sickness, wound, scar. Survival, surviving. Renewal of youth (forming a new skin). Symbiosis. Aptitude. Physiognomy. *Population:* sex, marriage, family, couple, kinship, brotherhood, cousinhood, virginity. Congenital, hereditary. Proliferation.

The *vegetable kingdom* gives us: spore, kernel, root (rooting, uprooting), sap, peduncle, verticil, trunk, stem, branch (to branch out), growth (to grow), foliation, boughs (ramification), nervure, vein, fibre, scale, bark, leaf (leaflet), pellicle, membrane, pore, bud (burgeoning), flower (flowering, inflorescence), fruit (fructify), bulb, bush, (bushiness), cluster, mould, to wilt.

From the *animal kingdom*: body (to embody), skeleton, hand, head (cephalization), face,[15] blood, heart, hair (skein), marrow, appendix, tentacle, antenna, sting, corpse, limb, horde, swarm . . .

ix THOUGHT

In man, thought, which has already been introduced by animal and even infra-animal, life, becomes *reflective.* The ego affirms itself and unifies itself in unifying the datum. Turning back upon itself, it makes contact with itself, determines itself, knows itself and creates for itself an interior universe.

Thus *existence* (ex-istence) is the emergence of the ego, which gives itself its freedom in relation to an external reality from which it is distinct. It is the person, the monad.

Human thought is deeply coloured by an *affectivity* to which Teilhard is very alive.

Need, tendency, disposition, aspiration, desire, wish, interest, zest, (disgust, nostalgia). Pleasure–pain. Joy–sorrow (unhappiness, insupportable). Sympathy (antipathy), affinity, sensitizing.

[15] The word 'face' is essential in Teilhard's theology (Christ being the face without which the world would be 'faceless').

Fear (alarm, to dread), anguish, disappointment, discouragement, bitterness, groaning, dejection; hope, despair, optimism, pessimism. Astonishment, surprise, excitement, dismay, stupefaction, shock, scandal, nightmare. Disconcerted, struck, reassured, concerned. Exaltation, rapture, intoxication, vertigo, fascination, bewitchment, dazzling. Admiration (unheard of, marvellous, captivated); charm, ravishing.

Teilhard expresses the acts of *thought* as follows:

Thought is the act of passing from ignorance to certain knowledge, from illusion (appearance, error, preconception) to truth.

Reality is initially hidden, masqued, disguised, blurred, indecipherable. It 'eludes'. It is multiple, confused, obscured: it is an enigma, a secret. It is sometimes commonplace, neutral, strange, bizarre, paradoxical, extravagant, unbelievable.

With all these qualifications, however, it emerges and appears: it is *phenomenon*.

Confronted by reality, man is curious, intrigued, perplexed, astonished.

To note data, to register, collect, make an inventory of, catalogue documents. To inspect, explore, scrutinize, consider, envisage: enquiry, investigation, sounding, description, experiment.

Problem, question, theme: to surmise, suspect, have a presentiment, imagine, take thought about.

Hypothesis, conjecture; draft, sketch, scheme.

Logic, method, process, procedure; knack, artfulness.

Signs, symptoms, indications (index), traces, bearings (landmarks), criteria.

To disentangle, discern, detect, disclose, discover, find, decipher, extract, reveal, clarify, specify, elucidate, explain, circumscribe.

To classify, range, insert, frame, reduce to, simplify, characterize, require, generalize.

To criticize, discuss, confront, debate.

To understand, explain, grasp, find a meaning or solution, assimilate, justify, establish a coherence.

To admit, adopt, hold; be certain, sure, convinced; give assent, recognize, concede, confirm. Evident, manifest, indubitable, exact, likely, plausible.

To express, note, mark, name (nomenclature, catalogue).

To express oneself, speak. Recall, evoke. Bear witness.

Choose, reject, omit. Dilemma, alternative. Hesitant, torn both ways.

Sophism, error, prejudice, subterfuge. Be misled, dupe. To correct, deny.

Attitudes of mind: trust (mistrust), seriousness, rigour, sincerity, loyalty, fidelity, tenacity, intransigence, persistence, obstinacy, adroitness, ingenuity, naiveté. Be circumspect, indifferent.

Categories (schemes) of truth: identity, coincidence, correspondence, analogy, participation, condition, proof, synthesis (unity, construction, coherence), consequence, finality, utility (convenience). Mystery (unfathomable, indecipherable). Chimerical, unreal.

Value of truth: capital, essential, fundamental, authentic, incontestable. Inevitable, inescapable, impregnable, implacable, irreconcilable, irreducible, inexpressible.[16]

Weltanschauung, culture, 'acculturation'.

These terms, taken from Teilhard, express in fact the approach and attitude of all thought, as it seeks for truth through a logical rationalization of the datum.

Man's *acts* are indefinitely multiple: we find the following terms in Teilhard:

To undertake, attempt (endeavour), be led to, prepare, begin, set oneself to, take upon oneself.

To handle, manipulate, feel, stir up, use, model, knead.

To dissect: unite, weld; encrust. Construct, build, constitute (reconstitute), forge.

To modify, transform, renew, recast, refashion, inhibit, remedy.

Collect (recollect), gather together, capture, hold, embrace, clasp, store up.

Keep, acquire, possess, let go.

To carry, raise, lead, urge on, throw (reject) (*jeter, rejeter*), place (displace, replace), pile up, amass, roll, turn, pull, catch hold of (tug), press, break, fragment, cut up (into fragments), fold, rumple, twist, stretch, close, dig out, empty, hollow out, bathe, plunge, drown, drive away, glean, hover, throw down, tear away.

---

[16] Teilhard is fond of superlatives: absolutely, admirably, particularly, prodigiously, tremendously, wildly; fantastic, tremendous, dizzy, incredible, maddening, mesmeric, terrifying, ineffable, gigantic, grandiose.

To give, abandon, surrender, transmit, communicate, exchange, waste, complete, conclude, accept.

To dominate, preside over, call, crush, extinguish, supplant, save, violate, subdue, obstruct.

Act, play (*jeu*), gesture, artifice, mechanism, design, plan, programme. Risk, stake, wager, drama. Easy–difficult. Useful–useless, adapted, brutal, violent.

Freedom is symbolized by the metaphor of the fork (bifurcation): sorting out, choice, selection, preference. Autonomy. 'Auto' (Greek), 'self' (English). To emancipate, liberate. Arbitrary.

Social realities: individual, person (ego)–other; function, association, organism, organization, solidarity, interdependence (cf. above, terms indicating synthesis); community–isolation (solitude); accord (concord), unanimity, conspiration; justice, alliance, invitation, visit; to cherish, caress, embrace, clasp, comfort; dissension, attack, siege, combat, strike (of workers), competition, rivalry, massacre, conquest, victory, rebellion, retrenchment, flight, to confront; emancipation, autonomy, domination, tyranny, monopoly, servitude, subjection (head), ascendancy, mechanization, coercion, termitary; poverty, wealth, costly, precious (price), rarity, wastage, resource, treasure. To ask, answer, inform, allow, favour, promise, impose, subjugate. Civilization.

Values: Good, evil (good, bad), 'eu' (Greek), better, optimum; failure, distortion, deviation, inanity. Hierarchy, privilege, importance, gravity, dignity, esteem, respect, contempt, love, hatred, demand. Beautiful, ugly.

Philosophical notions: possible, being, non-being (affirmation, negation); one, multiple (plural); absolute, relative; whole, part (participation); universal, element; necessary, contingent; finality, disorder; cause, consequence; analysis, synthesis, objective, subjective; love, hate.

x GOD

At the summit of being, the notion of God is attained through a total negation of the finite, and at the same time through an affirmation of perfection that confers on him absolute interiority and unity. Teilhard's Omega will be this interior unity which gathers together the final organisms of persons. The word 'absolute' contains precisely this image of a negation of every limit (*absolvere*) an image, accordingly, of independence. The same applies to the idea of *transcendence*.

The notion of *supernatural* is richer in meaning than the word itself would suggest: it is expressed in the spatial image it contains, which signifies separation, negation, rupture. Man's access to the supernatural order is expressed in images contained in the term which designates passage: in particular, therefore, by the prefix *trans* (transfiguration). In this can be seen a dialectic of continuity and discontinuity.

Teilhard's religious vocabulary makes extensive use of a symbolism drawn from the earlier levels of being or of human activity: body, pole, milieu, fire . . . What appear to be positive notions, such as plenitude, totality, mystery, contain in fact a negation. It is the same with the notion of communion, since man's union with God is effected through the mediation of an 'excentration', of a 'reversal', a 'metamorphosis', a 'traversing', an 'ecstasis', a 'detachment'.

xi CONCLUSION

The enumeration of the principal terms used by Teilhard shows how ambitious was his project and how wide the scope of his work. He overlooked nothing that was essential in the categories of the real and of truth, and in the degrees of being or the forms of thought. The description of experience immediately transcends itself in the absolute by disclosing the world's movement towards unity, in the affirmation associated with the disclosure, and in the action that both realizes it and shares in it.

Teilhard may not fully have appreciated the philosophical significance of his terms and imagery; but, like every great thinker, he attributed great importance to *language* and its power to express ideas. That language, we need hardly add, is animated by an individual style that reflects the soul of the person.

Teilhard's Style

Having examined Teilhard's vocabulary, we may conclude with a few observations about his style.

1. The thought is expressed with perfect *clarity* and *sharpness*, and, at his best, at least, with a sobriety that never degenerates into

abstract dryness. A continual illumination, a joy to the mind, emerges from the lucidity of the text.[17]

2. His thought is developed in sections, all of much the same average length, that are unified by a central axis: this is the master notion, announced, as it should be, in the opening sentence. These sections are grouped together in a wider unity, of which they are progressive elements. This gives his writing a feeling of coherence and logic, of vigour and mastery, of strength and balance. Teilhard's 'development' is, in this, a true child of his own scientific discipline, for the idea unfolds and matures in conformity with the laws of biology.

3. This intellectual coherence, which reflects an interior demand, is animated from within by an *affective impulse*, itself proceeding from a faith or 'generosity' of mind that is evidence of Teilhard's eager sensibility. He loves what he is expressing; he is passionately excited by his vision of the universe; his writing is committed. It often happens that he defends his position by an attack on contrary views, or is simply clearing his mind of illusion or appearance. In short, Teilhard's style always gives an impression of movement and vitality. Starting from a profound intuition, truth emerges step by step with the inner core of his thought and the release of his spiritual energy. A born writer, Teilhard seems to have had a passion for writing and is manifestly fascinated by a writer's problems.

4. Teilhard adapts his style to the different *types of literary work* he was successively engaged in: scientific papers, essays in general cosmology, theology, spirituality, prayer, correspondence. His lyricism, though sometimes restrained or muted, constantly breaks through, but never divorced from the idea or doctrine under discussion. From time to time it comes out in *Le Milieu Divin*, it runs through *The Mass on the World*, and rises to heights in his mystical meditations on matter.[18] Many, however, would give their preference (as I do myself) to his more restrained and less eloquent work, particularly the simplicity of *Letters from a Traveller*.[19]

[17] We should note Teilhard's great attention to exact punctuation: a discipline indicative of his respect for the precise shade of meaning expressed by a mental connexion or disconnexion.

[18] *Christ in the world of matter* and *The spiritual power of matter* (in *Hymn of the Universe*).

[19] In his introduction to Teilhard's *Lettres d'Egypte*, Père de Lubac analyses his style as follows: 'The literary talent seen in *The Making of a*

5. An abundant imagery illustrates and illuminates his writing. Teilhard combined a wide experience with an intimate knowledge of the resources of language. The images are contained primarily in the actual root of the words used, and, to be fully appreciated and understood, they should be related to their etymology: he uses the whole range of complementary synonyms to pin down cardinal realities. The imagery is expressed, too, in the use of symbols, and in analogies drawn from the sensory world (objects and qualities). Like every great writer, Teilhard makes great play with correspondences. Less frequently, he introduces comparisons and examples.[20] This wealth of imagery is often associated with their

---

Mind and *Letters from a Traveller*, is already beginning to assert itself in these letters from Egypt. Scenes of school life, or Moslem life, pictures of the city or desert, accounts of geological expeditions, descriptions of natural history —whatever the subject treated, the handling is always sure, the observation exact, the fruit of an unremitting curiosity served by an extraordinary sharpness of vision. As in Claudel's *Connaissance de l'Est* the minute precision of description gives the poetry a sort of scientific exactitude—whether he is writing of a pig or a pine tree—so in Teilhard, sometimes even in this first period, a similar process makes the scientific description blossom out into poetry' (p. 9).

[20] One example is the miners caught in a roof-collapse and trying to find a way out of the shaft (*Les conditions psychologiques de l'unification humaine*, 1949, in *L'activation de l'énergie*, p. 180). There is a similar comparison in *Un phénomène de contre-évolution*, 1949, *ibid.*, p. 200; 'the caterpillar whose substance, as its metamorphosis approaches, dissolves into a practically amorphous product' (*Du cosmos à la cosmogénèse*, 1951, *ibid.*, p. 263); the aircraft that, accelerating along the runway, 'finally transforms its speed on the ground into flight'; the bouquet in which it is no surprise to find some damaged flowers; 'God's operation moulds us like a plastic clay'... 'Imagine a deep-sea diver trying to get back from the sea-bed to the clear light of day. Or imagine a traveller on a fog-bound mountainside climbing upwards towards the summit clothed in light' (*Le Milieu Divin*, p. 107). 'Just as on certain days the sea lights up only as the ship's prow or the swimmer cleaves its surface, so the world is lit up with God only when reacting to our impetus' (*ibid.*, p. 118). 'Like those powerful rockets that the boldness of modern man is launching in the attack on interstellar space, so a cosmos in controlled progress cannot conceivably advance without leaving behind a more or less dense smoke-trail' (*Du cosmos à la cosmogénèse*, 1951, in *L'activation de l'énergie*, p. 268).

We should, however, note a certain narrowness, even perhaps poverty, in Teilhard's use of symbols. 'Fire' is given so much prominence that it excludes other less striking and dynamic, but still significant, symbolisms;

individual or combined power, and it is this that makes many of his formulas raise a corresponding echo in the reader, and gives his arguments an almost physical grip.

6. Although there are normally no signs of an attempt to achieve a melodious effect, Teilhard's style sometimes acquires a deep *musical* charm in the ordered balance of his sentences and his choice of words. The most characteristic example of this is *The Mass on the World*, which almost calls for declamation. In it one can recognize a deliberate essay in a solemn mode of cosmic liturgy. Successful though it was, the attempt could not be carried further without going too far and straining for effect.

7. It would appear that a *progress* can be detected in Teilhard's style, as he grew older and had more sense of economy of means and simplicity.[21] He seemed to become aware of his tendency to pile words one upon another. His war-time essays, and even *Le Milieu Divin* show a certain prolixity and over-amplification that were later corrected in his masterpiece, *The Phenomenon of Man*.

The sum total of these qualities, seldom combined in one mind, is some explanation at least of the mysterious attraction exerted by Teilhard's style and thought. The truth of a thought, we should remember, is inseparable from its form, and the poetry of its expression contributes to its value.

---

such as *night, water, sleep*. Teilhard made little use of the richness of biblical language, and it is to be regretted that he did not or could not profit from the example of St John of the Cross (cf. G. Morel, *Le sens de l'existence d'après Saint Jean de la Croix*, Vol. 3, *La symbolique*, Aubier, 1960), as also from those of Claudel and Péguy.

[21] When planning a theological essay, Teilhard wrote, 'I'd like to find a form (a setting) that's not too heavy or diffuse' (Letter of 1 January 1917, in *Making of a Mind*, p. 160). Some months later he criticizes Vigny's style as follows: 'I've been rather disappointed, I must say, to find him so pompous, such a phrasemonger at times, so loaded with metaphor—so much a slave to words that too often they govern the thought' (Letter of 14 August 1917, *ibid.*, p. 201). He goes on to wish for a more flexible type of poetry: 'A literary piece, if it is really felt and expressed, should be like a piece of music, with shades of emphasis, silences, themes, an over-all harmony, etc.'

Notes

CHAPTER I: FORMATIVE INFLUENCES

[1] 'The error of concordism lies in confusing the meridians in the region of the equator (the meridian of science and the meridian of Faith). They must, however, meet again somewhere, in a pole (if we consider the whole, from the scientific and religious point of view)—and that means that they must fulfil certain general structural conditions (such as the organic laws of union); and it is only this *coherence* (not concordance) that I defend' (Letter of 30 April 1948). 'We must take care not to confuse *"concordism"* with *"coherence"*' (*Comment je vois*, unpublished, August 1948).

[2] This is particularly apparent in *Christ in the World of Matter* (1916), a meditation before a picture of the Heart of Christ, and before the Host. 'It was as though the planes which marked off the figure of Christ from the world surrounding it were melting into a single vibrant surface whereon all demarcations vanished . . . I had then the impression as I gazed at the host that its surface was gradually spreading out like a spot of oil . . .' (*Hymn of the Universe*, pp. 43, 47). 'I have the faculty,' said Teilhard, 'of perceiving the undefined fringe that things have in common, more intensely than their exact, individual, kernel' (1917).

[3] 'I love irresistibly all that your continuous help enables me to bring each day to reality. A thought, a material improvement, a harmony, a unique nuance of human love, the enchanting complexity of a smile or a glance, all these *new* beauties that appear for the first time, in me or around me, on the human face of the earth— I cherish them like children and cannot believe that they will die entirely in their flesh' (*Le Milieu Divin*, p. 55).

[4] In *Christ in the World of Matter* (1916: *Hymn of the Universe*, pp. 53, 54) Teilhard, deliberately disguising his own identity, wrote, '"I had always," he went on, "been by temperament a pantheist . . . I live at the heart of a single, unique Element, the centre of the universe and present in each part of it: personal love and Cosmic Power."' Teilhard has a note justifying this statement by an appeal to St Paul's phrase, 'God, all in all'. The discovery, however, of God in the outward manifestation of the world, is made easier by his sensibility's feeling for the universe.

279

[5] 'Like the monist I plunge into the all-inclusive One . . . Like the pagan I worship a God who can be touched . . . like the quietist I allow myself with delight to be cradled in the divine fantasy' (*The Mass on the World*, 1923, in *Hymn of the Universe*, pp. 26–7). 'As for my innate "materialism" (I now fully realize), it is from roots in the tangible layers of the universe, that, in my eyes, all reality is illuminated and transfigured' (*L'étoffe de l'univers*, 1953, in *L'Activation de l'énergie*, p. 307).

[6] 'You're perfectly right in thinking that the sap of my thought is sentient rather than intellectual . . . Even though the distinction between the two powers, the "affective" and the "apprehensive", is much less sharp than at first appears, and that to feel intensely involves almost necessarily a very intimate vision of what is experienced . . . there are obviously temperaments in which intuition is born from an excess of tension or vital ardour much more than from methodical effort: and it's probably to this type that I incline. I am much more enthusiast than scholar' (Letter of 29 June 1916, *Making of a Mind*, pp. 106–7). The metaphor of *fire* occupies a central position in Teilhard's mysticism, and is equally characteristic of his own soul. Himself 'incandescent', he sees the universe, too, as such. 'Sometimes I feel as though I were one of those birds one sees tossed about in a great wind. Spiritual forces have a power and a mystery even greater than material forces' (Letter of 10 January 1926).

[7] To interpret Teilhard correctly, one should be careful to note that his feeling for material nature is not passive contemplation, an enraptured and naive sense of wonder, before a settled order of things. His correspondence, it is true, reflects an impassioned view of natural scenes, and in one of his letters to Fr Janssens he speaks of his 'feelings of wonderment' as he looks at the world (12 October 1951). This vision, however, is the dawn of a *quest*: '. . . nature is disturbing rather than satisfying: it's so obviously the basis of *something*, wears the face of *some one*, that you can't define: and you can find no rest in it . . . until you reach the ultimate term hidden in it . . . I'm so fascinated and intrigued by the riddle that I find in it a *sufficient stimulus* to search and thought. Perhaps this peculiarity of my sensitivity derives from the fact that things in the cosmos and in Life have always presented themselves to me as objects to be pursued and studied—never just as material for contemplation—the

lack of satisfaction I find in nature—to a point where it causes me physical suffering—is chiefly the inevitable *superficiality* of our experience of it here below. Anything *new* we can contrive to discover or extract is contained within a zone limited beforehand by our own faculties. As soon as we reach a certain depth, we're down to rock: we're ringed in by a barrier we can't break through, that can only be broken through by some *complete organic transformation* such as death alone can bring about' (Letter of 12 July 1918, *Making of a Mind*, pp. 213–14). In this we may note the *dialectical* character of Teilhard's sensibility, and the presence in it of a principle of negation.

[8] Cf. R. d'Ouince, *L'obéissance du Père Teilhard de Chardin* in *L'Homme devant Dieu*, Mélanges offerts au Père de Lubac, Paris (Aubier) 1964, p, 341.

[9] Nevertheless, as we shall see, Teilhard acknowledges the difficulty he found in making contact with others, outside certain privileged relationships. (Letter of 14 August 1917, *Making of a Mind*, p. 202). This spontaneous aversion—common enough, after all, to all of us— was, in any case, overcome; of this Teilhard's whole life gives evidence. At the same time the fact remains that he had a feeling of loneliness. 'So far,' he recognizes, 'not one of my best friends really understands me.' And it may be that the intensity of spiritual or scientific research, his own interior adventure or passionate interest in problems, sometimes obscured for Teilhard the very real suffering of the masses.

This withdrawal should not, however, be taken as indicating a habitual lack of compassion for men. Thus, in a letter describing a murderously costly offensive, Teilhard's first comment is, 'There is something implacable about all this, above all; it seems inanimate. You can see nothing of the agony and passion that gives each little moving human dot its own individual character and makes them all into so many worlds. All you see is the material development of a clash between two huge material masses.' But a few lines later, he goes on to describe the rescuing of the wounded: 'How could we leave these two poor fellows, half-mad with strain, and yet how could we get them away? . . . It's terrible, I can assure you, to be faced with so nerve-racking a dilemma. Finally, we managed with great difficulty, to carry them on our backs, to the shelter of a stranded tank . . . Yet how many other casualties were left lying

there, lost in the middle of those great cornfields, between the lines'
(Letter of 25 July 1918, *Making of a Mind*, p. 219). Later, Teilhard
has this to say about some Chinese peasants: 'They are poor
creatures, with no evil in them, quite defenceless, and their life is
hard. They live in what are no better than dens, have nothing to
eat but cereal pastes and millet—boiled—with a very occasional
dish of rice or corn, hardly ever any meat. It's a movingly pic-
turesque sight to see them travelling dozens of miles behind their
little donkeys, to the coal mines, where they hope to pick up a
hundredweight or two of coal. When you see such things you
understand the strength there can be in a really deeply experienced
feeling of pity' (Letter of 10 February 1924, *Letters from a Traveller*,
p. 111). Again: 'This was real village life, right among the simple
kindly folk, still smiling and unmoved after being plundered at least
twice this year, and spending every night with the threat of a bandit
raid hanging over them: poor things, they had lost nearly all their
livestock and are living off meagre plots of ground, painfully and
precariously saved from erosion' (Letter of 29 July 1926, *ibid.*,
p. 132). 'The population is entirely Moslem. I should like you to
see the women here, so that you could appreciate what our western
civilization has succeeded in winning for their sisters in Europe.
The poor creatures here are prematurely lined, buried in their
veils, and permanently cowed' (Letter to the Abbé Breuil, 21
October 1935, *ibid.*, p. 213). Finally, this war-time comment: 'In
the country, where the organization has broken down, it means
unspeakable misery. And on top of all this, there's the cold. If there
were a recorder of human suffering all over the face of the world
(a very real conception, after all) what would we not have to read
at this very moment!' (Letter of 25 January 1940, *ibid.*, p. 256).

10 'However far back I go in memory (to before the age of ten) I
recognize in myself the existence of one outstandingly dominant
passion: the passion for the Absolute . . . Ever since my childhood,
the need to possess, in everything, "some Absolute" was the axis of
my interior life. In the midst of the delights of that age I was never
happy (this I can remember perfectly clearly) except *in relation* to a
fundamental joy that consisted, generally, in the possession (or the
thought) of some object that was more precious, more rare, more
consistent, more incorruptible. Sometimes it would be some piece
of metal. Sometimes, going to the other extreme, my delight was in

the thought of God the Spirit (at that time the Flesh of our Lord seemed to me something too fragile and too corruptible!)' (*Mon Univers*, 1918, in *Ecrits du temps de la Guerre*, p. 269).

'Consistence—that, undoubtedly, has been for me the fundamental attribute of being' (*Le coeur de la matière*, unpublished, 1950). It is symbolized in Teilhard's passion as a child for stone and iron. 'All my life long, what would irresistibly (even at the expense of palaeontology) bring me back to the study of the great eruptive masses and continental plinths is simply an insatiable need to maintain contact (a contact in communion) with a sort of root or universal matter common to all beings' (*Ibid.*). Tied up with consistence, however, is Teilhard's 'rationalism': his passion for logic, coherence and rational continuity. The spiritual ambiguity of this symbol will be noted: the passion for the absolute is still contained in the impetus of *Eros*, and needs to be converted into, and opened up for, charity.

[11] 'I can recognize this enigmatic and importunate "me" that clings to its love of the front: it is the me of adventure and inquiry, the man who always wants to go to the furthest parts of the world, to see new and strange things, and to be able to say that he is "out in front".' (*La nostalgie du front* in *Etudes*, 20 November 1917, p. 460, and *Ecrits du temps de la Guerre*, p. 205). There is, he wrote, 'a real law or natural duty of pursuing research to the very end . . . Under pain of sin, we must try every road . . . (plumb all things, even since the coming of Our Lord)' (Letter of 4 August 1916, *Making of a Mind*, p. 116).

[12] 'As far as I can remember myself, I have always lived in a forward-looking tension' (Teilhard's comment on himself, quoted by Marguerite Teillard-Chambon—Claude Aragonnès—in the introduction to the *Making of a Mind*, p. 36). 'This appetite, this passion for living . . . this appetite and eagerness to be doing', he says of himself (Letter of 29 June 1916, *ibid.*, p. 106). Already in 1917 Teilhard was even beginning, quoting Blondel in support, to speak of God as the conditon of 'our appetite for action' and of the consistence of 'what our actions produce' (Letter of 13 October 1917, *ibid.*, p. 210). With George Steiner's fine *Tolstoy or Dostoevsky* (London, Faber, 1960 and New York, Knopf) in mind, it would not be unreasonable to include Teilhard in the group of minds represented by the former: a natural spiritual and emotional sound-

ness, optimism, an outlook directed towards the future, a body of work epic in design . . . (Cf. P. H. Simon's article on Steiner's book, in *Le Monde*, 27 November 1963).

[13] 'I've always been nervous about the possibilities the future holds for me—and the war had got rid of that worry for me' (Letter of 28 February 1919, in *Making of a Mind*, pp. 287–8). 'You know . . . how much I feel, at the moment, that the future is *yawning* before me' (Letter of 19 February 1919, *ibid.*, p. 285). '. . . the sort of divineness of the future, the future that is made up of terrifying inevitability, of no less frightening renewal, and at the same time of benign providence that can make itself manifest and modify itself in proportion to the intensity of our faith' (Letter of 17 August 1918, *ibid.*, p. 228). 'Flung into existence, we are forced to advance into a future which terrifies us by its novelty and disheartens us by the "chance" that seems to govern its development. We suffer equally from the *determinist* processes that involve us in their various phases, and from the forbidding indeterminism of chances whose multiplicity and slenderness makes it impossible for us to control them' (Letter of 12 September 1918, *ibid.*, pp. 234–5).

[14] The problem was solved by his attitude of hope, for it is this, in fact, that can give consistence and solidity to a future that is unknown. 'How difficult it is to fling oneself into the future; inevitably our sensibility sees in it only a dizzy void and restless fluidity: to give it solidity, we must have faith, mustn't we?' (Letter of 18 August 1918, *ibid.*, p. 231). 'What is said in the Epistle to the Hebrews, "*fides substantia sperandarum rerum*" may, I think, be translated so: faith is the element that stabilizes and divinizes our future' (Letter of 31 August 1918 *ibid.*, p. 232). ' . . . only God *ahead* and *around—thickening* (if I may use the word) as we advance' (Letter of 4 October 1917, *ibid.*, p. 207).

[15] Small, neat, simple, regular, rapid, controlled (signs of intelligence and mastery), dextrogyrous (a sign of activity directed towards ends to be attained and towards the future); rounded and smooth, and at the same time forceful. The regularity of the lay-out (disposition of text on the sheet), the straightness, vertically, of the margin and, horizontally, of the lines of writing, the carrying of the latter to the extreme edge of the paper, are evidence of the strength of a will that is capable of concentration and perseverance. The joining-up of letters within words (comparatively seldom broken up) is a sign of

mental consistency; his normal proportion of breaks in continuity is a sign of intuition. His sensibility comes through in two ways: in a slight up and down movement of the lines, but more particularly in a pronounced slope (30°–45°), that obviously indicates Teilhard's leaning towards the real and towards others. The initial T of his signature reflects both the strength of his personality and its openness, the final flourish the energy of vitality. Similar comments have been made by J. Mounot (*Analyse graphologique* in Jean Onimus, *Pierre Teilhard de Chardin ou la foi du monde*, Paris, Plon, 1963, pp. 169–73). In particular he finds in his hand signs of ambivalence and of the effort to overcome a feeling of anguish, a contradiction; the introversion he notes seems to indicate no more than richness of interiority and inspiration.

[16] 'It is to her,' wrote Teilhard at the time of his mother's death, 'that I owe all that is best in me' (7 February 1936). 'However unitive, however "communicating" and hence however charged with emotions my coming into contact with, and becoming conscious of, the universe may have been initially, it was bound, if left to itself, never to go beyond quite a moderate degree of intimacy and warmth . . . If the flame was to burst forth, a spark would have to fall on me. And it was, without any doubt, through my mother, and drawn from the main stream of Christian mysticism, that this spark illuminated and inflamed my child soul: it was through that that "my universe", still only *half* personalized, was to find its centre by becoming amorized . . . With my mother's milk, a "supernatural" sense of the divine flowed into me side by side with the "natural" sense of plenitude' (*Le Coeur de la Matière*, unpublished, 1950). It is to this tender maternal influence that we should, perhaps, attribute the co-existence with Teilhard's evident virility (strength, logic, coherence) of a certain feminine side to his soul (emotivity, intuition). The two 'principles', we know, normally exist side by side in the same individual, in the determined proportions.

[17] Teilhard finished his secondary schooling in 1898 and entered the novitiate in 1899, at the time of the Dreyfus affair. It is not difficult to guess the direction in which his own sympathies lay, and those of his fellow-students and teachers. The laws of 1901 were to condemn him to a sad period of exile, not calculated to increase his sympathy with the Republican regime. On the whole, the mentality of the

environment in which he was to live during his formative years was reactionary. It was against the general trend that, at the same time, Père Leroy aud Père Desbuquois, founded in 1903 the *Action Populaire* at Rheims.

[18] This essay was written at Strasbourg, during the opening days of 1919. It was dated (the choice was symbolic) the Epiphany, and sent to Père de Grandmaison on the 10th January.

[19] The influence of the *Spiritual Exercises* followed by Teilhard during his tertianship, in the 'long retreat' (October–November 1914) under the direction of Père Joseph Daniel, was not unconnected with his mystical fervour during the war. This final year of training, which he began on 20 September, and was to last ten months, was interrupted at the beginning of December by Teilhard's being called up, and was never completed.

[20] During his 'juniorate' first at Laval and then in Jersey, Teilhard was taught literature and French by the celebrated Père Longhaye, an excellent teacher and a fine classical scholar, though less receptive to modern literature. These two years of study (Latin, Greek, and French) gave Teilhard a solid intellectual training and developed his literary talent and his taste for writing. His reading of modern authors, however, was strictly controlled and more limited. His *licence*, which he passed at Caen in 1902, in one stage, as was the practice at the time, rounded off this educational period.

Though Teilhard's teachers of philosophy are no longer remembered, his theological teachers, on the other hand, were men of mark: in particular Père Xavier Le Bachelet, a first-rate patristic scholar, Père Albert Condamin, a great biblical expert, and Père Frédéric Bouvier, a specialist in the history of religions. This last, in 1908, succeeded in the chair of apologetics Père de Grandmaison, who had been appointed editor of *Etudes*. It was in this same year that Teilhard started his theological studies and was chosen for a formal defence of theses, an indication of the esteem in which his teachers held him and of his knowledge of scholastic disciplines.

[21] A year before Teilhard started his theology, the young Père Auguste Valensin, his fellow-student, was writing in his notes: 'Under the influence of an unwholesome rationalism, of an extravagant intellectualism, we have gradually become accustomed to see in faith no more than the mind's adherence to a truth. We have been frightened of the least appearance of Protestantism and, in

order to lessen the risk of swallowing-up faith in trust, we have denied that trust forms part of faith . . . We should be careful not to whittle it down to the point where it appears, to the eyes of the soul, with no more than the beggarly scantiness of a purely intellectual process' (*Textes et documents inédits*, Paris, Aubier, 1961, p. 53).

[22] Meanwhile, the biblical account of creation was being interpreted in a more or less literal way, and theories of evolution were regarded as materialism. Until his first contact with the thought of Bergson, Teilhard was to remain a believer in fixed species. As C. E. Raven has said, while Catholicism in France had had other subjects of controversy, the controversy between science and religion that had been started by Darwin in Great Britain found little echo in France (*Teilhard de Chardin, Scientist and Seer*, London, Collins, 1962, p. 33).

[23] *La Montée de l'autre*, 1942, in *L'activation de l'énergie*, p. 77. Père H. Bouillard, too, points out the shortcomings of normal teaching at that time on the fact of the 'supernatural'. It was expounded in an abstract, formal, way with insufficient attention on the one hand to man's ill-defined yearning and his liberty of assent, and on the other to Christ's mediation. 'The habit has been retained of concentrating in treatises on the Incarnation and Redemption all that we wish to say about Christ: until fairly recent times, no attempt has been made to introduce it into a wider field' (*L'idée de surnaturel et le mystère chrétien*, in *L'homme devant Dieu*, Mélanges offerts au Père de Lubac, Paris, Aubier, 1964, pp. 153-66).

More generally, Teilhard was to get over the difficulty caused by too narrow a concept of man: 'For a long time, like everyone else, I was nearly smothered by the antiquated habit of regarding Man as an anomaly in Nature . . . But now that my eyes have been opened . . . I can say that I have found myself and can breathe again, in the feeling, now at last vindicated, that I simply form one with all the rest' (*L'étoffe de l'univers*, 1953, in *L'activation de l'énergie*, p. 400).

[24] The only symbols he retained were, apparently: Elias's ascent to heaven in the fiery chariot (2 Kings 2:11-14) (*The spiritual power of matter*, 1919, in *Hymn of the Universe*, p. 59); Jacob's battle during the night with God (Gen. 32:23-33); and the Burning Bush scene. In April 1923, when he was passing close by Sinai, Teilhard wrote: 'I should have liked to land on those rocky slopes, not only to test them with my hammer, but also to find out whether I too could hear the

voice from the Burning Bush. But has not the moment gone when God spoke in the desert, and must we not now understand that "He who is" is not to be heard in this place or that, for the heights where he dwells are not inaccessible mountains but some more profound sphere of things? The secret of the world lies wherever we can discern the transparency of the universe' (Letter of 15 April 1923, *Letters from a Traveller*, p. 66). Teilhard also used the metaphor of the spark that is kindled in the reeds, *scintilla in arundineto* (Wisdom 3:7). It may well be that the symbol, of capital importance in his writing, of *fire*, came to him, as it did to Pascal, from the Bible; it is less certain that the Old Testament is the source of another symbol, no less important in Teilhard, that of the *hard* and *solid*. In connexion with the problem of evil, he introduces the figure of Job (*Le Milieu Divin*, p. 87). However that may be, he was very alive to the hope of Israel: 'Historically speaking, that hope has never ceased to guide the progress of our faith like a torch. The Israelites were continually "expectant"—and the first Christians too' (*Le Milieu Divin*, p. 151).

[25] It is all the more interesting to note that Teilhard's correspondence shows his aversion for the views of Maurras and Daudet—and that, later, his reaction to the Vichy regime was clear-sighted and sensible (Cf. Letters of 12 July 1940 and 20 November 1940 to his cousin, *Letters from a Traveller*, pp. 264, 267).

[26] The expression is not too strong, in view of the fact that up to that time Teilhard had been practically cut off from the world: he entered the novitiate almost immediately after leaving school, was then excused military service, and was away in England (this had serious disadvantages) for his studies. The only breaks were his three years of teaching (though these were spent in Cairo) and two years studying science in Paris (1912–14).

[27] 'Yes, the moral and social development of mankind is indeed the authentic and "natural" consequence of organic evolution . . . All moral perversions are found in embryo in the most "natural" of activities, the most passive (in appearance) in the hands of the first Cause; they are tamed therein, but not by-passed, nor surmounted, nor overcome' (Letter of 10 July 1916, *Making of a Mind*, p. 111).

[28] 'Activity culminates in a sort of intense but completely calm paroxysm, which dilates it to the scale of the vast work in which it is playing its part' (Letter of 23 September 1917, *ibid.*, p. 204). 'The

front has an irresistible attraction, because it is, in one way, the *extreme boundary* between what one is already aware of, and what is still in process of formation. Not only do you see there things that you see nowhere else, but you see emerge from within you an underlying stream of clarity, energy and freedom that is to be found hardly anywhere else in ordinary life' (Letters of 25 September 1919, *ibid.*, p. 205). See also the article, quoted above, *La Nostalgie du front*.

²⁹ Against the pessimism of his friend Boussac, who refused to link together the silent nobility of nature's transformations and the war-time brutality of men, Teilhard brought forward the optimistic vision of a universal continuity in progress (Letter of 10 July 1916, *Making of a Mind*, p. 110). Later, he thought that the front 'isn't simply the firing line; the exposed area corroded by the conflict of nations, but the "front of the wave" carrying the world of man towards its new destiny. When you look at it at night, lit up by flares, after a day of more than usual activity, you seem to feel that you're at the final boundary between what has already been achieved and what is striving to emerge' (Letter of 23 September 1917, *ibid.*, pp. 203–4).

From this angle, he speaks of the horror of war with a certain detachment. Thus he refers to the coming recapture of Douaumont as 'a magnificent, an almost fantastic exploit which will make and symbolize a definite world advance in the liberation of souls. And, I can tell you this—I shall go into this engagement in a religious spirit, with all my soul, borne along by a single great impulse in which I am unable to distinguish where human emotions end and adoration begins' (*Christ in the world of matter*, 1916, in *Hymn of the Universe*, p. 55). Similarly, he was later quite unmoved when he witnessed a huge forest fire in Annam that burnt up vegetation and animals. 'I realize that another era of the world is beginning and I believe that the new forms of life are more interesting than the old' (Letter of May or June 1926, *Letters from a Traveller*, p. 125).

At the same time we should remember that Teilhard's comparative silence in the face of human suffering arose from a very cogent sense of moderation in the expression of his feelings.

³⁰ 'I greatly admired the view of the castle you sent me. It seems to me like a proud affirmation of the need for an "élite", which is, I believe, one of the most decisive and enduring convictions I've

acquired from my experience in recent years. None but a race of men, strong and conscious of having outstripped their fellows, could have conceived and built those towers, proudly poised on the rock, overlooking the torrent. The whole difficulty (and secret) of real democracy is to encourage the renewal and the recruitment of the élite, and to make inclusion in it as universal as possible. But, *in itself*, the mass of humanity is profoundly inferior and repulsive. Don't you find it so?' (Letter of 8 September 1918, *Making of a Mind*, pp. 232–3). This aristocratic attitude, in a sense justifiable, but nevertheless somewhat crude, did not prevent Teilhard from forming friendships with humble folk: 'The war brought me, in the regiment, a group of unassuming and open-hearted friendships, in an atmosphere of complete disinterestedness and devotion, that I doubt whether I'll ever find again' (Letter of 12 February 1919, *ibid.*, p. 282).

[31] 'Reading Richet's article on alcoholism (I haven't yet read P. Bureau's on the fall in the birth-rate), I was greatly struck by the fact that it's necessary for so many people to be kept in or brought back to healthy and good conditions and ways *by force*. In the case of religion, of course, which calls for interior assent, and in which the things one can be certain of do not belong to the experiential order, the use of constraint is a matter of infinite delicacy . . . in any case, I am more and more convinced that mankind is not yet ripe (if it ever will be!) to be led by reason, and that for a long time still the masses will need to be kept on leading strings' (Letter of 10 July 1916, *Making of a Mind*, pp. 108–9).

'What will enable us to avoid a revolution and class warfare (at least in the immediate future), will be the joy with which the *poilus* will fall back into the pattern of familiar work and the new ardour with which most of them will throw themselves into it again' (*Ibid.*, p. 110). This is just an innocent simplicity of mind, or pure illusion —and precisely in relation to the social problems raised by work. In contrast to this, Teilhard showed a boldness that was unusual for his time in encouraging his cousin to adopt educational methods that allowed more freedom to the children. In practice, it is true, he restricted their application: 'there will always be a high proportion of unformed or defective minds that need to be *forced* into *the mould of truth*' (Letter of 18 September 1916, *ibid.*, p. 128).

[32] 'I'm interested at the liveliness of the feelings I'm experiencing in

myself of injured "right", of the *injustice* suffered, etc. There must be many hearts in the world—legions of them—grievously torn by revolt; and it must be doubly intolerable to feel that no one cares, that you can't expect consideration from any one, that there's nothing you can do. What a burden it must be for those who haven't the comfort of resigning themselves to God while waiting for some slow, laborious improvement in men and their selfishness' (Letter of 12 March 1917, *ibid.*, p. 187). Coming from an aristocrat like Teilhard, this passage is a very just and forceful diagnosis of the lot of the proletariat.

[33] Letter of 25 January 1917, *ibid.*, p. 174.

[34] Letter of 4 October 1917, *ibid.*, pp. 207–8.

[35] 'The new form that the soul then takes on is that of the individual living the quasi-collective life of all men, fulfilling a function far higher than that of the individual, and becoming fully conscious of this new state' (Letter of 25 September 1917, *ibid.*, p. 205).

[36] 'In spite of the friendliness I meet with everywhere, in spite of the peace and freedom I enjoy more and more, I don't like my new position. It doesn't *carry me with it*, it doesn't *bear me up* . . . I feel useless, a passenger. I assure you that I'd a thousand times rather be throwing grenades or handling a machine-gun than be a supernumerary as I am now. What I'm going to say may not be very orthodox—and yet I believe there's a core of truth in it: I feel that doing so I'd be more a priest. Isn't a priest a man who has to bear the burden of life in all its forms, and show by his own life how human work and love of God can be combined?' (Letter of 15 February 1917, *ibid.*, p. 183).

[37] 'So great was for me the fascination of the Impersonal and the Generalized' (*Le Coeur de la matière*, unpublished, 1950).

[38] Cf. J. Onimus, *op. cit.*, p. 50, note.

[39] 'In this very special situation, at the frontiers of two worlds, I found some exceptional friends to clarify my thought' (*Mon Univers*, unpublished, 1924). 'Through the influence of gifted friends who entered my life at certain moments to bring light and strength to my mind . . .' (*Mass on the World*, 1923, in *Hymn of the Universe*, pp. 25–6). 'One by one, Lord, I see and I love those whom you have given me to sustain and charm my life. One by one also I number all those who make up that other beloved family which has gradually surrounded me, its unity fashioned out of the most disparate

elements, with affinities of the heart, of scientific research and of thought' (*Ibid.*, p. 19).

40 Teilhard's close friendship with Auguste Valensin went back no further than 1919. Valensin was two years the older, and began his theology in 1903, in England. In 1908 he was sent for a rest to the theological house of studies of the German Fathers, at Valkenburg, just when Teilhard was arriving for his four years at Hastings. Brilliantly gifted, and with the advantage of never having been called up for military service, in 1918 Père Valensin's wide culture placed him well ahead of Teilhard. 'I feel that in Valensin I've indeed found a sure friend, all the more sure in that, with all his warm personal and intellectual sympathy he isn't quite at one with me' (Letter of 2 August 1919, *Making of a Mind*, p. 298). 'I hope that on the essential point we'll be in agreement: he admits in fact that the universe forms one natural whole, which finally can subsist only by dependence from our Lord. That's the main thing: and I think that, following on from that, we'll be able to part company only on questions of emphasis or shading. I can tell you, I was most surprised to find my friend so categorical on this point, and with such a predominant interest, too, in pantheism. With him, I believe, it's primarily an intellectual problem: what impels him is more, I think, the need to formulate a philosophy than the urgency of venerating an omnipresence. Even that, however, has the advantage that each of us complements the other' (Letter of 8 August 1919, *ibid.*, p. 300). Finally, after Père Valensin's death, Teilhard wrote: 'It was he who taught me to think. I could tell him everything and, without expressing it often, we loved one another deeply' (Letter of 5 January 1954, *Letters from a Traveller*, p. 348).

41 Teilhard's correspondence tells us something about Père Charles. 'I had a letter from my friend Père Charles, at Louvain, who is on the road to becoming an important figure in his own country. He told me that, for his part, he has succeeded in defining some ideas that he believes to be 'liberalizing', and wishes that we could meet soon. I am just as anxious for the meeting to take place: Père Charles is more of a theologian than I am, and more practical; he could give me valuable advice and strong moral support' (Letter of 5 March 1919, *Making of a Mind*, p. 289). After a conversation with Père Charles, at the beginning of August in the same year, Teilhard writes to his cousin: 'We agreed to keep in touch regularly.

And then, as I've long been thinking, we decided that the best way to spread our views was to start, first of all, from theology, from Scripture, from the Church's mystical practice. That's the basic foundation, the firmest, that all the philosophies can do no more than illustrate with more or less accuracy' (Letter of 31 August 1919. *ibid.*, p. 302). As a direct result of the development of his scientific thought, Teilhard was somewhat neglectful of this rule: his starting point was to be his reflexions on the history of the cosmos. Finally in 1954, he wrote: 'First there was our wonderful Auguste Valensin (a most beautiful death, almost childlike, calling on the sun and God at the same time . . .) then my other friend, who first opened my eyes, has also gone, Pierre Charles: he too must have ended with simplicity and style' (Letter of 28 February 1954, *ibid.*, p. 350).

[42] 'While reaching a more precise definition of my points of contact with my friends, I have also come to realize the turn of my mind that divides me from them. I'm less concerned than they are with the metaphysical side of things, with what might have been or might not have been, with abstract conditions of existence: all that seems to me inevitably misleading and shaky. I realize that, to the very marrow of my bones, I'm sensitive to the real, to what is made of it. My concern is to discover the conditions for such progress as is open to us, and not, starting from first principles, some theoretical development of the universe. This bias means that I'll always be a philistine to the professional philosophers; but I feel that my strength lies in the fidelity with which I follow it. So I'll continue to advance along these lines. Others will bring me into line with the principles, if they can' (Letter of 21 August 1919, *Making of a Mind*, p. 302).

[43] In 1910 Père de Grandmaison arranged for Teilhard, who was then one of his theological students, to attend a Catholic palaeontological congress in Belgium. In 1916 he wrote him a letter, from which Teilhard quotes several passages: 'Without disguising the difficulties of publishing anything that deals with the questions that interest me, he warmly encourages me to "integrate within Christian philosophy (even negatively such, that is, compatible with the Christian life) the results, suggestions, and interpretations, even hypothetical, that guide modern scientists". To do this "would be to render an immense service, one that a life would be well spent in". So you see that, fundamentally, I am understood and en-

couraged' (Letter of 28 December 1916, *Making of a Mind*, p. 157).[44]
In his well-known *The Intellectualism of Saint Thomas*) London, Sneed
& Ward, 1935). The kinship between this and the theories of
Maurice Blondel is an indication that the latter were beginning, in
spite of some resistance, to get through to Jesuit houses of study.

[45] On Père Victor Fontoynont, see an important note by Père H.
de Lubac, *The Religion of Teilhard de Chardin.*, appendix 1, p. 241.

[46] 'The great Bergson', Teilhard calls him in 1915 (Letter of 5–6
August 1915, *Making of a Mind*, p. 62). 'I can remember the eagerness with which I read *Creative Evolution* at that time . . . I can see
quite clearly that the effect on me of those burning pages was simply
to fan a flame that was already devouring my heart and mind'
(*Le Coeur de la Matière*, unpublished, 1950). 'While, in *Creative
Evolution*, the cosmos is seen as an irradiation that spreads as it bursts
from a centre, the picture of the universe given by creative union is
that of a compression, a confluence from some infinitely expanded
sphere. Each of these theories, both evolutionary, is the converse
of the other (*L'union créatrice*, 1917, in *Ecrits du temps de la Guerre*,
p. 179). In Teilhard's thought, says Claude Cuénot, Bergson acted
as a 'catalyst' ('*Situation de Teilhard de Chardin*', *Bulletin de la Société
Industrielle de Mulhouse*, No. 712, 111-1963).

[47] Auguste Valensin 'told me that Blondel has such strong views
on the consistence of the universe in Christ that he doesn't dare go
all the way with him—even though, he added, Rousselot didn't
hesitate to do so. I wasn't familiar with that side of Blondel's
thought, and I'm going to try to learn more about it' (Letter of
8 August 1919, *Making of a Mind*, p. 300). 'I had been in touch
(through Auguste Valensin) with Blondel for about a year (just
after the first war, about 1920). Some aspects of his thought undoubtedly affected me greatly: the value of action (which has
become for me a sort of semi-experimental energetics of the biological forces of evolution) and the notion of "pan-Christism"
(which I had arrived at independently but without daring, at the
time, to give it so appropriate a name)' (Letters of 15 February
1955, quoted by C. Cuénot, *op. cit.*, pp. 55–6).

[48] The revival of Hegelian and Marxist studies in France dates,
moreover, only from about 1930.

[49] Mgr. R. H. Benson's apocalyptic novels, Duhamel's *La possession
du Monde*, P. Bourget's *Le sens de la mort*, H. G. Wells' novels, C.

Farrère's *Histoires de guerre*, L. Daudet's *Salons et journaux*, H. Barbusse's *Under Fire* . . . Teilhard was not sparing, moreover, in his criticism of most of these. Nevertheless, one cannot but wonder a little when one sees a story by Benson suggesting the meditation *Christ in the World of Matter*. More profitable, it is true, was his reading of such works as Dante's *Divine Comedy*, Stendhal's *La Chartreuse de Parme*, Fromentin's *Dominique*, B. Constant's *Adolphe*, and Kipling's stories. Although the mysticism of Schuré's *Grands initiés* is questionable, it is still not without interest. Teilhard's reading, moreover, was always intelligent and selective. He looked constantly for what would serve his purpose and noted anything that coincided with his own thought. Thus he was glad to find in Wells and Kipling a mystical attitude to human effort (Letters of 5 and 14 January 1919, *Making of a Mind*, pp. 273, 277-9). We may note, too: 'I've just received your Plato, and even looking through a few pages has set my feeling for the spirit "vibrating" in me' (Letter of 11 October 1918, *ibid.*, p. 245).

[50] 'Today, after forty years of constant reflexion, it is still exactly the same fundamental vision that I feel the need to set forth and to share, in its mature form, for the last time' (March 1955, quoted in *Le Milieu Divin*, p. 155).

[51] It was during my theology years in Hastings (that is immediately after the marvels of Egypt) that there gradually grew in me—much less as an abstract notion than as a presence—until it filled my whole interior climate, the consciousness that all around me flowed the deep, all-embracing, ontological drift of the universe' (*Le Coeur de la Matière*).

[52] J. Madaule, *Initiation à Teilhard de Chardin* (Paris, Editions du Cerf, 1963, pp. 23-6). It may, however, be going too far to say that 'it was in the first place by coming up against the feminine that Teilhard was led to the person, in its aspect of being strictly individual and irreplaceable' (p. 25). Numerous human contacts, in his family and with friends, had already done that for him. In 1950, Teilhard was to pay 'a general tribute, almost with worship' to 'those women whose warmth and charm passed drop by drop into the blood of (his) most cherished ideas'. (*Le Coeur de la Matière*). 'Nothing,' he said, 'has developed in me except under the watchful gaze and influence of woman.'

[53] Teilhard's first year in the army was marked by an intellectual

quiescence; it was some mysterious affinity between himself and the Flanders countryside that roused him. 'You can't imagine what charm I find, looking back on it, in that time by the dunes and the Yser, which brought so lively a reawakening of the urge to think and write, dormant since a year of war. To find a comparable harmony (and reciprocal influence) of place and self, I think I'd have to go back in my past as far as the happy days when I felt the intoxication of the desert' (Letter of 1 January 1917, *Making of a Mind*, p. 159).

54 (Letter of 17 April 1923, *Letters from a Traveller*, pp. 66–7). Teilhard was to remember this war period as an 'intellectual honeymoon'.

55 'For the last two years in particular, I have had the feeling of being gradually drawn to the study of Mankind, not prehistoric man, but man of today. I am coming more and more to see Man as *the great terrestrial phenomenon*, that in which the greatest geological events and the most massive movements of life reach their peak. In other words, I am discovering human extensions of geology' (Letter of 31 December 1926).

56 'Until 1935, in the brief *Credo* placed at the head of *Comment je crois* (and even though that essay itself is explicitly based, as an argument, on the phenomenon of man) the word *Man* does not appear. Today I would say: . . . I believe that Evolution progresses towards the Spirit. I believe that Spirit, in *Man*, attains its fulfilment in the personal. Just one added touch, but it is enough to take us unmistakably out of metaphysics into the historic, the biological, the planetary' (*Le Coeur de la matière*). We should correct this remark on two points. The essay *Comment je crois* dates from 1934, and a number of indications show, in fact, that Teilhard post-dates by four or five years his awakening to the importance of the *person* as the type of being.

57 Already in 1919 Teilhard was saying, 'The future is finer than any past' (Letter of 5 September 1919, *Making of a Mind*, p. 306). And in 1923, 'I'd like, within a descriptive framework, to get across this idea that historical and geographical research is, in itself, empty and deceptive, the true science being that of the future as gradually disclosed by life itself' (Letter of 30 September 1923, *Letters from a Traveller*, p. 90). We find a similar passage in a letter of October, *ibid.*, p. 101: 'I am a pilgrim of the future, on my way back from a

journey made entirely in the past. But isn't the past, viewed from a certain angle, transformable into future? . . . is not my whole life as a palaeontologist sustained by the single hope of co-operating in a forward march?'

[58] In a letter to the Very Revd. Fr. Jansens, General of the Society of Jesus (12 October 1951, quoted by Père Leroy in *Letters from a Traveller*, p. 43), Teilhard writes, 'obviously I cannot abandon my own personal quest—that would involve me in an interior catastrophe and in disloyalty to my most cherished vocation; but (and this has been true for many months) I have ceased to propagate my ideas and am confining myself to achieving a deeper personal insight into them'. He goes on to say that the Wenner-Gren foundation has asked him to extend his stay in America: 'They want me to classify and develop the data obtained from my work in Africa. All this allows me a breathing space and gives a purely scientific orientation to the end of my career . . . and of my life.'

[59] *An intimate picture of Teilhard*

Teilhard's interior life lies outside the scope of the present study and has, moreover, been excellently treated by Père Henri de Lubac, in particular in his *La Prière du Père Teilhard de Chardin* (Paris, Fayard, 1964: English trans. *The Faith of Teilhard de Chardin*, London, 1965). Nevertheless, in order to fill out the objective picture given in this chapter, we may be allowed to suggest a more intimate, and so far little appreciated, aspect of the man.

First, there was the Teilhard who *suffered*, and at times expressed his feeling of bafflement and intense distress. On the day, for example, when he learnt that he must give up his teaching at the Institut Catholique, he wrote: 'So it's happened: I'm to be taken away from Paris. Do what you can, my dear friend, to help me a little. I haven't shown my feelings, but, inside me, it's something like real agony, a real storm . . . I can see that if I were to cut myself off or rebel, I should be disloyal to my faith that everything that happens is animated by Our Lord, and that He is worth more than anything that goes to make up this world' (Letter of 16 May 1925). And shortly afterwards: 'Pray that whatever happens I may not allow myself to desire anything else but the Fire' (30 May).

It is hardly surprising, again, that, like many mystics, Teilhard should have experienced the pain, even though it may have been transitory, of a sort of dark night of the soul. 'I've lost all interest in myself. If only Our Lord would give me a more concrete and more "consoled" faith in what lies at the end of life! . . . I feel that none of his harshness would distress me much so long as I *know* that he *exists*. But, for years, I have been living in the shadow of the fear of *not meeting him* in the end, the real *Him* . . . All I can do is to press on, blindly trusting in "being" ' (23 March 1930). Later, he repeats this confession: '*Advesperascit* (evening is at hand). If only, ahead of me, in the beyond, I could see more light! . . . But I think it is my fate (and perhaps my vocation) to have, and suffer from, this consciousness of a leap in the dark. My greatest comfort is the thought that I have always done my best to serve the Power that draws us into itself' (25 May 1938).

We should remember, too, Teilhard's steadfastness. A letter of 15 July 1929 speaks of the end of an interior crisis and his firm determination never to break with the Church and the Society of Jesus: 'I am conscious of feeling myself fundamentally bound to both, for new and even more cogent reasons—by which I mean that I believe I would be betraying "the World", if I deserted the post I have been assigned to. In this sense, I love them both, and I want to work, as an individual atom, to perfect them *from within*, with no trace of antagonism. You may be quite certain that the very idea of taking steps to leave the order has never even crossed my mind' (see note 69, Chapter 7).

The Teilhard, again, who was enamoured of the deepest essence of Christianity. Commonly presented as an enthusiast for the energies of the natural world and for the active life, he yet wrote, on the day after the death of his sister Marguerite, who had long been an invalid, 'O Marguerite, my sister, while I, in my devotion to the positive forces of the Universe, was roaming over continents and oceans, you, stretched out motionless on your bed of sickness, were silently transforming into light the most grievous shadows of the world. Tell me, in the eyes of the creator, which of us will have chosen the better part?'

And two days before his own death, on Good Friday, 8 April 1955, he wrote: 'In all history man has found no more powerful spiritual motive force than the crucified God.' (See the passages quoted in notes 63–7, Chapter 7.)

Finally, there was the Teilhard to whom we cannot deny the name of mystic, since he often had an extra-normal experience of

God and lived in an intimate friendship with Christ. 'Lord, enfold me in the depths of your heart, and there hold me, refine, purge and set me on fire, raise me aloft, until my own self knows utter annihilation.' And again, during a retreat: 'Jesus alone, only Jesus. I must be entirely dependent on him, in what I do, and even in my passion for him. Lord Jesus, I accept possession by You and the guidance of the inexpressible power of your Body, to which I shall be bound, towards solitary places whither I should never have dared, alone, to climb.'

CHAPTER 2: THE INTUITION AND THE PROJECT

[1] 'Everything finally concentrates on one single point to which, even though one might almost despair of so doing, one could approach more and more closely. In this point there is something simple, infinitely simple, so extraordinarily simple that no philosopher has ever succeeded in expressing it. That is why his whole life has been spent in talking about it. He could not put into words what was in his mind without feeling obliged to correct what he said; in correcting himself, while thinking that he was completing his expression, all he has done, in his added complication and in developments presented side by side with other developments, is to give the simplicity of his original intuition with increasing approximation. The whole complexity of his teaching is thus no more than the incommensurability between his simple intuition and the means he has of expressing it' (*L'intuition philosophique*, 1911, in *La pensée et le mouvant*, p. 137). Teilhard lived this intuitive unity. 'The whole of my thoughts and tastes, developed throughout so many pages of writing, seems to me more and more to be concentrated on one point, on one attitude, both extremely simple and fruitful: they come down in the end to a very small thing—and it's a thing that brings me a solution and consolation for everything (Letter of 30 July 1918, *Making of a Mind*, p. 223).

[2] '. . . a man who believes himself to feel deeply in tune with his own times' (*Le Milieu Divin*, p. 46).

[3] 'Until the sixteenth century men in general thought of space and time as though they were *limited* compartments in which objects were *juxtaposed* and *interchangeable*. They believed that a geo-

metrical envelope could be traced round the totality of the stars. They talked, thinking they understood, of a first and last moment discernible in the past and the future. They argued as though every element could be arbitrarily moved, without changing the world, to any point along the axis of time. The human mind believed itself to be perfectly at home in this universe, within which it tranquilly wove its patterns of metaphysics . . .' (*The grand option*, 1939, in the *Future of Man*, p. 48). In his *Introduction au Christianisme*, unpublished, 1944, Teilhard refers again to 'the strictly circumscribed, centred and neatly balanced cosmos of the ancients'. 'The universe was constructed in accordance with a qualitative hierarchy of increasing perfections, majestically rising from low to high, in which man occupied his central position: so much so, that the cosmos, filled with visible finalities, was a sort of perpetual feast that nature seemed to offer to man, as though in recognition of his sovereignty' (Etienne Borne, *De Pascal à Teilhard de Chardin*, Edit. de Bussac, Clermont-Ferrand, 1963, p. 37).

[4] *Le néo-humanisme et ses réactions sur le christianisme* (notes taken at a lecture to chaplains of the *Action catholique ouvrière*, Versailles, 21 September 1948, unpublished). *Un phénomène de contre-évolution en biologie humaine, ou la peur de l'existence*, 1949, in *L'activation de l'énergie*, p. 187. 'Formerly man had the illusion of living "out in the open" in a universe that was penetrable and transparent' in which 're-ciprocity between heaven and earth was natural'. 'The sight of the inhabited earth . . . had in it something inoffensive and soothing.' Man felt at home (*Ibid.*, pp. 192, 195).

[5] The history of the transformation of man's consciousness is sum-marized in the article *Du cosmos à la cosmogénèse*, 1951 (*L'activation de l'énergie*, pp. 261–5). The Galilean release (*lysis*) in the sixteenth and seventeenth centuries; the appearance in human thought of the first germs of evolution (eighteenth and nineteenth centuries); the emergence in our own days of the idea of evolution. Mankind's 'change of age' is described at the beginning of the chapter on 'The modern earth' in *The Phenomenon of Man*, pp. 213–15: it involves economic, industrial and social changes, with a trans-formation of consciousness.

[6] 'God no longer stands immediately above man: in between there is now an intermediate grandeur, with its accompaniment of promises and duties. While still remaining in the World, man now

finds that above him there lies something greater than himself, something that can, in a way, be "adored". I believe that we may trace the source of today's uneasiness to the appearance of this new star that draws to itself the religious energies of the world. To that, in any case, we may certainly attribute the irresistible rise of the great myths (communism, nationalism) whose emergence and impact are rocking the foundations of our ancient civilization. It is now not just a matter of mere heresies within Christianity but of what appears to be an entirely new religion in opposition to Christianity, that threatens to sweep everything away. We might call it the temptation on the mountain, but it is an infinitely subtle form of that temptation, since it no longer, at this present moment, involves adoration prompted by sensual enjoyment, but a disinterested domination, that quite certainly generates spiritual forces. It is charity replaced, in the consciousness of men, by the sense of the earth' (*La parole attendue*, in *Cahiers Pierre Teilhard de Chardin*, No. 4, p. 24).

'By structural necessity, a struggle was raging in the very depth of my soul (note: and, more widely, I am certain, in that of *every* modern soul) between the God of the Above and a sort of new God of the Ahead, which arose from the permanent co-existence and irresistible meeting in my heart of the cosmic sense and the Christic sense' (*Le coeur de la matière*, unpublished, 1950).

[7] *Note pour servir à l'evangélisation des temps nouveaux*, 1919, in *Ecrits du temps de la guerre*, p. 369. 'In taking on a sort of natural unity throughout duration, the world is not only acquiring one more dimension in the eyes of intellectual research, it is taking shape too, over against the human individual, as an object of higher value and dignity, to which it is clear he must submit and devote himself. With the irresistible magnetism of an immensity that is close at hand and tangible, it stimulates to resonance within us the strings, ever ready to vibrate, of adoration' (Answer to a questionnaire on modern reasons for unbelief, in *La vie intellectuelle*, 25 October 1933, in *Science et Christ*, p. 150).

'In a few generations Mankind has been literally *converted*, spontaneously, to a new sort of Religion of the World, ill-defined in dogma, but perfectly clear in its moral orientations. These are: the predominance accorded to the whole over the individual; a passionate faith in the value and potentialities of human effort; a very lively awareness of the sacred character of research *along every line*' (*Ibid.*, p. 151).

[8] *La route de l'Ouest*, unpublished, 1932. 'There is already a general realization that the universal turbulence, far from being an incoherent dream, disguises and paves the way to, a divine advent' (*Ibid.*). 'We have become conscious of the unitary magnitude of the cosmos and of the organic significance of time . . . in future we can see that the world has both past and future, in other words that it has growth' (*Science et Christ*, p. 150). 'The universe is not simply without end, spatially. It now reaches back limitlessly in all its constituent fibres, at the behest of a cosmogenesis that is constantly progressing' (*Christologie et évolution*, unpublished, 1933). 'Hitherto men have been living at once dispersed and closed in on themselves, like passengers who have met by chance in the hold of a ship without the least idea of its mobile nature or of the fact that it is moving. Living, therefore, on the earth that grouped them together, they could think of nothing better to do than quarrel among themselves or try to amuse themselves. And now, by chance, or rather by the normal effect of the passage of time, our eyes have just been opened. The boldest of us have made their way to the deck, and seen the ship that carried us. They have noted the creaming of the bow-wave. They have realized that there are boilers to be fed and a wheel to be manned. Above all, they have seen the clouds above them and smelt the fragrance of the islands over the circle of the horizon. The picture of men ceaselessly in agitation over the same spot has gone; this is no longer an aimless drifting, it is a *passage to be made good*. It is inevitable that some *other* sort of Mankind must emerge from that vision' (*La montée de l'autre*, 1942, in *L'activation de l'énergie*).

'If they wish to speak in language that will be understood by and, what is more important, will be convincing to our contemporaries, then the theoreticians of Christianity must understand, and accept, and love the new idea that man has been scientifically brought to the point where he builds himself by his own efforts. At an initial stage, this idea is the idea of an organic and genetic dependence that links Mankind directly to the rest of the world. Man is born, and grows historically, in dependence on the whole of matter and the whole of life . . . He is not born as an individual alone but *as a species*. We must therefore recognize in man not only the cycle of the individual but, beyond that, the cycle of the species, too. Through its axial, living, portion the universe is moving, simultaneously and in exactly the same way, towards super-complexity, the super-centre, super-consciousness (*Le Christ évoluteur ou un développement logique de la notion de rédemption,* unpublished, 1942).

'In addition to the space that mesmerized Pascal, we now have time: not a time that is simply a container in which years are stored side by side, but an organic time, measured by the development of global reality. Formerly, we used to look on ourselves and the things around us, as self-contained points. Now we see that beings are like insubstantial fibres woven into a universal process. Everything sinks back into the boundless depths of the past, and everything is flung into the boundless depths of the future. In its history, every being is coextensive with the whole of duration: and its ontogenesis is nothing but an infinitesimal element of a cosmogenesis in which the individuality—the face, I might say—of the universe is finally expressed' (*Du cosmos à la cosmogénèse,* unpublished, 1951).

[9] *Contingence de l'univers et goût de survivre,* unpublished, 1953. 'Until the dawn of the modern era, the problem of salvation, for man, could be formulated in only two terms, man's existence on earth and his final end, the brief years of his life and eternity: the human individual and God. Between the two there was nothing . . . Now man has simultaneously become conscious both of the almost incredible resources that have been accumulated in the human mass, and of the possibilities open to this energy for the *construction* of a concrete body of work for which nature has been waiting' (*La parole attendue,* 1950, in *Cahiers Pierre Teilhard de Chardin,* No. 4, p. 24).

'The centre of gravity of our most concrete interests has been forced almost an infinite distance ahead of us' under the compulsion 'of a total work that has to be accomplished' (*L'atomisme de l'esprit: un essai pour comprendre la structure et l'étoffe de l'univers,* 1941, in *L'activation de l'énergie,* p. 49).

'Man is dedicated to a common task, a task that we may call sacred—the idea that there is work to be finished and that in the effort to do so all men must be as one' (Third lecture to the Marcel Légaut group, 10 December 1930).

[10] In every field of research and discovery—medicine, flying, mountaineering, polar exploration—the risks taken by men are

evidence of this. 'Men give their lives that things may become better, that they may advance, that there may be some progress' (Third lecture to the Marcel Légaut group, 10 December 1930). 'They answer the call to co-operate in a great victory that is bigger than themselves' (*Le sens humain*, unpublished, 1929).

[11] *Ibid.*

[12] *Christologie et évolution*, unpublished, 1933.

[13] *Barrière de la mort et co-réflexion*, 1935 (in *L'activation de l'énergie*, p. 420). 'Thought on earth becoming conscious that it forms an organized whole, with the attribute of growth, capable of realizing, and responsible for, some future' (*Le sens humain*, unpublished, 1929). 'Mankind was at first a vague entity, felt rather than thought out, in which an obscure feeling of perpetual growth was allied to a need for universal fraternity. Mankind was the object of a faith that was often naive but whose magic, being stronger than all vicissitudes and criticisms, goes on working with persuasive force upon the present-day masses and on the intelligentsia alike. Whether one takes part in the cult or derides it, even today no one can escape being haunted or even dominated by the idea of mankind' (*The Phenomenon of Man*, p. 245).

[14] *Réflexions sur la probabilité scientifique*, in *L'activation de l'énergie*, p. 289.

[15] 'Puffed-up by a new ebullition of energies and desires, the modern world—disappointed and yet only too ready to take on some new form—is suffering and deeply disturbed by the need to adopt some spiritual orientation. Forcibly brought back to the initial sources of action, it is seeking for the essential idea and ideal that are necessary to enable it to reach unanimity' (*La route de l'Ouest, Vers une mystique nouvelle*, unpublished, 1932). 'The charms scattered throughout the universe give him (western man) some idea of the beauty that would, in giving full realization to them, bring them all together; and the recognition, in the universe, of this emergent beauty, redoubles his admiration and respect for the chosen substance hidden in the world's elements' (*Ibid.*).

[16] *Man's religious aspiration*

'It is you, Jesus, I now see, whom men, my brothers, even those without belief, feel and seek for, through the magic of the great cosmos' (*La vie cosmique*, in *Ecrits du temps de la guerre*, p. 59).

'Anyone, today, who has had much to do with unbelievers other-

wise than by reading about them in text-books, . . . will agree with
me that we meet in the best representatives of our race this fear that
Christianity is no longer *fine enough* to satisfy the desires of their
hearts . . . There are sincere and *religious* men among us, men who
live their lives in real effort and are ready to deny themselves, who
no longer find that our dogmas can meet their aspirations. In these
men charity—natural charity—is not dead; one cannot even say
that it is growing cold. It is being directed *elsewhere*, towards
some reality that is more pure, more human, more elevated, towards
some passionately loved "Anti-Christ"' (*L'âme du monde, ibid.*, p.
223).

'Replacing an assured geo-anthropo-europeo-centric illusion, a
more correct outlook on things is showing us today our existence
lost in such a reservoir of forces and mysteries, our individuality
subjected to so many attachments and extensions, our civilization
encompassed by so many other cycles of thoughts, that the feeling
of the world's crushing domination over our persons affects anyone
who shares the vision of his own time' (*Note pour servir à l'évangélisation des temps nouveaux*, 1919, *ibid.*, p. 369).

'For this is the supreme purpose of the present human phase of
terrestrial history; that the moral crisis which has struck us shall be
compensated by the renewal and growth of our beings, in the double
form of a necessity and an attraction, of a divine pressure emanating
from the Absolute' (*Hominization*, 1923, in *Vision of the Past*, p. 77).

'In a positive sense, men began to feel themselves bound together,
all united in a great task, and captivated, in an almost religious
sense, by its progress. To know more, to be able to do more.
Although many still take these words in a utilitarian sense, for the
great majority they are already tinged with sacred value. In our
days people constantly devote their lives to "the progress of the
world"' (*The Phenomenon of Man, ibid.*, p. 172).

'Like a bud from which the scales have been stripped away, the
religious kernel, in which the finest life-sap of man is concentrated,
is emerging at this very moment so that we can see it more clearly
defined and vigorous than ever' (*Le Christianisme dans le monde*, 1933,
in *Science et Christ*, p. 131).

'It has become a commonplace to speak of western civilization—
the home of the new mankind—as materialist. Nothing could be
more unfair. The West has overthrown many idols. But, by its

discovery *of the dimensions of the universe and of its forward progress*, it has stimulated a powerful mysticism . . . The whole question now is to determine the truth of the Presence we believe we feel behind the fire of the universe, and to give it a name' (*Ibid.*, p. 136).

'The humanist pantheisms we see around us represent a completely youthful form of religion—a religion that (apart from Marxism) has little or no exact formulation: a religion with no apparent God, and no revelation. But it is a religion in the true sense of the word, if by religion we mean contagious faith in an ideal to which one's life can be devoted . . . A rapidly increasing number of our contemporaries are agreed, from now on, in recognizing that the most important thing in life is to devote oneself body and soul to universal progress—that progress being expressed in tangible developments of mankind . . . This can only mean that under different forms (communist or national-socialist, scientific or political, individual or collective), for the last hundred years we have been witnessing the positive birth and the building up around us of a new faith: the religion of evolution' (*Comment je crois*, unpublished, 1934).

'You often hear it said that, from the religious point of view, the earth is definitely growing cold. In fact, it has never been so ardent . . . Under the influence of a number of convergent causes (the discovery of organic time and space, advances in the unification or "planetization" of man, etc.), man for the last century has, without any doubt, been realizing that he is caught up in a vast process of anthropogenesis, cosmic in dimensions and at the cosmic level.

'The direct result of this awareness has been to build up, above the juvenile, "magmatic", forces that lie deep within his being, the pressure, powerful though as yet ill-defined, of boundless hopes and aspirations. Whether it be the thunder of the waves on which society is tossed, the voice of the press or of literature, to the informed or practised listener, all this discordant hum rising up now from the mass of humanity, vibrates to the frequency of one single fundamental note: faith and hope in some salvation that is bound up with the evolutionary fulfilment of the earth. No, the modern world is not irreligious—far from it. We have to admit that there is in the world a sudden influx, massive in its proportions, of a new life-sap; this is, indeed, the religious spirit, in all its fullness and essence, surging up in a ferment and transforming itself and so transforming it.' (*Christianisme et évolution*, unpublished, 1945).

'Every conversation I have ever had with communist intellectuals has left me with a decided impression that Marxist atheism is not absolute, but that it simply rejects an "extrinsical" God, a *deus ex machina* whose existence can only undermine the dignity of the universe and weaken the springs of human endeavour—a "pseudo-god", in short, whom no one in these days any longer wants, least of all Christians' (*The Heart of the Problem*, 1949, in *The Future of Man*, pp. 266–7). 'The materialists of today are, in fact (as I have often felt when listening to them or reading them) simply followers of the spirit without realizing it' (*Barrière de la mort et co-réflexion*, 1955, in *L'activation de l'énergie*, p. 425).

[17] Cf. C. Tresmontant, *La métaphysique du christianisme et la naissance de la philosophie chrétienne*, Paris, Editions du Seuil, 1962.

[18] 'The secret of the strength of western mysticism lies in this, that it is the first mystical system whose subject is explicitly no longer the human monad but the world. It is essentially 'catholic'': by that characteristic alone, we could recognize that, in spite of a number of appearances to the contrary, it is the true daughter —or, more exactly, the present term and evolved expression—of Christianity' (*La route de l'Ouest*, unpublished, 1932).

[19] 'The God whom our century awaits must be: 1. As *vast* and mysterious as the cosmos. 2. As *immediate* as life. 3. As *bound up with* (in some way) our effort as mankind itself' (*Note pour servir à l'évangélisation des temps nouveaux*, 1919, in *Ecrits du temps de la guerre*, p. 370).

'We can no longer admit any control over *our activity that is not directed towards the fulfilment of a world*, and a world that, in attaining its own consummation, includes us integrally. The free and thinking energy that is released by the earth can no longer be dominated by the *ideal of any established order to be accepted or preserved*. Morality and religion (like the whole social order) have ceased to be for us something static: *we must have, to win our allegiance and save us, a dynamic*' (*Le christianisme dans le monde*, 1933, *Science et Christ*, pp. 135–6).

'In future, the only possible religion for man is the religion that will teach him *in the first place* to recognize, love and serve with passion the universe of which he is a part' (*Le sens humain*, unpublished, 1929). 'The idea of a "unity in convergence" *is the only one that can be the basis of the morality and religion of a universe which is being built on research and progress.* No conversion, accordingly (if we may so express it) will be so deeply rooted as that which is now coming about under the disguise of modern unbelief' (*La route de l'Ouest,* unpublished, 1932).

'As a result of the scientific discovery of the natural unity and immensity of the world, modern man can no longer accept God except as an extension (could one say "under the species of"?) some universal progress or attainment of maturity' (*L'incroyance moderne. Cause profonde et remède,* 1933, in *Science et Christ,* p. 151).

'Nothing can be admitted into our systems unless it first satisfies the conditions of a world in process of transformation . . . A Christ whose features are not moulded to the requirements of a world that is evolutionary in structure, will be progressively rejected without further examination—just as in any scientific institution today a treatise on perpetual motion or squaring the circle goes straight into the wastepaper basket, unread' (*Christianisme et évolution,* unpublished, 1933).

[20] 'As it became conscious of its true nature, the soul acquired a new dimension; it is as though, while still remaining itself, it had taken on a more complex and richer curvature.' 'We live in more dramatic times than those that witnessed the formation of any continent or mountain range, for what is happening now is without any doubt some sort of re-birth of the soul' (Third lecture to the Marcel Légaut group, 10 December 1930).

[21] *Le néo-humanisme moderne* . . . unpublished, 1947.

[22] 'Pascal's twin abysses, plumbed more deeply, and complicated by two more (the abysses of number and time) which in the seventeenth century, the great seer could not yet discern' (*Un phénomène de contre-évolution* . . . in *L'activation de l'énergie,* p. 192).

As mankind takes on form and unity, it becomes more sharply aware of its isolation in the cosmos: this is the theme developed in *La grande monade* (1918, in *Ecrits du temps de la guerre,* pp. 237-48). 'I suddenly became conscious of the incurable isolation in which the glory of mankind is lost . . . I felt as if we were all, clinging on to one another, floating in the void . . . Heavy on me, I felt the weight of a final, irrevocable, isolation—the agony a prisoner suffers when he explores the walls that shut him in and can find no way out. Man finds a companion in man—but mankind is *alone* . . . I saw the *boundaries* of mankind; I saw the blackness and emptiness that surrounds the earth . . . It will indeed be a critical hour when human beings awake, not simply here and there, but as one body, to a *collective* consciousness of their isolation in space—in which, as they raise their eyes to take in the whole picture of their world, they will see themselves imprisoned' (*Ibid.*, pp. 240–1, 243).

'It is a terrifying thing to have been born: I mean, to find oneself, without having willed it, swept irrevocably along on a torrent of fearful energy which seems as though it wished to destroy everything it carries with it' (*The Mass on the World* in *Hymn of the Universe*, p. 20). 'I am afraid, too, like all my fellow-men, of the future, too heavy with mystery and too wholly new, towards which time is driving me. Then like these men I wonder anxiously where life is leading me' (*Ibid.*, p. 30).

[23] 'Man, a closed being, is the notion reformulated by our modern existentialists,' pushing further Leibnitz's concept. Mankind, 'the gigantic and devouring organism by which one feels oneself sucked-up, absorbed, dominated, one might say, while still living' (*Un phénomène de contre-évolution . . . . op. cit.*, p. 196).

[24] 'Man now sees that the seeds of his ultimate dissolution are at the heart of his being. The *end of the species* is in the marrow of our bones! Is it not this presentiment of a blank wall ahead, underlying all other tensions and fears, which paradoxically (at the very moment when every barrier seems to be giving way before our power of understanding and mastering the world) is darkening and hardening the minds of our generation?' (*The End of the Species*, 1952, in *The Future of Man*, p. 300).

Earlier, in 1949, Teilhard was saying, 'A truly "mortal" fear tends to possess us: the fear that, in the course of the transformation we see heralded, we may lose the precious spark of thought, so painfully kindled after millions of years of effort—our own little ego: the essential fear of the reflective element when it faces an apparently blind whole, whose vast layers enfold it, as though to absorb it while still in the fulness of life' (*Man's Place in Nature*, p. 100).

[25] Man has the feeling of 'losing his footing in the world, at the very moment when, deep within himself, he thought he had finally come clear' (*Un phénomène de contre-évolution, op. cit.*, p. 190). This 'fear is at once physical, metaphysical and (in as much as it is shot through with an inexplicable feeling of guilt) moral' (*Ibid.*, p. 197). 'The great fear (so disturbing a threat to our nervous balance) that hangs

heavy over the world at this moment is surely more *cosmic* than political: by that I mean that it is caused more by the darkening of a sky from which God has been removed than by the formation of any atomic cloud' (*Le phénomène chrétien*, unpublished, 1950).

Thcse later passages express the same view as that we find in the following, which dates from the first significant awakening of Teilhard's thought: 'At one moment, the earth believed that it could *forget* or *deny* the essential need for the infinite presupposed by the quest for truth and its implementation . . . But when the first enthusiasm for the new and for independence had died down, and the earth sought to assess its work and estimate its hopes, the gaping void that, from its very depths, calls out for the absolute, seemed more sombre than ever' (*La maîtrise du monde et le règne de Dieu*, in *Ecrits du temps de la guerre*, 1916, p. 78).

26 For the consolation the individual can find in telling himself his 'effort is being exerted within a Human that is greater, more perfectly centred and more consistent than himself . . . seems unable to stand up to a serious examination of man's condition' (*Barrière de la mort et co-réflexion*, in *L'activation de l'énergie*, p. 421).

27 *The conditions for hope*

Any number of passages justify this statement. See, in particular, *Hominization*, 1923, in *Vision of the Past*, pp. 75 ff; *La crise présente*, *Etudes*, 20 October 1937, in *Science et Christ*, pp. 189–91; *The grand option*, 1939, in *The Future of Man*, pp. 41–3; *The Phenomenon of Man*, pp. 142–234, 254–7; *Some reflexions on progress*, in *The Future of Man*, pp. 61 ff.

Suffering from a 'terrible crisis of revolt and despair', mankind 'asks existence why it inflicts such sufferings on men . . . Faith in the world has just been born. It is that faith and that alone that can save the world from the hands of a mankind that is determined to destroy the universe if it cannot adore it' (*Le sens humain*, unpublished, 1929). This date, well before the appearance of existentialism, should be noted.

During the Citroën expedition, Teilhard observed that his companions (all unbelievers or non-practising Christians) found 'a real difficulty (in spite of a very pronounced need for religion) in rising above the level of immediate or individual attitudes, scepticism and pessimism checking an undisguised desire to believe and hope'. He writes, 'Outside the continually active influence of Christianity, men have the greatest difficulty in acquiring and preserving the perception of the great universal realities that are with us now, and still more those to come. In other words, the "world-citizens" I dream of cannot be met except among elements that have been *christianized in advance*' (Letter of 13 March 1932).

Teilhard seems to have been much concerned by present indications of scepticism and pessimism. What he dreaded above all was 'a world strike' (Cf. *The Phenomenon of Man*, p. 231). 'Is life a road or a blind alley? This is the question, scarcely formulated a few centuries ago, which is now explicit and on all men's lips. Following the short and violent crisis in which it became conscious simultaneously of its creative powers and its critical faculties, humanity has become rightfully awkward; and no spur drawn from blind instincts or economic needs will suffice for long to drive it forward. Only one motive, one true and important motive, a passionate love of life, will decide it to move any further. But where, on the empirical plane, can we find the bait (if not the actuality) of a justification for life?' (*The Phenomenon of Man*, 1930, in *Vision of the Past*, p. 172).

Teilhard was deeply affected by the death of his friend, the anatomist Davidson Black, and wrote: 'But what an absurd thing life is, looked at superficially: so absurd that you feel yourself forced back on a stubborn, desperate, faith in the reality and survival of the spirit. Otherwise—were there no such thing as the spirit, I mean—we should be idiots not to call off the whole human effort' (Letter of 18 March 1932, in *Letters from a Traveller*, p. 202).

'Man, the more he is man, can give himself only to what he loves. And ultimately he loves only the indestructible. Multiply the extent and duration of progress as much as you like. Promise the earth another hundred million years of growth and expansion. If, at the end of that time, it becomes apparent that consciousness must revert to zero, with its hidden essence nowhere preserved, then, I maintain, we down tools—and the world will be on strike' (*Comment je crois*, unpublished, 1934).

The crisis of the religion of science and progress is examined in an article written in 1939 (*La mystique de la science*, 1939, in *L'énergie humaine*, pp. 203–23): 'Humanity has no conceivable future without science; but the same is true of science without some religion to animate it. Christianity is an exemplary form of this religion in science. Should we add that it is the necessary form, as though the earth were unable to progress to the end in the true developments of its activities except by becoming converted? To judge from the disgust and despair in the face of effort, so openly admitted in our time by outstandingly clear-minded unbelievers, one would be obliged to think so' (*Ibid.*, p. 223).

'We may wonder whether it is not that (the irreversible summit of the world) that is destined, tomorrow, to rescue human progress by preserving in it its interior impulse, without which everything around us would come to a halt' (*Observations sur la signification et les conditions biologiques de la recherche*, unpublished, 1939). 'At the rate that consciousness and its ambitions are increasing, the world will explode if it does not learn to love' (*The Natural Units of Humanity*, 1939, in *Vision of the Past*, p. 214).

'It cannot be denied that, in a primordial form, human anxiety is bound up with the very advent of reflection, and is thus as old as man himself. Nor do I think that anyone can seriously doubt the fact that, under the influence of reflection undergoing socialization, the men of today are particularly uneasy, more so than at any other moment of history. Conscious or not, anguish—a fundamental anguish—despite our smiles, strikes in the depths of all our hearts and is the undertone of all our conversations' (*The Phenomenon of Man*, p. 227). 'And, what is more serious still, is that we have become aware that, in the great game that is being played, we are the players as well as the cards and the stakes. Nothing can go on if we leave the table. Neither can any power force us to remain. Is the game worth the candle, or are we simply its dupes?' (*Ibid.*, p. 231).

'Even when the intellectual difficulties of the mind in conceiving the collective and in visualizing space-time have been overcome, we are left with another and perhaps more serious form of hesitation, which is bound up with the incoherent aspect presented by the world of men today. The nineteenth century had lived in sight of a promised land. It thought that we were on the threshold of a golden age, lit up and organized by science, and warmed by fraternity. Instead of that, we find ourselves slipped back into a world of ever more extensive and tragic dissensions' (*Ibid.*, p. 254).

'Promise man as many million years as you will; let him glimpse at the end of that period as high (that is to say, as super-human) a peak as you will. If it is known beforehand that, once that summit is reached, we shall have to descend without any signs of our ascent surviving in the universe; then, I say plainly, we shall not have the heart to advance, and we shall not advance. Whatever Jeans and Langevin may say, man will never consent to work like a Sisyphus' (*Man's place in the Universe*, 1942, in *Vision of the Past*, p. 231).

'The evolutionary vigour of mankind can wither away although it be surrounded by mountains of coal, oceans of petroleum, and limitless stocks of corn; it can do so as surely as in a desert of ice, if man should lose his impulse or, worse, develop a distaste for ever-increasing growth "in complexity and consciousness"' (*The human rebound of evolution*, 1947, in *The Future of Man*, p. 205).

'How would it help man to accumulate mountains of wheat, coal, oil, and all the metals ready to hand, if he had unfortunately lost the taste (a "geometrically progressive" taste) for action, that is to say for becoming increasingly man by way of planetary totalization?' (*The singularities of the human species*, 1954, in *The Appearance of Man*, p. 261). We find a similar passage in *The Phenomenon of Man*, in *Les conditions psychologiques de l'unification de l'homme*, 1949 (*L'activation de l'énergie*, p. 179), *The phyletic structure of the human group*, 1951 (*The Appearance of Man*, p. 169) and *La réflexion de l'énergie*, 1952 (*L'activation de l'énergie*, p. 348).

'The world, our terrestrial world, is, as we cannot but see for ourselves, irresistibly taking on the form of a fantastically complicated engine ready for every sort of operation and ready to master everything; but at the same time it can function only if one condition is satisfied—that, to keep its working parts in motion, we find and burn exactly the right sort and quality of fuel. In other words, if the earth of man is today already hesitant in its motion, if there is ɐ danger that tomorrow it may grind to a halt, it is simply and solely for lack of a sufficiently wide vision, a vision commensurate with the vastness and variety of the effort to be produced' (*Les conditions psychologiques de l'unification humaine*, 1949, in *L'activation de l'énergie*, p. 185).

'Now that humanity has become conscious of the movement which carries it onwards it has more and more need of finding, above and beyond itself, an infinite objective, an infinite issue, to which it can wholly dedicate itself' (*Le Coeur de la matière*, unpublished, 1950; in *Hymn of the Universe*, p. 139).

'For all his discoveries and inventions, twentieth-century man is a sad creature. How shall we account for his present dejected state except basically by the fact that, following that exalted vision of species in growth, he is now confronted by a mass of scientific evidence pointing to the reverse—the species doomed to extinction' (*The end of the species*, 1952, in *The Future of Man*, p. 299).

Comparing man's situation to that of miners caught in an explosion, Teilhard comes to the conclusion that he must ask himself whether 'the light towards which humanity is drifting really denotes a way out into the open air, or if it is only caused by a momentary flash in the night; in which case there would be nothing left for us but to go on strike and, in spite of nature, come to a stop'. (*The singularities of the human species*, 1954, in *The Appearance of Man*, p. 264).

The temptation to lose heart by which man is threatened is aggravated by 'both the planetary magnitude of the interests involved (so hopelessly) in neo-anthropology, and by the continually increasing degree of renunciation demanded (with no reward!) from human workers . . . If the Weltstoff, now in motion, can ultimately find rest (and that is the very essence of materialism) only in total decomposition, i.e. in unconsciousness, then the paralysing venom of death irremediably permeates the whole structure of our works, and of our working . . . Tomorrow, mankind will be possessed by a sort of panic claustrophobia, simply at the idea that it may find itself hermetically sealed in a closed universe' (*Barrière de la mort et co-réflexion*, 1955, in *L'activation de l'énergie*, pp. 422–6).

[28] *L'atomisme de l'esprit*, 1941, *ibid.*, p. 62.

[29] Biblical anthropology, as expressed in the Psalms, the prophets and the sapiential books, includes, we find, two negative characteristics of man. First, his natural finiteness: his fragility, his conditional state, his subjection to time, his transitoriness . . . (man is but a 'breath'). Secondly, however, there is the violence of disruptions: in particular between man and man (individuals, groups, nations); the dominance of the strength of the stronger over the weakness of the weaker (many of the Psalms contain this theme). It goes without saying that these negative observations are balanced first by the optimistic concept of man as the image of God and as attached to the world or to men, and again, most of all, by the

concept of a possible salvation and hence of hope in an assurance of grace.

[30] *Pensées* (Ed. Brunschvicg) No. 82, p. 367. On force, Nos. 298ff. 'Justice is what is established, and so all our established laws will be accepted as just without examination, simply because they are established' (No. 312). On the origin of property: 'Mine, yours. This dog is mine, these poor children used to say; that is my place in the sun. There you have the beginning, and a picture of, the usurpation of the whole earth' (No. 295).

[31] 'The neo-humanist mysticism of an ahead clashes with the Christian mysticism of the above; it is precisely in this apparent conflict between the old faith in a transcendent God and a young "faith" in an immanent universe that we find the modern religious crisis: here we touch its inmost essence, expressed in a form at once scientific and social. The whole progress of the Kingdom of God ... depends at this moment on the problem of reconciling with each other, not superficially but organically, these two currents' (International conference of the Society of Jesus, Versailles, 1947).

'Instead of looking for salvation from above and outside himself, man thinks he can find a door that will let him out by pressing on ahead; a door has opened in front of him' (*Le néo-humanisme moderne*, unpublished, 1948).

[32] *L'incroyance moderne*, 1933, in *Science et Christ*, p. 149.

[33] *Un phénomène de contre-évolution*, 1949, in *L'activation de l'énergie*, p. 193.

[34] *Criticism of modern Christianity*

As early as 1916, in a war-time letter, Teilhard was writing: 'Some reasonable reconciliation must be made, I am sure, between God and the world, between the detaching aspirations of Christianity and the ineradicable passion that makes our whole being vibrate when we experience something of the soul of the mighty whole of which we are undeniably a part' (Letter of 2 February 1916, in *Making of a Mind*, p. 93).

Again, in 1918, when reading a book by Wells, he writes: 'Wells's judgment of us (he knows Christianity only through Protestantism) is most unreasonable. But even when he exaggerates, he's most instructive, because he shows us what we look like to outsiders and what, at the present moment, are the unforgivable "faults against

the world or against humanity" that a religion can be guilty of'
(Letter of 11 January 1919, *ibid.*, p. 276).

'It's very remarkable and very pronounced, this gulf between
thought that lives and thought that doesn't' (Letter of 2 August
1919, *ibid.*, p. 298).

'What continues rather to dominate my outlook is the realization
—constantly more vivid, I think—of a lack of proportion, sometimes overwhelming, between the greatness of the realities involved
in the world's forward progress (physical, biological, intellectual,
social, etc.) and the pettiness and narrowness, the make-shift nature,
of the philosophico-dogmatic solutions which we claim to have
built up as a permanent bulwark for the universe. We're trying to
put the ocean into a nutshell' (Letter of 16 March 1921).

'I am beginning to think that there is a certain aspect of the real
world as closed to some believers as the world of faith is to unbelievers' (Letter of 17 April 1923, in *Letters from a Traveller*, p. 66).

In a letter of 7 August 1927 Teilhard feels that he has made up his
mind to 'affirm his "belief" in the future of the world, in spite of
appearances, and in spite of a false orthodoxy that confuses progress
and materialism, change and liberalism, the perfecting of man and
naturalism' (*Letters from a Traveller*, p. 143).

After the Citroën expedition, Teilhard wrote to Père Valensin:
'In the chance group we made up there was not a single practising
Catholic; but on the other hand, in the headquarters unit alone (the
mechanics have less significance) there were six or seven men who
had had a Christian upbringing but had practically given it up,
because religion (as they understood it) had nothing positive to say
to them.' Realizing this 'confirmed me in the belief that at present
Christianity is losing ground in the living strata of society (don't
forget that as a body we formed a carefully selected élite): and the
reason for this is that the scribes and Pharisees have debased the
super-human that the Gospel rightly is (hence its attraction) into what
is, in appearance, *in-human* (and that means alien to the true and
lofty aspiration of man *continually in genesis*)' (13 March 1932).

'To those who do not know him *really well*, the Christian, *without
any doubt*, gives the impression of having escaped, and even of being
opposed to, the psychological "revolution" we have just been
analysing. He cannot make up his mind frankly to accept, in their
general application and in *their spirit*, the prospects of the future of

the cosmos—even though everyone except him recognizes them. He seems to delight in belittling human hopes and in pointing out the weaknesses of our society. He is either contemptuous of, or afraid of, progress and discovery. In short, he does nothing to consecrate or add grandeur to modern mankind's loftiest and most deeply felt aspirations. This is what it *looks like*: we, who see it from inside, know that it is a false picture, but it is tragically deceptive to those who see us from outside' (*L'incroyance moderne*, 1933, in *Science et Christ*, p. 150).

'The reason for the conflict between "faith and progress", whose developments have done more harm to Christianity than the most savage persecutions, seems to me to lie in a faulty adjustment that affects the three components (futurist, universalist, and personalist) of the Christian mind. Christianity is by definition universalist. But surely the danger lies in this, that Christians, false to these true attitudes, are clinging belatedly to a medieval cosmology, instead of resolutely facing the temporal and spatial immensities to which the facts demand that we extend our views of the Incarnation. Christianity is supremely futurist. But the very transcendence of the hopes it entertains is in danger of inducing some of its adherents to shut themselves up in an extra-terrestrial ideal (one that is therefore passive and soporific): whereas, by all the logic of dogma, this ideal should be supra-terrestrial (and therefore productive of maximum human effort). Tomorrow, we can be sure, the world will belong to those who bring the earth (even on this earth) a greater hope. Finally, Christianity is specifically personalist. But here again we have to take care that the predominance accorded to the values of the soul does not cause the Gospel to be presented as a juridical or moral system, at the expense of the organic and cosmic splendours we find in the Pauline doctrine of Christ "gathering up" all things' (*Sauvons l'humanité. Réflexions sur la crise présente*, in *Science et Christ*, p. 190).

'We who are Christians know that the saviour has already been born. But now that we have this completely new phase of mankind, should he not be *re-born*, in a way adapted to our present needs? . . . We find something too narrow and something lacking in the Gospel as it is now presented. Our soul needs stronger meat. The trial through which we are passing is not a crisis of weakness and spiritual frigidity, but one of metamorphosis and growth. Wider horizons

and not tighter control, that . . . is the only thing that can effectively
bring our generation back to the paths of truth' (*La parole attendue*,
1940, in *Cahiers Pierre Teilhard de Chardin*, No. 4, pp. 22–3). If we
refuse an organic conception of history, 'everything in the world of
man becomes "artificial" (in the worst sense of the word); everything is divested of its importance, urgency and interest; Christianity
itself becomes no more than a sort of alien proliferation, without
analogy or roots in the phenomenon' (*Turmoil or genesis*, 1947, in
The Future of Man, p. 226).

'Everything stems from the perception and acceptance of a new
sense of the value of the world. It is the absence of such a sense . . .
that leaves the admonitions of our missionaries so cold and unin-
spiring. On the other hand, once this sense emerges, then, I am
convinced, the Christian faith will once again find echo throughout
the world' (Letter of 3 January 1948).

[35] 'Is it not becoming more obvious every day that, for our generation, there is something essential lacking in a sub-manichean Gospel,
in which advances in knowledge and technology are still presented
not as a primary co-condition of the spirituality of man, but simply
as some sort of extra? in which failure is accorded just as much if not
more sanctifying value than success? in which the Cross is constantly
put before us to remind us of an initial miscarriage of the world we
live in, much more than as a fulfilment?' (*Le Christique*, unpublished,
1955).

After commenting on the present vigour of Promethean faith in
the world and its future, Teilhard adds: 'We see, or are in danger of
seeing, no other faith ready to serve the world. Hence the tendency
(which is also as old as the world) of the defenders of the spirit to
regard as diabolical, and to reject as being among the most formidable manifestations of pride, the irresistible desire for growth and
conquest, the unshakable sense of power and progress, which at
present fills the human breast' (*Faith in Man*, 1947, in *The Future of
Man*, p. 189.)

[36] 'Charity, as at present urged on us, is resigned and static. That is
why Nietzsche's superman is eclipsing the kindness of the Gospels'
(*L'atomisme de l'esprit*, 1941, *op. cit.*, p. 59).

[37] 'The time has gone when God could simply be imposed on us from
outside, like a master or a proprietor. The world will never again
fall on its knees, except before the organic centre of its evolution.

What, at the present moment we all lack, in varying degrees, is a new formulation of holiness' (*Le phénomène spirituel*, 1937, in *L'énergie humaine*, p. 136).

'With the utmost and deepest veneration for the words of Christ, may we not say that the Judaeo-Christian faith is still being expressed (how could it fail to be?) in the text of the Gospels, in terms of a typically neolithic symbolism? Neolithic—that is to say, the age of a mankind (and more widely, of a world) built up, from the sky above to the village below, on the model and (practically speaking) the scale of the family and the ploughed field. How can we imagine, without a psychological contradiction, that in such a universe monotheism could have emerged except in terms of a God who is the great paterfamilias and supreme landlord of the inhabited world? This is just the mental framework or background from which our modern consciousness is in process of emerging more and more completely' (*Le phénomène chrétien*, unpublished, 1950).

Similarly, J. Lacroix speaks of the necessity for a 're-furbishing' of the idea of God (*Le sens de l'athéisme moderne*, Casterman, 1958, p. 64).

[38] *Christology*

'In practice, if not in theory, our Lord has been too exclusively presented to our contemporaries in the form of a complement promised to their personality—a complement that is moral, extrinsic, *particularist*, and individual. They have been given a picture of Christ, dissociated from the universe, as a detached fragment which brings men into conflict with one another. Is it in any way surprising if the soul of the world, now that it has, in its turn, spontaneously disclosed itself to their consciousness, has appeared to them as an 'extra', or antagonistic, or stronger, absolute—a new Messiah more desirable than the old?' (*L'âme du monde*, 1918, in *Ecrits du temps de la guerre*, p. 227).

'The expression of our Christology is still exactly the same as that which, three centuries ago, was sufficient for men whose cosmic outlook has now become physically insupportable.' . . . 'the four thousand year-old world, encircled in its eight or nine spheres, for which our theological textbooks were written' (*Christologie et évolution*, unpublished, 1933).

'Without injustice to the Latin Fathers, could one not reproach them with having unduly developed the rabbinical and casuistic side of St Paul in their theology? Under their influence, the Christian history of the world has taken on the appearance of a legal battle between God and his creature. Forgetting a more noble tradition, our cosmology tended to become reduced to an argument about ownership: a humiliating and disheartening attitude. It is time to yield to the pressure of facts and return to a more scientifically physical, more organic, form of Christology' (*Ibid.*).

'By continually envisaging only "personal" relations in the world, the average Christian has ended by reducing the creator and the creature to the standard of "juridical man". By continually hearing the value of the spirit exalted and the supernatural nature of the divine, he has come to regard the soul as a passing guest in the cosmos and a prisoner of matter. From that moment the universe has ceased, for him, to extend the primacy of its organic unity over the whole of interior experience: the operation of salvation, now become simply a matter of individual success, proceeds with no concern for cosmic evolution. Christianity seems not to believe in human progress. It has not developed within itself the *sense of the earth*, or if it has, it has allowed it to become dormant' (*Comment je crois*, unpublished, 1934).

'For reasons of practical convenience and perhaps also of intellectual timidity, the city of God is too often described in pious works in conventional and purely moral terms. God and the world he governs are seen as a vast association, essentially legalistic in its nature, conceived in terms of a family or government. The fundamental outlook from which the sap of Christianity has risen from the beginning and is nourished, is quite otherwise. Led astray by a false evangelism, people often think they are honouring Christianity when they reduce it to a sort of gentle philanthropism. Those who fail to see in it the most realistic and at the same time the most cosmic of beliefs and hopes, completely fail to understand its "mysteries". Is the Kingdom of God a big family? Yes, in a sense it is. But in another sense it is a prodigious biological operation—that of the redeeming Incarnation' (*The Phenomenon of Man*, p. 293).

When speaking of the devotion to the Sacred Heart that he had acquired from his mother, Teilhard criticizes certain forms it assumes: 'Historically, as we all know, devotion to the Sacred Heart (or the love of Christ), which had always been latent in the Church found expression in France, during the seventeenth century, in a form that was astonishingly vivid but at the same time curiously limited: this is true both of the object towards which it was directed ("Reparation") and to its symbol (the heart of our Saviour represented in the most strangely anatomical forms)' (*Le coeur de la matière*, unpublished, 1950).

39 *Sin and Redemption*

'The Cross has always been a symbol of conflict, and a principle of selection, among men . . . Wherever it appears, unrest and antagonisms are inevitable. But there is no reason why these conflicts should be needlessly exacerbated by preaching the doctrine of Christ crucified in a discordant or provocative manner. Far too often the Cross is presented for our adoration, not so much as a sublime end to be attained by transcending ourselves, but as a symbol of sadness, of limitation and repression . . . Speaking in this way ends by conveying the impression that the kingdom of God can be established only in mourning, and by constantly thwarting and standing out against the current of man's energies and aspirations' (*Le Milieu Divin*, pp. 101–2).

On resignation, Teilhard writes: 'There are many reasonable men who honestly consider and denounce Christian resignation as being one of the most dangerous and soporific elements in the "opium of the people" . . . This accusation, or even suspicion, is infinitely more effective, at this moment, in preventing the conversion of the world than all the objections drawn from science and philosophy. A religion that is judged to be inferior to our human ideal, for all the marvels that surround it, is already *condemned*' (*Ibid.*, pp. 90–1).

'Christian detachment is still too often urged on us or understood as an attitude of contempt, indifference or mistrust towards the realities of the earth. The present world is nothing but clay and dust, and the less you have to do with it, the holier you are' (*Le sens humain*, unpublished, 1929).

'Original sin (as now pictured) continually obstructs the natural expansion of our religion. It clips the wings of our hopes. At every moment we are reaching out to the wide-open field of the good things that optimism can win, and every time it drags us back to the *over-riding* shadows of reparation and expiation.' It is a 'strait-jacket that checks any movement of heart or head'; it 'binds us hand and foot and drains the blood from us', 'because, *as it is now expressed,* it represents a survival of static concepts that are an anachronism in our evolutionist system of thought' (*Christologie et évolution,* unpublished, 1933).

[40] 'Indeed, when you come back to some of our religious circles after having for some time shared the interests and hopes and activities that animate the spear-head of mankind, you think you must be dreaming when you see what efforts are devoted to the beatification of some servant of God, to the success of some devotion, to the subtle analysis of some mystery . . . We are building castles in the air and we do not see that reality is pressing on without us . . . And yet reality needs us Christians to attain its fulfilment' (*Note pour servir à l'évangélisation des temps nouveaux,* 1919, *op. cit.,* p. 327).

'The Church has drifted into a backwater of abstract theology, quantitative sacramentalism, refinements of devotional practices, and has thus lost contact with the real. The guidance of the clergy and the interests of the faithful are gradually being confined within a little artificial world of ceremonies and practices and pious accretions that is entirely cut off from the true current of things. The Eucharist, in particular, is tending to become a sort of object treasured for its own sake, that absorbs religious activity into itself instead of making it work like a leaven for the salvation of all things in the universe' (*Le sens humain,* unpublished, 1929).

Elsewhere, again, Teilhard speaks of 'the slowness with which Christianity itself is transposing its precepts and counsels to the dimensions of a mankind that has become conscious of the historical immensity and the collective potentialities or requirements of its development' (*L'atomisme de l'esprit, op. cit.,* pp. 55–6).

'If Christianity has nothing to offer us but a pig in a poke, we'll soon end by jettisoning the whole thing, Christianity and all. A truth that has no immediate effective reaction on life, has no existence or validity' (Letter of 20 April 1948).

[41] 'It seems to me that if a man of our time is convinced that there is nothing beyond the earth, it gives him (1) a concrete and direct *compassion* for other men, (2) an eagerness for work, (3) a disinterestedness in his work . . . which makes up the moral idea of our day. Conversely, there is a danger that belief in God may (by a distortion, of course, but the danger is still there, in fact) make us lazy, preoccupied with our own "petty salvation", charitable only

as a matter of form' (Letters of 30 July 1918, in *Making of a Mind*, pp. 223-4).

[42] *Notes sur la notion de perfection chrétienne*, unpublished, 1942.

With the present development of mankind, 'a new section or, to put it more exactly, a further dimension has suddenly brought about an almost limitless expansion of man's destiny—a section and dimension of which there is no explicit mention in the Gospel. Until that happened, the Christian had learnt to think and act, to fear and to worship, on the scale of his own individual life and death. How, without breaking with his traditional background, will he or can he extend his faith and hope and charity to the proportions of a terrestrial organization that is destined to persist for millions of years?' . . . There is 'a lack of proportion between the insignificant mankind that still appears in our catechisms and the great mankind with which science is concerned'; 'a lack of proportion between the tangible aspirations and anxieties and responsibilities of life, according to whether they are expressed in a secular book or in a religious treatise' (*Le Christ évoluteur*, unpublished, 1942).

[43] *Lack of appeal*

'For centuries we have been examining and trying to define the mysteries of the supernatural world, the relations between the divine persons, the nature of the theandric compound or hypostatic union, the hierarchy of the angels and the saints, the mechanism of grace . . . We have built and embellished with loving care a universe of theology and piety. And we have not noticed, so engrossed have we been in this work of esoteric planning, that we are rapidly ceasing to make any appeal to the mass of human beings because we seem to have built our city in the clouds' (*L'âme du monde*, 1918, in *Ecrits du temps de la guerre*, p. 230).

'We should make no mistake about this: the *Christian ideal* (as ordinarily presented) has ceased to be, what we still blissfully continue to flatter ourselves it is, the common ideal of mankind. If they wish to be sincere, increasing numbers of men will have to admit to the man in the pulpit that Christianity seems to them irremediably inhuman and inferior, *as much in its promises of individual happiness* as in its *maxims of renunciation*. "Your Gospel", they are already saying, "ends up in creating souls who are interested in their own selfish gains and have no interest in the common task; and so we have no

use for it. Ours is a finer, and so a truer, concept". The pre-
eminence accorded to the whole in modern consciousness is rapidly
tending to produce a new moral ideal in which justice takes precedence over charity, work over detachment, an all-out effort to
develop over mortification. "Christian" and "Human" are tending
to drift apart. This is the great schism that now threatens the
Church' (*Note pour servir à l'évangélisation des temps nouveaux*, 1919,
op. cit., p. 370).

'Though the world is full of potencies, it is floundering and
suffocating: the reason is that there is no one at hand, not even the
Christian, to set an example and show how men may learn to act
and live in a way that will be human in the fullest sense, passionately
and actively receptive of everything and beautiful and true. There
is only one contact charged with an irresistible centripetal and unifying force, and that is contact of the whole of man with the whole of
man' (Letter of 20 February 1927, in *Letters from a Traveller*, pp.
138–9).

'Christianity has become antipathetic to humanity. Once it was
feared and persecuted because it was a force. Today people avoid
it or repel it, because they see it as an encumbrance or an
imprisonment. Its ideal no longer seems sufficiently lofty . . . The
sense of man believes in the magnificent future of the tangible world;
and the Gospel seems to disdain it. The sense of man urges the need
for avidity and effort in the conquest of things: Christianity calls for
indifference and renunciation. The sense of man discerns a universe
emerging in radiance from the midst of the struggle for being;
Christianity holds us down to the view of a fallen, static, nature . . .
There is now an unmistakable conflict between the Gospel as presented by some preachers and the sense of man. Temperamentally
and because of the way it is made up, mankind of today believes in
the world; and, if we are to judge from appearances, the Church of
Christ refuses to do so. The Church no longer gives the impression
of "feeling with mankind". There we have the underlying reason
for the attitude of hostility or contempt that surrounds her, even—
most of all—in the most progressive sections of society. Here, too, is
the explanation of the Church's present sterility. The proper characteristic of a true religion must be to spread irresistibly, like fire or
water. If at this moment the church is marking time or progressing
only with great difficulty and that in the least active strata of the

world, it is because something is lacking to the splendour of her truth, and that means lacking to the fullness of her power to meet the present requirements of mankind' (*Le sens humain*, unpublished, 1929).

After his visit to Somaliland (November 1928 to February 1929), Teilhard wrote: 'During this voyage alone I met, without going out of my way to do so, half a dozen completely different types of mind, for whom Christianity (as commonly taught) had become either a burden that makes life impossible, or a useless dead-weight, or the religion that you would never dream any longer of asking questions of, because it's perfectly clear that you can't expect anything from it that will answer the questions that *we* ask *today*' (Letter of 25 February 1929).

It will be noted that some of Teilhard's comments (quoted in this or earlier notes) date from a period of spiritual crisis, following his withdrawal from the Institut Catholique (1925).

'We have ceased to catch on' (Letter of 9 December 1933).

'Precisely because of this "eruption" (of modern aspirations) it is inevitable that deep-seated disturbances should appear within Christianity. Christian dogmatic teaching was formulated and systematized in a way that was adapted to and fitted the dimensions of an earlier (antecedent) state of man's religious energy; today it no longer functions in a way that accurately meets the demands of the *new-style "anima naturaliter christiana"*. It is to this, without doubt, that we must attribute the indifference to the teachings of the Church that is characteristic of our generation. As Nietzsche pointed out, it is not the arguments that have been rejected, it is the Gospel's *appeal* that has been lost, irresistibly drained off by a higher appeal . . . On one side we have, emerging from the depths of man's consciousness, an innate, tumultuous, surge of cosmic and humanitarian aspirations, whose rise cannot be checked, but which are dangerously imprecise and still more dangerously "impersonal" in their expression: the new faith in the world. And, on the other side, we have—inflexibly maintained by Christian dogma but more and more abandoned (it seems) by the main stream of religion—the vision and expectation of a universal pole, transcendent and loving: the ancient faith in God. On one side, in the form of modern humanism, we have a sort of neo-paganism, bursting with life but still lacking a head; on the other side, in the form of Christianity, a head in which the circulation of the blood has slowed down. On one side, the fantastically enlarged layers of a cone that are nevertheless powerless to close up together: a cone with no apex. And, on the other side, an apex that has lost its base. Can we possibly fail to see that these two halves are designed to be combined into one whole?' (*Christologie et évolution*, unpublished, 1935).

'The difficulty of a noble enterprise has always fascinated souls. But the truth about the Gospel today is that it has ceased, or practically ceased, to attract because it has become *unintelligible*. In a world that has been terrifyingly transformed, the same phrases are still being repeated to us that our fathers heard . . . The best of the unbelievers I know would consider they were falling short of their moral ideal if they took the step of conversion: they have told me so themselves' (*Ibid.*).

'In their quest to give a name to the unknown God whose existence they divine, the Gentiles look to us. And then they turn away from a Gospel that seems to have no answer, either to their outlook on the world, or to the questions they ask or to the things they look for. The resistance the Church comes up against nowadays in getting a footing, does not derive, as is sometimes said, from its dogmas being too lofty and its moral system too difficult. It is due to the fact that men no longer recognize in us their religious and moral ideal, and accordingly stand aside, waiting for something better' (*L'incroyance moderne*, 1933, in *Science et Christ*, p. 151).

Teilhard concludes a criticism (quoted, note 42 above) as follows: 'It is here, and only here, in this lack of balance (sometimes more, sometimes less distinctly felt) that we can hope to find the ultimate source of the uneasiness that today lies heavy on the mind and consciousness of so many Christians. Contrary to what is generally held, it is not the scientific discovery of man's humble origins but much more the equally scientific discovery of man's fantastic future that now troubles the hearts of men; and it is with this above all accordingly, that our modern apologetics should be concerned.' The crisis that is upon us is one 'of re-adjustment' (*Le Christ évoluteur*, unpublished, 1942).

'Because of the shortcomings of Christians, Christianity at the present time is losing its momentum. We are not offering a Christianity of the requisite quality for the world to be enriched by it. At the point the world has now reached we are impoverishing it by our

modern Christianity. This modern Christianity cannot, however, be
the whole of Christianity . . . What makes Christians sterile is that
they do not love the world' (*Le néo-humanisme moderne*, lecture
quoted above).

'The fact remains that for some obscure reason something has
gone wrong between man and God as in these days he is represented
to man. Man would seem to have no clear picture of the God he
longs to worship . . . Hence (despite certain positive indications of
re-birth which are, however, still largely obscured) the impression
one gains from everything taking place around us is of an irresistible
growth of atheism—or more exactly, a mounting and irresistible
de-Christianization' (*The Heart of the Problem*, 1949, in *The Future of
Man*, p. 260).

'Worldly faith, in short, is not enough in itself to move the earth
forward: but can we be sure that the Christian faith in its ancient
interpretation is still sufficient in itself to carry the earth upward?
. . . By definition and principle, it is the specific function of the
Church to Christianize all that is human in man. But what is likely
to happen (indeed, is happening already) if at the very moment
when an added component begins to arise in the *anima naturaliter
christiana*, and one so compelling as the awareness of a terrestrial
"ultra-humanity", ecclesiastical authority ignores, disdains and even
condemns this new aspiration without seeking to understand it?
This, and simply this, that Christianity will lose, to the extent that it
fails to embrace as it should *everything that is human on earth*, the keen
edge of its vitality and its full power to attract. Being for the time
incompletely human it will no longer fully satisfy even its own disciples.
It will be less able to win over the unconverted or to resist its
adversaries. We wonder why there is so much unease in the hearts
of religious and priests, why so few deep conversions are effected in
China despite the flood of missionaries, why the Christian Church,
with all its superiority of benevolence and devotion, yet makes so
little appeal to the working masses . . . My answer is simply this,
that it is because at present our magnificent Christian charity lacks
what it needs to make it decisively effective, the sensitizing in-
gredient of *human* faith and hope, without which, in reason and fact,
no religion can henceforth appear to man other than colourless,
cold and unassimilable' (*Ibid.*, pp. 265–6).

'In spite of some revival of its dominance in conservative (or undeveloped) [Teilhard uses the English word] areas, it remains true that Christianity is visibly and decidedly losing its appeal to the most influential and progressive portion of mankind. Not only to the Gentiles and simple layfolk, but even in the heart of the religious orders, Christianity is still to some extent a *refuge*, but it does not *embrace*, or *satisfy* or even lead the "modern soul" any longer. Something has gone wrong, and something, therefore, must be provided, on this planet, in the field of faith and religion—and that without delay. But what, exactly?' (*Le Dieu de l'évolution*, unpublished, 1953).

[44] Many Catholics, failing to find in their religion a 'complete vindication of their lives, adhere to Christianity but only *for want of anything better*, and only so long as a number of central points (in connexion with the origin and significance of the world) are discreetly left in the background. This is no longer a complete and fervent adherence to the light one has found. They are already—how many people have told me this—anxiously awaiting a new Gospel' (*Le sens humain*, unpublished, 1942).

[45] Cf. Daniel-Rops, *The Church in an Age of Revolution 1789-1870* (London, Dent and New York, Dutton, 1965) pp. 235-305 (with a balanced estimate of the Work of Pius IX). A. Latreille . . ., *Histoire du Catholicisme en France*, vol. 3, *La période contemporaine* (Spes, 1962) pp. 429, 444, 584. Régine Pernoud, *Histoire de la bourgeoisie en France*, vol. II (Ed. du Seuil, 1962) pp. 516-19, 563-4.

[46] 'Normal' though this mystical experience was, it nevertheless reached at times to a high level of exaltation in communion with God, in particular in the vision of 1916 he described in *Christ in the World of Matter* (*Hymn of the Universe*, pp. 42–55). In *Mon Univers* (1918, in *Ecrits du temps de la guerre*, pp. 209–79) in which he first disclosed his inmost thoughts, he brings out, among others, the fundamental idea in his life and thought: the coming together of the universe and God, the coexistence of Christ and the universe. Throughout his life he was to strive to unite, while still keeping them distinct, two absolutes: 'that of experience (the universe) and that of Revelation (the transcendent God)' (*Ibid.*, p. 278). Cf. also *Le milieu mystique*, 1917, and *L'union créatrice*, 1917, *ibid*. A more exact examination would show how intensely Teilhard meditated on the mystery of the Eucharist, the 'sacrament of matter'. Cf. *Christ in the World of Matter*, 1916; *The Mass on the World*, 1923 (both in *Hymn*

of the Universe); and *Le Prêtre*, 1918, in *Ecrits du temps de la guerre*, pp. 281 ff.

[47] The essentially *missionary* character of Teilhard's project (as it was of Pascal's) orientated him, from the outset and of set purpose, towards his fellow-men from *outside*. This extremely Pauline orientation explains his wish for a re-shaping of the Church's attitude and terminology.

If we are fully to understand Teilhard's attitude throughout his life as a priest, an apostle and a member of the Church, we must give first place to the religious training he received in the Society of Jesus during his youth, and which culminated in the 'long retreat' of thirty days, in October 1914 (when he was thirty-three). This initial training which, in one sense, lasted all his life, in the atmosphere of the religious communities he lived in, left a permanent mark upon him. It was from this basis and this accumulated store that there sprang, under the stimulus of the war from 1916 onwards, a more personal and original religious experience—one that was both in harmony with, and went beyond, what he had already learnt: the experience of the conjunction or coincidence of the universe and Christ. Ample evidence of this is provided (1916–20) by some twenty remarkable essays. As has been well demonstrated by Madame M. Barthélemy-Madaule, it is from this intuition that the whole body of Teilhard's work is derived (*op. cit.*, pp. 19–38, 474–93).

[48] Teilhard wrote, after a conversation with an unbeliever: 'However far-fetched the notion might seem at first, I realized in the end that, *hic et nunc*, Christ was not irrelevant to the problems that interest Professor Parker: it only needed a few intermediate steps to allow a transition from his positivist psychology to some sort of mystical outlook' (Letter of 19 June 1926, in *Letters from a Traveller*, pp. 127–8). Cf. G. Fessard, *La vision religieuse et cosmique de Teilhard de Chardin* in *L'homme devant Dieu*, Melanges offerts au Père de Lubac, *op. cit.*, p. 248).

[49] 'Left to themselves the new wise men of the West may well linger too long over the enjoyment of their conquests. They will probably limit their hopes to temporal and spatial horizons without realizing that such a restriction to an obsolete and lower form of matter is a logical contradiction of their passion for scientific research and of their vigorous optimism . . . At the level of concentration and

moral tension it has reached, mankind cannot afford to wait any longer before it takes the spiritual step that will give it a soul' (*La route de l'Ouest*, unpublished, 1932).

'If the impression we have is simply a dream (if, that is, there is nothing final at the end of our effort) then there is an end, once and for all, to the splendid flame of man . . . Otherwise, we down tools' (*Le Christianisme dans le monde*, 1933, in *Science et Christ*, p. 136).

'Either there is some way out, somewhere, for thought and personality—or the world is a ghastly mistake. And if that is so, we must call a halt' (Letter of 18 March 1934, written after the death of his friend Davidson Black, the anatomist, quoted in Cuénot, *op. cit.*, p. 193).

'Just look around you at the increasing number of people who are secretly weeping tears of boredom, or who commit suicide because they want to escape from life . . . The day will soon come when mankind will see that, as a direct result of its position in a cosmic evolution it has become competent to discover and judge, it finds that it is faced, biologically, with the choice of suicide or adoration' (*Comment je crois*, unpublished, 1934).

'Urged on by his growing awareness of forming part of an evolution that carries him along, man has come to the point where he must formulate to himself, with ever greater emphasis and clearness of mind, the question of his biological destiny . . . His first concern is to examine the solidity of the vessel that carries him, and its equipment. There will be no lack of physical strength. But on the other hand, what about courage? What about the vital impulse? What about psychic resources? Will we always have enough of those?' (*L'activation de l'énergie humaine*, 1943, in *L'activation de l'énergie*, pp. 410, 412).

50 *The Phenomenon of Man* ,1930, in *The Vision of the Past* p. 172. *The Grand option*, 1939, in *The Future of Man*, p. 37. *Man's Place in Nature*, 1932, in *The Vision of the Past*, p. 243.

Writing in a psycho-analytic review (*Psyché*, December 1948) Teilhard expressed a wish for a 'really sound and high-minded examination of the cosmic libido': 'psychoanalysis not in order to detach but to involve. Make man look into himself, not in order to dispel illusions, but to give consistence, orientation, and satisfaction to certain dominant requirements or essential demands that are stifled inside us (and that stifle us) for lack of being expressed and understood' (*Les conditions psychologiques de l'unification humaine*, in *L'activation de l'énergie*, p. 183).

Teilhard realized that his energetics of the spirit 'coincided unexpectedly with the existentialist problem in its very essence' (*Hominisation et spéciation*, 1952, *ibid.*, p. 379).

'Kant asked himself the question: "In what conditions is knowledge possible?" Teilhard transferred the enquiry to the plane of action: "In what conditions is human action possible?" (C. Cuénot, *Teilhard de Chardin*, in the series '*Ecrivains de toujours*', p. 131). Teilhard's approach, in fact, led to a vindication of knowledge too.

[51] 'How can one be more Christian than any man and yet be more man than any?' (Letter to Père Victor Fontoynont, 15 March 1916, quoted by H. de Lubac, *op. cit.*, p. 243).

[52] *Introduction au christianisme*, unpublished, 1944. 'The cause of Christianity and the world's cause are closely bound up with the present crisis. The world would be incoherent in its make-up if Christianity were not at hand to centre and consummate it. But Christ would not be divine if his spirit did not acknowledge his presence underlying movements that, at this moment, are re-creating the soul of the earth' (*Le sens humain*, unpublished, 1929). 'On one side (in the case of the Christian) a centre in process of expansion that seeks a sphere. And on the other side (in the human) an ever-deepening sphere that calls for a centre' (*Le Christique*, unpublished, 1955).

[53] 'In my own small way, Lord, I would wish to be the apostle, and (if I may be so bold) the evangelist *of your Christ in the universe . . . To bring Christ, in virtue of inter-connexions that are specifically organic, to the very heart of the realities that are considered the most fraught with danger, the most philosophically naturalistic, the most pagan*—that is my gospel and there lies my mission' *Le Prêtre*, 1918, in *Ecrits du temps de la guerre*, p. 298).

'And once again, I was conscious within myself of the inspiration that calls me to the great work of reconciling the supreme and absolute love of God with the lower (but still legitimate and necessary) love of life embraced in its natural forms' (Letter of 22 July 1916, in *Making of a Mind*, p. 114). 'Isn't it an odd situation that I'm in, of being reckoned (and in fact being) among the orthodox, and yet feeling with the heterodox? I hope that this dualism is allowed by our Lord in order that I may be able more easily to act as a link between the two. But you can well imagine that it doesn't make for interior tranquillity' (*Ibid.*, p. 277).

'I couldn't help thinking of the gulf that divides the intellectual world I was in and whose language I spoke, from the theological world of Rome with whose idiom I am also familiar . . . I told myself that now perhaps I was capable of so using the first language as to make it fairly express what the other contains but puts into words that most people can no longer understand . . . There I felt, lie the Indies that call me more strongly than St Francis Xavier's. But what a vast problem to be solved, no longer of ritual but of ideas, before one can really convert them!' (Letter of 19 June 1926, in *Letters from a Traveller*, pp. 127-8).

'The originality of my belief consists in its being rooted in two spheres of life that are generally considered antagonistic. By upbringing and intellectual training, I belong to the children of heaven: but, by temperament and professional studies, I am a child of the earth' (*Comment je crois*, unpublished, 1934).

Teilhard's apostolic project should not make us forget that his intellectual quest arose initially from a personal need for clarity. This is a point that he often makes.

[54] *Phenomenology*

The word 'phenomenology' is used only once by Teilhard in *The Phenomenon of Man* (p. 53), as a synonym for 'generalized physics'. It appears similarly in a letter to C. Cuénot, quoted below. The expression 'generalized physics' indicates not only a kinship with classical physics but a science of matter, or cosmology.

Hegel's phenomenology sought to construct a total logic of reality, a rational dialectical development of history and of the categories of the mind. The word 'phenomenology' was adopted again by *Husserl* (1859-1938), particularly in his *Logische Untersuchungen* (1900). Rejecting Cartesian dualism, in order to give more weight to the complex unity of aspects of being, and also to the possibility of a universal language and total understanding of reality, he is satisfied with a fragmentary and naive description of its many sectors and of the countless different attitudes that consciousness adopts towards the world; he seeks to bring out the significance and the *intention* of the projects of the ego, which he connects with the transcendental ego. In Paul Ricoeur's phrase, Husserl's aim is 'to get back to things themselves' and to 'let human experience speak in its integrity' (*Encyclopédie française*, vol. 19, 19–10–9). But while Husserl's phenomenology rightly rejects a psychological approach in order to produce a logical construction, it is still divorced from any notion of genesis and history. Moreover, it leaves to one side the question of the absolute. While agreeing with Hegel about the inseparable character of man and the world, Husserl is accordingly in conflict with him on many points.

Like Husserl and Merleau-Ponty, and in contrast with the abstract distinctions of materialism and spiritualism, Teilhard rejects the matter-spirit, body-soul dualism (*Le phénomène spirituel*, 1937, in *L'énergie humaine*, p. 118; *The Phenomenon of Man*, pp. 35–6, 53, 62, 308–9). He objects, however, to their phenomenology on the ground that it does not include consciousness in the objective reality of the universal movement of history (Letter to Claude Cuénot, 11 April 1955, in Cuénot, *op. cit.*, p. 311).

[55] 'Seeing' (*voir*) is the first word emphasized in *The Phenomenon of Man* and the title of the foreword. "To try to see more and better is not a matter of whim or curiosity or self-indulgence. *To see or to perish* is the very condition laid on everything that makes up the universe, by reason of the mysterious gift of existence. And this, at a higher level, is man's condition' (*ibid.*, p. 31). 'It was all very well for Leverrier to have worked out the existence of Neptune; but Neptune never really began to exist for us until we had *seen* it' (*Barrière de la mort et co-réflexion*, 1955, in *L'activation de l'énergie*, p. 426).

[56] 'Man *solely* as a phenomenon . . . but the *whole* phenomenon of man' (*The Phenomenon of Man*, Preface, p. 29).

'We are faced by a problem in nature: we have to discover, if such exists, the direction of evolution. And we must solve it without going outside the field of scientific facts' (*Esquisse d'un univers personnel*, 1936, in *L'énergie humaine*, p. 69). 'It is of course understood that in what follows I am expressly, and rightly, taking my stand on the ground of facts, that is to say in the field of the tangible and photographable' (*Man's place in the universe*, 1947, in *Vision of the Past*, p. 217).

This attempt is not an 'abstract metaphysics, but a realist ultra-physics of union. (*La Centrologie, essai d'une dialectique de l'univers*, 1944, *op. cit.*, p. 106). 'As for my innate "materialism" (I now see quite clearly) it was with the tangible strata of the universe as a

starting point that all reality became for me luminous and transfigured' (*L'étoffe de l'univers*, 1953, in *L'activation de l'énergie*, p. 397).
[57] Teilhard's preference for reflexion based on fact is in harmony
with his temperament. In 1919 he wrote, comparing himself with
some of his friends: 'I'm less concerned than they are with the metaphysical side of things, with what might have been or might not
have been, with the abstract conditions of existence: all that seems
to me inevitably misleading or shaky. I realize that, to the very
marrow of my bones, I'm sensitive to the real, to what is factual.
My concern is to discover the conditions for such progress as is open
to us, and not, starting from first principles, some theoretical
development of the universe. This bias means that I'll always be a
philistine to the professional philosophers: but I feel that my
strength lies in the fidelity with which I obey it' (Letter of 21 August
1919, in *Making of a Mind*, p. 302).

'The following pages do not seek to present any philosophy
directly; they set out, on the contrary, to draw their strength from
the careful avoidance of all recourse to metaphysics. Their purpose
is to express as objective and simple a vision as possible of humanity
considered (as a whole and in its connexions with the Universe) as a
phenomenon' (*Hominization*, 1923, in *Vision of the Past*, p. 23).

'During recent years, I have sought in a long series of essays, not
to philosophize in the absolute, but as a naturalist or physicist to
discover a general significance in the events in which we are materially involved' (*The New Spirit*, 1942, in *The Future of Man*, p. 82).

This use of the mind to examine the whole of reality, brings to
mind a saying of Descartes: '. . . and making up my mind to seek
no other knowledge than such as could be found in my own self, or
in the great book of the world' (*Discours de la méthode*, part 1).

[58] The following passage is evidence that Teilhard's thought was not
limited to the mere juxtaposition of facts and to the empiricism of
such juxtaposition: 'During the last fifty years or so, the investigations of science have proved beyond all doubt that there is no fact
which exists in pure isolation, but that every fact, however objective
it may seem, inevitably becomes enveloped in a complex of assumptions as soon as the scientist attempts to express it in a formula. But
while this aura of subjective interpretation may remain imperceptible where the field of observation is limited, it is bound to
become practically dominant as soon as the field of vision extends to

the whole. Like meridians as they approach the poles, science, philosophy and religion are bound to converge as they draw nearer to the whole. I say "converge" advisedly, but without merging and without ceasing, to the very end, to assail the real from different angles and on different planes' (*The Phenomenon of Man*, Preface, pp. 29–30).

The 'interpretation' of which Teilhard speaks, is synonymous with 'explanation'; and in *The Phenomenon of Man* the explanation is offered at two levels. There is first an explanation of the scientific or cosmological order, by transformism; this moves on to the philosophical or metaphysical plane, (cf. below) by reference to the Omega-Point, which is Absolute-God. In Teilhard's thought, however, the two approaches are inseparable.

[59] *The criterion of coherence*

'The cogency of a system lies much more in its effectiveness in explaining (i.e. giving unity to) intelligible reality, than in the way t enables one to see its isolated parts, and in particular its basis (which is a postulate)' (*L'union créatrice*, 1917, in *Ecrits du temps de la guerre*, p. 175). Cf. *The Phenomenon of Man*, p. 234.

'As I proceed, I shall be concerned only to follow out to their logical end the organic connexions that emerge—simply to see what happens—rather as though one was constructing a geometry. And it is whether the whole thing works in the end that will decide the matter. If the structure is not complete in itself, or if it contradicts some part of experience, then it means that the initial hypothesis is false and must be abandoned. But if, on the other hand, it succeeds in embracing the world and giving it a higher degree of harmony, then we shall be able to conclude that in recognizing a spiritual significance in evolution we have come closer to truth. Truth is simply the total coherence of the universe in relation to every point within itself' (*Esquisse d'un univers personnel*, 1936, in *L'énergie humaine*, p. 70).

'In a world whose whole point seems to be to become organized in relation to itself, that is the more *true* which more fully harmonizes, in relation to ourselves, the larger ensemble'. (*Le phénomène spirituel*, 1937, *ibid.*, p. 118).

'The essential criterion and specific mark of truth is the ability to develop itself indefinitely, not only without developing any internal contradiction, but also by forming a positively constructed whole, whose parts support and complement one another with continually fuller reciprocity' (*Comment je vois, Avertissement*, unpublished, 1948).

'When this further degree of the compression of things is reached, a sudden leap forward seems to me to be made in the coherence and simplicity—and hence in the verisimilitude and attractive power —of some structure of the world' (*L'étoffe de l'univers*, 1953, in *L'activation de l'énergie*, p. 397).

This ideal of coherence should be related to the necessity felt by Teilhard, and shared by every man, of attaining, through symbols, the solid and unchangeable, and felt so strongly that being is legitimately defined by consistence (Cf. appendix, note 14).

To the criterion of intellectual coherence, Teilhard adds the more existential criterion of coherence with life; in order to be, the world must not only be thinkable, but livable and breathable. It is this that ensures for it ultimate convergence in the absolute (*Un phénomène de contre-évolution . . .*) Nor does he underestimate the more practical criterion of fruitfulness, of the power to activate human energy.

⁶⁰ This fundamental choice is of the order of faith. 'On the strictly psychological plane, . . . I mean by faith any adherence of our intelligence to a general perspective of the universe and its future. We may try to define this adherence by certain aspects of liberty ("choice") or affectivity ("appeal") that accompany it. These features seem to me derivatory or secondary. In my view, the essential note of the act of psychological faith is to recognize as possible and accept as most probable, a conclusion that, in spatial extension or temporal prolongation, outdistances all analytical premises' (*Comment je crois*, unpublished, 1934). In spite of what Teilhard says, we retain the idea of choice, implicit in the heart of this faith in the whole.

Teilhard's thought seems to be diametrically opposed to that of Martin Heidegger, whose metaphysics is inspired by the initial question, 'Why is there being rather than nothing?' In fact, like every great philosopher, it seeks also a vindication of the being it has posited in an initial affirmation.

⁶¹ In *Le coeur de la matière*, Teilhard recalls his childhood memories of his passion for the hard and solid (crystal, iron).

⁶² There can be no doubt that Teilhard was aware of the thesis developed in Père Pierre Rousselot's study *The Intellectualism of St*

Thomas (1908). Above *ratio* (understanding) Rousselot found in St Thomas the reality of *intellectus*, that is to say of *mind*, thought-will, considered in its reality as an image of God, as being participating in Being, in fact a dynamic act, open to limitless being, with a dynamic relation to being and capable of affirming it freely: the secondary activity of understanding (*ratio*) being justified by its connexion with the mind (*intellectus*) and by the position as absolute achieved by the latter.

[63] 'Ultimately, then, I am closer to history than to metaphysics:' a history 'in which matter and spirit would be embraced in one and the same coherent and homogeneous explanation of the world' (Letter of 11 October 1936). With the human, 'we have just one added stroke—but it is enough to take us unmistakably out of metaphysics into history' (*Le coeur de la matière*, unpublished, 1950).

While rightly seeking to reject pure abstraction, Teilhard may here be deceiving himself about true metaphysics, which is always founded on facts (including the facts of history), and therefore about his personal claim, too, to work out a history that is independent of philosophy.

In *The Grand Option* (in *The Future of Man*, p. 37) Teilhard, after pointing out that philosophy consists in establishing or organizing a coherent network of intelligible relationships, asks us to consider the *mutation of consciousness* that, by introducing the notions of evolution and *history*, has profoundly modified the 'properties' of the real.

'The sense of history . . . Even for minds as acute and powerful as Spengler and Toynbee, history is reduced essentially to a periodic function, without beginning or end, whereas the problem in understanding history is to discover some basic current beneath the superficial cultural oscillations. Moreover, to make it worse, even for the most up to date historians, the human, taken as a whole, seems to constitute, in the heart of things, no more than a juridical microcosm, tossed to and fro, and shut in. And yet the whole problem faced by modern science is to include it, genetically and organically, in the domains of physics and biology' (*Transformations et prolongements en l'homme du mécanisme de l'évolution*, 1931, in *L'activation de l'énergie*, p. 320).

[64] 'To our predecessors, time was both extrinsic to beings and isotropic in relation to itself. To us, it is becoming more and more

dominatingly organic and convergent: the very stuff of things and the heart of their ontogenesis' (*Du cosmos à la cosmogénèse*, 1951, in *L'activation de l'énergie*, p. 266).

[65] 'For every modern mind (and the more modern the mind, the truer this is) *consciousness* has appeared once and for all—a *sense* is born—the sense of a universal, completely specific, movement, by virtue of which the totality of things shifts as one whole, from top to bottom, and in one block, not only in space and time but in a space-time (hyper-einsteinian) whose particular curvature has the faculty of *making what moves within it progressively more organized*' (*Du cosmos à la cosmogénèse*, 1951, in *L'activation de l'énergie*, p. 264). The idea of evolution is the perception of 'this fundamental dynamic unity' (*Ibid.*).

[66] This idea of a total phenomenology is not something reconstituted by the commentary offered in the text. It *emerges* unmistakably from Teilhard's most finished writings, *The Phenomenon of Man* and *Comment je crois* (unpublished, 1948). The phenomenon of man is constantly associated with the Christian phenomenon.

[67] In *L'atomisme de l'esprit* (1941) Teilhard speaks of the oscillation 'between a cult of the spirit that jettisoned nature and a cult of nature that led to a denial of the spirit' (*op. cit.*, p. 63).

'In order to preserve spiritual values, are we really reduced to seeking refuge in an impossible dualism, as if matter and thought formed two separate universes, mutually coextensive and yet sharing no common dimension?' (*Man's place in the universe*, 1942, in *Vision of the Past*, p. 222).

Matter and spirit, 'two terms integrated with one another in the unity of one and the same movement' (*Introduction au christianisme*, unpublished, 1944).

In *Le coeur de la matière* (unpublished, 1950, p. 9) Teilhard speaks of the joy with which he realized that 'the dualism to which he had hitherto been confined was evaporating like mist before the rising sun. Matter and spirit: no longer two things but two *states*, two aspects of one and the same cosmic stuff, depending on whether you look at it, or extend it, in the direction in which (as Bergson would have said) it is formed, or in the direction in which it loses form'.

[68] 'The human body is simply a super-molecule, in which we have the opportunity to distinguish the properties of every molecule' (*La centrologie*, No. 1, in *L'activation de l'énergie*, p. 106).

[69] This reconstruction is supported by Teilhard's avowed intention 'In this second part I shall try to reconstruct deductively, that is to say *a priori*, the system so observed (including its theological or revealed extensions), starting from certain general principles, taken as absolute' (*Comment je vois*, unpublished, 1948; part 2, *Métaphysique*).

Answering, in impersonal terms, a question about his thought, Teilhard explains that it is in the first place 'a sort of experiential phenomenology', secondly an 'apologetics' (identifying the Omega of reason with the universal Christ of revelation), and finally a 'mysticism'. 'Taken together, the three branches of the system suggest and without difficulty trace the outlines of a metaphysics of union, dominated by love' (*La pensée du Père Teilhard de Chardin par lui-même*, 1948, in *Les études philosophiques*, October–December, 1955).

[70] See Père Christian d'Armagnac's excellent study, *Philosophie de la nature et méthode chez le Père Teilhard de Chardin*, in *Archives de philosophie*, January–March 1957, in particular p. 30.

[71] *The Phenomenon of Man* and *Le Milieu Divin*, to which we should add *Man's Place in Nature*, which covers the same ground as the first.

[72] Cf. M. Barthélemy-Madaule, *op. cit.*, pp. 593–5.

[73] The whole progress of Teilhard's thought advances from appearance to truth, from the superficial to the profound, the less real to the more real (= solid = consistent), from less-being to more-being, from what has less 'substance' (interior unity) (material things) to what has more substance (the person, the organism of persons, God). This progress of thought is at once intellectual and mystical. The texts which illustrate this start with his earliest confidences. '. . . to find that other blue sky and that other sun that illuminate all things from within' (Letter of 24 April 1919, in *Making of a Mind*, p. 294). 'There's no doubt that there is a powerful educative force lodged in the world, which continually calls us to journey further into the deep layers of being: what attracts us in things is always withdrawing further from us, beyond every individual tangible reality, and finally beyond death' (Letter of 27 April 1919, *ibid.*, p. 296).

[74] 'For a Pascalian faced with the question that it has itself raised, science is continually developing; for a Teilhardian, science, not any particular science, but science considered as one whole, is not philosophically dumb; it speaks a language that is metaphysically

eloquent and, basically, raises only the problems that it is capable of solving' (Etienne Borne, *op. cit.*, p. 55). From another angle, Père G. Fessard shows the natural possibility, for positive and scientific language, of signifying, by analogy, ontological and theological realities (*La vision religieuse de Teilhard de Chardin*, in *L'Homme devant Dieu*, Mélanges offerts au Père de Lubac, Aubier, 1964, pp. 234–6). 'Ultimately, when it is a question in their dialogue of the "whole phenomenon of man", there is practically no difference between the technical language of the phenomenologist and the human or universal language of the philosopher and theologian' (*Ibid.*, p. 235).

75 *The Phenomenon of Man*, p. 29. 'This book . . . must be read not as a work on metaphysics, still less as a sort of theological essay, but purely and simply as a scientific treatise' (*Ibid.*, Preface, p. 29).

'To harmonize objects in time and space, without presuming to determine the conditions that can rule their deepest being: to establish an experiential chain of succession in nature, not a union of "ontological" causality; to see, in other words, and not to explain —this, let it not be forgotten, is the sole aim of this study' (*Ibid.*, p. 58).

Quite apart from the vagueness of the notion of 'depth' that Teilhard introduces, we may well wonder whether this sort of reflexion on experience is not, by nature and from the outset, on the plane of truth and philosophical explanation.

76 'In the first place, and in spite of certain appearances, the *Weltanschauung* I am putting forward in no way represents a fixed and closed system. It is not a question of (what, indeed, would be absurd) a deductive *solution* of the world in the manner of Hegel, of a definite framework of truth, but simply of a fascicle of *axes of progression*, such as exist and are gradually being disclosed in every evolutionary system: not a total absorption of truth, but lines of penetration that open up for us an unexplored immensity of the real'(*Comment je vois*, unpublished, 1948).

We may well conclude that Teilhard can have had only a distant and conventional idea of Hegel: had he been able to benefit from the revival of Hegelian studies he would no doubt have recognized the eminently concrete side of Hegel's philosophy.

Teilhard rather plays down the notion of *certainty*, as though truth were patient of no more than an 'approach' or of a greater probability. For example, in introducing the hypothesis of the world's movement towards the greatest degree of personalization, he puts it as follows: 'If (the structure) succeeds in embracing and harmonizing the world to a higher degree, then we can conclude that, in recognizing a spiritual significance in evolution, we have approached the truth' (*Esquisse d'un univers personel*, 1963, in *L'énergie humaine*, pp. 70–1). Similarly, he speaks several times later on of the conjectural character of Omega Point. This idea of certainty, which is influenced by the positive and scientific aspect of Teilhard's method, and seems never to go so far as an 'absolute' affirmation, is, no doubt, simply the expression of a feeling that all rational thought or language must necessarily fall short of the infinity of the real.

[77] The term *ultra-physics*, contradictory in appearance but dialectical in fact, indicates in the first place fidelity to positive and scientific experience, the indissoluble adherence of philosophical reflexion to facts, concern for rationality, and the desire to express the *laws* of the real and the *necessity* of the order of things. It implies also a *negation*, by which thought goes beyond the order of verifiable evidence, the measurable relations of phenomena, to express the secret of their being and the goal to which they are directed, the law of their essence and of their movement.

[78] 'A view of the world that is sufficiently profound may be called metaphysics, in as much as it opens a breach, and this opening is part and parcel of the whole outlook' (M. Barthélemy-Madaule, *op. cit.*, p. 409). 'For the last five hundred years the most important problem for philosophy has been the realization, acute and decisive, that time is truly constitutive of man, not simply a form of his experience but this actual experience in its deepest intensity and widest extension. That, moreover, is why philosophy is being recognized as essentially historical; this in no way prevents it from driving its roots into the eternal; far from it, since philosophy and phenomenology have a mutual attraction for one another, and eternity and history do not form a series'. (G. Morel, *Renouvellement de la philosophie*, in *Responsables*, January 1964, '*L'homme de l'an* 2000', p. 132).

[79] At a time when his thought had not yet been fully clarified, Teilhard, more concerned, as he ever was, to point out the continuity of things than the cleavages between them, called 'faith' the

first direct discovery of the Absolute-God in the perception of beings (but also perhaps in the rational development of truth): 'The "visibilia" are not for me only a logical premise to some process of reasoning that leads to the invisibilia. They constitute for me *a first world* of faith, of which the world of supernatural faith is simply the development' (Letter of 25 February 1929).

80 At this stage in its progress, and before reaching its consummation in loving communion through the mystical life, Teilhard's philosophy (or total phenomenology) is still in the *abstract* order of representation or idea; unified and coherent though it is, it falls short of a real possession.

81 *Bergson and Teilhard*

Here we find one of the fundamental differences between Teilhard and Bergson. For the latter, the grasping of being in its truth is operated integrally by a double direct *intuition*, involving 'torsion' and 'reversal', starting from abstract knowledge: intuition of the underlying ego (Cf. *Time and Free-will*) and intuition of the underlying movement of objective reality (Cf. *Creative Evolution*). Intuition which is 'philosophy' itself, concrete knowledge of being.

Teilhard entirely rejects this approach. Although he is no less eager for concrete possession of the real, he believes that it can be obtained only at *the term of a dialectical progress*, that goes through all the existential stages or moments of values: science, philosophy, art, social life, moral and religious life, theology, mysticism. And this, not only in the activity of the person, but in that of all mankind in its collective history. Short of the term (individual and social) there is nothing that is not at the same time *necessary and abstract*, and therefore insufficient: nothing is robbed of value but everything is integrated and gathered up again.

Madame M. Barthélemy-Madaule (*op. cit.,*) has well brought out Bergson's dependence on an interior and psychological concept of reality, on a desire to meet the real through a direct psychic intuition; as a consequence of this, in spite of the respect he has for abstract knowledge, he has difficulty in justifying it completely. Teilhard undoubtedly, and rightly, felt the *illusory and mythical* character of the Bergsonian intuition of the underlying ego and of movement. We are speaking, of course, of metaphysical intuition, and not of psychological, intuition, well-known and perfectly valid, which is in fact consciousness.

[82] *L'esprit de la terre*, 1931, in *L'énergie humaine*, pp. 56–7.

[83] *Teilhard's dialectic*

Finding again in facts, though without giving any metaphysical explanation of it, the Hegelian dialectic of the transformation of quantity into quality, Teilhard formulates the following law: 'In every domain, when anything exceeds a certain measurement it suddenly changes its aspect, condition or nature' (*The Phenomenon of Man*, p. 78). 'All growing magnitudes in the world (must) become different so as to remain themselves' (*Ibid.*, p. 166).

'There is a relationship in nature between quantity and quality. Change the spatial dimensions of bodies and their very properties change with them . . . Concentric with ourselves, there undoubtedly exist a certain number of critical spatial surfaces, passing through which physical values are reversed' (*L'atomisme de l'esprit*, 1941, *op. cit.*, p. 32). Cf. *Esquisse d'un univers personnel*, 1936, in *L'énergie humaine*, p. 76.

'Carried to a certain degree of convergence, the layers of a cone run together into a point with no extension. Raised to a certain temperature or pressure bodies change their *state*: they become liquid or gaseous. In all the movements of matter we find 'critical' or 'unique' points. Why should there not be the same in the transformations of life?' (*Man's Place in Nature*, 1932, in *The Vision of the Past* p. 179-80. Cf. *The Phenomenon of Man*, p. 101).

'If nature teaches us clearly that there is a universal struggle for life, it shows us equally unmistakably that in passing from one level of being to another, living properties can persist only in being transformed or transposed' (*The Natural Units of Humanity*, 1939, in *The Vision of the Past*, p. 213).

A characteristic example, and one to which Teilhard attributed the utmost importance, is provided by 'the change of curve which is suddenly obliging us to move from a Universe in which the divergence, and hence the spacing-out, of the containing lines still seemed the most important feature, into another type of universe which, in pace with time, is rapidly folding-in upon itself' (*Man's Place in Nature*, p. 103). Cf. *Hominization*, 1925, in *The Vision of Past*, pp. 64–5). '. . . People persist in trying, in order to explain the apparent genesis of the world, to contrast only two terms: complete stability and continuous change. We must make up our minds, under the pressure of facts, to introduce into natural history the notion of unique points or changes of state.'

Similarly, the rise of *reflexion* represents a critical point and change of state: 'Discontinuity in continuity: that is how, in the theory of its mechanism, the birth of thought, like that of life, presents itself and defines itself' (*The Phenomenon of Man*, p. 169). 'A knot whose strands have for all time been converging from the four corners of space,' and then 'at one single stroke the birth of intelligence' (*Ibid.*, pp. 170–1).

Death is conceived as an inevitable metamorphosis, since there comes a moment when persons can no longer become greater without changing (*Esquisse d'un Univers personnel*, 1936, in *L'énergie humaine*, p. 109).

The dialectic of history is symbolized by drawing a meridian from the lower pole to the equator and then on to the higher pole: 'The passage from expansion to contraction' (*The singularities of the human species*, 1954, in *The Appearance of Man*, p. 235. *Man's Place in Nature*, pp. 82, 102).

To this dialectic belongs also the differentiation of properties in the different sections of the universe, in the extremely small, the medium and the vast. (*Man's place in the Universe*, 1942, in *Vision of the Past*, pp. 217–21).

To symbolize the dialectic of attachment and detachment in the spiritual life, Teilhard uses the simile of two cones meeting at their apexes. 'The lower layer can pass into the higher only by inverting itself and reducing its volume until it is no more than a point. And yet at the same time everything that was in the lower layer has passed into the higher, and the higher has no existence without the influx of the lower' (Letter to Père Auguste Valensin, 12 December 1919, in *Archives de Philosophie*, January–March 1961, p. 139). Cf. *Le Milieu Divin*, p. 110: 'Immersion and emergence; participation in things and sublimation: possession and renunciation; crossing through and being borne onward; that is the twofold yet single movement which answers the challenge of matter in order to save it.' The progress of the spiritual life consists in passing through the intermediate stages, not in rejecting them: it is a passage (*Ibid.*, p. 139). Similarly Teilhard speaks of 'the psychological reversal (experienced by the Christian) whereby joy in action melts imperceptibly into desire for submission, and the exaltation of

being one's own self into the zeal to die in another' (*Ibid.*, p. 74).
Referring to an article in which Père M. de la Taille had shown
that, while differing in nature from ordinary prayer, mystical contemplation has its roots in it, Teilhard notes: 'His general principle,
which seems to me extremely sound, is precisely that of "creative
transformation"—the principle that explains, without removing it
from the cosmic framework, life after death, thought after instinct,
revelation after the labour of reason, the new earth after the old,
etc.' (Letter of 21 December 1919).

    C. Cuénot points out a three-termed dialectic in Teilhard;
divergence, convergence, emergence (afresh). (*Teilhard de Chardin*,
in the series 'Ecrivains pour toujours,' Editions du Seuil, p. 106).
These three terms, dovetailed together in a circuminsession, come
together in 'recurrence' at each phase or stage of progress.

[84] In a letter of 8 January Teilhard speaks of spirit as 'an un-
quenchable force that insists on the destruction of everything that
has outlived its time' (*Letters from a Traveller*, p. 150).

[85] *The Phenomenon of Man*, p. 169. 'That is how, in the theory of its
mechanism, the birth of thought, like that of life, presents itself and
defines itself' (*Ibid.*, p. 169).

Describing the evolution of life, Teilhard says: 'Something is
carried over: it grows, jerkily, but ceaselessly, and in a constant
direction' (*The Phenomenon of Man*, p. 148). This sentence expresses
both the continuous and discontinuous aspect of history.

'Modern science has made us familiar with the idea that certain
sudden radical changes occur inevitably in the course of every
development, provided it be carried far enough and always be in
the same direction. Once matter has reached certain extreme levels
of transformation then, at the cost of a trifling modification of its
arrangement, it is capable of suddenly modifying its properties or
even of changing its state. This notion of *critical thresholds* is commonly accepted today in physics, chemistry and genetics. Has not
the time come when we should use it to reconstruct the whole edifice
of anthropology on a new and solid foundation?' (*La convergence de
l'univers*, 1951, in *L'activation de l'énergie*, p. 297).

[86] 'Here again the mysterious notion of "transformation" must come
in—that doesn't cut out the "critical thresholds" but allows their
function—that links super-nature to nature, and spirit to matter—
that makes it possible to look for higher realities *through* the wretched

crust of every shape and every physical property' (Letter to Père Auguste Valensin, 8 December 1919).

[87] Teilhard was aware of this category, as we know from an unpublished ms. (Cf. M. Barthélemy-Madaule, *op. cit.*, p. 36).

[88] 'One must have clearly and forcibly realized the separation and antagonism of the elements of the cosmos, if one is to be intoxicated by the thought of their underlying connexion and the confluence we anticipate for them' (*La route de l'Ouest*, unpublished, 1932).

'All the rest of this essay will be nothing but the story of the struggle in the universe between the unified multiple and the unorganized multitude . . .' (*The Phenomenon of Man*, p. 61).

While holding that Teilhard's passion for unity prevented him from allowing full weight to the immanent contradiction of the real, Etienne Borne adds: 'And yet at the same time, and still because of his fidelity to the real, no one has more clearly brought out the full degree to which there is negation of the spirit in matter as it now is: adding that if the genius of man, the advance guard of life as it presses on, should (a catastrophe that is always possible) check its drive and, through laziness or pride, satisfy itself with what it has already built up—then, that in itself would be sufficient for an insoluble contradiction to be produced in the world, and to ensure the victory over reason of the absurd . . . the dialectic of the universe has a tragic reality, that can be overcome only in faith' (*Matière et esprit dans la philosophie de Teilhard de Chardin*, Recherches et débats du C.C.I.F., cahier No. 40, Fayard, 1962, p. 63).

In an article in the same number, Claude Soucy compares Teilhard's method with that of Hegel in his *Phenomenology of Mind*: he shows that Teilhard seeks to think the whole, in its concrete development. He notes, however, their divergence on the problem of religion (*Teilhard de Chardin est-il philosophe? ibid.*, pp. 38–42).

[89] *Comment je crois*, unpublished, 1934.

[90] Speaking of Teilhard, Jean Hyppolite went so far as to say, 'He was more Hegelian than I' (C. Cuénot, *op. cit.*, p. 311). C. Cuénot has worked out the terms of comparison between Teilhard and Hegel: both, basing themselves on the totality of the real, posited the identity of thought with being, as also the correspondence of the movement of thought with the movement of the real. Hegel, however, is blind to the fact of cosmogenesis and the progressive unification of spirit; he is less concerned with positive observation

than with the strictness of conceptual connexions; and finally, he reduces religion to philosophy, and seems to assimilate God to the deployment of the world (article quoted above, pp. 19–23).

[91] Cf. the well-known fragment about the three 'orders' (the flesh, thought, charity), Ed. Brunschvicg, No. 793.

[92] Cf. Edouard Le Roy, *Essai d'une philosophie première*, P.U.F., 1956. The passage that follows illustrates the epistemological realism of Teilhard. 'I'm firmly convinced (and in fact could any other philosophy be Christianizable?) that the substance of our states of consciousness—which is the stuff of the universe in so far as it's *experienced* by us—represents some absolute' (Letter of 12 July 1918, p. 214). While recognizing the value of a 'stable distribution' of degrees of being, as in the tradition of the ancient philosophers, Teilhard thinks that the 'particular slant of our thought today is to seek in this gradation . . . a road for life to follow, the shape of individual and collective being, in *course* of formation' (*Ibid.*, p. 215).

To Père Auguste Valensin, who also was urging him towards the 'idealist transposition', Teilhard wrote: 'I shall always be grateful to you for having shown it to me. But, because of what I naturally have a taste for and need, I don't feel at home in it. My intellectual position is more empirical and more modest—closer to the scientific approach. What attracts me is the construction of a linked series of phenomena extending, under the influence of a single fundamental evolutionary process, from the spiritual pole to the material pole of experience. In other words, I am working not so much in the direction of an "idealist transposition" as in that of a "spiritualist transposition" of the universe. You may be sorry for me, if you like, but you must forgive me. It's the only road that gives me confidence in the order of the real' (13 October 1933).

[93] 'However dispersed and seriated in time and space they may be, yet in their birth, through the operation of evolution, the particles of a universe in process of cosmogenesis enjoy the full property of being co-extensive, in an infinitesimal degree, with the totality of space and time' (*Du cosmos à la cosmogénèse*, 1951, in *L'activation de l'énergie*, p. 269).

[94] 'Indifference to what is *a priori* impossible is characteristic of intrepidity of mind. And in Teilhard, as in Bergson or even in Hegel, there is this confidence of the mind in mind, that sets out *solvere ambulando* and for which knowledge is not obsessed by its own

technique, that seeks to efface itself before the true or rather the real, so much so that the great adventure of knowing takes us straight to the heart of the real, and once the real has been attained the distinction between absolute and relative disappears . . . The real discloses itself, matter or spirit, or rather matter and spirit, or, still, better, matter-spirit; it points out the truth of that which is: being bears witness of being; the phenomenon is not an appearance that refers back to an unknowable thing within itself . . . That there is no truth but the real, which is in itself its own proper criterion, this sort of physical, and metaphysical, axiom is constantly pre-supposed in the whole of Teilhard's approach' (E. Borne, *Matière et esprit dans la philosophie de Teilhard de Chardin*, in *Essais sur Teilhard de Chardin, op. cit.*, p. 47).

Claude Cuénot rightly remarks that Teilhard's method 'is reason finding and recognizing itself again in everything' (*art. cit.*, p. 8).

[95] 'Whatever may still be said . . . the much vaunted "subjectivity" of history (like that of ethical systems) is in course of being irre-vocably transformed into objectivity, as man more clearly discovers an absolute significance (and therefore scale of values) in the pro-cesses of hominization and socialization' (*The singularities of the human species*, in *The Appearance of Man*, p. 243 n. 1).

[96] *The Phenomenon of Man*, pp. 221–2.

[97] *Ibid.*, pp. 32–3.

[98] 'When I try to picture the world before the dawn of life, or life in the palaeozoic era, I do not forget that there would be a cosmic contradiction in imagining a man as spectator of those phases which ran their course before the appearance of thought on earth. I do not pretend to describe them as they really were, but rather as we must picture them to ourselves so that the world may be true for us at this moment. What I depict is not the past *in itself*, but as it must appear to an observer standing on the advanced peak where evolution has placed us' (*Ibid.*, p. 35).

[99] *Esquisse d'un univers personnel*, 1926, in *L'énergie humaine*, p. 71. 'This duality of the cognitive order and the order of the real has always seemed to me, since that time, arbitrary and false. We have no serious reason for thinking that things are not made with the same rhythm as that with which our experience unfolds them. So far from that being true, this rhythm may very well reveal to us the underlying texture of the spirit' (*L'union créatrice*, 1917, in

Ecrits du temps de la guerre, p. 184). 'In constructing truth,' comments Madame M. Barthélemy-Madaule, 'we grasp reality, and in so doing we adhere closely to being' (*op. cit.*, p. 572).

[100] 'Long ago Kant (and the scholastics before him) had indicated the links that, within every universe, give indissoluble solidarity to the perceiver and the perceived. But this fundamental condition of knowledge disturbed only the rare and unapproachable metaphysical experts. To those who were interested in nature, it seemed established, without any discussion, that things project themselves for us "just as they are" on a screen on which we can look at them without being involved in them. Scientists used to contemplate the cosmos without suspecting that they could influence it in any degree by the contact of their thought or their understanding; they were not even aware of belonging intrinsically to the system which they analysed with such amazement. On one side was man, on the other the world. It now appears that, for decisive reasons, and reasons that come from within us, we are beginning to emerge today from this naive extrinsicism . . . the old realism of the laboratory is now, through the very logic of its development, tending towards a scientific idealism: matter is moulded by the intelligence that informs it' (*L'énergie humaine*, 1947, pp. 143–4).

[101] 'The universe and man confer on one another, reciprocally but not symmetrically, a consistence in relation to thought, a cohesion and a significance. Man confers a consistence on the universe, since the presence of man, his coming, puts out of court the idea of an evolution that is a vague, meaningless, drift; the history of the universe comes to a head for a first time in man, before receiving a plenitude and infinite significance in Christ. And reciprocally, the universe confers on man a first consistence . . . ' (C. d'Armagnac, *De Bergson à Teilhard, Etudes*, February 1964, p. 169).

[102] 'Teilhard's realism, marked though it is—his thought places him at the opposite extreme from all forms of idealism—has nothing naive about it. Teilhard, like every scientist, is certain that nature precedes thought; he refuses to make of it a representation or an obstacle to value, but he is not so ingenuous as to believe (and in this he is Kantian) that we can reconstruct the origins of the world while leaving out of account the thought that reconstructs them. This realism is a dialogue between the demands of nature (of the 'external world') and man's response—and this response is valid

because man himself has emerged from nature and because nature already contains thought. Teilhard . . . restores the cogito to the setting of a natural history of the world' (C. Cuénot, *Teilhard de Chardin*, in the series *Ecrivains de toujours*, pp. 115, 117).

[103] 'How can we acquire the concept of that which is the opposite of nothing, rejects nothing, and resembles nothing?' (P. Valéry, *Au sujet d'Eurêka*, in *Variété*, 18th edition, Paris, Gallimard, 1924, p. 136. Cf. *ibid.*, pp. 132-6).

[104] Père J.-Y. Calvez shows that Marx excludes 'the possibility of a dialectic of nature independent of any existence of man' (*La pensée de Karl Marx*, Editions du Seuil, 1957, pp. 380-2). Commenting on Engels' attempt, he adds that 'a dialectic of nature is not perhaps inconceivable. It would in every way differ in its significance from the dialectic of history and of society: it would be a dialectic of the movement of man's consciousness of it' (*Ibid.*, p. 383 note).

[105] Teilhard's view of the world has a very pronounced affective character; he is impressed by the immensity, the hugeness, the vastness beyond all measure, of the universe, by the multiplicity of its elements, by the depth of time and space. Cf. in particular, *Man's Place in the Universe. Reflexions on complexity* 1942, in *The Vision of the Past*, p. 216: 'I say "dizzy" advisedly: caught between the immense and the infinitesimal. Man is indeed, as Pascal felt, floating between two abysses.'

This lyrical feeling comes out most strongly in the papers collected in *Hymn of the Universe*, particularly in *The Spiritual Power of Matter* (pp. 59-71). He sees matter as a fire, as a whirlwind unleashed, a violent and untamed passion, a torrent of energies, or terrifying force: as challenging man to a struggle and driving him to anguish. It is an impressive description of the pagan forces of the earth, the more so in that Teilhard adds that they must be redeemed and brought to salvation (p. 61).

[106] 'Christ, no doubt, is not the centre whom all things here below could *naturally* hope to espouse. To be destined to Christ is an unexpected and gratuitous favour from the creator. It remains true that the Incarnation has so completely recast the universe in the supernatural that, concretely speaking, we can no longer try to imagine towards what centre the elements of this world would have gravitated had they not been raised up to

grace' (*L'union créatrice*, 1917, in *Ecrits du temps de la guerre*, p. 195).

[107] 'Nature is an image of grace' (Pascal, ed. Brunschvicg, No. 643). 'The form has been modelled on truth, and truth recognized in the form' (No. 673).

[108] 'Like the meridians as they approach the poles, science, philosophy and religion are bound to converge as they draw nearer to the whole. I say "converge" advisedly, but without merging, and without ceasing, to the very end, to assail the real from different angles and on different planes' (*The Phenomenon of Man*, Preface, p. 30).

'On a sphere it would be absurd (this is concordism) to run the meridians together at the equator; but (and this is coherence) these same meridians must, from structural necessity, meet at the pole' (*Comment je vois*, unpublished, 1948).

[109] *The influence of Christianity*

'Christianity so largely takes on its full value by virtue of the ideas related to creative union that this theory, instead of being regarded as a philosophy that is confirmed and strengthened by Christian views, should rather be called a philosophical extension of faith in the Incarnation' (*Mon univers*, unpublished, 1924).

'I should never have ventured to envisage the Omega Point or formulate the hypothesis rationally if, in my consciousness as a believer, I had not found not only its speculative model but also its living reality' (*The Phenomenon of Man*, p. 294).

'If elsewhere I may have given the impression, in other writings of mine, of leaping directly (from a reflexion on the phenomenon of man and its culmination in Omega) to Christ, it is either because, taking my readers to be sufficiently informed, I neglected to distinguish the stages (to put down the intermediate operations)—or because there is a positive difficulty for a mind that is already Christian, in thinking of Omega (even at its elementary stage) without realizing that its function of gathering together and unifying implies its being, in one way or another, partly involved in the world. Cf. Duns Scotus's views on the necessity for some Incarnation' (*Esquisse d'une dialectique de l'esprit*, 1946, in *L'activation de l'énergie*, p. 257).

'Although the ideas contained in this essay are (as is evident) influenced by the Gospel, they were not born in my mind from that part of me that is specifically Christian' (*Ibid.*, p. 112).

To these passages we should, however, add the following remark, which maintains the autonomy of scientific thought: 'As I am living at the heart of the Christian world, I might be suspected of wanting to introduce an apologia by artifice. But, here again, so far as it is possible for a man to separate in himself the various planes of knowledge, it is not the convinced believer but the natural scientist who is asking for a hearing' (*The Phenomenon of Man*, p. 292).

[110] In spite of its opening assertion, the following passage, from notes taken by Claude Cuénot of a lecture given by Teilhard at the École Normale Supérieure, conforms with the idea of a connexion between the natural order and the theological. 'There is no Christian philosophy, in the sense that would imply two opposed entities. Faith is born only from faith. It is not a question of reason on the one hand and faith on the other. There are only progressively higher acts of faith: the world has a significance, and that significance is spirit; spirit comes from unification, and unification comes through Christianity. Philosophy is pre-Christian, but it adopts the attitude of a faith' (*Teilhard de Chardin et les philosophes*, in *La Table Ronde*, June 1955, p. 37). Cf. E. Gilson, *Le philosophe et la théologie* (Fayard, 1960) pp. 191-216. C. Tresmontant, however, has shown that there are some philosophies that Christianity cannot take in (*op. cit.*).

CHAPTER 3: A PHENOMENOLOGY OF HISTORY

[1] 'A first multiple, followed by a first unification—a new plurality forming again at every successive stage of consciousness, to allow a higher synthesis: it is thus that we may express the law of recurrence in which we are involved' (*Esquisse d'un univers personnel*, 1936, in *L'énergie humaine*, p. 73). We should note that the 'first multiple' is for Teilhard only a figure of speech, since there is no pure multiplicity independent of any unity.

[2] Nor is history *cyclic*, as the ancients believed it to be, whose concept was based on relating the revolutions of heavenly bodies to human time.

[3] *The Phenomenon of Man*, p. 31. In the present unification of mankind, Teilhard sees 'the natural culmination of a cosmic process of

organization which has never varied since those remote ages when our planet was young' (*Ibid.*, p. 243).

[4] *Le Christique*, unpublished, 1955. Entropy is the mathematical formulation of the second law of thermodynamics, expressing the amount of necessarily unavailable energy in any closed thermodynamic system, as a result of its tendency to fall into a state where the scattered particles are homogeneously in motion. More precisely, Teilhard distinguishes in matter entropy, expansion, and attraction (electrical or gravitational) (*Man's Place in Nature*, p. 33).

[5] We should remember too, says Teilhard, that there is a proto-history of matter, in the form of the filiation of atoms and the genealogy of molecules, starting from 'an as yet unresolved simplicity, luminous in nature and not to be defined in terms of figures'. 'From its most distant formulations matter reveals itself to us in *a state of genesis* or becoming—this genesis allowing us to distinguish two of the aspects most characteristic of it in its subsequent stages. First of all, to begin with a critical phase, that of granulation, which abruptly (and once and for all?) gave birth to the constituents of the atom and perhaps to the atom itself. Next, at least from the molecular level, of going on additively by a process of growing complexity' (*The Phenomenon of Man*, pp. 47, 48-9).

[6] *Le coeur de la matière*, unpublished, 1950, p. 26.

[7] Letter of 19 January 1929, in *Letters from a Traveller*, p. 151. 'The universe in gravitation was falling towards spirit as though seeking its stable form, lying ahead of it' (*Le coeur de la matière*, unpublished, 1950, p. 10). 'The spirit of the philosophers and theologians' lies in a 'direct extension of the physical chemistry of the universe'. The *Weltstoff* counters entropy's dissipation of energy 'by striving, in its totality and in all its individual constituents, to reflect upon itself' (*L'étoffe de l'univers*, 1953, in *L'activation de l'énergie*, pp. 400-1).

This active presence of spirit in the material world, in spite of its partial aspect of dissipation, justifies Teilhard's passion for matter: 'In fact, even at the zenith of my spiritual trajectory, I shall never feel completely at home unless I am immersed in an ocean of matter' (*Le coeur de la matière*, p. 6).

[8] 'If the world is indeed a thing that is characterized by arrangement in one way or another, then we can better appreciate that life can no longer be regarded as a superficial accident in the universe; we must look on it as under pressure everywhere in the universe,

ready to seep through the narrowest fissure it can find anywhere in the cosmos' (*Man's Place in Nature*, p. 35).

'As soon as the earth can be said to have a surface, however far back in time that may be, that surface is inhabited, as though no heavenly body could arrive at a certain level in its sidereal evolution without blazing out into life' (*Le phénomène spirituel*, 1937, in *L'énergie humaine*, p. 120).

[9] In common with many biologists, Teilhard sees the rise of living forms as that of a central stem surrounded by divergent ramifications, scales or leaves, bulbous in form. The divergent lines represent incompletely successful attempts on the part of vital energy whose pressure is trying to force its way out. He also compares the ribs of this fan to the different colours of a spectrum.

On the phenomenon of ramification, by which 'Life propagates like a morphological fan, each line of which is capable of producing another fan, and so on indefinitely', see *The natural units of humanity*, 1939, in *Vision of the Past*, p. 193.

In 1949, we find Teilhard emphasizing the evolution, dispersive in character, and the fan-like mutations that give biological series the appearance not so much of a trajectory as of an 'explosive wave' of forms (*The Vision of the Past*, 1949, in *The Vision of the Past*, p. 239).

With the *dispersive* evolution that limits itself to the diversification of living forms in multiple groups, and the *instrumental* evolution that divides them into specialized morphological types (swimming, running, flying, etc.), Teilhard associates the *global* evolution towards fuller consciousness (*L'esprit de la terre*, 1931, in *L'énergie humaine*, pp. 33-4).

On *orthogenesis*, that 'orientates the sum total of individual variations in one special direction', see *The natural units of humanity*, 1939, in *Vision of the Past*, p. 195.

[10] Teilhard characterizes the *insects* thus: 'This could be called a paroxysm of consciousness, if you like, which spreads outward from within, to become materialized in rigid arrangements. The exact opposite of a concentration.' (*The Phenomenon of Man*, p. 155).

The *mammals* represent a key-stage in progress. 'If a furry quadruped seems so "animate" compared with an ant, so genuinely alive, it is not only because of a zoological kinship we have with it. In the behaviour of a cat, a dog, a dolphin, there is such suppleness, such unexpectedness, such exuberance of life and curiosity. Instinct is no longer narrowly canalized as in the spider or the bee, paralysed to a single function. Individually and socially it remains flexible. It takes interest, it flutters, it plays. We are dealing with an entirely different form of instinct in fact, and one not subject to *the limitations imposed on the tool by the precision it has attained.* Unlike the insect, the mammal is no longer completely the slave of the phylum it belongs to. Around it an "aura" of freedom begins to float, a glimmer of personality. And it is in that direction that the possibilities crop up, interminate and interminable, before it' (*Ibid.*, pp. 155-7).

Of the *primates*, Teilhard has this to say: 'They represent a phylum of *pure and direct cerebralization.* In the other mammals too, no doubt, the nervous system and instinct gradually develop. But in them the internal travail was distracted, limited, and finally arrested by easily achieved differentiations.' *Pari passu* with their psychical development, horse, stag and tiger became, like the insect, to some extent prisoners of the instruments of their swift-moving or predatory ways. *For that is what their limbs and teeth had become.* In the case of the primates, on the other hand, evolution went straight to work on the brain, neglecting everything else, which accordingly remained malleable. That is why they are at the head of the upward and onward march towards greater consciousness' (*Ibid.*, p. 159).

11 'To overcome the improbability of arrangements leading to units of ever increasing complexity, the involuting universe, considered in its pre-reflective zones, proceeds step by step by dint of billionfold trial and error' (*Ibid.*, p. 302).

12 *Ibid.*, pp. 122-40.

13 *Ibid.*, pp. 147-52. 'Right at its base, the living world is constituted by consciousness clothed in flesh and bone. From the biosphere to the species is nothing but an immense ramification of psychism seeking for itself by means of different forms' (p. 151). The most significant of the properties of organic arrangements is 'the gradual emergence of the effects of indetermination and choice' (*La convergence de l'univers*, 1951, in *L'activation de l'énergie*, p. 300).

14 'The smallest thing formed in the world is always the result of the most formidable coincidence—a knot whose strands have been for

all time converging from the four corners of space' (*The Phenomenon of Man*, p. 170).

[15] Teilhard locates the appearance of man in the heart of Africa (*Africa and Human Origins*, 1955, in *The Appearance of Man*, pp. 196–207). This theory has been largely confirmed by later palaeontological discoveries (Cf. E. L. Boné, *La paléoanthropologie*, in *Etudes*, July–August 1963; and *Olduvai Gorge, Tanganyika: Récentes découvertes et profondeurs nouvelles en paléontologie humaine*, in *Revue des questions scientifiques*, 20 July 1963). 'The antiquity now accepted as a reasonable estimate for man is of the order of 2,300,000 years. Another important conclusion: it is becoming increasingly apparent that even at that depth of time Australopithecus was already a tool-maker' (*Olduvai Gorge*, p. 337). Père Boné would be inclined to the view that here we have a true man 'conscious of his relationship to a world outside him and alien to him, on which he is capable of working' (p. 339). In fact, there is no break between the primitive tool-making of this Australopithecus and that of later times. 'Since Olduvai man develops throughout the whole range of specialized tool-making, it is in him that the promise for the future lies. Instinct invents nothing. It is complete from the outset, but tied to a single structure' (p. 339).

Comparing the human mutation with those that preceded it, Teilhard shows that it was unique of its kind: unique in its astonishing power of geographical expansion, its extreme rapidity of differentiation (and of progress), from Australopithecus to Homo sapiens, in the proliferation of its ethnic branches, and finally in their capacity to coalesce and synthesize (*Man's Place in Nature*, pp. 72–8).

[16] Teilhard rightly distinguishes in the evolution of man, a pre-hominian stage, characterized by a less marked involution, if not volume, of brain, as well as by the divergence of races. (*On the probable coming of an ultra-humanity*, 1950, in *The Future of Man*, pp. 270–80). Appearing in the middle of the quaternary, Homo sapiens is the 'definitive expression of the whole mass that lives and reflects' (*Man's Place in Nature*, p. 78). It is 'only after Homo sapiens that the cultural phenomena of *co-reflexion* acquire a decisive spread over the earth. Their importance, absolutely dominant in our modern civilization, suddenly flashes out in the middle Pleistocene, not only in the appearance of art, but also (a perhaps still more

significant fact) in a sudden expansion of the human species across the continents (*The singularities of the human species*, 1954, in *The Appearance of Man*, p. 232).

The 'second critical point of reflexion' does not mean, however, that the earlier men (Sinanthropus, Neanderthal) were not true men: 'How many species of man must we not suppose, behind Stellenbosch Man and Fauresmith Man, to nourish the long effort of elimination and phyletic concentration from which *Homo sapiens* finally emerged?' (*Notes de préhistoire sud-africaine*, unpublished, 1948).

On the successive waves of mankind, see *The Phenomenon of Man*, 1930, in *Vision of the Past*, pp. 163-4.

[16] *The Phenomenon of Man*, p. 163. 'The insignificance and the extreme importance of the phenomenon of man.' (*Ibid.*, p. 164). 'And what is so extremely instructive about the origins of this noosphere (if we know how to look) is to see how *insensibly*, by dint of being universally and lengthily prepared, the enormous event of man's birth took place. Man came silently into the world' (*Ibid.*, pp. 183-4).

Teilhard notes, too, that, externally imperceptible though the mutation may initially have been, we are forced to recognize that it must have been produced suddenly and decisively '*between* two individuals' (*Ibid.*, p. 171). 'A trans-experiential interval about which scientifically we can say nothing, but beyond which we find ourselves transported to a new biological plane' (*Ibid.*, p. 172).

In *La centrologie* (1944) Teilhard returns to the problem of man's apparent insignificance, which may well 'make us dizzy with the infinitesimal'; consciousness, he says, 'this unique essence of things, can appear only in the form of a *rarity* and an *accident*, though without thereby being merely an *accessory* or an *incident*' (No. 33, *op. cit.*, p. 133).

[17] 'The passage from a still diffuse consciousness to one sufficiently well centred to be capable of coinciding on itself . . . *consciousness* raised to the power of two . . . passage from simple to squared numbers' (*The singularities of the human species*, 1954, in *The Appearance of Man*, p. 224) (Cf. *The Phenomenon of Man*, 1930, in *Vision of the Past*, p. 161).

[18] 'The geometric perfection (of the animal) is not in the line of our

evolution, whose bent is towards suppleness and freedom.' (*The Phenomenon of Man*, p. 282).

[19] 'Taken in its true and scientific sense, the word *singularity* does not mean a more or less monstrous accident or exception or anomaly. On the contrary, it signifies (like the dot on the 'i') a fulfilment of expression, a paroxysm in its development, the completion of a line . . . the appearance of thought on earth in the Pliocene is on the contrary an event which (if we really know how to look at it) completes and illuminates the immense history of all matter' (*The singularities of the human species*, in *The Appearance of Man*, p. 228).

[20] 'Man is not the centre of the universe as once we thought in our simplicity, but something much more wonderful—the arrow pointing the way to the final unification of the world in terms of life (*The Phenomenon of Man*, p. 224). Man is 'only one attempt among many' but 'through him, through the breach he has made, the whole essential stream of terrestrial biological evolution is flowing' (*Turmoil or genesis?* 1947, in *The Future of Man*, p. 220).

[21] 'When for the first time in a living creature instinct perceived itself in its own mirror, the whole world took a pace forward' (*The Phenomenon of Man*, p. 181). 'With hominization, in spite of the insignificance of the anatomical leap, we have the beginnings of a new age. The earth gets a "new skin". Better still, it finds its soul' (*Ibid*', p. 182).

[22] *The Noosphere*

Ibid., p. 208. *Man's Place in Nature*, 1932, in *The Vision of the Past*, p. 180. *The singularities of the human species*, 1954, in *The Appearance of Man*, pp. 222 ff. 'From its position at the front of the line of advance of the cosmic wave, human energy acquires an interest out af all proportion to the apparent smallness of its dimensions. Compared with the magnitudes of celestial bodies, the noosphere is an almost imperceptible skin. In reality, however, this extremely shallow surface is nothing more nor less than the most progressive form in which we can grasp and examine the energy of the universe. Within this slender envelope is held the hidden essence of the immensities it borders upon: it is the highest note reached by the vibration of the worlds' (*L'énergie humaine*, 1937, in *L'énergie humaine*, p. 152).

'Something has been introduced into the general process of the vitalization of matter. Something so subtle that, when it first appeared it seemed to cause no stir. And nevertheless it is something so violently active at the heart of things that in a few hundreds of thousands of years it has transformed the face of the earth' (*La réflexion de l'énergie*, 1952, in *L'activation de l'énergie*, pp. 337–8).

In *Le coeur de la matière* Teilhard tells how his instinctive need to find something 'solid' was transferred from matter to the noosphere, which contains the 'peripheral layers—ridiculously thin but formidably active and complex—of the planet' (p. 14).

[23] *The growth of mankind*

It is, indeed, a matter for regret that Teilhard's phenomenology, leaving a gap here between the appearance of man and his present situation, does not include the analysis of the process of contradiction in social forces, so well analysed in the dialectic of master and slave and again by Marx (later, too, and in a different way, by Bergson in his dialectic of the closed and open, the static and the dynamic). Teilhard could have shown the unremitting struggle between the forces of 'mechanization' and 'conspiration' which he rightly pointed out in present-day developments. What is even more important, he could have included in the phenomenology of the *Phenomenon of Man*—but simply as observed evidence—the fact constituted by the growth of spirit (in pagan humanism, in Israel, and in Christianity): as Bergson sets out to do in *The Two Sources*.

We may, however, note a number of searching comments: In the animal world 'the stronger supplants the weaker and ends by stifling it . . . With man, . . . simple elimination tends to become exceptional, or at all events secondary. However brutal the conquest, the suppression is always accompanied by some degree of assimilation. Even when practically absorbed, the vanquished still reacts on the victor so as to transform him. We might borrow a geological word for the process—endomorphosis' (*The Phenomenon of Man*, p. 208). 'Basically, can we not say that the essential thing in history consists in the conflict and finally the gradual harmonization of those great psycho-somatic currents?' (*Ibid.*, p. 209). 'There was a time when life held sway over none but slaves and children . . . The half-confused struggle for a place in the sun, stepping over others, trampling them down if need be. The aggregate rose automatically and docile, as the resultant of an enormous sum of egoisms given rein. There was a time too, almost within living memory, when the workers and the disinherited accepted without reflection the lot which kept them in servitude to the remainder of society' (*Ibid.*, p. 230).

'It is easy for the pessimist to discount this period, so extraordinary among the civilizations that have fallen into ruins one after the other. Is it not far more scientific to recognize, yet once again, beneath these successive oscillations, the great spiral of life: thrusting up, irreversibly, in relays, following the master-line of its evolution? Susa, Memphis, and Athens can crumble. An ever more highly organized consciousness of the universe is passed from hand to hand, and glows steadily brighter' (*Ibid.*, p. 211).

24 *The Phenomenon of Man*, pp. 213—15. 'In the course of a few generations, almost without our realizing it, our view of the world has been profoundly altered. Under the combined influence of science and history, and of social development, the twofold sense of duration and collectivity has pervaded and re-ordered the entire field of our experience; with the twofold result that the future, hitherto a vague succession of monotonous years awaiting an unimportant number of scattered individual lives, is now seen to be a period of positive becoming and maturing—but one in which we can advance and shape ourselves only in solidarity' (*Faith in Man*, 1947, in *The Future of Man*, p. 186). *The Grand Option*, 1937, *ibid.*, pp. 58–60. *Some Reflections on Progress*, 1941, *ibid.*, pp. 67–8. *The New Spirit*, 1942, *ibid.*, pp. 82–96.

25 'The great superiority over primitive man which we have acquired is in the realm of self-knowledge: in our growing capacity to situate ourselves in space and time, to the point of becoming conscious of one place and responsibility in relation to the universe . . . We have discovered that there is a whole, of which we are the elements . . . In the domain external to our flesh our *real and whole body* is continuing to take shape' (*A Note on Progress*, 1920, *ibid.*, pp. 16–17).

'Mankind has just entered upon what is probably the greatest period of transformation it has ever known. The root of the evil from which we are suffering lies in the very foundations of thought on earth. Something is going on in the general structure of human consciousness. What is being inaugurated is another sort of life' (*Sauvons l'humanité*, 1937, in *Science et Christ*, p. 169).

'The fact of organo-psychic development seems to be clearly manifest in collective man: and this, whatever one may think of it, represents as true an advance as the acquisition of an added convolution by the brain' (*Some Reflections on Progress*, 1941, in *The Future of Man*, p. 69). Teilhard even goes so far as to use the term *Homo progressivus* (*The Planetization of Mankind, ibid.*, p. 137). He recognizes the specially favoured position of the West in the development of civilization (*The Phenomenon of Man*, pp. 211–12).

[26] *Le coeur de la matière*, p. 19. It may well be, Teilhard considers, that, as an individual, man is incapable of further progress (that he may be unable, for example, to surpass Plato or Beethoven); as a collective organism of thought, however, he attains greater perfection through what he inherits (*ibid.*, p. 18). 'What might appear to be the most static thing in nature, that is to say, man, is suddenly found to be the most mobile thing in the world—because he has been introduced into a new compartment of the universe (the "reflexive domain") where everything is still free, and everything has still to be created' (*La réflexion de l'energie*, 1952, in *L'activation de l'énergie*, p. 341).

[27] 'Towards the end of the nineteenth century it could seriously be asked whether hominization were not approaching, through pulverization and fragmentation, its final phase. At that time, in fact, corresponding historically to the full "expansional" deployment of the noosphere, the isolation one from another of human particles, their self-centred tendencies now heightened by the first establishment of a practically universal culture, reached, as one might expect, its maximum . . . this was the age of the rights of man (i.e. of the "citizen") against the collective: the age of democracy, naively conceived as a system in which everything is for the individual and the individual is everything: the age of the superman, envisaged and awaited as standing out in isolation above the common herd' (*Man's Place in Nature*, p. 94).

Cf. *Does mankind move biologically upon itself?* in *The Future of Man*, pp. 250–1. On the temptation to take refuge in isolation, cf. *The Phenomenon of Man*, p. 237.

[28] *The Formation of the Noosphere*, 1947, in *The Future of Man*, p. 176. 'Man has come to a *dead end*. May I remark once more how ill such a perspective (however much it is favoured by those who for all sorts of reasons do not want to see the world around them, and still less man, in process of movement) agrees with the extraordinary vitality of an animal group, which appears by all its characteristics to be, on the contrary, in the full flight of expansion and organiza-

tion? Never on earth before has such a quantity of living matter reached so high a state of fermentation. How then can they convince us that it is here, in this (human) mass precisely, raised to boiling-point that the forces of speciation have been suddenly extinguished? This is absurd' (*Reality and significance of human orthogenesis*, 1931, in *Vision of the Past*, p. 252).

'*Natural evolution* and *cultural evolution* are one . . . In man, as the psychological effect of reflexion, the technico-mental becomes additive (cumulative) to a degree never reached even by the insects' (*Hominization and Speciation*, 1952, *ibid.*, p. 263).

[29] Teilhard speaks of the great cosmic movements whose apparent slowness often disguises their real nature (*The formation of the Noosphere*, 1947, in *The Future of Man*, pp. 169–70). He speaks also of the basic movement in which the anomalies of detail disappear (*ibid.*, p. 181. Cf. *A Note on Progress*, 1920, *ibid.*, p. 14).

[30] *The Grand Option*, 1939, *ibid.*, p. 39.

[31] 'Seen as a whole, do not these multiple vortices of elements (creations of human thought) manifestly form one vast surge of thought, within which science is not nearly so much *deployed* as *folded back* into countless branches? . . . In us, us men, life is not marking time: not only has it ceased to split up into divergent phyla, but, still more, concentrating in the urge to know, it has, through the operation of that convergence, just arrived at a paroxysm of the power that characterizes it; it has now brought about a simultaneous and reciprocal rise in the universe of organization and consciousness; in other words it has, by complexifying matter, interiorized it. As I watched it, entranced, the Berkeley cyclotron had definitely faded away. And, in my imagination, it was the entire noosphere I saw instead, spiralling in the whirlwind of research, and forming one vast cyclone whose specific effect was to produce not nuclear energy, but psychic energy in an ever more reflective, that is ultra-human, state' (*En regardant un cyclotron*, April 1953, in *L'activation de l'énergie*, p. 375).

[32] *La centrologie*, 1944, No. 29, *op. cit.*, p. 126.

[33] *La montée de l'autre*, 1942, in *L'activation de l'énergie*, p. 71.

[34] *La grande monade*, 1918, in *Ecrits du temps de la guerre*, p. 239. See the commentary on this paper by a professor of law: André Tunc, *Planétisation du droit* in the *Revue de l'Action Populaire*, December 1963, p. 1187. Teilhard returned to this theme during the second world

war: 'There can no longer be any space for doubt: spiritually, at the same time as materially—by its conscious aspirations as much as by deterministic economic forces—at this moment we are watching the earth at war being thrown into the universal' (*Universalisation et union*, 1942, in *L'activation de l'énergie*, p. 88).

[35] The importance of concentration within a finite space and of the progress it stimulates plays a big part in Teilhard's philosophy: the curvature of the planet producing the effort required for life, and the numerical increase of primitive man encouraging the development of a stable civilization (*The Phenomenon of Man*, p. 204; *La montée de l'autre*, in *L'activation de l'énergie*, 1942). 'If we can imagine an earth whose radius continually increased, then the organisms would have remained loosely associated and would perhaps have never gone beyond the monocellular state (if, indeed, they had ever arrived at it), and certainly man, free to live in a scattered state, would never have reached even the neolithic stage of social development' (*Life and the Planets*, 1945, in *The Future of Man*, p. 115). 'That is how, step by step, through the simple multiplying effect of generations, we have come to constitute, as we do at present, an almost solid mass of hominized substance' (*The Phenomenon of Man*, p. 240).

[36] Teilhard compares the progress of mankind to the movement that starts at the lower pole of a sphere, reaches its fullest extension at the equator, and then closes in towards the upper pole. Thus a period of expansion is followed by a period of compression, which stimulates an inter-penetration of consciousness (*The Phenomenon of Man*, p. 225). With the geographical curve of the earth is associated the psychic curve of thought (*The heart of the problem*, 1949, in *The Future of Man*, p. 263. Cf. *The essence of the democratic idea*, 1948, *ibid.*, pp. 238–9).

'The more mankind is compressed upon itself by the effect of growth, the more, if it is to find room for itself, is it vitally forced to find continually new ways of arranging its elements in the way that is most economical of energy and space. This has the most remarkable result (though a biologist might well anticipate it) that, under the stimulus of this need and inspired by this search—as a result, too, of the new devices that are contrived—what appeared at first no more than a mechanical tension and a quasi-geometric arrangement imposed on the human mass, now takes the form of a rise in interiority and liberty within a whole made up of reflective particles that are now more harmoniously inter-related (*Man's Place in Nature*, p. 98).

Mankind is obliged 'to invent continually new schemes of mechanized industry and social organization', and hence 'to reflect' and 'reflect upon itself to yet a further degree'. We are submitted to the pressure of 'a closed mental dome whose walls inexorably force our intelligences together'. (*Comment concevoir et espérer sur terre l'unanimisation humaine*, unpublished, 1950).

In one of his last articles Teilhard deals with the problem of the *compression of man* (*Psyché*, September 1953, in *L'activation de l'énergie*, p. 357). Henceforth with the law of complexity-consciousness are associated the parallel forces of 'compression-consciousness' (p. 360) or, a better name for it, 'compression-love'. 'Convergence, by the very fact that it organizes and dynamises, releases tension' (p. 362).

In *La grande monade*, 1918, Teilhard looks to mankind's consciousness of its collective isolation to stimulate within it a concentration of souls (Cf. Chapter 2, note 22): 'If the pressure of some great common need should succeed in overcoming our mutual aversions and in breaking the icy barriers that isolate us, who can tell what well-being and tenderness would not emerge from our harmonized multitude? When men feel that they are really alone in the world, then (unless they turn and rend one another) they will begin to love one another' (pp. 242-3).

[37] *Faith in Peace*, 1947, in *The Future of Man*, p. 150-1. Here Teilhard concentrates on the fact of *race* which 'not only prevents the branches (of man) from falling apart, but also *uses* their diversity to obtain, by effects of combination, superior forms of consciousness' (*The natural units of humanity*, 1939, in *Vision of the Past*, p. 207).

'In all realms, organic union differentiates, but does not neutralize the elements it groups together. Applied to the case of races and peoples, this principle allows us to foresee a certain future growth in the uniformity of man's somatic and psychic characteristics; but in combination with a living richness in which the qualities belonging to each of the lines of convergence is recognizably carried to its maximum' (*Ibid.*, p. 292).

[38] *How may we conceive and hope that human unanimization will be realized on earth*, 1950, in *The Future of Man*, p. 281. *Sur la nature du phénomène*

social humain et ses relations cachées avec la gravité, 1948, in *L'activation de l'énergie*, pp. 173–4.

[39] 'I am not denying that with the coming of the collective and of mass-man, a first wave of enslavement and standardization, ugly and catastrophic, strikes us like a blow in the face. Nevertheless, behind us and hidden in the foam of the wave, surely we must discern a prodigious increase in the speed and flexibility of communications, in organization and penetrative depth in research, in efficiency and power in action—and, finally, in the breadth and depth of our vision of the world we live in (*Transformations et prolongements en l'homme du mécanisme de l'évolution*, 1915, in *L'activation de l'énergie*, pp. 321–2).

Elsewhere, Teilhard lists the defects of contemporary civilization: submergence of the élite, the loss of solitude and the over-running of nature by factories and towns, 'the disagreeable relationship, the continual friction between individuals who are the more alien and even hostile to one another the more numerous they are; the mechanization of the person through enslavement to forms of work that cannot but be collective; the complexity, the dead weight of daily life and its increasing lack of security—all these go a long way to explain what makes our own time seem so very strange and new to us, a source even, of neurotic distress. . . There are too many of us and too little room'. However, Teilhard takes advantage of this gloomy picture to put forward the ultimate solution of man's problem in the escape of the spirit into the absolute (*Réflexions sur la compression humaine*, *Psyché*, September 1953, in *L'activation de l'énergie*, p. 357).

[40] *The natural units of humanity* in *Vision of the Past*, pp. 210–11. 'Each nation desperately forges weapons to defend and isolate itself, and the weapons immediately become common property. Thus they are transformed into new bonds that add still a little more to the solidarity of man. It is the same with the inventions, sometimes industrially quite revolutionary, that each country is forced to develop in order to maintain a self-sufficient economy. And the same, again, with the psychological and social reforms in which each nation hopes to discover and win for itself the spiritual predominance that will give it a unique position among its neighbours. All that is progressive and useful in such inventions or newly developed ideas spreads by contagion, to be shared by

the whole human family. In short, every effort we make to isolate ourselves forces us still closer against our neighbours' (*Ibid.*, p. 295).

'Examined in the light of a general world science capable of giving spiritual energies their place in a third infinite, the crisis we are passing through bears the "positive sign". Its characteristics are not those of a break-up but of a birth. Let us not be frightened therefore of what at first sight might look like a final and universal discord. What we are suffering is only the price, the annunciation, the preliminary phase of our unanimity' (*Man's place in the universe*, 1942, in *Vision of the Past*, p. 233). 'We may, then, be of good heart. The vast industrial and social system that surrounds us is not going to crush us; it is not seeking to rob us of our soul.'

41 *The Phenomenon of Man*, p. 252.

42 'But if, on the other hand, we refuse to regard human socialization as anything more than a chance arrangement, a *modus vivendi* lacking all power of interior growth, then ... we find the whole structure of politico-economico-social relations reduced to an arbitrary system of conventional and temporary expedients. Everything in the human world becomes artificial in the worst sense of the word; everything is divested of importance, urgency and interest' (*Turmoil or genesis?* 1947, in *The Future of Man*, p. 226). 'We may delude ourselves with the idea that we are simply weathering a storm. The truth is that we are undergoing a radical change of climate' (*Does mankind move biologically upon itself?* 1949, *ibid.*, p. 249).

43 *Le Milieu Divin*, p. 153.

44 *Man's place in the universe*, 1942, in *Vision of the Past*, p. 232.

45 'What are the finest triumphs of life in the past compared with the floodtide of modern civilizations? What eruption can compare with the explosion of man?' (*L'énergie humaine*, p. 144).

46 *Socialization*

The theme of socialization on a planetary scale is adumbrated in some war-time notes and observations (Letter of 8 September 1916 in *Making of a Mind*, p. 125). We first find it expressed in the years 1930-9, in the essays published in *L'énergie humaine*; it becomes more prominent in *The Phenomenon of Man* (pp. 213–26) and assumes a position of predominance in all Teilhard's post-war essays (in particular *Man's Place in Nature*, pp. 96–112). This development was stimulated by the fantastic evolution of the contemporary world. The present short summary of this intuitive perception gives only a partial view of the analyses on which it was based. The subject, as we know, received a great deal of attention in *Mater et Magistra* (Nos. 59–67), an important section of which is devoted to it. Cf. *Hominization*, 1923, in *Vision of the Past*, pp. 58–61; *L'énergie humaine*, 1937, in *L'énergie humaine*, pp. 144–5; *L'atomisme de l'esprit*, 1941, in *L'énergie humaine*, pp. 144–5; *Some Reflexions on Progress*, 1941, in *The Future of Man*, pp. 68–70; *Life and the Planets*, 1945, ibid., pp. 113–15; *The Planetisation of Mankind*, 1945, ibid., pp. 124–39; *The formation of the Noosphere*, 1947, ibid., pp. 169–84; *On the probable coming of an ultra-humanity*, 1950, ibid., pp. 274–6; *Human unanimisation*, 1950, ibid., pp. 281–8; *From the pre-human to the ultra-human*, 1950, ibid., pp. 293–4; *The singularities of the human species*, 1954, in *The Appearance of Man*, pp. 255–9.

'In the narrow and inelastic world represented by the surface of the earth, under the pressure of population and the force of continually multiplying economic ties, we are now forming but one single body. And within that body, as a result of the gradual establishment of a uniform and universal industrial and scientific system, our thoughts are tending more and more to function like the cells of one common brain. That can only mean one thing, that if this transformation continues on its natural line, we may anticipate the time when men will come to know what it is, as with one heart, all as one man to desire, hope for and love the same thing at the same time' (*Réflexions sur le bonheur*, 1943, in *Cahiers Pierre Teilhard de Chardin*, No. 2, p. 63).

'The all-encompassing ascent of the masses; the constant tightening of economic bonds; the spread of financial and intellectual associations; the totalization of political regimes; the closer physical contact of individuals as well as of nations; the increasing impossibility of being or acting or thinking *alone*; in short, the rise, in every form, of the *other* around us. We are all constantly aware of these tentacles of a social condition that is rapidly evolving to the point of becoming monstrous. You feel them as I do' (*Life and the Planets*, 1945, in *The Future of Man*, pp. 113–14). Cf. also: 'Let us try to get some idea of the speed of this process of in-folding (of mankind) over the period of a single generation. Looking back to the turn of the century . . . and today . . . ' (*Does mankind move biologically upon itself?* 1949, in *The Future of Man*, p. 247).

[47] Letter of 1 September 1926, in *Letters from a Traveller*, pp. 132–3.

[48] 'When the stuff of the universe has reached the last stage of its evolution, the transformation it will go through will take the form of a sort of fragmentation, a granulation, into monads neutralized in their relations to one another. At this moment the blazing torch of the world is dying down, in us and outside us, in a shower of sparks. Evolution is reaching its climax in disintegration. That is how those think and act who find all that is most precious in life only in what the present moment has to offer' (*Esquisse d'un univers personnel*, 1936, in *L'énergie humaine*, p. 78).

[49] *Man's Place in Nature*, p. 118.

[50] Teilhard frequently refers to the law of the slowness of biological evolution and of history (*The Phenomenon of Man*, p. 255).

[51] 'Though the study of the past may give us some idea of the resources of organized matter in its dispersed state, *we have as yet no idea of the possible magnitude* of "noosphere" effects. We are confronted with human vibrations resounding by the million—a whole layer of consciousness exerting simultaneous pressure upon the future and the collected and hoarded produce of a million years of thought. Have we ever tried to form an idea of what such magnitudes represent?' (*The Phenomenon of Man*, p. 286). In a note on this passage Teilhard speaks of the increased clarity with which men in general, if not individually, can see things. 'To this progress in consciousness, could anyone dare to object that there has been no corresponding advance in the profound structure of being?' (*Ibid.*).

'We must look for and allow for a change of regime. We must assume that under the rapidly mounting pressures forcing them upon one another the human molecules will ultimately succeed in finding their way through the critical barrier of mutual repulsion to enter the inner zone of attraction' (*The human rebound of evolution*, 1947, in *The Future of Man*, p. 211).

[52] *L'esprit de la terre*, 1931, in *L'énergie humaine*, pp. 50-1. 'What new power may we not expect to spring from this modification of "spiritual matter"?' After one more period, and that a period of trial, the spirit of the earth will emerge with its specific individuality, its own proper character and configuration. And then, when the interests and passions of the noosphere have gradually been sublimated, when it concentrates on the solution of loftier problems and the achievement of grander aims, then its surface tension towards being will reach its maximum' (*Ibid.*, pp. 51-2).

'No obstacle can prevent human energy—the expression of a force as irresistible and infallible as the universe itself—from freely attaining the natural term of its evolution' (*L'énergie humaine*, 1937, in *L'énergie humaine*, p. 190).

'It would be easier, at the stage of evolution we have reached, to prevent the earth from revolving than to prevent mankind from becoming totalized' (*Directions and conditions of the Future*, 1948, in *The Future of Man*, p. 229). We find the same in other essays, *ibid.*, pp. 132, 152, 239.

'To attain the biological paroxysm to which, if our reckoning is correct, every noosphere is by nature *logically* destined' (*The singularities of the human species*, 1954, in *The Appearance of Man*, p. 246).

[53] 'Hominization can only end (if successful) in a paroxysm (= a higher critical point of reflexion = an escape point = a way out) (*Monde ouvert? Monde fermé?* unpublished, 1954).

[54] *Réflexions sur la compression humaine*, *Psyché*, September 1953, in *L'activation de l'énergie*, p. 357.

[55] *The Phenomenon of Man*, pp. 250-3. 'The noosphere tends to constitute itself a single closed system in which each element sees, feels, desires and suffers for itself the same things as all the others at the same time . . . In the direction of thought, could the universe terminate with anything less than the measureless, any more than it could in the direction of space and time?' (*Ibid.*, pp. 251, 252).

'The multitude, carried to its peak, of individual oppositions finding harmony in intimate association in the same desire: what does all that imply, if not the genesis of a *single collective act* in which the forces of personality contained in the noosphere will come out into the open as they approach maturity—in other words, at their final confluence—and in the only form in which we could conceive them, the form of love?' (*L'énergie humaine*, 1937, p. 191).

'Mankind will come to an end when, having finally *understood*, it has, in a total and final reflexion reduced everything in it to a common idea and a common passion' (*Man's Place in Nature*, 1949, p. 114).

Explaining in a note just what he means by 'union differentiates', Teilhard speaks of 'this evidence of a "creative" current that carries the megamolecules (and precisely through the statistical effect of their increasing liberties) towards an incredible almost "monocellular" state, in which (in obedience to the biological laws of union) each *ego* is destined to attain its paroxysm in some mysterious super-ego' (*Le coeur de la matière*, unpublished, 1950, p. 19).

'What crisis of consciousness (too dazzling for us to be able to "place") are we not justified in supposing the noosphere will reach when, as it approaches maturation, there will no longer be only a single physics on earth, or even a single ethic but also (by the polarization of spirits and hearts at a focus *finally in sight* of evolutionary convergence) a single passion, that is to say a single "mysticism"?' (*The singularities of the human species*, 1954, in *The Appearance of Man*, p. 267).

In his affirmation of a definitive end to history, Teilhard is in sharp contrast with Marxism. In Marxism there is a basic contradiction (already forcibly pointed out by Père Fessard in his *Le dialogue catholique-communiste est-il possible?* Grasset, 1937, and later by Père Calvez in his *La pensée de Karl Marx*, Editions du Seuil, 1956) in which both the continuance and the ultimate fulfilment of history are affirmed. While recognizing the need for an 'improvement in the economic conditions in which men live' Teilhard is at pains to distinguish between his ideal and a godless millenarianism, a materialist utopia of ease and abundance. 'It is not *well-being* but a hunger for *more-being* which, of psychological necessity, can alone preserve the thinking earth from *taedium vitae*' (*The end of the species*, in *The Future of Man*, p. 303).

[56] *Super-Humanité, Super-Christ, Super-Charité*, 1943, in *Science et Christ*, p. 196. This theme of the breath of the spirit that animates mankind today could be magnificently illustrated, though in non-Christian terms, in some of the poems of Saint-John Perse. 'I can hear the bones grow, from which a new age on earth is built . . . Leaf by leaf, vast structures are being raised up, vast structures rising up in silence in the hidden lairs of the future, in the pale dawn of blind begettings' (*Oeuvre poétique*, Gallimard, 1960, II. pp. 61, 62). 'From the four corners of this world the great winds were blowing . . . on every highway of this world forces of growth, great and greater still . . .' (*Ibid.*, pp. 11, 16).

[57] *Ibid.*, p. 206.

[58] *The singularities of the human species*, 1954, in *The Appearance of Man*. p. 267.

[59] *The formation of the noosphere*, 1947, in *The Future of Man*, p. 181. 'Not a gradual darkening but a sudden blaze of brilliance, an explosion in which thought, carried to the extreme, is volatilized upon itself: such, if I had to bet on it, is how I would depict the ultimate phase of a vitalized star' (*From the pre-human to the ultra-human*, 1950, *ibid.*, p. 295).

'A strange vision, no doubt, this vision of a universe in which each thinking planet would represent, at its term, by concentration of its noosphere, a point of penetration and escape from the temporo-spatial envelope of things' (*The phyletic structure of the human group*, 1950. *ibid.*, p. 171).

[60] *La grande monade*, 1918, in *Ecrits du temps de la guerre*, p. 246.

[61] 'There is but one possible way in which human elements, in-numerably diverse by nature, can love one another: it is by knowing themselves all to be centred upon a "super-centre" common to all to which they can only attain, each at the extreme of himself through their unity' (*Some reflections on Progress*, in *The Future of Man*, p. 75).

[62] Cf. the conclusion of *La religion du personnel* (quoted by C. Cuénot, *op. cit.*, p. 239): and that of *La réflexion de l'énergie*, *ibid.*, p. 429). 'At the term of this process of ultra-reflexion (which operates on a defined planetary "*quantum*") there can be distinguished a pole of maximum convergence—which, as an inevitable consequence of the irreversibility inherent in reflective life, cannot be regarded as a transitory state (or a "flash") but rather as a higher critical point (of reflection), beyond which the evolutionary curve of complexity-growth emerges, as far as we can see, from space and time.'

Elsewhere, Teilhard speaks also of 'a critical point in the maturing of man—the experimental aspect and point of impact of the Parousia' (Letter of 19 March 1948, quoted by C. Cuénot, *ibid.*, p. 352).

[63] *The Phenomenon of Man*, p. 272. 'A remarkable picture, indeed—a spindle-shaped universe closed at each end (to the rear and in front) by two peaks of diametrically opposite character' (*Man's Place in Nature*, p. 116).

[64] *The singularities of the human species*, Appendix (*The unique nature of the Christian phenomenon*) 1954, in *The Appearance of Man*, pp. 271ff.

[65] *The Phenomenon of Man*, pp. 268–72, 'The attributes of the Omega

Point'. 'Expressed in terms of internal energy, the cosmic function of Omega consists in initiating and maintaining within its radius the unanimity of the world's "reflective" particles. But how could it exercise this action were it not in some sort loving and lovable *at this very moment*? Love dies in contact with the impersonal and the anonymous . . . For love to be possible there must be co-existence. Accordingly, however marvellous its foreseen figure, Omega could never even so much as equilibrate the play of human attractions and repulsions if it did not act with equal force, that is to say with the same stuff of proximity' (*Ibid.*, p. 269). 'To be supremely attractive, Omega must be supremely present' (*Ibid.*).

'If Omega really exists, it is difficult to conceive that its supreme *ego* should not make an immediate impact as such, in some way, on all the inchoate egos (that is to say, on all the reflective elements of the universe)' (*Un sommaire de ma perspective phénoménologique*, unpublished, 1954).

On Omega Point and its attributes, see also *La Centrologie*, Nos. 19–26, *op. cit.*, pp. 117–20.

[66] Cf. in particular a passage in *The singularities of the human species* (appendix), as cited in note 64, and *L'énergie humaine*, chapter 6, *passim*, in which Teilhard finds in love the principle that 'totalizes' human energy.

'The planetization of mankind, if it is to come properly into effect, presupposes, in addition to the enclosing earth, and to the organization and condensation of human thought . . . the rise on our inward horizon of a cosmic spiritual centre, a supreme pole of consciousness, upon which all the separate consciousnesses of the world may converge and within which they may love one another: the *rise of a God*' (*The Future of Man*, p. 120).

[67] *Le phénomène spirituel*, 1937, in *L'énergie humaine*, p. 130. 'In his effort to escape the threats of disappearance that cannot be reconciled with the mechanism of a reflective activity, man seeks to include in an ever greater and more permanent subject the principle that brings together the results achieved by his activity: civilization, humanity, the spirit of the earth. Once he is integrated with these vast entities, in the incredibly slow rhythm of evolution, he feels that he has escaped from the destructive action of time. But in doing so, he only postpones the problem. The radical fault in all forms of faith in progress, as expressed in positivist terms, is that they do

not finally eliminate death. What use is it to be able to discern some centre at the head of evolution, if some day that centre itself must disintegrate?' (*Ibid.*, p. 300).

'Either there is, somewhere, some way out for thought and personality—or the world is a ghastly mistake. If that were so, we should have to call a halt' (Letter of 18 March 1934, about the death of Teilhard's friend Davidson Black, the anatomist, quoted by C. Cuénot, *op. cit.*, p. 193).

[68] *L'esprit de la terre*, in *L'énergie humaine*, p. 56. *Esquisse d'un univers personnel, ibid.*, pp. 84–5. 'A person cannot disappear by passing into another person.'

These arguments could have been rounded off by the following consideration, which is only implicit in Teilhard's exposition: if the absolute ideal, recognized by man as the term of his activity and of his project, is only 'ideal', then it is only a creation of man's, a goal that a finite being sets itself, and could never be more than something possessed or held; man, therefore, can avoid pride only if he recognizes that this absolute ideal is the sign (obscure) of a personal God, who calls him freely to communion.

[69] 'Universal energy, if it is not to be less evolved than the terms its action animates, must be a thinking energy . . . since everything, in the universe beyond man, takes place in personalized being, the final divine term, the term of universal convergence, must possess eminently the quality of a person (lacking which it would be less than the elements it dominates). To *super-animate* a universe made up of personal elements, *without destroying*, it must itself be a special centre' (*Sauvons l'humanité, Réflexions sur la crise présente*, 1936. The above fragment was published in *La Table Ronde*, June 1955, pp. 58–9).

'The personal elements of the universe would revert to disorder (that is to say, to nothingness) if they did not find something suprapersonal, already effectively present, to dominate them. To balance our action, therefore, not only must there be in the world around us the expectation of a universal personality, but its features must already be recognizable' (*Esquisse d'un univers personnel*, 1936, in *L'énergie humaine*, p. 152).

'As seen from our side of things, the apex of the evolutionary cone (Omega Point) stands out at first against the horizon as a purely immanent focus of convergence . . . But, on looking more closely, it is seen that if this focus is to hold firm, it presupposes behind it a transcendent, divine, core' (*Esquisse d'une dialectique de l'esprit*, 1946, in *L'activation de l'énergie*, p. 152).

On the problem of God, as approached by reason and facts, see also *Esquisse d'un univers personnel*, 1936, in *L'énergie humaine*, pp. 82–9; and *L'énergie humaine*, 1937, *ibid.*, pp. 172–80.

[70] 'If we seek to determine the position and analyse the properties of this supreme centre, it soon becomes clear that we must look far beyond and far above any mere aggregation of perfected mankind. If it is to be capable of joining together in itself the prolonged fibres of the world, the apex of the cone in which we move can be conceived only as something that is ultra-conscious, ultra-personalized, ultra-present' (*The New Spirit*, 1944, in *The Future of Man*, p. 92). This passage shows that for Teilhard the term *ultra* implies a dialectical negation.

In 1949, at the end of *Man's Place in Nature*, Teilhard tried to synthesize the two aspects of Omega: its finiteness (or incompleteness) and its divine infinity. 'Unless it is to be powerless to form the keystone of the noosphere, Omega can only be conceived as the *meeting-point* between a universe that has reached the limit of centration, and another, even deeper, centre—this being the self-subsistent centre and absolutely final principle of irreversibility and personalization: the one and only true Omega' (p. 121). There seems to be some ambiguity here (as, indeed, one might expect in so abstruse a context): Omega is presented both as a 'meeting-point' between two realities and as the absolute-God.

[71] *L'esprit de la terre*, 1931, in *L'énergie humaine*, pp. 52–7.

[72] The more so that man's planetary noosphere may be but one of the world's noospheres (*The singularities of the human species*, in *The Appearance of Man*, p. 268 note).

[73] *Un phénomène de contre-évolution*, 1949, in *L'activation de l'énergie*, p. 201. 'However tangled the undergrowth, however inhospitable the country, however black the life we journey through, warmth and friendship and shelter await us at the centre of the star, and there is no longer any fear that we may miss them' (*Ibid.*, p. 199).

Teilhard protests against the picture of the end of the world presented by Sir James Jeans in *The Universe Around Us*: 'Jeans' book . . . absolutely makes one despair: he believes that he is offering us hope and something to live for when he tells us that with a certain amount of luck we still have some million million years of humanity before the final and utter end (humanity petering out on a frozen earth where no problems exist any longer') (Letter of 4 May 1932, in *Letters from a Traveller*, p. 176).

[74] *Esquisse d'un univers personnel*, 1936, in *L'énergie humaine*, p. 111. Earlier, in *L'union créatrice*, 1917 (in *Ecrits du temps de la guerre*, p. 191) Teilhard wrote: '*The consistence of the future* is the indispensable condition of *the consistence of unity* . . . it is the future and not the past that becomes, in duration, the direction in which being acquires solidity, depth and stability.' Later, adopting a phrase of Maurice Blondel's, he added, 'Contrary to our usual impression, everything here below holds together from on high' (*La foi qui opère*, 1918, *ibid.*, p. 322).

[75] 'Recognize, on the other hand, that in the realm of our experience man, because he is the advancing front of one of the two most enormous waves into which tangible reality is for us divided, holds the fate of the universe in his hands: and you turn his face towards the great rising sun' (*The Phenomenon of Man*, 1930, in *Vision of the Past*, p. 172).

[76] *From faith in the world to faith in God*
Commenting on Blondel, Père H. Bouillard well brings out both the natural character of the desire for God and the transcendence of God's freedom in the answer he gives (*Blondel et le christianisme*, Editions de Seuil, 1961). Many passages in Teilhard show the influence on him of Blondel's thought. 'The Christian pheno-menon could well be what it claims to represent—and what, more-over, every theory of a personal universe demands as a final proof of its truth: the reflection of the supreme consciousness on the consciousness of the elements it brings together—a revelation' (*Esquisse d'un univers personnel*, 1936, in *L'énergie humaine*, p. 114). Earlier, in *L'union créatrice* (1917), Teilhard admitted that 'the ontological system' he was presenting 'would be extremely pre-carious and hypothetical without knowledge of Christ'. The more fully worked-out essay *Comment je vois* (unpublished, 1948) re-inforces this notion. 'If the evolutionary effort of hominization is to be maintained and animated, without faltering or slackening, until it reaches its term, must there not be something *besides this*: the explicit manifestation and intervention of the terminal focus of

biological involution? I believe this to be true, and it is here that Christic faith comes in, to take over from and consummate faith in man.'

In his *Esquisse d'une dialectique de l'esprit* (1946, in *L'activation de l'énergie*, pp. 149-58) Teilhard sets out clearly the 'successive phases of his apologetics or, if you so prefer it, dialectic: (1) discovery of Omega as the 'purely immanent focus of convergence'; (2) discovery of God as the personal centre of attraction, not only for the world but for free consciousnesses; (3) discovery of the Christian phenomenon and faith in the Incarnation; (4) discovery of the Church, the germ of the 'super-vitalization' of history. The distinction and dialectical connexion of the stages of the religious quest are well brought out by these phases, in particular the transition into the order of revelation. It is worth noting that the second phase opens with a question: that of 'knowing whether there are not hidden *messages*, as yet unnoticed by our observation' (*Ibid.*, p. 153). The enquiry, still rational, into the divine, is then continued by an *historical* enquiry. 'It is here, in the very midst of the human phenomenon that the Christian problem emerges and demands our attention. Historically, starting with the Man-Jesus, a phylum of religious thought appeared in the human mass' p. 154). We find that Teilhard, though without developing the interior analysis of the will, coincides exactly with Blondel's approach: this, too, leads to an historical enquiry, as soon as it realizes the impossibility of man's determining by himself the effective existence of revelation as well as its content (Cf. again Père Bouillard's book).

It is in this context that one should interpret the controversial passage from Teilhard: 'If, as a result of some interior revolution, I were to lose in succession my faith in Christ, my faith in a personal God, and my faith in spirit, I feel that I should continue to believe in the world. The world (its value, its infallibility and its goodness) —that, when all is said and done, is the first and the only thing in which I believe . . . I surrender myself to an ill-defined faith in a world that is one and infallible, wherever it may lead me.' (*Comment je crois*, unpublished, 1934). Père de Lubac, while admitting that there is some ambiguity in this passage, forcibly demonstrates that it expresses an approach both justified and classical. Teilhard, addressing himself to an unbeliever and adopting an existential point of view, seems to make a clean sweep of his religious faith; but he does this only to develop to its conclusion the basic affirmation of the world and unfold the dialectical stages that can lead the unbeliever to the recognition of God and of Christianity. Both on the objective and the personal level, the order of nature and that of the supernatural are connected by a dialectic of analogy and discontinuity. The passage from one order to the other is achieved by a gratuitous initiative on the part of God, which resumes and transcends nature, and subjectively by an act of faith that transcends, without denying, the initial affirmation of the world (H. de Lubac, *The Faith of Teilhard de Chardin*, London, 1965, pp. 136ff.). In a recent book the eminent theologian Père Guy de Broglie shows also that Christian faith appears not as the result of two different intellectual processes (one purely rational, the other purely mystical) but as the climax of a single spiritual activity, animated by grace and receptive of the good tidings that crown it (*Les signes de crédibilité de la Révélation chrétienne*, Fayard, 1964).

[77] *Super-Humanité, Super-Christ, Super-Charité* (1943, in *Science et Christ*, p. 211).

[78] Col. 1:15–17; 2:3.

[79] Rom. 8:15–23.

[80] 'And he has put all things under his feet and has made him the head over all things for the church, which is his body, the fullness of him who fills all in all' (Eph. 1:22–3). 'He who descended is he who also ascended far above all the heavens that he might fill all things . . . until we all attain to the unity of the faith and of the knowledge of the son of God, to mature manhood, to the measure of the stature of the fullness of Christ . . . from whom the whole body, joined and knit together by every joint with which it is supplied, when each part is working properly, makes bodily growth and upbuilds itself in love' (*Ibid.*, 4:10–16). 'When all things are subjected to him, then the Son himself will also be subjected to him who put all things under him, that God may be everything to everyone' (1 Cor. 15:28).

'For the Romans, the Corinthians, the Ephesians and the Colossians, this image (the Pleroma) no doubt had only a vague meaning, since at that time the world, the whole (with all the definite organization that these words now imply for us) did not yet exist in the consciousness of men. For us, however, who live under the spell of the newly discovered magnitude of the universe, it is an exact expression of the aspect of the God that our adoration is waiting for. Christ the king, the Christ of the universe: a mere matter of emphasis, maybe, but it is everything; it is the whole difference between an external power that could never be anything but juridical and static and an internal sovereignty that, inaugurated in matter and culminating in grace, operates on us by and through all the organic foundations of the evolving world' (*La parole attendue*, 1940, in *Cahiers Pierre Teilhard de Chardin*, No. 4, p. 427).

[81] *Le coeur de la matière*, unpublished, 1950, p. 28. Even if, at the present time, 'the individual and society are continually reinforced and fulfilled the one in the other', 'when the limit is reached, at the moment when the supreme meeting is brought about, the final step will be *from* the element *to* the whole; it is the whole that will have the last word . . .In the end the person is for the whole, and not the whole for the human person; but this is because at that final instant the whole itself has become person' (*L'atomisme de l'esprit*, 1941, in *L'activation de l'énergie*, p. 58).

'The only millenarianism I can entertain is that of an age in which men have finally become alive to their unity with all men, and to their intimate connexion with all the rest, and so will hold in their hands the *fullness of their soul*, freely to throw it into the divine centre' (Unpublished letter to Père Auguste Valensin, 29 December 1929).

[82] *La parole attendue*, 1940, in *Cahiers Pierre Teilhard de Chardin*, No. 4, p. 27.

[83] 'But this certainty, born as it is of a "supernatural" act of faith, is of its nature supra-phenomenal: which means, in one sense, that it leaves all the anxieties attendant upon the human condition, on their own level, still alive in the heart of the believer' (*The Directions and Conditions of the Future*, 1948, in *The Future of Man*, p. 237).

[84] 'For a Christian believer, it is interesting to note that the final success of hominization (and thus cosmic involution) is positively guaranteed by the "redeeming virtue" of the God incarnate in his creation' (*The Phenomenon of Man*, p. 308 note).

[85] *Social Heredity and Progress*, 1925, in *The Future of Man*, pp. 33–4.

[86] *Super-Humanité, Super-Christ, Super-Charité* (1943, in *Science et Christ*, p. 210).

[87] *The God of evolution and the Christian God*

The Phenomenon of Man, p. 300. 'The universe fulfilling itself in a synthesis of centres in perfect conformity with the laws of union. God, the centre of centres. In that final vision the Christian dogma culminates . . . coinciding perfectly with the Omega Point' (*Ibid.*, p. 294).

'If truly, in order that the kingdom of God may come (in order that the Pleroma may close in upon its fullness), it is necessary, as an essential physical condition (but not, of course, sufficient in itself), that the human earth should already have attained the natural completion of its evolutionary growth, then it must mean that the ultra-human perfection which neo-humanism envisages for evolution will coincide in concrete terms with the crowning of the Incarnation awaited by all Christians' (*The Heart of the Problem*, 1949, in *The Future of Man*, p. 268).

We find the same line of reasoning in the lecture (quoted earlier) on happiness (1943): 'Under the persistent effort of Christian thought, the terrifying vastness of the world is gradually converging upwards, until it becomes transfigured into a centre of living energy . . . We must surely recognize that these two powerful currents between which the impact of man's religious energies are at present divided—that of human progress and that of all-embracing charity—seek but one thing: to run together and complete one another.'

'How can these two super-entities, the one "supernatural", the other natural, fail to come together and harmonize in Christian thought; the critical point of maturation envisaged by science being simply the physical condition and experiential aspect of the critical point of the Parousia postulated and awaited in the name of revelation? . . . By this conjunction Christian cosmology, harmonized and effectively articulated at its peak with human cosmology, shows itself to be fundamentally and in real values homogeneous with the latter. Thus dogma is no mere flowering of the imagination but something authentically born of history; and it is in literal not metaphorical terms that the Christian believer can illumine and further the genesis of the universe around him in the form of a Christogenesis' (*Turmoil or Genesis?* 1947, in *The Future of Man*, p. 224).

There is 'correspondence, or even parity, between the complexions of these two Omegas, face to face with one another—that postulated by modern science and that experienced by Christian mysticism . . . The two Omegas (that of experience and that of faith) are certainly ready to react upon one another in the consciousness of men, and, ultimately, to form a synthesis: the cosmic being on the point of fantastically enlarging the Christic, and the Christic (incredible though it may seem) on the point of *amorizing* (which means energizing to the maximum) the entire cosmic' (*Le Dieu de l'évolution*, unpublished, 1953).

[88] *The Phenomenon of Man*, p. 297. 'Reset in an evolution interpreted as an ascent of consciousness, this phylum, in its trend towards a synthesis based on love, progresses precisely in the direction presumed for the leading-shoot of biogenesis' (*Ibid.*, p. 298).

[89] *Social Heredity and Progress*, 1921, in *The Future of Man*, p. 34. 'In short, Christ (provided he is seen in the full realism of his Incarnation) is a perfect parallel to the Omega Point our theory led us to anticipate, and tends *to produce exactly* the spiritual totalization we are awaiting' (*L'énergie humaine*, 1937, p. 192).

[90] *Le Christ évoluteur*, unpublished, 1942.

[91] *Le Dieu de l'évolution*, unpublished, 1953.

[92] 'Père Teilhard's assertions can, no doubt, seem disturbing, so rashly does he insist that the mystical Christ who "fills, consummates and gives consistence to the entire structure of matter and spirit", coincides "physically and literally" with the Teilhard Omega Point, which "because of its structure is supra-personal in nature". It is hardly surprising that more than one theologian, meeting these emphatically repeated adverbs or other similar expressions, should have taken them literally and accused Teilhard of having excessively naturalized dogma in his desire to make it intelligible. In our view, most of Teilhard's assertions, interpreted in the light of his fundamental project, can be perfectly acceptable. It must, however, be realized that they are essentially concerned with *historicity*, and a historicity that is specifically supernatural—so much so, indeed, that they impinge on *natural* historicity only through the medium of *human* historicity, and thus of our own present situation in history' (G. Fessard, *La vision religieuse de Teilhard de Chardin*, in *L'homme devant Dieu*, Mélanges offerts au Père de Lubac, *op. cit.*, p. 239). This passage agrees with our interpretation of Teilhard: a *dialectical* relation between nature and man, between the evolutionary history of the world and sacred history, and, finally between 'natural' phenomenology and 'supernatural'

phenomenology (which presupposes, goes beyond, and completes the former).

[93] Addressing the modern unbeliever, Teilhard tells him: 'As far as you are concerned (and it is here that you are not yet human enough, you do not *go to the limits* of your humanity) it is simply a matter of the success or failure of a reality which remains vague and precarious even when conceived in the form of a super-humanity. For us, it is a question in a true sense of achieving the victory of no less than a God' (*Le Milieu Divin*, p. 69).

[94] *Turmoil or Genesis?* in *The Future of Man*, 1947, pp. 214–26.

[95] A diagram may give some idea, even though very approximate and incomplete, of the problem presented by Omega.

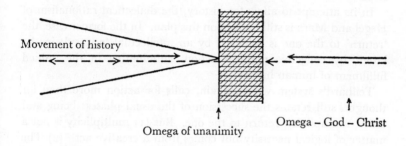

Omega of unanimity   Omega – God – Christ

Movement of history

The dotted line represents the action of Omega-Christ in a history that is, in fact, supernatural from its origin.

We may recall here a passage quoted earlier (Chapter 2, note 109): 'If I may have given the impression elsewhere, in other writings of mine, of leaping directly (from a reflexion on the phenomenon of man and its culmination in Omega) to Christ, it is either because, taking my readers to be sufficiently informed, I neglected to distinguish the stages (to put down the intermediate operations)—or because there is a positive difficulty, for a mind that is already Christian, in thinking of Omega (even at its elementary stage) without realizing that its function of gathering together and unifying implies its being, in one way or another, partly involved in the world. Cf. Duns Scotus's views on the necessity for some Incarnation' (*Esquisse d'une dialectique de l'esprit*, 1947, *op. cit.*, p. 157).

[96] Similarly: 'Unless it is to be powerless to form the keystone of the

noosphere, Omega can only be conceived as the *meeting-point* between a universe that has reached the limit of centration and another, even deeper, centre—this being the self-subsistent centre and absolutely final principle of irreversibility and personalization; the one and only true Omega' (*Man's Place in Nature*, p. 121).

[97] This final distance of man from God is the *essential distinction between Teilhard's rationalism and the rationalism of non-Christians.* Characteristic of the latter is, in fact, the plan, a classic legacy from Plato and Plotinus, by which being returns to oneness, starting from the 'procession' that projects it, disintegrates it, and multiplies it. Knowledge, dissociated in the subject–object opposition, seeks to attain unity. (Cf. Eliane Amado-Valensi, *Les niveaux d'être; la connaissance et le mal*, Paris, P.U.F., 1962).

In its attempt to allow for history, the dialectical rationalism of Hegel and Marx is still built upon this plan. In the former case, the 'return' to the one is achieved by an intellectual 'ecstasy'; in the latter, by collective political action, culminating in the unified fulfilment of human history.

Teilhard's system which, again, calls for action more than for thought, still retains the succession of the usual phases: being and unity, multiplicity, return to the one. But (1) multiplicity is not a matter of logical necessity but comes from a creative act. (2) The 'return' to the one is achieved by the coincidence of divine freedom and human freedom: it is 'given'. (3) Most important of all, the final unity of human history still lacks absolute consistence and is incomplete.

[98] Père Jeannière has appreciated this problem and goes so far as to ask, 'Should we duplicate Omega Point? Should we, in short, relate it to two modes of historical synthesis?' This hypothesis is entirely unacceptable: only one unique absolute can exist as the term of history. But the supernatural relation, which was more and more clearly perceived by Teilhard, particularly in *Le Christique*, completes the purely philosophical or cosmological line of thought, by introducing explicitly the notion of a fundamental *negativity* of God in relation to man. Omega-God, known as the super-person and final pole of consciousness; already postulated as 'self-subsistent' and autonomous, but seen primarily in his involvement in history— Omega-God is affirmed as even more transcendent. And, says Teilhard, man's access to communion with him implies an annihila-

tion, a reversal of the whole. The peak of historical evolution is a way out. 'Totalization can only be given, but it is as inevitable as it is gratuitous. While it is the legitimate object, for the human adventure, of a passionate quest inspired by a dynamic Promethean urge, it can be accepted in humanity only by faith' (A. Jeannière, *Approches christologiques*, in *Essais sur Teilhard de Chardin, Recherches et débats du C.C.I.F.*, cahier No. 40, Paris, Fayard, 1962, p. 95).

'Not only,' to quote Père Jeannière again, 'has Omega Point no duration, but it is not of the order of time. Nevertheless, if there is really such a thing as a totalization of history, if the end is not an artificial super-added salvation but it is indeed the history of men that is totalized, then the Pleroma must be formed in history' (*Sur le mal, l'union, et le point Oméga*, in *Esprit*, March 1964, p. 364).

From another angle, Père J.-Y. Calvez, criticizing the Marxist view of an end to history that is immanent in history, adds: 'History has a direction, which is contained in its relation to the absolute that constitutes it; it is related to a Logos; but this direction is never totalized in one single determination ... History has a direction that is immanent in it, but this direction is never fully developed in a moment of empirical history.' 'Such a view of man and the world ... does not recognize, in the conditions of history, a single fulfilment of history or a triumphant victory with no possibility of falling back ... Such a reading of history cannot promise that the relationship of otherness between finite and infinite can be fully bridged, that the infinite will be reunited with the finite; but it anticipates it as a free gift, as fully as it already recognizes the free gift that constitutes man's freedom and the possibility of realizing it' (*La Pensée de Karl Marx*, Paris, Editions de Seuil, 1957, p. 634).

[99] This point has been well brought out by Pierre Fruchon in *Création ou consentement*, Paris, Aubier, 1963, pp. 260-300.

[100] *Structure et herméneutique*, in *Esprit*, November 1963, in particular pp. 611-14.

[101] The words *synchrony* (*synchronie*) and *diachrony* (*diachronie*), are borrowed from Claude Lévi-Strauss (*La pensée sauvage*, Paris, Plon, 1962). See the article, quoted above, by Paul Ricoeur, who questions Lévi-Strauss's 'structuralism': the societies that lend themselves too readily to structural and purely objective analysis are not those that are most highly charged dynamically and in line with the movement of history.

[102] As we shall see, Teilhard attached great importance to scientific and technical factors. Similarly, he appreciated the economic and social solidarity and interdependence of modern mankind. He emphasized the importance of the growth of population on a limited surface. He called attention, too, to the problem of new collective requirements (*L'atomisme de l'esprit*, 1941, in *L'activation de l'énergie*, p. 43).

[103] Indispensable though this classification is for an exact study of Teilhard's thought, some excuse must be made for inevitable repetitions. Some ideas, already briefly noticed in the chapter on phenomenology, have had to be treated again. We shall try, too, as we proceed, to indicate the connexion and the breaks in continuity between the different levels, in particular in the theology. Similarly, on a few occasions, it has been necessary to repeat some quotations from Teilhard in the notes.

CHAPTER 4: COSMOLOGY

[1] *L'énergie de l'évolution*, unpublished, 1943.

[2] *The basis and foundation of the idea of evolution* in *Vision of the Past* p. 121.

[3] *Ibid.*, p. 130.

[4] 'Indeed we owe our knowledge of the macro-structure and the micro-structure of the universe far more to increasingly accurate measurements than to direct observation' (*The Phenomenon of Man*, p. 45). 'Fortunately, there are a number of different ways in which our minds can reach reality. What escapes the intuition of our senses we can encircle and define approximately by a series of indirect attacks' (*Ibid.*, p. 90). 'To a considerable extent, the representation of the atom accepted at this moment is nothing more than a simple means, graphic even while subject to revision, enabling the scientist to put together and to show the non-contradiction of the ever more various "effects" manifested by matter' (*Ibid.*, p. 39).

[5] 'Who can say to just what extent an attractive harmony is not the budding charm, the anticipatory sign, of the strictest truth?' (*The Phenomenon of Man*, 1930, in *Vision of the Past*, p. 162).

'The more I think about it, the less I can see any criterion for truth other than the establishment of a growing maximum of universal coherence' (*Comment je crois*, unpublished, 1934).

'Truth is simply the total coherence of the universe in relation to every point within it' (*Esquisse d'un univers personnel*, 1936, in *L'énergie humaine*, p. 71).

'In science (and elsewhere) the great test of truth is coherence and productiveness. For our minds, the more order a theory imposes on our vision of the world, and, at the same time, the more capable it shows itself of directing and sustaining the forward movement of our powers of research and construction, the more certain that theory is. (*True theory=the most profitable*)' (*Man's Place in the Universe*, 1942, in *Vision of the Past*, p. 227).

'The specific mark of truth is the power to develop indefinitely, not only without developing any internal contradiction but also by forming a positively constructed whole, whose parts give one another mutual support, and complement one another, ever more fully. (*Comment je vois*, unpublished, 1948). See also Chapter 2, note 55.

[6] Cf. René Boirel, *Théorie générale de l'invention*, Paris, P.U.F.,1961. 'Scientific method, in the strictest sense, implies that the notions introduced are capable of being defined positively and experimentally: to put it more exactly, the notions must be "operational", which means that they must be arrived at and brought into action by objective and material processes. As for theories, while they may no doubt introduce hypotheses that go far beyond the facts, they will never be recognized as valid unless they are checked by experiment. Such is the case with the theories of universal gravity and quantum mechanics' (F. Russo, *La méthode du Père Teilhard de Chardin*, in *Essais sur Teilhard de Chardin, op. cit.*, p. 15).

Cf. André Astier, *Rendre à César ce qui est à César, ou le matérialisme scientifique*, in *Science et matérialisme*, Cahier No. 41 of C.C.I.F., Paris, Fayard, 1963, pp. 85–117.

[7] 'The most solid part, the truly indestructible residue, of the conquests of science in physics and chemistry, is represented by the discovery and cataloguing of a vast family of natural units, centres, nuclei, defined by their specific properties and grouped in graded categories . . . Under the pressure of nature and truth, the combined influences of physics, chemistry and astronomy, are leading, through the most valuable of their speculative conclusions, to the

construction of a vast systematics of the inorganic world, into which, at the level of the biosphere, the classification of organic beings may readily be interpolated. The tree of inorganic unities (atomic and sidereal) is beginning to envelop and relay with its branches the tree of organic unities' (*The Natural History of the World*, 1925, in *Vision of the Past*, p. 112).

[8] Thus in arithmetic, the whole number is a particular case of the fractional number, the latter of the complex number, etc. Euclidean geometry is a particular case of n-dimensional geometries. A conic curve is intelligible through its classification in the series of more general curves, etc.

[9] *Transformism*

If Teilhard adopts, in biology, the theory of transformism, it is not only because it covers a continually increasing number of facts, but also because transformism is the *mental category* necessary to interpret the ordered sequences of evolution. 'Evolution . . . is a general condition to which all theories, all hypotheses, all systems must bow, and which they must satisfy henceforward if they are to be thinkable and true' (*The Phenomenon of Man*, p. 219).

'In *every* scientific field, it is unanimously recognized that there is only one possible way of understanding beings—*knowing their history*. Nature=development'. (Unpublished letter to Père Auguste Valensin, 4 July 1920).

'What modern natural scientists most fundamentally hold to— what they cling to as an unshakable conviction, a conviction that has continuously grown beneath their surface arguments—is the fact of a *physical connexion* between living beings. Living beings *hold together* biologically. They have organic command of their successive appearances . . . The successive growths of life can be the *substance of a history* . . . Every being in our universe is by its material organization part and parcel of a whole past. It is in essence a history. And by its history, by this chain of antecedents which have prepared and introduced it, it is joined with no severance to the milieu within which it appears to us. The smallest exception to this rule would upset the entire edifice of our experience . . . *Reduced to its essence*, transformism is not a hypothesis. It is the particular expression, applied to the case of life, of the law which conditions our whole knowledge of the sensible universe: the law that we can understand nothing, in the domain of matter, except as part of a sequence or collection' (*The transformist question*, 1921, in *Vision of the past*, pp. 22, 24–5).

'Is transformism fundamentally anything but the belief in a *natural* link between animal species?' (*The transformist paradox*, 1925, ibid., p. 87).

'In living organisms nothing is constructed without a preliminary sketch. Never do really viable and stable characteristics appear by chance, all take their place in a rigorously determined order' (*Ibid.*, p. 84).

'Nothing can enter our life or our field of vision except by way of birth, which means linked to the development of the whole.' 'In the realm of life, as in that of matter, the fundamental unity of the universe and the inexorable inter-relationship of the cosmic elements, which will allow any new being to enter our experience in the context of all the present and past states of the world known to science, appear to be ideas now definitely accepted by the human mind' (*The Natural History of the World*, ibid., p. 104).

'The biosphere presents itself as a *constructed whole*, the external structure of great adjusted blocks being repeated by an internal texture of smaller elements. One conclusion is inevitable: that it took shape progressively. (*Basis and foundation of the idea of evolution*, 1920, in *Vision of the Past*, p. 122).

All the above ideas are found again in *What should we think of transformism?* ibid., pp. 151–60.

'At this degree of generalization, it may be said that the problem of transformism no longer exists. The question is settled once and for all. To shake our belief now in the reality of biogenesis, it would be necessary to uproot the tree of life and undermine the whole structure of the world' (*The Phenomenon of Man*, p. 140). Teilhard adds in a note: 'As a matter of fact, in view of the impossibility of empirically perceiving any entity, animate or inanimate, otherwise than as engaged in the time-space series, evolutionary theory has long ceased to be a hypothesis, to become a (dimensional) condition which all hypotheses of physics or biology must henceforth satisfy. Biologists and palaeontologists are still arguing today about the way things happen, and above all about the mechanism of life's transformation' (*Ibid.*).

'In the space of two or three centuries, and under the converging influence of a number of factors (all connected with our growing

awareness of the importance, in all fields of knowledge, of history),
it has become impossible to present the universe to us in the form of
an established harmony: we now see unmistakably that it is a
system in movement. It is no longer an *order*, but a *process*. No
longer a cosmos but a cosmogenesis . . . This is an expression of the
structural law (both of "being" and of knowledge) by virtue of
which *nothing, absolutely nothing*, we now realize, can enter our lives
and our field of vision except by *way of birth*—which means, in other
words, the pan-harmony in space-time of the phenomenon—the
idea of evolution has nothing in common with a hypothesis' (*Réflexions sur la probabilité scientifique*, 1951, in *L'activation de l'énergie*,
p. 282).

'The idea of evolution (this is my second point) has not ceased to
universalize in the course of its progress. Appearing locally, in the
wake of zoology, evolution, after making gradual progress through
the neighbouring realms, has finally *invaded everything* . . . Let us be
done once and for all, therefore, with the naive conception of the
"evolutionary hypothesis"; it has long been out-of-date. No,
taken sufficiently broadly, evolution is no longer, and has not been
for a long time, a hypothesis—nor merely a simple method. It is in
fact a new and common dimension of the universe, and consequently affects the totality of elements and relations of the universe.
Not a hypothesis, therefore, but a condition which all hypotheses
must henceforth fulfil. The expression for our minds of the
world's passage from the state of "cosmos" to the state of "cosmogenesis" (*Evolution of the idea of evolution*, 1950, in *Vision of the Past*,
p. 246).

'And now we find that a true genesis of simple bodies is revealed
to us by physics. An "aphyletic" type of evolution, no doubt, . . .
but nevertheless a true evolution, since, in one way or another,
atomic additivity exists, starting with nuclear elements and electrons'
(*L'énergie d'évolution*, 1953, in *L'activation de l'énergie*, p. 383). The
mechanics of heavenly bodies has been transformed into 'an
embryology of heavenly bodies' (*Du cosmos à la cosmogénèse, ibid.*,
p. 263).

The objection from religion: Teilhard answers it as follows.
'Scientific transformism, strictly speaking, proves nothing for or
against God. It simply notes the fact of a chain of connexion in
reality. It presents us with an anatomy of life, certainly not a final

reason for it' (*The transformist question*, 1921, in *Vision of the Past* p. 23).

Moreover, 'Evolution is as capable as the theory of fixed species, if not more so, of investing the universe with that greatness, depth and unity which are the natural climate of the Christian faith' (*What should we think of transformism?* 1930, *ibid.*, p. 159).

Teilhard, again, and for sound reasons, accepts the transmission of 'acquired characteristics' (*The Singularities of the Human Species*, 1954, in *The Appearance of Man*, p. 240).

He describes three ways of evolutionary mutation: by dispersion, by radiation, by canalization. Particularly in the first two, the mutations are not continuous but periodical. 'Our straightest series are actually made up of a host of little overlapping shoots, corresponding each to a separate form; and these forms replace one another like tangents along the line of a curve' (*The movements of life*, 1929, in *Vision of the Past*, p. 146).

In answer to an objection against transformism, Teilhard often recalls the fundamental condition of experience, in virtue of which the beginnings of everything tend to become physically unavailable: it is the law found universally in history, which we shall later call 'the automatic suppression of evolutionary peduncles' (*The Phenomenon of Man*, pp. 90, 120, 125, etc.) (On this point, see also: *On the necessarily discontinuous appearance of every evolutionary series*, 1926, in *Vision of the Past*, p. 114-5; *The basis and foundations of the idea of evolution*, *ibid.*, p. 125; *The Vision of the Past*, *ibid.*, p. 243, etc.)

Teilhard speaks also of the law of succession, which brings about the sudden emergence of new species within lineages in which they had already been secretly active (*The Phenomenon of Man*, pp. 199–200).

He notes the phenomenon of *orthogenesis*, or controlled additivity (*ibid.*, pp. 108–9), 'biological efficiency in the struggle for life', 'the fundamental technique of *groping* . . . which combines the blind fantasy of large numbers with the precise orientation of a specific target. It would be a mistake to see it as mere chance. Groping is *directed* chance'; life's ingenuity, its indifference to the individual and its orientation towards the future and totality, the innumerable ramifications of the tree of life, with their dovetailed, fan-like character, the aristogenesis that seeks to produce more perfect beings, with larger brains . . . (*ibid.*, pp. 109ff).

This subject is excellently treated by Madame Barthélemy-Madaule, *op. cit.*, pp. 130–47.

10 *The Phenomenon of Man*, 1930, in *The Vision of the Past*, p. 166. The systematics of living species and, no doubt, that of the structures of matter, represents in fact a genesis in history (*The Phenomenon of Man*, p. 84). However, since it is founded on the Aristotelian logic of *inclusion* (the less general in the more general, the species in the genus) it does not allow us, by itself, to determine man's unique position in nature. 'It is not enough now (indeed, it would be unscientific and illogical) to continue to treat man as no more than one section *within* the animal kingdom. Because of his planetary situation man, physico-biologically, transcends classic systematics, for he belongs to another level, another form, another species of life in the universe' (*La convergence de l'univers*, 1951, in *L'activation de l'énergie*, p. 298).

11 Cf. Chapter 5, note 32.

12 'At that moment I seemed to be face to face with this thing, that seemed to be taking shape—like an animal, whose soul is stirring, that can see groups of linked realities but cannot grasp the relationship they represent' (*La nostalgie du front, Etudes*, 20 November 1917, in *Ecrits du temps de la guerre*, p. 214). In this connexion see (in the appendix) the logical order of the terms used by Teilhard to indicate the approach of thought to the true.

13 'During the last fifty years or so, the investigations of science have proved beyond all doubt that there is no fact that exists in pure isolation, but that every experience, however objective it may seem, inevitably becomes enveloped in a complex of assumptions as soon as the scientist attempts to express it in a formula. But while this aura of subjective interpretation may remain imperceptible where the field of observation is limited, it is bound to become practically dominant as soon as the field of vision extends to the whole. Like the meridians as they approach the pole, science, philosophy and religion are bound to converge as they draw nearer to the whole. I say "converge" advisedly, but without merging, and without ceasing, to the very end, to assail the real from different angles and on different planes' (*The Phenomenon of Man*, Preface). 'In its early, naive, stage science, perhaps inevitably, imagined that we could observe things in themselves, as though we were the starting point of the universe. Instinctively physicists and naturalists went to

work as though they could look down from a great height on a world upon which their consciousness could penetrate without being submitted to it or changing it. They are now beginning to realize that even the most objective of their observations are steeped in the conventions they adopted at the outset and by forms or habits of thought developed in the course of the development of research so that, when they reach the end of their analyses, they cannot tell with any certainty whether the structure they have reached is the essence of the matter they are studying, or the reflection of their own thought. And at the same time they realize that as a result of their discoveries, they are caught body and soul in the network of relationships they thought to cast upon things from outside: in fact, they are caught in their own net. A geologist would use the words metamorphism and endomorphism. Object and subject marry and mutually transform each other in the act of knowledge; and from now on man willy-nilly finds his own image stamped on all he looks at' (*Ibid.*, p. 32).

[14] The sense of the immensity of space, the sense of depth, number, proportion, quality or novelty, movement, the organic.

[15] *Comment je crois*, unpublished, 1934. 'Matter, the symbol of multiplicity and impermanence, can never be directly grasped by thought' (*L'esprit de la terre*, in *L'énergie humaine*, p. 29).

[16] *Creative Evolution*, pp. 232–237.

[17] *The Phenomenon of Man*, p. 74. 'Matter . . . with the same basic attributes of plurality, perceivability and inter-connexions' (*Le Milieu Divin.*, p. 106).

[18] *Le coeur de la matière*, unpublished, 1950, p. 15.

[19] 'It is matter that allows spirit to subsist, by constantly providing it with a focus of action and constantly feeding it' (*Mon univers*, 1924, in *Science et Christ*, p. 78).

[20] '*Real nothingness, physical nothingness*—the nothingness that stands at the threshold of being, on which all possible worlds, following their axes, must converge—is *pure multiplicity; it is the multitude* (*La lutte contre la multitude* 1917, in *Ecrits du temps de la guerre*, p. 114). 'At the lower extremity of things, so far below that we can never reach it (analysis) reveals to us an immense plurality—complete diversity combined with total disunity. This absolute multiplicity would, in fact, be nothingness, and it has never existed. But it is

the direction from which the world emerges for us' (*Mon univers*, 1924, in *Science et Christ*, p. 74).

[21] The word 'matter' is derived from *materia*, whose primary meaning is the trunk of the tree, which holds the branches and from which they spring: hence the idea of timber in general (cf. the French words *madrier*, *merrain*, *marmenteau*). There is an echo of *maternity* in the word, the trunk of the tree being the mother, *mater*, of the foliage (cf. A. Ernout and A. Meillet, *Dictionnaire étymologique de la langue latine*, Lille). This etymology fits in with Teilhard's concept of matter as the matrix of spirit, *materia matrix* (*Du cosmos à la cosmogénèse*, 1951, in *L'activation de l'énergie*, p. 267).

[22] Cf. R. Boirel, *op. cit.*, p. 365.

[23] 'Without the involution of matter upon itself, that is to say without the closed chemistry of molecules, cells and phyletic branches, there would never have been either biosphere or noosphere. In their advent and their development, life and thought are not only accidentally, but also structurally, bound up with the contours and destiny of the terrestrial mass' (*The Phenomenon of Man*, p. 273).

In a passage written in 1949, which may reflect a withdrawal from the affirmation of a physical connexion between matter and life, Teilhard calls material structures *pseudo-complexes*, as opposed to organic arrangements or *eu-complexes* (*Does humanity move biologically upon itself?* 1949, in *The Future of Man*, p. 253).

'According to the physicists—speaking with the authority derived from a complete system of successful experiments—cosmic energy, taken in the most primordial, the most extended, the most "radiant" form we know, appears already granulated (photons)' (*The singularities of the human species*, 1954, in *The Appearance of Man*, p. 211).

[24] 'In concrete reality, there are not both matter *and* spirit: there is only matter becoming spirit. There is neither matter nor spirit in the world: the "stuff of the universe" is spirit-matter. No other substance but this could produce the human molecule' (*Esquisse d'un univers personnel*, 1936, in *L'énergie humaine*, p. 74).

'Plurality, unity, energy: the three faces of matter' (*The Phenomenon of Man*, p. 40).

'Two different factors or terms are therefore necessary to denote the complexity of a system; one expresses the number of elements or groups of elements contained in the system; the other, much more difficult to represent, expresses the number, variety and closeness of the links (density) existing between these elements at a minimum volume' (*Man's Place in the Universe*, 1942, in *Vision of the Past*, p. 222).

[25] 'Aristotelian hylomorphism represents the projection of modern evolution on a world without duration. Transferred to a universe to which duration has added an extra dimension, the theory of matter and form becomes practically indistinguishable from our modern speculations on the development of nature' (*Basis and foundations of the idea of evolution*, 1922, in *Vision of the Past*, p. 129 note).

[26] 'The profoundly "atomic" character of the universe is visible in everyday experience, in raindrops and grains of sand, in the hosts of the living and the multitude of stars; even in the ashes of the dead. Man has needed neither microscope nor electronic analysis in order to suspect that he lives surrounded by and resting on dust . . . Indeed our sensory experience turns out to be a floating condensation on a swarm of the undefinable. Bewildering in its multiplicity and its minuteness, the substratum of the tangible universe is in an unending state of disintegration as it goes downwards' (*The Phenomenon of Man*, pp. 40-1).

[27] *The Phenomenon of Man*, p. 41ff. 'The mesh of the universe is the universe itself' (*Ibid.*, p. 45). 'The stuff of the universe cannot divide itself but, as a gigantic "atom" it forms in its totality (apart from thought on which it is concentrated and centred at the other end) the only real indivisible' (*Ibid.*, p. 43). 'The radius of action proper to each cosmic element must logically be prolonged to the utmost limits of the world itself. Since the atom is naturally co-extensive with the whole of the space in which it is situated—and since, on the other hand, a universal space is *the only space there is*—we are bound to admit that this immensity represents the sphere of action common to all atoms. The volume of each of them is the volume of the universe. The atom is no longer the microscopic closed world we may have imagined to ourselves. It is the infinitesimal centre of the world itself' (*Ibid.*, pp. 45-6).

In *La Centrologie* (1944, No. 6, in *L'activation de l'énergie*, p. 110) Teilhard distinguishes three complementary forms of the solidarity that exists between all the nuclei of the universe: tangential and superficial solidarity within their isosphere, radial solidarity (through participation in all the interconnexions of the different isospheres), and a further radial solidarity in their common orientation towards Omega Point. Thus unlike Leibnitz's 'doorless and windowless' monad, each individual being is partly itself and 'partly one with the whole to which it is open' (*Ibid.*).

[28] *The Phenomenon of Man*, pp. 45, 53.

[29] *L'esprit de la terre*, 1931, in *L'énergie humaine*, pp. 27–8.

[30] *Turmoil or genesis?* 1947, in *The Future of Man*, pp. 215–18. 'However improbable, in a mechanistic sense, the elaborate organic structure created by life may appear, it seems increasingly evident that the cosmic substance is drawn towards these states of extreme arrangement by a particular kind of attraction, which compels it, by the play of large numbers in which it is involved, to miss no opportunity of becoming more complex and thus achieving a higher degree of freedom' (*From the pre-human to the ultra-human*, 1950, in *The Future of Man*, p. 290).

On the biosphere, see *Basis and foundations of the idea of evolution*, 1926, in *Vision of the Past*, p. 117 note: 'By biosphere we do not mean "some great animal" that destroys individual spontaneity, but simply a natural association of individuals in some unity of a higher order, which cannot be conceived except *by analogy* with everything else we know about natural units.'

[31] *The Phenomenon of Man*, p. 39.

[32] However, Teilhard also says, 'The universe *had already begun to ramify* and it doubtless goes on ramifying indefinitely, *even below* the tree of life' (*The Phenomenon of Man*, p. 96).

[33] *Man's Place in Nature*, pp. 21–32. Teilhard enumerates the phases of increasing complexity as follows: the pre-atomic phase (nuclei and electrons); the atomic (the grouping of nuclei in atoms, in free spaces, fixed and limited in number); the molecular (the grouping of atoms in finite or indefinite chains); the cellular (the grouping of molecules in centred assemblies). Viruses, for example, contain something like a million atoms (*Turmoil or genesis?* 1947, in *The Future of Man*, p. 217 note). On the same page (note 2) he distinguishes between the involution (or coiling) of mass, and the involution of complexity. Cf. *Life and the Planets*, *ibid.*, pp. 105–8.

If viruses are defined by 10^8 simple elements, and large mammals by 10^{20}, biology may be defined as 'the physics of very large complexes', 'the physics of the third infinite'. Moreover, the coefficient of complexity gives us the 'basis for a truly natural classification of the elements of the universe' (*La Centrologie*, No. 2).

Man's place in the universe, in *Vision of the Past*, pp. 218ff. In this essay, Teilhard arrives at the following law. 'Everything happens as though at each end of the world certain properties of matter were exaggerated, and became dominant, that, at the other end, became so attenuated as to have no impact on our experience' (p. 221). Here, we may note, Teilhard shares Edouard Le Roy's views on the difference in the zones of the universe. Cf. Note 54.

[34] '... these two energies being linked to one another in the "arrangement", but even so powerless either to combine or to be transformed into one another directly, because they operate at different levels' (*L'activation de l'énergie humaine*, 1953, in *L'activation de l'énergie*, p. 416).

[35] 'The most metaphysical', says Bergson, 'of the laws of physics' (*Creative Evolution*, p. 256).

[36] *The phenomenon of man*, 1930, in *Vision of the Past*, p. 235. *L'esprit de la terre*, 1931, in *L'énergie humaine*, p. 28.   *The Phenomenon of Man*, pp. 50-2, 64-6. *The singularities of the human species*, 1954, in *The Appearance of Man*, pp. 264-6).

'Entropy, as is known, is the name that physics gives to that apparently inevitable fall by which collections of corpuscles (the scene of all physico-chemical phenomena) sink, by virtue of statistical laws of probability, towards an intermediate state of diffuse agitation, a state in which all exchange of useful energy ceases on our scale of experience. Everything around us seems to be descending towards this death of matter' (*The movements of life*, 1928, in *Vision of the Past*, p. 149). 'As a matter of fact, from the real evolutionary standpoint, something is finally burned in the course of every synthesis in order to pay for that synthesis. The more the energy-quantum of the world comes into play, the more it is consumed.' 'A price has to be paid for every synthesis.' The initial impulse is gradually exhausted. 'Laboriously, step by step, the atomic and molecular structures become built up and complicated, but the upward force is lost on the way. Moreover, the same wearing away that is gradually consuming the cosmos in its totality is at work within the terms of the synthesis, and the higher the terms the quicker this action takes place. Little by little, the *improbable* combinations that they represent become broken down again into more simple components, which fall back and are disaggregated in the shapelessness of *probable* distributions' (*The Phenomenon of Man*, pp. 51-2).

Teilhard is at pains, too, to show how the two forms of energy come to terms, in particular how science is not, in practice, hampered in its own field by the normal increase of radial or spiritual energy (*Ibid.*, pp. 65-6).

[37] *Ibid.*, p. 51.

[38] 'This absolute of physics has thus far not only resisted all attempts at "relativization", but, if I am not mistaken, it tends to find its counterpart in a current moving in the opposite sense, positive and constructive, which is revealed by the study of the earth's biological past: the ascent of the universe towards zones of increasing improbability and personality. Entropy and life; backward and forward: two complementary expressions of the arrow of time' (*The grand option*, 1939, in *The Future of Man*, pp. 48-9).

'In addition to this sharply defined and firmly established thermodynamic nucleus, should we not recognize in the *Weltstoff* the presence of certain structural elements, which, though negligible for physics and physical chemistry, take on a rapidly increasing importance in the case of the externally complex assemblies with which the biological sciences are concerned?' (*L'énergie de l'évolution*, 1953, in *L'activation de l'énergie*, p. 382).

[39] *The Phenomenon of Man*, p. 52.

[40] '. . . by showing preference in the use of chances' (*La convergence de l'univers*, 1951, in *L'activation de l'énergie*, p. 303).

[41] '. . . the radial increasing with the arrangement of the tangential, and the tangential only arranging itself when prompted by the radial' (*The singularities of the human species*, 1945, in *The Appearance of Man*, p. 265 note).

[42] Here Teilhard seems to adopt the view that movement comes before the thing that moves: 'In physics, we now know, acceleration produces mass, which means that what moves comes only after movement' (*Contingence de l'univers et goût humain de survivre*, unpublished, 1953). In fact, the close connexion between structure and energy is so essential in Teilhard that there can be no question of his conceiving an energy that lacked support, however mysterious the support might be.

[43] *Bergson and Teilhard*

'Without the slightest doubt, *there is something* through which material and spiritual energy hold together and are complementary. In the last analysis, *somehow or other*, there must be a single energy operating in the world' (*The Phenomenon of Man*, p. 63). 'In essence, we recognize, all energy is by nature psychic' (*Ibid.*).

'While in *Creative Evolution* the cosmos is seen as a radiation spreading out from a centre of emergence, the picture of the universe presented by creative union is one of reduction, of a confluence that starts from an infinitely distended sphere. The two theories, both evolutionary, are the converse of one another' (*L'union créatrice*, 1917, in *Ecrits du temps de la guerre*, p. 179).

'If we accept the idea of a world in which there are two currents, it would be more plausible to accept that only one current is fundamental, the current that runs towards the improbable. We can see no way at all by which there could be an ascent from a fundamentally determinist current, represented by large numbers and by lack of consciousness, to the other. We can more or less see how a world of matter could be born from a world of spirit, but not how a world of spirit could be born from a world of matter' (First lecture to the Marcel Légaut group, 19 November 1930).

'In spite of the appearance, so impressive to the physicist, of secondary phenomena of progressive dispersion such as entropy, there is only one evolution, the evolution *of convergence*' (*Christologie et évolution*, unpublished, 1933).

'The spiritual phenomenon, then, is one of the two most fundamental cosmic movements we can grasp experientially. And since, in all probability, these two contrary movements (vitalization and dissipation of energy) are but the two opposite poles of one single cosmic movement, whose positive or synthetic term is the more significant, then it is ultimately *the* one basic cosmic movement—it is from that that everything depends, and there is nothing that can explain it; it is indeed, we maintain, *the* phenomenon' (*Le phénomène spirituel*, 1937, in *L'énergie humaine*, p. 123).

'Matter and spirit: not two things—but two states, or two aspects, of one and the same cosmic stuff, depending on whether you look at it, or follow it, in the direction in which it is created, or conversely, in that which it ceases to be' (*Le coeur de la matière*, unpublished, 1950).

H. Gouhier, on the authority of at least the first of these passages, points out that both Bergson and Teilhard believe in the fundamental unity of the world and the uniqueness of the energy that moves it. He adds, however, that while Teilhard's thought is dominated by the notion of universal convergence, Bergson seems to assert the irreconcilable antagonism and divergence of the energies. In each case, he qualifies this by saying that these are only 'tendencies' (*Bergson et le Christ des Evangiles*, Paris, Fayard, 1962, p. 68).

Madame M. Barthélemy-Madaule's view agrees with this, in contrasting Bergson's concept of a fundamental and inevitable dispersion of historical reality with Teilhard's concept of its progressive convergence. In Bergson, the dominating images are of explosion, bursting, multiplication; in Teilhard, unification, construction, totalization, synthesis. Teilhard preserves the fundamental interconnexion and engagement of matter and life, while Bergson emphasizes their severance: all reality, however primitive, is matter-life, or matter-spirit, and, at the very heart of intellectual and moral life, matter's 'drag' is at once the obstacle to, the resistance against, and the object of unification.

As many passages show (particularly in *L'union créatrice*, 1917, in *Ecrits du temps de la guerre*, and in reading notes taken in 1942–5), Teilhard was very alive to this difference. Here, for example, is a passage from an unpublished letter to Père Auguste Valensin, 26 April 1928: 'The only remark of Le Roy's that made him wince (he is speaking of Père de Sinéty) is when Le Roy says that he and I have common roots in the philosophy of Bergson (which, in fact, isn't absolutely true, particularly so far as I'm concerned).'

Teilhard may have been thinking of Bergson when he wrote: 'Evolutionisms "of divergence", whether radically materialistic (that is to say placing the equilibrium of the world in multiplicity) or simply renouncing all hope in an ulterior unification of spiritual monads (regarded as a scattering of glowing sparks) are incapable of implanting a sense of universal responsibility and love. They may make all men and everything else in the world into brothers as firmly united in the womb of Demeter as in that of any Eve. But brothers can be enemies; and if they are not, it is for reasons other than their common origin. Birth, after all, is only a memory. The existence of love depends on a common growth in the womb of a single future' (*Basis and foundations of the idea of evolution*, 1926, in *Vision of the Past*, p. 138 note). On the convergence-divergence alternative, see *The New Spirit*, 1942, in *The Future of Man*, pp. 45–7.

It would seem that the Christian notion of the Church as the mystical body of Christ, moving towards total communion, influenced Teilhard by helping him to take as his hypothesis the universal unification of the world. The prospect of such a communion or such a church is foreign to Bergson, for whom the essential function of the universe is to be a 'machine for the making gods'. More exact in his observation of social facts, and more careful, too, in interpreting them, Bergson was chary of taking into account the progress of man's unity in history and of reading into it a dawn of unanimity; he limited himself to the more modest noting of the sporadic triumphs of spirit in the personalities of the élite. This did not prevent him from hoping, like Teilhard, and in the essential contexts, for the interventions of economic planning (*The Two Sources*, pp. 250–251) nor even from envisaging the possibility of some total transcendence of mankind (*Ibid.*, p. 273–275).

However, while Teilhard postulates, at the beginning of the universe, a matter that is impregnated with a potentiality for spirit (an idea that is foreign to Bergson) he retains, too, the view of a divergence and opposition between the two energies: 'Yet, seductive though it be, the idea of the *direct* transformation of one of these two energies into the other is no sooner glimpsed than it has to be abandoned. As soon as we try to couple them together, their mutual independence becomes as clear as their interrelation (*The Phenomenon of Man*, p. 64). For Teilhard as for Bergson, if spirit is concentration, matter, in as much as it is subject to entropy, is dispersion, disintegration. Teilhard even considers that at the end of history the two tendencies of energy will not be reconciled: matter has played its part if it has succeeded in producing the right conditions for the development of person and the emergence of spirit. After that, it walks off the stage and loses all interest, it seems to have no share in the final success of the world.

The kinship of Bergson and Teilhard is seen again in the notions of tension and relaxation, with their degrees: in one aspect, matter is relaxation, while spirit is creative tension.

Finally, while Bergson was not committed to the idea of an

historical unification of mankind, he did not forget that mankind forms a structural whole, as is evidenced in the well-known sentence that closes the third chapter of *Creative Evolution*. 'The animal takes off from the plant, man bestrides animality, and the whole of humanity, in space and in time, is an immense army galloping beside and before and behind each of us, in an overwhelming charge able to beat down every resistance and clear the most formidable obstacles, perhaps even death.'

[44] This proposition of Teilhard's is closely akin not only to that of Leibnitz, but still more to Bergson. François Heidsieck, in his *Henri Bergson et la notion de l'espace* (Paris, P.U.F., 1961) has admirably demonstrated (relating it to Plotinus) the 'ideal genesis of space' in Bergson (pp. 131-5) and has shown how space became for Bergson an instrument of creation for man (pp. 135-45).

[45] *Comment je vois*, unpublished, 1948, No. 2, note 3. *Esquisse d'un univers personnel*, 1936, in *L'énergie humaine*, p. 70.

'All the rest of this essay will be nothing but the story of the struggle between the unified *multiple* and the *unorganized multitude*' (*The Phenomenon of Man*, p. 61).

[46] A very slow over-all movement, a 'directed linear transformation' (*Vision of the Past*, 1949, p. 240) or general orthogenesis, a tide running below the surface waves (*Ibid.*).

[47] 'The current that raises matter up should be conceived not so much as a mere internal impulse but rather as a *tide*. The multiple rises up, drawn by and into what is "already one". This is the secret and warrant of the irreversibility of life. In a first phase— before man—the attraction was vitally but unseeingly felt by the world' (*L'esprit de la terre*, 1951, in *L'énergie humaine*, pp. 56-7).

'The "impetus" of the world, glimpsed in the great drive of consciousness, can have its ultimate source only in some moving principle *within it*, which alone could explain its irreversible advance towards higher psychism.' (*The Phenomenon of Man*, p. 149).

In *Le coeur de la matière*, Teilhard again explains his grounds for believing that he 'cannot be mistaken in attributing to the cosmic movement that had just become apparent to him a maximum of creative value and invariability' (p. 10).

[48] Teilhard can establish the law of the conservation of the world's global energy in the course of the transformation that brings about the progressive dominance of spiritual energy: 'nothing is lost, while

everything is created' *L'énergie humaine*, 1937, appendix, pp. 198–200).

[49] *Le coeur de la matière*, unpublished, 1950.

[50] On one occasion, however, Teilhard says that the movement of the world is reversible, and explains in a note: 'Reversible, in so far as, with no support to rest on ahead of it, it is structurally bound up with a precarious arrangement of particles that are all, by nature, completely and fundamentally liable to disintegrate' (*Man's Place in Nature*, p. 120).

[51] 'Life taken as a whole does not manifest itself to our experience only as an advance into improbability. It also appears in the light of our scientific investigation as a continuous ascent towards greater consciousness. Beneath the ups and downs of the countless waves of organic forms runs a constantly mounting tide towards greater freedom, inventiveness and thought' (*The movements of life*, 1928, in *Vision of the Past*, p. 150).

[52] '*Theoretically*, the spiritual phenomenon develops a magnitude that we conceive as indefinitely perfectible; *functionally*, it maintains itself by its own growth . . .' (*Le phénomène spirituel*, 1937, in *L'énergie humaine*, p. 124).

[53] *Comment je crois*, unpublished, 1934. *Le phénomène spirituel*, 1937, in *L'énergie humaine*, pp. 123–5; The spiritual phenomenon is irresistible, irreversible, totalizing.

[54] 'In a famous passage, Pascal imagined, within a cheese-mite, another universe with other mites. It is on lines that *contradict* this idea of a space that expands or contracts in its own likeness that we are now obliged to think. Just as the brightness and the forms of life are transformed in the eyes of an observer who moves along a meridian on the earth or plunges into the depth of the seas, so, and even more radically, must we conceive the universe as changing if we try to shift ourselves, mentally, either to the top or to the bottom of its furthest limits.' Teilhard points out, too, how, with the introduction of relativity, both the universe of the excessively small and that of the excessively large oblige us 'to say goodbye to common experience' (*L'atomisme de l'esprit, un essai pour comprendre la structure de l'étoffe de l'univers*, 1941, in *L'activation de l'énergie*, pp. 31–2).

[55] 'Biology is simply the 'physics of very large complexes, the physics of the third infinite (that of complexity, in which life

appears)' (*La centrologie, ibid.,* p. 107 note). 'Complexity' is distinguished from 'complication' by combining 'with the plurality and differentiation of its parts a maximum of lightness and simplicity' (*Transformations et prolongements en l'homme du mécanisme de l'évolution,* in *L'activation de l'énergie,* p. 316 note).

[56] *L'atomisme de l'esprit, op. cit.,* p. 25.

[57] *L'atomisme de l'esprit,* 1941, in *L'activation de l'énergie,* p. 36. 'When physics is baffled, it lays the blame on nature. But surely what really happens is that physics, mutilating nature, persists in constructing its universe exclusively along a spatial axis, and life does not appear along that axis. What we have to do is to make a break-through, above us, cutting across the very large and the very small, to allow the axis of the complex to pass through. As soon as we do that, an additional dimension is introduced which creates a new setting for the cosmos; the vitalizing of matter no longer seems inacceptable or inexplicable; on the contrary it seems as "natural" as variation of mass with high acceleration or the appearance, with very great distances, of the effects of relativity.' 'The molecular branch and the cellular branch of matter; these two sections, hitherto treated as divergent or heterogeneous, tend, as we examine them, to come together' (*Ibid.*).

'Every infinite, physics teaches us, is characterized by certain "special" effects proper to that infinite: not in the sense that it is the only thing to possess them, but in the sense that those effects become perceptible, or even dominant, at the particular scale of that infinite. Such for example are the quanta in the infinitesimal, and relativity in the immense. Once we admit this, we have to ask what can be the specific effect proper to the vast complexes we have just recognized as constituting a third infinite in the universe. Surely we must answer that the specific effect is in fact precisely what we call life' (*Man's Place in Nature,* p. 23).

[58] *The singularities of the human species,* 1954, in *The Appearance of Man,* p. 214. This connexion between *complexity* and *consciousness* is fundamental to Teilhard's theory (Cf., in particular, *L'étoffe de l'univers,* 1953, in *L'activation de l'énergie,* p. 599).

[59] *The singularities . . ., op. cit.,* pp. 214-15, 220-1. In *Le coeur de la matière,* Teilhard notes how he came to realize that the 'solidity' or consistence of things, which is to say their very being, went hand in hand with their complexity (p. 10). As a partial explanation of

complexity he suggests that if the particles are not to crush one another or be confused with one another on the *closed surface* produced by the gravity of matter, they must necessarily 'arrange themselves' (*The singularities, op. cit.*, p. 214). Later he put forward the same hypothesis for the phenomenon of socialization.

'This particular property possessed by terrestrial substances—of becoming more vitalized as they become increasingly complex—is only the local manifestation and expression of a trend as universal as (and no doubt even more significant than) those already identified by science: those trends which cause the cosmic layers not only to expand explosively as a wave but also to condense into corpuscles under the action of electro-magnetic and gravitational forces, or perhaps to become dematerialized in radiation: trends which are probably strictly interconnected, as we shall one day realize' (*The Phenomenon of Man*, p. 301).

[60] *La centrologie*, No. 3, *op. cit.*, p. 108.

[61] *Life, a universal property of the cosmos*

'Nothing really exists in the Universe except myriads of more or less obscure spontaneities, the compressed swarm of which gradually forces the barrier separating it from liberty. From top to bottom of the series of beings, everything is in motion, everything is raising itself, organizing itself in a single direction, which is that of the greatest consciousness' (*Hominization*, 1923, in *Vision of the Past*, p. 72).

'Life's windfalls are, partly at least, a statistical effect, by which I mean the result of an infinite number of attempts continually made to find a biological way out towards more-being or better-being— you might compare the result of such an attempt to the pressure exerted by a gas on a container' (*The natural history of the world*, 1925, in *Vision of the Past*, p. 109).

These ideas recur in *Le phénomène spirituel*, 1937 (in *L'énergie humaine*, pp. 118–23).

'Caught within the curve of space-time, the layers of matter (considered as separate elements no less than as a whole) tighten and converge in thought, by synthesis. Therefore it is as a cone, in the form of a cone, that it can best be depicted' (*The new spirit*, 1942, in *The Future of Man*, p. 88).

Matter and spirit are certainly not heterogeneous or antagonistic; each requires the other, 'like the two aspects of one and the same object or, better, like the *terminus a quo* and the *terminus ad quem* of one and the same movement . . . If matter is defined as a "thing" without any trace of consciousness or spontaneity, then it ceases to exist . . . There is nothing in the universe except spirit, at different degrees of organization or plurality. But, all the time, what are truly new centres are emerging as a result of centro-complexity, from successive syntheses or segmentations'. While we must distinguish in the stuff of the cosmos, the inanimate zone, the animate zone, and the thinking zone, at the same time 'these divisions are after all only secondary, since all they do is to mark off into compartments a continuous psychic ambience that is subject to a single general transformation (centrogenesis) and depends entirely on Omega' (*La centrologie*, 1944, No. 32, *op. cit.*, p. 132).

'For underlying these supposedly "exceptional" cellular arrangements we have first the far vaster world of molecules, and underlying this again the immense and decidedly cosmic world of atoms; two worlds, displaying, the first by its inter-atomic arrangements and the second by its nuclear groupings (each in its own order and by different procedures) *precisely the same tendency* to "fall" into increasingly organized states of complexity . . . So finally we find the universe from top to bottom brought within a single immense coiling movement of mass and complexity, successively generating nuclei, atoms, molecules, cells and metazoa—the special properties of life being due solely to the extreme (virtually *infinite*) degree of complexity attained at its level' (*Turmoil or genesis?* 1947, in *The Future of Man*, pp. 216–17).

'Life and consciousness are no longer chance anomalies in nature: rather we find in biology a complement to the physics of matter. On the one hand, the stuff of the world dispersing through the radiation of its elemental energy; and on the other hand the same stuff reconverging through the radiation of thought' (*The Formation of the Noosphere*, 1947, in *The Future of Man*, pp. 181–2.)

'Living beings, far from constituting a singular and inexplicable oddity in the world, are on the contrary the outcome of an entirely generalized physico-chemical process in virtue of which cosmic matter, by its very existence and structure, is not only in a state of spatial expansion (as in these days is generally accepted) but even more significantly, presents itself to our experience as actuated by a movement of qualitative in-folding (or arrangement, if you prefer) upon itself. (*Does mankind move biologically upon itself?* 1949, in *The Future of Man*, p. 251).

'Life is not a peculiar anomaly, sporadically flowering on matter, but on exaggeration, through specially favourable circumstances, of a universal cosmic property—life is not an epiphenomenon, but the very essence of phenomenon' (*Man's Place in Nature*, p. 18). Cf. *The Phenomenon of Man*, pp. 301-2.

'The phenomenon of the vitalization of large molecules, that we find so astonishing, is itself only an extension of the moleculization of atoms, and ultimately of the atomization of energy—in other words of a process that affects and defines the universe in the whole of its substance and history' (*La réflexion de l'énergie*, in *L'activation de l'énergie*, pp. 344-5).

'However localized and scattered life may be in the universe, it would immediately become unintelligible to science if we did not regard it as having been *from the beginning everywhere under pressure*' (*The singularities of the human species*, 1954, in *The Appearance of Man*, p. 229).

This theory enables Teilhard to determine his attitude in regard to the plurality of inhabited worlds: ' "planets with noosphere", far from being a curiosity in nature, would quite simply be the *normal and ultimate product of matter carried to its completion* . . . Today, when the galaxies are revealed in millions on our photographic plates—each with its tens of thousands (millions?) of solar systems more or less like the one in which we were born . . . there *must undoubtedly* be "other inhabited worlds" ' (*ibid.*, pp. 229—30).

[62] 'From top to bottom of the series of beings, everything is in motion, everything is raising itself, organizing itself in a single direction, which is that of the greatest consciousness' (*Hominization*, 1923, in *Vision of the Past*, p. 72). Earlier, in *L'union créatrice* (in *Ecrits du temps de la guerre*, 1917, p. 190) Teilhard had said, 'Leaving to that lower form we might call "material" the single attribute of multiplicity, we find ourselves obliged to recognize that *true matter* (that is, what had always been known and respected under that name) is *spirit*'.

[63] *Basis and foundations of the idea of evolution*, 1926, in *Vision of the Past*, p. 187. A remark of François Mauriac's is apposite: 'This first living cell, that held in embryo all love and all thought, and all music, and this human body, so beautiful when it is beauti-

ful, and all that it has inspired, would in itself be enough to bring
me to my knees' (*Le nouveau Bloc-Notes*, Paris, Flammarion, 1961,
p. 44).

Some passages in Teilhard (dating, it is true, from the formative
period of his thought) have, nevertheless, a somewhat dualist and
Platonic tone. This is particularly marked in the *Hymn to Matter*:
'Blessed be you, impenetrable matter: you who, interposed between
our minds and the world of essences, cause us to languish with the
desire to pierce through the seamless veil of phenomena' (*The
spiritual power of matter*, 1919, in *Hymn of the Universe*, p. 69). Cf.
E. Borne, *art. cit.*, p. 56.

[64] *Determinism*

The cardinal idea of determinism is expressed in numerous passages:

'Because life is a physical factor *of a higher order* than measurable
forces, it is quite as possible to analyse its productions without
meeting the thing itself as to explain a watch mechanically without
thinking of the watchmaker: at every instant the universe, even if
we assume it to possess psychic forces, takes the form of a closed
circuit of determinisms which mutually induce one another. But on
the other hand, because these psychic forces constitute the co-
ordinating factor of various determined systems the totality of which
forms the animate world, the successive transformations of this
world cannot possibly be explained without recourse to some imponderable forces of synthesis . . . Beside the properties resulting
from collective play of the parts, there must also be in every
organized whole certain other properties, measurable or not, belonging to the collectivity as such, which neither the analysis nor the
sum of the elementary forces could ever account for' (*The transformist paradox*, 1925, in *Vision of the Past*, pp. 96, 98).

'From the initial form of a cosmos, made up of elementary
"liberties" one may readily "deduce", as a statistical effect of large
numbers and of habits, all the apparent rigidity on which is based
the mathematical physics of matter' (*L'esprit de la terre*, 1931, in
L'énergie humaine, p. 29).

'The determinisms of matter are no more than traces that survive
of spirit's own subjection' (*Comment je crois*, unpublished, 1934). 'A
mass of liberties in disorder comes to the same thing as determinism'
(*Ibid.*).

'Freedom is simply the advanced and distinct expression of what is disguised or dissociated in physical determinisms' (*Esquisse d'un univers personnel*, 1936, in *L'énergie humaine*, p. 90).

'Under the superficial cloak of mechanisms thrown over it by the laws of large numbers, matter is seen to be a swarm of elementary consciousnesses ready to enter into the higher combinations of the organic world' (*Le phénomène spirituel*, 1937, *ibid.*, p. 138).

'The determinisms in which we are ready to locate the essence of the world are simply a cloak of rigidity thrown by statistical necessity over a mass of elementary liberties' (*L'énergie humaine*, *ibid.* p. 151).

'Thermodynamics might well be, after all, no more than a statistical echo of the current that feeds human energy in its axial, spiritualized form' (*Ibid.*, p. 172). 'Space in itself is something that overflows any formula; yet it is in terms of this inexpressible that a whole expressible world is interpreted and developed' (*The grand option*, 1939, in *The Future of Man*, pp. 57–8).

'The regularity of physical laws (the determinism of nature) is explained by the statistical effect of a multitude of unorganized, infinitesimal, liberties . . . Physical energy is simply psychic energy materialized' (*La centrologie*, 1944, *op. cit.*, p. 128, note).

'The reconciliation of the two ideas of determinism and indeterminacy . . . will no doubt be discovered to be an effect of great numbers combined with an "innate" (and therefore scientifically inexplicable) preference of the stuff of the universe for higher states of complexity and consciousness' (*Hominization and speciation*, 1952, in *Vision of the Past*, p. 259 note).

Material energy, the domain of statistics and entropy is 'only a minor product statistically engendered by the interactions of the elementary "centres" of consciousness, imperceptible in the "pre-living", but clearly discernible to our experience once matter has reached a sufficiently advanced degree of arrangement . . . This would finally amount to saying, as Léon Brillouin has recently suggested, that the physical (as still defined at present) would only be a "degradation of" (I would rather say "a first approximation to") the biological' (*The singularities of the human species*, 1954, in *The Appearance of Man*, pp. 265–6).

'As such coolly objective thinkers as Louis de Broglie and Léon Brillouin suspect, should we not, if we really wish to unify the real, completely reverse the values? Should we not, I mean, consider the whole of thermodynamics as an unstable, momentary, by-effect of the concentration upon itself of what we call consciousness or spirit?' (*Monde ouvert? Monde fermé?* unpublished, 1954).

No close and honest observer of things, moreover, can fail to feel their mystery. Thus, writing on board the *Angkor*, in which he was travelling to the Far East, Teilhard expresses his 'astonishment before the shape and the wonderful flight of the gull: how was that craft built? The worst failing of our minds is that we fail to see the really big problems simply because the forms in which they arise are right under our eyes. How many gulls have I seen, how many other people have seen them, without giving a thought to the mystery that accompanies their flight? . . . May God grant it to me ever to hear, and to make others hear, the music of all things so vividly that we are swept away in rapture' (Letter of 26 April 1926, in *Letters from a Traveller*, p. 123).

[65] 'Molecules, atoms, electrons—whatever the name, whatever the scale—these minute units (at any rate when viewed from our distance) manifest perfect identity of mass and behaviour. In their dimensions and their actions they seem to be graduated with astonishing regularity and to be extremely monotonous' (*The Phenomenon of Man*, p. 41). Here Teilhard agrees with the Bergson of *Matter and Memory*, who conceives the elementary movements of an energy not in tension as similar to one another.

[66] 'We cannot determine with certainty at what level in evolution the presence of a final purpose begins to be scientifically demonstrable. "Reflectively", however, even when the faculty of invention has not yet appreciably broken through the crust of determinisms, we are justified in saying that a final purpose is already present, hidden under the veil of determinisms. If that were not so, how could it ever manage to emerge unmistakably at a higher level in the domain of man' (Teilhard's preface to *Evolution et finalité*, an unpublished book by Jean Montassey—pseudonym of O. Costa de Beauregard—1948).

[67] *Comment je crois*, unpublished, 1934.

[68] *What should we think of transformism?* 1930, in *Vision of the Past* p. 158. 'Nevertheless the problem is presented—and inevitably so —by the case of man: we have to know whether a place should not be left open for the effects of consciousness in the mechanism of zoological evolution. We should rightfully remember this each time a

residuum appears in the analysis of this evolution, which is irreducible to the ordinary factors of chance, heredity and selection' (*Zoological evolution and invention*, 947, in *Vision of the Past*, p. 235).

⁶⁹ *The Phenomenon of Man*, p. 141. Teilhard compares the growth of consciousness, again, to a rise in temperature. 'Physicists and doctors use delicate instruments on living bodies. Let us do likewise, applying our "thermometer" of consciousness to this somnolent nature' (*Ibid.*, p. 153). He uses, too, the metaphor of colour: 'As we continue peering into the abysses of the past, we can see its colour changing. From age to age it increases in intensity. Something is going to burst out upon the early earth, and this thing is Life' (*Ibid.*, p. 74). 'We must not lose sight of that line crimsoned by the dawn. After thousands of years rising below the horizon, flame bursts forth at a strictly localized point. Thought is born' (*Ibid.*, p. 160).

⁷⁰ *La centrologie*, 1944, No. 31, *op. cit.*, p. 131.

⁷¹ 'Considered in the mass, the earth is veiled in geometry as far back as we can see. It crystallizes' (*The Phenomenon of Man*, p. 69). On the transition to polymerous molecules, *ibid*, pp. 70-1.

⁷² 'Pre-life is no sooner enclosed in the nascent earth than it emerges from the torpor to which it appeared to have been condemned by its diffusion in space. Its activities, hitherto dormant, are now set in motion *pari passu* with the awakening of the forces of synthesis contained in matter. And at one and the same stroke, over the whole surface of the new-formed globe, the tension of internal freedoms begins to rise' (*Ibid.*, p. 73). Among the favourable conditions Teilhard notes one to which he often referred in later essays, the constitution of a portion of matter in 'a closed volume' (*Ibid.*, p. 72).

⁷³ *The Phenomenon of Man*, p. 71. Teilhard illustrates this principle by showing the kinship of the living cell with physical chemistry (*ibid.*, p. 81). 'The mineral world and the world of life seem two antithetical creations when viewed by an overall glance in their extreme forms and on the intermediary scale of our human organisms; but to a deeper study, when we force our way right down to the microscopic level and beyond to the infinitesimal, or (which comes to the same thing) as far back along the scale of time —a single mass gradualy melting in on itself' (*Ibid.*, p. 77).

⁷⁴ *Ibid.*, p. 79. 'The explosion of internal energy consequent upon and proportioned to a fundamental super-organization of matter is

precisely the event which our theory could have led us to expect'
(*Ibid.*, p. 89). 'To judge by our repeated failures to find its equivalent around us or to reproduce it, the first apparition of living bodies
is clearly one of the most sensational of these events (*Ibid.*, p. 98).

[75] Just as modern physics, says Teilhard, has shown that there are
orders or levels (the very small, the intermediate, the vast) so we
should recognize several biologies distinguished by a difference of
order or level of complexity: a biology of viruses or genes, a biology
of cellular beings, and finally a biology of man. From this arises the
notion of an 'infinite of complexity' (*Comment je vois*, unpublished,
1948).

[76] *L'énergie d'évolution*, unpublished, 1943. 'If an animate (or even
inanimate) substance is to liberate or transform its potentialities
into "act", it must be patient of, and receive, the appropriate
stimulus . . . An animal behaves entirely differently according to
whether it is fed or is hungry, left in peace or hunted . . . Activation
of the living being calls, ever more undeniably, for the intervention
of some fear, some revulsion or, above all, some *attraction*' (*L'activation de l'énergie humaine*, 1953, *op. cit.*, p. 412).

[77] 'It has been said, often enough, that to speak of an "élan vital" in
evolution was almost as childish as to attribute the motion of a
locomotive to a locomotive force. This is not, in fact, a very good
joke. If you read the clear and perceptive pages that I am delighted to introduce, you will realize that the modern neo-finalist is
no less rigorous and exact than his determinist colleagues in the
mechanical dissection and re-assembling of living beings. There is
one thing, however: being rather more clear sighted, maybe, than
his opponents, he believes, once he meets the multiple adaptations
and coaptations of organized matter, that even in life's earliest
constructions, he can explain completely the design and assembly of
the parts of the machine, only if he can find *in the element the equivalent*
of an "engineer"—provided, of course, that he does not attribute to
this psychic homologue of the human brain any more than the
strict minimum of reality and influence required to overcome, at its
level, the indeterminisms of matter' (Preface to *Evolution et finalité*,
an unpublished book by Jean Montassey, 1948).

[78] *Marxism*

Marxism is imperceptive (R. Garaudy, *Perspectives de l'homme*,
Paris, P.U.F., 1959, p. 202) in failing to recognize a *negativity* in

Teilhard's philosophy of history. To avoid, however, the cancelling-out of the terms in the expression 'force of negation', Teilhard, in his realism, identifies this negativity with *spirit*: not a thing or sub-stance of which spirit is the quality or attribute, but a factual super-reality, inexpressible, and to be distinguished only in its effects. R. Garaudy admits, moreover, the 'awkwardness' of the Marxist position (*op. cit.*, p. 305). Although one would not wish to overlook the value of a dialectic that has won respect ever since the time of Hegel, it is impossible not to find great obscurity in the notion of a pure quantity that, at one point in its development, transforms itself unaided, into quality (p. 306). How are we to picture to ourselves, the presence in it of an ascensional impetus?

'It is one thing to assert the fecundity of nothingness, and quite another to assert that of negation; for it presupposes an active subject as the additional source of the being that results' (*Claude Soucy, Philosophies de la nature et philosophies de l'esprit,* in *Science et matérialisme, op. cit.,* p. 34). Soucy quotes Sartre, who very rightly says both 'we find in nature only the dialectic we have put there' and 'if there is dialectic, it is because certain areas of materiality are structurally such that it would be impossible for the dialectic not to exist . . . Thought has to disclose the necessity of its object in its own self, in as much as it is itself a material object' (=involved in nature).

Marx, not content with saying that 'reason has always existed, though not always in rational form' (*Oeuvres philosophiques,* ed. Costes, Vol. 5, p. 208, was fond of using Jacob Boehme's phrase about the 'torment' of matter. Diderot, again, in his controversy with Helvetius, did not hesitate to speak of a 'physical sensibility' in matter. The Abbé René Lavocat quotes some interesting passages from the *Shorter Dictionary of Philosophy* (Moscow, 1955) which show that Marxist materialism is a long way from rejecting the reality of thought (*Vrai et faux matérialisme* in *Science et matérialisme, op. cit.,* p. 130).

Teilhard is more scientific than the pure dialecticians when he says: 'Like a river that continually modifies its character as it flows, every *real* transformation, because it depends on a complex assembly of interdependent factors, inevitably changes its form (or even its *state*) through an *unequal* growth of the different variables it contains.' He refers, too, to the physical relation between mass and acceleration (*Transformation et prolongements en l'homme du mecanisme de l'évolution*, 1951, in *L'activation de l'énergie*, p. 314).

[79] 'When we see to our astonishment, teeth becoming reduced and sharper along the phylum of the carnivores (that is to say, alterations in the organs best constructed by their rigidity to escape the modifications resulting from usage), how can we avoid thinking of the accentuation of a temperament or a passion, that is to say of the development of a moral character rather than the evolution of an anatomical one?' (*The transformist paradox*, 1925, in *Vision of the Past*, p. 97).

[80] A difficult section in *The Phenomenon of Man* (pp. 63–4) examines the relations between the two sorts of energy, in man and in the world. The problem arises from their apparent quantitative disproportion, which excludes a direct transformation of one into the other, and from the evident fact of their interdependence. It arises secondly, from the need to retain the principle of the conservation of tangential (mechanical) energy in spite of increase in radial energy. Teilhard puts forward the following principles as the basis of a solution: (1) *Rejection of dualism*: all energy is by nature psychic; tangential or radial energy are only components. (2) The rise of radial energy is effected through the medium of a *structuration*; this may call for only an extremely small expenditure of tangential energy. (3) Until we reach the domain of man, the tangential energy of the cosmos remains practically constant: this is confirmed by science. (4) The rise of radial or spiritual energy, until it reaches its goal, is always *conditioned by tangential energy*, in spite of the dissipation of the latter. It will be noted that Teilhard has no hesitation in admitting the relativity of mechanical energy, which is the normal field of science.

[81] 'Matter and spirit do not present themselves as "things" or "natures" but as simple related variables, of which it behoves us to determine not the secret essence but the curve in function of space and time' (*The Phenomenon of Man*, p. 308).

'The spirit in question has a particularly well-defined nature. It in no way represents an entity that is independent of or antagonistic to matter (=the world of material substances), or some power locked up in or existing freely in the material world. By spirit I mean "the spirit of synthesis and sublimation", in which the power to become one, now scattered in the universal multiple, is painfully and through endless attempts and failures, concentrated: *spirit coming to birth within and as a function of matter*' (*Comment je crois*, unpublished).

[82] 'At every instant the universe, even if we assume it to possess psychic forces, takes the form of a closed circuit of determinisms which mutually induce one another. But on the other hand, because these psychic forces constitute the co-ordinating factor of various determined systems, the totality of which forms the animate world, the successive transformations of this world cannot possibly be explained without recourse to some imponderable forces of synthesis' (*The transformist paradox*, 1925, in *Vision of the Past*, p. 96).

'In the older universe of Laplace, the quantity of contingence, once initially posited, whatever may be its indefinite transformations, remains indefinitely the same in any subsequent state of the system. In the universe of Einstein, on the contrary, or Heisenberg, the quantity of indeterminacy (because it is continually fed by the action of each corpuscle) varies, and a better arrangement of the system may cause it to increase. In that case, wherever vitalization of matter is possible, would it not provide some sort of overflow for this continually increasing mass of indeterminate secreted by the universe?' (*Man's Place in Nature*, pp. 34–5).

[83] 'What is the numerical difference between the energies of two systems composed of the same object, with a higher or lower degree of skill in their arrangement? In other words, in what and why does the effort required to invent and construct a watch or an aircraft differ from the mere material work of making and assembling the various working parts? One thing is quite certain: *in a system of auto-evolution*, some such "organizing" form of energy—the energy that invents and combines—is appearing; and, in spite of its insignificance in ergs or calories, it is beginning to play an increasingly important part in the progress of the world. Moreover, it is going to raise unexpected problems for the engineers of tomorrow—and those problems include not only how best to increase the psychic forces of evolution and how to use them most fully, but also how to feed and conserve them' (*Note sur la réalité actuelle et signification d'une orthogénèse humaine*, unpublished, 1951).

[84] 'The conclusions of palaeontologists are often based on an argument of "convergence" that to some extent oversteps the boundaries of scientific method. When serious scientists look at evolution they

do not hesitate to speak of psychism and its progress in the ascending series of living beings. Moreover, in seeking to account for the behaviour of organized beings they, to a more or less marked degree, introduce the idea of a final purpose.' (F. Russo, *op. cit.*, p. 17).

On the subject of finality in Teilhard, see the answer of C. Cuénot to R. Garaudy (*Perspectives de l'homme, op. cit.*, pp. 181–2 for Garaudy, pp. 205–7 for Cuénot):

'Analysis is an admirable and effective instrument for dissecting the real; but it leaves us with terms that are continually less intelligible and with less content. It shows us the law by which things are constructed; but when it has done its work what is left does not give us the permanent essence of the world: on the contrary it increasingly approximates to nothingness' (*Mon univers*, in *Science et Christ*, 1924, p. 78).

In connexion with the development of languages, C. Lévi-Strauss speaks also of 'an unconscious teleology that, while taking place in history, stands right outside the history of man' (*La pensée sauvage*, Paris, Plon, p. 333). 'Language is a human reasoning, but one that man is ignorant of' (*Ibid.*, p. 334).

85 'Man has this special property that he is a transformer so made that a signal transmitted by a very weak material energy can produce unexpected qualitative and quantitative results, that are, energetically, out of all proportion to the force that stimulated their release . . . This qualitative energy is none the less real; and though our understanding is quite unable to comprehend it, our concrete unity gives us prima facie evidence, and we know perfectly well that ideas, through mysterious ways, possess an extreme energetic power whose quantitative results, at any rate, can be perfectly measurable' (C. Cuénot, *Teilhard de Chardin*, in the series *Ecrivains de toujours*, Paris, Editions du Seuil, pp. 119–20).

86 *Life and the Planets*, 1945, in *Future of Man*, p. 110. *The New Spirit*, 1942, *ibid.*, p. 88. *La centrologie*, 1944, No. 31; the method of 'groping' combines 'in harmony the play of (physical) chance and that of psychic finality' (*op. cit.*, p. 130).

'Far be it from me . . . to deny the important, indeed essential, role played by this historic working of material forms. As living beings, we feel it in ourselves. To jolt the individual out of his natural laziness and the rut of habit, and also from time to time to break up the collective frameworks in which he is imprisoned, it is indispensable that he should be shaken and prodded from outside. What would we do without our enemies? Though capable of flexibly regulating within organic bodies the blind movement of molecules, life seems still to exploit for its creative arrangements the vast reactions which are born fortuitously throughout the world between material currents and animate masses' (*The Phenomenon of Man*, pp. 148-9). 'It would be most rash . . . to underestimate the almost miraculous power of the play of large numbers' (Preface to J. Montassey's unpublished book, 1948). Teilhard admits the role of chance in the first stages of evolution, until it is relieved, to an ever increasing extent, by spiritual energy (Cf. *The Phenomenon of Man*, pp. 307-8; *Man's Place in Nature*, p. 108; *The singularities of the human species*, 1954, in *The Appearance of Man*, p. 253).

Teilhard admits the validity of the neo-Darwinian position in the pre-human areas of life, which recognizes 'nothing but the play of chance selection in the advance of the organized world' (*The human rebound of evolution*, 1947, in *The Future of Man*, p. 200). 'Complexification, which initially is principally brought about by chance . . .' (*Transformation et prolongements en l'homme du mécanisme de l'évolution*, 1951, in *L'activation de l'énergie*, p. 317).

This recognition of chance is accompanied in Teilhard, by the recognition of determinism. One might well wonder whether he does not sometimes exaggerate the influence of the former since he is logically obliged, from the outset, to introduce *spirit* as a factor in organization and progress. It is true that while Teilhard refers to the 'play of probabilities' and the 'eddies of the improbable', he also speaks of 'a preferential selection of chances', 'a controlled play of chances' (Cf. *La réflexion de l'énergie*, in *Revue des questions scientifiques*, 20 October 1952, pp. 484, 492, 494, 496).

87 *Man's Place in Nature*, p. 19.

88 'Comprehension of the principle and origin of life has long seemed impatient of materialist explanation. Between animate and inanimate matter the gulf seemed so wide that it was asserted that the latter could never in any way account for the former, at least in its essential nature. Today, we know, our ideas about this have been profoundly modified. The gap is progressively being narrowed. The difference is being reduced between highly organized molecules of

still inert matter and the fundamental structures of life: most notably in the famous tronihelicoid DNA, our knowledge of which is making such remarkable progress. We have not yet completely explained the behaviour of living matter starting from material processes but there is increasing hope that we shall one day succeed in doing so' (F. Russo, preliminary notes to *Science et matérialisme*, *op. cit.*, p. 11).

At Florida State University, Sydney W. Fox has succeeded in synthesizing giant organic molecules, to which he gives the name of proteinoids. They have the remarkable property of being morphogenous, grouping together to form true corpuscles, similar to the bacteria known as *cocci*. They are not, however, living beings, since the proteinoids have no antigenic power. For a long time now, scientists have been able to produce experimentally organic compounds similar to the bodies found in living beings; but, while the molecules of the latter are asymmetrical, the molecules so obtained are symmetrical.

Teilhard believed, however, that, the initial quantum of consciousness having passed entirely into the biosphere, matter was now 'exhausted, emptied, devitalized', and could no longer produce new life (*L'esprit de la terre*, 1931, in *L'énergie humaine*, pp. 32–3).

[89] Madame M. Barthélemy-Madaule rightly relates the spiritual forces of synthesis described by Teilhard to the 'phenomenon-envelope' suggested by François Meyer, in *Problématique de l'évolution* (*op. cit.*, p. 137).

[90] Cf. D. Dubarle, *Concept de la matière et discussions sur le matérialisme*, in *Science et matérialisme*, *op. cit.*, pp. 37–70.

[91] In this connexion we are not relying on any of the hypotheses of modern science, whether those of Einstein or those that involve the discontinuity of matter. They are patently illogical, and their precariousness will one day be appreciated. They interest us only in their widest philosophical propositions, and the universal and necessary categories (objective and mental) they make use of.

[92] This is Einstein's equation, $E = mc^2$ (where E is energy, in ergs, m is mass in grammes and c the velocity of light).

[93] This diversification of matter seems to be confirmed by the new theory of elementary particles, the result of a collaboration between French and Japanese scientists (see J. L. Lavallard's article in *Le Monde*, 1 November 1963). The distortions, caused by rotation and

expansion, of a single fundamental particle of known diameter, produce theoretically an infinite number of possible quantic 'states', and hence an infinite number of different particles, whose existence could be verified by experiment.

[94] Cf. the impossibility of grafting tissues, already differentiated, from one individual to another belonging to different or the same species.

[95] These views coincide, at least to some extent, with those of O. Costa de Beauregard (*Le second principe de la science du temps*, Paris, Editions du Seuil, 1963), for whom the underlying trend of nature is to struggle (so far as it can) against the tendency of its energies to sink towards homogeneity and lose organization in disorder. Following Bergson in this, Beauregard thinks that while life's creation of centres of consciousness or information, and their functioning, are brought about only by an expenditure of energy and an increase of entropy, the *action* at least of those centres towards a restructuration of the world combats and negatives entropy: as though the haemorrhage were provisionally arrested by a transfusion of new blood, and there were a restoration of the order that had been lost. It would certainly appear, then, that the world of matter, in order to check its collapse, necessarily demanded first life and then thought. Thus psychism intervenes at the heart of things, but in a reverse direction. O. Costa de Beauregard differs from Teilhard in not introducing the idea of collective complexification and of the world's progress towards final unity. At the same time, his conclusion seems to envisage, at the term of the universe, 'an implosion of finality' corresponding to the initial explosion of causality.

[96] A molecule of DNA, or desoxyribonucleic acid, is made up of two juxtaposed and parallel helicoidal chains, comprising a number of segments (adenine, guanine, cytosine and thymine desoxyribonucleotides). 'It is accepted that the only difference between the two desoxyribonucleic acids, and hence between two genes, lies in the number and order of assembly of the four nucleotides' (H. G. Hers, *Génétique biochimique humaine*, in *Revue des questions scientifiques*, 20 July 1963, p. 345). 'There is a strict correspondence between the two parts of the molecule, the adenine always facing the thymine, and the guanine the cytosine and vice versa. Thus each half contains the information required to reconstitute the whole molecule.' The gene serves as the model for the formation of a new molecule

of DNA identical with itself. Moreover, it determines 'the structure of a particular protein, a structure that results from the order in which its constituent amino-acids are arranged'; this is done through the medium of an RNA that acts as a messenger and uses a code. There are at least as many genes in an organism as there are proteins. 'There is every reason to believe that the mechanism that introduces the sequence Gene–Protein–Phenotypic Manifestations is generally applicable to all hereditary characteristics, both normal and pathological' (*Ibid.*, pp. 345–65).

[97] Several of the foregoing themes are borrowed from the works of Stéphane Lupasco, in particular his *Les trois matières* (Paris, Julliard, 1960) and *L'énergie et la matière vivante* (Paris, Julliard, 1962). Lupasco differs, however, from Teilhard on one essential point: while Teilhard is at pains to demonstrate the convergence of the spiritual history of the universe on an ultimate and absolute point, Lupasco believes that the universe's construction of systems, and of systems of systems, is indefinite.

Universal consciousness

[98] 'Below the level of our souls there are, no doubt, numerous inter-connexions that we call material. We are held together, one to another, by the fibres of the ether, by the impulse of the current of life . . . But these great fundamental connexions should not be regarded as due to our being rooted in matter. We should see them as the trace of wide pre-spiritual unions that were produced, before the appearance of thought, by some sorts of *formae cosmicae* successively imposed on the multiple by a breath from on high. The ether, life, mankind (?), these are great indistinct souls that are preliminary to more perfect concentrations. We should no longer say that transitivity is an effect of *matter*, but of *spirit*. What gives the monads cohesion is not the body; it is the soul' (*L'union créatrice*, 1917, in *Ecrits de temps de la guerre*, pp. 189–90).

In 1922 Teilhard wrote, 'it is arbitrary in itself, and, as a matter of observation, implausible, to attribute consciousness only to men, and to regard all other beings as deprived of any "within" . . . (without asking whether this notion of purely exterior or "transitive" being is even thinkable) . . . The world cannot exist except upon a basis of thought' (Letter of 17 December 1922).

'It is impossible to deny that, deep within ourselves, an "interior" appears at the heart of beings, as it were seen through a rent. This is enough to ensure that, in one degree or another, this "interior" must be recognized as existing everywhere in nature from all time. Since the stuff of the universe has an inner aspect at one point of itself, there is necessarily *a double aspect to its structure*, that is to say in every region of space and time—in the same way, for instance, as it is granular: *co-extensive with their without*, there is a *within to things . . .* In a coherent perspective of the world, life inevitably assumes a pre-life for as far back before it as the eye can see' (*The Phenomenon of Man*, pp. 56–7). 'From this aspect, one might say that, on the phenomenal plane, each being is constructed like an ellipse on two conjugate foci: a focus of material organization and a focus of psychic centering—the two foci varying solidarily and in the same sense' (*Ibid.*, p. 61 note).

'If we have already endowed the long chain of atoms, then molecules, then mega-molecules, with the obscure and remote sources of a rudimentary free activity . . .' (*Ibid.*, p. 88).

'Consciousness (defined experimentally as the specific effect of organized complexity) transcends by far the ridiculously narrow limits within which our eyes can directly perceive it . . . We are logically forced to assume the existence in rudimentary form (in a microscopic, i.e. an infinitely diffuse, state) of some sort of psyche in every corpuscle, even in those (the mega-molecules and below) whose complexity is of such a low or modest order as to render it (the psyche) imperceptible—just as the physicist assumes and can calculate those changes of mass (utterly imperceptible to direct observation) occasioned by slow movement' (*Ibid.*, pp. 301–2). 'At the end of its analyses, physics is no longer sure whether what is left in its hands is pure energy or, on the contrary, thought' (*Ibid.*, p. 281, cf. p. 308).

All corpuscles, 'somewhat like man, have a . . . minute "within", in which is reflected a particular, more or less rudimentary, representation of the world: in relation to themselves, these are psychic centres, and at the same time they are infinitesimal psychic centres of the universe' (*La centrologie*, 1944, No. 2, in *L'activation de l'énergie*, p. 106).

'Consciousness (like such phenomena as the variation of mass according to speed, or radiation as a function of temperature) is a universal property common to all the corpuscles constituting the universe, but varying in proportion to the complexity of any particular molecule; which amounts to saying that the degree of psychism, the "within" of the different elements composing the world, will be small or great, according to the place of the element in the astronomically extended scale of complexities at present known to us' (*The planetization of mankind*, 1945, in *The Future of Man*, p. 130).

'Absolutely inert and totally brute matter *does not exist*. Every element contains, at least to an infinitesimal degree, some germ of inwardness and spontaneity, that is to say of consciousness. In extremely simple and extremely numerous corpuscles (which only manifest themselves by their statistical effects) this property remains imperceptible to us, *as if it did not exist*. On the other hand its importance grows with its complexity—or, which comes to the same thing, with the degree of "centration" of the corpuscles on themselves' ((*Man's place in the universe*, 1949, in *Vision of the Past*, p. 225).

[99] *The Phenomenon of Man*, p. 56.

[100] *Ibid.*, p. 58.

[101] *Place de la technique dans une biologie générale de l'humanité*, unpublished, 1947.

[102] *La centrologie*, No. 8, *op. cit.*, p. 111.

[103] *Ibid.*, No. 12, *op. cit.*, p. 114.

[104] *The Phenomenon of Man*, p. 60. 'The higher the degree of complexity in a living creature, the higher its consciousness, and vice versa.' However, while the number of atomic elements incorporated may serve as a parameter for lower forms of organization, it is superseded, for higher forms, by 'the quality of the *links* established between the atoms' (*Life and the planets*, 1945, in *The Future of Man*, p. 111).

[105] It is also that of d'Holbach and Diderot: of Marx, who admits an orientation of matter towards man; of Julian Huxley, who admits the existence of a universal evolutionary matter that contains potentialities of spirit, and is tempted to associate with matter, *simpliciter*, something which meets the same definition as spirit in the higher animals (Quoted by J. Rostand, *Ce que je crois*, Paris, Grasset, 1956, p. 43). On the other hand, the interiority of matter contradicts the Cartesian concept, which reduces matter to extension.

[106] *La vie et l'oeuvre de Ravaisson*, in *La pensée et le mouvant*, Paris, Alcan, 1934, p. 305.

[107] In *Matter and Memory*, matter appeared in the metaphor of a

relaxation or drop in tension. Teilhard adopts this metaphor (*Le phénomène spirituel*, 1937, in *L'énergie humaine*, p. 127).

[108] 'If there were no real internal propensity to unite, even at a prodigiously rudimentary level—indeed, in the molecule itself—it would be physically impossible for love to appear higher up, with us, in "hominized" form. By rights, to be certain of its presence in ourselves, we should assume its presence, at least in an inchoate form, in everything that is . . . Driven by the forces of love, the fragments of the world seek each other so that the world may come into being . . . Whether as a force or a curvature, the universal gravity of bodies, so striking to us, is merely the reverse or shadow of that which really moves nature. To perceive cosmic energy "at the fount" we must, if there is a "within" of things, go down into the internal or radial zone of spiritual attractions' (*The Phenomenon of Man*, pp. 264-5). On Christian love, *ibid.*, p. 295.

[109] Letter from Père Joseph Maréchal, 26 November 1931, quoted by H. de Lubac, *op. cit.*, p. 258.

[110] *The Phenomenon of Man*, p. 61. C. Cuénot, *L'oeuvre du R. P. Teilhard de Chardin et le marxisme*, in R. Garaudy, *Perspectives de l'homme*, Paris, P.U.F., 1959, p. 207.

Teilhard notes, starting with the 'transit to reflexion', the 'equally decisive appearance between elements of true forces of attraction and repulsion (sympathy and antipathy), replacing the pseudo-attractions and pseudo-repulsions of pre-life or even of the lower forms of life, which we seem to be able to refer back to simple reactions to the curve of space-time in the one case, and to the bio-sphere in the other' (*The Phenomenon of Man*, p. 303).

[111] *Ibid.*, p. 281.

[112] *Art. cit.*, pp. 59-64.

[113] *The debated question of the consciousness of things*

Père d'Armagnac (*art. cit.* pp. 23-4, 36-41) criticizes Teilhard's notion of a universal consciousness, for which he substitutes that of an immanence of beings. Teilhard's proposition, it must be admitted, is an extrapolation that cannot be checked experi-mentally; it is a deduction, philosophic in order, and Teilhard might well have spoken of analogy or correspondence, maybe, rather than levels or degrees of intensity in consciousness. Science, however, often proceeds from facts to such deductions; and such an objection was not raised earlier against *Matter and Memory*. On the other hand, the notion of different degrees of universal immanence is very close to Teilhard's notion: it is even, it would appear, identical with it, even if it cannot be entertained philosophically except as a self-unification of being.

Similarly, in a short book of the highest value philosophically (*Le problème de Dieu inscrit dans l'évolution*, Paris, Editions du Cerf, 1963, pp. 53–63) Père Olivier A. Rabut, O.P., does not think it possible to accept the thesis of consciousness as the real spiritual energy of the organization and movement of things. He recognizes the problem raised by the structuration, coherence and converg-ence of forms and phenomena, and rejects the sufficiency of blind mechanisms. In order, however, to preserve the independ-ence of science in relation to philosophy, he attaches the *meaning* demanded by the world to a source of intelligibility, both trans-cendent and immanent in the universe, and the perception of that meaning to the activity of thought by which it is progressively revealed. This is another philosophical attitude, justified in its choice, but one that seems to overlook Teilhard's view of the indissociable totality of matter and spirit; and yet that attitude of Teilhard's has the great advantage of a simple conformity with the real, which it refuses to dissociate in an abstract dualism. It is perhaps science itself that should accept a conversion, recognizing that it is faced with a choice. The author recognizes, too, the astonishing fact of the objective aptitude of the elements for entering into higher syntheses; and does not aptitude imply something more, not only than pure mechanism and chance, but also than the total absence of spontaneity?

On the other hand, a contemporary logician, H. Boirel, in his valuable *Théorie générale de l'invention* (Paris, P.U.F., 1961, p. 366) supports the notion of a consciousness co-extensive in matter. 'On the material plane, every time one structure acts upon another, there is a reaction of one structure to the presence of the other, and, in consequence, contact is established with another structure. Already at this stage there is certainly reaction to a presence, and there is consciousness—not clear consciousness, indeed, but none the less consciousness of an extraneous power. If there were not, in one form or another, some feeling of that presence there would be no reaction: if matter were completely deprived of consciousness, the whole of the material universe would be completely inert; and nothing would happen in it.' In a more metaphysical, and even more religious, note, Boirel introduces an attraction, an appeal of the Absolute-Word, to explain the continual restructuration of the world (pp. 387-9). He quotes the opinion of the great biologist, J. B. S. Haldane to the effect that while we can find no evidence of thought or life in what we call matter, yet, if modern scientific views are correct, we must expect ultimately to find them, at least in a rudimentary form, throughout the whole universe (*The Inequality of Man*, p. 114; *op. cit.*, p. 364).

Similarly O. Costa de Beauregard believes that if we admit that living matter must have emerged imperceptibly from inert matter, then 'the very logic of the thesis obliges us to extend *potentially* the domain of "supra-consciousness" or "infra-psychism" to that of the whole of matter' (*Le second principe de la science du temps*, Paris, Editions du Seuil, 1963, p. 121).

[114] 'We cannot accept an area of chaos lying between science and our philosophy. Such a "gap" is improbable and dangerous. We must bridge it.'

'If we compare the domain of mind to a sphere, I hold that the mistake of concordism is that it runs the meridians together in the region of the equator (the meridian of science and the meridian of faith). However, these meridians must meet somewhere at a pole (if, from a scientific and religious point of view, you look at the whole)—they must, that is, obey certain general structural conditions (such as the organic laws of union) . . .' (Unpublished letter to Père Auguste Valensin, 20 April 1948).

[115] *The Phenomenon of Man*, prologue. *L'esprit de la terre*, 1931, in *L'énergie humaine*.

[116] 'Would you insist on placing the primacy of being in the plural and unconscious at the risk of making the world unthinkable and incapable of life? Then everything reduced to its lower terms becomes matter.

'Do you not understand, we ask, that on the contrary only union and synthesis make the universe blessed and stable? In order to be, would you not choose to seek the absolute sense of all growth in the direction of this upper pole? In that case, by virtue of the link between things established by evolution, everything is related to the highest; everything becomes, if not spirit, at least a distant preparation, "matter" for, spirit' (*Basis and foundations of the idea of evolution*, 1926, in *Vision of the Past*, p. 133).

What the scientist wishes to do, Teilhard says also, is 'to discover the secret of the real, and find its source. However positive he may claim it to be, his enquiry is modified, toned—or, rather, invisibly animated—by a mystical hope'.

[117] *Barrière de la mort et co-réflexion*, 1955, in *L'activation de l'énergie*, p. 426. Revelation complements this minimum of certainty by an added assurance, without in any way encroaching on the autonomous domain of science (*Ibid.*, p. 427). While admitting that Omega Point 'lies outside the scientifically observable process of which it marks the close', Teilhard rightly adds, 'at the same time, this transcendence does not prevent it from appearing to our scientific thought as necessarily endowed with certain perceptible properties' (*Man's Place in Nature*, p. 116).

[118] The movement (of universal convergence) is not 'relative, but truly absolute, in as far as it advances towards a state that is definable only in terms of itself' (*Du cosmos à la cosmogénèse*, 1951, in *L'activation de l'énergie*, p. 265).

[119] *Art. cit.*

[120] 'Nothing seems to be able to pierce the veil of phenomena,' says Teilhard, speaking of pure science (*Basis and foundations of the idea of evolution*, 1924, in *Vision of the Past*, p. 130).

[121] M. Lamotte, *La théorie actuelle des mécanismes de l'évolution*, in *Archives de philosophie*, January–March 1960, pp. 9–10.

[122] *Man's Place in Nature*, p. 64.

[123] *Le sens de l'espèce chez l'homme*, 1949, in *L'activation de l'énergie*, p. 205.

[124] F. Meyer, *Problématique de l'évolution*, Paris, P.U.F., 1954, p. 154. (Teilhard lived long enough to write a highly favourable appreciation of this book, published, after his death, in *Etudes*, May 1955, p. 279). In a shorter, more recent, book (*Teilhard et les grandes dérives du monde*, Paris, Editions Universitaires, 1963) F. Meyer has collected the mathematical data that make it possible to construct graphs of evolution. In the biological order (increase in number of species, evolution and biochemical orthogenesis), the demographic order (increase in life-span and population), and the technological order (increase in numbers of discoveries and in quantity of useful energy), these graphs show a regular increase, whose acceler-

ation at the present time seems enormous. They seem also to indicate that during the first half of the twenty-first century man will enter an important higher stage. We may note that though Meyer is an admirer of Teilhard he is more alive than Teilhard was to the dialectical antithesis between the two energies that divide the world between them, and is closer accordingly to Bergson.

[125] E. Callot, *Philosophie biologique*, Paris, Doin, 1957.

[126] M. Lamotte, *op. cit.*, p. 51.

[127] 'It is in terms of proteins, again, that we should think of the bio-chemistry of evolution . . . We are justified in expecting a great deal from the detailed study of the haemoglobins of vertebrates. But we should accept, too, that all the characteristics (from the shape of teeth to certain psychic characteristics) on which we rely to establish the filiation of species are determined by a particular protein, and that each mutation corresponds to a new substitution of amino-acid at the level of the primary structure of that protein' (H. G. Hers, *art. cit.*, p. 366). See also M. Lamotte, *La théorie actuelle des mécanismes de l'évolution*, in *Archives de philosophie*, January 1960).

[128] *Creative evolution*, p. 33.

[129] *The Two Sources of Morality and Religion*, p. 165.

[130] 'It is important to make it clear that some leading scientists (Grassé, Goldschmidt, Schindewolf, to mention but a few in different fields of geography and the biological sciences) question the ability of neo-Darwinist theory to give an exhaustive explana-tion of the history of the world of life' (E. Boné. *Polygénisme et polyphylétisme*, in *Archives de Philosophie*, January–March 1960, p. 135).

[131] C. d'Armagnac, *Epistémologie et philosophie de l'évolution*, in *Archives de philosophie*, January–March 1960, p. 161.

[132] 'If we wish to express the whole grandeur of the phenomenon of life, we are obliged to include some sort of "preferential" as integral with the "fortuitious"; palaeontology, in the schemes it constructs, must leave room for the idea of direction . . . If we now look at the countless phyla that palaeontology has disentangled, we might believe that life, whether feeling its way or achieving its objectives, seems to have tried everything. In reality, whatever phylum we are studying, life's efforts have always been made in the same direction, and that is towards a fuller degree of arrangement and of psychism'

(J. Pivetau, *Teilhard de Chardin*, in *Bulletin de la société géologique de France*, 6th series, Vol. 7, 1957; quoted by M. Barthélemy-Madaule, *op. cit.*, p. 144).

[133] Cf. C. d'Armagnac, *art. cit.*, p. 160. We should note here Jean Pivetau's *Des premiers vertébrés à l'Homme* (Paris, Albin Michel, 1964), which, on the whole, accepts Teilhard's ideas. The same may be said of André Leroi-Gourhan's *Le geste et la parole* (Paris, Albin Michel, 1965). While attributing more importance than Teilhard to the influence of mechanical forces of balance that brought about the flattening of the face and the freeing of the hand, he admits that 'the brain governs evolution but remains inexorably subordinate to the bodily structure's possibilities of selective adaptation' (p. 88).

CHAPTER 5: ANTHROPOLOGY

[1] 'If we are going towards a human era of science, it will be eminently an era of human science. Man, the knowing subject, will perceive at last that man, "the object of knowledge", is the key to the whole science of nature' (*The Phenomenon of Man*, p. 281).

[2] *Man's Transcendence*

'Simply by "anatomical" routine, man, inexplicably, is still being regarded by the majority of biologists as a mere filament (or sub-filament) within the fascicle of zoological forms: a "mere family" (just a few lines) in D.G.G. Simpson's monumental catalogue of *Genera*, an utterly insignificant leaflet on the imposing tree of life that illustrates Lucien Cuénot's scientific testament. And yet, as true scientists, is it not time for us to recognize that such a view is certainly wrong?' (*La convergence de l'univers*, unpublished, 1951).

'With a global reservoir of physical energy more or less equal to that of the animals of the same size he lives among, man shows a most surprising power of activating everything in nature around him.' 'In the human individual an extreme perfection of the nervous system co-exists with a sort of universality of knowledge' (*L'énergie d'évolution*, unpublished, 1953).

This is the answer Teilhard gives to the question of man's place in nature, the subject, in particular, of *Man's Place in Nature* (p. 13). In spite of the relatively slight morphological difference between man and animal, hominization represents a real *inversion* in relation to biological evolution. While the latter proceeded in its ascending search by the creation of different species, fanning out in groups, man represents a definite form that can be diversified only into original personalities or particular groups: and both persons and groups in this new history are subject to an involution which is forwarding their unity. Cf. *Reality and significance of human orthogenesis*, in *The Vision of the Past*, p. 252-3.

Using Bergson's exact words, Teilhard says that man's emergence constitutes 'not merely a matter of change of degree, but a change of nature resulting from a change of state' (*The Phenomenon of Man*, p. 166). Cf. *Hominization and Speciation*, 1952, in *The Vision of the Past*, p. 261. Bergson, 'From the limited to the unlimited there is all the distance between the closed and the open. It is not a difference of degree but of kind' (*Creative Evolution*, p. 278).

'Our brain, our society and our language are only the external and various signs of one and the same internal superiority. They tell, each after its manner, the unique exceptional success which life has won at a given moment of its evolution. They express the difference of kind, and not only of degree, which separates man from the rest of the animal world. They let us guess that, while at the end of the vast spring-board from which life has taken its leap, all the others have stepped down, finding the cord stretched too high, man alone has cleared the obstacle' (*Ibid.*, p. 279).

'We are happy to admit that the birth of intelligence corresponds to a turning in upon itself not only of the nervous system, but of the whole being. What at first sight disconcerts us, is the need to accept that this step could only be achieved *at a single stroke*' (*The Phenomenon of Man*, p. 171).

'What explains the biological revolution caused by the appearance of man, is an explosion of consciousness; and what, in turn, explains this explosion is simply the transit of a specially favoured filament of "corpusculization" through the hitherto impenetrable surface that separates the zone of direct psychism from that of reflective psychism. Once life, along this particular way, reached a critical point of arrangement (or, as we call it in this context, of convolution) it became hypercentred upon itself, to the point of becoming capable of foresight and invention. It became conscious "in the second degree"' (*Man's Place in Nature*, p. 62).

'Between the animal world of the Pliocene (so exuberant and expansive in the variety and dissemination of its forms) and the world of man that succeeded it (a world so astonishingly closed, structured, and dominating over—or excluding—every other sort of life) there lies, whatever may be said, not only a difference of degree but a change of order (or, if you so prefer it, a change of state)' (*La réflexion de l'énergie*, 1952, in *L'activation de l'énergie*, p. 337).

Teilhard speaks of the recent change in our concept of man: lost in the mass of the universe, adrift in the multiplicity of species, threatened by an interior abyss of the unconscious, man had seemed to have disappeared: but now he is 're-emerging, more strongly than ever, at the head of nature' (*The singularities of the human species*, 1954, in *The Appearance of Man*, p. 268).

'Initially, that is to say a century ago, man considered himself first of all as a simple observer; then after Darwin as a simple branch of evolution. But now, as a result of this incorporation in biogenesis, he is beginning to perceive that the principal shoot of the tree of earthly life passes through him. Life does not diversify by chance, in all directions. It shows an absolute direction of progress towards the values of growing consciousness; and on this principal axis man is the most advanced term that we know' (*Evolution of the idea of evolution*, in *The Vision of the Past*, p. 246).

Père C. d'Armagnac refers here to a passage from St Thomas, for whom, following the main stream of Christian tradition, man represents a perfection of the universe. 'The tendency of matter is towards the highest and most perfect form to which it can attain . . . since therefore the human soul is the summit of all generation, it is towards this that matter tends as towards the highest form which it can achieve' (St Thomas Aquinas, *Summa contra Gentiles*, III. 22) (*Etudes récentes sur le Père Teilhard*, Etudes, January 1963, p. 58). Cf. P. Smulders, *op. cit.*, p. 77.

[3] While the animal is completely absorbed in all that is involved in its biological activities, man 'because of his physiological organization continually—both in the space he allots himself and in the time he foresees—exceeds the work demanded by his animality. Through man, an ocean of free energy (an energy just as real and "cosmic" as any studied by physics) is spreading over the earth' (*Le christianisme dans le monde*, 1933, in *Science et Christ*, p. 132). From this

penetrating thought Teilhard was later to draw conclusions about the origin and function of morality and religion.

'In the termitary and the hive (as in the case of the cells of our own body) the union and therefore the specialization of the elements takes place in the field of *material functions*—intuition, reproduction, defence, etc.—which accounts for the transformation of the individual into a standardized part. But let us imagine another kind of association, within which a different possibility of mutual fulfilment is offered to the individuals composing it, this time a psychic grouping corresponding to what might be called a *function of personalization*' (*The grand option*, 1939, in *The Future of Man*, pp. 53-4).

[4] *L'activation de l'énergie humaine*, 1953, in *L'activation de l'énergie*, p. 409.

[5] *The Phenomenon of Man*, pp. 31-3. 'About "becoming": I'm just wondering at the moment whether the individual should not be looked on as an element of fixation or stabilization. In that case, movement—evolution—would be realized in a sort of surround, a sort of "sheath" enveloping and giving birth to individuals . . . the truth would lie in a synthesis of fixation and movement' (Letter of 4 August 1918, in *Making of a Mind*, p. 225).

'Each monad is the partial centre of the whole cosmos, whose network both supports it and rests upon it' (*Le prêtre*, 1918, in *Ecrits du temps de la guerre*, p. 288). We have to introduce the human layer 'to reconstitute the movement from which we emerged' (*L'hominisation*, unpublished, 1923). 'We must look at what is in the foreground of our world, and not at its distant horizons, if we are to see things in their correct perspective' (*Ibid.*).

[6] 'Sexual attraction, with the laws of reproduction; the inclination to struggle for survival, with the competition it involves; the need for nourishment, with the accompanying taste for seizing and devouring; curiosity to see, with its delight in investigation; the attraction of joining others to live in society . . .' (*The Phenomenon of Man*, p. 179). 'All these lower manifestations of life are reconstituted and super-animated in man, at once recognizable and unrecognizable' (*L'hominisation*, unpublished, 1923).

In a sense as profound as it bore for Aristotle or the Middle Ages the soul is for Teilhard 'the form of the body'. Of reflection, Teilhard says that it is the 'passage (as though in a second birth) from simple life to "life in the second power" ' *Le coeur de la matière,* unpublished, 1950, p. 17).

[7] 'What was then only a surface with a centre became a centre. With only a minute *tangential* increase, the *radial* turned back on itself, and took, we might say, an infinite forward leap.'

[8] 'From our experiential point of view, reflection is, as the word indicates, the power acquired by a consciousness to turn in on itself, to take possession of itself *as of an object* endowed with its own particular consistence and value; no longer merely to know, but to know oneself; no longer merely to know but to know that one knows' (*The Phenomenon of Man,* p. 165). Thus Teilhard, we see, makes a capital distinction between *consciousness* and *consciousness of self*: all beings, at different degrees, have the former; the latter is proper to man alone (*Ibid.,* pp. 168–9). 'Millions of years before man, the animal felt, discovered, and *knew*; but its consciousness remained simple and direct' (*On the probable coming of an ultra-humanity,* 1950, in *The Future of Man,* p. 279).

St Thomas Aquinas also defines spirit in terms of reflection: 'that it returns to its own essence in a complete return' ('*Quod redeat ad essentiam suam reditione completa*', *In Librum de Causis,* Lect. 15). 'To return to its essence means that a thing subsists in itself' ('*Redire ad essentiam suam nihil aliud est quam res subsistere in seipsa*' (*Summa Theologiae* I. Q. 14, art. 2, ad. I).

We may question how far, in defining man by reflection, Teilhard appreciated the significance of the transition from an *external* observation of the phenomenon of man and an observation *from within,* based on a witness of self to self, and of self to another. He seems, however, to have realized fully that reflection is exercized only in and on an objective act of knowledge. Reflection is the power that every human consciousness has of 'turning in on itself in order to recognize the conditions and mechanism of its activity' (*Hominization,* 1923, in *The Vision of the Past,* p. 60).

[9] Teilhard points out the essential distinction between *person* and *personality.* 'My life's work is, indeed, to some degree represented by what passes from me into all: much more, however, by the extent to which I succeed in creating within myself something that is incommunicable or *unique.* But it is in my personality, that is to say the particular centre of perceptions and love the development of which is the whole point of my life—it is there that what is most

truly precious in me lies. And there, accordingly, lies the only value
important enough to engage and justify my efforts to preserve it'
(*Comment je crois*, unpublished, 1934).

And, however manifold our 'personal qualities' may be, they are
made one by the act of the ego: they are not some top-dressing but
'coincide exactly with the substance of our being—for their very
fabric is woven by our consciousness of them' (*Ibid.*). Cf. *The
Phenomenon of Man*, pp. 261, 263.

Teilhard is struck by the richness and variety 'of the lives and
temperaments we try to force into the same mould' (Letter of April
or May, 1926, in *Letters from a Traveller*, p. 124).

[10] *Le Milieu Divin*, pp. 76–9. '. . . I went down into my inmost self,
to the deep abyss whence I feel dimly that my power of action
emanates. But as I moved further and further away from the
conventional certainties by which social life is superficially illuminated, I became aware that I was losing contact with myself . . .
We cannot either in theory or in practice lay our hands on the
sources of life. My self is given to me far more than it is formed
by me' (*Ibid.*, (p. 77).

'Man is accessible to us from within': if 'he represents in the
universe the appearance of some fundamental current in things, we
can explore that current not only by observation from outside but
also through a sort of introspection' (Second lecture to the Marcel
Légaut group, 27 November 1930).

[11] Note from Teilhard to Père Valensin, 12 December 1919
(*Archives de Philosophie*, January–March 1961, p. 142). Elsewhere,
Teilhard speaks of man's 'incurable' instability.

[12] Letter of 7 November 1915, in *Making of a Mind*, p. 78. In a letter
dated 21 January 1917, Teilhard speaks of his 'resolve to write
something on the aspiration of the individual to complete himself
by something that is all' (*Ibid.*, p. 173).

Similarly: 'Can you not see, then, that what is satisfied in you by
effort is precisely the passion "to be permanently more"? . . . In
each individual the "sense of the whole" may be atrophied or dormant. But matter could more easily escape from gravity than a soul
from the presence of the universe' (*Comment je crois*, unpublished,
1934). 'The only reality in the world is the passion to grow greater'
(*Ibid.*).

'Mythology and folklore are filled with symbols and fables

expressing the deeply rooted resolve of earth to find its way to heaven; from which it follows that we may in a perfectly legitimate sense accept the fact that a generalized, implicit faith of man in man is older than all civilization and that it is this, finally, which constitutes the basic impulse informing all our past history' (*Faith in Man*, 1947, in *The Future of Man*, pp. 185–6).

'You're not gettting to the bottom of your heart or of what's in your mind: and that's why the sense of the cosmos and faith in the world are still dormant in you' (A remark quoted by Père P. Leroy, in *Pierre Teilhard de Chardin tel que je l'ai connu*, Paris, Plon, 1958, p. 61).

[13] *The will towards the absolute*

'With Blondel and Le Roy, I answer this problem of action as follows: "To set in motion what appears so slight a thing as a human activity, calls for nothing less than the lure of a result that nothing can destroy. We can press on only if we have the hope of an immortal conquest" . . . In the case of a *true action* (by which I mean one in which a man gives something of his life) I commit myself to it only if I also have at the back of my mind the intention of making something that will last for ever . . . To release a little being for ever—anything else is intolerable emptiness . . . To fight, and conquer—that is what satisfies and lures you on. But can you not see that what is satisfied in you by that effort is precisely the passion to "be permanently more"?' . . . (*Comment je crois*, unpublished, 1934). 'Our will can be put into motion only towards an object in which it can detect a savour of indestructibility' (*La crise présente*, 1936, in *Science et Christ*, p. 175).

'Does not the end or confine of thought consist precisely in not having a confine? Unique in this respect among all the energies of the universe, consciousness is a dimension to which it is inconceivable and even contradictory to ascribe a ceiling or to suppose that it can double back on itself. There are innumerable critical points on the way, but a halt or a reversion is impossible: and for the simple reason that every increase of internal vision is essentially the germ of a further vision which includes all the others and carries still farther on' (*The Phenomenon of Man*, p. 231).

Elsewhere, Teilhard speaks of a 'radical determination in action not to undertake any work that will not be immortal', and of the pull towards more-being 'without which all science and all technology lose their impetus' (*Les conditions psychologiques de l'unification humaine*, 1949, in *L'activation de l'énergie*, p. 184).

'Once it is hominized . . . this operation (the vitalizing of matter) has an additional requirement necessary to its success: this is the imponderable, but decisive, influence of a certain "field", psychic in nature, that may be defined as an appetite or desire. If Jean Herzog had not had a passion for the high places, Annapurna would never have been climbed. If evolution is to continue in a hominized setting, it is a physical necessity that man shall believe, with all the force at his disposal, in some absolute value possessed by the movement whose continuance is in his hands. And, in consequence of this, we find, unexpectedly, a bridge by which our experience can connect two domains apparently so foreign to one another as Physical chemistry and religion. Faith is no longer simply a way of escaping from the world—but the very leaven and principle of the world's fulfilment' (*Contingence de l'univers et goût humain de survivre*, unpublished, 1953).

'All that I have been able to understand . . . about the true motives ultimately inspiring the human passion to know and do, has never failed to persuade me that what, despite all sorts of denials, sustained the most agnostic and sceptical scholars in their efforts was the obscure conviction of collaborating, in the words of old Thucydides, in a work that will never end' (*The singularities of the human species*, 1954, in *The Appearance of Man*, p. 263).

[14] *Le Milieu Divin*, p. 79.

[15] *L'atomisme de l'esprit*, 1941, in *L'activation de l'énergie*, p. 48.

[16] *Comment je crois* (unpublished, 1934) takes the form of an analysis of the successive, hierarchically arranged, stages in the affirmation of truth: positing of the world as a whole, an evolutionary movement, an ascent towards spirit; the primacy of the personal in which that ascent culminates; and finally the affirmation of the Universal-Christ, who is the supreme personal. In a much-quoted passage, Teilhard writes: 'If as the result of some interior revolution I were to lose in turn my faith in Christ, my faith in a personal God, and my faith in spirit, I believe that I would retain an invincible faith in the world.' This implies no more than the recognition of the basis of all truth, which is the spontaneous affirmation, consubstantial with man, of *being*. Cf. Chapter 3, note 76.

In a fine passage, Teilhard expresses the dynamic force behind truth: 'The whole of history is there to pledge to us that a truth once seen, even by a single mind, always ends up by imposing itself on the totality of human consciousness' (*The Phenomenon of Man*, p. 218). 'Ideas, like life of which they are the highest manifestation, never turn back.' *The transformist paradox*, 1925, in *The Vision of the Past*, p. 102). 'Nothing has ever been able to prevent an idea from growing and spreading and finally becoming universally accepted' (*Human unanimization*, 1950, in *The Future of Man*, p. 283).

[17] This notion of the world's *depth* is central in Teilhard's thought. His phenomenology is in fact a journey towards total and absolute knowledge of the real.

In 1918, he had been reading Schuré's *Les grands initiés*, and, criticizing his naturalist mysticism, he says: 'True esotericism, the true *gnosis*, have no impact on the scientific order, and (unfortuately) do not allow us to draw the exasperating veil of phenomena from before our eyes. *The mystery of every circle of the world* lies *in the next circle*: that's the principle that should protect the mystic from every fanciful dream and every absurdity' (Letter of 20 November 1918, in *Making of a Mind*, p. 256). 'I was able, in reading Schuré, to put my finger on the mistake of false mystical systems that, confusing the levels, look for mystery at the phenomenal level' (Letter of 13 December 1918, *ibid.*, p. 268).

[18] *La crise présente*, in *Cahiers Pierre Teilhard de Chardin*, No. 3, p. 77.

[19] *Essai sur la personne*, unpublished, n.d.; cf. Chapter 4, note 59.

[20] It is not, accordingly, strictly true to say that 'Teilhardism treats personalism only in terms of religion' (Claude Soucy, *Teilhard, les personalistes et l'Etat*, in *Esprit*, March 1954, p. 400). In fact, Teilhard rejects individualism only in order to safeguard the person and guarantee its existential vocation.

[21] First lecture to the Marcel Légaut group, 19 November 1930.

[22] 'We must of course be careful not to let ourselves be guided in these matters by questions of feeling or sensitiveness. As if it were more repugnant to feel oneself joined to an animal stock than to the earth itself! Nothing in nature is low and inferior once one considers it *in motion* towards being and the light of God' (*What should we think of transformism?* 1930, in *Vision of the Past*, p. 156 note).

'Thought would not be queen of the world, if it were not connected with the world by all the fibres of matter, even the most humble ones' (*The discovery of Sinanthropus*, 1937, in *The Appearance of Man*, p. 92).

[23] *Le Milieu Divin*, pp. 58–60. 'The labour of seaweed as it concentrates in its tissues the substances scattered, in infinitesimal quantities, throughout the vast layers of the ocean; the industry of bees as they make honey from the juices broadcast in so many flowers—these are but pale images of the ceaseless working over that all the forces of the universe undergo in us in order to reach the level of spirit' (*Ibid.*, p. 60). 'We know ourselves and set our course but within an incredibly small radius of light. Immediately beyond lies impenetrable darkness, though it is full of presences—the night of everything that is within us and around us, without us and in spite of us' (*Ibid.*, p. 75). '. . . the length and depth of the countless servitudes which make us servants far more than masters of the universe' (*Ibid.*, p. 74). 'My self is given to me far more than it is formed by me' (*Ibid.*, p. 77).

'Nothing, not even at the summit of our being, can escape this flux of space-time any longer, because it is only definable in increase of consciousness. The very act by which the fine edge of our minds penetrates the absolute is a phenomenon of *emergence*' (*The Phenomenon of Man*, p. 220).

As Père J. M. Le Blond points out, St Thomas Aquinas had already noted (*De unitate intellectus contra Averroistas*, par. 28–30) that man's transcendence is realized in the progressive 'emergence' of 'form' from 'matter' (*Le paradoxe de l'homme*, in *Revue de l'Action populaire*, July–August 1963, pp. 788–9).

[24] *The experience of discovery*
Hominization, 1923, in *The Vision of the Past*, pp. 71–2.

'Organic life under cover of the determinisms analysed by biological science is, like our conscious life, an infinite fumbling and perpetual discovery' (*Ibid.*, p. 72).

The principle that makes man the type of the universe is the key to Bergsonian metaphysics. 'Creation, so conceived, is not a mystery: we experience it in ourselves as soon as we act freely' (*Creative Evolution*, p. 262). (Cf. E. Rideau, *Les rapports de la matière et de l'esprit dans le bergsonisme*, Paris, Alcan, 1932, p. 128).

Cf. *The Phenomenon of Man* (1930) in *Vision of the Past*, p. 171: 'Let us observe ourselves; and we shall find by intuition, if not by calculation, something of all the past movements of the universe in the living creatures we are. Let us join and exalt our individual powers; and we shall glimpse the grandeur towards which the phenomenon of man is progressing. Let us then narrow our possibilities of perception and choice; and we find ourselves back on the dark roads that life climbed, up to thought, by way of a long series of instinctive "inventions". Lastly, let us observe the veil of determinism which tends incessantly to conceal the repetition and disorganized multitude of our actions: and we catch in the act, in this invasion of our being by the tendency to greater probability, a true birth of matter.' 'In order to know how life operates (if it is really life that operates in us), is it not enough to watch ourselves at work?' (*Zoological evolution and invention*, 1947, *ibid.* p. 235).

'In virtue of analogies that correspond . . . to a deep bond of nature, the development of a phylum is strangely parallel to the successive stages undergone by an invention made by men. We have been familiar with these for a century or more. The idea is first roughly embodied in a theory or a provisional mechanism. Then follows a period of rapid modifications. The rough model is continually touched up and adjusted until it is practically perfected. On the attainment of this stage, the new creation enters its phase of expansion and equilibrium. As regards quality, it now undergoes only minor changes; it has reached its ceiling. But quantitatively it spreads and becomes permanently established. It is the same story with all modern inventions, from the bicycle to the aeroplane, from photography to the cinema and radio' (*The Phenomenon of Man*, p. 116).

This comment on the correspondence between the psychological experience and objective fact of invention does not conflict with what Madame M. Barthélemy-Madaule has to say: 'Although the principle that explains this lies ultimately in the psychic factor, it can be seen also in the objective characteristics we find both in the world and in ourselves. It is an explanation through the psychic, not a psychological explanation: and still less an exclusively psychological process' (*op. cit.*, p. 276).

[25] 'Let N^1 be the number of grains of thought incorporated in Omega, and N^2 the number of non-reflective corpuscles necessary to produce N^1: then the ratio N^1/N^2 gives the "yield of cosmogenesis". It is the "cosmic constant" of the universe that represents

the "pain and labour of the world" ' (*La centrologie*, 1944, No. 31, in *L'activation de l'énergie*, p. 129).

[26] *The Phenomenon of Man*, p. 221.

[27] *The Phenomenon of Man*, p. 221. *Le coeur de la matière*, unpublished, 1950, p. 17. *La centrologie*, 1944, No. 16. *L'atomisme de l'esprit*, 1941.

[28] *Le coeur de la matière*, unpublished, 1950, p. 17.

[29] *La centrologie*, 1944, No. 27.

[30] *L'activation de l'énergie humaine* in *L'activation de l'énergie*, pp. 409-10.

[31] *Barrière de la mort et co-réflexion*, 1955, *ibid.*, p. 425. 'Man is not yet complete in nature, not yet fully created, but, in and around us, he is still in full evolution' (*Sur la valeur religieuse de la recherche*, 1947, in *Science et Christ*, p. 258). 'One of the most dangerous illusions that has invaded the heart of man in the course of history, is the fallacy of his completeness and permanence' (*La réflexion de l'énergie*, 1952, in *L'activation de l'énergie*, p. 340).

[32] *The discovery of the true*

This very Cartesian principle is often implicit in Teilhard's argument, and faithfully applied not only in an exhaustive phenomenology of the real but also in a constant effort to disclose the real under its outward appearances, and so to go beyond habit and 'intellectual routine' (*The Phenomenon of Man*, p. 305) or the obvious. 'What stares us in the face is often the most difficult to perceive' (*Ibid.*, p. 33). 'What we need most of all is not new facts—there are enough facts already, staring us in the face—but a new way of looking at facts and handling them. A new way of seeing, and with it a new way of acting—that is what we need' (*La convergence de l'univers*, in *L'activation de l'énergie*, p. 308). This explains why Teilhard's writing is often *polemical* in tone.

Numerous examples could be quoted: the awareness of socialization: 'our view of life is obscured and inhibited, by the absolute division we continually place between the natural and the artificial' (*Hominization*, 1923, in *The Vision of the Past*, p. 59, and *L'étoffe de l'univers*, in *L'activation de l'enereie*, p. 402). The re-appraisal that must be made if we are to have a correct view of man (*Ibid.*, p. 79, *The phenomenon of man*, 1930, in *The Vision of the Past*, p. 166). The dialectical notion of spirit-matter (*Esquisse d'un univers personnel*, 1936, in *L'energie humaine*, p. 74). The change of outlook necessary if we are to be alive to the spirit of the earth or noosphere (*L'energie humaine*, 1937, in *L'énergie humaine*, p. 149). The zones or levels of the material universe (*The Phenomenon of Man*, p. 44). 'The effort at perspective (that) is indispensable if we wish to probe the secrets or even the "space" of nascent life' (*Ibid.*, pp. 91-2). The recognition of a progressive all-embracing movement of the earth, not periodic, but directed towards an end (*Ibid.*, p. 101). 'Life is not a peculiar anomaly, sporadically flowering on matter, but an exaggeration, through specially favourable circumstances, of a universal cosmic property—not an epiphenomenon but the very essence of the phenomenon' (*Man's Place in Nature*, p. 18). The natural character of the appearance of man in the universe (*L'étoffe de l'univers*, 1953, in *L'activation de l'énergie*, p. 400). On other points, cf. *The Phenomenon of Man*, pp. 91, 133-4, 182-4, 216-17, 222, 226-7, 246, *Man's Place in Nature*, pp. 66-7).

[33] Although Teilhard admits, as we have seen, the possibility of introspection, he would appear, following the scholastic line and the theories of his friends (Pères Rousselot, Charles, and Maréchal), entirely to reject the Bergsonian theory of an 'immediate' and intuitive knowledge of the ego by itself: man knows himself, no doubt, but he does not know himself, nor does he ever have any knowledge, except through *representation*, in the subject–object relationship. Thus Teilhard would seem to be closer to Hamelin (*Essai sur les éléments principaux de la représentation*, 1907) and G. Bachelard (*La dialectique de la durée*, 1932), both of whom represent a reaction against the Bergsonian immediate and continuum.

We should note that Teilhard describes reflection as 'the power acquired by a consciousness to turn in upon itself, to take possession of itself *as of an object* endowed with its own particular consistence and values' (*The Phenomenon of Man*, p. 165). In italicising the word *object* Teilhard does not seem, nevertheless, to have brought out the condition of the human mind, essentially divided within itself, and doomed to know itself (as it knows all reality) only from a distance and in relationship of objectivity.

[34] *Le milieu mystique*, 1917 in *Ecrits du temps de la guerre*, p. 137.

[35] See the list of images used in Teilhard's terminology (appendix, pp. 258-73).

[36] 'It's interesting to note in oneself how much words, while they impoverish living thought, at the same time give it a strength that completes it and sometimes surprises it;' how much, too, 'the effort of composition (at least when the subject is something by which the

mind really lives) enriches one's understanding, and even one's power of expression, and makes it more lively' (Letter of 27 September 1918, in *Making of a Mind*, p. 239). In an earlier letter, Teilhard criticizes the intellectualist concept, according to which 'everything can be reduced, with nothing left over, to "language". That's exactly what Bergson most objects to. I find this concept of the world so impoverished, so empty, so trivial' (Letter of 16 January 1916, *ibid.*, p. 170).

[37] 'I want to discern more clearly this complex of regrets and desires that makes up our life and our most individually personal energy' (Letter of 13 January 1917, *ibid.*, p. 168).

[38] 'The man who is absorbed in the demands of practical life—the *exclusively* positive man—only rarely, or with difficulty, realizes this second phase in our perceptions—when the world that has impinged on us, withdraws from us, taking us with it. He is only mildly sensitive to the pervasive, emotive aura through which, in *every* contact, the unique essential of the universe is disclosed to us' (*Le milieu mystique*, 1917, in *Ecrits du temps de la guerre*, p. 138).

[39] 'The activation of the living being—the more living it is, and in virtue of what is most living in it—calls ever more insistently, if it is to become effective, for the intervention of some fear, some repugnance, or (most of all) for some *attraction*' (*L'activation de l'énergie humaine*, 1953, in *L'activation de l'énergie*, p. 413). 'Nothing, not even evolution, can withstand *boredom*' (*Du cosmos à la cosmogénèse*, 1951, *ibid.*, p. 273 note).

[40] *L'énergie d'évolution*, in *L'activation de l'énergie*, p. 387.

[41] *L'énergie humaine*, 1937, in *L'énergie humaine*, pp. 180–1. 'Every single thing, no matter how humble it be, *provided it keeps to the line of advance*, is warmed and illuminated and animated, and in consequence becomes an object to which *total* adherence is given. What was cold, and dead, and impersonal to eyes that were blind, takes on, for those whose eyes are opened, not only life, but a life more vigorous than their own—so that when they act they have a much stronger sense of being taken and assimilated than of themselves taking and assimilating. Where the man who cannot see meets only an object that produces a limited reaction, the others can deploy the full range of their powers—can love passionately, accepting it as a real contact, even a caress—the most humble of their tasks' (*Ibid.*, pp. 183–4).

[42] 'The mutual attraction of the sexes is so fundamental a fact that any explanation of the world (whether biological, philosophical or religious) that cannot find a *structurally essential* place in its system, is to all intents and purposes ruled out. Sexuality can be included, in this sense, with particular ease, in a cosmic system that is based on union' (*Esquisse d'un univers personnel*, 1936, in *L'énergie humaine*, p. 91).

[43] Letter of 8 October 1915, in *Making of a Mind*, p. 74.

[44] *Le Milieu Divin*, p. 49.

[45] *Un phénomène de contre-évolution*, 1949, in *L'activation de l'énergie*, p. 200. A wartime letter speaks of the fragility of the ego: 'One becomes a "war-monad" a depersonalized element in a supra-individual operation. One is no longer the person one was before' (Letter of 22 December 1916, in *Making of a Mind*, p. 154).

[46] Teilhard describes his first experience of the world as a totality: 'For all their slightness and transience, the whisper of the breeze, the subtle touch of the aether, the soul's expression, sank further into my being, to where man's faculties are so closely concentrated that they converge in a single point. With the sharp, triple arrowhead it sank into me, the world pierced its way into me, and took me back to itself' (*Le milieu mystique*, 1917, in *Ecrits du temps de la guerre*, p. 137).

Our personal qualities 'coincide exactly with the substance of our being—for their fabric is woven by our consciousness of them' (*Le coeur de la matière*, 1950).

We should note, however, that, unlike Bergson, Teilhard never uses the word intuition: though he frequently uses a word close to it in meaning—*sense* (*sens*), as for example *sense of the cosmos*, *sense of man*.

[47] 'For if our "artificial" constructions are really nothing but the legitimate sequel to our phylogenesis, *invention* also—this revolutionary act from which the creations of our thought emerge one after the other—can legitimately be regarded as an extension in reflective form of the obscure mechanism whereby each new form has always germinated on the trunk of life . . . In the same beam of light the instinctive gropings of the first cell link up with the informed gropings of our laboratories . . . The passing wave that we can feel was not formed in ourselves. It comes to us from far away;

it set out at the same time as the light from the first stars' (*The Phenomenon of Man*, p. 224).

⁴⁸ Twice, after reading Bergson—first during the 1914 war and again during the second world war—Teilhard criticizes him for neglecting the specific character of choice or option in favour of a questionable intuition of duration, and holds, with good reason, that fullness of freedom will be attained only at the term in history of personalization (Cf. M. Barthélemy-Madaule, *op. cit.*, pp. 542-4).

⁴⁹ No writer has analysed this more clearly than Jules Lequier (cf. Xavier Tilliette, *Jules Lequier ou le tourment de la liberté*, Desclée de Brouwer, 1964). A certain misunderstanding of the act of conversion will be noted later.

⁵⁰ We should, however, note a penetrating comment in a letter of 2 November 1916: 'All these horrors, I should add, are to me no more than the memory of a dream. I think that you live so immersed in the immediate effort of the moment that little of them penetrates to your consciousness or memory. And on top of that, the lack of proportion between existence on the battlefield and life in peacetime (or at any rate in rest billets) is such that the former, looked back on from the latter, is never anything but a fantasy and a dream' (*Making of a Mind*, p. 140). There is a similar comment in a letter dated 22 December p. 16. *ibid.*, p. 154.

⁵¹ 'Every operation, as it becomes effective, becomes mechanical. No sooner has the act been initiated than it encloses itself in the rudiments of a habit. Perception has hardly become conscious before it becomes dulled by growing familiarity, which robs it of its freshness and makes it insensitive. Thus, by a law inherent in life, two things happen simultaneously: in the first place we are driven irresistibly towards new forms of activity and perception (because that is the only way in which we can continue to be sensitive—and there we have a principle that governs progress in being); and secondly, every time we act, a new layer of determinism and unconsciousness is added to all the corporeal burden we carry around with us. The two processes, spiritualization and materialization, are intimately connected, in our evolution, as being two aspects of one and the same thing' (*Les noms de la matière*, 1919, in *Ecrits du temps de la guerre*, p. 427).

⁵² Here Teilhard's psychology agrees with modern psychology, according to which man comes into contact with himself only in

the significance of his acts or behaviour, and in the dymamic intention of the situations in which he finds himself.

53 *The sense of the person*
The singularities of the human species, 1954, in *The Appearance of Man*, p. 269. The following passage from a letter dated 5–6 August 1915 shows how early in his life Teilhard developed this sense of the person: 'It seems to me that once you pass from individual consciousness to collective phenomena you fall back into the inevitable, into blindness—as though the agglomeration of human societies ended by causing a new matter to crystallize around us . . . One thing at any rate I can see more clearly, that one of dogma's most precious properties is that it forces us to maintain the primacy and priority over everything of souls, that is, of individual centres' (*Making of a Mind*, p. 64). 'True progress never makes itself felt, is never realized, in any of the material creations we try to substitute for ourselves in the hope that they will survive our life on earth: it is in souls that the advance is made, the real sparks in which the inner fires of the world are concentrated and embodied, and it disappears with them' (Letter of 6 January 1917, *ibid.*, p. 163).

'It must never be forgotten that, as in the empirical spheres of the world, each man, though enveloped within the same universe as all other men, presents an independent centre of perspective and activity for that universe (so that there are as many partial universes as there are individuals), so in the realm of heavenly realities, however deeply we may be impregnated by the same creative and redemptive force, each one of us constitutes a particular centre of divinization (so that there are as many partial divine *milieux* as there are Christian souls) (*Le Milieu Divin*, p. 141).

In 1929 Teilhard experienced a fresh discovery of the 'person'. 'After the ideal of the spiritual, another, that of the "person" is rapidly becoming outstandingly important in my picture of the world. After a long odyssey, I am rediscovering these values in a way that makes them completely new to me and—if that's the word I want—delectable' (Letter of 15 July 1929). Later in the same letter Teilhard introduces the notion of the person of Christ as the face of the world. 'As I was telling you, my mind is entirely taken up with constructing a world for myself that is physically explained by spirit and the growing personalization of the monads (a world in which man is the key, not an anomaly) (Letter of 29 September 1929).

Whereas below man life itself was 'more real than living beings', the person introduces a unique absolute value. 'Until now it was enough to consider in nature a simple vibration on a wide front, the rise of consciousness. What we now have to do is to define and determine the laws of an ascent of individual centres of consciousness, a much more delicate phenomenon. We are dealing with the progress made up of other progresses as lasting as itself; a movement of movements' (*The Phenomenon of Man*, pp. 173-4).

[54] *Esquisse d'un univers personnel*, 1934, in *L'énergie humaine*, p. 70. 'The personal is a threshold, an innovation, an event', as Madame M. Barthélemy-Madaule rightly says (*La personne dans la perspective Teilhardienne*, in *Essais sur Teilhard de Chardin, op. cit.*, p. 73).

[55] *The Phenomenon of Man*, p. 258.

[56] *La centrologie*, No. 27, *op. cit.*, p. 28 note.

[57] Teilhard associates individuality both with the normal distinction between persons and with the immorality of their egoism: it is this ambiguity that has led him, quite mistakenly, to be accused of devaluing the notion of the individual (Cf. B. Charbonneau, *Teilhard de Chardin, prophète d'un âge totalitaire*, Editions Denoël, 1963).

[58] In particular through the analysis of *language*.

[59] 'Similarly, the reflective psychic centre, once turned in on itself, can subsist only by means of a double movement which is in reality one and the same. It centres itself further on itself by penetration into a new space, and at the same time it centres the rest of the world around itself by the establishment of an ever more coherent and better perspective in the realities which surround it. We are not dealing with an immutably fixed focus, but with a vortex which grows deeper as it sucks up the fluid at the heart of which it was born. The ego persists only by becoming ever more itself, in the measure in which it makes everything else itself. So man becomes a person in and through personalization' (*The Phenomenon of Man*, p. 172). It is not only modern man says Teilhard, but man in general who can 'see nothing, *not even himself*', other than in space-time (*Ibid.*, p. 219).

[60] *Palaeontology and the appearance of man*, 1923, in *The Appearance of Man*, p. 57.

[61] *Le Milieu Divin*, pp. 76-7. Cf. H. Bergson, *Essai* . . . pp. 97-8, 102-5, 130.

[62] *La lutte contre la multitude*, 1917, in *Ecrits du temps de la guerre*, p. 118.

[63] *Le Milieu Divin*, p. 82.

[64] *Ibid.*, pp. 136-7.

[65] *Ibid.*, p. 82.

[66] Letter of 19 June 1916, in *Making of a Mind*, p. 103.

[67] *Letters from a Traveller*, p. 183. 'The future seems to be abandoned to the forces of *chance* . . . Everywhere ahead of me, as far as the eye can reach, the future vacillates, like a treacherous mirage that eludes one's grasp. The only stability I can see in the picture is the in-human features of certain laws of probability . . . the abyss of necessity opening out below the abyss of contingence' (*La foi qui opère*, 1918, in *Ecrits du temps de la guerre*, pp. 310-11).

[68] *Le Milieu Divin*, p. 82. 'Seen as something awaiting us in the future, death contains within itself, and underlies, everything that terrifies us and robs us of security . . . a man must have felt the shadow of death pass over him if he is to appreciate the full loneliness, the hazards and terrors of the new and unknown, that come with our journey into the future' (*La foi qui opère, op. cit.*, p. 313).

[69] 'Man, with his freedom to lend or refuse himself to the battle, represents the fearful faculty of scanning and criticizing life' (*Hominization*, 1923, in *Vision of the Past*, p. 74).

'When the first spark of thought appeared on the earth, life found it had brought into the world a power capable of criticizing and judging it. This formidable risk, which long lay dormant, but whose dangers burst out with our first awakening to the idea of evolution' (*The Phenomenon of Man*, p. 230). Cf. Péguy's 'There is something peculiarly agonizing in the thought of the death of man-kind' (*Encore de la grippe, Oeuvres en prose*, 1898-1908, Gallimard, p. 114).

[70] *The Phenomenon of Man*, p. 229.

[71] *Man's place in the universe*, in *The Vision of the Past*, p. 221.

[72] Letter of 1 September 1926, in *Letters from a Traveller*, p. 133. He is commenting on Paul Morand's *Rien que la terre*.

[73] Letter of 15 November 1935, *ibid.*, p. 216.

[74] *Le Milieu Divin*, p. 78.

[75] *Le coeur de la matière. Prière au Christ toujours plus grand.*

[76] *Ibid.*

[77] Letter of 6 January 1917, in *Making of a Mind*, p. 163. Some months later, in *Le milieu mystique* (*op. cit.*, p. 159) Teilhard continues: 'One day, I remember, I could not find the words in which to express the thought in which my life was struggling to embody itself. Half of what I had to say, no one listened to and it was carried away by the wind. And the rest, no one understood. It was then that I felt that all of us, crammed together as we are on the face of the earth, are living, so far as such matters are concerned, in a state of wretched estrangement from one another.' 'Travelling among exotic people,' Teilhard thought about the problem of conversion: 'You feel that you come up everywhere against water-tight bulkheads between minds, and you have to dive down to the absolute depths if you want to make real contact with souls and "convert" them. "Conversion" always seems to me a very difficult problem to understand' (Letter of 26 April 1926, in *Letters from a Traveller*, p. 124).

[78] 'In any case, there is in this a most mysterious and profound source of pain. The soul dimly regrets the dignity and the insurmountable barriers that prevents it from bursting out and re-immersing itself in the whole. Sometimes it shudders at feeling alone with itself, never completely understood. Sometimes, it suffers the anguish of feeling lost in the midst of a multitude of strangers. Sometimes it is seized with giddiness, when it realizes that emancipation has made it sole master of its destiny: it would be so pleasant and comfortable to abandon oneself to a vast current shared by all. The monad suffers again at seeing the universe threatened by failure because its most noble elements, surrendering to anarchy, shirk the common tasks (this is the "cosmic crisis" brought about by the awakening of thought that I spoke of in one of my recent letters): what can one do that will effectively sanctify and co-ordinate this effervescent multitude? How heavily the burden of the world weighs upon the spirit that is tied so strictly to it and yet is powerless to animate the whole!' (Letter of 6 January 1917, in *Making of a Mind*, p. 164). 'I want, you see, to discern more clearly this complex of regrets and desires which in effect makes up our life and our most individually personal energy' (Letter of 13 January 1917, *ibid.*, p. 168).

[79] 'Who will come to relieve us from the pain of solitude? The

answer is obviously our Lord, who opens up to us in himself a beatifying centre of convergence and confluence. In him we find real fusion in a real unity, we find effective interaction and the inter-comprehension we need . . . both organically and morally, through the unifying activity of his body and the efficacious sanctity of his teaching. And so the monad finds solace and the crisis of the world is averted' (Letter of 6 January 1917, *ibid.*, p. 164).

[80] *Esquisse d'un univers personnel*, 1936, in *L'énergie humaine*, pp. 105–10. 'In the small number of effective encounters, there is still an incredible difficulty to be overcome if the external contact of men's lives is to be maintained. Too often those who love one another most have hardly come together before they are separated by the very chances that brought them into contact. Even in those exceptional cases when the bringing together runs smoothly, there are infinite difficulties and dangers in the development of contact from within: the labyrinths in which you hear, but cannot find one another; the dead ends you run up against; the roads that lead you apart—the souls that lose their way in one another . . . And even if, by some final godsend, one at last makes his way to the heart of the other, there is still the ultimate barrier of two minds that can never, however close they come together, be entirely transparent to one another—because they are not yet, and can never be, until the final consummation, interiorized in one another' (*Ibid.*, p. 106).

[81] *La lutte contre la multitude*, 1917, in *Ecrits du temps de la guerre*, p. 120.

[82] *Le prêtre*, 1918 (*ibid.*, p. 285). 'There are times when the world seems like an immensity of chaos' (Wedding address, 1918).

[83] 'When our soul comes hard up against the impenetrability that closes it and makes it a mystery to all other souls, powerless to communicate its ideas, to describe its suffering, to show the measure of its love . . . When it is cold and frightened by feeling lost all alone in the midst of a multitude of living beings . . . When our minds reel at the thought that we are lashed, all by ourselves, to the prow of the world as it plunges on, . . . then we fancy that what we hear is still the lament of our own petty self-centred being, begging for some sop of happiness. In reality, *what is groaning within us is something greater than ourselves*. The voice we then hear is that of the one single soul of the time to come, mourning its multiplicity. And it is the breath of this still nascent soul that is passing into us, in that fundamental,

lived, incurable yearning for *total union* that gives life to all poetry, all pantheism, all holiness' (*La lutte contre la multitude*, 1917, *op. cit.*, p. 118).

[84] *Le Milieu Divin*, p. 115. In *The Phenomenon of Man* (pp. 226-8), Teilhard sums up the reasons for our modern disquiet: 'Enormity of space, enormity of duration, enormity of number; sickness of the dead end—the anguish of feeling shut in.' Cf. *Man's Place in Nature*, pp. 100-1. Elsewhere, Teilhard analyses the three fundamental fears of modern man: the overwhelming of man's significance by the size of the universe, the definitive stabilization of the species, the possibility that even at the peak of his trajectory man may still fall back; 'fear of not being able to make oneself understood by anyone; fear of no longer being able to move; fear of not being able to get out' (*The singularities of the human species*, in *The Appearance of Man*, pp. 208-9). For an analysis of the forces of repulsion and materialization in our own time, see *The Phenomenon of Man*, pp. 254-7. And on this whole subject, cf. H. de Lubac, *op. cit.*, pp. 12, 92-3, 144.

[85] Jean-Marie Domenach, *Le personnalisme de Teilhard de Chardin*, *Esprit*, March 1963, pp. 340-2: and René Pucheu, *Teilhard et le pari*, *ibid.*, pp. 384-90. Pucheu holds it against Teilhard that he solves the problem of man's disquiet by the certainty of an absolute (final and already present), of definitive attainment of plenitude, of an ultimate answer that will set him at rest: in so doing Pucheu is, strangely enough, attacking the natural, innate desire to neutralize the present alienations inherent in man's condition and to find a way out into the eternal. Here the whole of Christianity is an answer to the evil of existence. No doubt, this striving for the eternal may be contaminated by the selfishness of a desire for security; at the same time true hope is a love and a way of living, and is justified only in the desire for a communion, and an active communion, with other men and with God. There is no reason to think that Teilhard conceived final immortality as consciousness relaxing into blissful sleep.

In *The spiritual power of matter* (1919, in *Hymn of the Universe*, in particular pp. 65-7), Teilhard speaks of the mystical illumination that revealed to him the all-embracing framework of the cosmos, and sent him back to earth a 'stranger', 'outside human society', a man now living 'on another plane'. We should not, I believe, push our interpretation of this too far. Not only may there well be a certain rhetorical exaggeration, appropriate to that particular type of composition, but what Teilhard says fits in with one aspect of the Christian experience, that aspect, in fact, which St Paul refers to (1 Cor. 7:29): '. . . . those who deal with the world as though they had no dealings with it'), as do many mystics whose detachment and hope have not prevented them from being ardently present in flesh and blood and active in the world. The editorial note, *Hymn of the Universe*, pp. 70–1, emphasizes more exclusively the purifications that are a necessary preliminary to mystical experience. We shall see that Teilhard did not deny their necessity.

[86] Cf. Chapter 1, note 9.

[87] 'Because I am conscious of feeling with great intensity the aspirations—as others feel the pitifulness—of the soul of my own time' (*Note pour servir à l'évangélisation des temps modernes*, 1919, in *Ecrits du temps de la guerre*, p. 380). Later, writing more confidentially, Teilhard said, 'If it was only a question of my own self . . . but in life it's generally for others that one suffers most' (Unpublished letter to Père Auguste Valensin, 10 January 1926).

[88] See the passages quoted in note 151 to this chapter.

[89] Letter of 8 April 1930, in *Letters from a Traveller*, p. 164. 'It is apparent, we must realize, that the world we live in, which is *essentially one*, is, in spite of its unity, as multiple as the monads it contains . . . By virtue of some divine foreknowledge that governs the progress of the whole as a function of the freedom of each individual, everything goes to show that, in the unique system of events that at any given moment constitutes the state of the universe, there are as many *independent providences* as there are souls in the world. Thus each one of us has in truth *his* universe, of which he is the centre, and which it is his duty to give harmony to as though he were alone, *in natura rerum* (*La foi qui opère*, 1918, in *Ecrits du temps de la guerre*, p. 321).

'Because of the spiritual nature of the noosphere, its elements are not strictly comparable to the anonymous and interchangeable particles of a gaseous mass. They correspond more to the cells of a supremely specialized organism, each one of which occupies, and alone is able to occupy, a determined place. This means that the perfection and usefulness of each nucleus of human energy in relation to the whole, depend ultimately on whatever is unique and incommunicable in the perfection of each. When, therefore, the technician has to handle human units there is one thing that should be his basic concern: it is, throughout whatever transformations he seeks to impose on them, to allow them the chance to determine themselves and the freedom to differentiate themselves, ever more fully. The organization of the energy of human elements, however generally its methods may be applied, must culminate in the production within each element of *a maximum of personality*' (*L'énergie humaine*, 1937 in *L'énergie humaine*, p. 164).

[90] The attempt to depersonalize or 'dis-humanize' ourselves, referred to on one occasion by Teilhard, brings us a new contact with reality: 'Of one thing we can be sure: that we shall be rewarded for merely attempting or outlining the action, by the powerful and dramatic interest that the human commonplaces will assume, rediscovered from this point of view' (*Hominization*, 1923, in *Vision of the Past*, p. 52).

[91] *The Phenomenon of Man*, p. 313. 'Yes, the more man becomes man, the more serious becomes the problem of evil and the more ingrained in his flesh, his nerves and his mind, the problem of understanding evil and of suffering it' (Preface to *L'énergie spirituelle de la souffrance*, by Marguerite-Marie Teilhard de Chardin, Editions du Seuil, 1951, p. 10, and in *L'activation de l'énergie*, p. 255). 'Although the problem of evil has not once more (as some people mistakenly hold) become the great problem of the day—that's a problem of power—yet it confronts the consciousness of today with a fundamental unknown quantity, an X'. (Letter of 20 April 1948).

[92] *Hominization*, 1923, in *The Vision of the Past*, p. 74. 'Evil inevitably appears in the course of the unification of the multiple, because it is the very expression of a still incompletely organized state of plurality' (*Christianisme et évolution*, unpublished, 1945).

'Like those powerful rockets that the intrepidity of modern man launches into the astronautic battle, a cosmos in controlled movement cannot advance as it is intended to without leaving behind a dense smoke-trail . . . Evil, then, is a *secondary* effect, an inevitable *by-product* of the advance of an evolving universe' (*Du cosmos à la cosmogénèse*, 1951, in *L'activation de l'énergie*, p. 268).

[93] 'Every advance in personalization has to be paid for: for so much union, so much suffering. This relation of value for value governs all the transformations of spirit-matter. And nothing can dispense

us from it' (*Esquisse d'un univers personnel*, 1936, in *L'énergie humaine*, p. 107).

In this connexion E. Borne suggests a distinction between two levels, or rather two modes, of evil. While some sorrows, that are in a way normal and foreseeable, can be overcome or 'mediatized', cured or made good, there are others that are permanently irreparable: 'through evils that cannot be mediatized, we can distinguish the features of an evil that is, it seems, the absolute of evilness' (*Le problème du mal*, P.U.F., 1958, pp. 16–30). And, in fact, it is only this mode of evil that presents itself to us as a real stumbling block, sheer opacity, an unjustifiable contradiction: the horror of contempt for innocence, of the tortured child, of permanent, hopeless destitution, of inexplicable injustice, of the great physical catastrophes or the great conflicts of history . . . It is only then that creation seems to break down and to be at the mercy of blind chance, or, what is worse, of some hidden malice. Teilhard does not shirk this problem. 'There are more difficult cases (and in fact they are the commonest) when human wisdom is altogether out of its depth. At every moment we see diminishment, both in us and around us, that does not seem to be compensated by any advantage on any perceptible plane' (*Le Milieu Divin*, p. 87). Nevertheless, some contemporary existentialists, whether Christian like E. Borne, or non-Christian like A. Camus, would think this view somewhat over-simplified, and still too intellectual in its insistence on the "horror' of the world (*Le Milieu Divin*, p. 138). Such thinkers would hardly accept Teilhard's statement that 'in a system of cosmogenesis, the problem of evil is not only soluble, but even ceases to exist as a problem' (*Du cosmos à la cosmogénèse*, 1951, in *L'activation de l'énergie*, pp. 267–8).

[94] The immortality of the person is envisaged by Teilhard not only at the term of history in the community of the whole human organism, but at the end of each individual biological existence. He sees this immortality as 'a property of our centre' (*Comment je crois*, unpublished, 1934, p. 28). 'All around us, one by one, like a continual exhalation, "souls" break away, carrying upwards their incommunicable load of consciousness. One by one, yet not in isolation' (*The Phenomenon of Man*, p. 272). The problem of personal immortality comes up again in a note to *The Singularities of the human species*, 1954, in *The Appearance of Man*, p. 266. Moreover the

disappearance in death of the bodily envelope leaves intact man's fundamental relation to the universe: Teilhard believes that the idea of the 'separated soul' is false (*Du cosmos à la cosmogénèse*, 1951, in *L'activation de l'énergie*, p. 269 note).

[95] *Immortality*

'In all sincerity, it seems to me more difficult to dissolve a soul than to smash an atom' (Letter to Père Auguste Valensin, March 1963).

'The world would inevitably, and justifiably, cease to function—from lack of heart—if it realized (in its thinking zones) that it was moving towards total death. Therefore there is no total death' (*L'esprit de la terre*, 1931, in *L'énergie humaine*, p. 49).

The existence of a 'limitless horizon ahead of us' is the indispensable condition for justifying the project immanent in evolution and conscious in man. 'The prospect of a total death would immediately dry up the sources of our effort' and the impulse of history would vanish in disgust (*Comment je crois*, unpublished, 1934).

A cosmos that is 'polarized towards an ever-increasing concentration on itself . . . can never disintegrate so long as time's pointer does not reverse. Incorruptibility, we now see, is not inherent in simplicity but in irreversibility' (*Esquisse d'un univers personnel*, 1936, in *L'énergie humaine*, p. 75).

'No term can be set to the growing series of molecules unless it is positive and maximum by nature. This means that, in one way or another, we can escape the tendency to decay of the star that bears us' (*L'atomisme de l'esprit*, in *L'activation de l'énergie*, 1941, p. 50). 'Everything collapses completely if this higher term turns out to be unstable or non-existent' (*Ibid.*).

Moreover, immortality is not simply a *condition* but an *experience* tied up with the appearance of man. 'Conscious both of his uniqueness and of the existence of a future, man sees that he cannot be reconcilable with a destruction that, in annihilating him, would annihilate an *irreplaceable* portion of the cosmic effort' (*La centrologie*, 1944, No. 15, *op. cit.*, pp. 115–16). While other living centres, for lack of internal unification, remain 'reversible and fragile', entirely subject to the laws of matter, 'it is only once the critical threshold of reflexion has been crossed that the human particles become capable through the spiritualized apex of their being (their "soul"), not only of effectively experiencing the action of Omega, but also of sharing in Omega's essentially personal consistence.' 'Released from the matrix of complexity that sinks back into the multiple, the reflective centre can at last, definitively, be unified upon itself, and meet the ultimate pole of convergence' (*Ibid.*, No. 30, *op. cit.*, pp. 128–9).

It is in fact at this culminating moment when mankind reaches its final point of communion and apparently finds it impossible to press on any further, that its necessary irreversibility, combined with its hunger for the absolute, will give it the added urge to 'impel it forward in yet another advance' (*The formation of the Noosphere*, 1947, in *The Future of Man*, p. 180).

Cf. the letter to C. Cuénot, 30 November 1952, reproduced at the beginning of his *Teilhard de Chardin* (in the series 'Ecrivains de toujours').

'Unless it is automatically to cease to be active in direct ratio to its hominization, the world cannot be of the "closed" type. Since it is inevitably energized, it must open out ahead (*Monde ouvert? Monde fermé?* unpublished, 1954).

We should, finally, note the difference between Teilhard's arrival at belief in immortality and Bergson's. In *Matter and Memory* it is treated as a possibility for a consciousness embodied only in gesture and language; in *The Two Sources* as experimentally verifiable by trans-natural communication with the dead.

[96] *Comment je crois*, unpublished, 1924. 'The whole is not the immensity in extension, and therefore potentially dissolving, in which you seek its image. It is essentially, just as we are, a centre, with the qualities of a centre. And does its centricity come from breaking down the centres subordinated to it? By no means: it comes by strengthening them into its own likeness. Its own particular way of dissolving is to unify even more deeply. For the human monad, to be absorbed into the universe is to be super-personalized' (*Ibid.*).

[97] 'Taken as static and in isolation, sorrow and perversity are an anomaly. Taken dynamically, in a system that is groping its way and moving forward, they are justified and transformed' (*L'atomisme de l'esprit*, 1941, p. 57).

'Evil, in all its forms—injustice, inequality, suffering, death itself —ceases theoretically to be outrageous from the moment, when, *evolution becoming a genesis*, the immense travail of the world displays itself as the inevitable reverse side—or better, the condition—or better still, the price—of an immense triumph. And in its turn earth, that microscopic planet on which we are crushed together, is seen to be no longer the meaningless prison in which we thought we must suffocate: for if its limits were less narrow could it be the matrix in which our unity is being moulded?' (*The new spirit*, 1942, in *The Future of Man*, p. 90). Cf. *The Phenomenon of Man*, p. 228.

'In the vast process of organization from which life emerges, every success, we realize, has necessarily to be paid for by a high percentage of failures. There can be no progress in being without some mysterious tribute of tears, blood and sin. It is hardly to be wondered at, then, that some patches of shadow grow deeper around us as the light grows brighter: for, from this point of view, sorrow, in every form and every degree, is (at least to some extent) only the natural consequence of the very movement by which we ourselves were produced' (Preface to *L'énergie spirituelle de la souffrance*, *op. cit.*, p. 10, and in *L'activation de l'énergie*, pp. 255–6).

[98] *Esquisse d'un univers personnel*, 1936, in *L'énergie humaine*, p. 89. 'To re-adjust, within a universe recognized as convergent, the whole range of human values' (*La convergence de l'univers*, in *L'activation de l'énergie*, p. 308). 'Science, art, morality, thought, mysticism: these are so many different forms of one and the same effort to achieve harmony; and in them is expressed, through our human activities, the destiny and even, one might say, the essence of existence' (Wedding address, 15 June 1953).

[99] *The Phenomenon of Man*, p. 261. As we noted earlier, Teilhard thus distinguishes, correctly, between person and personality: the first being, rather, a reality of the ideal or metaphysical order.

[100] Teilhard attributes a special position among the sciences to that of the past, history, whose individual character cannot be overlooked, since it determines the relationship of 'unique' events situated in an irreversible time-dimension (*The discovery of the past*, 1949, in *The Vision of the Past*, pp. 188–91).

[101] To 'dedicate oneself, body and soul, to the sacred duty of research' (*Le Milieu Divin*, pp. 69–70).

[102] 'Never before has the seeker after knowledge been what we are now beginning to see him as—a sort of priest.' Even so great a genius as Pascal 'blamed himself for studying science. Pascal reckoned the hours spent in scientific or mathematical research as time wasted on trivialities' (*Le sens humain*, unpublished, 1929).

[103] 'No scientist worthy of the name goes on working—or can go on

working—unless he is inspired by the idea of advancing the progress of the world around him, right to the extreme end' (*Recherche, travail, adoration*, 1955, in *Science et Christ*, p. 285). 'In the worker-priest, the "social" claim to *better-being* hides the neo-humanist aspiration for, or faith in, *more-being*, which is the chief and most vital element in the "new spirit" ' (*Ibid.*, p. 287 note).

[104] *The value of research*

L'énergie humaine, 1937, in *L'énergie humaine*, p. 170. *La mystique de la science*, 1939, *ibid.*, pp. 203–23. (In this article Teilhard gives an historical appreciation of science: antiquity, the discovery of time, religion of science, the intellectual and moral crisis of progress). *The Phenomenon of Man*, p. 278. *The formation of the noosphere*, 1947, in *The Future of Man*, pp. 172–3. *Man's Place in Nature*, pp. 105–6. *Recherche, travail et adoration*, 1955, in *Science et Christ*, p. 283.

As early as 1916 Teilhard was speaking of the nobility of scientific enquiry: 'Inspired by the vast hope of indefinitely increasing his stature, and gratifying his yearning to get a purchase on matter, man, in a new burst of ardour, is devoting himself to an impassioned study of the forces of the universe, and is absorbed in the search for the great secret: the strictness of his task is enveloped in the mystical glow that lit up the anxious features of the alchemists, haloed the foreheads of the magi, divinized the gesture of Prometheus' (*La vie cosmique*, in *Ecrits du temps de la guerre*, p. 25). In 1918, shortly after his religious profession, Teilhard wrote: 'I would like to remind those who are cowardly or timid or infantile, or, again, narrow in their religion, that the development of man is demanded by Christ for his body, and that, in relation to the world and to truth, the quest for knowledge is an absolute duty' (*Le prêtre, ibid.*, p. 299). Some months later, turning over in his mind a saying of Plato, and comparing it with something Pascal said, he came to the conclusion: 'Geometry is not the term of our intellectual effort, but is ordered toward divinizing us, by developing spirit in us and can therefore be given a "religious" impulse not only "by intention" but by reason of the work it performs in us' (Letter of 29 September 1918, in *Making of a Mind*, p. 242).

'It is the sacred need to know' that sustains the scientist and enables him to face danger (*The face of the earth*, 1921, in *The Vision of the Past*, p. 44).

In 1924, back from the Far East, Teilhard spoke of his conviction that 'without knowledge and research, there can today be no possibility of any human progress or real mystical life' (*Letters from a Traveller*, p. 119). In a letter dated 12 October 1926, quoted by C. Cuénot (*op. cit.*, p. 105), he goes so far as to say of research that 'it is a vital and sacred function—the source of all higher life and mysticism'. We find the same phrase in *La mystique de la science*, 1939, in *L'énergie humaine*, p. 219.

'For a long time past, research has been accepted by men as a secondary activity, an oddity, or a danger. The time has come, and is with us now, when we shall realize that it is the highest of all human functions—swallowing up in itself the spirit of war, and resplendent with the brilliance of all true religion. Constantly to exert pressure on the whole surface of the real—surely that is the outstanding manifestation of loyalty to being, and therefore of adoration?' (*L'esprit de la terre*, 1931, in *L'énergie humaine*, p. 47).

'Because some hidden instinct urges him on, and because long experience tells him so, man clings to this belief—that no fragment of truth is sterile; the most insignificant scientific discovery is an irreplaceable element without which man will never attain the full development of his consciousness, in other words the plenitude of his soul. The earth is a monstrous problem in which man is involved. He has flung himself into it. And who will dare to say that he has not emerged greater from this contact with the unknown?' 'In a very real sense, work that consists in developing, through knowledge, our awareness of the world, is linked, by making ready an object on which they can act, to the functions of the priesthood: to forward the progress, through its creative activity, of a universe, at the centre of which stands God.'

'That research is progressively entering more fully into human activity is neither whim, nor fashion, nor chance: it is simply and solely that man has now grown up, and feels an irresistible impulse to take over the evolution of life on earth, and that research is, in fact, the expression (at the reflective stage) of this evolutionary effort not only to subsist but to attain fuller being, not only to survive but, irreversibly, to attain super-life' (International conference of the Society of Jesus, 1947).

A year before his death Teilhard wrote, in connexion with the international geophysical year: 'As spiritual unification of man, it is still terribly superficial, but it is the first step, a finger at least, you might say, on the gear-lever of unification; and I am deeply moved by this great concerted movement in which for the first time in millions of years, a unanimous gesture—unanimous in orientation—will reach out to the ends of the earth: "Year I of the Noosphere" ' (Letter of 12 December 1954, in *Letters from a Traveller*, p. 346). Elsewhere Teilhard protests against 'the pettiness of spirit, poverty of means and general haphazardness with which we pursue truth in the world today' (*The Phenomenon of Man*, p. 278).

[105] *The phyletic structure of the human group*, in *The Appearance of Man*, p. 162.

[106] *La centrologie*, No. 17, *op. cit.*, p. 117.

[107] *The phyletic structure of the human group*, in *The Appearance of Man*, p. 162. Similarly, 'economics will soon count for very little in comparison with the ideological and emotional factors in the arrangement of the world' (*The Phenomenon of Man*, p. 306).

[108] *La montée de l'autre*, 1924, in *L'activation de l'énergie*, p. 76.

[109] *L'énergie humaine*, in *L'énergie humaine*, pp. 168-9. Teilhard is alive to the reckless squandering of the earth's resources; but he is counting, in fact, on a plan of rational exploitation, and also on the invention or discovery of new nutritional possibilities (*The singularities of the human species*, 1954, in *The Appearance of Man*, pp. 249-52). 'Concerted and methodical research' (*Man's place in nature*, 1932, in *Vision of the Past*, p. 179).

[110] *En regardant un cyclotron*, 1953, in *L'activation de l'énergie*, p. 370: 'The dividing line between laboratory and factory is disappearing.'

[111] *The Phenomenon of Man*, p. 248. Teilhard's views on the value and method of science are treated in Chapter 4 (Cosmology).

[112] *En regardant un cyclotron* . . . April 1935, *op. cit.*, p. 371. 'My guide went on talking about interacting fields. And all the time I could not help feeling and seeing beyond and around this imaginary electro-magnetic tornado, the concentric emission of another and no less formidable radiation: that of the human, swirling around me from the four corners of space. A whole range of knowledge and skills, and with it a whole spectrum of forces, converging on the spot where I stood, and running together into something specifically unique and alive with passion' (*Ibid.*, p. 369).

[113] *The Phenomenon of Man*, p. 249.

[114] *Ibid.*

[115] *The machine*

Man's Place in Nature, pp. 104–5. 'What has really let loose the machine in the world, and for good, is that it both facilitates and indefinitely multiplies our activities. Not only does it relieve us mechanically of a crushing weight of physical and mental labour, but by the miraculous enhancing of our senses, through its powers of enlargement, penetration and exact measurement, it constantly increases the scope and clarity of our perceptions. It fulfils the dream of all living creatures by satisfying our instinctive craving for *the maximum of consciousness* with a minimum of effort' (*Directions and conditions of the future*, in *The Future of Man*, pp. 229–30).

On being taken to see the cyclotron at Berkeley, Teilhard wrote: 'You really have the feeling in such a place of being out of your depth in this new human thing: in the complexity and power of one machine—mathematical speculation, laboratory research, the wide scope of industrial enterprises, military ambition, medical hopes of therapy—and even the secret hope of finding the ultimate explanation of things' (Letters of 28 July 1952, in *Letters from a Traveller*, p. 331).

Teilhard was very much alive to the problem of unemployment as a consequence of the leisure provided by the machine: he saw in it, however, a normal and transitory phenomenon, a symptom of the world's drift to a new and more interiorized order: 'As for leisure, mankind began to have leisure (or at least to be in a position to have it) from the first moment when its new-born mind emerged from immediate perception and action, to wander in the domain of what was distant or possible. Mankind never felt that it lacked employment, either in fact or because it was entitled to leisure, so long as much the greater proportion of men were still obliged to undertake work that absorbed most of their energies. Now, however, we see from numerous indications that unemployment is with us, and may well continue constantly to increase: for now the balance between material needs and productive capacity has definitely been upset, and, in theory at least, all we have to do is to put our hands in our pockets and let the machine that releases us from work run on.' The present crisis is 'the inevitable consequence of the loss of equilibrium introduced into animal life by the appearance of thought. Men are completely at a loss to know towards what universal and final goal they should direct the energy of their souls'.

(*Le christianisme dans le monde*, 1933, in *Science et Christ*, p. 134). 'Under the combined influence of the machine and the super-heating of thought, we are witnessing a formidable *upsurge of unused powers*. Modern man no longer knows what to do with the time and the potentialities he has unleashed. We groan under this burden of wealth. We are haunted by the fear of unemployment' (*The Phenomenon of Man*, p. 252). See also *The phyletic structure of the human group*, in *The Appearance of Man*, pp. 161–2.

The machine's introduction of leisure presents man with the difficult problem of distinguishing new valid goals. While the animal, being continually and fully occupied, is balanced and at ease, man is in danger of either 'running in neutral' or losing all sense of discipline. The present crisis is 'the inevitable result of the loss of equilibrium introduced into animal life by the appearance of thought. Men are completely at a loss to know towards what universal and final goal they should direct the energy of their souls' (*Le christianisme dans le monde*, 1933, in *Science et Christ*, p. 134).

It would be a mistake to be shocked by Teilhard's objective attitude to unemployment. The cool appraisal of the sociologist or philosopher of history does not, in itself, imply an insensitiveness to poverty.

[116] *Man's Place in Nature*, p. 111. *The phyletic structure of the human group*, in *The Appearance of Man*, p. 161.

[117] *The formation of the noosphere*, 1947, in *The Future of Man*, pp. 164–8. Human brains do not simply add up to a total; they form one continuous vault: 'The vision so produced goes beyond the individual, and cannot be exhausted by him . . . Our common technology is not simply the numerical total of commercial enterprises, a dead industrial weight, but the sum produced by processes that are combined reflectively with a view to maintaining in men the state of consciousness that corresponds to our state of aggregation and unity' (*Place de la technique dans une biologie générale de l'homme*, 1947, in *L'activation de l'énergie*, pp. 165–6).

Modern technology is not 'a sporadic and local type of technology; it is a real *geo-technology*, extending over the whole surface of the earth the closely interdependent network of its enterprises' (*The singularities of the human species*, 1954, in *The Appearance of Man*, p. 236).

[118] *Some reflections on the spiritual repercussions of the atom bomb*, 1946, in *The Future of Man*, p. 146.

[119] *The singularities of the human species*, 1954, in *The Appearance of Man*, p. 256. 'Indeed it is impossible habitually to keep one's eyes on the great horizons discovered by science without an obscure desire arising to see a growing knowledge and sympathy so linking men that, as a result of some divine attraction, there shall be only one heart and one soul on the face of the earth'. (*The face of the earth*, 1921, in *Vision of the Past*, p. 46).

'Structurally, each of these technical devices is, and cannot but be, the convergent result of countless disciplines and technical skills, so terrifyingly complicated that no single person working alone could ever master them. In design and manufacture these familiar objects presuppose nothing less than a *complex reflective organism*, acting, *per modum unius*, as a single subject. That means that it is not just man's work, but mankind's. Henceforth it is more impossible than it ever was before, for man to think alone. We have only to look at the range of modern concepts in science, philosophy and religion to see that each one of them, the more fruitful and generally applicable it is, the more it tends to assume the form of a collective entity: individually, we can indeed cover one aspect of it, absorb and develop one portion, but the whole concept rests in fact on a *vault of interlocking thoughts*' (*L'atomisme de l'esprit*, 1941, *op. cit.*, p. 44).

[120] *The Phenomenon of Man*, p. 282. *The human rebound of evolution and its consequences*, in *The Future of Man*, p. 197. *The Directions and conditions of the Future*, 1948, *ibid.*, pp. 232-6. *The singularities of the human species*, 1954, in *The Appearance of Man*, 254-5.

[121] *The Phenomenon of Man*, p. 250. *Le sens de l'espèce chez l'homme*, 1947, in *L'activation de l'énergie*.

[122] *Some reflections on the spiritual repercussions of the atom bomb*, 1946, in *The Future of Man*, p. 144. This article brings out the completely new character of atomic energy, compared with earlier inventions (pp. 142-4).

[123] *Ibid.*, p. 143.

[124] *Place de la technique dans une biologie générale de l'homme*, 1947, in *L'activation de l'énergie*, p. 167. In *La convergence de l'univers*, 1951 (*ibid.*, p. 307) Teilhard returns to the idea of the possible scientific measurement of mankind's 'psychic tension or temperature', its 'degree or gradient of reflection'.

[125] *The singularities of the human species*, in *The Appearance of Man*, p. 255–6. The close connexion Teilhard establishes between science and its applications is borne out by the present position in science: it holds good in every field, notably in economics, as is shown by H. Bartoli in his account of the work of François Perroux (*Revue économique*, No. 5, September 1961, pp. 818–19).

[126] *Barrière de la mort et co-réflexion*, 1955, in *L'activation de l'énergie*, p. 427.

[127] Cf. G. Fessard, *De l'actualité historique*, Desclée de Brouwer, 1960, Vol. 1, p. 166.

[128] 'Before man, practically the whole of vital energy was continually absorbed in the task of obtaining food, of reproduction and of morphological evolution. Like over-worked employees, animals were constantly overwhelmed by the enormous efforts they had to make. They had neither the time nor the interior capacity to look around and think. In man, on the other hand, as though a drill had bored down to some underlying stratum, a sudden gush of power came to the surface.'

[129] Teilhard notes the phenomenon of 'economic concentration' (*Some reflections on progress*, in *The Future of Man*, p. 69), but he does not develop his examination of the dialectic it introduces.

[130] At the same time Teilhard is not insensitive to human suffering: 'Never give up: try to attack it from another angle, the correct angle—where success is in proportion not to the development of the individual, but to constancy in the effort to make the world around oneself less harsh and more human' (Letter, 1934, in *Letters from a Traveller*, p. 265).

[131] Although Teilhard fully, and rightly, appreciated the value of thought, he did not make quite clear the insufficiency of the rational order (science and philosophy). He could have shown that it reveals a severance of the ego from itself in the subject-object relationship, that it is obliged to proceed by discontinuous abstraction and use signs as intermediaries, that it leads to an impersonal knowledge, and finally that it is tempted to question everything. At the same time he indicated very clearly the danger for life of individual reflexion.

[132] *Comment comprendre et utiliser l'art dans la ligne de l'énergie humaine*, 1939, in *Cahiers Pierre Teilhard de Chardin*, No. 3, pp. 101–3. Letter

of 29 March 1939, quoted by C. Cuénot, *op. cit.*, p. 275. *The Phenomenon of Man*, pp. 201-2.

Music and poetry 'do not lead us exclusively to pantheistic and pagan bursts of feeling. All they do is to arouse the soul *in a general way* to the search for the most beautiful and the greatest. They make it *sensitive* to the whole. They "cosmify" it, if you follow me, sometimes by causing it to lose itself in the lower nirvana, sometimes by causing it to unite itself ardently with the great effort towards the higher spheres' (Letter of 27 March 1916, in *Making of a Mind*, p. 97).

A letter written in 1917 (*Ibid.*, pp. 201-2) contains some apposite comments on poetic expression, which, according to Teilhard, is hampered rather than assisted by classical verse-forms.

Teilhard considers, too, whether art has a function in the progress of the world. 'The "true" undoubtedly grows with the passage of time: the "beautiful" must necessarily do the same if the world is organically integrated. But where, and how?' (Letter of 2 February 1953, in *Letters from a Traveller*, p. 337).

Finally, speaking of cave paintings: 'We can see in the artists of those distant ages a power of observation, a love of fantasy, and a joy in creation: flowers of a consciousness not merely reflecting on itself but rejoicing in so doing' (*The Phenomenon of Man*, p. 203).

[133] 'If even the most humble and most material of our foods is capable of deeply influencing our most spiritual faculties, what can be said of the infinitely more penetrating energies conveyed to us by the music of tones, of notes, of words, of ideas?' (*Le Milieu Divin*, p. 59). Teilhard then introduces the noble concept that the role of these higher values is to educate the soul of man to the vision of God. 'It can hardly be doubted that it is here below that we give ourselves the eyes and the heart which a final transfiguration will make the organs of a power of adoration, and of a capacity for beatification, particular to each individual man and woman among us' (*Ibid.*, p. 60).

[134] 'How can we account for that irresistible instinct which leads us towards unity whenever and in whatever direction our passions are stirred? A sense of the universe, a sense of the *all*, the nostalgia that seizes us when confronted by beauty, nature, music—these seem to be an expectation and awareness of a great presence. The "mystics" and their commentators apart, how has psychology been able so

consistently to ignore this fundamental vibration whose ring can be heard by every practised ear at the basis, or rather at the summit, of every great emotion? Resonance to the all—the keynote of pure poetry and pure religion' (*The Phenomenon of Man*, p. 266).

[135] Cf. Bergson's: 'Is not the world a work of art, incomparably richer than that of the greatest of artists?' (*Le possible et le réel*, in *La pensée et le mouvant*, p. 131).

[136] We should, however, note this stimulating passage: 'Thus, while the pursuit of an essential fulfilment of our nature concentrates us upon ourselves, and circumscribes and isolates us in individuation, every emotion we feel, *the more aesthetic* it is, the more it tends to break up our autonomy. The real constantly calls us back to an impassioned consciousness of a fuller development and a unity whose embrace is wider. It is in arousing this disquiet that the hallowed role of feeling is fulfilled' (*Le milieu mystique*, 1917, in *Ecrits du temps de la guerre*, p. 138). 'But happy above all is the man who has risen above superficial delight in the arts and the material appeal of the lower strata of life, and has heard real beings, one after another, and with one voice, answering him: "What you have seen going on, like a world, behind the song, behind the colour, behind the eyes in the face, is not in any of those things: it is a presence that fills all things"' (*Ibid.*, p. 139).

[137] Teilhard expresses the 'two basic assumptions' of *The Phenomenon of Man* as follows: 'The first is the primacy accorded to the psychic and to thought in the stuff of the universe, and the second is the "biological" value attributed to the social fact around us' (p. 30).

'Is there after all such a great difference from the point of view of the expansion of life between a vertebrate either spreading its wings or equipping them with feathers, and an aviator soaring on wings with which he has had the ingenuity to provide himself? In what way is the formidable and ineluctable play of the energies of the heart less physically real than the principle of universal attraction?' (*The Phenomenon of Man*, p. 222). 'The social phenomenon is the culmination and not the attenuation of the biological phenomenon' *Ibid.*, p. 223).

A science of sociology can exist only as an extension of physics and biology. Social groupings are 'the "hominized" extension of the same mechanism as that which produced the metazoa from isolated cells' (*La centrologie*, 1944, No. 26, in *L'activation de l'énergie*, p. 121 note).

'Since the older chromosomic heredity is now partnered by an "educational" extra-individual heredity, the preservation and accumulation of the "acquired" suddenly assumes an importance, in biogenesis, of the first order' (*Man's Place in Nature*, p. 87).

Teilhard recognizes three properties in the social sense, that give it a kinship with life: 'Of self-direction in arrangement (by invention); of additive transmission of the acquired (by education); and of convergence upon itself (by socialization and "planetization")' (*L'énergie d'évolution*, 1953, in *L'activation de l'énergie*, p. 384).

[138] As C. Cuénot points out (*Teilhard de Chardin*, in the series 'Ecrivains de toujours', Editions du Seuil, p. 41), it may well be that Teilhard's discovery of the vastness of China, with its countless types of humanity, widened his view of the world and introduced him to the idea of the collective.

In fact, as Teilhard shows in *Le coeur de la matière*, (p. 14, note) the notion of collective man came to him as early as 1917: and he points out that even if collective man cannot be directly seen as such, we can know him from the evidence of the effects he produces (*ibid.*) 'the "mega-man" with his psychic temperature and internal energy, becoming for me a magnitude just as evolutionarily real, and therefore just as biological, as a giant molecule of protein' (*Ibid.*, p. 13).

If collectivity has 'effects that are specifically proper to it', it is because the objects it creates presuppose 'a complex reflective organism, acting *per modum unius*, as a single subject' (*L'atomisme de l'esprit*, 1941, *op. cit.*, p. 44).

[139] 'In man, therefore, it is not simply an additional phylum branching off at the head of the primates. It is the world itself forcing its way into a physical domain hitherto closed, and falling back on itself for a new step forward. In man, fantastically enough, the whole of evolution rebounds on itself' (*The singularities of the human species*, 1954, in *The Appearance of Man*, p. 227).

[140] *La centrologie*, 1944, No. 16, in *L'activation de l'énergie*, p. 116. As early as 1917, Teilhard was writing, in *L'union créatrice* (*Écrits du temps de la guerre*, p. 193): 'Love does not simply set up an *external* relationship between beings, whose term would be no more than a mutual moral completion. Love is, in us, the conscious evidence of

the activity that creates us as it welds us together. It is a factor of *physical* organization and construction. Thus *social groupings*, for whose formation love is responsible, have a far higher reality than association for economic well-being or pleasure: collective units represent attempts, carried further and deeper according to circumstances, to cause the multitude of men to form themselves into a *physical unit* of a higher (more spiritual) order.'

141 'At our present level of evolution, we are still rudimentary sketches or fragments of persons looking for completion . . . Only the whole is finally and fully personal . . . We cannot become completely ourselves except by totalizing one another under Omega, in the universal' (*La centrologie*, No. 28, *op, cit.*, pp. 124–5).

142 'If charity has so far failed to reign in the world, is it not simply because it could not establish itself until the earth had first become conscious of its spiritual cohesion and convergence? If we are to be able to love one another, must we not first *move into another plane*? Everything, in short, hangs together and links up, provided we can detect, beneath the fever the world is now suffering from, evidence of the rising temperature of a sense of man' (*La montée de l'autre*, 1942, in *L'activation de l'énergie*, p. 81).

143 Letter of 14 July 1916, in *Making of a Mind*, p. 112.

144 *Esquisse d'un univers personnel*, 1936, in *L'énergie humaine*, pp. 79–80. *Le phénomène spirituel*, 1937, *ibid.*, pp. 129–31. *The grand option*, 1939, in *The Future of Man*, pp. 52–3. *The Phenomenon of Man*, p. 262. *Man's Place in Nature*, pp. 114–15.

First memorandum from Teilhard to Père August Valensin, 12 December 1919, in *Archives de Philosophie*, January–March 1961, note 16 (by Père de Lubac).

'True union does not stifle the elements nor lose them in one another: it super-differentiates them in oneness' (*L'esprit de la terre*, 1931, in *L'énergie humaine*, p. 52).

'True union (i.e. spiritual union, or union in synthesis) differentiates the elements it brings together. This is no paradox, but a law confirmed by the whole of experience. Are two beings who love one another ever more vividly conscious, each of their own self, than when they are utterly absorbed in one another?' (*Comment je crois*, unpublished, 1934).

'True union does not confuse the beings it brings together. On the contrary it differentiates them more fully: in other words, when it is acting on reflective particles, it ultra-personalises them. The whole is not the antipodes of the person, but its very pole' (*Sauvons l'humanité*, 1936, in *Science et Christ*, p. 178).

'It is the specific effect of love to strengthen the self-awareness of the beings it brings together' (*Introduction à la vie chrétienne*, unpublished, 1934).

On another occasion Teilhard distinguishes between 'unity through release of tension' which tends to obliterate difference in *identification*, and 'unity through tension' (ultra-differentiation), which tends to *unification*. (*Pour y voir clair: réflexions sur deux formes inverses d'esprit*, 1950, in *L'activation de l'énergie*, pp. 225–36). Cf. *Quelques remarques pour y voir clair sur l'essence du sentiment mystique*, unpublished, 1915.

[145] 'We may be reassured. The vast industrial and social system by which we are enveloped does not threaten to crush us, neither does it seek to rob us of our soul' (*The formation of the noosphere*, in *The Future of Man*, p. 183).

[146] *Esquisse d'un univers personnel*, 1946, in *L'énergie humaine*, p. 82.

[147] *L'énergie humaine*, 1937, in *L'énergie humaine*, p. 149. This vision of unity includes the unitary nucleus of spiritualized energy in the total mass of human energy (*Ibid.*, pp. 146–8).

The realization of unanimity of spirit is preceded and accompanied by a biological activity: this does not, as happens with animal species, bring divergence, but has the effect of at once diversifying and bringing together the human branches, and so allows them to react on one another 'either by sexual crossing or by moral and intellectual cross-fertilization' and produce many different types of combinations (*The natural human units*, 1939, in *The Vision of the Past*, pp. 201–3).

[148] *The Phenomenon of Man*, p. 239. *La centrologie*, 1944, No. 28, *op. cit.*, p. 124.

[149] 'It would be well to investigate every possible channel and see whether there may not, perhaps, be some physical or psychic means of detecting and measuring, at every moment (with a view to constructing a graph of it) the noosphere's degree of reflection (or what we might call its psychic temperature)' (*Un problème majeur pour l'anthropologie: y a-t-il, oui or non, chez l'homme, prolongation et transformation du processus biologique de l'évolution*, unpublished, 1951).

On another occasion Teilhard speaks of the 'perception—almost in terms of physical chemistry—of a certain extreme state attained in the thinking medium (as one might say uranium) by the stuff of the universe' *L'téoffe de l'univers*, 1953, in *L'activation de l'énergie*, p. 399).

[150] *The formation of the noosphere*, 1947, in *The Future of Man*, pp. 161-4. *The Phenomenon of Man*, pp. 178, 224-6. 'Transplanted by man into the thinking layer of the earth, heredity, without ceasing to be germinal (or chromosomatic) in the individual, finds itself, by its very life-centre, settled in a reflective organism, collective and permanent, in which phylogenesis merges with ontogenesis' (pp. 225-6). 'Here, as elsewhere in the universe, the whole shows itself to be greater than the simple sum of the elements of which it is formed. The human individual does not exhaust in himself the vital potentialities of his race' (*Ibid.*, p. 178). *Man's Place in Nature*, pp. 85-6, 91-2.

[151] After watching the victory parade at Strasbourg, on 9 December 1918, Teilhard noted: 'On such occasions, however little one consciously looks for it, one *feels* the reality of the extra-individual world, of the world which takes shape through a union of souls. The feelings you experience and that animate the crowd with one mind, are definitely of a higher order than those experienced in the private life of an individual. You would have to be blind not to see that such an expansion is possible for our individual souls, and what hopes it opens up for us' (*Making of a Mind*, p. 266).

'We need only recall those moments in time of war when, wrested out of ourselves by the force of a collective passion, we had a sense of rising to a higher level of human existence' (*A note on progress*, 1920, in *The Future of Man*, p. 21).

For Teilhard the social phenomenon, and in particular the present-day 'social wave', is much more than an accident or a juridical necessity: it belongs to the spiritual essence of history (*Comment je vois*, unpublished, 1948, No. 13).

[152] *Comradeship and friendship*
Teilhard was acutely alive to the part played by working-teams in bringing men together. 'I greatly enjoyed the contact that was established between such diverse elements; it was really natural and deep-rooted, and its sole basis was our common, dedicated, search for some small measure of truth. There's no doubt that the mind

has a far greater power of bringing people together than we can ever imagine. But if that power is to operate it must be under perfectly simple and natural conditions, and not under a cloak of formality and convention' (Letter of 4 December 1923, in *Letters from a Traveller*, p. 107). On the eve of setting out on one of his scientific expeditions (1927), he writes, 'There is only one contact charged with an irresistible centripetal and unifying force, and that is contact of the whole of man with the whole of man' (*Ibid.*, p. 139). He notes, too, that 'in isolation a man stops either thinking or advancing' (*Ibid.*, p. 74).

Esquisse d'un univers personnel, 1936, in *L'énergie humaine*, pp. 89–104. 'Great friendships,' being based on a common interest, 'are cemented in the pursuit of an ideal, in the defence of a cause, in the vicissitudes of scientific research. They develop not so much through the penetration of one by the other as through the advance of both together into a new world' (*Ibid.*, p. 98). 'Despite the egoistic crises which too often cause learned men to quarrel bitterly among themselves, nothing—and this is a fact—brings souls more closely together than a common pursuit (particularly a dangerous one!) of the same truth' (*The singularities of the human species*, 1954, in *The Appearance of Man*, p. 256). Speaking of the future tasks that the whole planet will have to share, Teilhard points out that 'these various actions . . . would after all only extend, on the scale of the phylum, the most humanizing moral quality we know: the team spirit' (*Ibid.*, p. 259). He shares Saint-Exupéry's belief that 'to be ardently intent upon a common object is inevitably the beginning of love' (*Spiritual repercussions of the atom bomb*, 1946, in *The Future of Man*, p. 147).

Nevertheless, there is an omission in Teilhard's enumeration of the forms of human relationship: it is that of the master-disciple, or of teaching, which is well analysed by Père Fessard in his *Autorité et bien commun* (Aubier, 1944, pp. 26–35), and by E. Levinas in *Totalité et infini* (The Hague, 1961). Teilhard did not go further than to bring out the importance of education.

[153] 'I can still hear Père Teilhard saying to me, with that keen, dreamy look in his eyes, after he had read my first story, 'Can an exclusively human love escape a selfishness shared by two?' (J. de Bourbon-Busset, *Les aveux infidèles*, Gallimard, 1962, p. 87).

[154] *Woman*

Without denying to woman the emancipation she is entitled to,

Teilhard sees in her a 'light-giving and idealisating' ('forgive that ghastly word' he adds) power, 'exercised by the mere act of being present, by just being quietly there', which 'sets her apart from the tumults and banalities of everyday activity' (Letter of 29 August 1916, in *Making of a Mind*, p. 121).

L'éternel féminin (1918, in *Ecrits du temps de la guerre*, pp. 253-7), is a poetical elaboration of the theme of *eros*. Love, which is a hidden energy immanent in the whole of the universe, an attractive force between material elements and between living beings, which is, in short, the soul of the world, presents itself to man as 'the attraction of the universal presence, and of the ceaseless ripple of its smile': [The reference is to κυμάτων ἀνήριθμον γέλασμα, Aesch. *Pr.* 90.] 'through me, he says, lies the road to the whole heart of creation; I am earth's gate—I am the initiation . . . He who takes me, gives himself to me, and is taken by the universe'. Love, however, has to bear the burden of sin in so far as man, instead of purifying it and heeding the call to rise to a higher plane, delights in the selfish idol of pleasure. Love then becomes material instead of divine, and wanders from reality. This essay begins with a phrase ('I am the eternal feminine') reminiscent of the famous verse from the book of Proverbs (8:23), 'the Lord created me at the beginning of his work': and this again suggests a kinship between Teilhard's thought and Claudel's. 'For me,' says Claudel, 'woman always stands for four things: the soul of man, the Church, our Blessed Lady, or divine wisdom' (*Mémoires improvisés*, Gallimard, p. 50). 'This figure of wisdom, this image of woman standing by the side of God at the beginning of the world and sharing in creation, plays a continually greater part in Claudel's work' (P. A. Lesort, *Paul Claudel par lui-même*, Editions du Seuil, 1963, p, 112).

'Woman stands before man as the appeal and symbol of the world. And because the world is ever greater and ever incomplete and ever lying ahead of us—man finds that if he is to possess her love he is committed to a limitless conquest of the world and of himself. In that sense man can obtain woman only in the consummation of the universe' (*Construire la terre*, unpublished). *L'esprit de la terre*, 1931, in *L'énergie humaine*, pp. 40-2: 'What makes its impact on man through woman is in truth, the universe. The whole problem —the vital problem for our planet—is that they shall recognize one another' (*Ibid.*, p. 42). Teilhard goes on to hope that 'man may see the universal reality that shines in spirit through the flesh. Then he will find what it is that had been frustrating and perverting his power to love' (*Ibid.*).

'Woman is, for man, the term that has the power to initiate forward progress. Through woman, and through woman alone, man can escape from the isolation in which his very perfection would be in danger of being imprisoned' (*Esquisse d'un univers personnel*, 1938, *ibid.*, pp. 93, 91–6). 'Love of the invisible aroused and nourished by the influence of the feminine.'

'And yet woman, for all that man needs her so much to reflect the world for him, is not the centre of the world' (*L'énergie humaine*, 1937, in *L'énergie humaine*, p. 186).

Teilhard's kinship with Blondel, again, comes out strikingly in the following comment: 'When two people come together as a couple they cannot, without emerging from themselves, maintain their balance except in a third who lies ahead of them. What name should we give to this mysterious "intruder"?' (*Esquisse d'un univers personnel*, in *L'énergie humaine*, p. 94). Unlike Blondel, however, Teilhard answers: 'Ultimately, it is the total centre itself, much more than the child, that seems essential to the consolidation of love. Love is an equation with *three* terms, man, woman, and God' (*Ibid.*, p. 95).

On this, see André-A. Devaux, *Le féminin selon Teilhard de Chardin*, in *La femme; nature et vocation* (*Recherches et debats du C.C.I.F.*, cahier No. 45, pp. 120–38, Fayard).

[155] *Le coeur de la matière*, unpublished, 1950.

[156] In the *Satin Slipper*, in particular, Prouhèze is, for Rodrigue, the impossible love that contributes, in a dialectic of passion and frustration, to the world of divine grace, as expressed in the Jesuit's prayer:

Already you have taught him desire, but as yet he cannot guess what is to be desired.

Teach him that you are not the only one who can be absent.

Bind him by the weight of this other being, so lovely and so far, who calls to him across the gulf.

Make of him a man whose wound is that once in this life he has seen the face of an angel.

Fill these lovers with such desire that, forgetting their wanderings in the contingence of everyday, it may embrace

The pristine oneness and the very essence in which God conceived them of old, in a contact that nothing can sever.

(*Théâtre*, Bibliothèque de la Pléiade, Gallimard, Vol. 2, p. 570).

[157] *Le mystère de l'histoire*, in *Recherches de science religieuse*, No. 2, 1948, pp. 182–225; *Esquisse du mystère de la société et de l'histoire*, 1960, in *L'actualité historique*, Desclée de Brouwer, Vol. 1, pp. 162–71.

[158] In *Le prêtre* (1918, in *Ecrits du temps de la guerre*, p. 297) Teilhard speaks of love's threefold dream: 'So to envelop oneself in the loved as to be overwhelmed in it: constantly to intensify the presence of the loved; to lose oneself in the loved and yet never to be sated.'

[159] *Le Milieu Divin*, p. 74. Cf. *Le coeur de la matière*, p. 28.

[160] There still remains the problem of Teilhard's attitude to *pity*. He seems, surprisingly, to have had such respect for the great imperatives of the historical future that he had little room for pity. Nevertheless, the moral ambiguity of this feeling has often been pointed out. Teilhard's attitude may be accounted for also by his reaction against certain individualistic forms of Christian charity: his own vocation was to call for a profound change in social structures from which mankind as a whole would benefit. In his dread of any narrowness or restriction in view or action, he constantly urged that charity should be universal. His personal attitude shows clearly enough the interest he took in individual cases. While that is true, it is still regrettable that Teilhard's system did not include sufficiently clearly the direct and all-embracing concern we should have for the manifold forms of human misery.

[161] 'Since I left Marseilles, my strongest impression is that the world is something even vaster and more formidably complicated than I imagined. True enough, a journey to the Far East does indeed represent a sort of "temptation of the multiple". How can we hope for the unification, in spirit and heart, of these fragments of mankind that cover every stage between barbarism and forms of neo-civilization themselves hardly reconcilable with our views as Christians?' (Letter of 23 May 1923).

[162] *The difficulty of loving*

L'esprit de la terre, 1931, in *L'énergie humaine*, p. 43. 'It is impossible sincerely to love everyone. The heart of each of us is full when it is given to one other. Therefore, if we set out to love the human mass, we are false to ourselves; or rather we deceive ourselves. We are making an effort against nature' (*Basis and foundations of the idea of evolution*, 1926, in *Vision of the Past*, p. 138).

'I confess, my God, that I have long been, and even now am, recalcitrant to the love of my neighbour . . . But "the other man", my God,—by which I do not mean "the poor, the halt, the crippled and the sick", but "the other" quite simply as "other", the one who seems to exist independently of me because his universe seems closed to mine, and who seems to shatter the unity and the silence of the world for me—would I be sincere if I did not confess that my instinctive reaction is to rebuff him? And that the mere thought of entering into spiritual communion with him disgusts me?' (*Le Milieu Divin*, p. 145). The tone of that passage is oddly reminiscent of some of J. P. Sartre's analyses. Only those who preserve the illusion of man's innate goodness will be shocked by what Teilhard reveals of himself or notes of others. The last chapter of *The Two Sources* has a more realistic clarity.

Love of others comes up against serious difficulties, 'harder to overcome than inertia; a sort of veil, or barrier, seems to grow up around our persons at the very moment when they take form. You have all experienced . . . the sort of repugnance we feel at having to come out of ourselves to give ourselves to another. It is as though our being, supple and flexible though it is, were enveloped, as soon as it appeared, in this insulating skin which makes it shrink from any intimacy of contact with others, and gives it a sort of feeling of revulsion from others (Second lecture to the Marcel Légaut group, 27 November 1930).

'Left to their own reactions (and apart from sexual forces) men would generally be more sensitive to mutual repulsion than attraction. To be more fully themselves, they seek prematurely to be alone' (*Esquisse d'un univers personnel, ibid.*, p. 81). 'It is not intersympathy, surely, but mutual repulsion that predominates within the human mass. Apart from some exceptional cases, "the other" appears as the greatest threat we meet on the road our personality follows as it develops. The other who impedes us, and must be rebuffed' (*Ibid.*, p. 97).

'The strange fact is that, in spite of the strength of these energies bringing men together, thinking units do not seem capable of falling within their radius of internal attraction. Leaving aside individual cases, where sexual forces or some extraordinary and transitory passion come into play, men are hostile or at least closed to one another. Like a powder whose particles, however compressed, refuse to enter into molecular contact, deep down men exclude and repel one another with all their might' (*The Phenomenon of Man*, p. 256). 'The fundamental obstacle to charity is the multitude.'

Teilhard admits, too, that 'despite the compressive and unifying conditions to which we are subject, mankind is still made up of terribly heterogeneous parts, unequally matured' (*The essence of the democratic idea*, 1948, *The Future of Man*, p. 243).

[163] Letter of 1 January 1917, in *Making of a Mind*, p. 160. The same idea will be found in *The Phenomenon of Man*, pp. 229-32. Already, however, Teilhard is introducing Christianity as the spiritual force that will be able to 'neutralize the risks of deviation inherent in the thought of our independence', and Christ as the safeguard against the temptation to fall back and disintegrate. For his part, Bergson considers static religion as 'a defensive reaction of nature against what might be depressing for the individual, and dissolvent for society, in the exercise of intelligence' (*The Two Sources*, p. 175).

[164] *Le sens de l'espèce chez l'homme*, 1949, in *L'activation de l'énergie*, p. 208. Teilhard explains this by urging that one should encourage 'the development of the affective energies, which are basically productive of union (a sublimated sense of sex and a generalized sense of man).'

[165] 'As a result of the effects of *foresight*, which are inseparable from reflexion, a disconcerting barrier, the barrier of death, rises ahead of us: it seems to restrict and discourage our hopes and therefore the impetus of emergent self-evolution' (*Barrière de la mort et co-réflexion*, 1955, in *L'activation de l'énergie*, p. 419).

'As the attraction of the future gradually replaces for us the simple effort to survive, we are all coming to appreciate the ever-increasing importance that is being assumed in our personal ideas and affections by the unrealized, the unexpected, the *ideal*'. At the collective level, Teilhard then goes on to speak of 'the still vague (but infinitely more developed than in neolithic times) conscious-ness that "something" awaits us in the depths of time to come. No longer is there simply the sting of death to be avoided (as we see in animal species): now there is the passionate desire to surpass oneself and reach a peak glimpsed through the clouds' (*L'énergie d'évolution*, 1953, in *L'activation de l'énergie*, pp. 387-8). 'In man, by harnessing forces that stem from the future, this general process of activation of living matter has entered a critical phase, characterized by an increasing predominance of the effects of fear or hope allied to the formidable gift of foresight' (*Ibid.*, p. 386).

166 *L'activation de l'énergie humaine*, 1953, in *L'activation de l'énergie*, p. 413. *L'énergie d'évolution*, 1953, *ibid.* Even though it is a waste of time to try to form an imaginary picture of the end of history, it is nevertheless essential to determine 'what conditions, governing the application of energy, mankind must in all cases and by every necessity satisfy if it is to continue its progress and at some time arrive at (if such a thing exists) the natural term of its development' (*L'énergie d'évolution, ibid.*, p. 389). The problem of thermodynamic supplies for man and his ever more voracious machines will no doubt be solved without difficulty: the real problem will be 'to discover how man can maintain and increase, with no check, throughout these vast periods of time, a passionate will not only to subsist, but to press on: without that will every physical or chemical force we dispose of will remain contemptibly idle in our hands' (*Ibid.*, p. 391).

167 *La réflexion de l'énergie*, 1952, in *L'activation de l'énergie*, p. 350

168 'Mankind was sleeping—it is still sleeping—imprisoned in the narrow joys of its little closed loves. A tremendous spiritual power is slumbering in the depths of our multitude, and it will awake only when we have learnt to *break down the barriers* of our egoisms, and, by a fundamental recasting of our outlook, raise ourselves up to the habitual and practical vision of universal realities' (*Le Milieu Divin*, p. 146).

169 *Une philosophie de contre-évolution en biologie humaine, ou la peur de l'existence*, 1949, in *L'activation de l'énergie*, p. 201.

170 *Transformations et prolongements en l'homme du mécanisme de l'évolution, ibid.*, p. 319.

171 *L'énergie d'évolution, ibid.*, p. 393.

172 'In what direction may we expect this further evolution of love to be realized? It will lead, without doubt, to a gradual decrease in what still, necessarily, constitutes the admirable but impermanent reproductive side of the sexual relationship. Life propagates itself not simply for the sake of doing so, but only in order to accumulate the elements necessary for its personalization. When, therefore, the earth approaches the maturity of its personality, men will have to

recognize that their problem is not simply the control of the birth-rate; the really important thing will be to allow full development to the quantity of love released from the duty of reproduction. Under the pressure of this new need, the essentially personalizing function of love will be more or less completely detached from what has hitherto had to serve as the instrument of propagation; in other words from "the flesh". Without ceasing to be physical—indeed in order to remain physical—love will become more spiritual. The sexual will be absorbed, for man, by the pure feminine. Is not that the very reality enshrined in the dream of chastity?' (*Esquisse d'un univers personnel*, 1936, in *L'activation de l'énergie*, p. 96).

Following up this line of thought, Père S. de Lestapis has em-phasized the urgency of the challenge presented to mankind by the normal growth of population; in 600 years time, with an average yearly increase of 1.6%, there will be one inhabitant to every square yard. This challenge can be met only by the practice of continence in marriage, inspired by the virtue of chastity, and controlled by an appreciation of the optimum population-level required for the common good (*Défi démographique et avenir de l'humanité*, in *Revue de l'Action Populaire*, April 1962, pp. 389–403).

[173] *Le coeur de la matière*, unpublished, 1950.

[174] Letter of 11 November 1934.

[175] *Le coeur de la matière*, unpublished, 1950. 'With the appearance of man, the activation of the energy required to maintain and forward evolution is effected by the stimulation of a centre of attraction lying continually higher and further ahead in time. This means that it gradually assumes the characteristics and dimensions of a faith.' (*Ibid.*).

[176] *Le sens de l'espèce chez l'homme*, 1949, in *L'activation de l'énergie*, p. 210.

[177] *On the probable coming of a Ultra-Humanity*, 1950, in *The Future of Man*. 'A purely conjectural Omega (deduced simply by "calcula-tion") would be far too precarious to maintain in the heart of man sufficient enthusiasm to impel him to carry his hominization to its limit' (*Un sommaire de ma perspective phénoménologique du monde*, un-published, 1954).

We have only to transpose this proof of God, which is concerned with the future of history, into a consideration of the condition *here and now* of the communion of persons, to reconcile Teilhard's thought on this point with existential personalism. The latter, though less receptive of a demonstration of God that starts with the world, is more so to a demonstration that unfolds the goal of co-consciousness. In this case, God is seen as the concrete *bond* in the reciprocity of persons, the ultimate intention of their mutual gift, the foundation and grace of their recognition of one another and of their dialogue.

[178] *Esquisse d'un univers personnel*, 1937, in *L'énergie humaine*, pp. 112-14. Madame M. Barthélemy-Madaule well brings out both the distinction between the three aspects under which Teilhard considers the person, and their unity: the speculative aspect of synthesis between universal and personal, the concrete aspect of political and social currents, and the religious and Christic aspect.

[179] *Esquisse d'un univers personnel*, 1936, in *L'énergie humaine*, p. 90.
'Love is, by definition, the word we use to designate attractions that are personal in nature. Since, in a universe that has reached the stage of thought, everything ultimately moves in and towards the person, it must necessarily be love, a sort of love, that forms, and will continue to form more and more exclusively, the stuff of human energy in its pure state' (*L'énergie humaine*, 1937, in *L'énergie humaine*, p. 181).

'Love has always been eliminated from realist and positivist concepts of the world: but sooner or later we shall have to acknowledge that it is the fundamental impulse of life, or, if you prefer, the one natural medium in which the rising course of evolution can proceed (*The grand option*, 1939, in *The Future of Man*, p. 54).

'Essentially, love is simply the specific energy of cosmogenesis' (*La centrologie*, 1944, No. 29, *op. cit.*, p. 126).

'For many years science has accustomed us to the idea that every physical energy, if we follow it evolutively "downwards", tends to be dissipated in heat in a world in which there is neither tension nor life. It is a remarkable thing, but we arrive at a concept that exactly fits in with and complements this, if we carry an integral energetics of the universe to its limit, towards a cosmic pole of unification, with every passion (and even every vision) displaying a singular "tendency" *to transform itself* into love. This means that love, which at first seemed to be no more than the appeal or the attraction and later the operative essence of all spiritual activity tends gradually to become, as experienced by us, its principal part;

and finally to emerge as the one unique and supreme form of that activity' (*Le coeur de la matière*, unpublished, 1950, p. 28).

'Thus,' says C. Cuénot (*op. cit.*, p. 132) 'in a very roundabout way Teilhard arrives, with Dante, at the concept expressed in the celebrated line that ends the last canto of the *Paradiso*: "L'Amor che move il sole e l'altre stelle." "Love, that moves the sun and the other stars." '

[180] *Life and the planets*, 1945, in *The Future of Man*, p. 119. 'Held in check by statistical necessity, a formidable affinity still lies dormant in the human mass' (*L'atomisme de l'esprit*, 1941, in *L'activation de l'énergie*, p. 54).

Although it is possible (though by no means certain) that cerebralization cannot be taken very much further, at the same time, in the field of collective organization, which we have hardly as yet started upon, 'our physical and spiritual future is almost limitless' (*The question of fossil man*, 1943, in *The Appearance of Man*, p. 125).

[181] *The Phenomenon of Man*, p. 265. There is a similar comment in *Du cosmos à la cosmogénèse*, 1951 (in *L'activation de l'énergie*, p. 274). From the coincidence of totality and personality, 'when it comes about, there will result in the near future the greatest of all phenomena: the life-sap that nourishes all things will pour into one single heart: the world will be cherished by man as something as precious or even more precious than a person, and, for the first time on earth, a love will be born as all-embracing and as mighty as the universe' (*L'énergie humaine*, 1937, in *L'énergie humaine*, p. 197).

[182] 'A world that is in a process of conscious concentration, should, you imagine, be an uniquely happy world. You would be very mistaken. It is precisely such a world that must, the most necessarily and naturally, suffer. Nothing brings greater bliss than the achievement of union, but nothing is more painful than the road to it. There are three reasons at least why a personalising evolution is necessarily painful: it is founded on plurality; it advances through differentiation; and it leads to transformations' (*Esquisse d'un univers personnel*, 1936, in *L'énergie humaine*, p. 105). Teilhard then proceeds to elaborate on those three reasons.

[183] *Social heredity and progress*, 1937, in *The Future of Man*, p. 35 (a remarkable article). In Teilhard's view, education is intimately connected with biological reality, which it extends, and the very seeds of which it permeates. As the new mould in which man is

formed, and as the storehouse of racial memory, it is of even more importance than the biological action of heredity (*The formation of the noosphere*, 1947, in *The Future of Man*, pp. 161-4). Teilhard urges his cousin to allow herself to be 'possessed by the "philosophic" and heavenly grandeur of even elementary teaching . . . It is your vocation, or at least your occupation, to mould the spirit, so far as you can, for eternal life: there are few more effective ways of collaborating for the fullness of Christ than cultivating the souls of children' (Letter of 20 November 1918, in *Making of a Mind*, p. 257).

[184] *The singularities of the human species*, 1954, in *The Appearance of Man*, p. 242.

[185] *Autorité et bien commun*, Aubier, 1943, pp. 26-35.

[186] *Racialism*

After condemning modern individualism, Teilhard adds: 'Less theoretical and less extreme, but all the more insidious, is another doctrine of "progress by isolation", which at this very moment is making a strong appeal to large sections of mankind: the doctrine of the selection and election of races. Flattering to collective egoism, which is keener, nobler and more sensitive than individual personal pride, racialism has the advantage in its attitude of accepting and extending, strictly as they are found, the lines in the tree of life' (*The Phenomenon of Man*, p. 238). 'Also false and against nature is the racialist ideal of one branch draining off for itself alone all the sap of the tree, and rising over the death of other branches. To reach the sun nothing less is required than the combined growth of the entire foliage'(*Ibid.*, p. 244).

As a biologist, Teilhard refused 'crudely to transfer the mechanical laws of selection into the field of man', and held that 'brotherly rivalry should take the place within men of hostile competition' (*The natural units of humanity*, 1939, in *The Vision of the Past*, p. 213).

Even so, it is surprising that Teilhard should have believed in racial inequality and the advantages of European colonialism. After a short stay in India, he wrote: 'As individuals, Indians are charming, but taken as a whole the country seems to be just as incapable of self-government as China or Malaya. Unfortunately, dislike of the English is general among the "natives". They want complete independence at all costs, even if it means death to the country. The English allow them as much rope as they can, but they don't let go: and I imagine they're quite right. The more I get around abroad, the more I fear that Geneva (of which I am in my heart a great supporter), numbers of liberal Catholics, and especially my "Missiologue" colleagues, are making a grave mistake in recognizing the equality of races in the face of all the biological evidence. "Universalism" is not democracy (=egalitarianism)' (Letter of 21 January 1936, in *Letters from a Traveller*, pp. 219–20).

In 1935 Teilhard was chary of condemning Italy's attitude to Abyssinia: 'It's clear that we must tend towards a moral and bio-logical organization of the earth: but what should be the attitudes of human groups in relation to one another, seeing that their social values and capabilities differ so greatly? . . . The more I see of the East, the more I distrust the demagogue in international matters' (Letter of 14 September 1935, *ibid.*, p. 209). In the article on racialism quoted above, Teilhard speaks both of their inequality and at the same time of their complementary character (pp. 212–4).

[187] *Fascism*

'These peaceful occupations (my studies) are not completely pre-venting me from watching, like everyone else, the strange develop-ments both in Europe and the Far East. I detest all forms of nationalism, and their apparently retrogressive tendencies. But I am keenly interested in the primacy they are restoring to the collective. Does the passion for "the race" perhaps represent a first step towards a sense of the earth?' (Unpublished letter to Père Auguste Valensin, 28 December 1933).

'Fascism opens its arms to the future. Its ambition is to embrace vast wholes in its empire. And, in the solid organization it dreams of, more care is given than you find anywhere else to maintaining and making good use of the élite (by which I mean an élite of mind and of personal quality). *Within the field it seeks to cover*, what it sets up, accordingly, satisfies more fully perhaps than any other system the conditions we have recognized as fundamental for the city of the future. The only regrettable thing—and it is a very important one— is that the field it is concerned with is ridiculously restricted . . . Fascism quite possibly represents a pretty successful blueprint for the world of tomorrow. It may even be a necessary phase during which men have to learn their business as men, on the reduced scale of the training ground' (*Sauvons l'humanité*, 1937, in *Science et Christ*, pp. 181–2). The limitations of Teilhard's outlook and the in-adequacy of his criticism cannot be disguised. Cf. J. M. Domenach, *Le personnalisme de Teilhard de Chardin*, in *Esprit*, March 1953, pp. 352–5).

While that remains true, Teilhard appreciated the conditions that governed the struggle against both fascism and communism: 'It seems to me essential that the Christian attitude should be at last presented in the form of an organized *Weltanschauung, that makes sense with* the modern world. How, otherwise, can one match the force of communist or fascist solutions to the problems of the earth? Our medieval galleys will never outgun their battleships' (unpublished letter to Père August Valensin, 25 May 1938).

Similarly, Teilhard is not taken in by the materialism of totalitarian mystiques: 'All their worship of material progress and race as an entity to be preserved will never produce freedom: they are inevitably absorbed and assimilated by the forces of determinism they build up. They become mechanized by their own mechanical institutions. And the only way now left for them to control the working elements of human energy is to use brute force—the force that, logically enough, they are now beginning again to try and make us worship' (*Sauvons l'humanité*, 1937, in *Cahiers Pierre Teilhard de Chardin*, No. 1, p. 26).

Teilhard puts it even more forcibly when he says of communism and national socialism that they are the 'most ghastly fetters' (*The Phenomenon of Man*, p. 257).

Finally, one should beware of misunderstanding Teilhard's language, for his *dialectic* is sometimes obscured by the very vigour of statements that represent only one of its aspects. Thus the article on the convergence of mystical systems quoted—and criticized, indeed—above (*Universalisation et union*, 1942) contains the following comment: 'Indeed, the quest for the universal, which can guide unerringly our progress toward union and automatically keep us on the right lines, has in addition the mysterious virtue of itself directly operating this union' (*op. cit.*, p. 100). There seems no doubt that the three adverbs, unerringly, automatically, directly, stress the 'inevitability' of the final victory of union only through an equally inevitable conjunction with the *freedom* of the media involved. When Teilhard affirms his faith in the power of spirit, he certainly has no intention—any more than Hegel had, let alone

Marx—of excluding the action of man, the rejection of error and the fight for truth.

[188] *Universalisation et union*, 1942, in *L'activation de l'énergie*, p. 100. 'I shall have occasion later to refer again to this torment of personality, and to discover what conditions the socialization of the world must satisfy if it is to save, and not kill, the human cell. The important point to note here is that if union does indeed super-personalize, then the collective entities whose birth and growth so alarm us *are being formed in the direction foreseen for evolution*. They are the first indications or primitive form of a higher spirituality and therefore of a higher freedom. This great mass is in full process of transformation and it is still impossible to distinguish within it what is a monstrous distortion, what is a definitive characteristic, and what is a transitory stage. One thing, however, is certain: for all our fears, it is in the direction of "wholes" that we must press on' (*Esquisse d'un univers personnel*, 1936, in *L'énergie humaine*, p. 81). 'Both in speculative theory and in practice, once they are taken to their extreme development *upwards*, all opposition disappears between a democracy, a communism, an axis-ism (and, I may add, a Christianity) that are *universalized* '(*Universalisation et union*, 1942, in *L'activation de l'énergie*, p. 100).

[189] Although there is some obscurity in Pope John's allusion, we may relate Teilhard's optimism to what the Pope said in *Pacem in terris*: 'The teachings, once they are drawn up and defined, remain always the same, while the movements, working on historical situations in constant evolution, cannot but be influenced by these latter, and cannot, therefore, avoid being subject to changes even of a profound nature. Besides, who can deny that these movements, in so far as they conform to the dictates of right reason and are interpretations of the lawful aspirations of the human person, contain elements that are positive and deserving of approval.' (C.T.S. translation, p. 58.)

[190] Cf. Pierre Fruchon, *Création ou consentement* (Aubier, 1963). In contrast with the reversal of values, maintained by Nietzsche, whose final effect is one of domination, the author shows that the whole of ethics is based on mutual agreement between persons.

[191] *Sauvons l'humanité*, 1937, in *Science et Christ*, p. 180.

[192] *Ibid.*

[193] *The essence of the democratic idea*, 1948, in *The Future of Man*, pp.

238-43. Also, *Some reflections on the rights of man*, 1947, *ibid.*, pp.
193-5. Teilhard quotes, too, in support of his view, a remark in the
New Yorker: 'The only conceivable way to catch up with atomic
energy is with political energy directed to a universal structure'
(*Spiritual repercussions of the atom bomb*, 1946, in *The Future of Man*,
p. 141). In 1938 he expressed the fear that 'the democracies are
dying for lack of constructive faith' (Letter of 25 May 1938).

[194] Cf. *Démocratie aujourd'hui*, *Action populaire*, Spes, 1963. *La Société
democratique*, 50th semaine sociale de France (Chronique sociale,
1964). Teilhard would certainly have agreed with Etienne Borne
when he wrote: 'Liberalism's opportunity, that nothing can stand
out against, lies in the progress of culture, without which there can
be no modern humanity or modern state; for to advance in the
sciences and liberal arts is to learn the critical spirit and objective
analysis; it enables intellectual groups or families to intercom-
municate; it breaks down the barriers of the contingent and brings
out the universality of the true' (*L'épreuve du libéralisme*, in *Le Monde*,
18 October 1963). It would, accordingly, be inaccurate and one-
sided to say of Teilhard's thought that it failed to recognize the
'slow influence of philosophy and politics' or that it 'short-circuits
mysticism and science' (J. M. Domenach, *Dieu et la dialectique*, in
Esprit, March, 1964). No doubt Teilhard's analysis of such influences, and in particular that of politics, was not always carried as
far as it might have been; however, the whole of this study brings
out the attention he gave to every aspect of man's condition. God
is attained only at the term of a journey.

[195] *The essence of the democratic idea*, *op. cit.*, p. 243. Cf. A. Jeannière,
Utopies du mondialisme politique (*Revue de l'Action populaire*, December
1963, p. 1157), and Eric Weil, *Philosophie politique* (Vrin, 1956,
pp. 225-61). There is an obvious kinship between these views and
those expressed in *Pacem in terris*.

[196] These dangers are explicitly recognized, particularly in *Esquisse
d'un univers personnel*, 1936, in *L'énergie humaine*, pp. 99-100: 'If there
is one universal heart-sickness in the world today, surely it is that of
the human person stifled by the collective monstrosities that a
remorseless demand to live forces us to surround ourselves with?
Huge towns, a vast industrial system, with economic organizations
on the same scale—these are heartless, faceless, Molochs. I feel as
much as anyone the gravity for mankind of the present moment—

and I feel less capable than anyone of saying what is going to happen tomorrow.' Here again, Teilhard's sensitiveness to the various aspects of socialization is in perfect agreement with the views of John XXIII in *Mater et Magistra* (c. 59–67).

[197] A passage quoted earlier shows how diametrically opposed Teilhard was to any reactionary social views: 'Morality and religion (and the whole social order, too) can no longer be regarded by us as static: *we need, to appeal to us and to save us, a dynamic*' (*Le christianisme dans le monde*, 1933). And even though Teilhard may not have distinguished sufficiently the terms 'total' and 'universal', it is abundantly clear that the society of persons which he urges and foretells excludes totalitarianism as altogether horrible.

[198] It is thus that advances in scientific research and invention produce, *from within*, and 'automatically', an ethic which is a necessary condition of their being made (*The human rebound of evolution*, in *The Future of Man*, pp. 204–6). Cf. the passages quoted by H. de Lubac, *op. cit.*, p. 109-10.

[199] Cf. *Le devoir* (Alcan, 1932), *Obstacle et valeur* (Aubier, 1935).

[200] 'However spiritualized we suppose its elements to be, every aggregate of consciousness, so long as it is not harmonized, envelops itself automatically (at its own level) with a veil of "neo-matter", superimposed upon all other forms of matter—matter, the "tangential" aspect of every living mass in course of unification' (*The Phenomenon of Man*, p. 256).

[201] *L'esprit de la terre*, 1931, in *L'énergie humaine*, p. 35.

[202] 'Morality is born very largely as an empirical defence put up by the individual and society. As soon as intelligent beings began to find that there was contact, and therefore friction, between them, they felt that they had to protect themselves against mutual encroachment. And as soon as an organization was found by experience to guarantee almost everyone what was due to him, then the system itself, they realized, had to be guaranteed against any changes that might be a challenge to the solutions already adopted, and so upset the established order of society. Hitherto morality has been chiefly conceived as a fixed system of rights and duties, designed to establish a static equilibrium between individuals, and concerned with *maintaining* it by a limitation of energies, in other words of force . . . This concept is completely revolutionized if one realizes that man exists on this earth only as an element destined

to a cosmic ascent within a growing higher consciousness . . . The loftiest morality is then seen to be the one that is the most capable of developing the phenomenon of nature to its higher limits. It is not a matter of preserving—but of developing the individual riches of the earth, by arousing them and leading them to converge upon one another' (*Le phénomène spirituel*, 1937, in *L'énergie humaine*, pp. 131–2).

Here Teilhard comes close to Bergson (*The Two Sources of Morality and Religion*) in the concept of static and closed morality as represented in the city; he parts company with Bergson by attributing the further development of this morality to the progress of modern consciousness, and so including it in his general theory, instead of relating it directly to Christianity.

[203] Speaking of transformism as a school of morality, Teilhard puts it as follows:

'Such a man would see in the first place the greatness of his responsibilities increasing almost to infinity before him. Hitherto he could think of himself in nature as a bird of passage, local, accidental, free to waste the spark of life that is given him, with no loss to anyone but himself. Suddenly he finds in his heart the fearful task of conserving, increasing and transmitting the fortunes of a whole world. His life, in a true sense, has ceased to be private to him. Body and soul, he is the product of a huge creative work with which the totality of things has collaborated from the beginning; if he refuses the task assigned to him, some part of that effort will be lost for ever and lacking throughout the whole future . . . When every man admits that his real being is not confined within the narrow limits of his own limbs and his own existence in history, then he will understand that, in order to remain faithful to himself he must devote himself to the task demanded of him by life as to a personal and sacred duty' (*Basis and foundations of the idea of evolution*, 1926, in *Vision of the Past*, pp. 137, 140–1).

[204] 'To determine man's choice, in his famous wager, Pascal loaded the dice with the lure of boundless gain. Here, when one of the alternatives is weighted with logic and, in a sense, with the promise of a whole world, can we still speak of a simple game of chance? Have we the right to hesitate? The world is too big a concern for that. To bring us into being it has from the beginning juggled miraculously with too many improbabilities for there to be any risk whatever in committing ourselves further and following it right to

the end. If it undertook the task, it is because it can finish it, following the same methods and with the same infallibility with which it began' (*The Phenomenon of Man*, pp. 233-4).

[205] *Le Christianisme dans le monde*, 1933, in *Science et Christ*, p. 132. 'Since the fundamental energy operative in the universe is simply a current of personalization, the whole mass of relations that we call moral, by which the thinking molecules react upon one another, ceases to constitute an artificial or secondary domain within nature . . .'(*Esquisse d'un univers personnel*, 1936, in *L'énergie humaine*, p. 90).

'Since man and in man (to the extent that he ultra-hominizes himself by collective cerebration) the mechanism of *ortho-selection* tends increasingly to give place to the effects of *ortho-election* in the expansion and accentuation of the life-phenomenon on the surface of the earth. *Since man and in man, simple evolution tends gradually to mutate into auto- (or self-) evolution (Human orthogenesis*, 1951, in *Vision of the Past*, p. 254).

[206] *Esquisse d'un univers personnel*, 1936, in *L'énergie humaine*, p. 90.

[207] *L'esprit de la terre*, 1931, *ibid.*, p. 36.

[208] *Basis and foundations of the idea of evolution*, 1926, in *Vision of the Past*, p. 137.

[209] Second lecture to the Marcel Légaut group, 27 November 1930.

[210] *Esquisse d'un univers personnel*, 1936, in *L'énergie humaine*, p. 79.

[211] *La morale peut-elle se passer de soubassements métaphysiques avoués ou inavoués?* (Unpublished, 1935).

[212] 'What name, still in the light of our system, should we give to this physico-moral energy of personalization to which all the activities exercised by the stuff of the universe can ultimately be reduced? Only one name will do, provided we give it the full scope and power that it must assume when it rises to the order of the cosmic—love' (*Esquisse d'un univers personnel*, 1936, in *L'énergie humaine*, p. 90).

'Love in all its subtleties, is nothing more and nothing less, than the more or less direct trace marked on the heart of the element by the physical convergence of the universe upon itself' (*The Phenomenon of Man*, p. 265).

[213] Second lecture to the Marcel Légaut group, 27 November 1930. 'It is possible to speak of morality in terms of physics. All these things that seem to us so juridical, so external to us, so much imposed from outside, are in fact lines of action that are

probably governed by some profound structure of things' (*Ibid.*).

'The man who thinks to stake the whole world on his own existence, and to stake his own existence on the moment, is bound to live every minute with extraordinary intensity. But if we look at it we can see that this brilliance, besides being pitifully limited in scope, is radically destructive of the spirit in which it springs to light . . . It robs the individual of the ineffable joys of conscious union and loss of self in that which is greater than self: the element burns up all its future in a flying spark . . . Here we part company with the whole-hearted indivividualists, the egoists who seek to grow by excluding or diminishing their fellows, individually, nationally or racially. Life moves towards unification. Our hope can only be realized if it finds its expression in greater cohesion and greater human solidarity' (*The grand option*, 1939, and *Some reflections on progress*, 1941, in *The Future of Man*, pp. 51, 72).

In thus placing selfishness at the root of sin, Teilhard agrees not only with the New Testament but also (unwittingly) with his contemporary, the philosopher Jean Nabert: the latter, particularly in his *Essai sur le mal* (P.U.F., 1955, pp. 90–112), rightly sees 'secession of consciousness' underlying all forms of evil.

[214] *A dynamic morality*
L'esprit de la terre, 1931, in *L'énergie humaine*, p. 46.

'At this very moment we are quite rightly beginning to realize what a *national effort* can be. Even so, now that mankind is adult, it must, if it is not to drift into destruction, educate itself up to the idea of an effort that is specifically and comprehensively *human*. For a long time it has been content to let itself live, but one day it will understand that the time has come when it must take charge of its own development and clear its own road' (*La grande monade*, 1918, in *Ecrits du temps de la guerre*, p. 243).

Some months later, on his return from the war, Teilhard was writing: '*We are still a long way from having released all our energies* . . . Another cause must emerge to exercise, *permanently and for good*, the activating force, the force of attraction and cohesion that the war exercised on us, *momentarily and as an answer so evil*. What was aroused in us for the time being by having to defend what was so dear and sacred to us—the knowledge, that is, that we were all collaborating together in a task as vast as the world—must now be produced again, never to fade, by the pursuit of a positive ideal' (*Terre promise*, 1919, *ibid.*, p. 393).

'Explain to men the greatness of the current of which they are part. Make them feel the immense weight of committed efforts for which they are responsible. Compel them to see themselves as conscious elements in the complete mass of beings, inheritors of a labour as old as the world, and charged with transmitting the accumulated capital to all those who are to come. Then, at the same time, you will have overcome their tendency to inertia and disorder, and shown them what they perhaps worshipped without giving it a name' (*Hominization*, 1923, in *Vision of the Past*, p. 77).

Juridical morality originated in a system of rights and duties designed for the protection of the individual, the defence of society and the reconciliation of conflicting forces: in future it must be supplanted by a morality of movement, defined by the following principles: 'Only that is ultimately good which assists the growth of spirit on earth. And *all* is good (at least fundamentally and in some degree) that brings about some spiritual growth of the earth. And that is ultimately *the best*, which ensures the development of the earth's spiritual energies . . . To try everything, and to push everything as far as possible in the direction of fuller consciousness, such, in a universe that we can see to be in a state of spiritual transformation, is the general and supreme law of morality: *to be sparing of strength*—unless it be thereby to acquire still greater strength—*that is what sin is*' (*Le phénomène spirituel*, 1937, in *L'énergie humaine*, pp. 131–5)

'Only one road lies open to us: to entrust ourselves to the infallibility and the infinitely beatifying power of the operation that embraces us. In us, the world's evolution towards spirit is becoming conscious . . . the basic need has now become to use our reason to ensure the progress of the world of which we form a part. How then—not simply, as it used to be, for our own petty individual selves, families and countries—not even for the whole earth—but for the salvation and success of the very universe—how, we must ask, are we men of today best to organize around us the maintenance, distribution, and advancement of human energy?' (*L'énergie humaine*, 1937, in *L'énergie humaine*, p. 156).

'Brotherly emulation must take the place of hostile competition within us, and war has no more sense except in relation to dangers or conquests outside humanity. Development of each one in sympathy with all. Graduated organization of spiritual energies in place of the mechanical balance of material forces. Law of teamwork replacing the law of the jungle' (*The natural units of humanity*, 1939, in *Vision of the Past*, p. 213).

'In matters of love or money or liberty, of politics, economics or society, we not only find our main line of conduct and criteria of choice laid down for us ("ever higher in convergence"), but furthermore our instinct for research and creation ("to consummate the universe in ourselves") discovers endless justification and sustenance. In short, everything makes sense, everything glows with life; and the flow of human sap rises to the very heart of the Christian faith' (*Turmoil or genesis?* 1947, in *The Future of Man*, p. 226).

'Tomorrow's engineers,' says Teilhard, 'will have to solve a whole series of unexpected problems, relating both to the optimum growth and utilization and the nourishment and preservation of the psychic forces of evolution'. Already, 'despite its incredible smallness in terms of "ergs" or calories', this spiritual energy 'begins to play an increasingly decisive role in the progress of the world' (*Human orthogenesis*, 1951, in *Vision of the Past*, pp. 254-5).

[215] *A note on progress*, 1920, in *The Future of Man*, p. 19.

[216] *L'énergie humaine*, 1937, in *L'énergie humaine*, p. 158. Cf. *Le Milieu Divin*, p. 154. 'We must try everything for Christ.' 'Under pain of sin, we must try every road' (Letter of 4 August 1916, in *Making of a Mind*, p. 116).

[217] *L'énergie humaine*, 1937, in *L'énergie humaine*, pp. 165-74. It is interesting to see Teilhard asking himself this question: 'Should not man's concern for his individual neighbour be balanced by a higher passion, born of faith in this other, higher, personality that, as we shall see, may be anticipated from the success on earth of our evolution? How far should the development of the strong (provided, of course, that one can define that accurately) take precedence over the preservation of the weak? In what exactly does true charity consist?'

In *The Phenomenon of Man*, (1939, in *Vision of the Past*) Teilhard lays down the main headings of a programme of human energetics: maintenance and increase in the vital tension of the human mass, unification of personalities, unification of mankind (pp. 172ff.).

[218] *The Phenomenon of Man*, p. 253.

[219] *La convergence de l'univers*, 1951, in *L'activation de l'énergie*, p. 305.

[220] *The Phenomenon of Man*, p. 233.

[221] 'When, therefore, a man suffers grief, or is sick, or dies, not one of us who witness it can say whether he grows less in his being or grows greater. For *under exactly the same outward appearances* the two diametrically opposed principles draw their adherents to them: *towards simplicity or multiplicity:* God and nothingness (*La lutte contre la multitude*, 1917, in *Ecrits du temps de la guerre*, p. 131).

'Now, invested as you are, Jesus, with the redoubtable power of selection which places you at the summit of the world as the principle of universal attraction and universal repulsion . . .' (*Le Milieu Divin*, p. 149).

[222] *Le prêtre*, 1918, in *Ecrits du temps de la guerre*, p. 300: *Le Milieu Divin*, p. 146.

[223] M. Blondel, *L'action* (conclusion): also, *Lettres philosophiques de Maurice Blondel*, Aubier, 1961, *passim*.

[224] Teilhard was already during the first war well aware of the importance of environment: 'Instead of working directly on souls, it would often be better to concentrate on transforming their environment, that is on gaining acceptance for, or bringing to the man in the street, certain points of view, certain ideological currents, that would win over and lead to God all who shared them, without there being any necessity to bring any external or other pressure on them' (Letter of 6 November 1916, in *Making of a Mind*, p. 142).

[225] The reader should not be misled by the comparatively limited importance attributed here to religion. As has been pointed out, the whole of Teilhard's thought is inspired by it, and his plan of action is apostolic. Until we come to deal with his theology and spirituality it will suffice simply to make it clear that the existential journey must necessarily culminate in the religious 'value', and that Teilhard's anthropology is completed by a mysticism.

[226] *L'atomisme de l'esprit*, in *L'activation de l'énergie*, p. 60.

[227] Cf. Pierre Fruchon, *Création ou consentement* (Aubier 1963).

[228] *L'esprit de la terre*, 1931, in *L'énergie humaine*, pp. 52-7. 'In a first phase—before man—the attraction (of unity) was vitally, but blindly, felt by the world. Since man it has become conscious, at least partially, in reflective freedom, and it is that which stimulates religion. Religion, which is not a strictly individual crisis, or choice, or intuition—but which represents the long unfolding of God's

being through the collective experience of the whole of mankind. God reflecting himself personally on the organized whole of thinking monads, and so guaranteeing a sure outcome, and laying down precise laws, for their hesitant activities. God, leaning over the mirror which is the earth, now endowed with intelligence, and imprinting on it the first outline of his beauty' (*Ibid.*, pp. 56–7).

'I believe that a properly conducted study of mankind would make it possible to bring out, almost scientifically, this truth—familiar though it is, it needs to be restated—that belief in some God is an almost physical factor in the correct adjustment and the progress of the human layer, of the noosphere . . . such a study would, I am sure, reveal interesting natural bases paving the way to Revelation and the Incarnation' (Letter of 3 December 1936).

[229] 'Religion, so often contemptuously relegated to metaphysics, has in fact the function of providing, in its turn, a basis for morality by providing the restless and undisciplined multitude of reflective atoms with a governing principle of order and a clearly marked line of advance. It gives them something supreme to create, to fear or to love. Religion then ceases to take the shape primarily of some sort of lazy way out, providing a screen against the insoluble or embarrassing difficulties the spirit comes up against as it develops. In its true essence, it is the counterpart biologically (one might almost say mechanically) required by the release of the earth's spiritual energy: man's being, by its appearance in nature, entails the revelation ahead of it of a divine pole to give it balance just as necessarily as, in the particular world explored by physics, the positive and negative elements of matter are linked together.'

'As soon as there is a lag between release of conscious energy and intensification of the sense of religion, disorder is introduced—and this is all the more dangerous now that mankind has come of age. Is this not precisely what we are now witnessing? . . . Material energy is not circulating with sufficient freedom because it cannot find a spirit strong enough to organize and harness its mass; and spirit is not strong enough to resist continual dissipation in restless disorder' (*Le christianisme dans le monde*, 1933, in *Science et Christ*, pp. 132–3).

[230] *Ibid.*

[231] Letter (1937).

[232] 'I feel, too, how much the exploration of the earth *in itself* fails to shed any light or point out any solution to the most fundamental questions of life. I feel as though I am going round and round an immense problem without getting to the heart of it. And I know, too, that the wider the problem seems to grow before my eyes, the more clearly I see that its solution can only be sought in a "faith" beyond appearances: never perhaps more than now has this veil seemed to me so "without seam"' (Letter of 11 May 1923, in *Letters from a Traveller*, p. 70).

'My life is now possessed by this indifference which I feel to be growing on me, while at the same time the deep-seated appetite that calls me to all that is real at the heart of the real, continues to grow stronger' (Letter of 30 October 1929, *ibid.*, p. 160).

While acknowledging his good fortune in having landed up, in India and Java, in 'two of the hottest sectors of the prehistory front', he adds 'fundamentally it gives me only moderate satisfaction. As a purpose in life, my science (to which I owe so much) seems to me to be less and less worthwhile. For a long time now, my chief interest in life has lain in some sort of effort towards a plainer disclosing of God in the world. It's a more killing task, but I see it's my only true vocation' (Letter of 21 January 1926, *ibid.*, pp. 218–19).

[233] 'If research is the very law of being advancing towards ever greater consciousness, we must find, in us and around us, in the world, something that justifies this effort ... If the world is to be able to maintain its effort of reflective research, it must preserve the results progressively obtained by that research. Otherwise, we are mere dupes, and, rightly enough, lose all desire to progress further' (*Observations sur la signification et les conditions biologiques de la recherche*, unpublished, 1939).

[234] *The Phenomenon of Man*, pp. 283–5. Always provided man extends his hope to its very limit, 'there is less difference than people think between research and adoration' (*Ibid.*, p. 250).

'I am aware of having striven, always and in everything, to attain the absolute. I would never, I believe, have had the courage to carry on for the sake of any other objective. Science (and that means every form of human activity) and religion have always, in my view, been one and the same thing—both being, for me, the pursuit of one and the same object' (*Mon univers*, 1918, in *Ecrits du temps de la guerre*, p. 270).

Teilhard ends his reflections on visiting the cyclotron at Berkeley as follows: 'The more I tried to extrapolate the course of the vast physico-psychic spiral in which history had caught me up, the more it seemed to me that what we still over-simply call "research" became charged with, or tinted by, or warmed by, certain powers (faith, adoration) hitherto regarded as alien to science. For the more closely I looked at this research, the more I saw that it was forced, by some internal necessity, ultimately to concentrate its effort and its hopes in the direction of some divine centre' (*En regardant un cyclotron*, April 1953, *op. cit.*, pp. 376–7).

[235] *Human unanimization*, 1940, in *The Future of Man*, p. 287. 'A veritable ego at the summit of the world for the consummation, without confounding them, of all the elemental *egos* of the earth' (*Ibid.*).

It is here that Teilhard conflicts with the concept of atheistic existentialism, particularly as found in Sartre: the fact that he is observed by a divine witness does not overwhelm man, for it is the observation of a loving and intimate Presence, who can transfigure contingence by an invitation to share in an infinite existence. Similarly the mutual relationship, impregnated with the spirit of love, between one consciousness and another rises above both their severance and their antagonism and allows them to recognize one another in communion.

[236] *Esquisse d'un univers personnel*, 1936, in *L'énergie humaine*, pp. 94, 95.
[237] *The Phenomenon of Man*, pp. 232–4.
[238] Letter of 9 September 1923, in *Letters from a Traveller*, p. 87. Earlier, in 1918, Teilhard spoke of mysticism as 'the science of sciences which is also the supreme art and the supreme work' (*Making of a Mind*, p. 268).

Leaving aside the question of mystical experience in Teilhard's own life, we may well ask what precise meaning he attaches to the word *mysticism*. It seems, for Teilhard, to coincide with the experience of God, but *in so far as* this experience strives to attain its extreme limit, to go beyond any still individual determinacy, and so arrive at a vision of one-ness, and coincide, in one unique act, with the universe (a universe itself filled with the divine presence of Christ: a universe which is a sign of God, and which God shines through).

Unlike mystical systems inspired by or in the tradition of,

Platonism, Teilhard's is characterized by its close relationship to the world and to activity exercized on the world, and also by the position it attributes to the person of *Jesus*. These two points are brought out with special clarity in an excellent essay, *Le milieu mystique* in *Ecrits du temps de la guerre*, 1917, pp. 137–67).

In this Teilhard describes the three stages of the spiritual ascent: the sense of the omnipresence of God in the consistence and energy of the world; the transition, through the activity and struggle that transforms the universe; and finally the access to the higher passivity of love. It is a dialectic whose successive stages overlap: although the mystic never ceases to be 'a great realist', he gradually ascends to the consciousness of a transcendent charity that descends from on high, to kindle all things in its flame.

[239] 'There must be some way, without leaving the field of experience, of recognizing around us, in the personalized zones of the universe, some psychic effect (radiation or attraction) that is specifically linked with God's operation, and that therefore provides positive proof of his existence. The definitive discovery of the spiritual phenomenon is tied up with the analysis—some day to be at length attempted by science—of the "mystical phenomenon", in other words of God's love' (*Le phénomène spirituel*, 1937, in *L'énergie humaine*, p. 139).

[240] Teilhard defines mysticism, in the widest term, as follows: 'In itself, the mystical emotion is a sense of, and a presentiment of, the total and final unity of the world beyond its present, sensibly experienced, multiplicity: a cosmic sense of "oneness" (Teilhard uses the English word). This holds good for the Hindu or the Sufi, just as it does for the Christian; and it allows us to measure the "mystical import" of a written document or a person's life' (*Quelques remarques pour y voir clair sur l'essence du sentiment mystique*, unpublished, 1951).

[241] *Comment je crois*, unpublished, 1934. Cf. *L'esprit de la terre*, 1931, in *L'énergie humaine*, p. 54. Here Teilhard was speaking from experience, as he does in his vivid war-time essays (*Christ in the World of Matter*, in *Hymn of the Universe*, pp.42–55, *Le milieu mystique*, *L'union créatrice*, etc.), which he elaborated shortly afterwards in *The spiritual power of matter* and *The Mass on the World* (in *Hymn of the Universe*, pp. 59-71 and pp. 19–37). Cf. M. Barthélemy-Madaule, *op. cit.*, pp. 485–91.

[242] *The basis and foundations of the idea of evolution*, 1926 in *Vision of the Past*, p. 132). A couple of sentences earlier we find: 'Science is certainly not going to discover a new God: all it is doing is to show us the matter that serves as a ladder leading up to God.' Speaking of his own continual travels, Teilhard asks on another cocasion: 'Are there any real journeys other than those that enable us not merely to go from one place to another in the universe but to enter a different sphere in it?'

'I am a little too absorbed by science to be able to philosophize much; but the more I look into myself the more I find myself possessed by the conviction that it is only the science of Christ running through all things, that is the true mystical science, that really matters. I let myself get caught up again in the game when I geologize' (Letter of 23 August 1923, in *Letters from a Traveller*, p. 86. Cf. Letter of 15 October 1923, *ibid.*, p. 91).

[243] The hierarchy of values is stressed in this sentence from *Le milieu mystique* (*Ecrits du temps de la guerre*, 1917, quoted in *Hymn of the Universe*, p. 86): 'But happy above all he who, rising above aesthetic dilettantism and the materialism of the lower layers of life . . .' Cf. 'Has not the moment passed when God spoke in the desert, and must we not now understand that "He who is" is not to be heard in this place or in that, for the heights where He dwells are not an inacessible mountain but a more profound sphere of things? The secret of the world lies wherever we can discern the transparency of the universe' (Letter of 15 April 1923, in *Letters from a Traveller*, p. 66).

[244] 'The world is building itself up . . . We may compare it not to a cluster of artificially juxtaposed elements but rather to an organized system, animated by a far-reaching growth-movement that is proper to it. In the course of the centuries an over-all plan is unmistakably being realized around us. Something is going on in the universe, some end-product is emerging, which we can best compare to a gestation or a birth: the birth of spiritual reality, which is produced by souls and by the material element they contain. Painfully and under the influence of human activity, the new earth is gathering itself together, emerging and shaking off its impurities. We cannot say that we are like flowers made up into a bunch: we are like the leaves or blossom of a huge tree, on which everything appears at its own proper time and place, as and when the whole

needs it . . . All those who suffer on earth uniting their sufferings in order that the pain of the world may become one vast, single, act of consciousness, sublimation and union—surely that is one of the loftiest ways in which we can look on the mysterious work of creation?' (*La signification et la valeur constructrices de la souffrance*, 1933, in *L'énergie humaine*, pp. 61-2. Cf. *Esquisse d'un univers personnel*.)

[245] The following passage, which expresses Teilhard's delight in the final vision suggested to him by the cyclotron at Berkeley, could be given a wider application: 'As a direct consequence of its vastness, and *therefore of its sureness*, the movement I could distinguish was allaying the terror of my mind. The vaster the cyclone, the less danger was there that the grain of sand that represented me would be lost in the universe. What I had been reading in existential literature for the last twenty years was a delusion: it is only an all-embracing view of evolution—and not an ever more isolated introspection of individual by individual—that can shield twentieth-century man from the terror he feels when he looks at life. Once again this was brought home to me by my own experience' (*En regardant un cyclotron*, 1953, in *L'activation de l'énergie*, p. 376). It should, however, be noted that Teilhard gives us here a somewhat over-simplified view of existentialism.

[246] Père Malevez considers that Teilhard's method is not phenomenological—using the word in the sense of existential—in that it overlooks the problems of interiority, and the drama of personal existence and puts forward 'no reduction or ascesis that allows the spirit to retrieve and discover itself' (L. Malevez, *La méthode du Père Teilhard de Chardin et la phénoménologie*, in *Nouvelle revue théologique*, June 1957, p. 592). This statement is based on a study of *The Phenomenon of Man* alone: even so the *Phenomenon* does refer to the conditions for man's existential fulfilment, in particular science and love (pp. 248-53), and also to the temptations of freedom (pp. 254-7).

CHAPTER 6: THEOLOGY

[1] 'Given a certain development of science, then a certain way of representing God and certain forms of adoration are ruled out, as

not being *homogeneous* with the dimensions of the universe known to our experience. This notion of homogeneity is certainly of capital importance in intellectual, moral and mystical life. If the various stages of our interior life do not form a strictly logical sequence, even so they must agree in scale, in nature and general tone. Otherwise, it would be impossible to build up any real spiritual unity within ourselves—and that is perhaps the most justified, most imperative and most categorical requirement for the man of today, the men we live among.' Teilhard then goes on to enumerate the modifications science has introduced into our concept of the universe (the total organicity of the world, the atomicity of its elements, the function of arrangement or unification) and adds, 'Metaphysics has over-emphasized the idea of abstract being, physically indeterminate. Science, on the other hand, using certain exact "parameters", defines for us the nature and the requirements, that is to say the physical stuff, of participated being. It is these parameters that, in future, every concept of Creation, Incarnation, Redemption and salvation, must respect—as, indeed, must every "demonstration" of the existence of God' (Letter to Emmanuel Mounier, for the Chatenay conference, 1 and 2 November 1947, in *Science et Christ*, pp. 291–3).

[2] Letter of 11 May 1923, in *Letters from a Traveller*, pp. 70–1. Speaking from a pragmatic angle, Teilhard says also 'If there is one thing we must cling to, it is indeed to this evident conclusion, this, the most reasonable of all postulates: that we must put our trust in being' (Second lecture to the Marcel Légaut group, 27 November 1930).

Teilhard writes, while making a retreat, to Père Auguste Valensin: 'And then, above, all, the appetite for being, and an overwhelming faith in being, have been preserved in me. For me, that is the whole of life' (28 December 1933).

In *Quelques réflexions sur la conversion du monde* (unpublished 1936) Teilhard speaks of an initial intellectual stage, preliminary to theology and mysticism: 'A correct physics and metaphysics of evolution . . . following the line of the "philosophia perennis": the primacy of being, act and potency.'

'The sub-division of what one may call "the human spiritual categories" begins logically with faith in being, and proceeds to faith in the further progress of the material world around us, that is to say, in the most fundamental terms, faith in the spiritual value of matter' (*The grand option*, 1939, in *The Future of Man*, p. 45).

³ 'Does the idea of being, in the universal human language, imply *any* kind of survival? Or rather does not the word signify (identically, and in every case) *to be for ever* and to *emerge completely*?' (*The singularities of the human species*, 1954, in *The Appearance of Man*, p. 263).

⁴ 'Either life is moving to no term that gathers up and consummates its work: and then the world is absurd, self-destroying, condemned by the first reflective glance which it has attained at the cost of immense efforts; and then revolt is with us again, no longer as a temptation but *as a duty*. Or else something (someone) exists, in which each element gradually finds, by reunion with the whole, the completion of all the saveable elements that have been formed in its individuality; and then it is worth while bending and even devoting oneself to labour; but with an effort that takes the form of adoration' (*Hominization*, 1923, in *Vision of the Past*, p. 78). 'If we study its most profound features, those of liberty, humanity seems certainly to have reached the stage of its evolution in which it cannot from any view-point face the problems presented to it by the growth of its inner energy without defining for itself a centre of love and adoration' (*The natural units of humanity*, 1939, in *Vision of the Past*, p. 215). 'In a world with three infinities we must, to save the *whole* phenomenon, introduce terms and values of action. *Since it has become human*, the world cannot continue to advance towards greater complexity and consciousness except by making an ever more explicit place for the spiritual forces of expectation and hope, that is to say for religion' (*Man's place in the Universe*, 1942, in *Vision of the Past*, p. 232).

⁵ 'What structural properties must the real possess, if this movement of the will is to be produced?' (*Comment je crois*, unpublished, 1934).

⁶ 'Consistence: that, without any doubt has, for me, always been the fundamental attribute of being' (*Le coeur de la matière*, unpublished, 1950). 'God is not a person of *the same order* as ourselves. He is a "super-person" a "hyper-centre", and that means someone deeper than ourselves.' 'At all costs (and because it is essential to the cosmos) we must preserve the primordial transcendence: for, if he had not pre-emerged from the world, how could God constitute for the world a way out and a consummation in the future?'

(*Du cosmos à la cosmogénèse*, 1951, in *L'activation de l'énergie*, p. 271).

In *Comment je vois* (unpublished, 1948), *Le coeur de la matière* (unpublished, 1950), and *Le Christique* (unpublished, 1955) Teilhard treats Omega as a conjecture, no more than postulated. This seems to indicate a withdrawal from the categorical assertions of *The Phenomenon of Man*. What he no doubt means is that rational knowledge of Omega does not, in itself, imply a religious possessing or spiritual communion. The affirmation of Omega remains a valid rational act, a movement of the whole man, who gives his assent to an absolute fact, as he discloses the sign under which it appears, involved in the movement of history.

[7] 'The laborious, personalising, unification in God, of a dust-cloud of souls, distinct from God and yet dependent from him' (*Introduction au Christianisme*, unpublished, 1944).

The same explanation appears in another form: 'In order to explain the presence, in and around us, of a field of physical energy sufficiently powerful to draw into itself the entirety of the human mass, it was not enough to adduce the collective pressure of myriads of elements driven in the same direction by the need to survive. In order to create the flood that, with increasing intensity and probably for hundreds of centuries still to come, is to draw us simultaneously upwards and forwards, one thing is demanded as a dynamic necessity: the pole of death, the pole that repels (or the negative pole) must be coupled with another, the positive pole or pole of attraction, of a super-life that is still to be attained: a pole that is capable of stimulating and satisfying continually more fully the two demands that characterize a reflective activity—the need for irreversibility and the need for total unity' (*En regardant un cyclotron*, April, 1953, in *L'activation de l'énergie*, p. 376).

Cf. Mgr. Bruno de Solages, *Les preuves teilhardiennes de Dieu*, in *L'homme devant Dieu*, Mélanges offerts au Père de Lubac, *op. cit.*, pp. 125–32. 'The two proofs to be found in their most developed form in the writings of Pere Teilhard are proofs from finality. They seek to demonstrate that the immense evolution of the universe would not make sense if it were not able to culminate in something whose character was definitive, but were fated to come to a complete dead-end' (*Ibid.*, p. 131). He adds that these proofs from finality provide the classic formulations with a 'notably wider basis'.

[8] *Comment je vois*, unpublished, 1948. If the summit of the world is to be real, it must be regarded as 'having emerged from all time into the absolute, since everything rests, with no other support, upon the absolute' (*Essai sur la personne*, unpublished, n.d.).

The following passage, though it does not deny God's efficient causality, bases itself (as we shall see) on a *psychological situation* of modern consciousness, and comes down more decidedly on the side of a proof of God from the convergent finality of history: 'While the creator (the efficient cause), in the case of a static world, remains, whatever one may say, *structurally* detached from his work and in consequence with no definable basis to his immanence, in the case of a world that is by nature evolving the opposite is true: God can then be conceived (both structurally and dynamically) only in so far as (like some sort of "formal" cause) he coincides, though without being confused with, the centre of the convergence of cosmogenesis.' 'If this were not so,' Teilhard adds, 'it would be towards some other "God" that our power to love would gravitate.' 'Since Aristotle men have almost continually been constructing "models" of God on the lines of an extrinsic prime mover, acting *a retro*. Since the emergence in our consciousness, of the "sense of evolution", it has been no longer physically possible for us to conceive, or adore, anything but a God who is an organic prime mover *ab ante* . . . only a God who is functionally and totally Omega can henceforth satisfy us' (*Le Dieu de l'Evolution*, unpublished, 1953).

It will be noted that Teilhard retains the essential idea of the 'prime mover', which is the affirmation of God as creator, but identifies it with the idea of God as the end of history and creation.

While the notion of creation must be *purified* from the contamination of imagery (in particular from a comparison with an initial 'flick', with a causality of the second order), it may be that here Teilhard overlooked the permanent value (outside his system) of the general notion of the creative act, situated in eternity, which confers finite existence upon beings (*ex nihilo* = beings not existing by right, who, being created, 'begin' an existence in time). It still remains to determine whether Teilhard's choice is better suited to modern mentality: he evidently believed that it is.

[9] Charity is not 'merely a secondary effect added as an extra to the creative process, but the operative factor and fundamental dynamic force' (*Introduction au Christianisme*, unpublished, 1944).

[10] Letter of 11 May 1923, in *Letters from a Traveller*, p. 70; *Comment je crois*, unpublished, 1934.

[11] Letter of 13 June 1936, in *Letters from a Traveller*, p. 226. 'Complete liberty is not only conceded but offered by the phenomenon to theology, so that it may add precision and depth to the findings and suggestions—always ambiguous beyond a certain point—furnished by experience' (*The Phenomenon of Man*, p. 313).

[12] 'Vast and innumerable as the dazzling surge of creatures that are sustained and super-animated by his ocean (God) nevertheless retains the concrete transcendence that allows him to bring back the elements of the world, without the least confusion, within his triumphant and personal unity' (*Le Milieu Divin*, p. 113).

'Pantheism attracts us by its vistas of perfect universal union. But ultimately, if it were true, it would give us only fusion and unconsciousness; for, at the end of the evolution it claims to reveal, the elements of the world vanish in the God they create or by whom they are absorbed. Our God, on the contrary, pushes to its furthest possible limit the differentiation among the creatures he concentrates within himself. At the peak of their adherence to him, the elect also discover in him the consummation of their individual fulfilment. Christianity alone, therefore, saves, with the rights of thought, the essential aspiration of all mysticism: *to be united* (that is, to become the other) *while remaining oneself*' (*Ibid.*, p. 116).

'. . . in the case of a *converging universe* such as I have delineated, how can we fail to see that, far from being born from the fusion and confusion of the elemental centres it assembles, the universal centre of unification (precisely to fulfil its motive, collective and stabilising function) must be conceived as pre-existing and transcendent. A very real "pantheism" if you like (in the etymological meaning of the word) but an absolutely legitimate pantheism—for if, in the last resort, the reflective centres of the world are effectively "one with God", this state is obtained not by identification (God becoming all) but by the differentiating and communicating action of love (God *all in everyone*). And that is essentially orthodox and Christian' (*The Phenomenon of Man*, pp. 309-10).

'We must, of course, maintain in the first place and at all costs—this is a matter of cosmic necessity—the primordial transcendence of this new *evolutive God*, who emerges from the very heart of the old worker-God; for, if he had not pre-emerged from the world, how could he serve the world as a way out and a consummation lying ahead of it?' (*Du cosmos à la cosmogénèse*, in *L'activation de l'énergie*, p. 271).

Similarly, Teilhard would frequently base the transcendence of God on personality's belonging to itself. 'The definitive peak of the fulfilled (that is to say the personalized world—and that means God) cannot possibly be conceived as being born from a sort of aggregation of elemental personalities (since these cannot, by nature, be de-centred). If a universe, made up of personal elements, is to be super-animated without being destroyed, it must itself be some special centre' (*L'esprit de la terre*, 1931, in *L'énergie humaine*, p. 56).

[13] *Le coeur de la matière*, unpublished, 1950, p. 32. 'God, who is eternal being-in-itself is, one might say, everywhere in process of formation for us' (*Christ in the world of matter*, 1916, in *Hymn of the Universe*, p. 54). '. . . the wonderful properties of this divine milieu which is all around us (and which is nevertheless beyond and underlying everything . . .)' (*Le Milieu Divin*, p. 47).

[14] This *logic* may be seen, in particular, in the following passage: 'By constructional necessity, when all is said and done, the personalization of the universe can be effected only by preserving for all time within a supreme person the sum total—distinct from it—of the "persons" produced in succession during its evolution. God can be defined only as a *centre of centres*. It is in this complexity that the perfection of his unity lies—the only culmination that can logically be attributed to the developments of spirit-matter' (*Esquisse d'un univers personnel*, 1936, in *L'énergie humaine*, pp. 85-6). To this Teilhard is at pains to add, some pages later, that the absolute term is 'outside the series' and 'finds its own consistence in itself'. 'Everything rises up in it towards a centre of immanence, but from it everything descends too, as though from a centre of transcendence' (p. 88).

[15] 'In virtue of their structure, the two points (the critical point of human maturity and the Parousia point) inevitably coincide, in the sense that the fulfilment of hominization through ultra-reflection appears as a necessary (though not sufficient) preliminary condition of its "divinization"' (*Comment je vois*, unpublished, 1948, No. 24).

'Unless it is to be powerless to form the keystone of the noosphere,

Omega can only be conceived as the *meeting-point* between a universe that has reached the limit of centration, and another, even deeper, centre—this being the self-subsistent centre and absolutely final principle of irreversibility and personalization: the one and only true Omega' (*Man's Place in Nature*, p. 121). There is a similar statement in *The Phenomenon of Man*, p. 298 note.

[16] *La centrologie*, 1944, Nos. 19–25, in *L'activation de l'énergie*, pp. 117–19. Teilhard says of Omega that it is personal, is individual (distinct from every other ego), is present here and now (and 'capable of acting upon us as an object that is present', 'for there can be no love that is not of the present'), that it is transcendent (for 'it is not subject to the conditions of time and space'), that it cannot be subject to entropy, that it possesses 'a supreme consistence' and 'the highest degree of cosmic centricity': at the same time he says also that it is 'partially present here and now', 'partially transcendent', that it has 'maximum complexity', that it has 'emerged since all time above a world from which nevertheless, seen from another angle, it is in process of emerging'.

Given the universal experiential law of unification 'no spirit (not even God, within the limits of our experience) exists or, by constructional necessity, can exist, without a multiple associated with it—any more than a centre can exist without its sphere or circumference' (*Esquisse d'un univers personnel*, 1936, in *L'énergie humaine*, p. 74).

[17] *La centrologie*, Nos. 23, 24, 26, in *L'activation de l'énergie*, pp. 115–20.

[18] An exact analysis of another passage produces the same conclusion. If the universe is extended in the direction of the personal, in other words of synthesis, 'God appears not in a diffusion but in a concentration of the stuff of the universe'. 'In the consummated universe, the richness and perfection of the synthesis being, as the hypothesis demands, carried to their highest point, consciousness, which is bound up with this very synthesis, must necessarily attain supreme values. In the final form assumed by the cosmos, personality, increasing with convergence, must be maximum.'

The ambiguity of Teilhard's explanation is apparent in the affirmation of a growth of consciousness up to its supreme form, which affirmation is accompanied by the phrase 'does not appear' and so makes it relative to human consciousness: it is a matter, therefore, of the progress that *man* makes in knowledge of and communion with God.

[19] 'By one of those strange inhibitory effects that prevent us from seeing what is staring us in the face, I did not realize that as God "metamorphosized" the world from the depths of matter to the heights of spirit, so, and in the same degree, the world in return must "endomorphize" God. Under the influence of the unitive operation that discloses him to us, God in some way "transforms himself" as he incorporates us. Thus what now seems to me to be the essential act and concern of hominized evolution is not simply to see God and allow oneself to be enveloped and penetrated by him . . . but at the same time (if not first of all) to disclose (or even in a sense to complete) him ever more fully. Around us and in us, through the encounter between his attraction and our thought, God is in process of changing. Through the rise of "the quantity of cosmic union", his radiance grows brighter and his colour richer. Here at last we find, here we have the expression of, the great event, the great tidings . . . Lord of consistence and union, you whose *mark of recognition and essence* are the power to increase indefinitely, without distortion or rupture, in step with the mysterious matter in whose heart you reside and of all whose movements you are the ultimate master—Lord of my childhood and Lord of my end—God, for himself ever complete, and yet, for us, ever and endlessly being born . . .' (*Le coeur de la matière*, unpublished, 1950). The precision of Teilhard's qualification will be noted 'around us and in us', and the dialectic of 'for himself' and 'for us.'

[20] *Knowledge and possession of God*

Teilhard's vindication of his approach, in *Esquisse d'une dialectique de l'esprit*, 1917, in *L'activation de l'énergie*, p. 149) makes it quite clear that he was alive to this problem and was anxious to find a solution.

'Omega Point appears as a centre at once single and complex, in which *three interlocking centres*, held together in the person of Christ, emerge ever more distinctly: externally, there is the immanent ("natural") apex of the cone of cosmic history; then inside, at the centre, the immanent ("super-natural") apex of the cone of Christ's Church—and lastly, right at the heart, the transcendent, divine centre, the complete Pleroma coming together under the mediating action of Christ-Omega.'

Teilhard then distinguishes the different phases in man's approach to God:

Phase I, reflection on the phenomenon of man, leading up to a transcendent Omega Point, the universal centre that brings spirit together, i.e. God (conceived as uniting the world to himself, rather than creating it).

Phase II, evolutionary creation, in which God is seen as the motive force of the universe and as revealing himself in it.

Phase III, the Christian phenomenon, the Incarnation.

Phase IV, the living Church. It is only at this point that Christ can be identified with Omega. 'Nothing now remains of the conflict that seemed, ever more dangerously, to range against one another the majesty of the universe and the primacy of God.'

Teilhard adds, 'the reason why some of my essays have seemed startling is generally that, writing for non-believers, I did not carry my argument beyond phase 1.'

In order to clarify the terms of the problem it may be well for us—though in this our agreement with Teilhard is not complete—to put forward the following propositions:

1. God is *complete in himself*, in the plenitude of his eternal act, and the communion, in the Trinity, of his Persons.

2. *From man's point of view*, God's creative action, which brings salvation and supernaturalizes, and so fulfils his loving plan, is operated, historically, in progressive phases.

3. *Man's knowledge of God*, the 'discovery' of God (to use Teilhard's expression we quoted above) also comes about in phases: in rational reflection on facts, and in particular on the finality of history (the approach used in *The Phenomenon of Man*); and then in faith's acceptance of historical revelation.

4. *Man's concrete possession of God* (his access or effective transition to God) comes about through good will's response to the gratuitous initiative of God, which summons man through signs (the greatest of which is Christ). For each individual person this happens in the present, for redeemed mankind at the end of history. History can lead in the end to the possession of God only if it is already permeated by a supernatural activity; but, in view of the *interlocking* of the phases of God's action (referred to by Teilhard) history is indeed, through Christ, supernatural. Phase 1, which provides the background and viewpoint of the *Phenomenon of Man*, is then seen to

be an abstraction: a necessary abstraction, from the point of view both of instruction and method.

[21] It is thus that Teilhard defines the 'two conditions that must, by structural necessity, be satisfied by the God we look for, if he is to be able to support and guide the phenomenon of the spirit. The first condition is that God shall gather together into his own simplicity the evolutionary extensions of all the fibres of the advancing world: he must be the God of cosmic synthesis, in whom we may realize that we are progressing and becoming united through a spiritual transformation of all the powers of matter. And the second condition is that this same God shall, in the course of that synthesis, act as a first nucleus of independent consciousness: a supremely personal God from whom we are all the more distinct the more we lose ourselves in him . . . A universal-God to be achieved through effort, and yet a personal-God to be experienced in love. (*Le phénomène spirituel*, 1937, in *L'énergie humaine*, pp. 135–6).

[22] 'Each element of the world, whatever it may be, only subsists, *hic et nunc*, in the manner of a cone whose generating lines meet in God, who draws them together (meeting at the term of their individual perfection and at the term of the general perfection of the world which contains them)' (*Le Milieu Divin*, p. 114).

[23] 'God, who cannot in any way be mixed with or lost in the participated being he sustains, animates and knits together, lies at the birth, the growing, and the term of all things. (*La vie cosmique*, 1916, in *Ecrits du temps de la guerre*, p. 37).

God is 'a Being which mingled with things yet remained distinct from them; a Being of a higher order than the substance of things with which it was adorned, yet taking shape within them' *The spiritual power of matter*, 1919, in *Hymn of the Universe*, p. 68).

The Mass on the World (1923) contains a magnificent exposition of the transcendence of God the creator: 'In the beginning was *power*, intelligent, loving, energizing. In the beginning was the *word*, supremely capable of mastering and moulding whatever might come into being in the world of matter. In the beginning there were not cold and darkness: there was the *fire*. And the truth. So, far from light emerging out of the womb of our darkness, it is the light, existing before all else was made, which patiently, surely, eliminates our darkness. As for us creatures, of ourselves we are but emptiness and obscurity' (in *Hymn of the Universe*, p. 21).

Teilhard rightly brings out to what degree the notion of a triune God is a (supplementary) basis of God's transcendence, and consequently of the free character of creation: 'The concept of the Trinity that serves only to confirm our idea of the oneness of God, by giving it the *structure* (or, more exactly, the structural, or constructed character) which is the mark, in our experience, of every real, living, unit. If God were not triune (which means if he did not confront himself) we could not conceive the possibility of his subsisting upon himself, independently, and without experiencing the reaction of some world around him' (*Introduction au Christianisme*, unpublished, 1944).

24 'Where there is complete disunity of the stuff of the cosmos (at an infinite distance from Omega), there is nothing' (*La centrologie*, 1944, No. 7, in *L'activation de l'énergie*, p. 122).

25 *The beginning of the universe*

'. . . at no moment in its duration (i.e. however far back in its internal experience) can the world show us an absolute beginning (in other words, give evidence of a production "*ex nihilo subjecti*"). If we start from within, we can never, I believe, reach the *confines of the whole*, either in time or in space, because *every such exploration amounts to an analysis*, and it is the *proper function of analysis to break up the real into real components*, indefinitely' (Letter of 20 October 1919).

'Our mind finds it impossible to conceive any absolute beginning *in the order of phenomena*.' (*The transformist question*, 1921, in *Vision of the Past*, p. 24).

'An absolute beginning in the very least thing (that is to say, the experiential reality of a being, however small, one of whose faces yawned on temporal nothingness) would as surely ruin the entire edifice of our perceptual universe, that is to say would as radically contradict its inner structure, as the existence of a cosmic boundary along which objects would present one face to spatial nothingness' (*Basis and foundations of the idea of evolution*, 1926, *ibid.*, p. 130).

'The perception of organic time of which we are speaking . . . does not offer in itself any explanation of things, but only a more correct view of their quantitative integrity . . . An immense progress in our consciousness of reality and mapping of the world, a more pronounced and justified taste for unitary views and theories; but, directly, no new access to the hidden levels of structures and causes. This is what the birth of a historical sense in human thought means to us . . . When we begin to speak of a universe in which the spatial and temporal series radiate without limit around each element, many minds take fright and we begin to speak of eternal matter. The absence of all empirical beginnings, an essential postulate of transformism and all history, has a more modest and very different meaning. It in no way entails the existence of a universe invested with divine attributes. All it means is that our world is so constructed that our perceptions are the absolute prisoners of its immensity. The further our mind penetrates, the further its shores seem to recede. Far from tending to discover a new god, science only goes on showing us matter, which is the footstool of the divinity. One does not draw near to the Absolute by travelling, but by ecstasy.' A footnote to the words 'divine attributes' makes it clear that 'such a universe has in fact none of the plenitude of being, or the eternal quality that Christian philosophy recognizes in God. Its necessity is a consequence of the free will of the Creator, and its "unbounded" character has nothing to do with infinity. From the fact that our mind does not perceive any first link in the chain of phenomena, one cannot conclude the non-existence of an ontological beginning of duration' (*Ibid.*, pp. 130–2).

'On the empirical and phenomenological plane, a given universe and each of its parts can have only one and the same duration, to which there is no backward limit. Thus each thing extends itself and pushes its roots into the past, ever further back, by that which makes it most itself. Everything, in some extremely attenuated extension of itself, has existed from the very first. Nothing can be done in a direct way to counter this basic condition of our knowledge' (*The Phenomenon of Man*, pp. 77–8).

In common with Père Smulders (*op. cit.*, p. 32 note) one must reject a concordist view that seeks to identify a scientific hypothesis of the origin of the universe with the empirical discovery of the creative act: 'A primordial explosion is not creation.'

[26] Unpublished letter to Père Auguste Valensin, 20 October 1919. In the same letter Teilhard suggests that the reference to the *whole* should be extended to other spheres (inspiration, the Fall, the Incarnation, Redemption): 'The "whole" would be like a new dimension to which all our concepts would have to be adapted, and in which alone they could become truly meaningful . . . no concept holding strictly true except for the whole.'

'For the universe, to be created means that it is in a transcendental relationship to God, which makes its being secondary, participated, dependent through and through on the divine. We have got into the habit (despite our repeated affirmations that creation is not an act in time) of connecting this state of "participated" being with the existence of an experiential zero in duration, that is to say with a *registrable* temporal beginning. But this alleged requirement of orthodoxy can only be substantiated by an illegitimate contamination of the phenomenal plane by the metaphysical . . . whether our space and time have an ascertainable limit or not in no way affects the operation of a higher force, the property of which is precisely that it is applied to the global totality of the world, past, present and future.' 'It does not at all follow from the fact that the temporal beginning of the world is, from the phenomenal point of view, not to be found, that the notion of an ontological beginning of the universe has no reality' (*Basis and foundations of the idea of evolution*, 1926, in *Vision of the Past*, pp. 134-5).

[27] *Christianisme et évolution*, unpublished, 1945. Also, *Comment je vois*, Nos. 26-9: 'The self-subsistent unity lies at the pole of being, and as a necessary consequence the multiple occupies the whole circumference around it—I mean by that *pure* multiple: "Creatable nothingness", which is nothing, and yet, in virtue of a passive potentiality for arrangement (that is to say, union) is at the same time a possibility of, or a yearning for, being—and here our intelligence is completely at a loss to distinguish, in such depths, supreme necessity and supreme freedom, for this potentiality or possibility of yearning is such that it is just as though God were powerless to resist it' (No. 28).

[28] 'To admit that no being is physically possible (that is to say, fully intelligible) except as emerging, for example, from a multiple is not to give the multiple the consistence that belongs to an antagonistic co-eternal, but the consistence of an essential *primordial stage* (*ex ipsa essentia entis realis*). At the very origin of the creative act, we should not see a substantial purchase-point, a "stuff" or "matter", but a "gateway", an *unavoidable entry* or channel' (Letter of 29 November 1919).

[29] *Creation as both free and necessary*
When his thought was first taking shape, in 1918, Teilhard wrote: 'I've also felt that the problem of creation, looked at not in its

present (evolutive) phase but in its first (involutive), is taking on increasing importance in my mind. What is the origin of the lower multiple? What "need" is filled by the fundamental fragmentation of being—driven from its source before returning to it? Until this problem is more or less coherently cleared up, one can't, I think, understand the worth of souls and the value of the Incarnation' (Letter of 13 December 1918, in *Making of a Mind*, p. 268).

'Then the organic complex will have been constituted of God and the world, the Pleroma—the mysterious reality of which we cannot say that it is more beautiful than God, since God could have done without the world; yet we cannot conceive the world as being merely accessory without rendering creation incomprehensible, the passion of Christ an absurdity—and our own struggle meaningless' (*Mon univers*, 1924, quoted in *The Future of Man*, p. 308).

'From the human point of view, a doctrine that *no longer justifies in our eyes* the vastness and the laboriousness of the evolution in which we can *see* that we are now caught up, does more than violently contradict the evidence of our minds—it strikes at the very motive power behind our action. What is the point of attaining "beatitude" if, in the final reckoning, we have made no absolute contribution, through our lives, to the totality of being? At the same time, from the Christian point of view, we can no longer understand why a God could have committed himself, out of mere "benevolence", to such a flood of sufferings and vicissitudes. You may, by a dialectic of pure act, silence our reason as much as you please, but you will never now convince our hearts that the vast business of the cosmos, *as we now see it*, is simply some gift or plaything of God's. And why, again, if that were so, do the most unmistakable scriptural texts attach so much importance to the fulfilment of the mysterious Pleroma? God is entirely self-sufficient: nevertheless the universe brings him something that is vitally necessary: there you have the two conditions, apparently contradictory, that must in future be satisfied explicitly by any theory of participated being' (*Christianisme et évolution*, unpublished, 1945).

'Christian faith, through its mysteries of the Incarnation and even of the Redemption, adorns this world with many charms, but does it not, on the other hand, rob it of all interest—even, maybe, make it contemptible to us—by insisting on God's self-sufficiency and, in consequence on the complete contingence of creation? . . .

It is sound scholastic philosophy, we all know, that being, in the form of *Ens a se*, is posited exhaustively and super-abundantly, and immediately, at the ontological origin of all things. After this, in a second phase, all the rest (which means the world) appears only as an addition, or an extra granted entirely by favour: we are guests at God's banquet . . . Unless at the term of existence we seek only an individual happiness (and that is a form of happiness we have definitely rejected), how could the self-styled revelation of man's radical uselessness fail to make him *lose all heart for action*? . . . This is a time when man is becoming conscious—as, apparently, he will now never cease to be—of his planetary responsibilities and future: and Christianity (for all the beauty of its gospel) would cease to have any religious value for us if we could suspect that it was depriving our universe of its zest; for that alone would exclude it from the domain of vitalizing faiths. . . . If I allow myself here to criticize so sharply the scholastic notion of "participation", it is not only (as will have been apparent) because it degrades the man in us, but also because it angers the Christian in me. "God creates by love" is a fine scholastic phrase: but what is this love, then, inexplicable in its subject and degrading for its object, that is *based on no need* (unless it be the pleasure of giving for the sake of giving)?' (*Contingence de l'univers et goût humain de survivre*, unpublished, 1953).

³⁰ *The problem of creation*
Comment je vois, unpublished, 1948, Nos. 25–31 (this is an essential source).

This line of thought had appeared earlier, in *L'union créatrice*, 1917 (in *Ecrits du temps de la guerre*, pp. 184–8), a personal reflexion, not intended for publication. In this we find that Teilhard has already arrived at his fundamental idea that being is defined by *union*, whether active or received, and is trying to envisage an interconnexion between God and the world that goes beyond the notion of efficient causality. He imagines 'a primitive substratum of spirit' which he sees as an 'extremely attenuated and reduced substance', and even as 'a sort of positive non-being'. 'I cannot pretend,' he says, 'that there are not grave objections to this concept . . . It suggests that the creation was not absolutely gratuitous but represents a work of almost absolute involvement.' He adds, however, 'why should we not admit that the necessary existence of absolute unity entails as a secondary consequence, *ad extra*, as an antithesis or a shadow, the appearance at the antipodes of being of an infinite multiplicity?'

We find the same idea in a paper dating from 1919: 'The time has now come, in every branch of sacred science, to examine, in prayer and study, the zone *where God and the cosmos meet*. In dogmatic theology, our scholars, who have long studied God's relationships *ad intra*, should now at last *embark on a sympathetic* study of the *relationship ad extra* that determine the subordination of the universe to God ... If you look around you, you cannot help being astonished that the Christian way of presenting the origins and vicissitudes of the world should be so artificial and even infantile. In making God both personal and free, making non-being absolute, the creation gratuitous, and the fall accidental, are we not in danger of making the universe insupportable and the value of souls, which we so emphasize, inexplicable?' (*Note pour servir à l'évangélisation des temps nouveaux*, 1919, in *Écrits du temps de la guerre*, p. 337). It is hardly necessary to add that Teilhard abundantly stresses the personality and freedom of God.

In 1936, writing from an evolutionary point of view, Teilhard is at variance with the 'extratemporal metaphysics of being' and admits his difficulty in finding 'in the God of evolution an exact equivalent of the attributes accorded by medieval philosophers to the *"Ens a se"* ' (*Esquisse d'un univers personnel*, 1936, in *L'énergie humaine*, p. 88). Teilhard realizes that making God the unity of human persons leads him to the notion of the 'complexity of God', the 'perfection of whose unity' is to be a 'centre of centres'. He is careful, however, to point out that while God 'constitutes a special term at the head of all the series', 'he is also in a way outside any series. Everything rises up in him as towards a centre of immanence; but everything comes down from him, as from a centre of transcendence' (*Ibid.*, p. 88). These reflexions occur in a paper which presents 'a sort of ultra-physics, linking together as coherently as possible the sum total of our experiences' (*Ibid.*).

In the same connexion, we find in *La centrologie* (1944, No. 26, *op. cit.*, p. 120) the following: 'The fundamental ontological relationship between being and the universe may be expressed in two converse and no doubt complementary forms. The first is passive, *"Plus esse est plus a* (or *ex*) *pluribus uniri"* (i.e. evolution that is undergone), the second is active: *"Plus esse est plus plura unire"* (i.e. active evolution.)' *Le coeur de la matière* (1950) tells us (p. 30), 'Classic metaphysics has accustomed us to seeing in the world—the object of the "creation"—some sort of extrinsic production, that emerged, in his super-abundant goodness, from God's supreme *efficiency*. In keeping with the spirit of St Paul, I am now irresistibly driven to seeing in it—because otherwise I could neither act nor love fully—a mysterious product that represents completion and fulfilment for absolute being itself: no longer *participated being lying outside and diverging*, but *participated being entering the Pleroma and converging*—creative causality, yes, but *towards* unity'.

Teilhard returned to this problem in 1953: 'This affirmation, a strict deduction from a particular metaphysics of potency and act, of the complete gratuitousness of a static universe in which creation had no part to play other than to accept itself and work out its own salvation [the sentence would appear to be incomplete in the ms.]. On the other hand, there can be something most dangerous, even virulent (because disheartening) in this proposition. This comes out as soon as, within cosmogenesis, the "participated being" which we all are, begins to wonder whether the radically contingent condition to which theologians reduce it really justifies the labour involved in evolution . . . Let us forget the *"Ens a se"* and the *"Ens ab alio"* and get back to the really authentic and concrete expressions of Christian revelation and mysticism. What we find at the heart of that teaching and those inspired outbursts is none other than the affirmation and the experience of a strictly bilateral and complementary relationship between God and the world . . . We should read St John again, and St Paul. They accept the existence of the world (in too summary a fashion, maybe, for our taste) as an initial datum. But on the other hand, what a feeling they both have for the absolute value of a cosmic drama, in which it is just as though God, even before his Incarnation, were ontologically involved. And, in consequence of this, how forcibly they stress the Pleroma and pleromization. Indeed, what really gives life to Christianity is not the sense of the contingence of the created, but the sense of the mutual completion of the world and God. So, if what is lacking in Aristotelian ontology is precisely this spirit of "complementarity", we must do what the physicists do when mathematics lets them down—change our geometry. When we see, for example that from the point of view of dynamics [footnote: and by analogy with what happens in physics, in which, as we now know, acceleration creates mass—which means that the motive force comes only after the movement] what comes first in the world, as apprehended by our thought, is not "being" but "the union that generates that being"—when we see that, we should try to replace a metaphysics of *Esse* by a metaphysics of *Unire* (or of *Uniri*). If it is approached from this genetic angle, the problem of the co-existence and complementarity of the created and the uncreated will to some extent, surely, be solved—in so far, that is, as the two terms that confront one another must both, each in its own way, exist in themselves and join together, so that, *in natura rerum*, the absolute maximum possible union may be realized' (*Contingence de l'univers et goût humain de survivre*, unpublished, 1953).

[31] 'In the light of creative union, the universe takes on the shape of a vast cone whose base opens out indefinitely backwards, into the night—while the apex rises up and closes up ever further into the light. Throughout the whole, the same creative influence makes itself felt, but always more conscious, more purified, more complex' (*Mon univers*, unpublished, 1924).

'From the modern point of view, as determined by the idea of evolution, the one is not simply opposed to the multiple, as a total perfection to a sum of imperfections: it is, to some degree at least, *born* of the multiple. Its unity is, to some extent, *woven* from the plurality whose fulfilment and synthesis it operates. Therein, for human activity, lies *the basic reason for devoting oneself passionately to effort. If life is to mean anything to us, we must have nothing less and nothing more than an awareness of this responsibility*' (*La route de l'Ouest*, unpublished, 1932).

[32] Teilhard's thought is diametrically opposed to Valéry's:

> O Vanity! First Cause!
> He who reigns in the heavens,
> With a voice that was the light,
> Opened up the wide universe of space.
> As though weary of gazing upon himself
> God himself has broken the barrier
> Of his perfect eternity.
> He made himself the Being who wastes
> In the derived, his own principle,
> In stars, his oneness.

The heavens are his error! Time, his ruin!
And the abyss of animality yawns!
What a fall in the source,
A spark in place of nothingness!
(*Ebauche d'un serpent, Poésie*, Gallimard, p. 168.)

[33] 'While the self-sufficiency and self-determination of absolute being are preserved intact in a metaphysics of union (the reason being, I repeat, that the pure multiple at the antipodes of unity is no more than potentiality and pure passivity)—on the other hand the creative act takes on a sharply defined significance and structure. The pleromization (as St Paul would have said), that is to say the realization of participated being through arrangement and totalization—which is the fruit, in some way, of a reflexion of God not within, but outside, himself—this is seen to be a sort of echo or symmetrical reduplication of trinitization' (*Comment je vois*, unpublished, 1948).

These propositions of Teilhard's are well discussed by Père Smulders (*op. cit.*, pp. 90–7). He is right in pointing out that the word 'trinitization', in spite of its grammatical form, 'does not imply a real *becoming* in God. It means that in the mystery of God trinity and unity are not a crude, static, datum, but something full of life . . .' (p. 93). It would seem that though Teilhard's metaphysics, is on this point, inevitably open to criticism, one should not press too far the 'positive' character he seeks to attribute to the 'absolute multiple' which is nothingness. When he 'insists' on its being 'no more than pure potentiality and passivity', or 'a void', Teilhard still remains this side of mythology. Moreover, Père Smulders adds, perceptively: 'Teilhard's metaphysical considerations should not be given too much weight in the whole body of his work, even though he himself attributed a great deal of importance to them. Only a few dozen of the thousands of pages he wrote cover this ground (in *Comment je vois* the whole treatment, from the first notion of being up to and including the mysteries of sin and the Incarnation, amounts to only four pages in all)' (*Op. cit.*, p. 97).

[34] The metaphysics of *Esse* implies, underlying it, a metaphysics of *Unire*; since, as Père Charles had clearly shown a long time ago (in an unpublished course in metaphysics) being must be conceived as an act of unification of self by self.

[35] References in some official texts to a 'need' in God obviously mean no more than a superabundance of gratuitous love: 'And yet it is also certain, surprising though it may seem, that Christ requires his members (*Attamen hoc quoque retinendum est quamvis mirandum prorsus videatur, Christum nempe requirere membra sua*) . . . this is not due to any need or insufficiency in him, but rather because he has so ordained it' (Pius XII, encyclical *Mystici Corporis*, C.T.S. trans., London, p. 27).

[36] In a comment on Père Morel's *Le sens de l'existence chez saint Jean de la Croix*, Père Henri Brouillard refers to the traditional doctrine, taught by mystics and theologians, 'of the exemplary causality of the divine Word'. He is at pains to add that they are careful to affirm also the dependence of the world in relation to God (*Mystique, métaphysique et foi chrétienne*, in *Recherches de science religieuse*, January–March, 1963, pp. 43-4). Later, in connexion with the mystic's experience of some sort of communication with the creative act, he makes it clear that this feeling implies an assent to re-creation, the fruit of the redemption (*ibid.*, p. 76). With this reserve, Teilhard's theological enquiry into creation could be given authenticity, *but only as a description of mystical experience.*

One might add a comment that is perhaps too far-fetched. The difficulty would vanish from the real problem put forward by Teilhard, if we accepted an eternal pre-existence of the creature in God. That, however, is impossible and the hypothesis is untenable. Teilhard went a little way in this direction when he spoke, as we saw earlier, of a 'pure potentiality', 'at the antipodes of God' and 'a yearning for being'.

[37] *Le Milieu Divin*, p. 122.

[38] *Ibid.*

[39] *Le coeur de la matière*, unpublished, 1950, p. 28. 'The fire has penetrated the earth . . . without earthquake, or thunderclap, the flame has lit up the whole world from within. All things individually and collectively are penetrated and flooded by it, from the inmost core of the tiniest atom to the mighty sweep of the most universal laws of being: so naturally has it flooded every element, every energy, every connecting link in the unity of our cosmos; that one might suppose the cosmos to have burst spontaneously into flame' (*The Mass on the World*, in *Hymn of the Universe*, pp. 23-4).

This might introduce the problem of the possibility of other races of men in the universe. Teilhard did not shirk this problem, and answered it by a positive acceptance of its probability. 'There is nothing to prove that in accordance again with some statistical law, many obscure stars, many other earths beside our own are not already scattered, or may be expected to be, among the galaxies. On this hypothesis, which is perfectly feasible, the phenomenon of life and, in particular, the phenomenon of man would lose something of its heart-breaking loneliness . . . But the law of recurrence remains the same. And there can never be but one single Omega' (*La centrologie*, No. 33, *op. cit.*, p. 34).

[40] 'There is a logic in things to which everything must submit . . . It is one of the weaknesses of Christian philosophy that it so emphasizes the omnipotence of God as indefinitely to multiply contingence and the arbitrary in the universe' (*Christologie et évolution*, unpublished, 1933).

Teilhard distinguishes between 'intellectual possibility' and 'physical possibility'; the former considers only the non-contradiction of a being and its abstract characteristics, it isolates it and looks at it as one whole. The latter considers 'the physical conditions in which it can be realized', its connexions with the totality of being, and of the structural requirements of the real. 'One can see that the various developments of participated being are not absolutely arbitrary or independent of one another. It is possible that they are all subject to some common general laws, by which I mean that there may be only *one single* process of creation conceivable for participated being (for example, the progressive simplification of a multiple, the emergence of, or of some kind of, matter).'

[41] 'Even when we accept the transformist theory, the place remains open—indeed it yawns more widely than ever—for a primal creative power. And even better, a creation of evolutionary type (God *making things make themselves*) has for long seemed to some very great minds the most beautiful form imaginable in which God could act in the universe. Was it not St Thomas who, comparing the viewpoint (fixist as we should call it today) of the Latin Fathers like St Gregory, to the evolutionary viewpoint of the Greek Fathers and St Augustine, said of the latter, '*Magis placet*'—it is more *acceptable* (II Sent, d. 12; g.1.a.2)—'Let us be glad to strengthen our minds by contact with this great thought!' (*What should we think of transformism?* 1930, in *Vision of the Past*, p. 154).

'To create, even for omnipotence, should not be understood by us as an instantaneous act, but as a process or act of synthesis . . . In spite of—or, rather, by reason of—his perfections, the creator cannot communicate himself immediately to his creature, but must make the creature capable of receiving him.' 'The creative act takes the form, for those who are its object, of a transition from a state of initial dispersion to a state of final harmony . . . The multiple has its natural place underlying things, since it represents, at the opposite pole from God, the diffused potentialities of participated being: not the fragments of a broken pitcher, but the elementary clay from which everything will be moulded' (*Christologie et évolution*, unpublished, 1933).

[42] *Mon univers*, unpublished, 1924. 'The general concept of an "evolutionary creation", understood as a free creation (free, at least, in Leibniz's restricted sense), a creation that is possible only on one occasion (since it extends gradually to the totality of "compossible" beings), a creation that is possible only through a continuous linking of ascending phases—such a concept (which is not mine) has the attractive aspect of a modernized and more flexible neo-platonism. It does not seem to be incompatible with Catholic teaching nor, in particular, with the doctrine of the original fall' (Letter from Père Maréchal to Teilhard, 3 July 1934).

[43] 'It is a perfectly correct view of things—and strictly consonant with the Gospel—to regard providence across the ages as brooding over the world in ceaseless effort to spare that world its bitter wounds and to bind up its hurts. Most certainly it is God himself who, in the course of the centuries, awakens the great benefactors of mankind, and the great physicians, in ways that agree with the general rhythm of progress. He it is who inspires, even among those furthest from acknowledging his existence, the quest for every means of comfort and every means of healing' (*Le Milieu Divin*, p. 84).

[44] *The creation of Man*
'The letter of the Bible shows us the creator forming the body of man from earth. Careful observation of the world tends to make us see today that by this "earth" we must understand a substance slowly developed from the totality of things, so that man has been drawn not precisely from a little amorphous matter, but by a prolonged effort of "earth" as a whole' (*Fossil men*, 1921, in *The Appear-*

ance of Man, p. 32)' 'We must be more logical than the scientists who teach us, and must carry the lesson to its conclusion: by which I mean that we must accept that man is born in his entirety from the world—not simply his flesh and blood—but his incredible capacity for thought' (*L'esprit de la terre,* 1931, in *L'énergie humaine,* p. 26).

'Many people think that the superiority of the spirit would not be safe unless its first manifestation were accompanied by some interruption of the ordinary course of the world. Just because it is spirit, one should say in refutation, its appearance must have taken the form of a crowning or blossoming. But let us put aside all systematic considerations. Is it not true that every day immunerable human souls are "created" in the course of an embryogenesis so continuous that no scientific observation will ever find the smallest break in the chain of biological phenomena? There we have daily before our eyes the example of a creation, absolutely imperceptible and undetectable by pure science. Why should we make difficulties in the case of the first man? . . . Why not admit, for example, that the absolutely free and special action by which the Creator decided that humanity should crown His work so influenced and pre-organized the course of the world before man, that he now appears to us (as a result of the Creator's choice) to be the fruit naturally expected by the developments of life? *Omnia propter hominem.*' (*Basis and foundations of the idea of evolution,* 1928, in *Vision of the Past,* p. 135).

Discussing the question of monogenism, Teilhard says that it is essentially for 'theological' reasons ('the Pauline conception of the fall and redemption') that 'the Church clings to the historical reality of Adam and Eve' (*What should we think of transformism?* 1930, in *Vision of the Past,* p. 156). He adds: 'On the other hand, for reasons of probability and also comparative anatomy, science, left to itself, would never (to say the least of it) dream of attributing so narrow a basis as two individuals to the enormous edifice of humankind'. And he anticipates that more profound theological research may solve the problem (*Ibid.*).

'For anyone who knows how to interpret the diagram of facts registered by science, mankind is no longer an accidental phenomenon, appearing by chance on one of the smallest stars in the heavens. It represents the highest expression known to our ex-

perience of the urge that has been directing the whole progress of
matter and life.' Teilhard adds a note: 'Is there any need to
emphasize how greatly the believer is enriched by realizing this
deliberate, directed, continuity of the work of creation? As the
finished prototype, whose perfection is developed from earlier
attempts, as the keystone on which the architectural lines of the
complete building converge, man can more fully appreciate, from
this new point of view, his right to a sovereign position in the
universe' (*La crise présente*, 1937, in Cahiers Pierre Teilhard de
Chardin, No. 3, p. 74, and in *Science et Christ*, p. 173).

Teilhard returns to this same problem in *Monogénisme et mono-
phylétisme: une distinction à faire* (unpublished, 1950) and repeats the
argument from scientific improbability. He adds that, as the most
recent developments in exegesis would accept, 'theologians are
realizing, in one way or another, that in a universe as organically
structured as that we are now coming to recognize as ours, they can
find a solidarity of man much more integral even than that they seek
in "the bosom of our mother Eve". It is provided by the astonishing
internal bond that holds together the world in which we live—a
world in process of cosmo- and anthropo-genesis'. In *The Phenomenon of Man*, Teilhard is inclined to believe in monophyletism,
but adds that 'the science of man can say nothing directly for or
against monogenism' (p. 188 note).

There is a long note by Karl Rahner on monogenism, in *Theological Investigations*, London, Darton Longman and Todd and
Baltimore, Helicon Press, 1963, vol. I, pp. 229-296 and an appendix
in Père Smulders, *op. cit.*, pp. 201. See also an article by the palaen-
tologist Hurteler, in *Orientierung*, September 1964.

[45] Letter of May 1920. Teilhard then develops the problem of the
separation by biological death, of the soul from the body: 'When
an animal dies, there is not simply a disintegration of its bodily
elements; it is its soul becoming incapable of any longer maintaining their unity. In the case of man, death represents a *metamorphosis*
in which there is a rejection of a merely apparent, provisional, form
of the universe (provisional and impermanent, because still tied to
and diluted with "animal" and "inert" forms of the universe's
unification); but it is no more than a metamorphosis. The
"separated" soul *continues to* exist *only in so far as it unifies the
universe*—but in a new way (and one that will be fully realized only

at the resurrection). Strictly speaking, there are no separated souls; there are only souls that are changing their "sphere" in a world in which everything holds together' (*Ibid.*). 'If I die, I shall change my state, that's all,' said Teilhard during the 1914 war.

[46] Problems of the causality of phenomena also belong logically to science: 'The surprising and indefinite connexions by which living species are grouped both in order of succession and, so to speak, organically, confront us with a *positive* scientific problem (as positive as the relative movement of the earth and the sun), which consequently demands a *positive* solution *of a scientific order*' (*What should we think of transformism?* 1930, in *Vision of the Past*, p. 152).

[47] This problem, however, engaged Teilhard's attention when he was first formulating his thought, in an unpublished note on the 'idea of creative transformation' (1916–20): 'Creation . . . is not a periodic intrusion of the first cause: it is an act co-extensive with the whole duration of the universe. God *has been creating* ever since the beginning of time, and, *seen from within*, his creation (even the initial creation?) has taken the form of a transformation. Participated being is not constituted in chunks that are later differentiated through some non-creative modification by God: God is continually breathing new being into them—of course, all along the curve followed by being as it grows, there are levels or individual points, at which the creative action becomes dominant (the appearance of life and thought). But strictly speaking, *every* good movement is, in some part of itself, creative.'

[48] 'Not, indeed, that the concentration and arrangement of the centres suffice *in themselves alone* to augment the being of the world but they undoubtedly achieve that under the radiated influence of Omega' (*La centrologie*, 1944, No. 27, *op. cit.*, p. 122).

[49] *The transformist question*, 1921, in *Vision of the Past*, p. 25. This 'consistence' and autonomy in relation to nature have been well brought out, in terms of Thomistic theory, by Père Chenu in his *Saint Thomas et la théologie* (Editions du Seuil, 1959). Jules Lequier, that ardent lover of freedom, used to say, 'God is the maker of making' (*Oeuvres complètes* ed. by J. Grenier, pp. 395, 397).

[50] *The Transformist Paradox*, 1925, in *Vision of the Past*, p. 102. 'What gives many people the impression that in a universe of evolutionary structure the Christian God disappears, is that they have not sufficiently reshaped the idea of creation in their minds.

They continue to believe that divine epiphanies will take the form of localized and tangible intrusions, like those accompanying the action of material and secondary causes. Now such violations of our sensible universe by an activity of a higher order would not only be, to use scholastic language, *contra leges naturae, in essendo et in percipiendo* (since they would take the form for us of the appearance of realities that have no antecedents, which is as we have seen an "experimental monstrosity"); but they would add nothing to the power of the creative act' (*Basis and foundations of the idea of evolution, ibid.*, p. 134).

'For transformism to be dangerous to reason and faith, it would have to claim that the action of a Creator fills no purpose, to reduce the development of life to a process purely immanent in nature, to state that "the greater can automatically arise from the less". Too many evolutionists have, in fact, committed this serious mistake of taking their scientific explanation of life for a metaphysical solution of the world . . . No, scientific transformism, strictly speaking, proves nothing for or against God. It simply notes the fact of a chain of connexion in reality. It presents us with an anatomy of life, certainly not with a final reason for it. It affirms that "something organized itself, something grew". But it is incapable of discerning the ultimate conditions of that growth' (*The transformist question, ibid.*, pp. 22-3).

[51] *Man's place in the Universe*, in *The Vision of the Past*, p. 231.

[52] It is precisely because it is *transcendent* and above all physical causality that this direct 'coaction' with God's works can give a real participation in his creative activity. '*It is precisely because* he is the centre that he fills the whole sphere' (*Le Milieu Divin*, p. 114).

[53] By supernatural Teilhard means the intimate mystery of the life of God, a mystery into which man cannot enter, but one revealed by Christ and in which man is invited to participate. Transcendence and gratuitiousness are the two essentials in the term. Teilhard says, for example: 'What determines the supernatural character of this unification (of man's being by our Lord) is that it is realized gratuitously around the Word and not around an infra-divine centre' (*Notes sur quelques représentations historiques du péché originel*, unpublished, 1924?).

[54] Cf. Chapter II, in which emphasis is laid on the difference, essential in Teilhard's view, between the two sources of the approach

to being, to truth and to existence. See, too, the analysis of his *Esquisse d'une dialectique de l'esprit*, chapter III, note 76.

[55] *The Phenomenon of Man*, epilogue, p. 298. In the following passage the theological accuracy of the term 'descent' will be noted: 'Nevertheless, however efficacious this newly born faith of man in the ultra-human may prove to be, it seems that man's urge towards *something* ahead of him cannot achieve its full fruition except by combining with another and still more fundamental aspiration—one descending from above, urging him towards *Some One*' (*Human unanimization*, 1950, in *The Future of Man*, pp. 287-8).

[56] *Le Milieu Divin*, p. 152. '*Et Verbum caro factum est.* That was the Incarnation. By this first and fundamental contact of God with our kind, by virtue of the penetration of the divine into our nature, a new life was born, an unexpected enlargement and "obediential" prolongation of our natural capacities: grace' (*La vie cosmique*, 1916, quoted in *The Future of Man*, p. 304).

[57] Second note to Père Auguste Valensin, 1919. *Archives de philosophie*, January–March 1961, p. 151. *Social heredity and progress*, 1938, in *The Future of Man*, pp. 35-6.

There are, moreover, many passages in which Teilhard forcibly emphasizes both the gratuitousness of the supernatural order and its absolute transcendence. (Cf. H. de Lubac, *op. cit.*, pp. 127-31). For example: 'Christ, indeed, is not the centre whom all things here below could *naturally* hope to be united with. That Christ should be our term is an unlooked-for and gratuitous favour of the creator's. It remains true that the Incarnation so completely *re-cast* the universe in the supernatural that, as a matter of *concrete fact*, we can no longer try to imagine towards what centre the elements of this world would have gravitated, had they not been raised up to grace' (*L'union créatrice*, 1917, in *Ecrits du temps de la guerre*, p. 195).

Similarly, in *Le milieu mystique* (1917) Teilhard brings out the dialectic of man's communion with God: 'The glittering trail of individual beauties and partial harmonies finds its centre *at one single point*, in one single person—yours, Jesus'. This person, however, has 'both name and face: but it is only he who can unveil his face and pronounce his name . . . Jesus' (*Ibid.*, p. 164).

[58] *Le Milieu Divin*, p. 74.

[59] *Ibid.*, p. 138.

[60] *Le coeur de la matière*, unpublished, 1930, p. 21.

[61] Letter to Père Auguste Valensin, 12 December 1919, *Archives de philosophie*, January–March, 1961, pp. 140, 142.

[62] Letter of 29 December 1919.

[63] *Social heredity and progress*, in *The Future of Man*, pp. 35–6.

[64] 'I believe that my position or tendency is pretty well as follows: to bring out, and restore the significance of the bases—pre-material, material, natural—to be found in all things. These bases are important only in so far as they lead up to a peak, and in so far as this peak is pre-contained in them. There is no question, then, of materialism. They are the medium through which higher being comes to us and draws us on—and through which we can react on it. That is why it is so important that we should be careful to recognize those bases and not, rashly and prematurely, cut ourselves off from them (which is what a soul would do if it tried to attain contemplation without the laborious effort of recollection) (Letter of 21 December 1919).

[65] *The value of nature*

This appraisal of nature is already to be found in a war-time letter, in which Teilhard discusses a book by Dom Chautard, *L'âme de tout apostolat.* 'It's all very well to run a young people's club only with supernatural resources; I'm quite ready to do without brass bands . . . At the same time that shouldn't make us forget the natural aspects of education (physical training, domestic science, cultural development . . .) which, normally, makes souls more fit to know God and serve him. Within such education there must be a hierarchy (the one complementing the other) but no abrupt divisions, no cutting off short. Christianity should form and "inform" (as the scholastics say) the whole man' (Letter of 8 January 1916, in *Making of a Mind*, pp. 86–7).

'It is precisely because of this cantilever-support (of the world by Christ) that there is in Christ *something* of the demiurge. If the new cosmos is indeed not a creation *side by side* with the old, but proceeds from a transformation of our order of things—if indeed, moreover, our *present* universe is supernaturalized in its entire being (i.e. has no direction or centre except *in Christo*) it follows automatically that our Lord has physically the function of giving stability to the world at all its levels. Christ became incarnate *solely* for our supernaturalization: but this very fact means that he must at the same time sustain and bring to their ultimate perfection the natural strata of the world (rather as scholasticism shows us the rational soul replacing lower substantial forms). And this again makes his action upon us even more inevitable, closer, and enveloping' (Letter to Père Auguste Valensin, 12 December 1919, as quoted in note 61, p. 521).

'When man has no belief, but is captivated by the revelation of the cosmos (cf. W. James), is he not already adumbrating the gesture of the elect who surrenders himself to God and is captivated by him? Surely the supreme lesson of all life is that we must die if we wish to live (so much so that Greek humanism should be accounted a true natural heresy)? Before the final and decisive metamorphosis there is, as a preparation for it, a repeated sloughing-off of the old; these serve as preliminary attempts, even though they are of a much lower order. There is a sort of continuity in the discontinuities through which being passes in turn in order to reach God. I am wondering whether this "gradation" will not prevent us (more and more, indeed!) from characterizing by a *single* word —which would be valid *only* for this act—the *"excessus"* (passing over) of our life into God' (Letter to Père Auguste Valensin, 29 December 1919, *ibid.*, p. 152).

'In one sense, grace does not introduce man into another universe, but into an extension of our universe in which nothing of what we are remains *ut sic*, but in which each element is used *ut sic*, and into which it enters through something of its own self (= the resurrection of the body). Everything retains, in the present world, its own form and natural appearance (apart from certain aspirations, a certain bias towards the divine). But everything is already basically animated by the divine' (*Ibid.*). 'It is true to say that it is the "void" in ourselves (being filled by God) that is enriching and beatifying. But there are three things that we should not forget: 1. The void (which draws God) can be created only at the heart of a pre-existing fullness. 2. Of this fullness there remains something more than a hollow shell (there is "assimilation"). 3. Finally, the notion of the full may well, in formal logic, exclude the notion of the empty, but in *life* it is different. There are fulls that prolong themselves (complete themselves) organically in emptiness, *fulls that are the initial form of a void* (such are the essential cavities in an organism that often appear in the embryo, in the form of solid masses that later become hollow). It is by the very logic of his development that man, I believe, is forced to *seek to* move into a greater than himself (and it is precisely there that we see the "spiritual power" of matter.) If the fruit is to split and open, it must first be ripe' (*Ibid.*, p. 155).

For Teilhard, moreover, the problem of the natural and supernatural is primarily a *practical* problem. 'Theologians are so taken up by speculative discussions that they forget this—*to reconcile* in practice *the natural and the supernatural* in one single harmonious orientation of human energy is an infinitely more acute problem than the whole accumulated mass of difficulties about the essence o grace. If it is to be solved, we must be shown that renunciation does not mean an impoverishment of nature nor that the Christian turns away from the universe in disgust: it proceeds essentially from *human effort*; true chastity and true contemplation are augmented forms, carried further in their original direction, of human activity and human love. The Christian option, therefore, should be presented as the choice not so much between earth and heaven as between two efforts, to fulfil the universe either *intra* or *extra Christum*' (*L'évangélisation des temps nouveaux*, 1919, in *Ecrits du temps de la guerre*, p. 379).

It will be noted that, in contrast with an earlier over-formal theology, Teilhard, with a sure instinct that is in line with tradition, reintroduces into this notion the concrete and historical reality of Christ, dimly, no doubt, looked for by an expectant creation but essentially new in relation to it (Cf. H. Brouillard, *L'idée de surnaturel et le mystère chrétien* in Mélange offerts au Père de Lubac, vol. 3, pp. 160–6).

[66] ' 'Science alone cannot discover Christ—but Christ realizes the wishes that are born in our hearts in the school of science' (*Science et Christ*, 1921, in *Science et Christ*, p. 62). Christian faith makes it possible to illuminate and distinguish more clearly many features 'in the structure and general progress of the universe' (*Comment je vois*, unpublished, 1948, No. 22).

Here we meet the influence, noted earlier, of Maurice Blondel on Teilhard.—For all the analogical nature of the expression, the conclusion of St Luke's genealogy of Christ's ancestors is here most apposite: 'The son of Adam, the son of God' (Luke 3:38), an affirmation of the astonishing link between God and man that lies behind both man's impulse towards God and his capacity for God.

Quoting the *Summa theologiae* (I. 93. 4) and the *De veritate* (XIII. 1. 1), Père J. M. Le Blond expresses the thought of St Thomas as follows: 'St Thomas, who often emphasizes the trinitarian reflection in every intellectual *act* (in as much as such an act implies a "principium verbi", a "verbum" and an "amor") characterizes the very *substance* of the spiritual creature even more profoundly by the urge, which constitutes spirit, to know God and love him . . . This he means in the very exact sense of the perfect knowledge that God gives in the vision of himself. This indeed introduces, in a universal definition of man, aptitude for, and being destined for, the supernatural' (*Mystique et théologie chez saint Jean de la Croix*, in *Recherches de science religieuse*, April–June 1963, p. 227).

[67] *Introduction au Christianisme.*

[68] *Ibid.*

[69] On first coming into contact with the Far East, Teilhard writes: 'When I look at this extraordinary variety and this vast mass, seeing it as it really is, I feel more strongly than ever that we must free our religion from everything in it that is specifically Mediterranean. I don't believe, mind you, that the majority of oriental "ways of thinking" are anything but obsolete and worn out, and must disappear with the human type that uses them. But I do say that if you look at these forms, worn out though they may be, you will find such a proliferation of "possibilities" in human philosophy, mysticism and morals that you can hardly continue to see mankind entirely and finally shut up in the narrow network of precepts and dogmas in which some people imagine they have expressed the whole broad sweep of Christianity. Our Christianity is the axis along which the religion of the future is developing' (Letter of 27 May 1923).

[70] The chief texts on which Teilhard relies are the following: Rom. 8:22 (the yearning of creation 'groaning in travail'); I Cor. 15:28 ('when all things are subjected to him, then the Son himself will also be subjected to him who put all things under him, that God may be everything to everyone'; Eph. 1:10 ('to unite all things in him, things in heaven and things on earth'); Eph. 1:19–22 (Christ is above all, 'the head over all things for the Church, which is his body, the fullness of him who fills all in all'); Eph. 2:20–22 (the building up and growth of the Church); Eph. 3:18 (the dimensions of the ransomed world, 'breadth and length and height and depth'); Eph. 4:13 ('until we all attain to the unity of the faith and of the knowledge of the Son of God, to mature manhood, to the measure of the stature of the fullness of Christ'); Eph. 4:16 (the organic

growth of the body of Christ); Phil. 3:20–21 ('But our common-wealth is in heaven, and from it we await a saviour, the Lord Jesus Christ, who will change our lowly body to be like his glorious body, by the power which enables him even to subject all things to him-self'); Phil. 4:8 (Christian humanism: 'whatever is true, whatever is honourable . . .'); Col. 1:15–20 (Christ's cosmic function: 'in him all things were created . . . all things were created through him and for him. He is before all things, and in him all things hold together . . . For in him all the fullness of God was pleased to dwell, and through him to reconcile to himself all things'); Col. 2:3 ('Christ, in whom are hid all the treasures of wisdom and know-ledge'); Apoc. 1:8 (Christ, the Alpha and Omega); and finally in the prologue to the Gospel of St John the statement that all things were made through the Word. (John 1:3–10).

[71] *Science et Christ ou analyse et synthèse*, 1921, (in *Science et Christ*, p. 60). It is 'impossible to understand a Christ organically *central* in the supernatural universe and physically *juxtaposed* in the natural universe' (Letter of 10 January 1920).

[72] *Christologie et évolution*, unpublished, 1933.

[73] Referring to astronomical discoveries, Teilhard writes: 'I can't understand why astronomy should still be regarded as a "conser-vative" science. It is more revolutionary than any of the sciences that study the history of life. Spirit is, of course, a greater thing than all dimensions, but such incredible dimensions as we find in stellar space force us to recognize that there is incomparably more "spirit" in the world than we generally imagine. In one sense, this doesn't matter, since the material immensities of the cosmos are "syn-thesized" by our simple powers of vision and our feeble calcul-ations, and so there is no shock in the *spiritual* immensities of the cosmos being destined to organize themselves around one and the same Christ. At the same time, however, we have to enlarge Christ indefinitely, by which I mean extend our view of him until we see that he is the organic centre of everything. This is urgently necessary . . . If only we could realize the variety and power represented by the totality (at one single moment) of all individual human souls, and the totality of all human psychic currents (and how impossible it is to contain them in some petty "Latinism") we would be utterly overwhelmed' (Letter of 28 February 1920).

[74] *Le Milieu Divin*, p. 76. 'In the first place, Christ immediately

becomes coextensive with the vastness of space . . . Once in that position, Christ is then seen, equally readily, to coincide with the depths of time into which the roots of space reach back ' He is 'the axis and the peak of a universal matter . . . In that position, finally, Christ, for all that his domain is ultimately supernatural, gradually radiates his influence throughout the entire mass of nature. Since there is, in concrete fact, only one single process of synthesis in operation, it follows that throughout the whole universe, no element, no movement can exist at any level in the world, without the "informing" action of this chief centre of things.' Christ is 'co-extensive with the scale of values that stretch from the heights of spirit to the depths of matter . . . In him, all things were launched, and all holds together, and all maintained' (*Christologie et évolution*, unpublished, 1933).

[75] Letter of 29 December 1919. 'It is as a result of our being plunged into this universal conflagration that we are (fortunately) obliged (as I see it) to say, "Christ gives us solidity as one whole, *etiam naturaliter*—because we can acquire solidity as individuals only through the whole—and because the whole holds together, throughout its entirety, only in virtue of its final cohesion, and because there is only one Centre-Omega, our Lord Jesus Christ' (*Ibid.*).

[76] *Le coeur de la matière*, unpublished, 1950.

[77] *Le Milieu Divin*, p. 62.

[78] The word 'biological' is used in a sense determined by the context of what follows: the Incarnation is in no way identified with the natural impulse of life, but the latter, already subject to Christ, attains through him a superanimation and sublimation that it was in itself incapable of; and the whole of history attains its unity.

[79] 'Who can fail to perceive the great symbolic gesture of baptism in this general history of matter? Christ immerses himself in the waters of Jordan, symbol of the forces of the earth. These he sanctifies; and in the words of St Gregory of Nyssa, the water streaming from him as he rises, he raises up the whole world with himself' (*Le Milieu Divin*, p. 110). It is an interesting comment, that shows how sensitive Teilhard was to the 'mysterious and sacramental' aspects of the facts of sacred history. Recent theology, in its study of the Fathers, has again brought out these aspects.

[80] *The Phenomenon of Man*, p. 294. 'The whole point of the world is the physical incorporation of the faithful with the Christ of God.

This capital task is carried out with the inevitability and smoothness of a natural evolution. At the source of its developments there had to be an operation, transcendent in order, that would—under conditions that were mysterious, but physically regulated—graft the person of a God upon the cosmos of man ... that operation was the Incarnation ... The Incarnation is a renewing, a reconstitution of *all* the forces and powers of the universe: Christ is the instrument, the centre, the end, of all animate *and* material creation; through him, all things are created, sanctified, given life ...' (*La vie cosmique*, 1916, in *Ecrits du temps de la guerre*, pp. 39–40, 48). 'If he is to be Alpha and Omega, Christ must, without losing his exact human definition, become co-extensive with the physical immensities of duration and space. If he is to reign over the earth, he must super-animate the world' (*Esquisse d'un univers personnel*, 1936, in *L'énergie humaine*, p. 113).

[81] *Le Christique*, unpublished, 1955.

[82] Teilhard criticizes an article on Pantheism contributed by his friend Père Augustin Valensin to the *Dictionnaire apologétique de la foi catholique*, as follows: 'You leave the reader with the impression that Spinoza's position, for example, is *simpliciter mala, falsa*. How is it that you have not suggested that between Spinoza's "Incarnation", in which the whole is hypostatically divine, and the "Incarnation" of the over-cautious, extrinsicist theologians, in which the Pleroma is no more than a social aggregate, there is room for an Incarnation that culminates in the building up of an organic whole, in which physical union with God is at *different levels*? You contrast Christian morality with the morality of Spinoza by saying that the former tells us only that we must become "like unto God'.' I don't accept the distinction. For the Christian, to be *summorphos Christo* is to participate, under a similarity of behaviour, in a common being; it is really "to become Christ", "to become God" ' (Letter of 17 December 1922).

Since that time, and especially as a result of the writings of Père E. Mersch, theologians have returned to views that are more physical and organic; and these have found their way into the encyclical *Mystici Corporis Christi*.

[83] In another passage, what is here noted as appropriate, is regarded as *necessary*: 'The Christian Universal-Christ would be inconceivable if the universe, which it is his function to gather into himself, did not,

in virtue of some evolutionary structure, have a natural centre of convergence from which the Word, becoming incarnate, could radiate its influence over the whole of the universe' (*Introduction au Christianisme*, unpublished, 1944).

[84] *The New Spirit*, in *The Future of Man*, p. 94. Père Fessard, quoting St Thomas and stressing the factual reality of the Gospel miracles, brings out excellently the cosmic role of Christ, not only as the Word, transcendent and immanent to his creation, but also through his humanity. (*La vision religieuse de Teilhard de Chardin* in *L'homme devant Dieu, op. cit.*, pp. 238-47). 'Christ as the centre of all history, and above all the Alpha and Omega of *supernatural* historicity, acts in the first place upon our *human* historicity, with which, moreover, his sojourn upon earth constantly links him: thereby, he attains also a *natural* historicity' (p. 246). He makes it clear that Teilhard never had a mythical view of Christ acting materially upon the cosmos 'in the way in which one *body* can act upon another' (p. 242).

[85] 'A criticism that is more and more frequently levelled against Christians by Gentiles is that, by the very fact of the interposition of Jesus between man and God, we find that the development of the idea of God is arrested—one might say atrophied. In consequence, they say, a modern mind finds that Christianity does not satisfy but paralyses our urge to adore . . . A Christ who reduced God's stature . . .' (*Le coeur de la matière*, unpublished, 1950, p. 30).

[86] *La parole attendue*, 1940, in *Cahiers Pierre Teilhard de Chardin*, No. 4, p. 26. It is, too, the prospect of the Incarnation that, through its influence on the metaphysics of being and the multiple, confers in fact an absolute value upon the latter. 'In the first place, by virtue of the Incarnation, God can no longer (at least *hic et nunc* and for ever) dispense with the multiple in which he has immersed himself. And secondly, the reality, God+Multiple, in *Christo Jesu*, seems both in Christian practice and in Pauline mysticism, to represent a perfection that, however extrinsic to God we may hold it to be, brings with it a real completion in the equilibrium of universal being. Implicit in that, without doubt, is the concept of the multiple as fundamentally good, and in some degree, necessary' (*La route de l'Ouest*, unpublished, 1932, appendix).

Speaking of Christ as the head of the Church, St Thomas holds that 'the whole humanity of Christ, soul and body, exerts an influence on men both as to the soul and (secondarily) as to the body' (*Summa theologiae* IIIa, p. 8. art. 2). In view of the solidarity of body and world, this means that Christ's influence extends to the entire universe.

87 *The historical Christ*

'Next, in order to win our love and secure our faith, Christianity unveils to our eyes and hearts the moving and unfathomable reality of the historical Christ in whom the exemplary life of an individual man contains this mysterious drama: the master of the world leading, like an element of the world, not only an elemental life, but (in addition to this and because of it) leading the total life of the universe, which he has shouldered and assimilated by experiencing it himself' (*Le Milieu Divin*, p. 102).

'The immense enchantment of the divine milieu owes all its value in the long run to the human-divine contact which was revealed at the Epiphany of Jesus. If you suppress the historical reality of Christ, the divine omnipresence which intoxicates us becomes, like all the other dreams of metaphysics, uncertain, vague, conventional—lacking the decisive experimental verification by which to impose itself on our minds, and without the moral authority to assimilate our lives into it. From this it follows that, however dazzling the expansions which we shall try in a moment to discern in the risen Christ, their beauty and their stuff of reality will always remain inseparable from the initial and verifiable truth of the Gospel event. The mystical Christ, the universal Christ of St Paul, has neither meaning nor value in our eyes except as an expansion of the Christ who was born of Mary and who died on the cross. The former essentially draws his fundamental quality of undeniability and concreteness from the latter. However far we may be drawn into the divine spaces open to Christian mysticism, we never leave behind the Jesus of the Gospels. On the contrary we feel a growing need to enfold ourselves ever more firmly within his human truth' (*Ibid.*, p. 117). 'For God, to become incarnate in an evolving world, is to be born into it. And how can he be born into it except through some individual as a starting-point? . . . To suppress the historical reality of Christ (and that means his divinity) would be immediately to dissipate in the unreal all the mystical energy that has been accumulating for the last two thousand years in the Christian phylum' (*Introduction au Christianisme*, unpublished, 1944). Teilhard immediately, however, relates Christ's historical reality to his universality 'I believe in the divinity of the child of Bethlehem *because it is included, and in so far as,* and *under the form in which* it is included, historically and biologically, in the reality of the universal Christ to whom my faith and adoration are more directly extended' (*Ibid.*).

'The more one thinks about the underlying laws of evolution, the more is one convinced that the Universal-Christ could not, at the end of all time, appear at the summit of the world if he had not previously entered it, in the course of its development, *by way of birth,* in the form of an *element.* While it is indeed the Christ-Omega who maintains the universe in motion, on the other hand it is from his concrete seed, the man of Nazareth, that (both in theory and in historical fact) the Christ-Omega draws for us his whole consistence. The two terms are intrinsically part and parcel of one another and, in a Christ who is truly total, they cannot vary except simultaneously' (*Christianisme et évolution,* unpublished, 1945). 'I find myself so placed that I cannot breathe apart from our Lord—and that I realize that, without the historical and traditional revelation, our Lord vanishes' (*Ibid.*).

'In the course of a conversation Teilhard, on 23 September 1950,' says C. Cuénot, 'spoke more or less as follows: "We may regard the historical Christ as the point from which a Christic religious movement springs. The historical Christ may be compared to a shaft on which the vault of the Christic religion is built. If you take away from Christ his quality of having existed as a real element, the Christian movement collapses. The historic Christ contributes an element of reality, of concrete involvement in the cosmos. There must be a cell, or a seed, for the structure to hold together biologically. If you take away from Christ the fact of having been an initial spark, a biological cell, then the whole structure is undermined" ' (C. Cuénot, *op. cit.,* pp. 147–8).

[88] Teilhard uses the word 'physical' to mean *real,* sometimes with an experimental or scientific overtone. He would not have rejected the notion of the 'juridical', too, which, in one sense, is also physical, and which conforms to the evidence of scripture, in both the Old and the New Testaments (the Incarnation is a 'covenant').

[89] *Teilhard and Péguy*

This subject was discussed by Péguy, in whom Teilhard was pleased to find a similarity of ideas: 'I was surprised to find Péguy so close to me (it would be less conceited to put it the other way round).

His concern to defend and praise the "fleshly cradle" of Christ fits in with my own personal preoccupations. And, just for the moment, I have a slight grudge against him for having taken the subject of Eve. *Eve*, the "natural" mother, whose face, so full of mystery, blends into the distant past, shrouded in symbol and legend: what an admirable personification of the ties, so essential and so vital, which indissolubly bind our human fascicle to nature's laborious and patient advance' (Letter of 1 January 1917, in *Making of a Mind*, p. 159).

Jean Onimus has given a good assessment of the resemblances and differences in Péguy and Teilhard: 'Péguy, resolute in his hostility to the modern world, was much too close to Pascal to be willing even to consider any relation between the progress of mankind and the manifestation on earth of the divine. Horrified by today's rising flood of universal evil and by the signs he found on all sides of a basic disaster, he saw in hope no more than a completely gratuitous aspiration, a gesture, he believed, that belied the scene presented by reality: in Teilhard, on the other hand, temporal hope tends to coincide with the virtue of hope' (*Pierre Teilhard de Chardin, ou la foi au monde*, Paris, Plon, 1963, p. 26). One should perhaps add that Péguy was more alive than Teilhard to the horror of damnation (of which temporal misery was the image). The aspect of redemption, emphasized by Péguy (particularly in the symbolism of the passion of Joan of Arc) is, again, stressed more lightly by Teilhard. Cf. H. Urs von Balthasar, *Les métamorphoses de l'enfer* in the special Péguy number of *Esprit* (August–September 1964).

[90] The latter is quoted by name in *Le Milieu Divin* (p. 110). St Irenaeus would have recognized his own influence in this passage from *Mon univers* (in *Science et Christ*, 1924, pp. 89-90; quoted in *Hymn of the Universe*, pp. 76-8). 'The prodigious expanses of time that preceded the first Christmas were not empty of Christ: they were imbued with the influx of his power. It was the ferment of his conception that stirred up the cosmic masses and directed the initial development of the biosphere. It was the travail preceding his birth that accelerated the development of instinct and the birth of thought upon the earth. Let us have done with the stupidity which makes a stumbling-block of the endless eras of expectancy imposed on us by the Messiah; the fearful, anonymous labours of primitive man, the beauty fashioned through its age-long history by ancient Egypt, the

anxious expectancies of Israel, the patient distilling of the attar of oriental mysticism, the endless refining of wisdom by the Greeks all these were needed before the flower could blossom on the rod of Jesse and of all humanity. All these preparatory processes were cosmically and biologically necessary that Christ might set foot upon our human stage. And all this labour was set in motion by the active, creative awakening of his soul in as much as that human soul had been chosen to breathe life into the universe When Christ first appeared before men in the arms of Mary he had already stirred up the world.'

In this context a famous passage from St Augustine is apposite. In his commentary on the multiplication of loaves he reminds us of the never-ceasing miracle of God's creative work, of which the germination of a grain of corn is an illustration: the miracle of God's extraordinary interventions being not 'greater' but 'unusual' (*ut non majora, sed insolita vivendo stuperent, quibus quotidiana viluerant, Tract. 24 in Joannem*).

After reading *Christologie et évolution*, Père Maréchal wrote to Teilhard: 'I believe, as you do, that progress in natural philosophy, if "properly understood", must enrich our knowledge of the mystery of the Incarnation and give a real content to some very fine sayings of St Paul and St John that we have retained without sufficiently "realizing" their primary significance. Since the later middle ages we have lacked, in scholasticism, a real "philosophy of nature": the few wretched propositions of our academic cosmologies cannot fill the gap; and on more than one point this philosophic poverty entailed a considerable impoverishment of theological speculation. Writing such as yours helps to give us back the feeling for what we have lost and to open the way to the adaptations that are now necessary. That is why I welcome it so sincerely, even on points where some of my own philosophical preferences lie elsewhere' (3 July 1934). Maurice Blondel, too, though parting company with Teilhard in his emphasis on the transcendence of the spiritual life, regards the Incarnation as the touchstone of a true cosmology and an integral metaphysics: 'Let us press on then, with no hesitation, in the direction in which, as the world and man grow greater in man's eyes, so does Christ grow greater, in our eyes and our hearts' (*Premier mémoire* from Maurice Blondel to Teilhard, *Archives de philosophie*, January–March 1961, pp. 129–30). On Blondel's 'pan-christism' see the passages collected in Maurice Blondel and Auguste Valensin, *Correspondance* (Aubier, 1957), Vol. 1, pp. 43-8.

[91] 'In the first place, Christ experienced in himself the *individual* human heart, the heart that is all our agony and our joy. In Christ, however, there was more than just a man—there was a man who was not only the perfect man, the ideal man, but also the total man, the man who gathered up, in the depths of his own consciousness, the consciousness of all men. In virtue of that, he must have experienced the universal' (*Mon univers*, in *Science et Christ*, 1924, p. 90).

[92] Cf. Henri Oster, *Le mystère pascal dans la pastorale* (Editions du Cerf, 1964, pp 33-5). Teilhard would have subscribed to such a theology of the Redemption as that put forward by Karl Rahner: the latter sees in the death of Christ not primarily the separation of body and soul or a way to moral merit, but the existential act of fulfilment that, by consummating his human life in an unsurpassable sacrifice, thereby establishes it in a state of glory: the infinitely loving sacrifice of Calvary is then, for Christ, the beginning of an eternal transfiguration, of a transition to God, but at the same time of a permanent and ever present position of saving mediation (or in St Paul's word 'intercession') (*Ibid.*).

[93] *Super-Christ*

In a paper dated 1945, and entitled *Super-Humanité, Super-Christ, Super-Charité* (in *Science et Christ*) Teilhard explains more exactly what he means (p. 193, note). 'In these three expressions the prefix "super" is used to indicate, not a difference in *nature* but a more advanced degree of realization or perception' . . . 'By Super-Christ I certainly do not mean *another* Christ, a second Christ different from and greater than the first; I mean the same Christ, the Christ of all time, revealing himself to us in a form and in dimensions, with an urgency and an area of contact, that are augmented and made new.' Later, Teilhard adds that by Super-Christ he means, 'the increase in stature, assumed in our consciousness, by the person of Jesus, proportionate with the awakening of our thought to the super-dimensions of the world and of mankind'. These passages confirm our interpretation, i.e. that we are dealing with a *subjective progress of religious consciousness*, not with the objective reality of Christ or God-Omega.

'Not simply infinitely extensible and adaptable to the new dimen-

sions of the world, but inexhaustibly charged for our hearts with evolutionary energy—so rises over our horizon, and grows greater, to the
scale of and to meet the needs of, the ultra-human, a true Super-Christ,
filled with the radiance of super-charity' (*Le coeur de la matière*, unpublished 1950, p. 30). Teilhard, we see, refers to a modification of
the religious consciousness of modern humanity, which calls for a
presentation of Christ better adapted to itself. Such a possible presentation, however, can be drawn only from a better development of
the tradition of Christ's relation to the world. In the preceding
paragraph Teilhard had said, 'In a governed plan of creative union,
it is inevitably not the universe alone but God himself that "is
Christified" in Omega, at the upper limits of cosmogenesis. In
other words, "evolved" monotheism, around which all that is best
in the earth's religious energies is concentrating, is logically and
biologically being fulfilled in the direction of some form of Pan-
Christism'. This comment would seem to mean, as pointed out in
the text, that in the eyes of the new man of today, the whole truth of
God, the one and triune God, appears in the form of Christ.
Similarly, when Teilhard says, 'Christ saves. But must we not
hasten to add that Christ, too, is saved by evolution?' (*Le Christique*,
unpublished, 1955), he does not mean that Christ is in some way
dependent on an evolving world   He is referring to the fact that the
growth of Christ's mystical body is necessary to him, and also
perhaps to the apostolic value derived from Christianity's acceptance of the idea of evolution.

A final passage that calls for explanation: in the same essay (*Le
Christique*) Teilhard says that 'in one sense Christ has a third
nature, not human, nor divine, but cosmic'. This cannot, evidently,
be reconciled with dogma; but if we look at it in the context of
Teilhard's thought and compare it with a similar statement in
Comment je vois, we shall see that it amounts to this: the Incarnation
of Christ in the flesh of man and his glorious Resurrection enabled
him, by forming one with the cosmos, to be the God of the cosmos,
the ultimate centre of 'universal concentration' (Cf. Roger Leys,
S.J., *Teilhard dangereux?* in *Revue Teilhard de Chardin*, No. 14, March
1963, pp. 28–9). In a long note, Père Smulders points out, without
attempting to reconcile, the dogmatic 'enormity' of this 'third
nature' of Christ; it would appear that here, as elsewhere, Teilhard's language should not be interpreted literally but in the light

of the intention beyond it: and he was certainly not so presumptuous as to intend to overlook or supersede the definitions of Chalcedon.

94 'When man has awoken to the idea of "man's function in the universe", the higher his appreciation of the part played in the world by the forces of choice and consciousness, the more clearly will he understand that the appearance on earth of reflective thought necessarily entails, to complete it and balance it, another "reflexion"—the reflexion of the whole upon the monad, following that of the monad upon itself: in other words, a revelation' (*Le sens humain*, unpublished, 1929).

'We may say, without in any way derogating from the gratuitousness of God's action, that the Creation, the Incarnation and the Redemption were necessary: necessary for us, not for God' (Roger Leys, *art. cit.*).

95 On the one hand, says Karl Rahner, there is in God the possibility, without renouncing his own self, of *becoming other*, of assuming man as his own reality, by stripping himself of himself, and veiling his majesty. This implies no lack, but a perfection. On the other hand, the mystery of man is defined by his 'obediential potentiality' for the infinite, his movement towards God, his capacity to be fulfilled by God. What Christ does is simply to display, at its highest degree, this tendency of man to fulfil himself in the infinite by abandoning his own self: he is the *truth of man*, the truth of the universe. The finite, in consequence, takes on an infinite depth, and is no longer the contrary of the infinite ('On the Theology of the Incarnation' in *Theological Investigations*, Vol. iv, London, Darton, Longman and Todd, and Baltimore, Helicon Press, 1966, pp. 105-121. Cf. 'Current Problems in Christology', *ibid.*, Vol. i, 1961, in particular pp. 136, 160, 162–5).

96 'We should note also that God's project, the project of love that first manifests itself in the creation, is *in itself* all of one piece; that supernatural "grace" and Christ are present in it from the very beginning; that everything was made, and is perpetually being made, for Christ, the total Christ, head and members, and for the participation of the world, within Christ, in union with the Father' (J.-M. Le Blond, *art. cit.*, p. 234).

Teilhard was not in a position to make sufficient use of the results of the renascence in biblical studies. Nevertheless, in his recognition of the eminent place occupied by Christ he at the same time re-disclosed the *concrete* character of a mystery of encounter and covenant, in history, between God and man.

[97] Cf. K. Rahner, *Réflexions théologiques sur l'Incarnation*, *op. cit.*, Vol. III, p. 96. The idea expressed here may be paralleled with Père Morel's commentary on St John of the Cross: *Le sens de l'existence d'après saint Jean de la Croix*, Aubier, 1960, Vol. II, *Logique*, pp. 256 ff.

[98] 'For all the transcendence and self-sufficiency of the absolute Being, some part of his characteristics is inevitably impressed upon nature, since he in some degree informs the latter and causes it to emerge "from nothingness". And on the other hand, too, some sort of complement is necessarily added to the absolute Being by the creative act, since that act can be expressed in terms of union. Creation becoming a union that generates!' (*Du cosmos à la cosmogénèse*, 1951, *L'activation de l'énergie*, p. 271 note). This remark is made in connexion with the Christology-theology nexus, *ibid*. 'The "trinitarian" being seen now not as a higher extension but as the very heart, of the "christic"' (*Ibid.*, p. 272 note).

[99] A. Jeannière, *Approches christologiques*, in *Essais sur Teilhard de Chardin*, *op. cit.*, p. 91. 'The Redemption has, indeed, a sorrowful side to it, for Christ suffers for the sin of the world, but at the same time it can be recognized as a correction of the line of advance of the whole of cosmogenesis. We should not, however, simply juxtapose the two aspects: it is the redeeming that transforms and irradiates new forces, and it is the salvation that, through Christ's victory over the forces of evil, transfigures the world and gives new life to its potentialities' (*Ibid.*, pp. 91-2).

[100] 'The essence of Christianity is simply and solely belief in the unification of the world in God through the Incarnation' (*La religion du personnel*, unpublished, quoted by C. Cuénot, *Pierre Teilhard de Chardin*, p. 239).

'Until the very end, I suppose, I shall be tied to a work of research that provides my platform—and is also my fate. But I am feeling more strongly than ever that the real interest of my life is wandering elsewhere—towards the renascence of a religion that will really make faith in a personal God an essential *working part* of an active world (and not just an extra ornament—or burden) (Letter of 18 January 1936).

[101] *Les deux sources de la morale et de la religion*, Alcan, 1932, p. 249.

[102] This is no more than a tendency, perhaps, and rests upon an 'abstraction' that, as noted earlier, Teilhard refuses to make. On this point it would seem, too, that Père Smulders, generally so sympathetic to Teilhard's thought, pushes his criticism too far when he says that his metaphysics 'makes the mistake of regarding man's real destiny of affiliation to God as the only possible destiny' (*op. cit.*, p. 147).

[103] Unpublished letter of 3 July, 1934, written after reading Teilhard's *Christologie et évolution*.

[104] Cf. G. Crespy, *La pensée théologique de Teilhard de Chardin*, *op. cit.*, on the Gospel problem, see X. Léon-Dufour, *Les évangiles et l'histoire de Jésus*, Editions du Seuil, 1963.

[105] *Introduction au christianisme*, unpublished, 1944.

[106] *Le coeur de la matière*, unpublished, 1950.

[107] *Original sin*

Teilhard was deeply interested in the problem of original sin; in particular he was very conscious of the difficulty, from the apostolic point of view, that arose from the way in which it was generally represented. 'I am daily becoming more and more convinced *by experience*, that our "catechetical" picture of the Fall bars the way for an extensive religious current that asks no more than to be absorbed into Christianity, but which turns aside because it feels, I think, that you cannot enter without discarding all the most valuable and important fruits won by recent efforts of men's minds' (Unpublished letter to Père Auguste Valensin, Holy Saturday, 1922).

Teilhard left some important notes on this problem: *Note sur le péché originel* (at the end of *Le Christ évoluteur*, unpublished, 1942): *Réflexions sur le péché originel*; a paragraph in *Introduction au christianisme*. From these the following ideas emerge:

1. The *scientific difficulties* in the traditional picture: the notion of a sin of absolute gravity, at the origin of mankind, which is improbable on the transformist hypothesis, is not patient of experiment or verification.

2. The *greatness* and the *gravity*, the extension and depth, of man's sin in history, a sin whose scope is revealed in the mystery of the Redemption: for the fault must be as cosmic as Christ. 'The most essential aim and criterion of Christian orthodoxy may be reduced

to this one point: to preserve Christ *on the scale of and at the head of* creation: however vast the world is found to be, the figure of the risen Christ must enclose it. Such, since St John and St Paul, is the fundamental rule of theology.' If original sin were only an accident, 'the Christic power could never directly, organically, formally, extend beyond a short, slender, human spindle' (*Réflexions sur le péché originel*).

3. A *constructive theory*, in conformity with Teilhard's system, which seeks to explain *if not the fact of the sin* (the mystery of freedom) at least its possibility or quasi-necessity: in biblical imagery, original sin symbolizes the law of a humanity in whose growth in time the fault is involved.

'The origin of evil does not present the same difficulties, nor call for the same explanations, in a universe whose structure is evolutionary as it does in an initially perfect static universe. It ceases then to be necessary for reason to suspect or look for a "culprit". Physical and moral disorders arise spontaneously in a self-organizing system, *so long as* that system is not completely organized. *Necesse est ut eveniant scandala.* From that point of view, original sin—considered in its cosmic basis, if not in its historical occurrence among the first men—tends to merge into the actual mechanism of creation, in which it appears as the activity of the negative force of "counter-evolution"' (*Note sur le péché originel*, at the end of *Le Christ évoluteur*).

'If we transpose the original fault to the dimensions of the universe as it now appears to us in the organic totality of time and space, it tends (at least in its roots) to link up with the law by which, in an evolving world, a fall is always possible and punishment always present' (*Introduction au christianisme*).

Realizing the difficulty in winning acceptance for his theory, Teilhard wrote: 'I don't think that in the history of the Church anyone has "pulled off" such an adjustment (in the way of representation) of dogma as that of which we're speaking—though similar attempts have been made and carried half-way, for example when geocentrism was abandoned. More precisely, one should say that the reformulation of historical views on original sin has been *virtually* achieved ever since the end of geocentrism; but it is only today that we have come explicitly to realize it'. Teilhard quotes, too, the abandonment of the idea of a world-wide Flood (Letter of 14 May 1922).

We should add that some aspects, at least, of the problem of original sin have been removed by the principles of the encyclical *Divino afflante spiritu* (1943) and by advances in exegesis. Thus Teilhard's statement of the problem is to some extent out of date. In one of his very last essays, he notes: 'It has taken us time, and a very long time, to realize that some ways of conceiving such a phenomenon (Revelation) were disastrous and impossible. All through a long initial stage (from which we are still hardly emerging) were not people looking in the Bible for answers to questions raised by astronomy, geology or biology? . . . As though in the domain of experience we could use (from the same angle and for the same facts) two different sources of illumination—the discovered and the taught' (*Barrière de la mort et co-réflexion*, 1955, in *L'activation de l'énergie*, p. 427).

[108] 'Above all, by revealing an original Fall, Christianity provides our intelligence with a reason for the disconcerting excess of sin and suffering at certain points' (*Le Milieu Divin*, p. 102). 'Of its nature, and as a result of original sin, it is true that matter represents a perpetual impulse towards failure' (*Ibid.*, p. 107). Cf. *Ibid.*, pp. 84–5.

'Is it really sure that, for an eye trained and sensitized by a light other than that of pure science, the quantity and the malice of evil *hic et nunc* spread through the world, does not betray a certain *excess*, inexplicable to our reason, if to the normal effect of *evolution* is not added the *extra-ordinary* effect of some catastrophe or primordial deviation?' (*The Phenomenon of Man*, p. 313).

[109] *Comment je vois*, unpublished, 1948, No. 30, note 32.

[110] Evil is the 'very expression of a state of still incompletely organized plurality. In a world that is in process of formation, this transitory state of imperfection is manifested, no doubt, in detail, in the form of a certain number of culpable actions: the very first instances of these, and the most decisive (although the least conscious in human history) could well be taken separately and described as a "primitive fault". But what constitutes the original weakness for the creature, is in reality the radical condition that causes it to be born from the multiple, so that it continually retains in its fibres (so long as it is not completely spiritualized) a tendency to sink back into the dust . . . In such conditions, evil is not an unforeseen accident in the universe. It is an enemy, a shadow that God inevitably raises up simply by the fact that he decides on the

Creation . . . Creation is no trifle for omnipotence, no afternoon picnic. It is an adventure, a risk, a battle to which he commits himself entirely' (*Christologie et évolution*, unpublished, 1933). 'In this new setting, evil, without losing any of its bite or horror, ceases to be an unintelligible element, and becomes a *natural feature* of the world's structure' (*Ibid.*). Cf. also *La route de l'Ouest*, unpublished, 1932, appendix.

[111] *Note sur le péché originel*, at the end of *Le Christ évoluteur*, unpublished, 1942.

[112] While rejecting a mythological concept of original sin, and making it a real event and an historical drama, Père Jean Daniélou interprets it as a *religious* reality lying 'in a domain that is inaccessible to empirical enquiry': 'To minimize the reality of the historical origin of original sin and its effects on the condition of man, is at the same time to destroy the significance of Christ's death and Resurrection. But it is the very gravity of this revelation that requires us to be pitiless in bringing it out in its naked truth and in not identifying the substantial content and the secondary representations' (*Au commencement, Genèse* 1-11, Editions du Seuil, 1963, p. 76). Père Daniélou rightly points out, too, that suffering and death are part of man's condition as such: the biblical account simply indicates that henceforth physical life 'pursues its normal course', but that man is deprived of access to the supernatural order to which he is called (pp. 73-5).

[113] The influence of Christ on man's fallen nature is seen again in this passage: 'By nature, too, and as a result of the Incarnation, matter has a tendency towards (feels the stimulus or allurement of) heightened being, and this counter-balances and even dominates the *fomes peccati*' (*Le Milieu Divin*, p. 107).

Similarly, at the end of his discussion of original sin (in *Le Christ évoluteur*) Teilhard says, 'Whatever step forward Christian thought may decide to take, we may say that it will be in the direction of a close organic link (both in co-extension and in mutual contact) between the forces of death and the forces of life that operate within an evolving universe—and that ultimately means between Redemption and evolution.'

[114] The reference is to the well-known passage in St Paul (Rom. 5:12-21) and to the canon of the fifth session of the Council of Trent, in 1546 (Denzinger-Bannwart, No. 790). The near-co-

incidence in date with Copernicus's book from which a complete change in man's awareness was to stem, will be noted (1543).

Père Leys shows that the Church's fidelity to Scripture and tradition does not rule out the possibility 'of a fuller development of the meaning of dogmas or of a later improvement in their expression': 'in the interpretation both of Scripture and of Conciliar pronouncements, we must remember that the formulas used are human words, and that it is important to know the cultural background, both in order to understand them in their true sense and to appreciate what they leave unsaid. Neither Scripture nor the Councils prepared in advance answers to questions that were not being asked of them'. 'The development of Semitic studies' has initiated us 'into types of literature that are proper to the genius of those peoples' and has made us recognize 'in the story of Adam and Eve an admirable parable of man's condition, which illustrates both the ideal that God envisaged for his creature and the constant inadequacy of the latter's response'.

Of the hereditary transmission of original sin (of which it will be noted that canon 790 of the Council of Trent simply says that it is *propagatione transfusum*) Père Leys says, 'original sin is not localized in chromosomes. What the picture of hereditary transmission seeks to uphold is the unity of the human race and the solidarity of all men in sin, that is to say, the need for redemption . . . Sin is transmitted by generation. Speaking strictly, we should put it more exactly: generation produces being-in-the-world, and since this world is sinful it infects man with its sin. Sin is a human, not a biological, reality: it affects the being through the world of man, not through the purely vital world'. In support of this interpretation Père Leys quotes Origen, who says that 'sin is transmitted not only by generation, but also by education and culture' (Commentary on Romans, P.G. 14. 1017. Cf. *art. cit.*). See, too, C. Tresmontant, *Note sur le péché originel*, included in R. Garaudy, *Perspectives de l'homme*, P.U.F. 1959.

Père Smulders includes in his book an appendix on original sin, in which he describes the progress of theological thought on the subject, which would doubtless have been accepted by Teilhard with whose thought it is fundamentally more or less in agreement.

In answer to a comment from a correspondent, Teilhard wrote: 'I am completely in agreement with you about the disadvantages in "rationalizing" dogma—it comes down to impoverishing and vulgarizing it. All the same, there are some legitimate ways of reconciling the two, which in no way sacrifice the transcendent developments of the Creed (it is in those, specifically, that the mystery lies)' (Letter of 14 May 1922).

[115] Here Teilhard seems not to have been sufficiently careful to distinguish accurately man's ontological condition and his contingent situation, which, by an accident in history, has made him a fallen being. Compact of weakness and finiteness, of enslavement to nature and mortality, man's structural condition has been no more than the occasion of his fall; but the fall aggravated that condition by creating an *estrangement* that did not exist by right. In fact, however, we have to admit that, in man's present state, the two phases are difficult to distinguish.

In a letter quoted earlier, which is most sympathetic, too, to Teilhard and to some of his theories, Père Maréchal pointed this out to Teilhard. He prefaces this by saying: 'I would certainly not go so far as to be shocked by your running the two things together in this way—including, in some undefined way, in personal sins some deliberate ratification of an innate fall, and in the original fault itself some anticipation of the series of personal sins it initiated. Without returning to the position of Catharinus, one might perhaps conceive a theory that would divide original sin less sharply from the sins we commit now.' Père Maréchal continues, 'But this new explanation [he is referring to Teilhard's theory of original sin] modifies, it seems to me, the essential basis and not simply the formulation of the "defined" dogma. More precisely still, it suppresses the dogma, by declaring that it is superfluous. What in fact it does is to replace original sin by the distant ontological root of physical and moral evil. Now, this root, this metaphysical possibility of evil, inherent in the creature qua creature, neither calls for nor rules out the state of supernatural justification, and therefore cannot take on, with the "privation of original justice", the relationship of active principle with effective consequence which the Council of Trent asserts so clearly of the sin of Adam. The whole Christian economy of "justification" is upset. The hypothesis put forward would lead to saying that mankind as such has never lost its initial right to grace and that the deprivation of grace is to be seen, in each individual, simply as the effect of a fault of which he is now guilty. All that would remain under the name "original sin" would be simply the natural imperfections of the created being, "the radical condition that causes the creature to be born from the multiple" (p. 10 of the ms. of *Christologie et évolution*)—in other words, a philosophical truth' (3 July 1934).

[116] On the problem of evil, see *Le Milieu Divin*, pp. 85-9. 'In virtue of his very perfections, God cannot ordain that the elements of a world in course of growth—or at least of a fallen world in the process of rising again—should avoid shocks and diminishments, even moral ones' (*Ibid.*, p. 86). Teilhard adds a footnote: 'Because his perfections cannot run counter to the nature of things, and because a world, assumed to be progressing towards perfection, or "rising upward", is of its nature precisely still partially disorganized. A world without a trace or threat of evil would be a world already consummated.' The theme of an imperfect creation and of the necessity for man to be progressively educated to use his freedom, was familiar to St Irenaeus.

'We soon see, under the veil of security and harmony which—viewed from on high—envelops the rise of man, a particular type of cosmos in which evil, as extensive and as grave as you please, necessarily appears, following in the wake of evolution—not by accident (which would not matter greatly) but through the very structure of the system. A universe which is involuted and interiorized, but at the same time and by the same token a universe which labours, which sins, and which suffers . . . Suffering and failure, tears and blood: so many by-products (often precious moreover and with a new purpose to serve) begotten by the noosphere on its way' (*The Phenomenon of Man*, p. 313).

'Not from any lack of power, but in virtue of the very structure of nothingness upon which he will act, God, in order to create, can proceed in only one way: by arranging, by gradually unifying, a multitude of elements, through the influence of a power of attraction and making use of the hesitant but persistent work of statistical causation; initially, those elements are infinite in number, extremely simple and barely conscious; then they gradually become much less numerous, more complex, and finally attain the power of reflexion. What, then, is the inevitable counterpart to any success that is won in the course of such a process, if not that it must be paid for by some proportion of wastage? Lack of harmony or physical decomposition in the pre-living, suffering in the living, and, in the domain of freedom, sin: there can be no order that does not involve at every level, as it takes form, some disorder. In this ontological (or, more correctly, ontogenic) condition of participated being there is nothing that derogates from the dignity or limits the omnipotence of the Creator: nothing, moreover, that contains the least suggestion of Manicheanism' (*Comment je vois*, unpublished, 1948, No. 30).

[117] Cf. *The Phenomenon of Man*, appendix. 'Yes, the moral and social development of mankind is indeed the authentic and "natural" consequence of organic evolution . . . All moral perversions are found in embryo in the most "natural" of activities, the most passive (in appearance) in the hands of the first cause: in these activities, perversions may be dormant, but they are not left behind, surmounted, nor overcome' (Letter of 13 July 1916, in *Making of a Mind*, pp. 110–11). As Pastor Crespy has perceptively noted, Teilhard is careful to distinguish the 'thresholds' of evil: 'Lack of harmony and physical decomposition in the pre-living, suffering in the living, and, in the domain of freedom, sin' (*Comment je vois*, as above). Note 33 in the same essay distinguishes 'statistical disorders' and 'the ontological slope, or inertia, that causes participated being constantly to fall back towards multiplicity'. Teilhard adds: 'It is one thing for us to explain the compossibility of evil and God, and quite another to bear physical and spiritual suffering. In the first case, a dialectic may, indeed, provide a sufficient answer; but to cure the second we need nothing less than the transforming power of what I shall later describe as "super-charity"' (*Ibid.*, note 31).

[118] 'But this nether darkness which we sought to flee, could equally well have been a sort of abyss opening on to sheer nothingness. Imperfection, sin, evil, the flesh, appeared to us mainly as a retrograde step, a reverse aspect of things, which ceased to exist for us the further we penetrated into God. Your revelation, O Lord, compels me to believe more. The powers of evil, in the universe, are not only an attraction, a deviation, a minus sign, an annihilating return to plurality . . .' (*Le Milieu Divin*, p. 147).

[119] 'If we read the Gospel boldly, we shall find that no idea expresses more clearly, to our minds, *the redemptive function of the Word*, than that of unification of all flesh in one and the same

spirit' (*La lutte contre la multitude*, 1917, in *Ecrits du temps de la guerre*, p. 124).

'We may well be inclined, perhaps, to see on the Cross no more than the suffering of an individual, an act simply of expiation. We fail to appreciate the creative power of that death. If we take a wider view, we shall see that the Cross is the symbol and the focal point of an action whose intensity is inexpressible. Even from the earthly point of view, Jesus crucified, if we understand him fully, is not rejected nor vanquished. It is he, on the contrary, who bears the burden and leads the course of universal progress ever higher towards God' (*La signification et la valeur constructrice de la souffrance*, 1933, in *L'énergie humaine*, pp. 65-6).

'The essence of Christianity is simply and solely belief in the unification of the world in God through the Incarnation' (*Esquisse d'un univers personnel*, 1936, *ibid.*, p. 113).

'Christ's essential message is not to be found in the Sermon on the Mount, nor even in the significant act of Calvary: it consists entirely in the proclamation of a "divine fatherhood": to put it in another way, in the affirmation in which God, a personal being, offers himself to man as the term of a personal *union*' (*L'énergie humaine, ibid.*, p. 193).

'In conformity with the deepest aspirations of our age, the Cross becomes the symbol, the way, the very act of progress' (*The new spirit*, 1942, in *The Future of Man*, p. 95).

'In an "Alexandrian" type of universe Creation and Redemption correspond to two independent and distinct operations and phases; but we should note that in the second type of world Creation, Incarnation and Redemption are seen to be simply three complementary aspects of one and the same process: creation (*because* it is unifying) entailing a certain involvement of the creator in his work, and at the same time (*because* it necessarily produces evil as a secondary statistical effect) involving a certain redemptive compensation' (*Réflexions sur le péché originel*, unpublished, 1947).

[120] This point has, of course, been noted by Pastor Crespy. We might say that the abasement, or even annihilation, of Christ is not sufficiently emphasized.

[121] *Le Milieu Divin*, pp. 103-4. The concept of evil as a by-product of evolution is one of the points on which Teilhard conflicts with Gabriel Marcel (Cf. C. Cuénot, *op. cit.*, pp. 308-9).

'The Cross is the supreme adoration of the Father by the incarnate Son in loving reparation for the sin of the human family, in a reversal, in a total offering, of even the greatest of men's crimes; it is also the mystery of love for men, in giving one's life for those one loves' (J. M. Le Blond, *Consacrer l'effort humain*, Etudes, January 1948, p. 65).

[122] The Church's never-dying Pascal joy is always tinged by the memory of Good Friday and continually looks back to the mystery of Christ's death: it is in virtue of his crucifixion that he judges the world and draws all to him (John 12:31-32). See the fine comment of St Leo (sermon 8, on the Passion) quoted in the breviary on the feast of the Exaltation of the Holy Cross (September 14).

[123] 'We must abandon this quarrel. It is generally presented as a conflict between a "plus" (religion) and a "minus" (atheism). It should, in fact, be presented as a conflict between two positive forces. Human faith is as justifiable as religious faith, and both may be reconciled if we admit (as is theologically sound) that the kingdom of God does not necessarily act upon a humanity that has come to rest; to attain its zenith, it awaits an adult humanity' (*Le néo-humanisme moderne, et ses réactions sur le christianisme*, notes taken at a lecture given by Teilhard to chaplains of the *Action catholique ouvrière*, Versailles, 21 September 1948).

[124] 'If we are dynamically orientated towards this total Christ, tomorrow China and the whole working class will be ours' (*Ibid.*).

[125] *Le Christ évoluteur*, unpublished, 1942. 'The Cross takes on a value which is the same, but with something new added, in the sense that its shadow is gradually illuminated.' The Cross 'is the symbol of the creative but painful effort of a mankind that rises up to the Christ that draws it to him' (Third lecture to the Marcel Légaut group, 10 December 1930).

'Flung as we are into a universe in which the struggle against evil is the *sine qua non* of existence, the Cross takes on for us a new gravity and new beauties, such, indeed, as have the greatest appeal for us. Jesus, it is true, is still he who bears the sins of the world, and evil is mysteriously paid for by suffering. But, more essentially still, Jesus is he who structurally in himself and for all of us, overcomes resistance to the spiritual ascent inherent in matter. It is he who bears the burden, structurally inevitable, of every species of creation. He is the symbol and the significant act of progress; the full and

definitive meaning of the Redemption is no longer precisely that it
is an expiation, but that it is a transition and a victory. The full
mystery of baptism is not simply that it is a cleansing, but (as the
Greek Fathers understood so well) that it flings us into the cleansing
struggle for "being". What we now see is not the shadow but
the blazing light of the Cross' (*Christologie et évolution*, unpublished,
1933).

If 'the specific function of Omega Point is to cause the conscious
particles of the universe to converge upon it', and if on the other
hand, 'the Christic function (in its traditional form) is essentially to
raise up, to restore and save man from the abyss', then the question
arises: 'Can one, without distorting the Christian attitude, pass from
the notion of humanization by redemption to that of humanization
by evolution?' . . . 'In the dogma of the Redemption Christian
thought and piety has hitherto *primarily* concentrated (for obvious
historical reasons) on the idea of expiatory reparation . . . Right
from the beginning, however, the picture included another element
—and this a positive one—of reconstruction and re-creation. For
Augustine, the fruit and the reward of the sacrifice of the Cross were
a new heaven and a new earth.' 'Christ exerts his attraction upon
us, as guide and king, no less than as restorer of the world. His
function is to make peace for us, but also to bring us life, and the
two functions are linked together.' 'For all her divinity and immortality the Church can never entirely escape from the universal
need of periodic rejuvenation by the infusion of new elements, that
is experienced by all organisms, whatever they be. And where shall
we find the principle of rejuvenation if not in the ardent stream,
now flowing freely, of humanization?' (*Le Christ évoluteur*, unpublished, 1942). The original heading to this essay sums up his
view as follows: 'A cross that has become an emblem of growth as
well as of our ransoming, is the only cross with which the world can
now sign itself.'

'When Christians consider Christ's work as saviour, they are now
coming, though without losing sight of the aspect of "expiation", to
concentrate on that of "re-casting and building-up" . . . For
believers, the suffering Christ, without ceasing to be he who takes
away the sins of the world, and precisely because of so being, will
become more and more "he who bears and holds up the burden of a
world in evolution". The Cross will be the symbol not only of the

shadowed, retrogressive, side but also, and primarily, of the conquering luminous side of the universe in process of genesis. It will
be the symbol of progress and of victory won through mistakes,
disappointments and hard work: the only Cross, in truth, that we
can honestly, proudly and passionately offer for the adoration of a
world that has become conscious of what it was yesterday and
what awaits it tomorrow' (*Introduction au christianisme*, unpublished,
1944).

In 1934, after reading *Christologie et évolution*, Père Maréchal wrote
to Teilhard: 'If, then, instead of saying "the full and definitive
meaning of the Redemption is *no longer* precisely that it is an
expiation but that it is a transition and a victory", you said "is not
simply an expiation, but . . .", I should have no objection in principle to make against such a "redemption", at once a victory and a
reparation' (3 July 1934). Teilhard's *Introduction au christianisme*
shows that he took notice of this comment.

Elsewhere Teilhard puts it with less qualification: 'It is impossible to think of Christ the "evolver" without thereby having to
rethink the while of one's Christology. A functional completion of
the one and the multiple takes the place of the creative paternalism we were accustomed to. The twofold notion of *static evil* and
evolutionary redemption correcting and filling out the idea of catastrophic sin and redemptive expiation; and the final Parousia
appearing more as a development of maturity than a destruction'
(*L'étoffe de l'univers*, 1953, in *L'activation de l'énergie*, p. 405).
[126] Lecture given by Père G. Martelet to school chaplains, Trier,
8 September 1963.
[127] Letter of 30 September 1937, in *Letters from a Traveller*, p. 231.
It is fair to say that Teilhard did not go sufficiently deeply into this
idea of God's fatherhood, which makes man, if he consents, an adopted son of God in and through Christ. At the same time he gave
God an almost maternal tenderness, coexisting with his greatness.
[128] We should note, too, that the Church has allowed theologians
great freedom in interpreting the mystery of the Redemption, and
that theology has gradually moved away from an over-juridical
concept of the redemptive act towards one that emphasizes the
element of love.
[129] Teilhard holds that the appearance of man caused a drop of
evolutionary pressure in the non-human branches of the tree of

life; he also held, however, that, with the opening of the field of mental and social transformations, 'bodies no longer change appreciably; they no longer need to . . . Evolution is henceforth occupied elsewhere, in a richer and more complex domain, constructing, with all minds joined together, *mind*'.

We should, however, note this statement: 'If you tell me that as time goes on man is becoming "better" or "worse" I hardly know or care what the words mean. But if you tell me that mankind can be regarded, at the present moment, as a species that is disintegrating or has reached its ceiling, then I deny it absolutely.' He refers also to the 'driving force of *co-reflexion*, that is to say *ultra-reflexion*, and that is to say *ultra-hominization*' (*L'étoffe de l'univers*, 1953, in *L'activation de l'énergie*, p. 403).

[130] During a discussion (21 January 1947) with Gabriel Marcel, Teilhard said, 'At this present moment, the world is divided into two: those who believe in man and those who do not.' To which Marcel answered: 'I do not believe in man . . . it may well be that man has in him what is needed to make everything come crashing down.'

[131] 'In its present state the world would be unintelligible and the presence in it of reflection would be inexplicable, unless we supposed there to be a secret complicity between the infinite and the infinitesimal to warm, nourish and sustain to the very end—by dint of chance, contingencies and the exercise of free choice—the consciousness that has emerged between the two. It is upon this complicity that we must depend. *Man is irreplaceable.* Therefore, however improbable it might seem, he *must reach* the goal, not automatically, doubtless, but infallibly' (*The Phenomenon of Man*, p. 276).

[132] *The infallibility of progress*

'My purpose is not to show that a necessary or *infallible* line of progress exists, but simply to establish that, *for mankind as a whole*, a way of progress is offered and awaits us, analogous to that which an individual cannot reject without falling into sin and damnation' (*A note on progress*, 1920, in *The Future of Man*, p. 19 note).

'But if, as history suggests, there is really a quality of inevitability in the forward march of the universe—if, in truth, the world cannot turn back—then it must mean that individual acts are bound to follow, *in the majority and freely*, the sole direction capable of satisfying all their aspirations towards every imaginable form of higher consciousness' (*The grand option*, 1939, in *The Future of Man*, p. 57).

Pointing out that cosmic energy 'finds itself intrinsically influenced in its effects by two uncertainties related to the double play—chance at the bottom and freedom at the top', Teilhard goes on to say, 'in the case of very large numbers (such, for instance as the human population) the process tends to "infallibilize" itself, in as much as the likelihood of success grows on the lower side (chance), while that of error and rejection diminishes on the other side (freedom) with the multiplication of the elements engaged' (*The Phenomenon of Man*, p. 308).

'Nothing, as it seems, can prevent the universe from succeeding— nothing, not even our human liberties, whose essential tendency to union may fail in detail but cannot (without "cosmic" contradiction) err "statistically"' (*Faith in Peace*, 1947, in *The Future of Man*, p. 152).

'By a sort of "infallibility of large numbers" mankind, the present crest of the evolutionary wave, cannot fail in the course of its guided probings to find the right road and an outlet for its higher ascent. Far from being stultified by overcrowding, the cells of individual freedom, in a concerted action growing more powerful as they increase in numbers, will rectify and redress themselves when they begin to move forward in the direction towards which they are inwardly polarized. It is reasoned calculation, not speculation, which makes me ready to lay odds on the ultimate triumph of hominization over all the vicissitudes threatening its progress' (*The directions and conditions of the future*, 1948, *ibid.*, pp. 236–7).

'The statistical effect of a vast number of liberties is to diminish their chances of error and of losing the way. They take the right road. Nothing can prevent mankind from advancing towards its term; but the determinacy lies in super-liberty and not in infraliberty' (*Le néo-humanisme moderne et ses réactions sur le christianisme*, lecture given in 1948).

'The higher reflection rises and the more it builds up its strength (as a result of combined reflections) within the human mass, the more too, as an effect of organized vast numbers, do the chances of mistakes (both deliberate and involuntary) decrease in the noosphere . . . A living system (provided we take it to be, as is the case with man, polarized towards a determined point) tends to correct and stabilize its progress to the extent that the twofold faculty of foresight and choice arises within its elements at the same time as a sharper awareness of the end to be attained' (*Man's Place in Nature*, p. 119).

Mankind 'is destined in future, *in virtue precisely of the operation of its countless individual choices*, to complexify and integrate upon itself, ever more rapidly and more fully' (*Transformation et prolongements dans l'homme du mécanisme de l'évolution*, 1951, in *L'activation de l'énergie*, p. 321).

'Indeed, there can be doubt that our future lies in our hands. Human evolution is both conscious and self-directed. Nevertheless it is, at the same time, *statistically* determined in this sense: 1. that there are natural through-roads and dead-ends about which our freedom can do nothing; and 2, there are in the Human, currents of unanimity against which the individual's reaction is fruitless or impotent' (Letter from Teilhard to the author, 13 June 1953).

'The type of evil we meet is becoming more and more serious. And this means that the success of the universe is in the balance. The statistical infallibility of our liberties, however, is such that nothing can prevent a truth from emerging' (A remark of Teilhard's, quoted by C. Cuénot from the person who noted it down, *op. cit.*, p. 313).

[133] *Progress*

'Crushed into the narrow and inelastic mould represented by the closed surface of the world, under the pressure of an ever-growing population and ever-increasing economic links, we already form but one single body. And within that body, as a result of the gradual establishment of a uniform and universal system of industry and science, our minds are beginning more and more to function as cells of one and the same brain. This can mean only one thing, that if this transformation continues along its natural line, we can foresee the time when men will know what it is to desire, all at the same time, and hope and love as though with one single heart' (*Réflexions sur le bonheur*, 1933, *Cahiers Pierre Teilhard de Chardin* No. 2. p. 63).

'Is there any cataclysm, other than the complete destruction of our planet, that could now rob man of what his mind has won? In short, by becoming common to the totality of all people, civilization seems to me to have passed a critical point: it is becoming invulnerable. What is merely national can disappear: what is human can never fail' (*Sauvons l'humanité*, 1937, in *Science et Christ*, p. 172). In this connexion Teilhard could not take into account the atom bomb, even though its invention was imminent.

'It is easy for the pessimist to reduce this extraordinary period to a number of civilizations which have fallen into ruins one after the other. Is it not more scientific to recognize, yet once again, beneath these successive oscillations, the great spiral of life: thrusting up, irreversibly, in relays, following the master-line of its evolution?' (*The Phenomenon of Man*, pp. 211–12).

'Under cover of realism (or sometimes of metaphysics) we are ceaselessly reminded that man is by nature held in a certain number of circles which he will never be able to break: the eternal conflict between master and slave—the organic necessity of wars—the functional inconceivability of a humanity not divided within itself. But how can one fail to see that, to justify conservatism and pessimism, all these alleged "iron laws" systematically ignore the possibility of a transformation *modifying the psychological circumstances* in which history has hitherto developed' (*The singularities of the human species*, 1954, in *The Appearance of Man*, pp. 257–8).

We should note, too, that Teilhard saw present-day atheism as a religious phenomenon (though a deviation), but failed perhaps to appreciate sufficiently its satanic character (particularly in *Christianisme et évolution*, unpublished, 1945).

134 'Little by little, we may rest assured, the work is being done. Thanks to the multitude of individuals and vocations, the spirit of God insinuates itself everywhere, and is everywhere at work. It is the great tree we spoke of a moment ago, whose sunlit branches refine and turn to flowers the sap extracted by the humblest of its roots . . . As humanity becomes Christianized, it feels less and less need for certain earthly nourishment. Contemplation and chastity should thus tend, quite legitimately, to take precedence of anxious work and direct possession. *This is the general "drift" of matter* towards spirit. This movement must have its term: one day the whole divinizable substance of matter will have passed into the souls of men: all the chosen dynamisms will have been recovered: and then our world will be ready for the Parousia' (*Le Milieu Divin*, p. 110).

'We are sometimes inclined to think that the same things are monotonously repeated over and over again in the history of creation. That is because the season is too long by comparison with the brevity of our individual lives, and the transformation too vast and too inward by comparison with our superficial and restricted outlook, for us to see the progress of what is tirelessly taking place in and through all matter and spirit. Let us take the word of Revelation for this, once again the best confirmation of what, on purely human grounds, we have a presentiment of. Under the commonplace envelope of things, of all our purified and salvaged efforts, a new earth is being slowly engendered' (*Ibid.*, p. 150).

'A certain pessimism, perhaps, encouraged by an exaggerated conception of the original fall, has led us to regard the world as decidedly and incorrigibly wicked . . . But how many of us are genuinely moved in the depths of our hearts by the wild hope that *our* earth will be recast? Who is there who sets a course in the midst of our darkness towards the first glimmer of a *real* dawn?' (*Ibid.*, p. 152).

'Everything that is true comes to light, and all that is best happens in the end.'

[135] *Comment je vois*, unpublished, 1948, No. 16. 'Having been initially the fundamental choice of the individual, the Grand Option, that which decides in favour of a convergent universe, is destined sooner or later to become the *common choice* of the mass of mankind. Thus a particular and generalized state of consciousness is presaged for our species in the future: a "conspiration" in outlook and intention' (*The grand option*, 1939, in *The Future of Man*, p. 57).

[136] *L'atomisme de l'esprit*, 1941, in *L'activation de l'énergie*. 'Brought to a halt in collectivity, mankind, that in the last two centuries has risen to such heights, is now a ghastly Moloch. We can neither love it, nor love ourselves as part of it: and that is why instead of fulfilling us, it is mechanising us' (*Ibid.*, p. 54).

Although Teilhard held that 'the future is finer than any past' (Letter of 5 September 1919, in *Making of a Mind*, p. 306), he admitted to the Abbé Breuil that 'the rise of the collective' is characterized 'by an initial wave of enslavement, of levelling-down, of ugliness and disaster' (27 November 1923).

He puts this more vigorously in *The Phenomenon of Man* (pp. 256-7). 'We have "mass movements"—no longer the hordes streaming down from the forests of the north or the Steppes of

Asia, but "the million" scientifically assembled. The million in rank and file on the parade ground; the million standardized in the factory; the million motorized—and all this ending up only with Communism and National-Socialism and the most ghastly fetters. So we get the crystal instead of the cell; the ant-hill instead of brotherhood. Instead of the upsurge of consciousness which we expected, it is mechanization that seems to emerge inevitably from totalization.'

'On first consideration, this idea, depressingly pessimistic though it be, of a decline or ageing of the spirit through a general anchylosis of the human mass, has some appearance of truth. The first effects, entailing unmistakable slavery, of factory work; the first forms, brutally herding men together, assumed by political state control . . . all these impressive symptoms justify, up to a point, the instinctive reaction of apprehension and recoil that, as we can see for ourselves, forces so many human beings in desperation, when faced by the inexorably rising pressure of the noosphere, to take refuge in what are now obsolete forms of individualism and nationalism' (*Man's Place in Nature*, pp. 100–1).

'We cannot possibly, indeed, fail to see that the rise of the collective and of mass-man is accompanied by a first wave of slavery, of levelling-down, of ugliness and disaster' (*Transformation et prolongements en l'homme du mécanisme de l'évolution*, 1951, in *L'activation de l'énergie*, p. 321).

Cf. *The singularities of the human species*, 1954, in *The Appearance of Man*, p. 234. *Le coeur de la matière*, unpublished, 1950, p. 27. *L'étoffe de l'univers*, 1953, in *L'activation de l'énergie*, p. 403: 'The horrors of the phase of totalization.'

[137] Cf. *The Phenomenon of Man*, p. 257. In an article written in 1947 Teilhard referred to the influence of demographic pressure in the 'formation of the noosphere'. A year later he was writing: 'I am very much less disposed to believe today that the tightening of the human mass will *of itself* suffice to warm the human heart'; he then introduces the idea of 'the radiations of some ultimate centre (at once transcendent and immanent) of psychic congregation' (*The directions and conditions of the future*, 1948, in *The Future of Man*, pp. 235–6).

'Despite the compulsions which oblige men . . . to live and think in an ever closer community, they do not necessarily love each

other more on that account—far from it': and this because of a
'separation of head and heart' (*Human unanimization*, 1950, in *The
Future of Man*, p. 284).

[138] *The directions and conditions of the future*, 1948, in *The Future of Man*,
pp. 236–7. 'Progress is not immediate ease, well-being and peace.
It is not rest. It is not even, directly, virtue. Essentially progress is a
force, and the most dangerous of forces. It is the consciousness of all
that is and all that can be' (*A note on progress*, 1920, in *The Future of
Man*, p. 19). Similarly the peace that can and must be established
in mankind is not the tranquillity of repose, but a 'cohesion in
tension', a 'unanimity in quest and through conquest' (*Faith in
peace*, 1947, in *The Future of Man*, p. 153).

[139] *Man's Place in Nature*, p. 119. 'Does the universe concentrate itself
above as assuredly and infallibly as it "entropizes" itself below?
The answer the facts give is "No"' (*Ibid.*, p. 117). 'A fatal mistake:
to be blind to evil and absorbed in one's own role. Underestimating
the forces of evil = danger of collapse for evolution in earth' (quoted
by C. Cuénot, *Teilhard de Chardin*, Editions de Seuil, in the series
Ecrivains de toujours, p. 159).

[140] *Faith in man*, 1947, in *The Future of Man*, p. 188. 'Here we have
the modern version of the heroic temptation of all time, that of the
Titans, of Prometheus, of Babel and of Faust; that of Christ on the
mountain; a temptation as old as earth itself; as old as the first
awakening of life to the awareness of its powers. But it is a temptation that is only now entering its critical phase, now that man has
raised himself to the point of being able to measure both the
immensity of the time that lies before him and the almost limitless
powers made available to him by his concerted efforts to seize hold
of the material springs of the world.' (*Ibid.*).

[141] 'A great yearning possessed me, I think, to go and find, far from
man, far from toil, the place where dwell the vast forces that cradle
us and penetrate us, the place where my over-tense activity might
relax, continually and indefinitely . . . And all my sensibility then
became alive, as though at the approach of a god of ready happiness
and intoxication, for there lay matter, and thence it was calling me.
To me, in my turn, as to all the sons of man, it was repeating the
summons that every generation hears. It was begging me to
surrender myself without reserve and worship it' (*La vie cosmique*,
1916, in *Ecrits du temps de la guerre*, p. 20).

[142] 'To an observer with perfect insight who looked for a long time at our earth from a great height, it would first of all appear blue from the oxygen that envelops it; and then luminous—ever more luminous—from the intensification of thought on its surface; but at the same time it would appear dark—ever darker—from suffering that increases in quantity and poignancy, in step with the rise, throughout the ages, of consciousness' (Preface to *L'énergie spirituelle de la souffrance*, 1951, *op. cit.*, p. 9 and *L'activation de l'énergie*, p. 255).

[143] *The Phenomenon of Man*, p. 288. Similarly, 'Born with the intellect, the temptation to revolt must constantly change and *grow* with it' (*Hominization*, 1923, in *Vision of the Past*, p. 75).

[144] 'The evolutionary process (so strongly suggested to us by the study of external nature) stops short at the level of man . . . Evolutionary becoming seems to me to be specifically the concrete way of synthesis (in the Hegelian sense) between form and matter. That would mean that the peak, or limit, is the human compound in its perfection as compound, in other words in the complete, conscious, assimilation of matter by form. I would, accordingly, be ready to accept that the "perfect man", if realized, would have a cosmic significance. But I must confess that I do not see how, in man himself, *completely* to reduce to evolutionary terms the essence and finality either of each individual mind or of the "society of minds". Must we not recognize for the spiritual soul, beyond its function as "the form of the universe", a destiny that is specifically its own, its own as being "person" (end in itself, image of God), and one that calls for a higher form of becoming, different in nature from evolutionary becoming? I am more ready to see in human nature the meeting of two worlds, than the first spiritual stage of a continuous natural evolution . . . The principal aspect, entirely supernatural and divine, of Christ's mission, is not intrinsically subject to any "cosmic" law of evolution, I mean the inner sanctification of souls, the gift of God's friendship' (Unpublished letter to Teilhard, 3 July 1934).

Père Smulders, sympathetic though he is to Teilhard's thought, also cannot accept the notion of a statistical infallibility in progress towards unanimity (*op. cit.*, pp. 158–61). 'The personal yes or no cannot be the object of mathematical calculation' (p. 159); the truth would seem to be that Teilhard's probabilist and mathematical language should not be taken too literally: it disguises a spiritual element, faith in the energy of spirit working in history, and in the power of God's love (though at the same time respecting man's liberty). 'It is just as though', perhaps, mutual compensation of chances, or preferential odds, were working for the victory of the good: this outward appearance, however, hides the concerted influence of God and human freedom.

[145] 'History is inevitably an ascent towards unity . . . The progress of unity is such that by its very existence it arouses an opposition commensurate with the unity produced. Evil is proportionate to the good to which it is opposed, and the need for unity exaggerates the sharpness of divisions. There is progress, but progress towards a paroxysm. The master-slave dialectic expands without limit its disjunctive force, while the forces making for solidarity rise on a world-scale. We should be as much concerned with the new radicalness of confrontations as with the growth of socialization . . . It is dangerous to dream of the time when an angelic mankind would definitively fold back upon itself. There is indeed an Omega Point, but it lies in supernatural history, where it is the term of all history. While it is well to bring out its significance for today, it is useless to dream of terrestrial approximations to it' (Abel Jeannière, *Utopies du mondialisme politique, art. cit.*, pp. 1167, 1169).

The great Swedish economist Gunnar Myrdal shows that the present age is characterized by 'a constant tendency towards international economic disintegration', through 'the weakening of international law' and 'the relative failure of nearly all attempts at organizing economic co-operation' (*Planifier pour développer*, Editions Ouvrières, 1963, pp. 134-5, 254-5).

Henri Lefebvre's 'non-orthodox' marxist discussion brings out vividly the inhuman aspects of our time: the stagnation of personal relationships, the exorbitance and megalomania of man's projects, the alienation of work, the over-organization of totalitarian, and anarchy of liberal states, the increasing inequalities in distribution . . .' (*Introduction à la modernité*, Editions de Minuit, 1963).

[146] These passages have received comparatively little exegetical attention. There is no reference to them, for example, in O. Cullman's great *Christologie du Nouveau Testament*, in spite of the title.

[147] 'Strictly speaking, the future of the world is not running up against a term. Its end is not one event following upon others, the

last event—for Teilhard a fortunate one—that links two worlds, while others see it simply as catastrophic. The term of history is not the last event of the series of events: Omega Point is much more the plenitude of reflection, the totality of the spirit's folding back upon itself, the perfection of planetization: it is the noosphere unified by personalization, the totalization of history' (Abel Jeannière, *Approches christologiques, art. cit.*, p. 80).

[148] In fact, when Teilhard appears to attribute the signs of man's progress to a biological energy, he is referring to a spiritual and even divine energy, which operated in the first radical mutation, at the same time establishing its historical roots in it. In the words of Pastor Crespy, Teilhard's optimism is 'an act of faith that leads him to consider evil as the reality swallowed up in Christ's victory' (*op. cit.*, p. 127).

It is, also, well worth comparing Teilhard's practical hope with that which animates the Old Testament, in particular the Psalms, constant reading of which coloured his whole thought: in them a most faithful and unvarnished account of human suffering and anguish constantly leads up to the certainty of hope based on the fidelity of God.

[149] E. Borne, *De Pascal à Teilhard de Chardin, op. cit.*, p. 66.

[150] Although Teilhard emphasizes certain passages in St Paul dealing with the final unity of the Church or the presence of God in all things, it should be added that many others (in the Gospels and the Apocalypse for example) present the general history of the world as a dramatic conflict, whose issue is a forcible division of mankind. We shall see, however, that Teilhard is at pains to include this view: nor should it be forgotten that it is impossible to conceive the Church without the Beatitudes.

[151] This conclusion agrees, in fact, with Teilhard's own thought. 'For a Christian . . . the eventual biological success of man on earth is not merely a probability but a certainty: since Christ (and in him virtually the world) is already risen. But this certainty, born as it is of a "supernatural" act of faith, is of its nature of a higher order than the phenomenal: which means, in one sense, that it leaves all the anxieties attendant upon the human condition, on their own level, still alive in the heart of the believer' (*The directions and conditions of the future*, 1948, in *The Future of Man*, p. 237).

[152] *The formation of the noosphere*, 1947, *ibid.*, p. 178.

[153] In *In the Beginning*, Baltimore, Helicon Press, 1964, Père Daniélou has well brought out the difference of viewpoint in the inspired authors: comparing, first, the first chapter of Genesis with the two following, and then the tenth (community of nations) with the eleventh (the story of the tower of Babel). Similar alternatives and points of view may be seen in the New Testament, both in the Gospels and the Epistles.

[154] Better organization of work and working conditions, progress in legislation, a clearer recognition of the rights of the person, general acceptance of democracy, acquisition by nations of political auto-nomy, man's realization of his limitations and of the two-sided character of material forces: 'For, if man becomes conscious of his rights, he must become equally aware of his duties. Thus he who possesses certain rights has likewise the duty to claim those rights as marks of his dignity, while all others have the obligation to acknow-ledge those rights and respect them.

'When the relations of human society are expressed in terms of rights and duties, men become conscious of spiritual values, under-stand the meaning and significance of truth, justice, charity and freedom, and become deeply aware that they belong to this world of values. Moreover, when moved by such concerns, they are brought to a better knowledge of the true God who is personal and transcendent, and thus they make the ties that bind them to God the solid foundations and supreme criterion of their lives, both of that life which they live interiorly in the depths of their own souls and of that in which they are united to other men in society . . .

'There is reason to hope that by meeting and negotiating, men may come to discover better the bonds that unite them together, deriving from the human nature which they have in common' (Pope John XXIII, *Pacem in Terris*, Vatican Polyglot Press trans., pp. 20, 46).

[155] *La parole attendue*, 1940, in *Cahiers Pierre Teilhard de Chardin*, No. 4, p. 27.

[156] *Le Christ évoluteur*, unpublished, 1942.

[157] Cf. Colossians 1, and Ephesians 1:4-5, 9-10. 'Even as he chose us in him before the foundation of the world . . . he destined us to be his sons through Jesus Christ . . . He has made known to us the mystery of his will . . . to unite all things in him (Christ).'

[158] 'In fact, from the beginning of the Messianic preparation, up till

the Parousia, passing through the historic manifestation of Jesus and the phases of growth of his church, a single event has been developing in the world: the Incarnation, realized, in each individual, by the Eucharist' (*Le Milieu Divin*, p. 124).

'The ancient cosmos was static, limited, and at any moment patient of re-arrangement; the modern universe is organically knit together into one evolutionary whole by its space-time. If we transpose these same mysteries from the former to the latter, they begin to form but one mystery. Without an initial creation, there would, it seems, be something absolutely lacking to God, considered in the fullness not of his being but of his unitive act. For God, then, to create is by definition to unite himself with his work, in other words in some way or other to involve himself, by incarnation, in the world. But is not "to be incarnate" *ipso facto* to share in the sufferings and evils inherent in the multiple as it painfully makes its way towards a convergence? Seen in the light of this new Christology the three mysteries of the Creation, the Incarnation and the Redemption, become in truth no more than three aspects of one and the same fundamental process: of a fourth mystery, in fact, which ultimately is the only mystery that is intellectually justifiable and valid in itself. To that, in order clearly to distinguish it from the other three, we should give the name of the mystery of the creative union of the world in God, or of the *pleromization*. Is not that consideration both extremely Christian and extremely coherent? In classic theology one might say that dogma was presented to our reason as a series of independent circles drawn on a plane surface. Today, with a new dimension behind it (that of the universal Christ), the same design is coming to be developed and grouped organically on one single sphere, in space' (*Christianisme et évolution*, unpublished, 1945).

'In a system of convergent cosmogenesis, to create is, for God, *to unite himself*. To unite himself is to immerse himself. But to immerse oneself (in the plural) is to "corpusculize" oneself. And to corpusculize oneself, in a world whose arrangement statistically involves disorder (and mechanically, effort) is to plunge—in order to overcome them—into error and suffering' (*Du cosmos à la cosmogénèse*, 1951, in *L'activation de l'énergie*, p. 271). 'God cannot appear as the prime mover (ahead) without becoming incarnate and redeeming—in other words with *christifying* himself for us; and, as a complement to this, Christ can no longer "justify" man except by at the same time super-creating the entire universe' (*Ibid.*, p. 272).

[159] *Constitution on the Catholic Faith*, Chap. IV. Denzinger-Bannwart, No. 1796: '... *analogia* ... *e mysteriorum ipsorum nexu* ...'

[160] *L'âme du monde*, 1918, in *Ecrits du temps de la guerre*, p. 231. In order to stress the absolute gratuitousness of God's plan, Teilhard very rightly adds, 'Does not this appearance itself answer a need more exact than the simple emotion of a *Bonum diffusivum sui*?'

[161] *Teilhard's passionate interest in the future*

'The only true knowledge of things lies in foreseeing and building up the future gradually as life gradually brings it into being' (Letter of October 1923, in *Letters from a Traveller*, p. 100). 'The world holds no interest for me unless I look forward, but when my eyes are on the future, it is full of excitement' (23 October 1923, *ibid.*, p. 104). 'What is imponderable in the world means much more than what we can put our hands on. What has not yet come to pass is more precious than what is already born' (Wedding address, 1928).

'The scientific solution of the human problem will never be attained by the study of fossils, but by a more careful consideration of the properties and possibilities that permit us to foresee in the man of today the man of tomorrow' (*Sinanthropus pekinensis*, 1930, in *The Appearance of Man*, p. 67).

'It is almost as though, for reasons arising from the progress of my own science, the past and its discovery had ceased to interest me. The past has revealed to me how the future is built; and pre-occupation with the future tends to sweep aside everything else' (Letter of 8 September 1935, in *Letters from a Traveller*, p. 207).

The whole of the article dated 20 November 1925 (*The discovery of the past*, in *The Vision of the Past*, pp. 183–9) is devoted to examining this dialectical transition:

'One day, I am convinced, the movement which launched our generation towards the shores of the past will appear like the rush towards an Eldorado whose promise was *final* knowledge. We set out for the past not as amateurs but as conquistadors, to discover the secret of the world, hidden in its origins ... Then at last man will have understood the essential word whispered to him by the ruins, the fossils and the ashes: "The only thing worth the trouble of finding is what has never yet existed. The only task worthy of our efforts is to construct the future"' (*Ibid.*, pp. 185–6, 191). In connexion with this essay, Teilhard writes: 'This is not a passing "mood"—it is a definitive forward projection that has been taking shape for a long time . . . What is past is dead, and no longer interests me' (18 January 1936).

It is interesting to note that this direction towards the future, originating in study of the past had, as an intermediate stage, an interest in contemporary mankind. 'Intellectually, I am still very interested, even absorbed in technical geological research, in a field and a country that still has many things to be discovered. Nevertheless, particularly during these last two years, I have been feeling gradually drawn to the study not of pre-historic mankind but of mankind *today*. I am seeing man more and more clearly as the *great terrestrial phenomenon*, in whom the great processes of geology and the most far-reaching of life's movements reach their peak. In other words, I am discovering *how geology is continued in man* (Letter of 31 December 1926)

[162] 'One day, the Gospel tells us, the tension gradually building up between humanity and God will touch the limits prescribed by the possibilities of the world. And then will come the end. Then the presence of Christ, which has been silently accruing in things, will suddenly be revealed—like a flash of light from pole to pole. Breaking through all the barriers within which the veil of matter and the water-tight isolation of souls have seemingly kept it confined, it will invade the face of the earth. And, under the finally liberated action of the true affinities of being, the spiritual atoms of the world will be borne along by a force generated by the powers of cohesion proper to the universe itself, and will occupy, whether within Christ or without Christ (but always under the influence of Christ) the place of happiness or pain designated for them by the living structure of the Pleroma . . . Like lightning, like a conflagration, like a flood, the attraction by the Son of Man will lay hold of all the whirling elements in the universe, to reunite them or subject them to his body' (*Le Milieu Divin*, pp. 150-1). See also the notes and comments attached to the section on Teilhard's phenomenology of history.

[163] *In Epist. Joannis*, tract. X, No. 3; P. L. 35, 2055.

[164] *Comment je crois*. This analogy between the Virgin Mary and the consummated humanity of the end of all time is theologically sound, if humanity is considered in its supernatural aspect as the

perfection of the Church, of which Mary is the type and anticipation.

[165] 'When Christ appears in the clouds, he will simply be manifest-
ing a metamorphosis that has been slowly accomplished, under his
influence, in the heart of the mass of mankind' (*Le Milieu Divin*,
p. 128). See the passages quoted by Père de Lubac, *op. cit.*, p. 176.

'Christ delays his reappearance until collective humanity shall
have finally become capable, in virtue of having fully realized its
natural *potentialities*, of receiving from him its supernatural consummation' (*Trois choses que je vois*, unpublished, 1948).

Cf. Y. Congar, *Pour une théologie du laïcat, Etudes,* January and
February 1948, and in particular the latter, pp. 213–17. 'What, then,
is our world? What does its development amount to, and what does
our effort represent, in relation to this kingdom? The Fathers of the
Church used to speak of a "pedagogy". By that they meant a
system of preliminary trials. These were not to be retained as such
in the final realization, but represented necessary stages essential to
further progress. It would be no distortion of their thought to put
it as follows: A master gives a pupil a series of difficult problems to
work out; the pupil will not solve them, even though he may come
comparatively close to doing so, and accordingly multiplies his
attempts. The solution will be given to him by the master but only
when the pupil, by working on it, has developed his mind and his
powers in a way that he would never have imagined to be possible
if the solution had been given to him immediately. The disciple will,
in some way, have raised himself to the level of the solution; but he
will *truly* possess it only because, in striving to attain it, he will have
grown to its measure' (p. 214).

[166] 'We continue from force of habit to think of the Parousia,
whereby the kingdom of God is to be consummated on earth, as an
event of a purely catastrophic nature—that is to say, liable to come
about at any moment in history, irrespective of any definite state of
mankind. But why should we not assume, in accordance with the
latest scientific view of mankind in a state of anthropogenesis, that
the parousiac spark can, of physical and organic necessity, only be
kindled between heaven and a mankind which has biologically
reached a certain critical evolutionary point of collective maturity?'
Teilhard adds a footnote: 'And, it may be added, in perfect
analogy with the mystery of the first Christmas, which (as everyone

agrees) could only have happened between heaven and an earth which was *prepared*, socially, politically and psychologically, to receive Jesus' (*The heart of the problem*, 1949, in *The Future of Man*, p. 267).

'Nothing seems more feasible and fruitful (and accordingly more imminent) than a synthesis between the above and the ahead in a becoming of the "Christic" type, in which access to the transcendent hyper-personal would be seen to be conditioned by the previous arrival of human consciousness at a critical point of collective reflection. The supernatural, in consequence, would not exclude but, on the contrary, call for, as a necessary preparation, the complete maturing of an ultra-human' (*Réflexions sur la probabilité scientifique*, in *L'activation de l'énergie*, p. 289).

[167] *The Phenomenon of Man*, p. 298. *Man's Place in Nature*, p. 121: 'Unless it is to be powerless to form the keystone of the noosphere, Omega can only be conceived as the meeting-point between a universe that has reached the limit of centration, and another, even deeper, centre—this being the self-subsistent centre and absolutely final principle of irreversibility and personalization: the one and only true Omega.' Similarly, at the end of *Le Milieu Divin*, Teilhard, emphasizing that the supernatural cannot dispense with the matter that nature offers it, speaks of it as 'transforming' nature (p. 152).

[168] *The grand option*, 1939, in *The Future of Man*, p. 56. Earlier, in 1919, Teilhard had written, '*Fundamentally*, I admit that the fulfilment of the world cannot be consummated except through a death, a "night", a reversal, an excentration and almost a de-personalization of the monads' (Note to Père Auguste Valensin, 12 December 1919, in *Archives de philosophie*, XXIV, 1961, p. 135).

[169] *Le Prêtre*, 1918, in *Ecrits due temps de la guerre* (extract in *Hymn of the Universe*, p. 152).

[170] *The Mass on the World*, 1923, ibid., p. 31. Cf. *Le Milieu Divin*, p. 88. 'We have not yet crossed the critical point of our excentration, of our reversion to God.'

'In a converging universe, each element achieves completeness, not directly in a separate consummation, but by incorporation in a higher pole of consciousness in which alone it can enter into contact with all others. By a sort of inward turn towards the other its growth culminates in an act of giving and in excentration ... Before passing

into the beyond, the world and its elements must attain what may be
called their point of annihilation' (*The grand option*, 1939, in *The
Future of Man*, pp. 55-6). In that same paragraph Teilhard distinguishes this act from the ideal of the mysticisms of escape, for 'this
mystical night or death can only be the end and apotheosis of a
process of growth'.

The above quotations may well be taken in conjunction with the
conclusion of Père de Lubac's *Catholicisme*: 'However authentic and
pure the vision of unity that inspires and directs man's activity, it
must, to attain reality, first be dimmed. It must fall under the great
shadow of the Cross. Mankind will never come together as one
except by ceasing to regard itself as its own end . . . Humanism is
not spontaneously Christian. Christian humanism must be a *converted* humanism. There is no human love from which we can pass
on the same level into supernatural love. To find ourselves, we must
lose ourselves. This is a dialectic of the spirit, imposed as rigidly on
mankind as on the individual, that is to say imposed on my love of
man and men as rigidly as on my love of my own self. It is a law of
exodus, a law of *ecstasis* . . . If no man may escape from mankind,
mankind must die to itself in each of its members in order to live,
transfigured, in God. There is no final and permanent brotherhood
except in a common adoration. *Gloria Dei vivens homo:* but man
attains life in the only total society that can ever exist, only through
Soli Deo gloria. Such is the universal passover, that makes ready the
city of God' (pp. 291-2).

[171] *Turmoil or genesis*, 1947, in *The Future of Man*, pp. 223-4.

[172] Letter of 29 December 1919.

[173] Here Teilhard admits that the quantity of biological potential,
or even the 'planetary human quantum' is limited, and is being
exhausted (Cf., in particular, *Réflexion sur l'énergie*, in *Revue des
questions scientifiques*, 20 October 1952, p. 487). But can life be compared with entropy? Is it not, rather, capable of developing fresh
bursts of energy?

'In affirming the existence of this supreme convergence, we are
going beyond the evidence of pure experience, for observation of our
daily setbacks would suggest that its realization must be postponed
so indefinitely into the future as to be quite unattainable. It is only
the Christian dogma of the mystical body, faith in a spiritual
organism, whose unity precedes the coming together of its members,

that can assign a real term to our journey towards "catholicity"'
(*La crise présente*, 1937, in *Cahiers Pierre Teilhard de Chardin*, No. 3,
p. 95).

[174] *The Phenomenon of Man*, p. 27. *Man's Place in Nature*, pp. 113–14.
We may then ask whether this crowning of human effort includes,
whether it can include, biological victory over death.

[175] *The Phenomenon of Man*, p. 249. 'The concentration of the whole
human in one single co-reflective system planetary in dimensions'
(*Réflexions sur la probabilité scientifique*, 1951, in *L'activation de l'énergie*,
p. 287). 'A complete reflection of the noosphere upon itself' (*La convergence de l'univers*, 1951, *ibid.*, p. 302). It is true that Teilhard did not
shrink from envisaging the possibility that Thought might 'artificially improve the actual organ of its thought' (*Ibid.*, p. 278). In
a letter of 1917, however, he writes: 'I don't think that transformation of organs holds out any hope to us, in fact, of any appreciable
development of psychisms in the future. What advance could there
be on thought?' (9 January 1917, *Making of a Mind*, p. 166).

[176] *The Phenomenon of Man*, p. 250. 'It was by the law of "consciousness and complexity" that we set our course: a consciousness
becoming ever more centred, emerging from the heart of an
increasingly vast system of more numerous and better organized
elements. But now we are faced by an entirely new situation: for
the first time we have no multiple material under our hands' (*The
formation of the noosphere*, 1947, in *The Future of Man*, p. 179). 'If man
is to reach his own centre, must he not have made his way to the
farthest limit of all things?' (*Man's Place in Nature*, p. 113 note).

[177] *The Phenomenon of Man*, p. 253. 'We are faced with a harmonized
collectivity of consciousness equivalent to a sort of super-consciousness. The idea is that of the earth not only becoming covered by
myriads of grains of thought, but becoming enclosed in a single
thinking envelope so as to form, functionally, no more than a single
vast grain of thought on the sidereal scale; the plurality of individual
reflections grouping themselves together and reinforcing one another in the act of a single unanimous reflection' (*Ibid.*, pp. 251–2).

[178] *Le Milieu Divin*, p. 150. 'I smile to myself when I hear people
speaking of the coming end of the world . . . unless they simply mean
the end of the earth, which, in relation to the great end, is not more
than the death of one man here below is to the end of mankind'
(Letter of 21 December 1919).

[179] Teilhard envisages 'some millions of years' before mankind reaches 'the polar regions of the symbolic hemisphere in which it is concentrating', or before the terrestrial noosphere arrives at its focal point (*Man's Place in Nature*, pp. 112–14). He adds, it is true, 'that to attain Omega (by the very act, indeed, of attaining it) we step out of space and time' (p. 116).

'... the intensity of psychic concentration attained by the species after another couple of million years of co-reflexion' (*The singularities of the human species*, 1954, in *The Appearance of Man*, p. 268)

This double reference, to the tangible and to its disappearace, is paralleled by Père Fessard's comment on Christ's ascension: 'Though hope sees its surety vanishing into the infinite, it receives the assurance of a return, of the *Parousia*: the future, the still-to-come, even though extended into infinity, is still a real advent (coming)—something that will come about. Our hope, then, is much more than a mirage that offers the possibility of an indefinite progress. Moreover, this still-to-come will not be this future or that future, this or that kingdom of Israel, but the still-to-come, identical with the principle seated at the right hand of the Father, which will then, after having destroyed all non-being and gathered up into itself all being, offer itself as an eternal present, so that God may be all in all. Hope has asserted itself first as *presence*, the presence of the future, through the maintenance of confidence in essential union with Christ and through anticipation of the return of what it has lost—presence, again, of the future, with the disappearance for ever of the palpable element it contained' (*La dialectique des Exercises spirituels de Saint Ignace de Loyola*, Aubier, 1956, p. 146).

[180] *Approches christologiques*, in *Essais sur Teilhard de Chardin, op. cit.*, p. 80. 'Teilhard does indeed believe that, in its own order, history is on the road towards some sort of totalization. But it is, in fact, a totalization. And, in contrast with what happens at other significant thresholds, it is impossible in this case to distinguish a continuity and a discontinuity within cosmogenesis; it is the whole of history meeting reversal in the antihistorical. And even though Teilhard anticipates, with more conviction and enthusiasm than I could ever feel, that even on the plane of human history there will be a great advance in the process of unification and spiritualization, yet the term must belong to an order other than the human' (*Ibid.*, p. 85).

'The natural fulfilment of man serves only as a preparatory stage and, as we have pointed out, Teilhard does not believe in a totalization of history on the plane of human history. The gratuitousness of salvation remains intact whether one believes, as he does, in the necessity for a preparation on earth, or whether one does not. But supernatural history and human history are not separable: we work for the kingdom of God. *The Parousia does not only enlighten, but already shines throughout the whole of history*' (p. 94).

[181] 'The term of creation is not to be sought in the temporal zones of our living world, . . . the effort required of our fidelity must be consummated *beyond a total transformation*, of ourselves and of everything surrounding us' (*Le Milieu Divin*, p. 103).

'The end of a "thinking" species: not disintegration and death, but a new break-through and a re-birth, this time outside time and space, through the very excess of unification and co-reflection' (*The end of the species*, 1952, in *The Future of Man*, p. 302).

[182] 'Those who think on Marxist lines believe that all that is necessary to inspire and polarize the human molecules is that they should look forward to an eventual state of *collective* reflection and sympathy, at the culmination of anthropogenesis, from which all will benefit through *participation*: as it were, a vault of interlocking thoughts, a closed circuit of attachments in which the individual will achieve intellectual and affective wholeness to the extent that he is one with the whole system' (*Human unanimization*, 1950, in *The Future of Man*, p. 287).

[183] *The Phenomenon of Man*, p. 287. Similarly: 'The end of the world: the overthrow of equilibrium, detaching the spirit fulfilled at last, from its material matrix, so that it will henceforth rest with all its weight on God-Omega' (*Ibid.*, pp. 287–88). 'An ecstasy transcending the dimensions and framework of the visible universe' (*Ibid.*, p. 289).

'One day, the whole divinizable substance of matter will have passed into the souls of men; all the chosen dynamisms will have been gathered up: and then our world will be ready for the Parousia' (*Le Milieu Divin*, p. 110). 'When all else has passed away, concentrated or dispersed, spirit will still remain' (*Comment je crois*, unpublished, 1934).

'. . . with one proviso: that the world in question shall have reached a stage of development so advanced that its "soul" can be detached without losing any of its completeness, as something wholly formed' (*The grand option*, 1939, in *The Future of Man*, p. 50).

'Is it not conceivable that mankind, at the end of its totalization, its infolding upon itself, may reach a critical level of maturity where, leaving earth and stars to lapse slowly back into the dwindling mass of primordial energy, it will detach itself from this planet and join the one true, irreversible essence of things, the Omega Point? . . . An escape from the planet, not in space or outwardly, but spiritually and inwardly' (*Life and the planets*, 1945, in *The Future of Man*, pp. 122–3).

'The curve of consciousness, pursuing its course of growing complexity, will break through the material framework of time and space, to escape somewhere towards an ultra-centre of unification and wholeness, where there will finally be assembled, and in detail, everything that is irreplaceable and incommunicable in the world' (*The formation of the noosphere*, 1947, *ibid.*, pp. 180–1).

'Not a gradual darkening, but a sudden blaze of brilliance, an explosion in which thought, carried to the extreme, is volatilized upon itself: that, if I had to bet upon it, is how I would depict the ultimate phase of a vitalized star . . . The critical point of planetary reflection, the fruit of socialization, far from being a mere spark in the darkness, represents our passage, by translation or dematerialization, to another sphere of the universe: not an ending of the ultra-human, but its accession to some sort of transhumanity at the ultimate heart of things' (*From the pre-human to the ultra-human*, 1950, *ibid.*, pp. 295, 296–7).

We can 'assume that, in the intense psychic union which another million or two years of co-reflexion will bring to the species, the difference will tend to vanish between man's will to survive and his anxiety to escape (even at the cost of an apparent death) from the temporo-spatial phase of his evolution' (*The singularities of the human species*, 1954, in *The Appearance of Man*, pp. 267–8).

'In the perspectives of cosmic evolution, not only does consciousness become co-extensive with the universe, but the universe rests in equilibrium, in the form of thought, on a supreme pole of consistency' (*The Phenomenon of Man*, p. 309). In this context, however, is the universe, in Teilhard's mind, synonymous with matter? Similarly: 'At a given moment in the future . . . it is inevitable that the two branches (geogenesis and noogenesis) should separate.

However convergent it be, evolution cannot attain to fulfilment on earth except through a point of dissociation' (*Ibid.*, p. 273).

In a letter of 9 January 1917, Teilhard had already written: 'The spirit cannot free itself except by some clean break, some escape, *of a completely different order* from the slow organization of matter that led up to the elaboration of the brain . . . The liberation of matter is an extra-transformist phenomenon (concept) which belongs more to idealist philosophy than to a scientific examination of things' (*Making of a Mind*, pp. 165–6).

[184] *The singularities of the human species*, 1954, in *The Appearance of Man*, p. 264.

[185] *L'atomisme de l'esprit*, 1941, *op. cit.*

[186] On the other hand there is the following, written in 1917: 'Attractive and easy though it is to envisage a total spiritualization of the cosmos, it remains true that the *risen flesh* and the new earth (the body of Christ, in fact) will form one *physically integrated* whole' (Letter of 26 July 1917 to Père Victor Fontoynont, quoted by Père de Lubac, *op. cit.*, p. 248).

Again: 'We hardly know in what proportions and under what guise our natural faculties will pass over into the final act of the vision of God. But it can hardly be doubted that, with God's help, it is here below that we give ourselves the eyes and the heart which a final transfiguration will make the organs of a power of adoration, and of a capacity for beatification, particular to each individual man and woman among us' (*Le Milieu Divin*, p. 60).

[187] Karl Rahner uses arguments drawn from philosophy and theology to show that biological death gives the soul a relationship to the totality of the universe, and access to its centre. Christ's death was for him, in fullness, this entry into possession of the world. The glorified body of the just, united in this way with the cosmos, appears as the perfect expression of this relation to the whole of the universe enjoyed by the glorified person (*The Theology of Death* in *Questiones Disputatae*, London, Nelson, 1961.

[188] Rom. 8:18–23. Again, should we interpret the 'new heaven' and 'new earth' of which St John (Apoc. 22:1), following Isaiah, speaks, in a realistic sense, as an effective transfiguration of the cosmos? Although we cannot understand how it happens, the physical solidarity of Christ and man with the material universe means that we should do so.

[189] Cf. Christian Duquoc, O.P., *Eschatologie chrétienne et mystiques humaines du progrès*, in *Cathéchistes*, October 1961, pp. 309–12; and *L'Eglise et le progrès*, Editions du Cerf, 1964.

[190] 'I thought that as soon as men saw the great Monad, *their work*, towering above them as the prize of battle, they would first bow down in adoration and pride in the power they had tamed. Man is already so proud when he is able to master the forces contained in his own poor person . . . How boldly will he salute his independence when he has been able to concentrate into a single sphere the power included in the whole of his species!' (*La grande monade*, 1918, in *Ecrits du temps de la guerre*).

'A more realistic and more Christian view shows us Earth evolving towards a state in which Man, having come into the full possession of his sphere of action, his strength, his maturity and his unity, will at last have become an adult being: and having reached this apogee of his responsibility and freedom, holding in his hands all his future and all his past, will make the choice between arrogant autonomy and loving excentration. This will be the final choice: a world that rebels or worships. And then, justice will set its seal upon an act which will sum up the toil of centuries, on an act finally and for the first time completely human, and all things will be made new.' (*A note on progress*, 1920, in *The Future of Man*, p. 19).

'The men of the future will in some sort form a single consciousness; and because, their initiation being completed, they will have measured the power of their associated minds, the immensity of the universe and the narrowness of their prison, this consciousness will be truly adult, truly major. May we not suppose that when this time comes mankind will for the first time be confronted with the necessity for a truly and wholly human act, a final exercise of choice, the yes or no in face of God, individually affirmed by beings in each of whom will be fully developed the sense of human liberty and responsibility? . . . As the end of time approaches, a terrifying spiritual pressure will be brought to bear on the limits of the real, born of the efforts of souls desperately straining in their desire to escape from the earth. This pressure will be unanimous.

'But the Scriptures teach us that at the same time it will be rent by a profound schism between those who wish to break out of themselves that they may become still more masters of the world, and those who, accepting Christ's word, passionately await the death of the world that they may be absorbed with it into God' (*Mon univers*, 1924, quoted in *The Future of Man*, pp. 306–7).

The grand option, 1939, *ibid.*, pp. 57–8. *The Phenomenon of Man*, pp. 288–90.

[191] *The Phenomenon of Man*, appendix, pp. 311–13.

'It is in the grip of the most powerful organic attraction conceivable (the force which held the universe together) that the monads will pour into that place whither they are irrevocably destined by the total maturing of things and the implacable irreversibility of the whole history of the world—some of them spiritualized matter in the limitless fulfilment of an eternal communion, and others materialized spirit in the conscious agonies of an interminable decomposition' (*Mon univers*, quoted in *The Future of Man*, p. 307).

A lengthier treatment of this question will be found in *Le Milieu Divin*, pp. 146–9. 'The whole process out of which the new earth is gradually born is an *aggregation* underlaid by a *segregation* . . . The powers of evil, in the universe, are not only an attraction, a deviation, a minus sign, an annihilating return to plurality. In the course of the spiritual evolution of the world, certain conscious elements in it, certain monads, deliberately detached themselves from the mass that is stimulated by your attraction. Evil has become incarnate in them, has been "substantialized" in them. And now I am surrounded by dark presences, by evil beings, by malign *things*, intermingled with your luminous presence. That separated whole constitutes a definitive loss, an immortal wastage from the genesis of the world. There is not only *nether* darkness; there is also *outer* darkness. That is what the Gospel tells us . . . You have told me, O God, to believe in hell. But you have forbidden me to believe with absolute certainty of any one man that he has been damned. I shall therefore make no attempt to consider the damned here, nor even to discover —by whatsoever means—whether there are any. I shall accept the existence of hell on your word, *as a structural element of the universe*' (*Le Milieu Divin*, pp. 147–8). 'If, more unfortunately, the world contains perverted energies and elements which are slowly separated from it . . .' (*Ibid.*, p. 109).

Much earlier (1916) in *Christ in the world of matter* (in *Hymn of the Universe*, p. 49) Teilhard had written in similar terms of damnation: 'As the host closed in on itself like a flower closing its petals, certain refractory elements in the universe remained behind, outside it, in the exterior darkness. There was, indeed, something which still lit them, but it was a heart of perverted light, corrosive, poisonous; these rebellious elements burned like torches or glowed red like embers.'

It is interesting that Teilhard, who made such use of fire as a symbol, should not have thought of using cold to symbolize the state of the damned. Here, Bernanos was a better theologian, especially in his *Sous le soleil de Satan* and *Monsieur Ouine*: 'I am cold, says Satan, cold itself: the essence of my light is an unbearable cold' (*Sous le soleil de Satan*, Plon, 1926, p. 168).

[192] *Introduction au christianisme*, unpublished, 1944.

[193] Origen was not responsible for later distortions of his thought. Scientific exegesis of his writings seems now to have vindicated his reputation.

[194] *Le Milieu Divin*, p. 149.

[195] 'Assuming success—which is the only acceptable assumption . . .' (*The Phenomenon of Man*, p. 277). 'Some sort of unanimity will reign over the entire mass of the noosphere . . . Such an outcome would, of course, conform most harmoniously with our theory' (*Ibid.*, p. 288).

Teilhard tried to reconcile the two (damnation and the Pleroma) by saying 'only sin is excluded from the Pleroma. And yet, since the damned are not annihilated, who can say that this eternal loss does not in some mysterious way complement the body of Christ?' (*Le Prêtre*, 1918, in *Ecrits du temps de la guerre*, p. 293).

[196] I Cor. 15:22-28; Eph. 2:21-22.

[197] In his letter (quoted earlier) to the General of the Society of Jesus, Teilhard speaks of 'three convictions which are the very marrow of Christianity: the unique significance of man as the spearhead of life; the position of Catholicism as the central axis in the convergent fascicle of human activities; and finally the essential function as consummator assumed by the risen Christ at the centre and peak of creation' (in *Letters from a Traveller*, pp. 42-3).

[198] 'After two thousand years, so many of our views have been modified that, in religion, we have to slough off the old skin. The formulas we have been using have become too narrow and unyielding. We find them irksome and they have ceased to move us. If we are to go on living we must make a fresh start. By constant repeti-

tion of dogma in the same form and by developing it only abstractly, we are losing ourselves in the clouds, where we are completely out of touch with what agitates the world, with what it seeks, and with what feeds its vigour. From the religious point of view we are living cut off from the world, both intellectually and emotionally. Here we have an indication that the time for a renascence is not far distant' (*Christologie et évolution*, unpublished, 1944).

[199] The demands both of reason and science led Teilhard to regard the different orders of the real as *homogeneous*. In answer to a criticism made by Père Maréchal, he wrote to Père Auguste Valensin 'There is another point that strikes me: it is to notice how many minds, better equipped than mine, are hardly aware of the need for a homogeneous world—both as the object of our thought and as the medium in which we live. And yet (this is one of the fundamental lessons taught us by familiarity with the sciences) there is *nothing* real *other than* the homogeneous (I mean that "homogeneity is an essential pre-condition of reality")' (24 August 1934). On the other hand Teilhard himself was not, perhaps, sufficiently alive to the at least partially heterogeneous character of the supernatural.

[200] Towards the end of his life, Teilhard summed up his theological views as follows: 'It is impossible to think of Christ as the "evolver" without thereby having to re-think the whole of Christology . . . A functional completion of the one and the multiple takes the place of the creative paternalism we were accustomed to. The twofold notion of *static evil* and *evolutionary redemption* corrects or complements the idea of catastrophic sin and reparative expiation. The final Parousia becomes more a maturing than a destruction' (*L'étoffe des choses*, in *L'activation de l'énergie*, p. 405).

[201] 'What are we entitled to ask from Scripture and to claim for it, if its sacred value is to be preserved? Two things, only. The first is that the intellectual and moral directions contained in revelation shall, when applied to the new curve followed by human spirit, retain without distortion those aspects that delineate the essential figure of Christ and the Christian; and the second is, that in this new situation, Christ and the Christian faith shall continue to assert themselves as elements that are of a different order from, but structurally necessary to, the development of human spirit' (*Le sens humain*, unpublished, 1929). This passage is a useful illustration of Teilhard's attempt to provide modern man with a theology adapted to

his new intellectual make-up, without doing violence to the mystery.

[202] 'Like you, I am openly convinced of the need, both practical and theoretical, frankly to adopt an evolutionary concept of the material universe, up to and including man, so far, at least, as man represents a centre of union and an "end" for matter. And to that same extent I admit the necessity, which sooner or later will assert itself, for a better adjustment of some theological formulas' (Unpublished letter from Père Maréchal to Teilhard, 3 July 1934).

[203] 'Our duty is not simply to preserve this precious treasure (Catholic teaching) as though we were concerned only with the past. We must also, fearlessly and with resolute will, give ourselves to the work that our age calls for, and so follow the road that the Church has been following for the last two thousand years . . . This sure and immutable doctrine, which we must faithfully accept, will have to be studied and presented in the ways that our time demands. The deposit of faith and the truths contained in our venerable doctrine are one thing, and the way in which they are proclaimed is, even though it preserves their meaning and scope, quite another. Our chief concern must be the way in which doctrine is presented, and to give to this work all the patience it calls for. The form of exposition to be used must be one that is more fitted to the Church's magisterium, which has a pastoral character.'

CHAPTER 7: SPIRITUALITY

[1] In a letter of 14 May 1922, Teilhard quotes a saying, 'Warm or cold, we still have to cross the water,' by which he probably means to stress the primacy of action over thought, and the duty, in any case, of not stopping short at thought. It inevitably suggests a comparison with Marx's celebrated comment on Feuerbach. 'It's not a question any more of interpreting the world but of transforming it.'

'There had been plenty of aerodynamic calculation before the Wright brothers and Blériot; but, for all that, aviation did not really come in and conquer the earth until men actually got down to flying' (*Sur la valeur religieuse de la Recherche*, 1947, in *Science et Christ*, p. 262).

[2] This spirituality is to be found mainly in *Le Milieu Divin*, but also,

as the quotations in these notes will show, in many other writings, especially the letters (*Making of a Mind*, *Letters from a Traveller*).

What Teilhard says in *Le Milieu Divin* about his intended audience would not appear to be fully justified. He is writing, he says, 'for the waverers, both inside and outside, that is to say for those who, instead of giving themselves wholly to the Church, either hesitate on its threshold or turn away in the hope of going beyond it' (p. 43). We may accept that, but to understand and appreciate the book thoroughly, the reader should in the first place be a faithful member of the Church and familiar with her teaching, and already advanced in intimacy with God.

[3] 'To some, the world has disclosed itself as too vast: within such immensity, man is lost and no longer counts; and there is nothing left for him to do but shut his eyes and disappear. To others, on the contrary, the world is too beautiful; and it, and it alone, must be adored . . . There are others who are alarmed by the agitation or the attraction invincibly produced in them by this new rising star' (*Le Milieu Divin*, pp. 45–6).

[4] In *Le Milieu Divin* (p. 108) Teilhard introduces this image of a distance, a specific path, a road.

[5] As put forward and practised by Teilhard, this spiritual relation to Christ concentrates on his theological aspects, on the all-embracing mystery of the redemptive Incarnation. Teilhard does not overlook Christ's sensible aspects as recorded in the Gospel account, any more than does St Paul; but they are relegated to the background. They are, moreover, presupposed, and sometimes brought to mind.

[6] *Le prêtre*, 1918, in *Ecrits du temps de la guerre*, p. 293.

[7] Although Teilhard does not dismiss the social symbolism of the mystical body, he prefers the *realism* of the *physical* symbolism. 'Without rejecting anything of the forces of freedom and consciousness which form the *physical reality* proper to the human soul, we must perceive the existence of links between us and the incarnate Word no less precise than those which control, in the world, the affinities of the elements in the building up of "natural" wholes' (*Le Milieu Divin*, pp. 57–8).

[8] *Le Milieu Divin*, pp. 134–7.

[9] Letter from Teilhard to Père Auguste Valensin, 8 December 1918, in *Archives de Philosophie*, January–March 1961, p. 134. 'The just man has eyes only for God. *Things*, for him, *have lost their superficial*

multiplicity' (*La lutte contre la multitude*, 1917, in *Ecrits du temps de la guerre*, p. 126).

'All the external appearances of the lower world remain the same . . . the man who *dares* to believe enters a sphere of the created in which things retain their normal texture but seem to be made of another substance. Everything in phenomena remains unchanged, and yet everything becomes luminous, animated, loving. It is Christ who appears, through the operative power of faith, born, without doing violence to anything, in the heart of the world' (*La foi qui opère*, 1918, in *Ecrits du temps de la guerre*, p. 327).

'I feel, too, how much the exploration of the world *in itself* fails to bring any light or point out any solution to the most fundamental problems of life. I feel as though I am going round and round an immense problem without getting to the heart of it . . . its solution can only be sought in a "faith" beyond all experience. We must break through and go beyond appearances: never perhaps more than now has their veil seemed to me so "without seam"' (Letter of 11 May 1923, in *Letters from a Traveller*, p. 70).

'Before, the light used to make the whole surface of things sparkle for me, and I found immediate delight in everything. Now it is as though the light were dimmed. The veneer of colour and scene bores me to tears; what I love is hidden. In all men, no doubt, it is thus that the first steps are made towards the migration from one sphere to the other. It is a pull towards another zone that draws us towards maturity and death' (26 April 1926, *ibid.*, p. 123). We should note the importance attached by Teilhard, as by the mystics, to the imagery of *surface* and *depth*.

'Let us get away from the *surface* and, without leaving the world, plunge into God' (*Le Milieu Divin*, p. 115). 'None of these things will be able to separate me from your substantial love, because they are only the veil, the "species", under which you take hold of me, in order that I may take hold of you' (*Ibid.*, p. 127).

[10] 'If anyone, then, wishes to erect in himself, for God, the framework of a sublime love, the first thing he must do is to train his sensitivity; by prudent but unremitting contact with the most affectively powerful realities, he must diligently foster in himself the feeling for, the appreciation of and zest for the omnipresence that encloses as in a halo everything in nature. Even under this stuff of matter that alone our senses can know, Lord, you make yourself

manifest to us, you fill us with delight and little by little reveal to us the wonders of your presence among us' (*Le Milieu Mystique*, 1917, in *Ecrits du temps de la guerre*, p. 141).

'The heights where God dwells are not an inaccessible mountain but a more profound sphere of things. The secret of the world lies wherever we can discern the translucency of the universe' (Letter of 15 April 1923, in *Letters from a Traveller*, p. 66).

'Like those translucent materials which a light within them can make into a luminous whole, the world appears to the Christian mystic bathed in an inward light which intensifies its relief, its structure and its depth. This light is not the superficial glimmer that can be realized in coarse enjoyment; nor is it the violent flash which destroys objects and blinds our eyes. It is the calm and powerful radiance engendered by the synthesis of all the elements of the world in Jesus . . . If we may slightly alter a hallowed expression, we could say that the great mystery of Christianity is not exactly the appearance, but the transparence of God in the universe. Yes, Lord, not only the ray that strikes the surface, but the ray that penetrates: not only your Epiphany, Jesus, but your diaphany' (*Le Milieu Divin*, pp. 130-1).

'The diaphany of the divine at the heart of a universe afire' (*Le coeur de la matière*, unpublished, 1950).

[11] *Le milieu mystique*, 1917, in *Ecrits du temps de la guerre*, p. 143.

[12] 'I, too, am pretty vividly aware of the limitations of my strength, and of a certain inability to master things and keep hold of them. So far as my own life goes, I mostly live with a sort of "day is done" feeling. And then it seems to me that the only way out (and you know this better than I do) is a blind and absolute faith in the *meaning* taken on by all things, even diminishments, for the man who *believes* in God's universal animation of all that happens. With his help, we must, don't you agree, develop this faith in ourselves? The further I go, the more convinced I am that the only knowledge— the knowledge that can be acquired even with all our weakness and ignorance—lies in seeing the unity "in becoming" under and in the incoherent multiplicity of things' (Letter of 27 May 1923).

[13] '(God) must reach and act upon us, not only indirectly, through the universal network of physical synthesis, but also, and even more, directly from centre to centre (that is to say, from consciousness

to consciousness), by touching the most sensitive point in ourselves' (*The new spirit*, 1942, in *The Future of Man*, p. 92).

[14] *Le Milieu Divin*, pp. 136–7.

[15] This is a topic that occurs frequently in Teilhard's letters to his cousin. (Cf. letter of 20 September 1915 in *Making of a Mind*, p. 69).

[16] Providence, at once benevolent and powerful: 'Who shall find words, Lord, for the violence the universe undergoes once it has fallen under your domination! Christ is the spur that urges the creature along the road of effort, drives it to the top, forces it to develop. He is the sword that mercilessly cuts off the unworthy or decayed members. He is the full strength of life that inexorably slaughters all base egoisms, to take to himself all their powers of love' (*Le prêtre*, 1918, in *Ecrits du temps de la guerre*, p. 288).

[17] 'When it's a question of union with God, it's in carrying along with us the whole world that we can advance further into the bosom of God; and that bosom itself is in all things; and all things, purified and concentrated, meet and are found again in God's innermost self' (Letter of 14 July 1916, in *Making of a Mind*, p.112).

'What peace it is to know that there is a living centre of all things, through whom our desires and insights can unerringly make their way and reverberate in the very depths of souls, of each individual soul—anonymously but divinely' (Letter of 18 September 1916, *Ibid.*, p. 128).

'Unchanging throughout the generations, I am here at hand, ready to save, for those who come to me, the treasure that today may be lost, but the future will inherit—one day I shall pass on your thought to another, whose name I know. And when he speaks and is heard, it will be your voice that will be heard. Do you yourself know whence comes the idea that moves you so deeply and which you cherish as though it were your own? It is I who am the true bond that holds the world together. Without me all beings, even if they appear to be in contact, are separated by an unbridgeable abyss. In me they meet, in spite of the chaos of endless time and space' (*Le milieu mystique*, 1917, in *Ecrits du temps de la guerre*, p. 160).

'In your breast, my God, better than in any embrace, I possess all those whom I love and who are illumined by your beauty and in their turn illumine you with the rays of light (so powerful in their effect on our hearts) which they receive from you and send back to you. That multitude of beings, so daunting in its magnitude.

that I so long to help, to enlighten, to guide to you: it is already there, Lord, gathered together within you. Through you I can reach into the inmost depths of every being and endow them with whatever I will—provided that I know how to ask you, and that you permit it' (*Le prêtre*, 1918, in *Hymn of the Universe*, p. 147).

'Jesus came to bring us . . . not only a new life, higher than the life we are conscious of possessing, but also, in a very real sense, a new physical power of acting upon our *temporal* world' (*La foi qui opère*, 1918, in *Ecrits du temps de la guerre*, p. 319).

'Let us get away from the surface, and, without leaving the world, plunge into God. There and from there, in him and through him, we shall hold all things and have command of all things . . . In this place the least of our desires and efforts is harvested and preserved, and can at any moment touch the deepest chords of the universe . . . all the external energies of the world are co-ordinated and harmonized at that privileged point' (*Le Milieu Divin*, p. 115).

[18] *Le Milieu Divin*, p. 135. 'The inward tension of the mind towards God may seem negligible to those who try to calculate the quantity of energy accumulated in the mass of humanity. And yet, if we could see the "light invisible" as we can see clouds or lightning or the rays of the sun, a pure soul would seem as active in this world, by virtue of its sheer purity, as the snowy summits whose impassive peaks continually breathe in for us the roving powers of the high atmosphere' (*Ibid.*, p. 134).

[19] Letter of 12 September 1918, in *Making of a Mind*, pp. 234–6. It is not surprising that an observant eye can discern, beneath the appearance of chance, the action—sometimes even the miraculous action—of providence. Teilhard often acknowledges the graces he had received even in carrying out his scientific work (Letters of 12 September 1923, 15 November 1935, 24 January 1936, in *Letters from a Traveller*, pp. 88, 215, 221).

'The successful realization of the Christian life, as effected by faith, has three characteristics: 1. It is produced without doing violence to or interrupting any individual determinism: events are not (in general) diverted from their course by prayer, but integrated in a new combination of the whole. 2. It is not necessarily apparent in the plane of man's natural success, but in the order of supernatural sanctification. 3. It has God *in absolute reality* as the principal agent, source and ambience of its developments' (*La foi qui opère*, 1918, in *Ecrits du temps de la guerre*, pp. 324–5).

[20] *Le Milieu Divin*, pp. 142–6. Teilhard rather unexpectedly admits that he is temperamentally more sensitive to affinities with things than with persons, at any rate if they are strangers to him. 'The "other" (which means everybody except a handful of human beings allowed to move in our orbit) is an importunate intruder. At least, that's how I feel sometimes. Instinctively, I'd much rather have an earth full of animals than one inhabited by men. Every man forms a little world on his own, and this pluralism is essentially distasteful to me' (Letter of 14 August 1917, in *Making of a Mind*, p. 202). (Cf. Chapter 5, note 162).

The war-time letters collected in *The Making of a Mind* shows us a Teilhard deeply conscious of the duty of charity towards the unfortunate, but still insufficiently responsive to the demands of justice as part of the problem of society (Letter of 15 October 1916, *ibid.*, pp. 132-3). He gives, however, some excellent advice on the supernatural exercise of charity, pointing out that it must reconcile the normal attraction of natural affinities and affection for 'unattractive or even repulsive creatures' (Letter of 20 October 1916, *ibid.*, p. 135).

[21] *The new spirit*, 1942 in *The Future of Man*, pp. 88–9, 95–6: 'In such an order of things, no man can love his neighbour without drawing nearer to God—and, of course, reciprocally. But it is also impossible . . . to love either God or our neighbour without assisting the progress, in its physical entirety, of the terrestrial synthesis of the spirit: since it is precisely the progress of this synthesis which enables us to draw closer together among ourselves, while at the same time it raises us towards God. Because we love, and in order that we may love even more, we find ourselves to our delight compelled to participate more fully than others in all the endeavours, all the anxieties, all the aspirations and also all the affections of the earth— *in so far as these embody a principle of ascension and synthesis* (*Ibid.*, p. 95).

'Christian faith manifests itself as an extremely real and comprehensive cosmic energy' (*La foi qui opère*, 1918, in *Ecrits du temps de la guerre*, p. 325).

'If it is psychologically impossible for man to surround each being with the distinct and overflowing affection characteristic of human love, he can at least cultivate towards all things that general warmth (inchoate but genuine) which will make him cherish in each object (over and above all sensible qualities) its very being. Being, that is to say that indefinable and chosen portion of each thing which becomes little by little, through God's influence, the flesh of his flesh.

'Love of this kind is not exactly comparable with any attachment known in ordinary social relations. Its "material object", as the schoolmen would say, is so vast, and its "formal object" so profound that it can only be translated into complex terms of espousals and adoration. In it all distinction between egoism and altruism tends to disappear. Each man loves and seeks himself in the consummation of all the rest: and the smallest urge to possession extends into an effort to attain, in the most distant future, that which is the same in all' (*Basis and foundations of the idea of evolution*, 1926, in *Vision of the Past*, p. 140).

[22] *L'atomisme de l'esprit*, 1941, *op. cit.*

[23] *Le milieu mystique*, 1917, in *Ecrits du temps de la guerre*, pp. 137–67.

[24] This is on the same lines as Teilhard's meditation before the host, in its third phase: the host eludes him, 'leaving (him) at grips with the entire universe', which has become 'like a wonderful prey'. 'From the host which I held in my fingers I was separated by the full extent and density of the years which still remained to me, to be lived and to be divinized' (*Christ in the world of Matter*, 1916, in *Hymn of the Universe*, p. 53).

[25] Letters of 4 August 1916 and 8 September 1916, in *Making of a Mind*, pp. 116, 126–7. Teilhard took the death of a friend at the front as an occasion to focus his thoughts: 'Man's labour, whatever form it may take, must be essentially tenacious, patient, gentle—and it's by uncomplainingly putting right the disorders and obstacles that a new order is doubtless taking shape, and painfully clearing a place for itself in the world—an order by virtue of which the brutal shocks and blind disasters . . . will be reduced to a minimum' (Letter of 8 September 1916, *ibid.*, pp. 123–4).

[26] *Le Milieu Divin*, p. 72. 'In building up the earth, an honest workman not only surrenders his calm and peace once and for all, but must learn continually to jettison the form which his labour or art or thought first took, and go in search of new forms. To pause, so as to bask in or possess results, would be a betrayal of action. Over and over again, he must go beyond himself, tear himself away from

himself, leaving behind him his most cherished beginnings' (*Ibid.*).

[27] *Christianisme et évolution*, unpublished, 1945. In 1918, a visit to the cathedral at Strasbourg suggested to Teilhard the question, 'Why was the mystical drive of the Middle Ages pulled up short? Was it only because a great influx of new elements cooled a fire that in extent covered hardly more than half Europe? or, was it also because the religious world, as seen by our ancestors at that time, was placed by them on too immediate a plane that failed to allow the natural universe its own proper scale of grandeur and its own particular development? . . . I can't help wondering how in these days we should envisage a cathedral?' (Letter of 2 December 1918, in *Making of a Mind*, p. 261).

[28] *What should we think of transformism?* 1930, in *The Vision of the Past*, p. 160.

[29] 'On the one hand, matter is the burden, the fetters, the pain, the sin and the threat to our lives. It weighs us down, suffers, wounds, tempts and ages us. Matter makes us heavy, paralysed, vulnerable, guilty. Who will deliver us from this body of death? But at the same time matter is physical exuberance, ennobling contact, virile effort and the joy of growth. It attracts, renews, unites and flowers. By matter we are nourished, lifted up, linked to everything else, invaded by life. To be deprived of it is intolerable . . . Who will give us an immortal body?' (*Le Milieu Divin*, p. 106). One part of the spiritual life consists in 'harnessing jealously for (God) the spiritual power of matter' (*Ibid.*, p. 107), and in 'touching and handling matter with a proper sense of reverence' (*Ibid.*, p. 107).

[30] Second memorandum from Teilhard to Père Auguste Valensin, 29 December 1919, *op. cit.*, p. 151.

'The totality of all perfections, even natural perfections, is the necessary basis for that mystical and ultimate organism which you are constructing out of all things. You do not destroy, Lord, the beings that you adopt for your building; but you transform them while preserving everything good that the centuries of creation have fashioned in them' (*Le Prêtre*, 1918, in *Hymn of the Universe*, p. 152). 'We are the foundation that is indispensable to your expansion. You do not annihilate us when you take possession of us. But you jealously preserve the essential core of our natural qualities, in order to make of them the axis, the nucleus, the bulwark of your growth. Under your action, which transforms and does not destroy, all the good in us passes, for all eternity, into the perfection of your body' (*Ibid.*, p. 290).

'The world will never be vast enough, nor will humanity ever be strong enough, to be worthy of Him who created them and incarnated Himself in them' (*What should we think of transformism?* 1930, in *Vision of the Past*, p. 160).

'The progress of the universe, and in particular of the human universe, does not take place in competition with God, nor does it squander energies that we rightly owe to him. The greater man becomes, the more humanity becomes united, with consciousness of, and master of, its potentialities, the more beautiful creation will be, the more perfect adoration will become, and the more Christ will find, for mystical extensions, a body worthy of resurrection' (*Le Milieu Divin*, p. 154).

[31] 'Those who adjust their sails to the winds of the earth will always find themselves borne by a current towards the open seas. The more nobly a man wills and acts, the more avid he becomes for great and sublime aims to pursue. He will no longer be content with family, country, and the remunerative aspect of his work. He will want wider organizations to create, new paths to blaze, causes to uphold, truths to discover, an ideal to cherish and defend. So gradually the artificer of the earth no longer belongs to himself. Little by little the great breath of the universe has insinuated itself into him through the fissure of his humble but faithful action, has broadened him, raised him up, borne him on' (*Le Milieu Divin*, p. 72).

'One can never stress too much the degree to which Christianity is a doctrine of, and offers the prospect of, universal transformation. Through the Incarnation, God came down into nature to superanimate it and gather it to himself: in that you have the real substance of Christian dogma' (*La mystique de la science*, 1939, in *L'énergie humaine*, p. 220).

[32] *Le Milieu Divin*, p. 153. 'The supernatural subsists by transforming (re-creating or creating further, "ultra creando") a sap that *must* be continually supplied by the natural effort of life.'

[33] Letter to Père Victor Fontoynont, 22 July 1916, quoted by H. de Lubac, *op. cit.*, p. 247.

[34] 'To the value of the work done is added the value of the actual doing, which by its fidelity creates in us the personality expected of

us by Christ. Our own soul—in itself and in its being at the heart of the universe—is the first of the tasks calling for our efforts' (Letter of 8 April 1930, in *Letters from a Traveller*, p. 164).

[35] Letter of 9 January 1917, in *Making of a Mind*, pp. 166-7.

[36] *Christologie et évolution*, unpublished, 1933.

[37] *A note on progress*, 1920, in *The Future of Man*, p. 22. 'Sharing in the enterprises and aspirations of men is by no means a mere accessory in the work of salvation: it is the psychic nucleus on which, in each man, falls (or from which is born) faith and the gift of self to the supernatural' (*Le sens humain*, unpublished, 1929).

[38] 'So long as the world is to me no more than an opportunity to win merit, and not some κτῆμα ἐς ἀεί to be constructed and perfected— I shall live only half-heartedly among men, and they will look on me, because of my religion, as a broken reed, or a deserter' (Letter to Père Victor Fontoynont, 15 March 1916, quoted by H. de Lubac, *op. cit.*, p. 243).

[39] 'In human effort, we have the sacred marrow of the universe. And it's there that we have to strike' (Letter of 6 November 1916, in *Making of a Mind*, p. 64).

[40] *Le Milieu Divin*, p. 64.

'In the life of each one of us an immense and indispensable part is earmarked for positive action, for man's natural social *effort*. This effort is imposed on us as an unavoidable burden by external conditions. But it has a spiritualizing value, too, of the first order, both in the moral "training" it gives our activity, and *also* in the positive results it brings us—in the *work* it produces. Who can say how much our mystical life, even at its most supernatural, owes to Plato, to Leibniz, Pascal, Newton, and countless others (many of them much more unexpectedly) whom each one of us, if he looked into his heart, could name? Who would be so bold as to prophesy all that the human soul is still in fact capable of acquiring in the way of natural powers that can be directly supernaturalized—to the extent, for example, that it becomes fully conscious of its solidarity with the universe, and of the still unexplored areas of the spirit that await man's spiritual unanimity? Who could deny that if charity is cut off from man's struggle and the pulse of his life, it would find itself shut up in a world that had been transformed into a cloister, and so perish? In the development of every individual life and in the history of the whole human race, there is an enormous mass of positive achievements that it is impossible, that it would be disloyal, to allow to come to nothing. If Christ is to fill my life—*all* my life—it is absolutely essential that I should be conscious of growing in him not only through the restrictions of asceticism and the detachments (supremely unifying though they are) of suffering, but even more through all the positive effort contained in my life, through my own natural perfection and duty as a man. This must be so—otherwise Christianity *robs* me of the courage I need for action, and I turn away in disgust from one whole side of my life which religion degrades and yet will not allow me to abandon' (Letter of 12 December 1919).

'We think of work as primarily a way of earning a living. But its essential virtue is on a higher level: through work we complete in ourselves the subject of the divine union, and through it, again, we somehow add to the greatness, in relation to ourselves, of the divine term of that union, our Lord Jesus Christ. Hence, whatever our function as men may be, artists, workers or scientists, we can, if we are Christians, speed towards the object of our work as though towards an opening into the supreme fulfilment of our being' (*Le Milieu Divin*, p. 63). 'In a universe within which everything contributes towards the gradual formation of spirit that God lifts up to final union, all work acquires, in its tangible reality, a value of holiness and communion' (*La mystique de la science*, 1939, in *L'énergie humaine*, p. 222).

[41] *Le Milieu Divin*, p. 62. 'All things become physically, and literally, lovable in God . . . It is the general ascent of life towards fuller consciousness, it is man's effort in its entirety, that must, by strict necessity, enter organically into the cares and aims of charity. If we are to love the super-Christ, we must at all costs forward the progress of the universe and of mankind in ourselves and in each of our fellow-elements (and, most of all, in the other grains of thought, our fellow-men)' (*Super-Humanité, super-Christ, super-Charité*, 1943, in *Science et Christ*, pp. 213–14). 'For the reflective element flung into a cosmogenesis directed towards a Christic pole, time and space (and that means every positive step and every event, everything done and felt, every growth and every diminishment) are dynamically Christified in the very stuff of their fundamental reality' (*Du cosmos à la cosmogénèse*, in *L'activation de l'énergie*, p. 274).

[42] Letter of 10 December 1918, in *Making of a Mind*, p. 264. 'The

Christian should even be ashamed of allowing himself to lag behind
the enemies of God in the keenness of his work, in the spirit of
enterprise and even of sacrifice' (Pius XII's Christmas broadcast,
1957).

[43] *Le Milieu Divin*, p. 118. 'There is only one possible place for each
one of us at any given moment, the one we are led to by unflagging
fidelity to the natural and supernatural duties of life' (*Ibid.*).

[44] *Ibid.*, p. 108.

[45] Letter of 12 December 1919.

[46] Unpublished letter to Père Auguste Valensin, 29 December 1919.

[47] *Super-Humanité*, etc., 1943, in *Science et Christ*, p. 215.

[48] 'Even now I am still experiencing the dangers to which a man is
exposed who, by internal law and necessity, sees himself forced to
leave the well-beaten track of a certain traditional ascesis that is
now insufficiently adapted to human requirements; he then has to
try to find another road that will lead to heaven, by which the
entire dynamism of matter and flesh is channelled into a genesis of
the spirit—and it must not be a mean between the two but a
synthesis of them' (*Le coeur de la matière*, unpublished, 1950, p. 25).
Teilhard speaks, too, of the 'novelty, the boldness and at the same
time the paradoxical possibility in the attitudes' that must be
adopted by man who 'in his quest for holiness' has decided to
'allow the free interaction within himself of the upward impulse of
faith in God and the forward impulse of faith in the ultra-human'.

'If we had to wait for mystical union with Christ before we could
face the problems of the earth, we should probably never get started
on our work as men. Reaching out towards things and concentration *in Christum* must always be two simultaneous processes. As soon
as man first became mystically awake and discovered the convergence of the universe—in other words discovered Christ as the end
of all things—there was no longer any danger of his wandering
adrift in his effort to dominate the real, since he realized that everything, in its interiority, had become one: but what was even more
important, he found the secret that would give him spiritual detachment without in any way impairing his activity (Letter of
29 December 1919).

[49] Memoranda to Père Auguste Valensin, *op. cit.*, pp. 139, 155. Teilhard justifies a friend's engaging in a business enterprise as follows:
'Because your undertaking—which I take to be perfectly legitimate

—is going well, a little more health is being spread in the human mass, and in consequence a little more freedom to act, to think and to love. Whatever we do, we can and must do it with the strengthening and broadening consciousness of working, individually, to achieve a result which (even as a tangible reality) is required, at least indirectly, by the body of Christ' (Letter of 8 April 1930, in *Letters from a Traveller*, p. 164). The justification would have been more complete if it had occurred to Teilhard to propose Catholic action to his friend and suggest that he should work for a fuller measure of social and economic justice.

[50] *Le Milieu Divin*, p. 97.

[51] *Ibid.*, p. 62.

[52] *Introduction au Christianisme*, unpublished, 1944.

[53] Letter of 6 November 1916, in *Making of a Mind*, p. 142.

[54] *Le Milieu Divin*, pp. 68–70.

[55] Many passages show how sensitive Teilhard was to suffering, and the nearness of death, and how clearly he appreciated the problem of evil. 'At any moment the vast and horrible thing may break in through the cracks,' and he speaks even of the 'universal horror' (*Le Milieu Divin*, p. 137). 'Few men,' says Claude Cuénot, 'have had so lively a sense of human suffering and of the Cross' (*op. cit.*, p. 483).

[56] 'Believing is not seeing. As much as any man, I imagine, I walk in the shadow of faith . . . If God allows us to suffer, to sin and to doubt, it is because he cannot without further ado cure us and show himself to us here and now. And if he cannot do so, it is simply and solely because, at the stage the universe has now reached, we are still incapable of more complete organization and fuller light. That being so, I am ready to persevere to the end along a road of which I am ever more certain towards horizons that are ever more deeply shrouded in mist' (*Comment je crois*, unpublished, 1944, epilogue). 'I know we cannot forestall, still less dictate to you, the smallest of your actions; from you alone comes all initiative—and this applies in the first place to my prayer' (*The Mass upon the World*, 1923, in *Hymn of the Universe*, p. 22). Earlier, in *Le milieu mystique*, Teilhard had said, 'It is more than a simple union that seeks to be effected, it is a *transformation*, and all that human activity can contribute to the process is a humble disposition and acceptance' (*op. cit.*, p. 161).

[57] 'If souls are to share in this joy and vision they must first have had the courage to smash their own petty individuality; they must in some way depersonalize themselves, to centre themselves on Jesus Christ. Underlying renunciation is purity: and charity even more' (*La lutte contre la multitude*, 1917, in *Ecrits du temps de la guerre*, pp. 129–30).

'It's a good thing, when you come to think of it, to be the pebble tossed by the divine ocean' (Letter of 10 July 1916, in *Making of a Mind*, p. 109). Teilhard devoted much thought to the mystery of the *future*, 'the future that is made up of terrifying inevitability, of no less frightening renewal, and at the same time of benign providence that can make itself manifest and modify itself in proportion to the intensity of our faith' (Letter of 17 August 1918, *ibid.*, p. 228). 'Yet how difficult it is to fling oneself into the future: inevitably, our sensibility sees in it only a dizzy void and restless fluidity: to give it solidity we must have faith' (Letter of 28 August 1918, *ibid.*, p. 229). 'What is said in the Epistle to the Hebrews, "*fides substantia sperandarum rerum*," may, I think, be translated so: faith is the element that stabilizes and divinizes our future—it creates it, for each one of us, to the measure of our own salvation and our own particular chosen destiny' (Letter of 31 August 1918, *ibid.*, p. 232).

After reading G. Duhamel's *La Possession du Monde*, in 1919, Teilhard commented: 'He makes his readers feel that they are in touch with the divine, and then he leaves them there, without pointing out to them the inexorable necessity of renunciation, the basic condemnation of selfishness and following the line of least resistance entailed in possession of the world.'

'The upward impulse of detachment remains unimpaired. The Cross and its symbol of annihilation still dominates the earth, but at the same time it sanctifies and completes all the constructive toil of man's effort. It is still annihilation, but positive annihilation; annihilation subordinated to a growth, corresponding to an excess of growth; annihilation that, to be legitimate and fruitful, requires that both individuals and world be ready and ripe for this final step of turning back and excentration. To be able to give oneself completely, one must be fully oneself.' Detachment must be effected by 'super-attachment' (*Note sur la perfection chrétienne*, unpublished, 1942).

'Christian detachment subsists wholly in this wider attitude of mind; but instead of "leaving behind", it leads on; instead of cutting off, it raises. It is no longer a break-away but a way through; no longer a withdrawal but an act of emerging' (*The new spirit*, 1942, in *The Future of Man*, p. 96).

[58] 'The intermediaries . . . are not rejected but outstripped' (*Le Milieu Divin*, p. 139). 'Detachment is now not a break but a way through and a sublimation. Spiritualization now comes not through a negation or withdrawal from the multiple, but through an emergence' (*L'atomisme de l'esprit*, 1941, in *L'activation de l'énergie*, p. 63). 'Spirit has ceased to be for us anti-matter or extra-matter, to become trans-matter . . . Spiritualization, as we now see it, can no longer be effected in a break-away from or in conflict with matter, but in a transition or emergence from it' (*Note sur la notion de perfection chrétienne*, unpublished, 1942).

[59] Teilhard identifies purity with love, and impurity with selfishness (*Le Milieu Divin*, p. 133). For Teilhard 'the Immaculate Conception is the feast of "passive action", the action that functions simply in the transmission through us of divine energy. Purity, in spite of outward appearances, is essentially an active virtue, because it concentrates God in us and on those who are subject to our influence' (Letter of 5 December 1916, in *Making of a Mind*, p. 149). Of the love of man and woman Teilhard was later to write, 'Purity simply expresses the degree of distinctness with which the ultimate centre of their coincidence emerges recognizably above two beings who love another' (*Esquisse d'un univers personnel*, 1936, in *L'énergie humaine*, p. 95).

[60] Memorandum of 12 December 1919, in *Archives de philosophie*, XXIV, 1961, p. 136. 'In the first place I have no difficulty in accepting that the universal effort of the world can be understood as the making ready of a holocaust' (Memorandum of 29 December 1919, *ibid.*, p. 151). 'The effort of mankind, even in realms inaccurately called profane, must, in the Christian life, assume the role of a holy and unifying operation. It is the collaboration, trembling with love, which we give to the hands of God, concerned to equip and prepare us (and the world) for the final union through sacrifice' (*Le Milieu Divin*, p. 97). 'When once a man has made up his mind unstintingly to practise love of God and of his neighbour, he sees that to rectify his own interior unity by selfless renunciation does not really mean that he has yet done anything.

Before that unity of his can be re-born in Christ it must pass through an eclipse that will seem to annihilate it. Those in fact will be saved who boldly transfer the centre of their being outside themselves and are not afraid to love Another than self: in some way they will then become Other, that is to say they will pass through death in their quest for life' (*La lutte contre la multitude*, 1917, in *Ecrits du temps de la guerre*, p. 130).

61 *Le milieu mystique*, 1917, *ibid.*, p. 154. 'I feel really at home in the hands of our Lord—and never perhaps have I been so conscious of the joy of allowing myself to sink into the future as though into the depths of his very being' (Unpublished letter to Père Auguste Valensin, 16 January 1927). 'My life consists, more and more simply, in a sort of act of boundless confidence in being, in the figure of Our Lord . . . I feel that I have emerged into a *state of sheer force* that presses on ahead without really knowing where, without *enjoying* anything, but with supreme faith in spirit—and in unity' (Letter of 15 July 1929).

'After many hesitant attempts, I have found no better phrase, from my own point of view, to define and direct my interior life than this (in which the whole context of the divine ambience is summed up): "To be in communion with becoming", in so far as becoming expresses at any moment the entirety of God's loving and personalizing action on us through the universe' (Letter of December 1942 to Madame Claude Rivière, quoted in her *Teilhard, Claudel et Mauriac*, Editions Universitaires, 1963, p. 47).

62 Letter of 12 January 1916, in *Making of a Mind*, p. 88.

63 *Le Prêtre*, 1918, *op. cit.*, p. 296. 'The only essential thing surely, is to cling to the divine action, present at every point, and the more worthy to be adored the more our destiny outruns our anticipation and control' (Letter of 13 October 1916 in *The Making of a Mind*, p. 132).

'Personal success or personal satisfaction are not worth another thought if one does achieve them, or worth worrying about if they elude one or are slow in coming. All that is really worth while is action—faithful action, for the world and in God. Before one can see that and live by it, there is a sort of threshold to cross, or a reversal to be made in what appears to be men's general habit of thought: but once that decisive step has been taken, what freedom is yours, freedom to work and to love!' (Letter of 30 October 1929, in *Letters from a Traveller*, p. 160). 'Stick to the hand of God' (Letter of 6 March 1933, *ibid.*, p. 196).

'(We must) accustom ourselves to that gesture, essential not only in death but in life, which consists in allowing ourselves to rest, as upon an invisible support, upon Him who sustains and upholds us right outside all the tangible things to which we feel so strong an instinct to cling' (Letter of 9 May 1940, *ibid.*, p. 264). 'To be in communion with becoming' (Letter of 19 May 1941, *ibid.*, p. 283).

[64] 'The great victory of the creator and redeemer, in the Christian vision, is to have transformed what is in itself a universal power of diminishment and extinction into an essentially life-giving factor. God must, in some way or another, make room for himself, hollowing us out and emptying us, if he is finally to penetrate us. And in order to assimilate us in him, he must break the molecules of our being so as to recast and remodel us. The function of death is to provide the necessary entrance into our inmost selves. It will make us undergo the required dissociation. It will put us into the state organically needed if the divine fire is to descend upon us. And thus its sinister power to decompose and dissolve will be harnessed to the most sublime operations of life. What was by nature empty and void, a return to plurality, can in every human existence, become fullness and unity in God (*Le Milieu Divin*, p. 89).

The 1914 war, naturally enough, made Teilhard think deeply about death (Letter of 13 November 1916, in *Making of a Mind*, pp. 144–5). 'Death surrenders us totally to God; it makes us enter into him; we must, in return, surrender ourselves to death with absolute love and self-abandonment—since, when death comes, all we can do is completely to accept the domination and guidance of God.' 'Death, through the great invasion and intrusion of everything new that it represents in our individual development, brings freedom and solace . . . it would be so stifling to feel oneself ineluctably confined to this superficial and experiential facet of our cosmos' (p. 158). 'Death *releases*, and if there were no death, the earth would doubtless seem a stifling place' (Letter of 5 August 1917, *ibid.*, p. 199).

Although Teilhard delighted in quiet recollection in natural surroundings, he found nature 'disturbing rather than satisfying'; 'you can find no rest in it, until you reach the ultimate term hidden in it'; he saw in it not so much an object to be contemplated as an opportunity for a quest, a pursuit of knowledge. 'The lack of satisfaction I find in nature lies in the inevitable superficiality of our knowledge of it here below. Anything *new* we can contrive to discover or extract is contained in a zone limited in advance by our faculties. As soon as we reach a certain depth we're down to rock: we're ringed in by a barrier that we can't break through, that can only be broken through by some *complete organic* transformation such as death alone can bring about. Nature makes us want to die, so that we may at last see what lies within her . . . to reach a new level of the absolute we have to throw off our present physical form' (Letter of 12 July 1918, *ibid.*, p. 214).

[65] Letter of 7 October 1915, in *Making of a Mind*, p. 74.

[66] After saying that ,'The man who is filled with an impassioned love of Jesus hidden in the forces that bring increase to the earth, him the earth will lift up like a mother, in the immensity of her arms, and will enable him to contemplate the face of God', Teilhard adds: 'The man who is filled with an impassioned love for Jesus hidden in the forces which bring death to the earth, him the earth will clasp in the immensity of her arms as her strength fails, and with her he will awaken in the bosom of God' (*The Mass on the World*, 1923, in *Hymn of the Universe*, pp. 30, 32).

'In God's hands the forces of diminishment have perceptibly become the tool that cuts, carves and polishes within us the stone which is destined to occupy a definite place in the heavenly Jerusalem. But he will do still more, for as a result of his omnipotence coming down to meet our faith, events which appear in our experience of life to be pure loss will become an immediate factor in the union we dream of establishing with him' (*Le Milieu Divin*, p. 88).

[67] *The consecration of suffering*
'The troops are suffering more than ever and accumulating the substance of an inexpressible sacrifice. Why must it be that their agony should lack the element of adoration and oblation through which the wearisome task of co-operating with life is transfigured and made intelligible?' (Letter of 2 February 1916, in *Making of a Mind*, p. 92).

'Why was my soul filled with joy? Because, when the direct supports on which I so rashly built my life, failed me, I realized in a

quite unique way, that I was resting only on your consistence . . .
Enjoyment and receptiveness are indispensable to the awakening
and preservation of mystical fervour. But all the exaltation they
bring, put together, has nothing like the power of the cold shock of
disappointment to make us understand that you alone have real
solidity. It is through sorrow, my God, and not through joy that
your reality gradually comes home to our sensibility' (*Le milieu
mystique*, 1917, in *Ecrits du temps de la guerre*, p. 146).

'That Christ may enter deeply into us we need alternately the
work that dilates the heart and the sorrow that brings death to it,
the life that enlarges a man in order that he may be sanctifiable, and
the death that diminishes him in order that he may be sanctified . . .
The universe splits in two, it suffers a painful cleavage at the heart
of each of its monads, as the flesh of Christ is born and grows. Like
the work of creation which it redeems and surpasses, the Incarnation, so desired of man, is an awe-inspiring work; it is achieved
through blood (*Le Prêtre*, 1918, in *Hymn of the Universe*, pp. 123-4).

'The consecration of the world would have remained incomplete,
a moment ago, had you not with special love vitalized for those who
believe, not only the life-bringing forces, but also those which bring
death. My communion would be incomplete—would, quite simply,
not be Christian—if, together with the gains which this new day
brings me, I did not also accept, in my own name and in the name
of the world as the most immediate sharing in your own being, those
processes, hidden and manifest, of enfeeblement, of ageing, of
death, which unceasingly consume the universe, to its salvation or
its condemnation' (*The Mass on the World*, 1923, in *Hymn of the
Universe*, pp. 31-2).

'Seen on the scale of our experience, the world is an immensity of
hesitant advances, a vast quest, a massive offensive: any progress it
makes must be paid for by many failures and casualties.' Although
resignation is the very opposite of capitulation, the sick 'have a
special function to fulfil . . . They have to co-operate with the
transformation—one might well call it the conversion—of human
suffering . . . The upward impulse of the world is hidden, under
extreme pressure, in suffering. The whole problem is to release it,
by making it conscious of its meaning and potential force. What a
vast leap towards God the world would make, if all the sick simultaneously concentrated their sufferings into one common wish that

the kingdom of God should rapidly mature through the conquest and organization of the world! Supposing all those who suffer on earth should unite their sufferings in order that the pain of the world should become one great single act of consciousness, sublimation and union—could we imagine any higher form that might be assumed by the mysterious work of creation?' (*La signification et la valeur constructrice de la souffrance*, 1933, in *L'énergie humaine*, pp. 61–6).

'Before our hearts can submit to this stern law of creation, one thing is psychologically necessary: in the painful negation involved in the operation that produces us, we must be able to discern an additional positive value that transfigures it and so makes it unarguably acceptable. It is here, of course, that there comes in, to supply what nothing else can, the astonishing Christian revelation of a suffering that can be transformed—provided it be *rightly* accepted—into an expression of love and a principle of union: suffering that in the first place is treated as an enemy to be overcome; suffering fought to the bitter end; and yet at the same time suffering that is accepted rationally and even welcomed in as much as it tears us away from self-love, compensates for our faults, and so is able to super-centre us upon God. There can be no doubt about it: that this very suffering, hidden, repulsive, should be exalted, for even the humblest sufferer, into a supremely active principle of universal humanization and divinization—in that we see the climax of the prodigious spiritual energy born of the Cross' (Preface to *L'énergie spirituelle de la souffrance*, 1950, *op. cit.*, p. 11, and in *L'activation de l'énergie*, p. 256). This preface and the passages quoted above should be compared with Claudel's letter to Suzanne Fouché, *Les invités à l'attention*, 1928, in *Positions et Propositions*, Vol. 2.

[68] Letter of 25 November 1942, in *Letters from a Traveller*, p. 285. On one occasion when circumstances made him turn his thought to 'the fragility of human hopes' and the possibility of some sort of social catastrophe, Teilhard nevertheless could not help feeling 'buoyed up with a sort of triumphant joy . . . based on a conviction of the transcendence of God' (Letter of 9 April 1916, in *Making of a Mind*, p. 98). Again, faced with an unknown future, that no human powers could determine, he had the feeling that God was '*ahead* and *around*, *thickening* (if I may use the word) as we advance' (Letter of 4 October 1917, *ibid.*, p. 207).

[69] *The Church*

Le Christique, 1955.

'I hope, with the help of God, never to do anything contrary to the Church, for outside her I can see no life-current that has any chance of success' (Letter of 4 July 1920). 'I believe in the Church as "mediatrix" between God and the world, and I love her. This, it seems to me, brings me great peace' (Letter of 22 August 1925).

'If Christianity, as it professes and believes, is indeed destined to be the religion of tomorrow, there is only one way in which it can hope to come up to the measure of today's great humanitarian trends and assimilate them; and that is through the axis, living and organic, of its Catholicism centred on Rome' (*Introduction au christianisme*, unpublished, 1944).

'For reasons that are built into the very structure of my habit of thought, I am deeply convinced that religious thought can develop only in tradition, collectively, "phyletically"; my only hope and wish, accordingly, is, in writing what follows, to *sentire*, or, more precisely, *prae-sentire cum Ecclesia*' (*Christianisme et évolution*, 1945, unpublished).

'A sort of ultra-socialization is going on in the heart of the social phenomenon: in it the Church is gradually developing, as its influence animates and brings together in their most sublime form all the spiritual energies of the noosphere: the Church, which is the consciously Christified portion of the world; the Church, the main focus-point at which the affinities that link men together meet in super-charity; the Church, the central axis of universal convergence, and the exact meeting-point that emerges between the universe and Omega Point' (*Comment je vois*, 12 August 1948, unpublished).

In 1948, when Teilhard was in Rome, he felt an 'awareness of the extraordinary focus of spiritual radiation concentrated by the two thousand years of history these places have witnessed: in these days, it is here in Rome that we find the Christic pole of the earth; through Rome, I mean, runs the ascending axis of hominization' (Letter of 7 October 1948, in *Letters from a Traveller*, p. 299). 'The Eternal City has made no violent *impact* on me . . . but I have been impressed (and heartened) by Christianity's extraordinary, really imperturbable, confidence in the unshakable solidity of its faith and truth. There is a remarkable phenomenon there, unique, in fact, in the world' (Letter of 28 October 1948, *ibid.*, p. 302).

'In fact I had the good fortune to be born into the heart of the Catholic "phylum": by that I mean into the centre of the specially favoured zone in which the ascending cosmic force of "complexity-consciousness" joins up with the descending (but magnetic) stream of personal and personalizing attraction generated between heaven and earth as an effect of hominization' (*Le coeur de la matière*, unpublished, 15 August 1950, p. 20).

'Only in the Roman stock, *taken in its integrity*, can I see the biological support sufficiently massive and differentiated to effect and maintain the transformation we look for' (Letter of 4 October 1950). 'Were Christic monotheism to disappear (collapse of the Church), monotheism (and cosmic love) would *never be born again* on earth, any more than man himself (thought) would—if the noosphere were to perish' (1950). 'If the Church falls, all is lost' (about 1945). The two preceding sentences are quoted by C. Cuénot in *Teilhard de Chardin* (Editions du Seuil, in the series 'Ecrivains de toujours', p. 163). 'I am so convinced (and continually more so) that the world cannot attain fulfilment without Christ and that there can be no Christ without loyalty to the Church, that I could not possibly have felt the least hesitation when I heard your decision' (Letter to the Very Revd. Fr. Jansens, 25 September 1947, quoted by R. d'Ouince, *L'obéissance du Père Teilhard de Chardin*, in *L'homme devant Dieu*, Mé'langes offerts au Père de Lubac p. 342). 'In sober truth (and in virtue of the whole structure of my thought) I feel myself today more indissolubly bound to the hierarchic Church and the Christ of the Gospels, than I have ever been at any moment in my life' (Letter quoted earlier, to Very Revd. Fr. Jansens, 12 October 1951). 'I am more and more convinced that some great thing is being born at the heart of the Church: something whose contagion will convert the earth. And it is to this that I feel myself really dedicated' (unpublished letter to Père Auguste Valensin).

[70] 'The Church, in whom and around whom Christ unceasingly develops in the world his total personality' (*Introduction au christianisme*, unpublished, 1944). 'The Christian group contains in itself, and at a higher degree, the hidden impulses and potentialities that enable it, through countless tentative gropings, to find its way to maturity and fulfilment' (*Ibid.*).

[71] Letter of 6 November 1916, in *Making of a Mind*, pp. 141-3.

Teilhard believes that, following the law of cephalization, the permanent organs of spiritual unification are 'localized', in particular in the Councils and the Pope (*Introduction au christianisme*, unpublished, 1944).

[72] *Le Milieu Divin*, pp. 142–6.

[73] In his spiritual autobiography, Teilhard notes that his religious experience was 'inaugurated *by upbringing*': 'Before the fire could blaze up, a spark had to fall on me'—the fire and the light without which he would never have gone beyond 'some comparatively moderate degree of intimacy and warmth' (*Le coeur de la matière*, unpublished, 1950).

[74] At the same time, Teilhard's very silence on the subject is an indication that he somewhat overlooks, in the history both of the Church and of mankind, the dynamic and stimulating role of great personalities, as though the influence of the spirit could make itself felt without specially favoured intermediaries.

[75] 'That star leads each man differently, by a different path, in accord with his vocation. But all the paths it indicates have this in common: that they lead always upward.'

Teilhard makes no secret of his personal vocation: 'Let others, fulfilling a function more august than mine, proclaim your splendours as pure spirit: as for me, dominated as I am by a vocation which springs from the inmost fibres of my being, I have no desire, I have no ability, to proclaim anything except the innumerable prolongations of your incarnate being in the world of matter; I can preach only the mystery of your flesh, you the soul shining forth through all that surrounds us' (*The Mass on the World*, 1923, in *Hymn of the Universe*, pp. 36–7).

[76] 'There are, of course, certain noble and cherished moments of the day—those when we pray or receive the sacraments. Were it not for those moments of more effective or explicit commerce with God, the tide of the divine omnipresence, and our perception of it, would weaken until all that was best in our human endeavour, without being entirely lost to the world, would be for us emptied of God' (*Le Milieu Divin*, pp. 65–6). Teilhard goes on to speak of 'jealously safeguarding our relation to God encountered, if I may dare use the expression, in "his pure state".'

[77] In *Le prêtre* (1918, *Ecrits du temps de la guerre*, pp. 285–302) Teilhard treats of the value and function of the priestly vocation. In 1917, he

writes to his cousin: 'Isn't the priest a man who has to bear the burden of life in all its forms, and show by his own life how human work and love of God can be combined?' (Letter of 15 February 1917, in *Making of a Mind*, p. 183).

78 'Some, maybe, when they see the mystic motionless, on the cross or in prayer, will think that his activity is dormant or has left the earth. How wrong they would be. Nothing in the world is so intensely alive and active as purity and prayer, poised like a steady beam of light between the universe and God. Through their serene translucency, the creative wave flows with its charge of natural virtue and grace. Is not that precisely what the Virgin Mary does?' (*Le milieu mystique*, 1917, in *Ecrits du temps de la guerre*, p. 162).

'And yet, if we could see the "light invisible" as we can see clouds and lightning or the rays of the sun, a pure soul would seem as active in this world, by virtue of its sheer purity, as the snowy summits whose impassive peaks breathe in continually for us the roving powers of the high atmosphere' (*Le Milieu Divin*, p. 134). 'All those different roles are necessary. The Church is like a great tree whose roots must be energetically anchored in the earth, while its leaves are serenely exposed to the bright sunlight. In this way she concentrates in herself a whole rhythmic range in a single living and all-embracing act, each vibration corresponding to a particular degree or possible form of spiritualization' (*Ibid.*, p. 101).

79 *Sur la valeur religieuse de la recherche*, 1947, in *Science et Christ*, pp. 255–63; *Recherche, travail et adoration*, 1955, *ibid.*, p. 288.

'We are familiar with the example of men who devoted themselves to science specifically in order to exalt or defend religion. But when are we going to see priests or religious deciding no longer to stand outside but joining in the quest for knowledge and discovery— and do so *because* of religion and *in a religious spirit*: by which I mean distinctly and deliberately realizing that even the smallest fragment they win from nature provides nourishment for souls and so produces a positive, permanent, augmentation of the body of Christ? I dearly hope that more and more people will come to see that a priest can, *as a priest*, devote himself to science and sociology; and that in so doing he is fulfilling his true function just as much as in the specialized duty of taking a funeral service. What a pity it is, and what a disaster, that we have allowed the minister of life to become for most people "the man who buries you" (*Note pour servir à l'évangélisation des temps nouveaux*, 1919, in *Ecrits du temps de la guerre*, p. 375).

[80] Letter of 12 December 1919, and *First Memorandum, op. cit.*, p. 141.

[81] *Le Milieu Divin*, pp. 99 ff.

[82] Letter of 12 December 1919.

[83] *First Memorandum* to Père Auguste Valensin, *op. cit.*, pp. 141, 143.

[84] *L'évolution de la chasteté*, unpublished, 1934, III: *La valeur de la virginité*. 'Virginity is added to chastity as thought is to life: through a reflected movement, or a concentration on one central point . . . It is biologically evident that to master passion and put it at the service of spirit is an essential condition of progress. Sooner or later then, whether we believe it or not, the world will take that step; for the greater truth will always come to light, and the greater good be realized' (*Ibid.*).

'Man and woman are designed to advance the highest degree of the earth's spiritualization; but there is no direct contact between them—there is convergence from on high . . . Virginity is added to chastity as thought is to life: through a reflected movement, or a concentration on one central point . . . Within the noosphere love is going through a "change of state"; and it is in this new direction that mankind's collective transition to God is being prepared. . . . Theoretically, such a transformation of love is possible. To effect it all that is needed is for the pull of the divine personal centre to be strong enough to master natural attraction' (*Ibid.*).

[85] 'The world undergoes a vast "ontogenesis" in which the development of each soul, assisted by the perceptible realities on which it depends, is but a diminished harmonic. Beneath our efforts to spiritualize our own lives, the world slowly accumulates, starting with all matter, that which will make of it the heavenly Jerusalem or the new earth' (*Le Milieu Divin*, p. 61).

[86] *Ibid.*, p. 151.

[87] 'We are making our way *in the dark* towards a luminous point; and unless we fight desperately to keep it in sight, unless we pin it down at every moment, the star that guides us will be lost . . . That is why a Church that did not (to suppose what is impossible) seek her God as though she might lose him (I was on the point of saying as though she did not already possess him) would be a dead Church, destroyed forthwith by human thought' (*Note pour servir à l'évangélisation des temps nouveaux*, 1919, *op. cit.*, p. 376).

[88] As early as 1918, addressing himself to soldier-priests, Teilhard had said, 'You are the leaven that Providence has spread out along the whole "front", so that the whole great mass of our work and agony may be transformed by the *mere fact of your presence*' (*Le prêtre*, 1918, in *Ecrits du temps de la guerre*, p. 302). Profoundly true though that may be, it does not of course rule out the missionary witness of the word. 'Christianity will never throw off its torpor and again begin to expand with all its primitive vigour, until it "gears itself" to the earth's natural aspirations' (*Le sens humain*, unpublished, 1929).

[89] *La crise présente*, 1937, in *Cahiers Pierre Teilhard de Chardin*, No. 3, p. 97.

[90] 'In future faith in Christ will never hold its own or gain ground except through the medium of faith in the world' (Letter of 4 May 1931, in *Letters from a Traveller*, p. 177).

'What we have to do is to make it clear that the universe, as revealed by contemporary research, is not pushing the Christian God into the background: it is only waiting to receive its crowning transfiguration from him. To be consummated is to be Christianized. To effect this transformation calls for more than a purely intellectual or negative act of judgment that discards false forms of materialism and pantheism. Our mission is to put on (*induere*) the religious soul of the modern world, in its natural fullness of development, and to live it, fully and sincerely, *on the Christian plane*. The religious aspirations of modern humanitarianism are distressingly vague and incomplete. It is for us to show, *verbo et exemplo* that there is nothing in sight to strengthen, concentrate and safeguard them, except the concrete reality of Christ. When, precisely in virtue of their Christianity, through the constructive activity of their charity, through their richly productive detachment and through the confident boldness of their supernatural vision, Christians have been shown that they are the first men to spiritualize terrestrial values and to press on towards the future—then the very soul of all that is best—and that means most dangerous—in human unbelief will stand defenceless. What is happening to the world now is that it is being spontaneously converted to a sort of natural religion of the universe which is, mistakenly, turning it away from the God of the Gospel; and it is in that that its unbelief lies. We must carry that conversion one degree further by making our whole lives show that only

Christ, *in quo omnia constant*, is capable of inspiring and directing the universe's newly appreciated line of advance; thus, from an extension of the very thing that produces modern unbelief, there may emerge the faith of tomorrow' (*L'incroyance moderne. Cause profonde et remède*, 1933, in *Science et Christ*, pp. 152–3).

[91] *Le Christique*, unpublished, 1955.

[92] Letter of 25 May 1923, in *Letters from a Traveller*, p. 73.

[93] Letter of 11 November 1929, *Ibid.*, p. 162.

[94] *The Eucharist*

It is essential to note this last, limitative, point, which Teilhard may have omitted to emphasize sufficiently, if we are to guard against too 'physical' or 'phenomenal' a view of the real presence.

Teilhard's eucharistic doctrine is presented in *Le Milieu Divin*, pp. 124 ff., and with even more lyrical fervour, in *The Mass on the World* (in *Hymn of the Universe*) and other passages in that volume. *The Mass of the World*, 1923, is a more elaborate handling of ideas and themes noted earlier in *Le prêtre* (1918).

'When Christ descends sacramentally into each one of his faithful, it is not only to commune with him. When, through the priest, he says *Hoc est corpus meum*, those words go beyond the fragment of bread over which they are said: they give birth to the whole mystical body. Beyond the transubstantiated host, the priest's effective act extends to the cosmos itself. The whole of matter, slowly and irresistibly, undergoes the great consecration' (unpublished). 'It seems to me that in a sense the true substance to be consecrated each day is the world's development during that day—the bread symbolizing appropriately what creation succeeds in producing, the wine (blood) what creation causes to be lost in exhaustion and suffering in the course of its effort' (Letter of 26 August 1923, in *Letters from a Traveller*, p. 86). This letter was written at about the same time as *The Mass on the World*. Cf. also *Le Christique* (1955).

'If, then, the Eucharist has a sovereign influence on our human natures, then its energy necessarily extends, by natural continuity, into the less luminous regions on which our existence is based . . . At every moment the eucharistic Christ controls—from the point of view of the organization of the Pleroma, which is the true point of view that makes the world intelligible—the whole movement of the universe . . . As our humanity assimilates the material world, and as the host assimilates our humanity, the eucharistic transformation goes beyond and completes the transubstantiation of the bread on the altar. Step by step it irresistibly invades the universe. It is the fire that sweeps over the heath, the stroke that vibrates through the bronze. In a secondary and generalized sense, but in a true sense, the sacramental species are formed by the totality of the world, and the duration of creation is the time needed for its consecration' (*Le Milieu Divin*, pp. 125–6).

Although Teilhard bears both aspects in mind, he is perhaps more alive to the mystery of consecration and the real presence than to the notion of a sacrifice through which a new presentation of the Redemption is effected.

For another, more dialectical and interiorized, approach, see G. Fessard, *La dialectique des Exercices spirituels de saint Ignace de Loyola*, Aubier, 1956, pp. 110–11: 'This eucharistic presence is itself not a new determination in objective existence, but the beginning of the *conversion* of the world of nature into a world of spirit, the abolition of the separation between God and his creature effected by sin . . . the eucharistic *hoc* is the hinge on which turns the revolution or conversion that the whole life of Christ causes the world to undergo.'

Père Smulders gives a lengthy vindication of Teilhard's eucharistic doctrine. In particular, he rightly notes that the consecration of the whole world 'is effected in a sacramental way', a way, therefore, that is imperfect and calls for completion . . . Christ has fulfilled this definitive act of oblation. For the human community and for the Church the sacrifice will not be accomplished until the end of time (*op. cit.*, p. 265). 'The Eucharist, which gives definitive consecration to the first-fruits of the old earth, is the starting point of the consecration of mankind and the world of mankind, a consecration that is effected slowly and painfully, and generally imperceptibly, but at the same time irresistibly' (p. 266).

[95] It is thus, at least, that we may interpret Teilhard's fine meditation before the eucharistic monstrance and pyx (*Christ in the world of matter*, 1916, in *Hymn of the Universe*, pp. 46–55).

[96] *Mass on the World*, 1923, in *Hymn of the Universe*, pp. 19, 20.

[97] *Le Milieu Divin*, p. 67.

[98] *Ibid.*, p. 124. 'The Eucharist is *the* central sacrament to which all the others are related: and this for the good reason that through it runs directly the *axis* of the Incarnation, that is to say of creation . . .

All the communions of our lives are in fact but successive moments or episodes of one single communion, in other words of one single process of Christification. All the communions of all men, of all times, taken as one great whole, also add up to one single and even vaster communion, coextensive in this case with the history of mankind . . . The Eucharist, taken in the entirety of its operation, is nothing other than the experience and manifestation of God's unifying energy applied individually to each atom of the universe. Adherence to Christ in the Eucharist must inevitably, *ipso facto*, incorporate us a little more fully each time in a Christogenesis which itself is simply the soul of universal cosmogenesis' (*Introduction au christianisme*, unpublished, 1944). Thus the Eucharist might well be seen by Teilhard as the visible and effective mode of Christ's invisible and transfigured presence in the universe.

[99] 'There is a communion with the earth (the first phase), and a communion with God (the second phase) and a communion with God through the earth (the third phase); and this last does not rule out but introduces and justifies our journey through darkness' (Letter of 8 December 1919). 'Phase' is used in this context with its dialectical, not its chronological, significance.

'The whole of human activity (both all that man undergoes and all that he does, the whole *opus* and the whole *operatio*) is thus animated and given a special character, without loss, by Christ. *"Omnia convertuntur in Christum"*. In spite of our attachment to things, we detach ourselves from them; and, in one sense, our very attachment detaches us, since there is in nature, if we appreciate it correctly, a logic or power of renunciation, of expansion, or creative dying—which in fact is an elementary form of the organic renunciation imposed by Christ on his supernatural members' (Letter of 12 December 1919).

'Thus, in the general rhythm of Christian life, development and renunciation, attachment and detachment, are not mutually exclusive. On the contrary, they harmonize—like breathing in and breathing out, in the movement of our lungs. They are two phases of the soul's respiration or two components of the impulse by which it uses things as a spring-board from which to mount beyond them' (*Le Milieu Divin*, p. 99). In a footnote, Teilhard shows that there is no opposition between asceticism and mysticism. '(Christian mysticism) shows an astonishing equilibrium between the active and the passive, between possession of the world and its renunciation, between a zest for things and an indifference to them' (*Ibid.*, p. 119).

¹⁰⁰ *Love of God and love of the world*

Le coeur de la matière, unpublished, 1950. In his very first essay, Teilhard had written: 'There is a communion with God, and a communion with the earth, and a communion, through the earth, with God' (*La vie cosmique*, 1916, heading).

'I believe that the kingdom of God would profit if an alliance could be effected, deep in our hearts—an enthusiastic, dynamic, alliance—between passion for the world and passion for God. It may well be that such a change of climate, repeated in thousands of living cells, is essential if the organism is ultimately to assimilate a loftier and wider truth' (Letter of 27 June 1926). 'Particularly during the last ten years, I have instinctively been offering myself to our Lord, as a sort of experimental field in which he can effect, on a small scale, the fusion of the two great loves, of God and of the world—without which fusion I am convinced there can be no possible kingdom of God' (Letter of 31 December 1926).

'I can see more distinctly how much my life is dominated by these twin peaks: an unbounded faith in our Lord, as animator of the world; and a clear faith in the world (particularly in the world of man) as animated by God' (Letter of 7 August 1927, in *Letters from a Traveller*, pp. 142-3). '. . . to reach heaven through cultivation of the earth' (Letter to Max Bégouën, 8 April 1930). 'To increase one's knowledge and power, in order to be more fully assumed by God' (*La route de l'Ouest*, unpublished, 1932). 'To make one's way to heaven through the earth' (*Christologie et évolution*, unpublished, 1933)

'Even in the most conservative circles it is beginning to be recognized that as a halo round the Eucharist there is a communion with God through the earth—a sacrament of the world' (*L'évolution de la chasteté*, unpublished, 1934).

'It is in no way metaphorical to say that man finds himself capable of experiencing and discovering God in the whole length, breadth and depth of the world in movement. To be able to say literally to God that one loves him, not only with all one's body, all one's heart and all one's soul, but with every fibre of the unifying universe, that is a prayer that can only be made in space-time' (*The Phenomenon of Man*, p. 297).

'If it is to be super-spiritualized in God, must not mankind first be born and grow in conformity with the entire system of what we call evolution? Whence, for the Christian in particular, there follows a radical incorporation of terrestrial values in the most radical concepts of his faith, those of divine omnipotence, detachment and charity' (*Some reflexions on progress*, 1941, in *The Future of Man*, p. 89).

'Christian detachment subsists wholly in this wider attitude of mind; but instead of "leaving behind" it leads on; instead of cutting off, it raises. It is no longer a break-away but a way through; no longer a withdrawal but an act of emerging' (*The new spirit*, 1942, *ibid.*, p. 96).

The following, obviously somewhat questionable passage, shows that Teilhard was alive to the dangers in certain deviations of Christian spirituality. After saying that the only valid mysticism is the Christian, he adds, 'Nevertheless we must recognize that as a result of a certain anthropomorphic trend (or a form of primitive nationalism) the Judaeo-Christian mystical current has had some difficulty in getting rid of an approach in which *oneness* (= absolute unity) is sought too exclusively in individuality rather than in *God's synthetic power*. This accounts for a certain "thinness" in the mysticism of the prophets and many of the saints; their mysticism becomes too "Jewish" or "human" in the restrictive sense of the words—not sufficiently universalist and cosmic. (There are exceptions, of course, Eckart, Francis of Assisi, St John of the Cross . . .) I need only mention a mistaken way of looking for *oneness* (Teilhard uses the English word) in destruction and death, death removing the multiple and leaving only God to subsist. It is doubtful whether this morbid interpretation has ever stimulated a true, real, mystical current. However, as a distortion or perversion, it is something to be guarded against as a danger that is *always possible* (the suffering of annihilation being confused, with *suffering of transformation*). Can we be quite sure that traces of this "illusion" are not still to be found in some interpretations of the meaning of the Cross?' (*Quelques remarques pour y voir clair sur l'essence du sentiment mystique*, unpublished, 1951).

While admitting the temptation, inherent in Christianity and constantly found in history, to succumb to Platonist influence, we should at least point out the inaccuracy of Teilhard's view of the prophets of Israel. They had a vivid sense of the universe, a great love for earthly things and a passion for justice.

'The "creature" is much more than a "tool to be used": it is a "co-element to be integrated" by mankind in genesis—and the ancient contrast of earth-heaven disappears (or is corrected) in the new formula "heaven through fulfilment of earth"' (*Recherche, travail et adoration*, unpublished, 1955).

[101] *La parole attendue*, 1940, in *Cahiers Pierre Teilhard de Chardin*, No. 4, p. 28.

[102] *Le sens humain*, unpublished, 1929. 'I sometimes think that the Church, after being so convinced of the imminence of the Parousia as almost to jettison the whole of human organization—and then, as time went by, after putting its hand again to the plough of earthly effort, without much conviction and protesting that all this work is not worth a single Hail Mary (which is true enough, though not in the sense that is often intended)—that the Church will come, in a third phase, to see that its appeal to the transcendent does not dispense it from this duty, but imposes on it a special obligation to work harder than others for the fulfilment of man's natural consciousness. That may be rather too crude and cut and dried a way of putting it, but I am sure there is truth in what I am saying' (Letter of 21 December 1919).

'Spiritual detachment will take the form of a conquest: we must, if we are to be raised up again and are ourselves to raise things with us, plunge into the flood of created energies—*including* the first and most ardent of them' (sexuality) (*L'évolution de la chasteté*, unpublished, 1934). 'There can be only one sun in the heaven of our hearts—but why should there not be lesser stars?' (*Ibid.*).

[103] Letter of 21 June 1921. 'Where, then, shall we find at last the *ideal Christian*, the Christian at once new and old, *who will solve in his soul the problem of vital equilibrium*, by channelling *all the life-sap of the world into his effort to attain the divine Trinity*?' (*La maîtrise du monde et le règne de Dieu*, in *Ecrits du temps de la guerre*, p. 81).

[104] Letter of 10 June 1917, in *Making of a Mind*, p. 195. The whole of this spirituality is characterized by strength and virility. Inspired by a passion for God and the world, it is free of any preciousness or sentimentality (*Ibid.*, pp. 190–1).

[105] 'There's no doubt that there is a powerful educative force lodged

in the world, which continually calls us to journey further into the deep strata of being: what attracts us in things is always withdrawing further from us, beyond every individual tangible reality, and finally beyond death. I am becoming continually more conscious of this rhythm: we're forced (by a compulsion rooted in ourselves) to pass through the world—and we're forced (by a compulsion rooted in the world) to leave it' (Letter of 27 April 1919, in *Making of a Mind*, p. 296).

'The sense of the earth opening and exploding upwards into a sense of God; and the sense of God sending roots downwards to take nourishment from the sense of the earth. The transcendent personal God and the evolving universe no longer forming two hostile centres of attraction, but entering into hierarchic conjunction to raise the human mass on a single tide' (*Some reflexions on progress*, 1941, in *The Future of Man*, p. 80). See also the whole of the preceding paragraph.

[106] *Le Milieu Divin*, p. 47.

[107] *Faith in man*, 1947, in *The Future of Man*, p. 188. 'Like Jacob wrestling with the angel, man ends by adoring what he was struggling against' (*Le Milieu Divin*, p. 74). 'We shall not be allowed to give up, any more than was that man who wrestled to exhaustion with the angel' (*Christologie et évolution*, unpublished, 1933). Teilhard was fond of this biblical image, whose significance was well brought out some time ago by Père Rouquette (*Tu as été fort contre Dieu, Etudes*, September 1952).

[108] 'It is an accumulation of desires that will cause the Parousia to burst upon us' (*Le Milieu Divin*, p. 151).

[109] 'The beauties and individual gradations of souls acquire their *definitive significance* only as the traits and touches that make up the celestial visage of the great and unique ultimate reality ... The most exquisite distillations of knowledge, of the beautiful, of the good life, are needed to achieve this task of life. One by one, through human effort aided by God, souls are distilled, precious drops—and the nectar that comes at the end has not the same savour as that which flowed first' (Letter of 5 February 1917, in *Making of a Mind*, pp. 180–1).

'No one lifts his little finger to do the smallest task unless moved, however obscurely, by the conviction that he is contributing infinitesimally (at least indirectly) to the building of something definitive—that is to say to your work, my God' (*Le Milieu Divin*, p. 56).

Teilhard shows how those 'rare creatures' who have the privilege of God's love are linked with 'the totality of beings engaged with him in the unifying work of the cosmos', and how even 'the humblest levels of belief in God' are already directed towards their End (*Basis and foundations of the idea of evolution*, 1926, in *Vision of the Past*, p. 139).

[110] 'Christ has conquered death, not only by suppressing its evil effects, but by reversing its sting . . . However marred by our faults, or however desperate in its circumstances, our position may be, we can, by a total re-ordering, completely correct the world that surrounds us, and resume our lives in a favourable sense' (*Le Milieu Divin*, pp. 82–3).

[111] Maurice Blondel, *L'action*, 1893, end.

[112] *Réflexions sur le bonheur*, Cahiers Pierre Teilhard de Chardin, No. 2, p. 53.

[113] 'Anyone whose only aim, in conquering the earth, has been to subject a little more matter to spirit has surely begun to take leave of himself at the same time as taking possession of himself. This is also true of the man who rejects mere enjoyment, the line of least resistance, and the lazy possession of things and ideas, and sets out courageously on the path of work, inward renewal, and the ceaseless broadening and sublimation of his ideal. And it is true, again, of the man who has given his time, his health, or his life, to something greater than himself—a family to be supported, a country to be saved, a truth to be discovered' (*Le Milieu Divin*, pp. 97–8).

'In its highest and most general sense, the doctrine of the Cross is that to which all men adhere who believe that the vast movement and agitation of human life opens onto a road which leads somewhere, and that that road *climbs upward*. Life has a term: therefore it imposes a particular direction, orientated, in fact, towards the highest possible spiritualization by means of the greatest possible effort. To admit that group of fundamental principles is already to range oneself among the disciples—distant, perhaps, and implicit, but nevertheless real—of Christ crucified. Once that first choice has been made, the first distinction has been drawn between the brave who will succeed and the triflers who will fail, between the elect and the condemned' (*Ibid.*, p. 102).

[114] In 1950 Teilhard had another look at his *Milieu Divin* and found in it, he thought, a certain narrowness of attitude. 'Originally, in order to "make and experience" Christ in all things, I could make use of only the *detail* of the events and beings I found around me.' He then notes the broadening of outlook he acquired from the discovery of the world's ascent towards Omega Point. He realized, in consequence that 'it is not metaphysically speaking, but *physically*, that the energy of the Incarnation flows, and so illuminates and warms them, in an ever more far-reaching and vaster embrace' (*Le coeur de la matière*, p. 26). He adds, 'the inspiration and writing of 'the Mass on the World' and the *Milieu Divin* clearly belong to that still somewhat ego-centric and closed-in period of my interior life' (p. 29).

[115] 'Reading Newman's *He and I* for the first time, I had the same impression as you, and applied the same corrective. "I" is not an entity isolated from all relations: it is, in a way, the whole universe centred on me, *whose destiny* (in a very true sense) *is played out in me* (in God's eyes isn't every soul worth the whole world, isn't it the whole world?) . . . Thus, in this essential confrontation of God and me, I feel *every* creature *behind* me . . . And so the fundamental primacy of individual salvation leaves the soul all its fullness, as far-reaching as the universe' (Letter of 5 January 1917, in *Making of a Mind*, p. 167).

[116] The Latin derivation of the word 'obedience' brings out the metaphor of listening (*ob-audire*).

[117] 'I can, I think, attribute the origin of the possession and envelopment by Christ, to the rapidly increasing importance assumed in my spiritual life by the sense of "the will of God"—loyalty to the divine will, that is to say to a directed and embodied omnipresence, actively and passively to be found in every element and every event in the world' (*Le coeur de la matière*, p. 25). 'Unless I do everything I can to advance or resist, I shall not find myself *at the required point*—I shall not submit to God as much as I might have done or as much as he wishes' (*Le Milieu Divin*, p. 92).

[118] 'If any words could express that permanent and lucid intoxication (of the soul in the divine milieu) better than others, perhaps they would be "passionate indifference"' (*Le Milieu Divin*, *p*. 120).

[119] The following passage reproduces almost the exact wording of

the *Foundation* in the *Spiritual Exercises*: 'At the heart of our universe, each soul exists for God, in Our Lord. But all reality, even material reality, exists for our souls. Hence all sensible reality, around each one of us, exists, through our souls, for God in our Lord' (*Le Milieu Divin*, p. 56). The syllogism is developed in the following pages.

120 We should not look to Teilhard for an analysis of interior movements, as found in the 'rules for the discernment of spirits', but he has sound advice to give, both prudent and generous, about the use of creatures or renunciation (*Le Milieu Divin*, pp. 99–101).

121 'It is God, and God alone, whom he pursues through the reality of created beings. For him, interest lies truly *in* things, but only in so far as God is present in them; he can see and attain the light of heaven only as it shines through the transparency of beings. But he wants only this light, and if the light is extinguished, whether because the object is out of its accustomed place, or has gone, or is moving away, then even the most precious substance is no more than ashes in his sight. Similarly, even within himself and his most personal development, it is not himself that he is seeking, but that which is greater than himself, to which he knows he is destined. In his own view he himself no longer counts, no longer exists; he has forgotten and lost himself in the very endeavour which is making him perfect' (*Ibid.*, p. 73).

122 This combination of obedience in trifles and grandeur of over-all aims recalls Ignatius's maxim: '*Non coerceri maximo, contineri tamen a minimo.*' Cf. G. Fessard, *op. cit.*, p. 173: 'However extensive the field it controls, is not freedom, even more profoundly than intelligence, a capacity for the possible, an "impulse for going further" and a denial of limitations? *Non coerceri maximo.* And on the other hand, the vaster and more distant its objective, the more, if it is to attain it or even advance towards it, must freedom determine itself with regard to what is nearest and most immediate. *Contineri a minimo*'.

The spiritual dialectic of the mysteries of Jesus' life at Nazareth and his flight to the temple, very consciously developed by Ignatius in the second week of the *Spiritual Exercises*, symbolizes this rhythmic balance of great and small, of prudence, too, and excess. The two phases appear also in Teilhard, whose *Milieu Divin* links the most commonplace duties (pp. 64–7) with the grandest of enterprises.

123 Teilhard refers in *Le Milieu Divin* to 'the force of gravity that drags us down into the abyss of self-indulgence and selfishness' (p. 109). On the evidence, however, of his own personal experience, he notes a more profound temptation, 'a subtle tendency to drift into a lower form (the vulgar, facile, form) of the pantheist spirit: the pantheism of effusion and dissolution . . . Possession of the world through surrender, passivity, and fading into a formlessness that has no limits: a movement of "centrifugal communion", animated by the instinct to extend and spread out, below all the plurality of individuals and their isolation, into the dimensions and homogeneity of the total sphere' (*Le coeur de la matière*, unpublished, 1950). 'A structurally necessary struggle was going on deep in my soul, between the God of the above and the new God of the ahead: it was brought about by the permanent coexistence and irresistible conjunction in my heart of the cosmic sense and the Christic sense' (*Ibid.*).

124 *Le Milieu Divin*, p. 148.

125 'I felt that, in common with all the beings I lived among, I was caught up in a higher movement that was stirring up the elements of the universe and grouping them in a new order. Then, when my eyes were opened and I saw where the dazzling trail of individual beauties and limited harmonies was leading, I realized that it all converged to centre itself *on one single point*, on one person—your person, Jesus' (*Le milieu mystique*, 1917, *op. cit.*, p. 164).

126 'Sometimes people think that they can increase your attraction in my eyes by stressing almost exclusively the charm and goodness of your human life, in the past. But truly, O Lord, if I wanted to cherish only a man, then I would surely turn to those whom you have given me with the bloom of their charm here and now. Are there not, with our mothers, brothers, friends, and sisters, enough irresistibly lovable people around us? Why should we turn to the Judea of two thousand years ago? No, what I cry out for, like every being, with my whole life and all my earthly passion, is something very different from an equal to cherish: it is a God to adore . . . Tear away, O Jesus, the clouds with your lightning! Show yourself to us as the mighty the radiant, the risen! Come to us once again as the Pantocrator who reigned alone in the cupolas of the ancient basilicas! Nothing less than this Parousia is needed to counter-balance and crown in our hearts the glory of

the world that is coming into view. So that we may triumph over the world with you, come to us clothed in the glory of the world' (*Le Milieu Divin*, pp. 127-8).

In relating his spiritual evolution, Teilhard admits that the discovery of the Sacred Heart, with the symbolism it expresses, was 'the means he had been looking for to enable him finally to escape from all that pained him so deeply in the organization of the body of Jesus, an organization at once so complicated, fragile and individualized' (*Le coeur de la matière*, unpublished, 1950, p. 22).

127 'The Christian option should be presented as the choice not, in fact, between heaven and earth, but between two ways of working to fulfil the universe, *intra* or *extra Christum*' (*Note pour servir à l'évangélisation des temps nouveaux*, 1919, in *Ecrits du temps de la guerre*, p. 379).

128 'There is no limit in *respect of the work done* or the diminishment undergone, because we can always sink ourselves deeper into the perfecting of work to be achieved, or into the better utilization of distressing events. We can always be more industrious, more meticulous, more flexible . . . Nor is there any limit in *respect of the intention* which animates our endeavour to act or to accept, because we can always go further in the inward perfecting of our conformity. There can always be greater detachment and greater love; still less, much less, is there any limit *in respect of the divine object*, in the ever-closer espousal of which our being can joyfully wear itself away' (*Le Milieu Divin*, pp. 138-9).

129 'A tremendous spiritual power is slumbering in the depths of our multitude, which will manifest itself only when we have learnt *to break down the barriers* of our egoisms and, by a fundamental recasting of our outlook, raise ourselves up to the habitual and practical vision of universal realities' (*Ibid.*, p. 146).

130 'Uniting oneself means, in every case, migrating, and dying partially in what one loves. But if, as we are sure, this annihilation in the other must be all the more complete the more we give our attachment to one who is greater than ourselves, then we can set no limit to the tearing up of roots that is involved in our journey to God' (*Ibid.*, p. 88).

Possession of the world can be achieved only through a preliminary detachment. 'If we are to attain you, matter, we must first have universal contact with everything that moves here below; then

we must feel that the individual forms of what we hold are gradually
fading away, until we are left confronted with the single essence of
all consistence and all union' (*The spiritual power of matter*, 1919, in
Hymn of the Universe, p. 70).

131 'The Lord appeared to Moses in a flame of fire' (Exodus 3:2).
'God is a devouring fire' (Deut. 4:24; Heb. 12:29; Cf. Mal. 3:24,
Psalms, *passim*). 'He will baptize you with the Holy Spirit and
with fire' (Matt.3:11). 'I came to cast fire upon the earth' (Luke
12:49).

We should note Teilhard's devotion to the heart of Christ. 'It
would be difficult to make anyone understand how deeply, and
constantly, and vigorously my spiritual life developed before the
war under the sign, and in wonderment before the heart of Jesus'
(*Le coeur de la matière*, unpublished, 1950). 'A spark had to fall
upon me before the fire could blaze up. It was through my mother
that it lit up my infant soul' (in private conversation with Père
Leroy).

The metaphor of fire appears in *Christ in the world of matter*:
'Through the mysterious expansion of the host, the whole world had
become incandescent' (1919, in *Hymn of the Universe*, p. 48). Again,
in *The Mass on the World*: 'Upon all that in the world of human flesh
is now about to be born or to die beneath the rising sun I will
call down the fire' (*Ibid.*, p. 21). 'Once again the fire has penetrated
the earth' (*Ibid.*, p. 23). The metaphor appears again in *Le
Milieu Divin*, and in the heading to *Le coeur de la matière*, the introduction to which has the title 'The Burning Bush', and in which it
occurs several times, ('The diaphany of the divine at the heart of a
universe afire'—'The divine radiating from the depths of a matter
ablaze').

The family motto of the Teilhards de Chardin was *Igneus est ollis
vigor et celestis origo*, 'Of fire is their strength and from heaven their
source' (Vergil, *Aeneid*, 6. 730). At a difficult moment in his life,
Teilhard wrote to Père Auguste Valensin, 'Pray that in any case I
never let myself seek anything but "the fire"' (unpublished letter,
30 May 1925).

132 'All my joy and all my triumph, my very reason for existence and
my zest for life, depend upon this fundamental vision of your
coming together with the universe' (*Le coeur de la matière*, unpublished, 1950).

[133] 'God reveals himself everywhere, beneath our groping efforts, *as a universal milieu,* only because he is *the ultimate point* upon which all realities converge. Each element of the world, whatever it may be, only subsists *hic et nunc* in the manner of a cone whose generators meet in God who draws them together (meeting at the term of their individual perfection and at the term of the general perfection of the world which contains them). It follows that all created beings, every one of them, cannot be looked at, in their nature and action, without the same reality being found in their innermost being—like sunlight in the fragments of a broken mirror—single beneath its multiplicity, unattainable beneath its proximity, and spiritual beneath its materiality. No object can influence us by its essence without our being touched by the radiance of the focus of the universe. Our minds are incapable of grasping a reality, our hearts and hands of seizing the essentially desirable in it, without our being compelled *by the very structure* of things to go back to the first source of its perfections. This focus, this source, is thus everywhere. It is precisely because he is at once so deep and yet so akin to an extensionless point that God is infinitely near, and dispersed everywhere. It is precisely because he is the centre that he fills the whole sphere' (*Le Milieu Divin,* p. 114).

In a letter to the General of the Society of Jesus (12 October 1951), Teilhard speaks of 'his absolute inability to contain his feeling of wonderment' (quoted by Père Leroy in *Letters from a Traveller,* p. 42).

In a comment on Père Morel's interpretation of St John of the Cross, Père J. M. Le Blond writes: 'Through these symbols the journey is shown as ending in a total possession of the world, even the world of sense, and that is seen as the ultimate destiny and final truth attained by human sensibility. "Yes," cries St John of the Cross, "the heavens are mine, the earth and all its peoples are mine; the just are mine, and the sinners; the angels are mine, and mine the mother of God; all things are mine": and in that we have the answer to the well-known opening lines of the *Ascent of Mount Carmel,* in which moreover, the "Nada" should not be divorced from the "Todo" which is its light. It is true that "he who seeks his life shall lose it", but it is also true that "he who loses it shall find it", in a total regeneration and elevation of man. This takes us beyond any Manicheanism or mistaken Platonism' (*Mystique et théologie chez saint Jean de la Croix*, in *Recherches de science religieuse*, April–June 1963, p. 204).

[134] Here Teilhard recognizes that Ignatius's view is to some degree only relative but he does not emphasize sufficiently the readiness with which it can be extended to the historical dimensions of a cosmogenesis. He acknowledges the uneasiness he feels at the concept, as represented by Bossuet, of a static universe and of a man in whose nature there is never any change, and 'whose only function is to relate to God in an intellectual act of homage and by using them with moderation, the multiplicity of objects that creation has once and for all harmoniously ordered'. 'It is', adds Teilhard, 'precisely the concept contained in the celebrated *Foundation* of St Ignatius's *Exercises*' (*Le sens humain*, unpublished, 1929).

Writing, later, about the spiritual training necessary to a religious who takes up science, he says: 'The Foundation, the Kingdom, the Two Standards . . . since these essential meditations were conceived at a time when man was still regarded as placed fully-fledged in a static universe, they make no allowance (in their present form) for the pull exerted on us, quite legitimately, by what lies ahead. They do not accord to the advances made in hominization their full value as agents of sanctification and communion. In consequence, they do not give either the seeker for knowledge or the worker what each of them looks first for in his faith—that is, as one of the Jocists (young Catholic workers) said, the right to tell themselves that *in working* they are in direct contact with the total Christ and contribute to his consummation. The "creature" is not simply "a tool to be used" but a "co-element" to be integrated by a mankind still in genesis, and in which the ancient contrast between heaven and earth disappears (or is corrected) in the new formula "to heaven through fulfilment of the earth"' (*Recherche, travail et adoration*, 1955, in *Science et Religion*, p. 289).

The *Exercises*, it is true, are necessarily coloured by the culture of their time, and St Ignatius could not have foreseen the change in modern man's consciousness. He offers a method of personal conversion and is not concerned with theological exposition. Nevertheless, an attentive reading brings out an *historical universalism* that accords well with Scripture: the meditation on the triple sin, the Kingdom and the Two Standards, the contemplation of the Incarnation (in particular the first introduction, which appears to aduell to the divine plan described in the Epistle to the Ephesians). The *Foundation*, too, should be read from this angle.

[135] Cf. the prayer 'to the ever-greater Christ' that concludes *Le coeur de la matière* (unpublished, 1950): 'Nothing, Lord, can in fact make you more lovable to my mind and heart, more uniquely lovable, than to see that you, the centre always *open* even to your utmost depths, are constantly growing more intense—your colour growing continually more vivid—as you gather more of the universe to yourself and bring it under your power ("until the time comes when you return, you and the world in you, to the bosom of him from whom you came"), and so effect your Pleroma' (p. 32). 'To such a degree that henceforward you have become, in my eyes and in my heart, much more than he who was and is, *he who is to be*' (p. 31).

[136] 'The pagan loves the earth in order to enjoy and confine himself within it; the Christian in order to make it purer and draw from it the strength to escape from it. The pagan seeks to espouse sensible things so as to extract delight from them: *he adheres to the world*. The Christian multiplies his contacts with the world only so as to harness, or submit to, the energies which he will take back, or which will take him, to heaven. *He pre-adheres to God*. The pagan holds that man divinizes himself by closing in upon himself; the final act of human evolution is when the individual, or the totality, constitutes itself within itself. The Christian sees his divinization only in the assimilation by another of his fulfilment; the culmination of life, in his eyes, is death in union. To the pagan, universal reality exists only in so far as it is projected on to the plane of the perceptible: it is immediate and multiple. The Christian makes use of exactly the same elements: but he prolongs them along their common axis, which links them to God: thereby, too, the universe is unified for him, although it is attainable only at the final centre of its consummation' (*Le Milieu Divin*, p. 119).

[137] 'What is most divine in God is that, in an absolute sense, we are nothing apart from him. The least suspicion of Pelagianism would suffice to ruin immediately the beauties of the divine milieu for those whose eyes are open to them' (*Le Milieu Divin*, p. 49). 'Of course, as God takes possession of man, the creature finally becomes passive (because it finds itself super-created in the divine union). But that passivity presupposes a subject that reacts, and an active

phase. The fire of heaven must come down on something: otherwise there would be nothing consumed and nothing consummated' (*Ibid.*, p. 99 note).

[138] A remark in a confidential letter shows that Teilhard was not concerned solely with a theological commitment: 'It has only been with occasional individuals, officers particularly, that I have been able to act as a priest; it is true that a single minute of such occasions, when you feel as needed, and, through his help, as strong as Our Lord, makes you forget the long periods of inactivity and justifies weeks of waiting and of life apparently turned to no account' (Letter of 28 May 1915, in *Making of a Mind*, p. 54).

[139] It would be a great mistake to interpret the *Exercises* as no more than a subjective essay in individual conversion: the key meditations, in particular the Kingdom and the Standards (and in this they are strictly faithful to the Bible), have a strong sense of the universal, and position man's commitment within a cosmic history in which the confrontation of God and his adversary develops.

[140] Teilhard's frequent use of the images of 'layer' or 'zone', or surface and depth (cf. 'Let us leave the surface and, without leaving the world, plunge into God' (*Le Milieu Divin*, p. 115; 'As soon as we leave the zone of sensible appearances . . .', *Ibid.*, p. 112) recalls the 'vertical' symbolism of the mystics. He, too, is concerned to go beyond, in height or depth, the inauthenticity of the surface world of appearances (cf. G. Morel, *Le sens de l'existence selon saint Jean de la Croix*, Aubier, 1960).

[141] In *Le coeur de la matière*, which is his spiritual autobiography, Teilhard speaks of his longing for plenitude and solidity, for the immutable and incorruptible, for consistence (which he regards as an essential attribute of being): a longing that dates back to his childhood and was aroused by various objects that symbolized those qualities. Without, probably, realizing it, in this he coincides with the fundamental biblical notion of solidity (expressed in the Hebrew word for truth or fidelity): throughout the Bible, God is the stone or rock. It is probably no exaggeration to see in Teilhard's bent for geology a transference of this spiritual attitude (*Ibid.*, p. 5).

[142] 'I live at the heart of a single, unique, element, the centre of the universe and present in each part of it: personal love and cosmic power' (*Christ in the world of matter*, 1916, in *Hymn of the Universe*, p. 54).

'In the life which wells up in me, and in the matter which sustains me, I find much more than your gifts. It is you yourself whom I find, you who make me participate in your being, you who mould me. Truly in the control and initial orientation of my vital impulse, in the continually beneficent play of secondary causes, I touch, as near as possible, the two faces of your creative action; and I encounter, and kiss, both your wonder-working hands: the one which holds us so firmly that it is merged, in us, with the sources of life, and the other, whose action is so wide that, at its slightest pressure, all the forces of the universe respond harmoniously together.' (*Le Milieu Divin*, pp. 78–9).

'To have access to the divine milieu is to have found the "one thing needful", *him who burns* by setting fire to everything that we would love badly or not enough; *him who calms* by eclipsing with his blaze everything that we love too much; *him who consoles* by gathering up everything that has been snatched from our love or has never been given to it. To reach those priceless layers is to experience, with equal truth, that one has need of everything and that one has need of nothing. Everything is needed, because eager though we are to be active, the world can never satisfy us by enabling us to attain God; and avid though we are for fulfilment, it can never sufficiently offer us the possibility of being possessed by him. And yet nothing is needed; for since the only reality that can satisfy us lies the other side of the transparent appearances through which we can see it, the more that veil which separates us from it is drawn or fades away, the purer the form in which we attain reality. Everything means both everything and nothing to me; everything is God to me and everything is dust to me: that is what man can say with equal truth, whichever way the divine ray falls' (*Ibid.*, p. 120).

'To adore . . . that means to lose oneself in the unfathomable, to plunge into the inexhaustible, to find peace in the incorruptible, to be absorbed in defined immensity, to offer oneself to the fire and the transparency, deliberately and knowingly to annihilate oneself as one becomes more conscious of oneself, to give of one's deepest to that whose depth has no end' (*Ibid.*, pp. 127–8).

[143] *Ibid.*, p. 74. Teilhard speaks, too, of the 'psychological reversal whereby, in the Christian as in every intelligent creature, joy in action melts imperceptibly into the desire for submission—and the

exaltation of becoming one's own self into the zeal to die in another'
(*Ibid.*).

[144] 'The magnificence I hold in my eyes,' wrote Teilhard, shortly
before his death. Cf. his profession of faith (March 1955) quoted at
the end of *Le Milieu Divin* (p. 155).

[145] Although Teilhard never experienced, as did Augustine or Pascal,
a conversion, he did meet certain, sometimes even revolutionary,
developments in his interior life. Cf. *Le coeur de la matière*, unpublished, 1950.

[146] Letter of 13 November 1918, in *Making of a Mind*, p. 252.
Shortly before, after having 'some things said to me in confidence',
he had written: 'I know few things that impel me more powerfully
towards an exact care for sanctification and a passionate (I'd almost
say desperate) reliance on Our Lord's strength, than this awareness
of the need for the treasures of the world to be purified' (27 September 1918, *Ibid.*, p. 239).

[147] *Le coeur de la matière*, pp. 24, 27.

[148] It is, moreover, advisedly that Teilhard adopts an 'illuminative'
approach. 'The reader need not, therefore, be surprised at the
apparently small space allotted to moral evil and sin: the soul with
which we are dealing is assumed to have already turned away from
the path of error' (*Le Milieu Divin*, preface, p. 44).

'If, in speaking of evil, we do not mention sin more explicitly it is
because, the aim of the following pages being solely to show how
all things can help the believer to unite himself to God, there is no
need to concern ourselves directly with bad actions, that is with
positive gestures of disunion' (*Ibid.*, p. 80 note).

[149] Père Fessard (*op. cit.*) gives an excellent analysis of this dialectic
of conversion in the *Exercises*, through transition from what lies
ahead to what lies after.

[150] 'Thus, in the depths of my heart, through a marvellous substitution, *the host was eluding me* by means of its own surface, and leaving
me at grips with the entire universe, which had reconstituted itself
and drawn itself forth from its sensible appearances' (*Christ in the
world of matter*, 1916, in *Hymn of the Universe*, p. 53).

'As long as I could see—or dared see—in you, Lord Jesus, only
the man who lived two thousand years ago, the sublime moral
teacher, the Friend, the Brother, my love remained timid and constrained. Friends, brothers, wise men: have we not many of those

around us, great souls, chosen souls, and much closer to us? And then can man ever give himself to a nature which is purely human? . . . How strange, my God, are the processes your spirit initiates! When, two centuries ago, your Church began to feel the particular power of your heart, it might have seemed that what was captivating men's souls was the fact of their finding in you an element even more determinate, more circumscribed, than your humanity as a whole. But now on the contrary a swift reversal is making us aware that your main purpose in this revealing to us of your heart was to enable our love to escape from the constrictions of the too narrow, too precise, too limited image of you which we had fashioned for ourselves. What I discern in your breast is simply a furnace of fire; and the more I fix my gaze on its ardency the more it seems to me that all around it the contours of your body melt away and become enlarged beyond all measure, till the only features I can distinguish in you are those of the face of a world which has burst into flame' (*The Mass on the World*, in *Hymn of the Universe*, pp. 33–4). Cf. the passage quoted from *Le Milieu Divin* in note 126.

'Christ is becoming more and more indispensable to me, . . . but at the same time the figure of the historical Christ is becoming less and less substantial and distinct to me' (Letter of 8 January 1936). 'I have never felt myself so full of my "gospel" and at the same time more wholly and entirely dependent, body, mind, and soul, on Christ Jesus. I have a bitter-sweet feeling of being completely powerless without him. And at the same time I am terrified when I realize that my view of him is continually carrying him further and higher along the axis of (I hope!) orthodoxy. It is not unlike what the astronomers tell us of the stars—that while they are ever more closely integrated in our system, they are also ever more breath-takingly distant than we imagined. In fact, my pan-Christism is in some way "trans-Christic". And it is only there that it coincides with my humanism, which, biologically, is one that posits a humanity still *very imperfectly* centred upon itself, both individually and collectively' (Letter of 20 April 1948).

Of the events in Christ's life on earth, the Transfiguration in particular meant a great deal to Teilhard: the vision he describes in *Christ in the world of matter* borrows certain elements from it (in *Hymn of the Universe*, pp. 42–6).

Some justification of Teilhard's attitude may perhaps be found in St Paul's words, 'even though we once regarded Christ from a human point of view, we regard him thus no longer' (2 Cor. 5:16), though St Paul is probably doing no more than to express the right to preach Christ granted to those who had not been witnesses of his life.

151 Cf. François Roustang, S.J., *Une initiation à la vie spirituelle*, Desclée de Brouwer, 1963, in the series *Christus*, pp. 208, 211, 229–33. 'While contemplation of Christ's humanity is an excellent standby for beginners in the life of the spirit, the greatest Christian mystics have often said that it is equally profitable for those who have already progressed in the intimacy of the Word' (p. 22 9).

152 Paul Claudel, on the other hand, writes: 'But the great book whose pages were open to me and from which I could learn, was the Church. Blessed for ever be that great majestic mother at whose knees I learnt all I know!' (*Ma conversion*, 1909, in *Contacts et circonstances*, Gallimard). Claudel's devotion to the Bible, too, is well known: 'It is not enough to let your eyes take in the words or your lips pronounce them—you have to make the text part of yourself, live in it, soak yourself in it, as the ancient fathers did: you have to dwell in it, not in a spirit of idle curiosity but of devotion, store it up within you, sleep with it and wake up with it' (*Introduction au livre de Ruth*, pp. 20–1). 'It is *something you have to eat*, to devour, so that through teeth and tongue and palate, it passes into the bowels' (*Ibid.*, p. 20). Cf. Père André Blanchet, *Paul Claudel, Pages de prose*, Gallimard, 1954, p. 269).

153 'I mean, brethren, the appointed time has grown very short; from now on, let those who have wives live as though they had none, and those who mourn as though they were not mourning, and those who rejoice as though they were not rejoicing, and those who buy as though they had no goods, and those who deal with the world as though they had no dealings with it. For the form of this world is passing away' (1 Cor. 7:29–31).

Again, Teilhard does not neglect this point: 'By the crucifixion and death of this adored being, Christianity signifies to our thirst for happiness that the term of creation is not to be sought in the temporal zones of our visible world, but that the effort required of our fidelity must be consummated *beyond a total transformation* of ourselves and of everything surrounding us' (*Le Milieu Divin*, p. 103).

Similarly, the death of a colleague made Teilhard 'realize the utter vanity of human effort unless there is a both natural and super-natural emergence of the universe towards some immortal con-sciousness' (Letter of 10 April 1934, in *Letters from a Traveller*, p. 202).

[154] 'The sensual mysticisms and certain neo-pelagianisms (such as Americanism), by paying too much attention to the first of these phases (attachment to the world), have fallen into the error of seeking divine love and the divine kingdom *on the same level* as human affections and human progress' (*Le Milieu Divin*, p. 110 note).

[155] 'My sole ambition now is to leave behind me the mark of a logical life, directed wholly towards the grand hopes of the world. There lies the future of man's religious life. I am as sure of it as I am of my own existence' (Letter of 7 August 1927, in *Letters from a Traveller*, p. 143). That was written at about the same time as *Le Milieu Divin*. Similarly: 'All that is really worth while is action—faithful action for the world, and in God' (30 October 1929, *ibid.*, p. 160).

After reading *Christologie et évolution* (unpublished, 1933) Père Maréchal wrote to Teilhard (in a letter quoted several times earlier) '*Evangelism:* if the author of this note simply wishes to emphasize the apostolic duty—perhaps more urgent now than ever before—we have of clearing away the artificial obstacles that our conservatism and narrow-nindedness have placed in the way of supernatural faith, then I am in agreement with him. All I ask of him is not to destroy the road when he blows up the obstruction. And that, I think, is what he would do, if he were so to exalt, in the "super-natural order", the perfection he attributes to nature itself as to make one forget the interior death, the total renunciation of our innate egoism, the surrender of our rational autonomy, the frank acceptance of a "re-birth" and of a new childhood, that must be our answer to the gift of grace. The supernatural will never, I think, cease to be a "stumbling-block" for scientists, because it can "save" and perfect science only by revolutionizing their normal outlook' (3 July 1934).

[156] 'This crisis of human activity is, by its nature, as old as man. It is abundantly clear that we must not confine it to a few brief instants or only to the origins of our race. Born with the intellect, the tempta-tion to revolt must constantly change and *grow* with it. And this is

why it has never appeared more acute and more universal than today. Within this human era *we are actually passing through a singular critical epoch*. At each epoch in history, the last men to arrive have always found themselves in possession of an accumulated heritage of knowledge and science, that is to say faced with a more conscious choice between fidelity and infidelity to life, between Good and Evil' (*Hominization*, 1923, in *Vision of the Past*, p. 75).

'Here we have, on the scale of today, the heroic temptation of all time, that of the Titans, of Prometheus, of Babel and of Faust; that of Christ on the mountain; a temptation as old as the earth itself; as old as the first reflective awakening of life to the awareness of its powers. But it is a temptation which is only now entering its critical phase, now that man has raised himself to the point of being able to measure both the immensity of the time that lies before him and the almost limitless powers made available to him by his concerted efforts to seize hold of the material springs of the world. Is the dilemma insoluble or (as we would rather believe) only a temporary one, destined to vanish like so many others, when we have reached a higher level of spiritual evolution? We may be in two minds about this' (*Faith in man*, 1947, in *The Future of Man*, p. 188). The duality, we believe, is built into history, and therefore permanent.

[157] 'No,' says Teilhard, 'those of us who are disciples of Christ must not hesitate to harness this force, which needs us and which we need. On the contrary, under pain of allowing it to be lost and of perishing ourselves, we should share those aspirations, in essence religious, which make the men of today feel so strongly the immensity of the world, the greatness of the mind, and the sacred value of every new truth. From this school our Christian generation will gain new and wider hopes and ambitions' (*Le Milieu Divin*, p. 153).

'Only a strange lack of faith can fear or despise or even condemn "the spirit of today". The awakening of the sense of man must inevitably herald a new Epiphany' (*Le sens humain*, unpublished, 1929).

'Now that the spirit of the earth has attained a higher degree of self-mastery, it is experiencing a constantly more urgent need to adore: we are conscious of God's emerging from universal evolution as greater and more indispensable than ever' (*L'esprit de la terre*, 1931, in *L'énergie humaine*, p. 53).

'In short, as science outgrows the analytical investigations which constitute its lower and preliminary stages, and passes on to synthesis—synthesis which naturally culminates in the realization of some superior state of humanity—it cannot but anticipate and commit itself to . . . the *future* and the *all*. And with that it goes beyond its own frontiers and emerges as option and adoration' (*The Phenomenon of Man*, p. 284).

[158] On the leisure produced, nevertheless, by industrialism, cf. *Man's Place in Nature*, pp. 104–5. The leisure of the future, however, will be invaded by the constant quest for knowledge: 'We can envisage a world whose constantly increasing leisure and heightened interest would find their vital issue in fathoming everything, trying everything, extending everything . . . a world in which, as happens already, one gives one's life to be and to know, rather than to possess' (*The Phenomenon of Man*, pp. 279–80).

[159] *Au nom de quoi? Esprit*, February 1964, p. 189.

[160] *Le Milieu Divin*, p. 110.

[161] 'What might have been taken in my attitude for the last thirty years for obstinacy or disrespect, is simply the result of my absolute inability to contain my feeling of wonderment' (Letter to Very Revd. Fr. Jansens, General of the Society of Jesus, 12 October 1951, quoted by Père Leroy in *Letters from a Traveller*, p. 42).

[162] 'It is perfectly true that the Cross means going beyond the frontiers of the sensible world and even, in a sense, breaking with it. The final stages of the ascent to which it calls us compel us to cross a threshold, a critical point, where we lose touch with the zone of the realities of the senses . . . That is exactly where the folly of Christianity lies in the eyes of the "wise", who are not prepared to stake the good which they now hold in the hands, on a total beyond' (*Le Milieu Divin*, p. 103).

'The supernatural awaits and sustains the progress of our nature. But it must not be forgotten that it purifies, in the end, only in an apparent annihilation' (*Ibid.*, p. 101).

[163] *Le Milieu Divin*, p. 103.

[164] Evode Beaucamp, *La Bible et le sens religieux de l'univers*, Editions du Cerf, 1959.

[165] Brunschvicg, No. 553, p. 567.

[166] Although this aspect is not, of course, denied, it is never more than implicitly accepted. 'Teilhard's mysticism is centred on the

risen Christ and the glorious mysteries' (C. Cuénot, *Teilhard de Chardin*, Editions du Seuil, in the series 'Ecrivains de toujours' p. 59).

It is interesting that Teilhard's quotations from St Paul are chiefly taken from humanist or cosmic passages: the speech to the Areopagus (*Le Milieu Divin*, p. 46), the Epistles to the Colossians and Romans, the 'groaning in travail' of the whole of creation to produce the 'glorious liberty of the children of God' (Rom. 8:18-23), rather than from the dialectic of the first chapters of Romans.

'If Christ is commensurate with the cosmos, I am perfectly happy about it—but it means nothing to me . . .' (F. Mauriac, *Ce que je crois*, Grasset, 1962, p. 139; cf. p. 37). 'It is each one of us whom the Lord addresses through Pascal. It is precisely for us and in language proper to us that he tells us what I hesitated one evening to repeat before a vast audience, so much did the words spring from the most intimate and secret depths of being: "In my agony it was of you that I thought . . ." It is in the context of friend speaking in confidence to friend that one should bring out what those words have, from generation to generation, given to those to whom they were spoken, and what they have given to me myself, and what they will continue to give to minds of a certain temper' (*Ibid.*, p. 148). Nevertheless, François Mauriac gave a warm welcome to *The Making of a Mind*.

[167] 'The Kingdom of Christ, to whose cause we have devoted ourselves, can never be established, either peacefully or through conflict, except on an earth that has been carried by *the development of every intellectual and technological resource*, to the extreme limit of its humanization' (*Sur la valeur religieuse de la recherche*, 1947, in *Science et Christ*, p. 263). We find the same type of idea in a letter written in 1948: 'Christian faith in God must develop a component that keeps pace with human progress—and that incidentally is the necessary and sufficient condition that will allow Christian faith to transmit on the right frequency and so once again make the world vibrate in resonance.'

[168] 'We have had enough talk about lambs—I should like to see more of the lion. Too much meekness and too little strength . . . At one particular time, it was possible to sum up the preaching of the gospel in the words of the Epistle: *Religio munda et immaculata haec est: Visitare pupillos et viduas, et immaculatum se custodire ab hoc saeculo—* "Religion that is pure and undefiled before God is this: to visit

orphans and widows in their affliction, and to keep oneself un-
stained from the world"—but that time has gone for good. In
earlier days, to love your neighbour meant to do him no wrong and
to bind up his wounds. Henceforth, charity, without ceasing to be
compassionate, will find its fulfilment in a life given for the common
progress of all. Such a Christianity is no longer simply the oil that
soothes the wounds of humanity or allows the gears to run smoothly'
(*Christologie et évolution*, unpublished, 1933).

169 *La route de l'ouest*, unpublished, 1932.

170 'Your summons, my God, has countless different tones, and the
duties you call us to vary in their essence. Each country, each
nation, and each social category, has its own apostle. For my very
humble part, Lord, I would choose to be the apostle and (if that be
not too bold an ambition) the evangelist of *your Christ in the universe* . . .' (*Le prêtre*, 1918, quoted in *Hymn of the Universe*, p. 151).

171 Teilhard was well aware of these dangers: 'It is not difficult to
see that there is a double danger in the tendency I would like to see
prevail in the Christian economy and in the interpretation of
dogma: 1. it may so aggrandize the universe as to eclipse or
"materialize" God, and 2. it may allow its use of life's natural
resources and affections to develop into a pagan enjoyment and
personal acquisitiveness. These two aberrations are both *exaggerations*, such as any truth may suffer. Their avoidance is a matter of
Catholic good sense and Christian prudence' (*Mon univers*, in
Ecrits du temps de la guerre, 1918, p. 279).

'Who then will at last be the ideal Christian, the Christian at once
new and old, who will solve in his soul the problem of life's balance
by allowing all the life-sap of the world to flow into its effort to
attain the divine Trinity?' (*La maîtrise du monde*, 1916, in *Ecrits du
temps de la guerre*, p. 81). Cf. H. de Lubac, *op. cit.*, p. 204.

172 'In each of these three great theological and spiritual terms we
find a similar structure: a universal diaphany of Christ, resting on
the concrete form of the epiphany of the gospels; a cosmic construction of the body of Christ, around an axis which is the body of
the Church; a consecration of the whole world, radiating from the
sacramental consecration of bread and wine at mass. And in each
of these themes we find a clear-cut eschatological prospect. The
homogeneity of this structure, which Teilhard himself did not
emphasize and of which he may have been quite unaware, says

much for the authenticity of his spiritual vision. We have to recognize that he had little contact with contemporary theology, but even so the central ideas in his spirituality are in perfect harmony with the most popular themes of that theology' (P. Smulders, *op. cit.*, p. 266).

[173] On this point Teilhard's thought agrees with certain ideas put forward by Pope Pius XII, who insists that Christianity is indispensable for the development of modern man and the success of modern civilization, and who, while pointing out the ambivalence of human industry and technology, also accords them a high value. 'Destroy faith in God, and you deal freedom a mortal blow.' 'Without the support of religion the rights and duties of man have no reliable or stable basis.' 'It cannot be denied that technical progress comes from God and therefore can and must lead back to God. In fact, it very often happens that the believer admires the conquests of technology, and uses them to acquire a more profound knowledge of creation and the mysteries of nature and to master them, with the help of modern machinery and scientific equipment, so that they may contribute to man's needs and enrich life on earth; and in so doing the believer feels impelled to worship the author of all these good things he admires and uses: so clear is it that all technology's quest for knowledge and discovery of natural forces is fundamentally simply the quest for and discovery of the greatness, wisdom and harmony of God. Who could disapprove of, or condemn, technical progress seen in this light?' 'Man's labour, too, constitutes a high moral value, and mankind at work is not simply a society that produces goods but one that glorifies God. Man can therefore regard his work as a real instrument of his own sanctification, because by working he perfects in himself the image of God, satisfies his duty and right to provide a living for himself and his family, and makes himself a useful member of society' (Allocutions of 4 December 1949 and 27 December 1945; Christmas broadcasts, 1953 and 1955). Cf. F. Russo, *Technique et conscience religieuse*, Bonne Presse, 1961. The passages quoted above should be complemented by some of Pope John XXIII's utterances, in particular *Mater et magistra*.

[174] On 15 February 1917, Teilhard wrote to his cousin: 'Did you read, last Sunday, the long epistle in which St Paul says to the Jews: *Hebraeus sum? Et ego! . . .* etc. For the new era that is now opening—

has, indeed, already begun—I believe the best self-discipline and the most effective apologetic will, for the Christian, consist in being able to present the world, through the example of his own life, with this new challenge. They say *Homo sum*—I say *Plus ego*' (*The Making of a Mind*, p. 183).

'When, precisely in virtue of their Christianity, through the constructive activity of their charity, through the effective fruitfulness of their detachment, and the confident boldness of their supernatural views, Christians show that they are the first men to spiritualize earthly values and press on towards the future, then all that is best—and that means most dangerous—in modern unbelief will stand weaponless, its very soul exposed (*L'incroyance moderne*, 1933, in *Science et Christ*, p. 153).

[175] A purely 'natural' history can never get away from a repetition of the same facts within a framework of laws (physical, psychological, social, etc.): what is more, under the influence of evil, it must lose momentum and finally disintegrate. To be real and authentic history must be able to progress towards a transcendent end, in which man passes into a higher stage. Moreover, that end must already be present, in the person of Christ and the pouring-out of the spirit in the Church.

During the 1914 war Teilhard had occasion to come into contact with country parishes that had lost all sense of Christianity: he wrote of these, 'You can't imagine the revolting state of selfishness, ill-nature, meanness and human pettiness to which these peasants are reduced, deprived of religion and educated in the State's republican principles! . . . One feels that one's in the presence of a veritable organic taint, as real as a disorder that attacks the tissues of the body. There's no doubt that morality has a "biological" value' (Letter of 25 January 1917, in *The Making of a Mind*, pp. 174–5).

[176] 'Once our minds have grasped first the existence of the Noosphere and then the vital urgency of our preserving it, the voice that calls out rings out more imperiously. It does not simply say "Love one another, that you may be perfect"; now it adds "Love one another, or you perish" "(*L'énergie humaine*, 1937, in *L'énergie humaine*, p. 189).

'Already we know enough (and this is a great deal) to affirm that this exploration will only reach its goal on one condition, that the entire work be conducted under the sign of unity. The very nature of the biological process taking place requires this. Unless they are put forth in an atmosphere of union glimpsed and desired, the most legitimate demands can lead only to catastrophes. We have more than enough evidence of this at the present time. Indeed, at the rate that consciousness and its ambitions are increasing, the world will explode if it does not learn to love. The future thinking of the earth is organically bound up with the transformation of the forces of hatred into forces of Christian love. If we study its most profound features, those of liberty, humanity seems certainly to have reached the stage of its evolution in which it cannot from any viewpoint face the problems presented to it by the growth of its inner energy without defining for itself a centre of love and adoration' (*The natural units of humanity*, 1939, in *Vision of the Past*, pp. 214–15).

'On mounds of wheat, coal, iron, uranium—under any sort of demographic pressure you like—the man of tomorrow will lie down and sleep if he ever loses his taste for the ultra-human. And not just any sort of taste, but a strong and deeply rooted taste; a taste constantly growing with the increase in his powers of vision and action; a taste, in other words, capable of becoming paroxysmal on the approach of the final paroxysm that he is charged to prepare' (*The phyletic structure of the human group*, 1951, in *The Appearance of Man*, p. 169).

On present-day anxieties and their remedy, see *The Phenomenon of Man*, pp. 226–32; *Man's Place in Nature*, pp. 100–2; *The Appearance of Man*, pp. 250–2.

177 *Eastern Religions*

Comment je crois, unpublished, 1934. Teilhard travelled extensively in the Far East, and wrote a good deal about eastern religions.

In *The Grand Option*, 1939, in *The Future of Man* (p. 43) he says of Hindu mysticism: 'It asks us to persuade ourselves of the non-existence of all surrounding phenomena, destroy the grand illusion by asceticism or mysticism, create night and silence within ourselves: then, at the opposite extreme of appearance, we shall penetrate to what can only be defined as a total negation—the ineffable reality.'

In *The Phenomenon of Man* (p. 211), he says of India and China: 'While China, already encrusted in its soil, multiplied its gropings and discoveries without ever taking the trouble to build up a science of physics, India allowed itself to be drawn into metaphysics, only to become lost there. India, the region *par excellence* of high philosophic and religious pressures ... we can never make too much of our indebtedness to the mystic influences which have come down to each and all of us in the past from this "anticyclone". But however efficacious these currents for ventilating and illuminating the atmosphere of mankind, we have to recognize that, with their excessive passivity and detachment, they were incapable of building the world. The primitive soul of India arose in its hour like a great wind but, like a great wind also, again in its hour, it passed away. How indeed could it be otherwise? Phenomena regarded as an illusion (Maya) and their connexion as a chain (Karma), what was left in these doctrines to animate and direct human evolution? A simple mistake was made—but it was enough—in the definition of the spirit and in the appreciation of the bonds which attach it to the sublimations of matter.'

In *La route de l'Ouest* (unpublished, 1932), Teilhard refers to 'the mystical cyclone over the plains of the Ganges'. 'At one particular moment, the finest part of mankind reached a unanimous belief in the essential unity of nature, and agreed that it could be effected only by a *relaxation* of the universe. The multiplicity of beings and desires is no more than a bad dream from which we must wake ... Phenomena do not show us the substance but hide it from us.' Teilhard speaks of the 'buddhist intoxication with emptiness'. 'To attain this emptiness we must divest ourselves of every concept, every image, and every desire ... It is literally the death of constructive activity; it is the radical futility of the universe of experience ... sanctity consisting in breaking the envelope of things in order to escape from them.'

The values of Indian, Chinese and Japanese religious systems are analysed more methodically in *L'apport spirituel de l'Extrême-Orient* (unpublished, 1947).

India is characterized by a 'predominant sense of the One and of the Divine', by the quest for a 'universal essence underlying all things', which only awaits our return to it, to absorb us and identify us with itself. 'It is the world, not God, whose existence raises difficulties for the intelligence, and requires justification.' 'Identification, however, is not union.'

China, on the contrary, is 'fundamentally naturist and humanist'.

It maintains 'the primacy of the tangible over the invisible'; it represents 'the persistent passion for man and the earth', and its moral system is essentially practical. This passion, however, is far from being a real faith in man: moreover, it is satisfied with a static equilibrium, with reasonable control in the possessing of things, and has no care for nor need of the future.

Japan, too, is humanist, but makes the individual 'the servant of society': it has the heroic sense of the collective, from which is derived its mysticism of war, its dehumanizing racialism, and its code of 'violence and chivalrous self-denial'.

These three spiritual currents, centred respectively on God, on the individual and on society, are only specialized, and hence incomplete, solutions of the problem of spirit. 'Their waters rise silently in land-locked lakes.'

Teilhard then contrasts with these the '*Western road*', the European option for the world, for rational and creative activity. Although this option appears to have no religious basis, it is in fact inspired by a Christian humanist mysticism. 'The West could not take and hold the lead in science, if it were not at the same time the leading-shoot of the religious creative effort.' Asia is now drawing closer to the West, but the West must also draw riches from Asia: 'It is only in union with all other men that each man can hope to reach the term and real essence of his own self . . . What we have to do is not to initiate ourselves into a higher form of spirit but rather to make a twofold effort—to produce sympathetic attunement and to perfect a total community—and so swell and enrich the new mystical note of Christian humanism now sounded in the West.'

In *Quelques remarques pour y voir clair sur l'essence du sentiment mystique* (unpublished, 1951) Teilhard returns to this theme. After distinguishing between the way of identification with an impersonal God, and the way of union with an ultra-personal God, he adds: 'It would seem that the second way—the "way of the West"—the fruit of the meeting of Christianity and the modern world, is the true road to adopt "towards and for" *Oneness* (Teilhard uses the English word) .. absolute unity. In its structure (theology) and in its practice (the primacy of charity) Christianity follows the second road'.

At a time when eastern mysticism was making a considerable appeal to Europeans, Teilhard wrote, 'There is something odd in the fascination exercized by a religious approach that is so little coloured by love of God' (Letter of 13 May 1952).

Teilhard's appraisal of eastern religions (which agrees with Bergson's, *The Two Sources*, pp. 188–193) should be qualified—as indeed Teilhard did qualify it on other occasions—by noting that both Vedantism and Buddhism can accept the notion of personality and encourage human activity. Moreover, they can take many different forms (cf. E. Gathier, *La Pensée hindoue*, Editions du Seuil, 1960). Chinese Buddhism and Hinduism, however, gave Teilhard an impression of inertia (Letters of October 1923 and 19 December 1935, in *Letters from a Traveller*, pp. 101–2, 216). At the same time, although he believed that the light of Asia had passed into other hands, he recognized that it was Asia that kindled it and that 'while a few wise men have it in safe-keeping' it is not extinguished (*Ibid.*, p. 102).

178 'If we turn to the Islamic group, we find that nothing subsists, everything is dissolved, even more completely. Islam has preserved the idea of the existence and greatness of God (and so contains the seed, it is true, from which everything might one day be born again); at the same time, however, it has achieved the seemingly impossible feat of making this God as ineffective and sterile as a negation of being, from the point of view of knowing and improving the world. After destroying much and creating a localized and ephemeral beauty, Islam now appears as a principle of fixation and stagnation. Powerless though it is in fact, it is perfectly conceivable that it could be restored to vigour: indeed, this, *which amounts basically to a convergence with Christianity*, is already happening among some more advanced and up-to-date minds. Until that renascence comes about the Allah of the Koran will remain a Bedouin God; he will never be able to attract to himself the energies of any really civilized man' (*La route de l'Ouest*, unpublished, 1952).

In another passage, Teilhard explains why he has devoted little attention to Islam: 'In spite of the number of its adherents and its continual progress (though we should note that this is among the less evolved strata of mankind) *Islam* is not considered here, because in my opinion, it has no particular solution—at least in its original form—to offer for modern religious problems. It seems to me to represent the residue of Judaism, and to have no character of individuality. And it cannot develop unless it becomes humanist or

Christian' (*Ibid.*). There is much to be said, no doubt, for that verdict, but it may well overlook the valuable spiritual, and sometimes mystical resources of a religion centred on a single God.

[179] *Ibid.* 'Modern positivists almost inevitably conceive God as a shoreless ocean . . . an immensity of diffused extension' . . . Unlike primitive men, who give a human countenance to everything that moves—or even the early Greeks, who divinized all the aspects and forces of nature, modern man is obsessed by the need to depersonalize (or impersonalize) what he most admires' (*The Phenomenon of Man*, p. 257). Teilhard calls the two 'antipodal' religions he treats of in this context 'the eastern road' and 'the western road'. The former represents 'release of tension and expansion', the latter 'tension and centration'.

[180] 'By showing us the summit that crowns the world, evolution makes Christ possible—just as Christ, by giving meaning and direction to the world, makes evolution possible. In other words, Christ must find a summit to the world for his consummation, just as he had to find a woman for his conception' (*Comment je crois*, unpublished, 1934).

[181] 'The world I live in becomes divine. And yet these flames do not consume me, nor do these waters dissolve me; for, unlike the false forms of monism that impel us through passivity towards unconsciousness, the pan-Christism I am finding places union at the term of an arduous process of differentiation. I shall become the Other only by being absolutely my own self. I shall attain the spirit only by releasing completely and exhaustively all the powers of matter.' 'I recognize that, following the example of the incarnate God revealed to me by the Catholic faith, I can be saved only by becoming one with the universe' (*Ibid.*).

[182] *Apologetics*

Teilhard's apologetics, like that of Maurice Blondel, to which it owes a great deal, is based primarily on Christianity's correspondence with man, on the answer it gives to the problem and mystery of his existence, and its ability to meet the demands of nature.

Thus Teilhard develops Christianity's 'conformity' with 'the subtle movements of our human ideal': 'For the last two thousand years, millions of lives—among them the best—have been spent, and are still being spent, in applying to this mysterious thing the most subtle and penetrating checks that psychological experience can devise. Countless minds and hearts have looked to this Christ to satisfy their most demanding and exact aspirations: and *he has never been found wanting* . . . This thing is, indeed, something quite extraordinary; it can be grasped as an element of experience, can be pursued as an ideal, can be cherished as a person, can be adored as a world. *This unlimited capacity to meet the needs of the whole physical and psychological order of our universe* can have only one explanation: Christ, as gradually disclosed to Christian thought, is not an image or a symbol (*if he were, his power would become exhausted or he would in some way be found wanting*): he is, or at least he introduces, the reality of what, in virtue of the very structure of human activity, we have been awaiting . . . *The curve then* (of the religious phenomenon) *is not individual, nor national, nor racial, but human*' (*Le christianisme dans le monde*, 1933, in *Science et Christ*, pp. 142–3; cf. *Comment je crois*, unpublished, 1934).

'Thus it is that our humanism, renewed in its love of living and spurred on in its aspirations by the discovery that there is a peak to the arrow-flight of time comes logically to perfect itself in an attitude of self-abandonment and adoration' (*The New Spirit*, 1942, in *The Future of Man*, pp. 92–3).

'The criterion by which the truth of a religion is finally determined can only be the capacity it shows to give a complete meaning to the universe as it emerges into our consciousness.' True religion may 'be recognized by this characteristic, that under its influence and illumination the world, as a whole, presents the maximum coherence to our intelligence, and the maximum importance to our love for action . . . Can we say categorically whether Christianity has or has not what is needed to make it *the* religion of progress the world is now waiting for? . . . God reveals himself to us not from outside, as an intruder, but from *within* (= in evolution), by stimulating, sublimating, and enriching the human psychic current—we can recognize the sound of his voice above all in the fullness and coherence it gives to our individual and collective being' (*Introduction au christianisme*, unpublished, 1944).

In Teilhard's view, the *miraculous* is still 'a criterion of truth'; it even seems to him all the less abnormal in that 'the determinisms of matter are no more than the unliberated residue of spirit', and that 'the principal axis of spiritualization', represented by Christianity, 'displays (to a more marked degree than elsewhere) a progressive emancipation from the body'. The miraculous 'does not have the character of a clean break, amounting to a tearing apart by God of the seamless veil of phenomena'. At the same time this criterion is 'subordinate and secondary' (*Comment je crois*, unpublished, 1934).

'There is, of course, a *faith that stems from the miraculous*; but it should not obscure for us the true nature of our spiritual sovereignty over the cosmos. The *prodigy*—which amazes us because, *over a limited area*, it does violence to determinisms and "*locally*" reverses the march of time—has always been, and, it appears, must always remain, an exceptional mode of action. It is an anticipation, or a reflection, of a form of life that transcends our own, and could not in any way be the dawn of a period on earth of emancipation and well-being. It heralds no millenium' (*La foi qui opère*, 1918, in *Ecrits du temps de la guerre*, p. 232).

The '*polyvalence*' of a cosmos which is simultaneously but distinctly a universe of nature and a universe of grace, is used by Teilhard to show that prayer does not interfere 'in a way that is *scientifically* demonstrable, with the course of natural events'. 'Empirical science, whose field is limited to individual determinisms, cannot conflict with faith, whose activity modifies the overall design of the embroidery without breaking any individual thread' (*Ibid.*, p. 321).

'What gives a miracle its force, is that it is produced within, and assists, a movement that, *quite apart from that*, shows a capacity to justify the religious development of the earth. If you take away from Christianity its power to direct human activity and keep it on an even keel in the new courses to which its destiny commits it, then the raising of Lazarus has hardly more power to command our adherence than the wonder-working of Buddha or Mahomet' (*Le sens humain*, unpublished, 1929).

'Nature, we know, can be super-animated under the influence of the divine ratification, and this may bring an unexpected relaxation of determinisms. That this can happen, or is even likely to happen, in close association with true religion, I am far from denying. We must, nevertheless, recognize that miracles have ceased seriously to influence our judgment. Their acceptance involves so many historical and physical difficulties that there are probably numbers of Christians today who continue to believe not *because of*, but in spite of the wonders recorded in Scripture' (*Le christianisme dans le monde*, 1933, in *Science et Christ*, p. 142).

Teilhard deals again with miracles, at greater length, in his *Introduction au christianisme*, unpublished, 1944: 'Some miracles are not only beyond but *in contradiction of* natural possibilities. Others are not so impressive, because we are beginning to suspect that organic determinisms, born of habit and subject to the control of life, are more amenable than we thought to the powers of the "soul" . . . The Christian miracle (by which I mean the manifestation of a personal divine influence in Christianity) is tending, quite naturally, to move in our eyes from the domain of "the individual prodigy" into that of "the general victory of life" which we now recognize in the faith of Jesus. Today—as yesterday, no doubt, but more explicitly—the capacity that Christianity shows of steadying, directing, animating and fulfilling human evolution (Anthropogenesis), is making us feel and recognize the hand of God in the world, more clearly than any individual extraordinary circumstance can do. At the same time it remains true that Christianity would cease to be Christianity if we found it impossible to believe (in however vague and general a way) that chance and determination in the cosmos was feeling the influence of God—that it was making them more flexible, setting a term to them, animating them recognizably, as our union with him grows closer and our prayer more urgent. The objective reality, however, of such interventions is more a matter of personal intuition than of demonstrability.' 'In a certain number of cases (the virginity of Mary, Christ's bodily resurrection, the Ascension) we have the impression that the gospel miracles are a material expression (like Genesis) of what is incapable of representation in such profound events as the embodiment of the Word in the human phylum or Christ's transition from his individual human state to his "cosmic" state as the centre of evolution. It is not simply a matter of symbols: it is the expression, in an image, of what is inexpressible' (*Ibid.*).

[183] Letter of 13 May 1952. 'Life becomes an increasingly heavy burden . . . this is what is "providentially" arising to sustain our courage—the hope, the belief that some immense fulfilment lies ahead of us . . . If evolution were to reach its highest point in our small, separate lives, then indeed the enormous travail of terrestrial organization into which we are born would be no more than a

tragic irrelevance. We should all be dupes. We should do better in that case to stop, to call a halt, destroy the machines, close the laboratories, and seek whatever way of escape we can find in pure pleasure or pure nirvana' (*Life and the planets*, 1945, in *The Future of Man*, pp. 117–18).

[184] *The human rebound of evolution*, 1947, in *The Future of Man*, pp. 206–9. 'Faith, not simply as a way of escaping from the world, but as the leavening co-principle of the very fulfilment of the world. As an instrument of evolutionary activation, Christianity, in as much as it "personalizes" cosmogenesis is unquestionably irreplaceable, and invincible' (*Contingence de l'univers et goût humain de survivre*, unpublished, 1953).

[185] *Les conditions psychologiques de l'unification humaine*, 1949 (*L'activation de l'énergie* p. 185). 'In spite of a number of inevitable mistakes, Christianity has hitherto made us not *in-human* but *super-human*, and still seeks to do so: this is what makes it acceptable.' It is 'the religion of universal progress' and is 'still today the only religion that can cope with the intellectual and moral world inaugurated in the West by the Renaissance'. 'We can now see a single intellectual current capable of meeting the demands and ambitions of modern thought; one single religion is today both *possible* and *embodied in the human phylum*: Christianity . . . If Christianity is at the moment the only possible religion *de facto*, it is because it is the only one that exists *de iure*.' 'Christianity in the world is not only what it sometimes appears to be, the religious side of an impermanent civilization localized in the West. It is much more, like the spirit of the West itself, (whose mysticism and hopes it expresses) an all-embracing phenomenon that marks the appearance of a new vital order in the human stratum' (*Le christianisme dans le monde*, unpublished, 1933).

[186] 'Christian love is incomprehensible to those who have not experienced it' (*The Phenomenon of Man*, p. 295). 'I have also noted, I think (in visiting some of the large Catholic centres of social work in Hong Kong and Shanghai) that Catholicism has an extraordinary power of penetrating and re-shaping souls (I have met children, old people and nuns, Chinese men and women, who really seemed to look at me with that man-to-man communication which I might have expected to find in Europeans')) (Letter to the Abbé Breuil, Tientsin, 23 May 1923, in *Letters from a Traveller*, p. 73).

[187] Teilhard shows too that the rivalry between Christianity and other religious ideologies must result in the victory of the former; for 'by the very fact of the new dimensions assumed by the universe as we see it today, Christianity reveals itself both as inherently more vigorous in itself and as more necessary to the world than it has ever been before . . . At the present moment Christianity is the *unique* current of thought, on the entire surface of the noosphere, which is sufficiently audacious and sufficiently progressive to lay hold of the world at the level of effectual practice in an embrace, at once already complete and yet capable of indefinite perfection, where faith and hope reach their fulfilment in love. Alone, unconditionally alone, in the world today, Christianity shows itself able to reconcile in a single living act, the All and the Person' (*The Phenomenon of Man*, pp. 296–8).

'Sooner or later, souls will be won by the religion that offers them the highest human fulfilment. In other words, Christian faith can hope to dominate the earth of tomorrow only if it proves to our reason that besides being already the only religion that can "*amorize*" the universe, it is also the only one that can "*valorize*" the stuff of the world and its evolution' (*Contingence de l'univers et goût humain de survivre*, unpublished, 1953).

'These three currents—the eastern, the human, and the Christian —still conflict in the great river of man. Nevertheless, there are unmistakable signs that show they are beginning to flow together. The East seems almost to have forgotten the original passivity of its pantheism. Those who worship human progress are continually becoming more aware, in their cosmogonic views, of the forces of spirit and freedom. Christianity is beginning to accept the value of human effort. In these three branches the same spirit that has made me what I am is obscurely at work' (*Ibid.*).

[188] *Sauvons l'humanité*, 1937, in *Science et Christ*, pp. 184–7. In the light of these views, Teilhard's thought is shared by all who, even without explicit adherence to the Church, seek to group men in large economic or political aggregations, or under the banner of a universalist ideal. It is not surprising, therefore, to find Léopold Sédar Senghor, for example, claiming the support of Teilhard, in his plan for an African socialism in which '*negritude*' plays a large part (*Pierre Teilhard de Chardin et la politique africaine*, in *Cahier Pierre Teilhard de Chardin*, No. 3).

[189] 'Peace is not the opposite of war. It is war carried above and beyond itself in the conquest of the trans-human. Always the same solution, so simple, so radically dependent on synthesis, for the problems that ravage us' (Letter of 20 September 1940, in *Letters from a Traveller*, pp. 267-8).

In letters written about the same time, Teilhard records his distrust of the ideology put forward in Vichy propaganda: 'Vichy's copy-book maxims for good children seem to me entirely to lack the fire which alone can bring out the virtues so rightly advocated' (*ibid.*, p. 267). 'It is not a Restoration that we want but a Renaissance—not discretion but a passionate faith in some future' (20 November 1940, *ibid.*, p. 271).

[190] Letter of October 1923, *ibid.*, p. 102. On many occasions, Teilhard says that the great cleavage at present is between those who do and those who do not believe in the progress of history (*Note on Progress*, 1920; *Some reflexions on Progress*, 1941; *The planetization of mankind*, 1945; in *The Future of Man*, pp. 20, 76-7, 138-9).

Within the first of these two groups there is a further cleavage, between those who worship God and those who worship the world (*Some reflexions on the spiritual repercussions of the atom bomb*, 1946, *ibid.*, pp. 147-8).

[191] *L'énergie humaine*, 1937, in *L'énergie humaine*, pp. 196-8; *Some reflexions on progress*, 1941, in *The Future of Man*, p. 79; *Turmoil or genesis?* 1947, *ibid.*, p. 225.

'The Upward and the Forward: two religious forces, let me repeat, now met together in the heart of every man; forces which weaken and wither away in separation . . . forces, therefore, that await one thing alone—not that we should choose between them, but that we should find the means of combining them' (*The heart of the problem*, 1949, in *The Future of Man*, p. 226). Teilhard believes that modern man can be satisfied only by a Christ who combines the qualities of indefinite growth and present completeness (*Le coeur de la matière*, unpublished, 1950).

[192] *Le néo-humanisme moderne et ses réactions sur le christianisme* (Notes taken at a lecture to *Action Catholique Ouvrière chaplains*, Versailles, 21 September 1948).

[193] *Le phénomène chrétien*, unpublished, 1950. The following passage, too, may present some difficulty. 'The great event that is in preparation, and which it is our duty to assist, is this: that these two

spiritual currents (faith in the world and faith in Christ) shall feed, augment and *fructify* one another, and so enable Christianity, *by their synthesis*, to emerge into a new sphere. That sphere will be none other than the one in which Revelation, combining in itself the energies of heaven and earth, will stand, supernaturally—and be so recognized by our faith—at the meeting point on which, as science shows us, the rays of evolution naturally converge' (*Le Christ évoluteur*, unpublished, 1942).

Here, again, is another passage also written towards the end of his life:

'A hitherto unknown form of religion—one that no one could yet have imagined or described, for lack of a universe large enough and organic enough to contain it—is burgeoning in men's hearts, from a seed sown by the idea of evolution. God is no longer sought in an identification with things that annihilates personality, nor in an escape from things that de-humanizes man. God is attained (and this is infinitely more energizing and brings infinitely truer communion) by entry into the centre of the total sphere that embraces all things—a centre that itself is in process of formation. Far from being shaken in my faith by so profound a revolution, it is with irrepressible hope that I welcome the rise and anticipate the triumph of this new mysticism. For if in the end nothing, absolutely nothing, can prevent man from finally coming to rest in the form of belief that activates in him the forces of convergence *to their maximum* —then, indeed, we have the finest proof of the transcendence of Christianity. We see it in its unique power to find within itself and present to us, at the very time we need it, what at this precise moment in history, is absolutely indispensable to our nature if it is to develop its power to act and adore to the full: and that is a Christ who can be and is commensurate with the universe, in other words a God—the God we look for—of evolution.' Then will be effected 'the meeting between the Above of heaven and the Ahead of earth, between a "cosmified" God and a "personalized" evolution' (*L'étoffe de l'univers*, 1953, in *L'activation de l'énergie*, p. 406).

'Since his appearance Christ has never ceased to emerge from every crisis of history more present, more urgent, more assertive than ever. What, then, does he lack to be able to appear once more to our new world as the "new God" we look for? 1. He must no longer be limited, *constitutionally*, in his operation to no more than the "redemption" of our planet. 2. We now realize that everything in our universe follows a single axis of co-reflexion: we must, therefore, avoid that subtle confusion of "supernatural" and "extra-natural", so that Christ will no longer be offered to our adoration as a peak distinct from and in rivalry with the summit to which the slope of anthropology, extended biologically, ultimately leads' (*Ibid.*).

In these paragraphs the form of expression sometimes, we can recognize, goes beyond what the thought behind it will bear, so that they would seem to suggest that we must look for something that will re-fashion or complement Christianity. They may, however, be interpreted in a way that reduces them to a more classic theme. The 'synthesis' in question is not an augmentation of Christianity *in itself*, but an enriching of 'our faith' by a better *appreciation* of its mystery, by an assimilation and integration of human values into the transcendence of its catholicity. And if the 'future' Teilhard speaks of is capable, through the action of the Spirit in the Church, of bringing about a better practical understanding of their faith among Christians, that future is already present in all who are already, in contrast with any form of Jansenism, fully living the mystery of the Incarnation.

[194] 'How are we to envisage coming developments of faith on earth? In the form, we may be sure, of a slow concentration of the power of adoration around a Christianity that has gradually become a "*Religion for quest and effort*". The first great event to come about—it is already, no doubt, happening—will be the cleavage between those who believe and those who do not believe in the future of the world . . . The world must be converted as one whole or by physiological necessity it will perish. And if it is to be converted, it will be by convergence around a *Religion of Action*, which will gradually be recognized as identical with, and subordinate to, a Christianity that has been *extended*, in a spirit of faith, *to its extreme limit*' (*Le christianisme et le monde*, unpublished, 1933).

[195] *Le phénomène chrétien*, unpublished, 1950.

[196] *La parole attendue*, 1950, in *Cahiers Pierre Teilhard de Chardin*, No. 4, p. 28.

[197] *Le phénomène chrétien*, unpublished, 1950.

[198] *Le sens humain*, unpublished, 1929. 'Everything that justly vindicates the sense of man can find a home' in Christianity: 'With-

out Christianity, the sense of man and all his aspirations must fall to the ground' (Third lecture to the Marcel Légaut group, 10 December 1930). 'Christianity can, without sacrificing anything of its integrity, without distortion or any harmful modification, accept the new line followed by the soul it guides and contains . . . It is continuing its role as the supreme educator of Christian souls' (*Ibid.*). 'The new religion will be exactly the same as our old Christianity, but with a new life drawn from the legitimate evolution of its dogmas as they come into contact with new ideas.'

CONCLUSION

[1] Teilhard's attempt would thus appear to conform with two of the essential canons of the Vatican Council: that which deals with the *signs* of credibility, and that which asserts the supra-rational and mysterious character of Revelation (Denzinger-Bannwart, 1812 and 1816). The signs, no doubt, refer to Christ's miracles, but, in a more general way, the possibility of a rational approach to Christianity is involved. One should note, too, the canon on the certain knowledge of God by the light of reason (*Ibid.*).

[2] Teilhard re-stated the ancient problem of the one and the multiple which could never be fully solved in an abstract form. The multiplicity of material elements, and later of conscious, personal centres, always unified and structured, and always to some small degree penetrated by spirit, converges and ascends towards the supreme unity, which is unanimity.

[3] 'Teilhard's thought is in the Thomistic tradition: reinstatement of a nature in itself trustworthy and good, rational description of man and the world according to concepts derived from an experimental and positive science, proof of the existence of the absolute from the movement of things, which points to a prime mover or Omega Point—all these features are common to St Thomas Aquinas and Teilhard de Chardin' (E. Borne, *De Pascal à Teilhard de Chardin*, *op. cit.*, p. 67). It is true that even St Thomas's theory itself represents an option: 'St Thomas', says one of his disciples, 'gives evidence of a rational optimism that could no doubt be revised. He seems to have little of the modern sense of contingence, or at least to have paid little attention to it. He hardly seems to have under-

stood the part played by crisis (as in Hegel, for example). He may well have underestimated the difficulties of knowledge, and failed adequately to appreciate the epistemological position of the mind). The instrument of reason is too simple, in spite of its overall validity' (O. A. Rabut, O.P., *Valeur spirituelle du profane*, Editions du Cerf, 1963, p. 8).

[4] Atomic physics (and in this it differs widely from Descartes), by emphasizing the action of the observer on the observed phenomena and the involvement of the experimenter in his own experiment, is an example at its own level of the general inter-dependence of what we are still obliged to call subject and object. Man's involvement is even more marked in the social sciences. It reaches its maximum when science, reflecting on the totality of experience, becomes philosophy.

[5] In conceiving the real as determined by our desires, and taking the latter as 'the measure of the real' (*The singularities of the human species*, 1954, in *The Appearance of Man*, p. 262), Teilhard is akin to the author of *L'Action*. 'Trust—complete and inexhaustible—in the great movement of "being" which has made us and carries us along: that is the only attitude of which we can be sure that it is never deceived and never deceives us' (Letter of 9 January 1955, in *Letters from a Traveller*, p. 360). In 1919, Père Auguste Valensin confided to Teilhard that Blondel had 'such strong views on the consistence of the universe in Christ that he doesn't dare to go all the way with him' (8 August 1919, in *The Making of a Mind*, p. 300).

[6] Péguy sees in *Polyeucte* the perfection of a loyalty of grace towards human nature, and in the humanism of the ancients the admirable nobility of a chivalrous combat. 'God himself is a gentleman, and if he has to judge his own case there will be no favouritism on his side. What is most impressive and important in *Polyeucte* is without doubt the complete absence of pious chicanery . . . Jesus Christ does not degrade the world in order to elevate himself. He renders to the temporal what is due to the temporal. Those who keep aloof from the world, and those who proudly spurn the world, do not really elevate themselves by debasing the world . . . It is not enough to degrade the temporal in order to raise oneself into the category of the eternal; it is not enough to degrade nature to raise oneself into the category of grace; it is not enough to degrade the world in order

to rise into the category of God . . .But Jesus Christ himself was man. He assumed Incarnation in all its exact detail and fullness: with no prudent hedging and no fraudulent reservation. He became a man among men' (*Note conjointe*, 22nd edition, Gallimard, 1935, pp. 103-215).

[7] It is easy to understand Teilhard's sympathy with Péguy's work, centred as it was on the mystery of the Incarnation, as pointed out by A. Béguin, J. Onimus and A. Rousseaux. M. L'abbé Pierre Grelot agrees with our own view that in Péguy's *Eve* 'the centre of gravity is provided by the Incarnation, not by the Cross and Resurrection. The emphasis is on the assumption of human and temporal values by Christ, who saves them, rather than on the death of the sinful world' (*Sens chrétien de l'Ancien Testament*, Desclée, 1963, p. 91). At the same time Péguy, even more no doubt than Teilhard, had an acute sense of human misery and of the necessity for a redemption.

[8] *Lettre sur l'humanisme*, Gallimard, p. 161.

[9] While it was essential that a first generation of scientists should relate man to animality and thereby to 'the general evolution of matter', it 'would be unscientific and absurd to continue to treat man any more as a mere compartment within the animal kingdom' (*La convergence de l'Univers*, unpublished, 1951).

'It might seem that after Galileo man lost his privileged position in the universe . . . he is now in process of recapturing his leadership' (*Evolution of the idea of evolution*, 1950, in *Vision of the Past*, pp. 246-7).

[10] On Marx and Marxism, see in particular *The Phenomenon of Man*, p. 261 and *Sauvons l'humanité*, 1937, in *Science et Christ*, p. 180. 'Christianity covers the whole of man; and you, you who are Christians, do not know the whole of man. And you Marxists, you do not go far enough, because you carry the development of man only towards the Ahead' (*Le néo-humanisme moderne*, unpublished, 1948). 'However powerful its impetus in the early stages of the course of biological evolutionism into which it has thrust itself, the Marxist anthropogenesis, because it rules out the existence of an irreversible centre at its consummation, can neither justify nor maintain its momentum to the end' (*The Heart of the problem*, 1949, in *The Future of Man*, p. 265). See also *Human unanimization*, *ibid.*, p. 286. 'The human set-up on this side (the extreme left) always

interests me enormously. I can recognize all its undercurrents and tributary streams—but their keenness! it really makes one jealous!' (Letter of 14 February 1928).

The interest in Teilhard's thought shown by some leading Marxists may be explained by his respect for positive facts, and by his concept of a history, cosmic and human, that advances towards its temporal end. Teilhard's unanimity of individuals has analogies with the 'generic' universality predicted by Marx, in which the 'conflict between man and man', and hence 'between man and nature' will be brought to an end. Moreover, Teilhard's dialectic is akin to at least Marx's (though not to that of his followers after and including Engels) in that it embraces 'one single indivisible reality, man–nature' (J.-Y. Calvez, *op. cit.*, p. 414). However, the under-lying solidity of Teilhard's position soon makes it impossible to carry on any dialogue initiated with Marxism: the latter cannot accept the primacy accorded to spiritual energy (rather than to the con-tradiction between economics and society) as the motive force in history, the affirmation of God as creator and as the term of history, man's existential vocation to the fullness of religious relationship, and man's access (both as person and as a community) to super-natural life, with history emerging into a transcendent reality—in short the coincidence of the *ahead* and the *above*. The notion of a final term to history releases Teilhard from the contradiction of a purely 'natural' history that claims both to attain its fulfilment and to continue (Cf. J.-Y. Calvez. *op. cit.*, pp. 616–19). While, accord-ingly, the road 'ahead' cannot be neglected, there is still a radical opposition between an atheist system that in denying God cuts away the foundation of the person and of interiority, and a doctrine that makes man reach his term by a transition into God.

[11] Preface to Jacques Rivière's *À la trace de Dieu*. 'In short, the Catholic religion must be proved by a catholic, that is to say, a total, demonstration, and by this totality itself. It is true because it is Catholic, that is to say complete, because it is the key to and the crown of all. It can triumph only by continually opposing its indivisible mass to every fractional criticism' (*Ibid.*, in *Positions et propositions*, Vol. 2, p. 73).

[12] 'The world should realize that the Church looks at it with deep understanding, and sincere admiration. She is truly concerned not to master it but to serve it, not to depreciate it but to recognize its

value' (Pope Paul VI, opening address to the second session of Vatican 2).

Père Joseph Thomas makes this comment: 'Our concern is no longer simply with the world's misery. What matters now is its values. The Church does not seek either to defend itself against the world nor to use it as a support, as though she was bound always to be alien to it. She seeks to integrate it and take it to herself' (*L'avenir de l'Eglise catholique*, in the special number of *Responsables*, *L'homme de l'an 2000*, January 1964, p. 142). On the need for dialogue with the world and the difficulties involved, see also the encyclical *Ecclesiam suam* (6 August 1964). In one sense, therefore, Teilhard's message is in line with the aims of the Church of today, as expressed by the Council. The battle that he and so many others fought is now bearing fruit. Without abandoning any part of her transcendent aim the Church is finding her way back into a world which she seeks to serve, and into a human history whose value she recognizes as capital.

[13] 'Jerusalem, lift up your head. Look at the immense crowds of those who build and those who seek. All over the world, men are toiling—in laboratories, in studios, in deserts, in factories, in the vast social crucible. The ferment that is working through them in art and science and thought is for your sake. Open, then, your arms and heart, like Christ your Lord, and welcome the streams, the flood of the life-sap of humanity. Accept it, this sap—for, without its baptism, you will wither, without desire, like a flower without water; and tend it, since, without your sun, it will disperse itself wildly in sterile shoots' (*Le Milieu Divin*, p. 154).

'To sum up, in order to match the new curve of time, Christianity is led to discover the values of this world *below the level of God*, while humanism finds room for a God *above the level of this world*' (*The New Spirit*, 1942, in *The Future of Man*, p. 96).

[14] Cf. P. Emmanuel, *art. cit.*

[15] There is much in this that explains why a large number of young people today, lost in a fog of myth, upset by the instability of our times, and often cut off from adults, look to and rely on Teilhard for something that will counter nihilism, for something on which to bite, other than the cold rationalism of science and technology or unsatisfying emptiness of money and a good time.

[16] Cf. O. Rabut, O.P., *Dialogue with Teilhard de Chardin*, London,

1961. While crediting Teilhard's thought with much positive value, Père Rabut would like to see his views more fully and accurately developed on the following points: the originality of the supernatural order and its values, and the conflicts between those values and the disordered movements of fallen nature. Similarly, while saying that in Teilhard the Church gave birth to 'an authentic witness of Christ, such as our age was sadly in need of', Père de Lubac ends his book with 'a certain number of critical comments'. These agree with our own. 'Did Teilhard succeed in keeping a correct perspective in his universe? Is the distinction between the orders sufficiently emphasized? Has he a strong enough appreciation of the revolution introduced by the revelation of the supernatural mystery —this "paradoxical mystery" as St Clement of Alexandria calls it?' (*op. cit.*, p. 202ff.). Another sympathetic critic, Pastor Crespy, says, among other remarks, that he regrets that Teilhard failed sufficiently to show that in the Cross of Jesus there is a rupture with the sinful world—it is a radical judgment passed on the world. He criticizes him, too, for a certain confusion of planes ('Teilhard tries to make evolution say what only faith can say,' *op. cit.*, p. 224). (Cf. Jacques Natanson, *Un point de vue protestant sur Teilhard de Chardin*, in *Esprit*, January 1963.)

Here we should note the objection made by those, particularly in existential philosophy, who are specially alive to the fact of liberty. They are disturbed by the view of a world whose infallible and inevitably successful advance threatens to diminish man's responsibility and neutralize his distress in the certainty of his future. Teilhard, however, is far from denying liberty. He simply believes that it is assisted, if it consents, by a Spirit that, since all time but more particularly since Christ, has animated the world and man in order to advance them towards their transition. The coexistence of liberty and spiritual energy, which is another name for grace, is undoubtedly a mystery. Grace, however, which is the effective sign of a transcendent love, does not cancel man's complete responsibility for himself and his future. There is the further mystery of a hope whose certainty coexists with anxiety and concern for a salvation promised to men of good will, but effected in fear and trembling.

[17] 'I have come to see more clearly the only things I now believe in, and the only thing I could be—"my gospel and my vocation" if I may put it so. The things in which I believe: there are not many of

them. They are: first, and fundamental, the value of the world; and secondly, the indispensability of some Christ to give this world a consistence, a heart and a face . . . I have no desire to live now except "desperately in faith", twofold faith in the world and in Christ . . . You will note the interesting apologetical approach I feel driven into. *Visibilia* are to me no longer simply a logical premise to some chain of reasoning that leads to the *invisibilia*. They now constitute for me an *initial world* of faith of which the world of supernatural faith is only the development. I wonder whether that is not the only legitimate apologetics. A faith can be born only from a faith (not from reasoning): otherwise the process would not be homogeneous. Spiritual operations must be homogeneous (as the mathematicians would say). That is one aspect of the fundamental law of evolution' (Letter of 25 February 1929).

Again: 'We cannot dedicate ourselves to a "faceless" world. And it is because we have, historically speaking, no face to give it but that of Christ, that I feel myself bound until the very end . . .' (Letter of 15 July 1929).

'Religion can become an opium. It is too often taken to be no more than an anodyne. *Its true function is to maintain and spur on the progress of life*' (*L'esprit de la terre*, 1923, in *L'énergie humaine*, p. 53). There is a kinship between this conception and that of Bergson; but Bergson confined the role of opiate to 'static religion' (the religion of natural conformity, the religion of the city) (*The Two Sources*, in particular pp. 109, 175).

'The value (of Christianity) as a "component" in humanity is evident; but it seems to provide only part of the solution. The world of human life seems to *dwarf it*' (Letter of 11 November 1934).

In fact, the supernatural, the world of Christian faith, animates the world of nature. Nevertheless, the dialectic of nature and the supernatural should, perhaps, be more clearly expressed. 'In the Bible,' says Père F. Varillon, 'the man-nature relationship is strictly bound up with the creation-alliance relationship. The alliance is the objective of creation, but the creation is the condition of the alliance' (*Travail et foi*, in *Revue de l'Action populaire*, May 1958, p. 516). Père J. Thomas, again, says, 'the fulfilment of the cosmos is not in itself identical with the coming of the kingdom of God'; it is rather 'the union of man with God that will have as its consequence the fulfilment of the world' (*Une théologie de travail?*, *ibid.*, January 1963, p. 15).

In a short publication, preliminary to a thesis, Père B. Besret shows that the dialectical terms of incarnation and eschatology contain ambiguities, and can give rise to one-sided options, even heresies: excessive regard for or indifference to temporal realities and values, emotional or over-simple optimism or pessimism. The paradoxical complexity of the Christian mystery is a warning not to separate the two essential aspects, but to maintain an intimate union between attachment to and detachment from the world: this again is the root problem of nature and the supernatural (*Incarnation ou eschatologie?* Éditions du Cerf, 1964). See also E. Rideau, *Les Chrétiens et le monde*, in *Revue de l'action populaire*, May, 1965, pp. 517–30).

[18] In the introduction to *La centrologie* (1944, *op. cit.*, p. 105), Teilhard speaks of 'this instinctive persistence of human thought in seeking to reduce the world to unity'.

We should, however, add that Teilhard, in direct contrast with the geometric spirit and abstract logic, does not *deduce* the history of the world from pre-existing principles. On the contrary, he confines himself to a *reading*, which gives a *directive significance* to the real in the unpredictable newness of its projects and its indeterminacy from moment to moment. While this real is subject to a law of increasing unity, nothing pre-exists the future, nothing is 'implied' or contained in the origins: the relative freedom of life, man's liberty, the liberty of grace, all emerge at a given moment as creations. And the synthesis of the overall view respects the 'datum' of the difference of orders.

[19] Letter of 17 April 1923, in *Letters from a Traveller*, p. 66.

[20] *The Two Sources*, pp. 256–62.

[21] Teilhard agrees, moreover, that 'the end of the world defies imagination' (*The Phenomenon of Man*, p. 273). At the same time he speaks of 'the biologically appointed hour' (*ibid.*, p. 276). Père Jeannière concludes his *Liberté et Pouvoir* as follows: 'Is there a term to the advance of freedom? Is there a point where man is in full possession of himself, where he is completely under his own power? a point where mankind achieves its freedom as pure transparence, as equality, with self, with nature and with others; a point at which freedom and power are each a justification of the other? Since this

question embraces the trans-historic, and since this realization totalizes history and makes it subside into the an-historic, it ceases to be a question of human politics. A truly organic and unifying totality is not the sum of its elements, but gives them a new significance. History cannot become total and yet remain human history. Only one real totality exists, the mystical body of Christ; but that is a completely different problem' (*Démocratie aujourd'hui*, in *La liberté et le pouvoir*, p. 73).

[22] '... so that, even on our refactory planet, the essential function of the universe, which is a machine for the making of gods, may be fulfilled' (*The Two Sources*, p. 275).

[23] The reference is to Omega Point, as the ultimate concentration of men, preparatory to their gratuitous divinization.

[24] This 'beyond' of which Père de Lubac says that it is 'infinitely closer than the future' (*Catholicisme*, Editions du Cerf, 1938, p. 285).

Eschatological expectation 'is not the desire to witness the coming of more or less prodigious events, some new golden age: it is simply and solely the desire—but how intense a desire—for the presence of Christ, who, alone, is *the principle and the end* of all, apart from whom there is no existence and no life. And this desire is not to be projected into the future: it is with us here and now . . . It is meaningless unless it is embodied in the moment, unless it is part and parcel of the rhythm of our lives, giving them a value "outside time". Any other attitude would empty the desire of its substance' (Jean-Marie Fenasse, *Terme et début, voilà ce que Je suis*, in *Bible et vie chrétienne*, No. 54, November–December 1963, p. 46).

[25] This first stage would include an initial consideration of the categories of human thought and the laws that govern its *expression*. At least until recently, this fundamental reflexion on *language* has been lacking in our time, and Teilhard's thought shared that lack. His statement of the religious problem, in particular, was to some extent impaired by insufficient attention to the relations between image and idea, word and meaning.

[26] We noted earlier (Chap. 3, pp. 70-3) the gap in Teilhard's phenomenology between the appearance of man and our own time. This lack is paralleled by his neglect of the preparations of Christ in the history of Israel. It is interesting that Bergson's approach, on the other hand, starting with a purely positive examination, discloses,

through a religious enquiry, the meaning and progressive stages of a revelation: in *The Two Sources* the prophets of Israel appear as an approach towards Christ. If the Incarnation is constitutive of history and the notion of history, it must also include the whole economy of the stages that preceded it.

[27] In this religious philosophy, which both combines and distinguishes the orders of reason and faith, *science* is present in three ways: in the phase of existential reflexion, as a moment, necessary but insufficient, of the progress of consciousness—in the history of nature and man—and finally in human action consecrated by the supernatural. No philosophy or theology can henceforth leave this out of account: Teilhard's merit will prove to have been that he made it impossible to dissociate it from philosophical and religious speculation. The succession of phases noted above is very similar to the 'plan for a course in apologetics' suggested by Père H. Bouillard (*Logique de la foi*, Aubier, 1964, pp. 39-44), but it places more emphasis on the place of Christianity in the general history of the world.

[28] *Monitum* of the Holy Office, 30 June 1962.

[29] It sometimes happens that Christian readers, who are justifiably attracted by Teilhard's optimism and his enthusiasm for man's possible triumph, but who read his books too rapidly, are inclined to confuse their planes and fail to recognize both the transcendence of Christian hope and the mortifying conditions that govern action in time and of the consecration of the world (Cf. H. de Lubac, *op. cit.*, p. 203-4). From another angle H. Urs von Balthasar stresses the primordial character of the divine initiative and the objective evidence of God's radiating intervention into history particularly in the very condescensions of the Word. While recognizing the value of the method of immanence, which clarifies man's appetite for the supernatural, he holds that 'it should not be overestimated at the expense of God's power, which expresses and affirms itself in its historical witness' (*La gloire et la croix*, Aubier, 1965, p. 169).

[30] Letter of 1 February 1919, in *The Making of a Mind*, p. 281.

[31] 'Pascal, moreover, is more conscious in the God-Man of the mystery of God making himself man and having, by an inconceivable condescension, become a single individual existence, incarnate; while Teilhard sees in Christ more the divinized man, and

divinizes the whole. Here again it is as though there were two ways of reading this central mystery of Christianity, which can be apprehended either by descending from above or by ascending from below. There would appear to be in this a Christological dualism, that characterizes the whole history of Christian theology: and neither Pascal nor Teilhard de Chardin can be dissociated from that history' (E. Borne, *De Pascal à Teilhard de Chardin, op. cit.,* p. 81).

[32] 'The Church, while constantly bearing witness to Jesus Christ, does not seek to deprive man of anything. She does not refuse him the possession of what he has won, nor the merit of what his efforts have accomplished. But she seeks to help him to find himself again and to know himself for what he is, to attain the fullness of knowledge and conviction which it has always been the ambition of wise men to acquire, even outside divine revelation' (John XXIII, Whitsun address, 1962, in *Documentation catholique,* July 1962, col. 837).

[33] Joshua, Ch. 2. On one occasion Père Maréchal tried to demonstrate to Teilhard how essential it was that this pioneer role should always be accompanied by a strict fidelity to the common mind of the Church. 'I have the feeling that we are experiencing the difficulties of a transition period. On the subject of original sin (and the divine inspiration of the Scriptures) "dogmatic development" is not sufficiently advanced to provide an answer to questions that science raises for educated people today. Normally speaking, while the development of dogma is, up to a point, based on the preliminary researches of experts, in the end it rests on the common reaction of the Christian mind: it takes time for this to get hold of a new problem and sort out the right solution. This is not the first time in the history of the Church that the intellectuals, too far ahead of the rank and file, have had the uncomfortable feeling of being left "high and dry"—not understood and afraid that they themselves have ceased to understand. The best thing they can do is to wait patiently on God's good time (it may not come in their lifetime) and meanwhile to carry on with their mission as "advanced patrols" . . . but never to lose contact with the main army; it is, you see, in the universal and hierarchic Church, and not necessarily first to us poor philosophers or scientists, that Christ pronounces the *verba vitae aeternae.* In spite of our ardent, sometimes agonizing,

concern for the apostolate, we have no right, if we wish to be reasonable, even to regret that those who represent the teaching authority are somewhat slow to adapt themselves (we could even say, to understand). Heavens above! What would happen if they were too eager to drink the new wine! What absurd mistakes might be made—what unfortunate and ephemeral "brilliancies"?'

[34] The reference is to the dream of Innocent III and his meeting with St Francis in 1210 (Daniel-Rops, *Cathedral and Crusade*, pp. 140-1) and also to the intellectual mission of St Thomas Aquinas (1226-74) under Clement IV and St Gregory X.

'I am struck by the fact that the Church has practically no *organ of research* (unlike her whole living and progressive environment). Yet she will never keep the faith as an illumination for her children and for outsiders unless she *seeks*, unless she engages in a quest that is felt to be a matter of life or death . . . At present there are crying problems that nobody, except in a few private conversations, either expresses clearly or faces boldly' (Letter of 26 July 1917 to Père Victor Fontoynont, quoted in H. de Lubac, *op. cit.*, p. 248).

[35] In its main outline Teilhard's work is comparatively simple; there is nothing esoteric in it. Although he coins many neologisms, his language is clear. The whole problem of his interpretation arises from the difficulty of arranging and classifying, determining the relative importance and position, of combining and distinguishing, themes that belong sometimes to natural philosophy and sometimes to theology.

[36] Christ is 'the Alpha and Omega, the beginning and the end, the foundation and the key-stone, the fulfilment and the fulfiller. He is the consummator and the giver of consistence to all things. It is towards him and through him, the inner life and light of the world, that, with pain and labour, the universal convergence of all created spirit makes its way. He is the unique, precious and consistent centre, which shines at what will be the summit of the world, at the opposite extreme from the dim, eternally shrinking, regions into which our science ventures when it goes down the road of matter and of the past' (*Science et Christ*, 1921, in *Science et Christ*, p. 60).

[37] 'Would it be wise to guide Christians away from the direction indicated in the writings of Teilhard? Would it be wise, for example, to work towards a complete separation between science on one side and philosophy and theology on the other? There is, it is true, a

discontinuity between science and philosophy, and still more between science and theology. There is also a connexion. St Thomas Aquinas (and in this he follows Aristotle) did not wish to separate his metaphysics from physics, and, even in theology, he accepted the use of arguments drawn from natural science. We should remember, too, Pope Pius XII's address to the Pontifical Academy of Science (22 November 1951) in which he drew attention to the assistance that modern science can give in demonstrating the existence of God. E. Gilson, again, has rightly said that "metaphysical systems grow old in their physics". We should, therefore, at least resume Teilhard's attempt to integrate theology with a scientific view of the world that is not obsolete, giving it back its true orientation and if necessary re-shaping it . . . Teilhard's thought meets a deep-rooted need in modern man: to see the world from the scientific standpoint is no longer the prerogative of a few scientists, and the application of all sorts of technical processes raises a problem of values that must be faced by all. The tendency, in fact, of Teilhard's work is to move from science and technology to religion: the general direction is "religious"' (J. M. Le Blond, *Mise en garde contre le P. Teilhard de Chardin*, in *Etudes*, September 1962, pp. 282–3).

Teilhard's synthesis has a further unrivalled merit, in the *language* he developed to make the Christian mystery accessible and easily grasped, in terms adapted to the men of our own day. While theology is rightly intransigent so far as traditional teaching and the deposit of faith are concerned, it must also, under the guidance of the Church, continually re-adapt its verbal expression by a systematic use of appropriate equivalent terms, in order to make itself intelligible to a humanity that is constantly changing. Deeply involved in the modern world himself, Teilhard was familiar with modern needs; he rejected, therefore, a conventional form of expression, in the belief that true fidelity is not a parrot-like repetition, that filial obedience in the best sense has nothing in common with intellectual inertia, and that dogma cannot be clamped down on the minds of living beings by an external authority. In his respect and love for the real man, he sought to make himself heard and to stimulate an echo or answer. For Teilhard, as for his fellow-men, there is a God above all things, transcendent and free, a God ho calls man to intimate union with him; there is a revelation, a Christ, a Church, and an eternal life. But what Teilhard had was the power to bring out the importance of this 'datum', by showing that God's intervention in history was *grafted on to* or geared into the evolution of things and mankind's progress through history, that it activated a fundamental movement in the world, that it filled a need and answered an expectation. He told man that Christianity enabled him fully *to achieve his own success*, and to reach his goal and exist in fullness more completely even than he could possibly wish. He tried to give *meaning and direction* to the world—not a phantom world, but a full, solid, world, as known and lived in by twentieth-century men of flesh and blood. He could accept the horizontal dimension of the terrestrial world, but combined it with a vertical dimension. Further, he addressed himself to men who are in the world and who approach it with passionate enthusiasm as a vast enterprise to be carried through, showing them its profound significance, its final orientation and term. It is hardly surprising that his language, which seeks to construct a dialogue, 'gets across'. Finally, it is most interesting that the very wide audience Teilhard reached and his effective power of conversion show that modern man is dissatisfied with his materialism and thirsts for God. It is *religious* truth that attracts them in Teilhard.

[38] This point concerns the *catholic* character of a truth that can accept any intellectual structure that is not manifestly contradictory of it. Comparing dogmatic formulas with the fullness of the Christian mystery, Karl Rahner says that they are 'a beginning, not an end; a means and not an objective', '*a* truth that discloses something of *the* truth, which is always vaster'. The transcendent character proper to each formula 'draws its value precisely from the very progress of the formula which supersedes itself to attain another' (*Schriften zur Theologie*, Vol. 1, p. 169).

[39] 'I am completely convinced that there is infinitely more truth in the Church's empirical and complex attitude than in all our simplifying philosophies. The practice of the saints, even when difficult to rationalize, is the real that is "imposed", the concrete truth. It is this concrete truth then that should mould our attempts at systematizing, and they will always fail to contain the whole of it. As for our speculations, they will always be sterile, both for ourselves and for others, unless we can make them into an example by living in

conformity with them' (Letter to Père Auguste Valensin, 29 December 1919).

Teilhard was aware of the shortcomings in his work, which he hoped might be taken over, corrected and carried further. 'The view of the world I am putting forward here does not in any way represent a fixed and fully-formed system. No attempt is made, indeed such an attempt would be absurd, to provide, as Hegel sought to do, a deductive solution of the world, a definitive framework of truth. All I am concerned with is a fascicle of axes of progress, such as exists and gradually comes to light in every analysis in depth, through which a vast and still unexplored expanse of the real opens up for us' (*Comment je vois*, unpublished, 1934, introductory note).

Shortly before Teilhard's death, his friend Max Bégouën told him that his 'work in emancipating men's minds could never die'. Teilhard answered, 'If I have had a mission to fulfil, it will be possible to judge whether I did so only by the extent to which I am superseded' (Max Bégouën, *Témoignage*, in *Cahiers Pierre Teilhard de Chardin*, No. 2, p. 35).

So reasonable a hope and such admirable modesty remind one of a passage from Péguy: 'The vulgarity, in a philosophical discussion, of scoring a debating point! The real philosopher knows very well that he is not standing up against an opponent; he is standing side by side with him and his fellows confronted by a reality that is continually vaster and more mysterious . . . a great philosophy is not one that pronounces final judgments or establishes a final truth: it is a philosophy that disturbs the mind and inaugurates a revolution' (C. Péguy, *Note conjointe*, pp. 36, 43).

[40] This is an appropriate place to give an extract concerning Teilhard from a press-conference given by the Very Revd. Fr. Arrupé, General of the Society of Jesus, 14 June 1965.

Question: What do you think of the fact that, in spite of the *Monitum* of 30 June 1962, in which the Holy See pointed out the 'grave errors', philosophical and religious, that 'swarmed' in the writings of Teilhard de Chardin, Catholic writers and journalists still hold up Teilhard de Chardin, without the necessary reservations, as one of the very great masters of Christian religious thought in the modern world?

Answer: I would answer that by two observations. The first concerns the writers and journalists who speak of Père Teilhard. There are some who praise him unreservedly, but these are not members of the Society. The two most recent books written by Jesuits about Père Teilhard—Pierre Smulders's *La vision de Teilhard de Chardin*, and Emile Rideau's *La pensée du Père Teilhard de Chardin*—while sympathetic to his ideas, are both careful to make 'the necessary reservations' on a number of ambiguous or erroneous points.

The second concerns the difficulty of arriving at the exact and definitive content of Père Teilhard's thought. He wrote a great deal in the course of his long life, but he continually went back over his ideas, revising and correcting them. In consequence, you find a large number of different and even contradictory passages dealing with the same problem. Many of his writings that are now published were never meant for publication. They were simply tentative essays in enquiry, in which some questions had not been fully thought out and others were still imperfectly expressed. Moreover, you find in Père Teilhard ambiguities and errors that were certainly not intentional, since he was determined always to be completely faithful to the teaching of the Church; they may be explained by the fact that, first, the field in which he was developing his thought was so far unexplored and the method he was using was untried; and, secondly, he was not a professional theologian and philosopher, so that it was possible for him to be unaware of all the philosophical and theological implications and consequences attached to some of his intuitions.

Nevertheless, it remains true that the positive elements in Père Teilhard's work outweigh the negative or questionable elements. His view of the world is exerting a most wholesome influence in scientific circles, both Christian and non-Christian. Père Teilhard is one of the great masters of contemporary thought, and his success is not to be wondered at. He carried through, in fact, a great attempt to reconcile the world of science with the world of faith. Starting from the evidence provided by scientific investigation, he used a phenomenological method now popular with contemporary thinkers, and completed his system by a spiritual teaching: in this, not only does the person of Christ stand at the centre of every Christian's life, but he stands, too, at the centre of the world's evolution, as St Paul meant when he spoke of the Christ 'in whom all things hold together'. It is impossible not to recognize how rich a contribution to our time has been made by the message of Père Teilhard.

Further, the spiritual depth of Père Teilhard, admitted by all, is rooted in his religious life, lived in the school of St Ignatius. His work followed exactly the line of the apostolate of the Society of Jesus: to show how all created values attain a total synthesis in Christ and work together for the glory of God.

Index

Above, see Ahead

absolute, 57, 140; affirmation of, 65-6; and appetite for living, 142; knowledge of, 44; man's need for, 34, 35, 101-2; materialist and pantheist illusion, 59; Omega Teilhardian a., 42-3; the personal, 247; recognition of divine a., 38; Teilhard's passion for, 16, 282; universal movement towards, 64; the will towards, 432-3

abysses: infinitely great and infinitely small, 112; Pascal's twin, 22

action: Christian, 195-6, 200, 204-5, 283-5; crisis of human activity, 624-5; extension of God's creative power, 199; free act, 106-7; human, 224, 230, 232, 605; risk in, 199, 588. *See* effort.

Adam, 170, 517, 542, 543

Ahead: and Above, 233; and Beyond, 248, 652; conflict between God of Above and God of A., 218, 301, 315, 613; synthesis with Above, 216, 565, 642

amorization: progressive, 207; total, 61, 196

analogy, notion of, 42

anthropogenesis, 53, 120, 175, 306, 569

anthropology: *def.*, 40; carried on into Christology, 142; Teilhard's (critique), 144-5

apologetics, Teilhard's, 239, 251-2, 635-8

Aristotle, 75, 92, 429, 498, 656

art, function of, 124-5, 461-2

ascesis, 199, 200-1, 222, 230

atheism: consequences of modern, 34, 231; Teilhard's attiitude to contemporary, 173, 221, 240, 242, 547

Augustine, St., 17, 18, 136, 227, 515, 533, 548, 621

Barthélemy-Madaule, Mme M., 329, 342, 390, 398, 416, 436, 443, 475

Beauregard, O. Costa de, 417, 423

being: affirmation of, 39, 41, 336: Being-God, 147; conception in depth, 42; concrete possession of, 44; defined by union, 509; degrees of, 45; ontological relationship between b. and

universe, 510; participated, 152, 154, 155, 180, 504, 507, 508, 511, 513, 515; precariousness of created, 157; primacy of, 146-7, 495-6

Bergson, Henri, 70, 72, 76, 86, 106-8, 116, 129, 148, 167, 202, 417, 652-3; and animation of matter, 91, 92; and art, 462; and belief in immortality, 452; and central intuition, 31; and contradiction in social forces, 359; criticism by Teilhard; and dissipation of energy, 84; and divine transformation of persons, 248; and extension of positivity to spiritual phenomena, 23; and free act, 106-7; influence on Teilhard, 25, 294; and intuitive knowledge of ego, 17, 438; kinship and differences between Teilhard and, 342, 397-400; and 'laws of twofold frenzy', 247; and man's emergence, 427; and master-disciple relationship, 132; and morality, 483; and organic and inorganic matter, 97; realism shared with Teilhard, 46-7; and spiritual energy, 241; and static religion, 472

Bernanos, Georges, 116, 228, 574

Bible: problem of language of, 20; Teilhard and, 167, 220, 223

biology, 75, 401, 404, 410; and acceptance of Teilhard's scientific laws, 92-3; and analytical method, 86; and technology, 121

biosphere, 53, 235, 387, 394

Blondel, Maurice, 17, 109, 140, 144, 148, 183, 200, 645; apologetics, 635; and encounter with God, 152; and existence of God, 147; influence on Teilhard, 25-6, 128, 375-6; and love, 469; pan-Christism, 294, 534; and phenomenology of man, 250; philosophic humanism, 239; and revelation, 20; and Incarnation, 533; and will towards happiness, 208

boredom, 35, 117

Borne, Etienne, 92, 450, 481

Bouillard, Henri, 375, 653

Boule, Marcellin, 25

Breuil, Henri, 25, 554

Broglie, Louis de, 88, 407

Camus, Albert, 450
centration, 81, 186, 209, 420
centrogenesis, 108
cephalization, 81
cerebration, 78, 81
charity, 36, 194-5, 464; exercise of,
    582; victory of, 141, 229, 627-8
Charles, Pierre, 24, 292-3, 438, 513
chastity, 131, 203, 225, 474, 553, 601
Chauchard, Dr. Paul, 86
Christ, 72, 73, 213; Alpha and Omega,
    655; centre of universe, 162-3, 526-7;
    cosmic role, 165, 529, 534; and
    creation, 153, 160, 163; creative and
    animating function, 179; crucial
    option for man, 213, 614; an
    'element' of the world, 164, 213; the
    evolver, 549, 575; the historical,
    60-1, 168, 530, 622; human features
    of, 165; immersion in things, 164,
    527; Incarnate Word, 155; Kingship
    of, 61, 62, 164, 165, 179, 378;
    mediator of absolute, 142; and
    modern world, 623-4; personal centre
    of convergent cosmos, 62-3; place in
    Teilhard's spirituality, 192-3, pri-
    macy of, 213, 613-14; Sacred Heart
    of, 219, 320-1, 614, 615; Super-, 534-
    6, 587; total, 156, 235. See Christo-
    genesis, Incarnation, Omega.
Christian phenomenon, 48, 160, 236
Christianity, 48, 69, 131; dialectic of,
    45, 221, 223; and God as term of
    history, 64; lack of contact with
    modern world, 36, 322; and man,
    63; and man's new requirements, 36,
    189, 206-7, 243, 253, 574-6, 602-3,
    642-4; only salvation of world, 37;
    original contribution of, 222; present-
    day lack of appeal, 37, 323-8; re-
    lation between natural reality and,
    45; source of modern neo-humanism,
    33; supremacy, 233-4, 235, 639-40,
    642; Teilhard's criticism of modern,
    36-37, 315-19; uniqueness, 210, 236.
    See Church.
Christification, 587; of history, 196,
    213
Christogenesis and cosmogenesis, 62
Christology, 240, 251, 319-20, 525-6,
    575; Teilhard's (critique), 162-9
Church: axis of concentration, 63, 202,
    203; collective centre of love, 202;
    continues mission of Christ, 61;
    educative aspect, 202; and Eucharist,
    179; expansion, 205; and fruit of
    human effort, 654; need for organ of
    research, 655; priestly vocation, 599-

600; progress of, 176; Teilhard's
    views on 220, 597-9, 601; variety of
    vocations within, 202-3; and world,
    242, 243, 647-8
Claudel, Paul, 24, 128, 144, 623; and
    love, 468-70
Clement of Alexandria, St., 649
Coeur de la matière, Le, 619
coherence: and concordism, 279; cri-
    terion of, 39, 335-6, 384-5
collective, Teilhard's sense of, 21, 23,
    27
Comment je crois, 433
communism, 234, 301, 479, 555
complementarity, logic of, 89
complexity: and consciousness, 86, 91,
    93, 186, 402-3, 404, 420; criterion of,
    84; infinite of, 80; organized, 78,
    394-5; structural c. and spiritual
    reality, 42
complexity-consciousness, law of, 27,
    64, 567
comradeship and friendship, 466-7
concentration, universal property of,
    80-81
concordism, 279, 423, 506
consciousness, 52, 338, 432; centration,
    108: and consciousness of self, 430;
    a cosmic property, 90; final com-
    munion of, 181, 183; interpenetra-
    tion of, 127; levels in man, 106;
    mutations of human, 104; phenome-
    non of, 81; progress of, 176; problem
    of communion of, 142; super-, 567;
    transformation of man's, 300; uni-
    versal, 418-21
conspiration, 127, 554; and 'mechani-
    zation', 175, 359
conversion, problem of, 218-19
co-reflexion, 55, 126, 130, 520, 550,
    569; ultimate point of, 131
cosmogenesis, 32, 62, 103, 156, 179, 388,
    511
cosmology: def., 40; Teilhard's (cri-
    tique), 84-88, 98-99
cosmos: organized, 76, 77; transfigura-
    tion of, 186, 571; unity through con-
    vergence, 27. See cosmogenesis.
creation: and Alexandrians, 157; con-
    tinuous and multiple, 158, 519; co-
    operation with God, 159; 'to create
    is to unite', 561; creative transforma-
    tion, 519; creative union, 535, 561;
    evolutionary, 515, 516; free and
    necessary, 507-9; historical char-
    acter, 157; and historical origin of
    man, 66; and infinite love, 156; re-
    creation, 219, 514; Teilhard and

problem of (critique), 152-6, 240; and unification, 154

Crespy, Georges, 545, 546, 559, 649

Cross: meaning of, 173, 225-7, 547-9, 626; mystery of, 36, 171-2, 173

Cuénot, Claude, 348, 414, 463, 476, 531, 589

Cuénot, Lucien, 86, 426

Cullmann, Oscar, 558

damnation, 188. See hell

Daniélou Jean, 94, 541, 560

Darwin, Charles, 31, 97

Darwinism, 96; neo-, 415, 425

death, 35, 102, 112, 117, 593; acceptance of, 201; anticipation of, 130, 472; collective, 34, 309; spiritual value, 225; transition through, 222-3; victory over, 38, 60

decentration, 209, 239

democracy, 133-4, 234, 481

Descartes, René, 26, 42, 74, 92; knowledge of reality, 334; laws of extension and movement, 85; and matter, 420; spatial infinity, 80

detachment, 195, 200, 321, 590-1, 614; and attachment, 198, 605

determinism, 51, 52, 70-1, 82, 86, 406-10; appearance of fatality-sequence, 70; and chance, 415; importance attributed to by Teilhard, 87; man negation of determinisms, 100; science and principle of, 85. See freedom

dialectic: of Christianity, 221, 223; of continuity and discontinuity, 83, 89, 93, 102, 143, 172, 181; expression of tension by Teilhard's, 45-6; of finite and infinite, 150; of Jew and pagan, 219, 247; of love and justice, 172; of man and woman, 128, 247; of man and world, 184; of master and disciple, 72, 247; of master and slave, 73, 172, 247, 558; of nature, 48; of potentiality and act, 89; of relation and rupture, 83; Teilhard's, 45-6, 343-7

Diderot, Denis, 411, 420

divine milieu: def., 193-4; 195, 207, 217, 500, 592, 611, 618, 620

divinization, 198-9; of history, 207; of world, 216

Divino afflante Spiritu, encyclical, 20

Doncoeur, Paul, 25

dualism, Teilhard's rejection of, 40, 49

East, road of the, 229, 635

Eastern religions, see religion

education: connection with biological reality, 476-7; role of, 132

effort: human, 181, 199, 204, 564, 586, 591; scientific, 54; world's threefold, 196. See action.

ego, 106, 119, 440; intuitive knowledge of, 438; Teilhard's exploration of, 109-10; two sorts of, 90

Einstein, Albert, 64, 413, 416

élite: control of social structure by, 132; of mankind, 210; role of élites in history, 73, 129; Teilhard's viewpoint, 22, 290

Emmanuel, Pierre, 225

energetics: human, 487; spiritual, 140, 331

energy, 51-2; cannot be dissociated from thought, 74; dissipation of, 84, 88, 397; increase of psychic, 54; transformation of material, 414; two forms, 78-9, 396; unity and duality of two forms, 79-80, 84, 412. See human, radial, spiritual, tangential.

Engels, Friedrich, 48

entropy: def., 353, 51, 79, 395-6, 407; escape from, 186; negative, 89, 417

Epicurus, 208

estrangement, 72; and man's fall, 543; modern man's, 35; problem of man's social, 21, 219; universal, 222

Eucharist: Incarnation and, 206; and transformation of Christian and world, 205; Teilhard's eucharistic doctrine, 603-5

evil, 72; by-product of evolution, 544-5, 546; increase of, 175; and multiplicity, 170-1, 540; non-theological interpretation, 170; persistence of, 176; problem of, 116-7, 449-50; regeneration of, 202. See original sin.

evolution, 52, 354-5, 387-90; biochemistry of, 425; crowning of, 184s expression of creation, 159; graph of, 424-5; painfulness of personalizing, 476; and present-day mankind, 53-4; process of personalization, 104; progressive, 174, 175, 557

excentration, 183, 201, 565-6

existential values, Teilhard's theory of, 118-9

existentialism, 241-2, 494; and man's isolation and distress, 113-6

faith: act of, 63; is love, 194-5; and realization of Christian life, 581-2; total, 193-5; in the world and in Christ, 641-2, 650; in the world and in God, 235-6, 375-81, 433

Fathers, Greek, 164, 165, 515, 548; Latin, 319-20, 515

Fessard, Gaston, 128, 132, 370, 529, 568-9, 604

fire, 30, 163, 193, 205, 214, 280, 288, 615

Fontoynont, Victor, 25, 294

Foucauld, Charles de, 18

Francis of Assisi, St., 207, 607, 655

freedom: basis of man's, 102; dangers inherent in, 175, 556; grand option, 554; and life: three choices, 208-9; and its objective conditions, 140; Teilhard's analysis of, 107; Teilhard's stress on, 135; transcendence of and Teilhard's philosophy of history (critique), 68-70

Freud, Sigmund, 31

fulfilment: of all things in God, 61; of man, 59, 60

future: mystery of, 590; Teilhard's orientation towards, 27, 180, 562-3

Galileo, 31

Garaudy, Roger, 411, 414

genetics, 96-7

Gide, André, 26, 208

God: action of living, 71; awaited by modern man, 33, 307-8; centre of universal contact, 194, 580-1, 616; and conic view of history, 151; and creation, 59-60; existence demanded as necessity, 59; diaphany, 193, 211, 217, 577-9; final intimacy with, 181-2; Kingdom of, 225, 228, 229, 231; knowledge and possession of, 502; is love, 60, 215; man and universe attain end in and through G., 60; man's tendency towards, 101-2; moving force in history, 59; necessary existence end of history, 147; notion of, 36; omnipresence, 194, 579-80; personal revelation of, 60; supreme absolute unity, 80; Teilhard and problem of existence of, 147-52, 496-9; temporary loss of, 33; transcendence of, 65-8, 149, 499-500, 504; unifying of world by, 164; universe body of, 214

Grandmaison, Léonce de, 24-5, 293

gravity, two forms of, 80

Greek Fathers. See Fathers, Greek

Gregory of Nyssa, St., 165, 527

Habit, danger of, 107

Haldane, J. B. S., 423

Hamelin, Octave, 42, 46, 438

happiness, problem of, 209

heart of Christ. See Christ, Sacred Heart of

Hegel, Friedrich, 26, 41, 42, 53, 70, 87, 116, 126, 147, 340, 479, 654; dialectic, 45, 46; dialectical rationalism, 382; phenomenology, 51, 231, 332

Heidegger, Martin, 241, 336

Heisenberg, Werner, 413

hell, 188, 213, 228, 573-4

Helvetius, 411

heredity, 463; educative, 127-8, 132, 466

history: affirmation of end to, 56-7, 370-1; difficulties in Teilhard's concept of, 247-50; fundamental idea of h. in time, 49; progress of, 235, 641; role of great personalities in, 72, 129; synchrony and diachrony in, 72; Teilhard's scheme of unification and the complexity of h., 70-1; totalization of, 568-9; transcendent end of, 65, 180, 183, 630

Holbach, d', 420

Holy Spirit, 169

hominization, 63, 101, 103, 126, 139, 141, 375, 378, 500; and biological evolution, 427; preparation for Parousia, 182

human energy: activation of, 83-4, 110, 130, 473; organization of, 139-40

humanism: atheistic, 233; Christian, 210, 245, 566; modern, 36; neo-, 33, 305-8; Teilhard's religious, 244

humanization, 179; completion of, 228, 627

Husserl, Edmund, 332-3

Huxley, Sir Julian, 26, 47, 420

Ignatius Loyola, St., 203, 214, 215, 217; and conception of cosmos, 215, 617; essence of thought, 213. See Spiritual Exercises

immortality, 117, 451-2

Incarnation, 36, 48, 67, 155, 162, 179; all-embracing dimensions, 165, 532-3; and concept of evolution, 167; of divine absolute, 38; and eschatology, 651; freedom and necessity of, 155, 536; gratuitous intervention, 167; linked with Redemption, 180; physical character of, 164, 165, 527-8; prodigious biological operation, 163, 527; Teilhard's emphasis on, 173-4

indeterminism, quantic, 82

individuation, penalty of, 35

infinite, concrete. See complexity

information, notion of, 92

interiority, 90
invention, 82; creative, 106; experience of, 435-6
involution, 127
Irenaeus, St., 165, 532
iron, 30, 283
Islam. *See* religion
Israel, symbolism of people of, 71-2
issue: need for, 35, 330, 638-9; life i. or dead end?, 38; expectation of i. for world, 204

Jansenism, 36, 215, 643
Jeannière, Abel, 185, 382-3, 651-2
Jeans, Sir James, 374-5
John, St., 216; affirmation of Word as mediator, 221; and Christogenesis, 62; and creation, 157; unifying of world by God, 164
John the Baptist, St., 229
John of the Cross, St., 193, 203, 607, 616
John XXIII, Pope, 178, 190, 480, 482
Judaism. *See* religion
judgment, last, 187, 572-3
juridicism, 36, 319-20

Kant, Immanuel, 26, 42, 47, 147, 331
Kantism, 74
Kierkegaard, Sören, 17, 18, 141, 246
knowledge, scientific, 74-6, 390-1

Lamarckism, 96
language: analysis of Teilhard's vocabulary, 258-273; clarity of Teilhard's expression, 273-4, 655; expression of the idea by, 105; Teilhard's l. and style, 241, 245, 253, 656-7; and thought, 652; variety of Teilhard's style, 274-6; 'vertical' symbolism of mystics and Teilhard, 619
Laplace, 413
Latin Fathers. *See* Fathers, Latin
Le Blond, J. M., 616
Lefebvre, Henri, 558
Leibnitz, 91, 309, 394, 400, 586
leisure, 54, 122, 136, 224; of the future, 626; and unemployment, 457
Leroi-Gourhan, André, 426
Le Roy, Edouard, 24, 395, 398; and free act, 106; idealism, 46; influence on Teilhard, 26
Leys, Roger, 542
liberty, 31, 33, 640; action of, 48; affirmation of, 50
life, 52, 354, 401, 404-5; central phenomenon of evolution, 63; life-matter whole, 90; material effect of

complexity, 87; and matter, 78, 87; modern scientific views, 89-90; originality of, 81; phenomenon of, 81; principle and origin of, 415-6; stability of, 96
love: creation and direction of universe by, 62; evolution of, 473-4; forces of, 56; and friendship, 54-5, 128; necessity for, 631; purity identified with, 591; and research, 102; sexual, 128; supreme form of spiritual activity, 475-6; symbol of spiritual energy, 199; and Teilhard's attitude to pity, 470; unifying action, 29, 463-4; and universal solidarity, 132; of the world and of God, 235, 606-10
Lubac, Henri de, 376-7, 566, 649, 652
Lupasco, Stéphane, 89, 418

man: affectivity, 105-6; agony of isolation, 113-14, 445-6; appearance, 52, 356-7; break entailed by emergence of, 69; collective, 463; completion of, 221; creation of, 157, 158-9, 516; creative subject of evolution, 56; crowning success of evolution, 53; distress, 114, 446-7; existential view of, 100; final choice of, 61; fulfilment of, 59, 60; incompleteness of, 70, 101, 135; involvement in history of universe, 103; ontological condition of, 35; phenomenal observation of, 108-10; planetary responsibilities, 32, 33, 303-4, 509; power of invention, 71; a problem of freedom inside time, 118; a species, 302-3; temptation and sin of, 56, 175, 212, 222, 556; tragic dilemma of, 38; transcendence of, 47, 100, 109, 241, 426, 646; transition to God, 115. *See* action, anthropogenesis, effort, noosphere.
Manicheanism, 33, 36, 153, 215, 221, 230, 616
mankind: common spiritual front, 234, 640; communion of, 70; compression of, 55, 363-4; consummation of, 564; crisis of growth, 56; growth and progress of, 359-66; and hope of transcendent outcome, 34, 310-14; isolation of, 34, 308; present stage of development, 53-4
Man's Place in Nature, 426
Marcel, Gabriel, 546, 550
Maréchal, Joseph, 24, 91, 109, 168, 175, 438, 533, 575, 624; on Church and pioneers, 654; and original sin, 543; and redemption, 549

Marx, Karl, 26, 41, 53, 70, 72, 73, 116, 200, 242, 480, 576; and contradiction in social forces, 359; dialectic, 45, 46; dialectical rationalism, 382; and matter, 420; phenomenology, 51; social violence, 219; view of an end to history, 383

Marxism, 241, 306, 307, 370, 410-12; and dialectical power of negation; Teilhard and, 224, 646-7

Mary, 177, 181, 563-4

Mass on the World, The, 28, 211; style of, 276

Mater et magistra, encyclical, 178, 482

materialism, 117, 241

mathematical method, 85

matter, 77, 391, 392; ancients' concept of, 84; animated by consciousness, 91, 92; concept of pure, 76-77; contradictory tendency to entropy, 51-2; diversification, 416-7; expression of spiritual energy in, 82-3; goodness, 196, 584; matter and life: disorder and order, 88-9: primary elements, 77, 393; principle of maximum arrangement of, 80; and spirit, 81, 84, 338, 392, 412; 'tangential' aspect, 482

Mauriac, François, 227, 405

mechanism, 97-8

mechanization. *See* conspiration

memory, 107

Mendeleyev, Dmitry, 89

Merleau-Ponty, Maurice, 333

metaphysics; *def.*, 40; dissociation of Teilhard from, 42-3; Teilhard and traditional, 137; of union, 510-11, 513

Milieu Divin, Le, 49, 114, 218, 225, 577, 611; style, 276; treatment of evil in, 171

millenarianism, 183, 378

miracles, 636-8

monogenism, 517-8

morality, 482-3, 484; dynamic, 485-7; and emergence of thought, 135-6; general principle of, 130; and human effort, 138-9; metaphysical basis of, 136-8; and religion, 140-1, 488-90; spirit of, 138; transformism a school of, 483

Mounier, Emmanuel, 30

multiple, 507, 516; evil and the m., 540, God and the m., 529; organized by energy, 78; problem of the one and the m., 27, 77, 644; pure m. nothingness, 76, 513; unification, 159, 400

multiplicity, 135, 391; and man, 110; physical evil linked with, 116-17; and unity, 510

Myrdal, Gunnar, 558

mystery, expression of, 162; unity of mysteries, 179-80, 560-1

mystical body, 62, 149, 166, 187, 195, 566, 577; consummation of, 180-1; growth of, 189, 215, 221, 248; influence of Christian notion, 399; unification and totalization, 177, 190

Mystici Corporis Christi, encyclical, 528

mysticism, 491-3; Christian m. and pagan attitude to world, 215, 618; Eastern, 33, 633-4; new, 642; sensual, 624; supremacy of, 142; Teilhard's, 37, 626-7; Western, 33, 307

Nationalism, 234, 301

nature: basis of supernatural, 161, 522; and grace, 49, 523; image of supernatural, 63; value of, 522

Negation, 44-5

New Testament, 178, 224; Teilhard's knowledge incomplete, 20

Newman, Cardinal, 26, 611

Newton, Sir Isaac, 586

Nietzsche, Friedrich, 55, 200, 242, 318, 480

noogenesis, 62, 103, 104

noosphere, 53, 235, 358-9, 448-9, 567, 568, 630; convergence of, 65; maturing of, 185; possible schism in, 68, 187; rising pressure and n., 555; temperature of, 56, 465

Objectivism, 49

Old Testament, 73, 178; and figure of poor man, 226; Teilhard's lack of knowledge of, 20

Omega, 45-6, 57, 66, 69, 81, 82, 99, 108, 115, 182, 199, 248, 372-4, 382-3, 498; access to, 187; affirmation of, 148-9; assembler of consciousness, 147; attributes, 58-9; contested by scientific method, 93-4, 424; final transcendent centre, 117; finite and infinite, 149-50, 501; focus of convergence, 58; and history, 185; identical with Christ, 61, 180, 186, 233, 380, 527, 531; keystone of noosphere, 565; necessity for science, 94; origin of term, 58; phenomenological approach, 160-1; Teilhardian absolute, 42; world's ascent towards, 611

ontology, 40

optimism: Teilhard's, 213, 224, 252, 263; supernatural, 177, 215, 559
Origen, 542, 574
Origenism, 188
original sin, 36, 321-2; cosmic basis, 169-70; and Council of Trent, 542, 543; Teilhard and problem of, 538-44
orthogenesis, 96, 127, 389

Pacem in terris, encyclical, 178, 244, 480, 481, 560
paganism, 71
Paliard, Jacques, 147
pan-Christism, 294, 534, 622, 635
pantheism, 117, 149, 217, 221, 233, 499
Parousia, 151, 182, 206, 371, 500, 549, 553, 564-5, 575; importance emphasized by Teilhard, 168; not inevitable, 181; and science, 183; 379; temporal, 182, 248-9, 584
participation, 67
Pascal, Blaise, 17, 18, 34, 35, 42, 115, 144, 401, 454, 586, 621, 627; and God-Man, 653-4; 'Mystery of Jesus', 227; and research, 453; spatial infinity, 80; symbolism of fire, 214; and Teilhard's dialectic, 46; wager, 483-4
passivities, 223, 227; fruitfulness of, 203, 225; and man, 111; passivity of suffering God, 217, 620
Paul, St., 92, 114, 213, 216, 219, 448, 529; and Christ, 165, 176; and Christogenesis, 62; and dialectic of death, 226; epistles, 61, 155, 188; Teilhard's quotations from, 627; on unification of Church, 176; and unifying of world by God, 164; and universal Christ, 530
Pauli, Wolfgang, 88, 89
Péguy, Charles, 26, 239, 645-6; Teilhard and, 531-2, 646
Pelagianism, 215, 618; neo-, 624
person: importance attributed by Teilhard to, 108, 116, 296, 442-3; interconnexion of persons, 126-7
personal, religion of the, 24
personalism, 49-50, 108-10, 115, 434; Teilhard's theory (critique), 133
personalization, 104, 108, 117, 126; energy of, 128
pessimism, existentialist, 28
phenomenology, 39-40, 51, 64, 332-5; all-embracing aim of, 237-8; deficiencies, 70-3, 250; existential character of, 41; expressed in a dramatic and tragic dialectic, 44-5;

influence of Christianity, 49, 351-2; originality and method, 339; Teilhard's notion of certainty, 340-1; reconstruction of, 40, 339
phenomenon of man, 53, 56, 100, 119, 357-8
Phenomenon of Man, The, 49, 95; and problem of evil, 170; scientific viewpoint, 109, 115, 149; style, 276
philosophy: boldness of Teilhard's ph. of history, 64; existential, 238; extension of scientific laws into, 92, 423; Teilhard's ph. unitary, 23
physics, 75, 402, 410; atomic, 645; ultra-, 43, 341
Pius XII, Pope, 629, 656
Piveteau, Jean, 426
planetization, 55, 365-6, 372
Plato, 49, 85, 92, 106, 382, 454, 586
Pleroma, 61, 155, 161, 197, 198, 377-8, 379, 508, 563, 603; and creation, 163; and damnation, 574; and Incarnation, 528; integration in, 201; synthesis of uncreated and created, 165
Plotinus, 49, 382, 400
poverty, 229
prayer, 203, 225
progress, 139, 552-60; economic, 33; infallibility of, 550-2; metaphysical laws of, 550-2; scientific and technical, 54, 117, 123, 224, 629; Teilhard's view of progress in history (critique), 174-8
Psalms, 35, 176, 224, 314, 559

Quietism, 215

Rabut, Olivier, 422, 649
racialism, 132, 477-8
radial energy, 79
Rahner, Karl, 166, 518, 534, 536, 657
Ravaisson, Félix, 91
real: and discovery of the true, 437-40; homogeneity, 575; inter-dependence of elements in, 74-5; intuition of the concrete, 107-8; knowledge of, 43-4, 75, 105, 231-2; and spiritualism and materialism, 87; structures of, 76-8; Teilhard's concept of, 43, 143; Teilhard's dialectic and, 45
realism: Teilhard's fundamental, 46-7, 347-8; solution to opposition between r. and idealism, 48
reason, appearance of, 129
Redemption: and Incarnation, 173, 179. 225; interpretation of, 174, 549; and man's development, 172-3; re-

Redemption (*cont'd*)
creation and reparation minimized, 171, 545-6
reflexion, 105, 429-30, 438; in man, 101; and vitalization, 63; and world of phenomena, 40
religion, 488-91, 650; Eastern, 24, 229, 232, 631-4; Islam, 232, 634-5; Judaism, 222; phenomenon of, 141-2; problem of, 131
research, 54, 139, 490; cardinal importance and role of, 119, 120-2; comradeship of, 126; the priest and scientific r., 203; value of, 454-6
Resurrection: of the body, 186, 571; importance stressed by Teilhard, 166, 213
revelation, and 'natural' history, 62-3
Ricoeur, Paul, 71, 383
Rostand, Jean, 96
Rousselot, Pierre, 25, 109, 336-7, 483

Sacraments, 206
salvation, 36, 69
sanctification: of man, 196-7; of the real, 196
Sartre, Jean-Paul, 411, 491
Scheler, Max, 126
Schelling, Friedrich, 91
Schopenhauer, Arthur, 208
Schrödinger, Erwin, 89
Schuré, E., 434
science, 33, 69, 120, 122; approximation between faith and, 63; fertility of, 42; and modifications to concept of universe, 495; omni-, 184; operational character of modern, 75; and philosophical and religious speculation, 653; progress of, 54; and religion, 122; and synthetic approach, 94
Sens humain, Le, 28
sense, use of word by Teilhard, 440
Sertillanges, A. D., 26, 109
sexuality, 106, 130-1, 142, 440
Simpson, George Gaylord, 97, 426
sin, 61, 72, 117, 175, 219; and morality, 138-9, 485; reparation for overshadowed, 171; Teilhard's views (critique), 169-73; word rarely used by Teilhard, 18
Smulders, Pierre, 506, 513, 535, 538, 557-8, 604
socialization, 27, 55, 63, 366-79; final stage, 56-7; present, 69
society: importance, 72; organization of modern, 175; unification, 126-30

sociology, 462; political (critique), 134-5, 482
Soucy, Claude, 411
soul, 40, 429; and death of body, 518-9, 571; unifying action, 157
space-time, 88, 103
Spinoza, 528
spirit, 57, 68, 71; genesis of, 87; phenomenon of, 81. *See* matter.
spirit of the earth, 121, 185
spiritual energy, 80, 136, 400, 413; activation of, 130-1; and dynamism of life, 98; expressed in matter, 82-3; a physical reality, 86; of the real, 92; and science, 84-5
Spiritual Exercises: and faith, 193; influence on Teilhard, 19; and loyalty to divine will, 211-12; and meditation 'to obtain love', 214; mystical experience of, 37; orientation towards God, 212, 612; and problem of conversion, 218, 621
spirituality: *def.*, 41; apostolicity, 216, 242, 619; approach intended for all men, 208; defects and merits, 230-31, 252, 628-9; incomplete, 218-20; mystical character, 216-18; necessity for ardent acceptance, 208-9, 610; of Teilhard (critique); 221-36; Teilhard's essentially Christic, 192-3
structuration, 52
suffering: acceptance of, 201; human, 106, 116, 460, 589; increase in, 175, 557; spiritual value, 200, 225, 494
super-centration, 209, 210
super-life, 129, 136
super-mankind, 57
supernatural: gratuitousness and transcendence, 520-1; and natural: correspondence and distinction, 160-2, 245; neglect, 230, 628; problem of, 182, 230, 628; and science, 624
systematics, 75, 386, 390

Tangential energy, 78-9
technology, 458-9; and conquest of universe, 184; and the machine, 457; nature, 33, 69; role of, 120-1
Teilhard's life and character: apostolic vocation, 19; ardent piety, 18; capacity for friendship, 29; double vocation, 38, 331-2; dynamic energy and strong will, 16; educational influences, 18-20; exceptional sensibility, 16, 28; extraversion and realism, 17; family background and influences, 18, 285; influence of First World War, 21-2; influence of

Society of Jesus, 19-21, 329; intellectual need for coherence, 15; interior life, 297-9; intrepidity, 16; lack of awareness of social problems, 18, 21; loyalty to Church, 37; mystical experience, 37, 328; passion for truth and absolute, 16-17, 282; philosophical and theological studies, 19-20, 286-7; physical and mental make-up, 15-17; problem of sex, 18, 27; reactionary element in education, 22, 287; science, 15-19, 23, 28; symbolism of iron and fire, 30; sympathy with the real, 16, 279; vivid imagination, 15

Teilhard's thought: awareness of world's crisis of consciousness, 31; and Bergson, see Bergson; bias towards 'general' and 'universal', 29, 115; and Blondel, see Blondel; central intuition springs from existential experience, 31, 299; continuous development of, 27; difficulties in, 245-51, 659; essential core of, 21; growing emphasis on man's future, 180; influence of biology and geology, 23; integration of theology with scientific view of world, 656; and Le Roy, see Le Roy; mainly expressed in essays, 41; mission to restore contact between humanism and Christianity, 38; and Monitum of Holy Office, 250-1, 658; originality of philosophy, 23, 124; and Pascal, see Pascal; passion for the rational, 23; a philosophy of history, 116; positivity, 23; primacy accorded to universe, 220; problem of interpretation, 635; and problem of opposition of God and world, 29; sense of the collective, 21, 23, 115; shift of emphasis of, 28; stages in, 28-9; status as thinker, 30; and study of mankind, 27, 296; theological contribution, 240; in Thomistic tradition, 644; universal humanism, 24; use of philosophical categories, 43

Teilhard de Chardin, Marguerite-Marie, 298

Teillard-Chambon, Marguerite, 283

theology: def., 40; of Teilhard (critique), 188-91; Teilhard's faithful to tradition, 188-9, 574; and theory of convergence, 251

theosphere, 235

thermodynamics, 407, 408; laws of, 79, 82

Thomas Aquinas, St., 203, 529, 655, 656; and evolutionary creation, 515; and nature and human nature, 221, 239; and reflexion, 430

Thomism: proofs of existence of God, 42; Teilhard and, 644-5

thought, 53, 103-4, 567; and attainment of the true, 104, 184; concrete, 90; reflective, 52; scientific effort and, 54; value of, 460. See noosphere; Omega; Teilhard's thought

thresholds, critical, 45, 51, 55, 64, 72, 83

time: conic, 185; convergence of, 64; and eternity, 38; evolutionary, 39-40; 337-8; and man, 111-2; organic, 303, 306, 505

tool, man's use of, 105, 109

totalitarianism, 54, 132-3, 478-80, 482, 555

totalization, 174, 570

transformation, 181, 198, 218; synonymous with transfiguration, 45

transformism, 75, 386-90, 515; and creation, 159, 520; theory of, 95-8

Trinity, 61, 222, 505; and creation, 155; trinitization, 154, 513

turning about, 44, 183, 201

Ultra-human, 28, 565; and superhuman, 235; and trans-human, 182, 570

ultra-physics, see physics

unconscious, discovery of the, 34

unification, 69, 352; growth of, 51-2, 92-3; of mankind, 54-5, 126-9, 139, 176, 184; spiritual, 184; and Teilhard's concept of history, 247

union: creative, 512, 535, 561; metaphysics of, 510-11, 513; 'union differentiates', 115, 127, 369-70, 464-5

unity: and spirit, 91; reduction of world to, 651; Teilhard's insistence on, 245

universe: beginning of, 505-7; coincidence of u. in movement and Christ, 27; convergent structure of, 51; expression of God, 207; magnitude, 112-13; man its consciousness and fulfilment, 47, 349; relation between man and, 45; static concept of, 31-2, 37, 299-300, 323; Teilhard's concept of, 45

Upward and Forward, 641

Valensin, Auguste, 24, 109, 183, 200, 292, 293, 398, 575, 645; and 'idealist

Valensin, Auguste (*cont'd*)
    transposition', 347; and pantheism,
    528
Valéry, Paul, 47, 512
Vatican Council: First, 148, 180, 644;
    Second, 21
Vincent de Paul, St., 203
vitalization, 63

War, 120, 641
west, road of the, 229, 633, 635
whole, discovery of the, 143-4
'within' and 'without', 90, 91, 419
woman, role of, 128, 467-9
Word, *see* Christ
work: and redemption, 226-7; reflexive

freedom of human, 122, 460;
    sanctification of, 196, 231, 630;
    sanctity of, 197, 212, 587; Teil-
    hard's philosophy of (critique), 122-
    4; value of, 200, 585, 629
world: Christianity and, 36-7; con-
    summation of, 182-3; crisis of con-
    sciousness of, 31; end of, 185, 188,
    567, 651; man-world dialectical re-
    lationship, 47; modern intrusion
    between God and man, 32; notion of
    depth of, 434; perpetual genesis of,
    80; spiritual value of, 32, 301-2;
    Teilhard's concept of, 48; temporal
    reality of, 51
World-God, 33, 36